Lecture Notes in Computer Science 14025

The series Lecture Notes in Computer Science (LNCS), including its subseries Lecture Notes in Artificial Intelligence (LNAI) and Lecture Notes in Bioinformatics (LNBI), has established itself as a medium for the publication of new developments in computer science and information technology research, teaching, and education.

LNCS enjoys close cooperation with the computer science R & D community, the series counts many renowned academics among its volume editors and paper authors, and collaborates with prestigious societies. Its mission is to serve this international community by providing an invaluable service, mainly focused on the publication of conference and workshop proceedings and postproceedings. LNCS commenced publication in 1973.

Adela Coman · Simona Vasilache
Editors

Social Computing and Social Media

15th International Conference, SCSM 2023
Held as Part of the 25th HCI International Conference, HCII 2023
Copenhagen, Denmark, July 23–28, 2023
Proceedings, Part I

Springer

Editors
Adela Coman
University of Bucharest
Bucharest, Romania

Simona Vasilache
University of Tsukuba
Tsukuba, Japan

ISSN 0302-9743 ISSN 1611-3349 (electronic)
Lecture Notes in Computer Science
ISBN 978-3-031-35914-9 ISBN 978-3-031-35915-6 (eBook)
https://doi.org/10.1007/978-3-031-35915-6

This Springer imprint is published by the registered company Springer Nature Switzerland AG
The registered company address is: Gewerbestrasse 11, 6330 Cham, Switzerland

Foreword

Human-computer interaction (HCI) is acquiring an ever-increasing scientific and industrial importance, as well as having more impact on people's everyday lives, as an ever-growing number of human activities are progressively moving from the physical to the digital world. This process, which has been ongoing for some time now, was further accelerated during the acute period of the COVID-19 pandemic. The HCI International (HCII) conference series, held annually, aims to respond to the compelling need to advance the exchange of knowledge and research and development efforts on the human aspects of design and use of computing systems.

The 25th International Conference on Human-Computer Interaction, HCI International 2023 (HCII 2023), was held in the emerging post-pandemic era as a 'hybrid' event at the AC Bella Sky Hotel and Bella Center, Copenhagen, Denmark, during July 23–28, 2023. It incorporated the 21 thematic areas and affiliated conferences listed below.

A total of 7472 individuals from academia, research institutes, industry, and government agencies from 85 countries submitted contributions, and 1578 papers and 396 posters were included in the volumes of the proceedings that were published just before the start of the conference, these are listed below. The contributions thoroughly cover the entire field of human-computer interaction, addressing major advances in knowledge and effective use of computers in a variety of application areas. These papers provide academics, researchers, engineers, scientists, practitioners and students with state-of-the-art information on the most recent advances in HCI.

The HCI International (HCII) conference also offers the option of presenting 'Late Breaking Work', and this applies both for papers and posters, with corresponding volumes of proceedings that will be published after the conference. Full papers will be included in the 'HCII 2023 - Late Breaking Work - Papers' volumes of the proceedings to be published in the Springer LNCS series, while 'Poster Extended Abstracts' will be included as short research papers in the 'HCII 2023 - Late Breaking Work - Posters' volumes to be published in the Springer CCIS series.

I would like to thank the Program Board Chairs and the members of the Program Boards of all thematic areas and affiliated conferences for their contribution towards the high scientific quality and overall success of the HCI International 2023 conference. Their manifold support in terms of paper reviewing (single-blind review process, with a minimum of two reviews per submission), session organization and their willingness to act as goodwill ambassadors for the conference is most highly appreciated.

This conference would not have been possible without the continuous and unwavering support and advice of Gavriel Salvendy, founder, General Chair Emeritus, and Scientific Advisor. For his outstanding efforts, I would like to express my sincere appreciation to Abbas Moallem, Communications Chair and Editor of HCI International News.

July 2023 Constantine Stephanidis

HCI International 2023 Thematic Areas and Affiliated Conferences

Thematic Areas

- HCI: Human-Computer Interaction
- HIMI: Human Interface and the Management of Information

Affiliated Conferences

- EPCE: 20th International Conference on Engineering Psychology and Cognitive Ergonomics
- AC: 17th International Conference on Augmented Cognition
- UAHCI: 17th International Conference on Universal Access in Human-Computer Interaction
- CCD: 15th International Conference on Cross-Cultural Design
- SCSM: 15th International Conference on Social Computing and Social Media
- VAMR: 15th International Conference on Virtual, Augmented and Mixed Reality
- DHM: 14th International Conference on Digital Human Modeling and Applications in Health, Safety, Ergonomics and Risk Management
- DUXU: 12th International Conference on Design, User Experience and Usability
- C&C: 11th International Conference on Culture and Computing
- DAPI: 11th International Conference on Distributed, Ambient and Pervasive Interactions
- HCIBGO: 10th International Conference on HCI in Business, Government and Organizations
- LCT: 10th International Conference on Learning and Collaboration Technologies
- ITAP: 9th International Conference on Human Aspects of IT for the Aged Population
- AIS: 5th International Conference on Adaptive Instructional Systems
- HCI-CPT: 5th International Conference on HCI for Cybersecurity, Privacy and Trust
- HCI-Games: 5th International Conference on HCI in Games
- MobiTAS: 5th International Conference on HCI in Mobility, Transport and Automotive Systems
- AI-HCI: 4th International Conference on Artificial Intelligence in HCI
- MOBILE: 4th International Conference on Design, Operation and Evaluation of Mobile Communications

List of Conference Proceedings Volumes Appearing Before the Conference

1. LNCS 14011, Human-Computer Interaction: Part I, edited by Masaaki Kurosu and Ayako Hashizume
2. LNCS 14012, Human-Computer Interaction: Part II, edited by Masaaki Kurosu and Ayako Hashizume
3. LNCS 14013, Human-Computer Interaction: Part III, edited by Masaaki Kurosu and Ayako Hashizume
4. LNCS 14014, Human-Computer Interaction: Part IV, edited by Masaaki Kurosu and Ayako Hashizume
5. LNCS 14015, Human Interface and the Management of Information: Part I, edited by Hirohiko Mori and Yumi Asahi
6. LNCS 14016, Human Interface and the Management of Information: Part II, edited by Hirohiko Mori and Yumi Asahi
7. LNAI 14017, Engineering Psychology and Cognitive Ergonomics: Part I, edited by Don Harris and Wen-Chin Li
8. LNAI 14018, Engineering Psychology and Cognitive Ergonomics: Part II, edited by Don Harris and Wen-Chin Li
9. LNAI 14019, Augmented Cognition, edited by Dylan D. Schmorrow and Cali M. Fidopiastis
10. LNCS 14020, Universal Access in Human-Computer Interaction: Part I, edited by Margherita Antona and Constantine Stephanidis
11. LNCS 14021, Universal Access in Human-Computer Interaction: Part II, edited by Margherita Antona and Constantine Stephanidis
12. LNCS 14022, Cross-Cultural Design: Part I, edited by Pei-Luen Patrick Rau
13. LNCS 14023, Cross-Cultural Design: Part II, edited by Pei-Luen Patrick Rau
14. LNCS 14024, Cross-Cultural Design: Part III, edited by Pei-Luen Patrick Rau
15. LNCS 14025, Social Computing and Social Media: Part I, edited by Adela Coman and Simona Vasilache
16. LNCS 14026, Social Computing and Social Media: Part II, edited by Adela Coman and Simona Vasilache
17. LNCS 14027, Virtual, Augmented and Mixed Reality, edited by Jessie Y. C. Chen and Gino Fragomeni
18. LNCS 14028, Digital Human Modeling and Applications in Health, Safety, Ergonomics and Risk Management: Part I, edited by Vincent G. Duffy
19. LNCS 14029, Digital Human Modeling and Applications in Health, Safety, Ergonomics and Risk Management: Part II, edited by Vincent G. Duffy
20. LNCS 14030, Design, User Experience, and Usability: Part I, edited by Aaron Marcus, Elizabeth Rosenzweig and Marcelo Soares
21. LNCS 14031, Design, User Experience, and Usability: Part II, edited by Aaron Marcus, Elizabeth Rosenzweig and Marcelo Soares

22. LNCS 14032, Design, User Experience, and Usability: Part III, edited by Aaron Marcus, Elizabeth Rosenzweig and Marcelo Soares
23. LNCS 14033, Design, User Experience, and Usability: Part IV, edited by Aaron Marcus, Elizabeth Rosenzweig and Marcelo Soares
24. LNCS 14034, Design, User Experience, and Usability: Part V, edited by Aaron Marcus, Elizabeth Rosenzweig and Marcelo Soares
25. LNCS 14035, Culture and Computing, edited by Matthias Rauterberg
26. LNCS 14036, Distributed, Ambient and Pervasive Interactions: Part I, edited by Norbert Streitz and Shin'ichi Konomi
27. LNCS 14037, Distributed, Ambient and Pervasive Interactions: Part II, edited by Norbert Streitz and Shin'ichi Konomi
28. LNCS 14038, HCI in Business, Government and Organizations: Part I, edited by Fiona Fui-Hoon Nah and Keng Siau
29. LNCS 14039, HCI in Business, Government and Organizations: Part II, edited by Fiona Fui-Hoon Nah and Keng Siau
30. LNCS 14040, Learning and Collaboration Technologies: Part I, edited by Panayiotis Zaphiris and Andri Ioannou
31. LNCS 14041, Learning and Collaboration Technologies: Part II, edited by Panayiotis Zaphiris and Andri Ioannou
32. LNCS 14042, Human Aspects of IT for the Aged Population: Part I, edited by Qin Gao and Jia Zhou
33. LNCS 14043, Human Aspects of IT for the Aged Population: Part II, edited by Qin Gao and Jia Zhou
34. LNCS 14044, Adaptive Instructional Systems, edited by Robert A. Sottilare and Jessica Schwarz
35. LNCS 14045, HCI for Cybersecurity, Privacy and Trust, edited by Abbas Moallem
36. LNCS 14046, HCI in Games: Part I, edited by Xiaowen Fang
37. LNCS 14047, HCI in Games: Part II, edited by Xiaowen Fang
38. LNCS 14048, HCI in Mobility, Transport and Automotive Systems: Part I, edited by Heidi Krömker
39. LNCS 14049, HCI in Mobility, Transport and Automotive Systems: Part II, edited by Heidi Krömker
40. LNAI 14050, Artificial Intelligence in HCI: Part I, edited by Helmut Degen and Stavroula Ntoa
41. LNAI 14051, Artificial Intelligence in HCI: Part II, edited by Helmut Degen and Stavroula Ntoa
42. LNCS 14052, Design, Operation and Evaluation of Mobile Communications, edited by Gavriel Salvendy and June Wei
43. CCIS 1832, HCI International 2023 Posters - Part I, edited by Constantine Stephanidis, Margherita Antona, Stavroula Ntoa and Gavriel Salvendy
44. CCIS 1833, HCI International 2023 Posters - Part II, edited by Constantine Stephanidis, Margherita Antona, Stavroula Ntoa and Gavriel Salvendy
45. CCIS 1834, HCI International 2023 Posters - Part III, edited by Constantine Stephanidis, Margherita Antona, Stavroula Ntoa and Gavriel Salvendy
46. CCIS 1835, HCI International 2023 Posters - Part IV, edited by Constantine Stephanidis, Margherita Antona, Stavroula Ntoa and Gavriel Salvendy

47. CCIS 1836, HCI International 2023 Posters - Part V, edited by Constantine Stephanidis, Margherita Antona, Stavroula Ntoa and Gavriel Salvendy

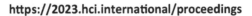

https://2023.hci.international/proceedings

Preface

The 15th International Conference on Social Computing and Social Media (SCSM 2023) was an affiliated conference of the HCI International (HCII) conference. The conference provided an established international forum for the exchange and dissemination of scientific information related to social computing and social media, addressing a broad spectrum of issues expanding our understanding of current and future issues in these areas. The conference welcomed qualitative and quantitative research papers on a diverse range of topics related to the design, development, assessment, use, and impact of social media.

A considerable number of papers focused on presenting advancements and recent developments in online communities and social media, discussing machine learning, artificial intelligence and algorithmic approaches for understanding social interactions, user behavior, as well as language and communication. Acknowledging and embracing cultural diversity in the field, several works focused on exploring cultural diversity and cultural influences in the design of social computing, fostering the design of technologies that are culturally sensitive and inclusive. Furthermore, a theme that emerged pertains to digital transformation in business and industry 4.0, highlighting the role and the importance of social computing to facilitate connectivity, communication, and collaboration, allowing organizations to adapt and remain competitive in the rapidly evolving digital landscape of Industry 4.0. An additional topic that is addressed this year is the prominence of SCSM in understanding consumer behavior, allowing businesses to tailor their marketing strategies, product and service development, and customer experience to address the needs and preferences of their target audience. Another field that can be revolutionized by social computing is that of learning and education, with contributions discussing new avenues for collaboration, knowledge sharing, and interactive learning experiences. Moreover, many papers targeted the topic of social computing for well-being and inclusion, presenting advancements that promote mental health, support individuals with developmental and learning disorders, and enhance rehabilitation efforts. In the health domain, discussions focused on the role of social computing during the pandemic and post-pandemic era. Finally, a significant number of papers elaborated on innovations in the design and evaluation of social computing platforms to create user-centric and socially meaningful digital spaces that enhance communication, collaboration, and information sharing.

Two volumes of the HCII 2023 proceedings are dedicated to this year's edition of the SCSM conference. The first volume focuses on topics related to developments in Online Communities and Social Media, SCSM in multi-cultural contexts, digital transformation in business and Industry 4.0 through Social Computing, as well as consumer behavior in SCSM. The second volume focuses on topics related to Social Computing in learning and education, Social Computing for well-being and inclusion, Social Computing in the pandemic and post-pandemic era, as well as advancements in the design and evaluation of Social Computing platforms.

The papers in these volumes were included for publication after a minimum of two single-blind reviews from the members of the SCSM Program Board or, in some cases, from members of the Program Boards of other affiliated conferences. We would like to thank all of them for their invaluable contribution, support, and efforts.

July 2023

Adela Coman
Simona Vasilache

15th International Conference on Social Computing and Social Media (SCSM 2023)

The full list with the Program Board Chairs and the members of the Program Boards of all thematic areas and affiliated conferences of HCII2023 is available online at:

http://www.hci.international/board-members-2023.php

HCI International 2024 Conference

The 26th International Conference on Human-Computer Interaction, HCI International 2024, will be held jointly with the affiliated conferences at the Washington Hilton Hotel, Washington, DC, USA, June 29 – July 4, 2024. It will cover a broad spectrum of themes related to Human-Computer Interaction, including theoretical issues, methods, tools, processes, and case studies in HCI design, as well as novel interaction techniques, interfaces, and applications. The proceedings will be published by Springer. More information will be made available on the conference website: http://2024.hci.international/.

General Chair
Prof. Constantine Stephanidis
University of Crete and ICS-FORTH
Heraklion, Crete, Greece
Email: general_chair@hcii2024.org

https://2024.hci.international/

Contents – Part I

Contents – Part II

Developments in Online Communities and Social Media

Detecting Public Spaces and Possibilities of Risk Situations in Them via Social Media Data

Aleksandr Antonov(✉), Lyudmila Vidiasova, and Andrei Chugunov

ITMO University, Saint-Petersburg, Russia
{asantonov,lavidiasova,chugunov}@itmo.ru

Abstract. Obtaining feedback from citizens is essential for the efficient and useful functioning of public spaces. The paper examines the case of St. Petersburg, a city with a population of 5.5 million. According to official data, over 2000 requests are received daily from residents to the portal for solving urban problems. The study hypothesized the possibility of using big data arrays to assess the demand and discontent with urban public spaces in St. Petersburg.

The research aim is identifying both the most important spaces and the major risks related to them, via user complaints and messages in social media.

The paper presents a method for identifying public spaces and citizens' reactions on them, as well as predicting social risks associated with those public spaces. The method is based on the application of natural language processing (NLP) methods to text messages of citizens received through feedback channels and official web-sites, and social media. First NLP method is a text classifier based on the pre-trained language model. Here we divide messages into 12 main categories. Then the second method, natural entities recognition combined with the approximate string matching, is used to identify approximate locations of events in messages.

The research was focused on the public spaces of Saint-Petersburg (Russia). The data for calculating the model was compiled by a corpus of more than 70 thousand citizens' appeals from social media communities and e-participation service. Based on the data in citizens' appeals about a specific issue of public agenda, location and any feedback being received, the model identifies points of public activity and assesses the risks associated with each specific object.

The method is based on the development of a classifier of thematic areas, automatic recognition of objects and problematic aspects. Further, the risks associated with public space are identified, and the polarity of users' sentiments to those risks is defined. The research group developed a model using Python and specific libraries. The classifier was developed with use of nltk and spacy libraries. NER method was applied with help of pymorphy2 and spacy. The accuracy metrics for the model are as follows: precision 86, recall 71, F-score 78.

Keywords: e-participation · public spaces · entities recognition · risk detection · social media

A. Coman and S. Vasilache (Eds.): HCII 2023, LNCS 14025, pp. 3–13, 2023.
https://doi.org/10.1007/978-3-031-35915-6_1

1 Introduction

The introduction of the "Government as a Platform" concept in the Russian Federation has stimulated the demand for research and development focused on the use of data by authorities, which can act as indicators of "feedback" and indicate the reaction of citizens to problems arising in various spheres of life. In recent years, in large cities, there has been a tendency for the general penetration of digitization and, as a result, the formation of a digital space for interaction between the population and city authorities. Since 2021, St. Petersburg has been actively implementing the concept of urban digital services ecosystem [5] as a space for the interaction of public and commercial services with residents aimed at developing the digital environment of the city, as well as creating new services based on open data.

This approach is based on the idea that a city can fully meet the needs of citizens only in cooperation with partners and third-party developers. Obtaining feedback from citizens is essential for the efficient and useful functioning of public spaces.

At the same time, citizens' appeals represent a large flow of poorly structured information, which contains important value assessments and judgments. But at the same time, with the ever-increasing volume of such messages, it is not always possible to get to their essence by automated means. In particular, the task of an automatic classifier of messages by topics and objects of the urban environment based on machine learning is quite acute [2].

This paper considers the case of using citizens' appeals as a data source for building a model for the development of urban spaces. The research was aimed at identifying both the most important spaces and the major risks related to them, via user complaints and messages in social media.

2 Literature Review

The research agenda for the analysis of civic e-participation forms is quite broad. Attempts to evaluate e-participation through various channels are being made in international indices. However, their criticism in recent years shows the need for new methods for analyzing data from e-participation platforms, publishing appeals and complaints by citizens [12].

On practice the incoming stream of requests from citizens is essentially a large array of textual data, often poorly structured [6]. Scientists emphasize successful cases of using these citizens' appeals in response to emergency situations, for example, during the COVID-19 pandemic in China [19]. Such use of citizens' appeals is developing within the framework of complain-oriented policy [8].

In another concept, the category of 'lay people' or 'sensing people' is used, which is opposed to the expert community, but can give a lot to the management of the city and specific public spaces [16]. City management is often associated with the assessment and management of risks that may arise in various areas, including urban facilities. According to Van Asselt and Ortwin [17], risk governance is "a translation of the substance and core principles of governance to the context of risk-related decision-making". In relation to urban objects, risk forecasting is not always unambiguous and can be determined by a mathematical function, in view of the large number of stakeholders that have one or another relationship with it, as well as social and cultural aspects [11].

Traditional risk management approaches involve extensive and costly ongoing monitoring, including the use of additional labor [14]. For many years, researchers have used traditional tools (questionnaires, interviews, focus-groups etc.) to study the urban environment and collect people's opinions on this matter.

With the development of Internet technologies and social networks, this need has disappeared and now big data is used for many studies. People use various social media platforms and share opinions and emotions, which helps in revealing the hidden characteristics of urban spaces [18]. And the application of deep learning and natural language processing provide a framework for further analysis of emotional information in social media data [5].

The field of natural language processing originated at universities in the UK and the US back in the mid-1950s [3]. However, since the end of the 20th century, database mining, which can be used in various fields of science, has caused a stir among researchers with the possibility of discovering new knowledge in unstructured text sources.

Computational linguist M. Hearst [7], in his pioneering text mining article "What Is Text Mining?" defines text mining as a search for new information using computer systems by automatically extracting it from various text resources. A key feature of text mining is the machine learning of processed information to form new intellectual results - facts and hypotheses, which can then be analyzed and investigated by more traditional methods.

Text mining is defined as the discovery and extraction of interesting, non-trivial knowledge from free or unstructured text. The application of this method involves a number of processes from directly searching for information, to text classification, subsequent clustering, extraction of entities, relationships and events [13].

Text mining and natural language processing become important where the size of the studied text materials does not allow for manual analysis. Unstructured data created by users of digital platforms every second around the world needs tools and methods that will automatically extract useful information from texts [4]. It is in connection with this that researchers began to apply automatic text analysis systems using artificial intelligence methods for the intellectual analysis of big data, combining achievements in the field of computer science, mathematics, management and other branch sciences [10].

To date, many methods have been developed for analyzing texts. Huang C-Y., Yang C-L. and Hsiao Y-H. [9] write about the use of latent Dirichlet distribution (LDA), 5-point Likert-type scale, random forest algorithm (RF), DEMATEL for the analysis of social networks.

Thus, the analysis of the literature emphasizes the relevance of developing a method for structuring social data and identifying situations on their basis that potentially form a state of risk.

3 Research Methodology

The method is based on the application of natural language processing (NLP) methods to text messages of citizens received through feedback channels and official web-sites, and social media. First NLP method is a cascade of classifiers based on the pre-trained language model. Here we divide messages into main categories and functional subcategories. Then the second method, natural entities recognition, is used to identify approximate locations of events in messages.

The research was focused on the public spaces of Saint-Petersburg (Russia). For the model development and experimentation, we used 2 datasets correspondingly:

1. Datasets of citizens' appeals and messages from social media and e-participation data portal containing 71 thousand records for the period of 30.12.2021–23.02.2022.
2. Dataset of citizens' messages from social media in one district of Saint-Petersburg containing 18168 records for the period of 05.06.2017–25.01.2023.

The dataset structure includes submitted messages with their attributes. This parameter set contains the following characteristics:

- Date of creation
- Text
- Block
- Location (district)
- Address of the object
- Streets of the facility

The classification includes 767 combinations divided into the following columns:

- Block
- An object
- Parameter
- Aspect
- Message subject
- Topic for the report
- Objects of Risk
- Risk processes

The classification includes such blocks as urban land improvement, roads, housing and communal services, health care, education, social protection, construction, waste disposal, transport, environment protection, energy and safety.

To classify messages into categories, we used the pre-labeled set described earlier. It was first preprocessed with the re python regex package. Punctuation signs, hashtags, duplicate spaces were separated. Next, a list of stop words in Russian language was loaded from the nltk library, and the words were also filtered from the texts.

In this work, the spacy-ru model [20] was used as the initial language model for training, as well as for lemmatization and morphological analysis. With this approach words related to nouns, adjectives, verbs and adverbs were highlighted and lemmatized. These sets formed the basis for further model training.

For training, the categories attribute was converted into separate attributes using the one-hot encoding procedure. The resulting set of text and the corresponding vector was randomized and divided into a training set, which is 0.9 from the original, and a test set, which is 0.1 from the original. A similar ratio is widely used in training with a limited amount of data. Training was performed with batches size equal to 32 and dropout rate = 0.2. The resulting model has the following accuracy characteristics by category, presented in Table 1.

Table 1. Model characteristics.

Category	Precision	Recall	F-score
Security	0.90	0.79	0.84
Urban land improvement	0.84	0.75	0.79
Roads	0.75	0.66	0.71
Housing and communal services	0.71	0.66	0.69
Healthcare	0.94	0.82	0.88
Education	0.94	0.79	0.86
Social protection	0.97	0.79	0.87
Construction	0.60	0.48	0.53
Waste disposal	1.00	0.61	0.76
Transport	0.91	0.88	0.90
Environmental protection	1.00	0.75	0.86
Energy	0.75	0.56	0.64
Average accuracy	**0.86**	**0.71**	**0.78**

It should be noted that the low accuracy for some categories may be described due to the similarity of some topics within them. So, for example, the energy category can often overlap with housing and communal services.

With the help of this step, we can identify problematic areas and spheres in the the city. Next, it is necessary to identify the location of the phenomena described in the messages. The spacy library was used for this task. Based on the addresses specified in the pre-allocated data, a language model was trained from scratch at 100 iterations to determine the NER, in this case, the streets. The text was not preprocessed for this step. The resulting model has the following characteristics: 0.65 precision, 0.67 recall, 0.66 F-score.

Next, we compared the street names obtained using this model with the official names downloaded from the open data service OpenStreetMaps. With this mapping, each post that mentions a location was assigned a linear geometry. Thus, after two steps of processing unstructured social data, it is possible to obtain appeals that have functional, spatial and temporal characteristics. On their basis we studied the dynamics of situations both in time and space, and to determine the risks that form as a result of these situations.

Based on the data in citizens' appeals about a specific issue of public agenda, location and any feedback being received, the model identifies points of public activity and assesses the risks associated with each specific object.

The method is based on the development of a classifier of thematic areas, automatic recognition of objects and problematic aspects. Further, the risks associated with public space are identified, and the polarity of users' sentiments to those risks is defined.

4 Results

For the experiment, a set of comments from the social network VK from the official group of the Admiralteisky district (Saint Petersburg, Russia) was used. Such groups are often used by residents as a platform for appealing to the authorities on various issues. The initial volume of messages was 18250 records from June 05, 2017 to January 25, 2023.

Next, the texts of the addresses were preprocessed: stop words were removed from the list of Russian stop words nltk, punctuation marks. The remaining words were lemmatized and presented in lower case. The resulting set of texts was classified using a pre-trained spacy model. Those texts that could not be assigned to any category with a probability greater than 0.6 were removed from the set, reducing it to 18168 hits. The distribution of calls by category at this moment is shown in Fig. 1.

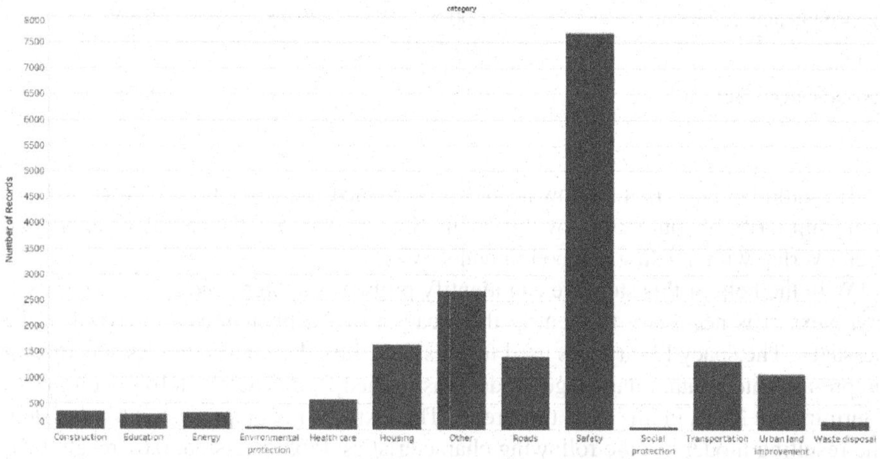

Fig. 1. Distribution of calls by categories in dataset after the classification.

Next, the geolocation algorithm was applied to the resulting set: first, toponyms were identified from the texts using a pretrained NER model. Messages without defined toponyms, as well as with incorrectly defined ones (the result length was more than 5 words) were filtered out. As a result, the set was reduced to 3845 entries. Then, using the method of fuzzy name matching for each toponym in circulation, geometries taken from OpenStreetMaps were added. Thus also filtering out some messages with toponyms that were not found in the city's address system (2727 messages). Moreover, if several places were mentioned in one appeal, it was duplicated for each of them. So the total amount of data was 16293 records.

The distribution of messages by the most popular toponyms is shown in Fig. 2 (map and diagram together). Based on certain functional and spatial characteristics, as well as initially available temporal characteristics, the data outliers in distributions were identified. The following are cases with spatial outliers and temporal dynamics. The spatial distribution of messages is displayed on the map in Fig. 2

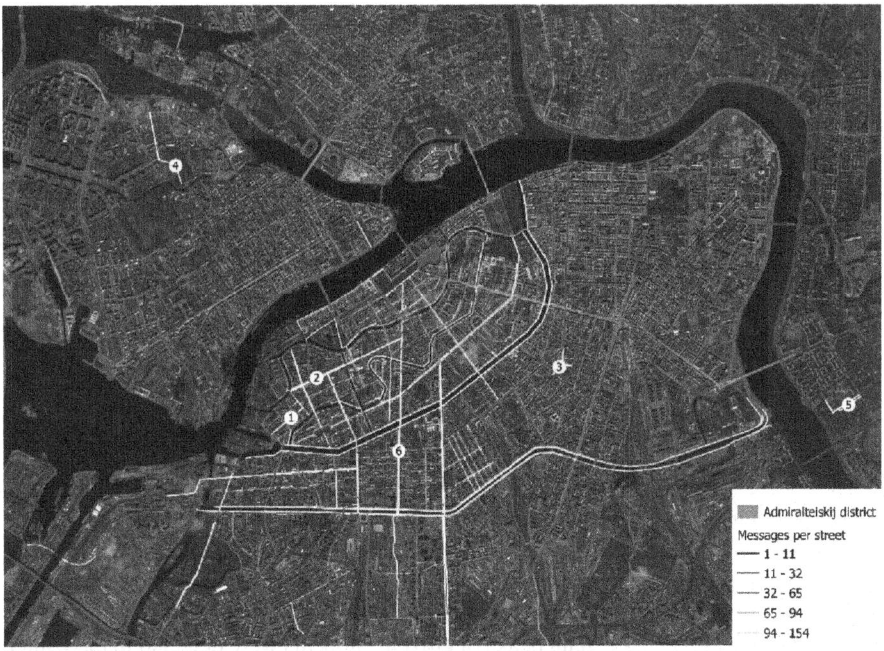

Fig. 2. Map of Admiralteisky district with geolocated messages grouped by streets.

Here, the gradient shows the number of mentions of streets in messages from the Admiralteisky district administration group. Based on the visual assessment, we can say that the algorithm correctly highlights the geolocation of messages. At the same time, outliers in the data corresponding to such locations as Pskovskaya street, Dekabristov Street, Bolshaya Moskovskaya street, Dekabristov lane, Rizhskaya Street, Rizhsky Avenue. The presence in this list of Bolshaya Moskovskaya Street, Dekabristov Lane and Rizhskaya Street can be explained by the lack of algorithm, where, due to the weakly formalized wording of the toponym in the message ("fix the sidewalk on Dekabristov", "the pipe burst on Bolshaya"), the message can be attributed to both one and the other street.

From the point of view of the functional distribution of messages on these streets (shown in Fig. 3), some problems specific to them were be identified.

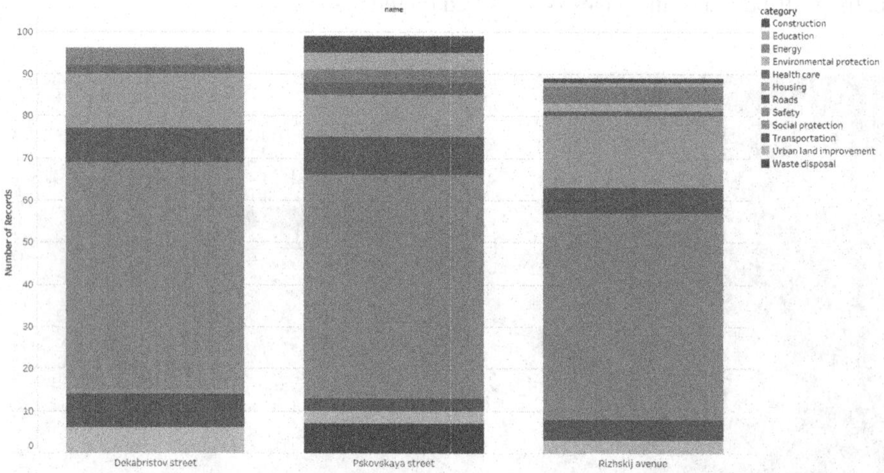

Fig. 3. Distribution of messages in categories for three streets of case study.

So, for example, only on Pskovskaya Street there are problems with the processing of municipal waste. The citizens from Dekabristov Street did not encounter any problems in the field of education and construction.

Also we identified the trends in the temporal distribution of appeals. For several years, on all three streets, the main peaks of citizens' appeals were detected in the winter months, related to the security sector (Fig. 4). This can be explained by a large flow of complaints about low indoor temperatures.

This distribution is also consistent with the general dynamics of messages in the Admiralteisky district, which is shown in Fig. 5.

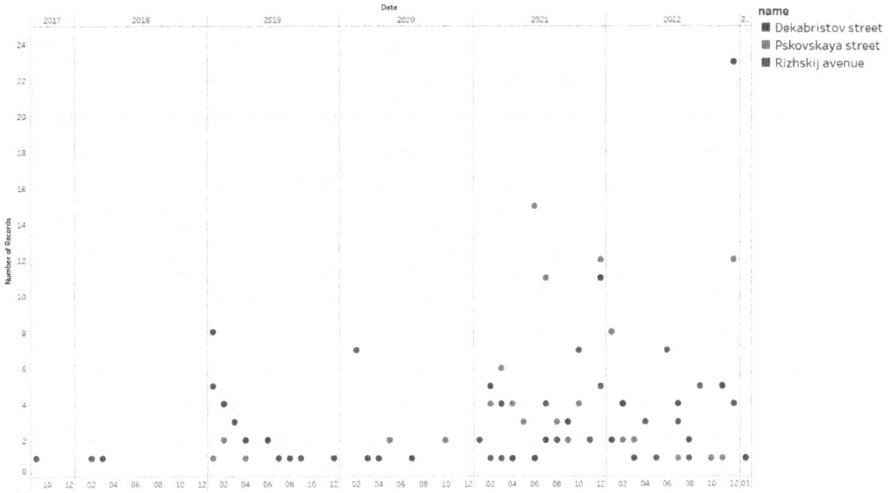

Fig. 4. Temporal distribution of messages per month for three streets of case study.

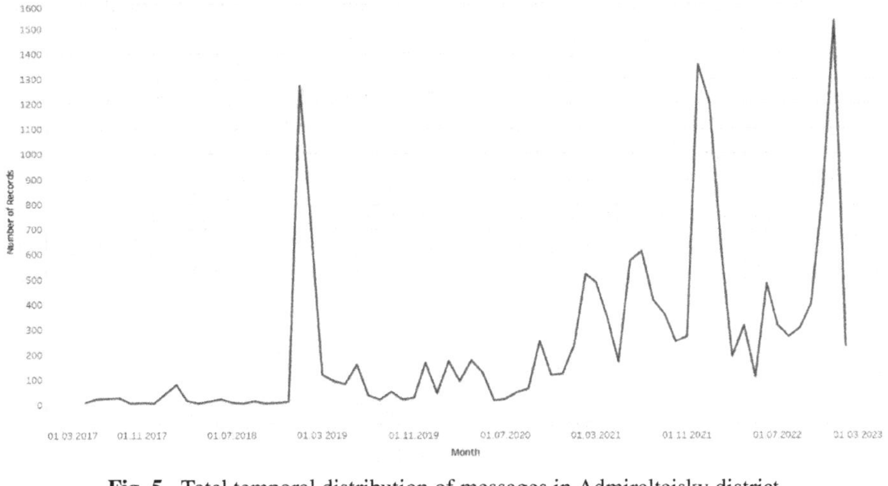

Fig. 5. Total temporal distribution of messages in Admiralteisky district.

5 Discussion and Conclusion

The proposed method of structuring social data and identifying on their basis situations that form a state of risk makes it possible to study the subjective assessment of the quality of city services in a historical perspective. Also the proposed method helps to quickly obtain structured information about emerging problems that need to be addressed.

However, in the current version, the algorithm has some limitations. At this stage of the study, it is difficult to accurately determine the address on the basis of one appeal text in the case of similar place names. In addition, there are difficulties with the definition of narrower topics of appeals. These questions will form the basis of further research.

At the present stage of digitalization of state and municipal government, the issue of forming a data-based decision-making system using big data technologies and artificial intelligence is one of the most relevant.

The results of the study open up prospects for the development of a risk model for public facilities. Within the framework of the model, risk detection is possible through the detection of citizens' appeals to determine those objects, the situation on which can lead to potentially risky social situations. Above all, this model is important for objects of socially significant infrastructure (schools, clinics, stadiums, playgrounds, etc.). The method presented in the article will allow you to quickly process large data arrays for the model development.

The development of a risk model based on citizens' appeals is of particular interest for research project "Institutional Transformation of E-Participation Governance in Russia: a Study of Regional Peculiarities", because the authorities are mastering new electronic channels of interaction with citizens and groups of activists. At the same time, the thematic content of e-participation channels is steadily shifting from socio-political discourse to appeals on the quality of the living environment, including public spaces. It is planned to receive answers to these questions in the context of specific e-participation channels (including existing and new, active and passive, state and civil initiatives). This will provide detailed information about the factors and effects of electronic interaction between the authorities and citizens.

Acknowledgements. The study was supported by the Russian Science Foundation, project No. 22–18-00364 "Institutional Transformation of E-Participation Governance in Russia: a Study of Regional Peculiarities" (https://rscf.ru/project/22-18-00364/) and project No. 622264 «Development of a service for identifying objects of the urban environment of social activity and high-risk situations based on text messages from citizens» (ITMO University research project).

The data collection and processing, the model development were employed in terms of the project No. 622264, the article concept and theoretical review – the project No. 22-18-00364.

References

1. Antonov, A.: Anomalies in feedback: detection of hidden events in dynamics of cite service complaint reporting. Procedia Comput. Sci. (2022)
2. Begen, P., Chugunov, A.: Intellectual classifier development of citizens' messages on the "Our St. Petersburg" portal: Experience in using machine learning methods. In: CEUR Workshop Proceedings : SSI 2019 - Proceedings of the 21st Conference on Scientific Services and Internet, Novorossiysk-Abrau, vol. 2543, pp. 82–92 (2020)
3. Dale, R.: Classical approaches to natural language processing. In: Indurkhya, N., Damerau, F.J. (eds.) Handbook of Natural Language Processing, 2nd edn. Chapman and Hall/CRC (2010). https://doi.org/10.1201/9781420085938
4. Fan, W., Wallace, L., Rich, S., Zhang, Z.: Tapping the power of text mining. Commun. ACM, 76–82 (2006)
5. Frias-Martinez, V., Frias-Martinez, E.: Spectral clustering for sensing urban land use using Twitter activity. Eng. Appl. Artif. Intell. **35**, 237–245 (2014)
6. Göbel, C., Li, J.: From bulletin boards to big data: the origins and evolution of public complaint websites in China. J. Curr. Chin. Aff. **50**(1), 39–62 (2021). https://doi.org/10.1177/1868102621992144

7. Hearst, M.: What Is Text Mining? (2003). https://people.ischool.berkeley.edu/~hearst/text-mining.html
8. Herring, C.: Complaint-Oriented policing: regulation homelessness in public space. Am. Sociol. Rev., 1–32 (2019)
9. Huang, C.-Y., Yang, C.-L., Hsiao, Y.-H.: A novel framework for mining social media data based on text mining, topic modeling, random forest, and DANP methods. Mathematics **9**(17), 2041 (2021). https://doi.org/10.3390/math9172041
10. Humphreys, A., Wang, R.J.: Automated text analysis for consumer research. J. Consum. Res. **44**(6), 1274–1306 (2018)
11. Johnson, B., Covello, V.: The social and cultural construction of risk. Essays on Risk Selection and perception. Technol. Risk Soc. **3** (1987)
12. Kabanov, Y.: Refining the UN E-participation Index: introducing the deliberative assessment using the varieties of democracy data. Gov. Inf. Q. **39**(1), 101646 (2022). https://doi.org/10.1016/j.giq.2021.101656
13. Kao, A., Poteet, S.R.: Natural Language Processing and Text Mining. Springer, London (2006). https://doi.org/10.1007/978-1-84628-754-1
14. Mead, M., et al.: The use of eletrochemical sensors for monitoring urban air quality in lowcost, high-density netwroks. Atmos. Environ. **70**, 186–203 (2013)
15. Sirakaya, A., Cliquet, A., Harris, J.: Ecosystem services in cities: towards the international legal protection of ecosystem services in urban environments. Ecosyst. Serv. **29**, 205–212 (2018). https://doi.org/10.1016/j.ecoser.2017.01.001
16. Suman, A,B.: Challenging risk governance patterns through citizen sensing: the Schiphol airport case. Int. Rev. Law **32** (1), 155–173 (2018)
17. Van Asselt, M., Ortwin, R.: Risk governance. J. Risk Res. **14**(4), 431–449 (2011)
18. Yang, L., Wu, L., Liu, Y., Kang, C.: Quantifying tourist behavior patterns by travel motifs and geo-tagged photos from flickr. ISPRS Int. J. Geo-Inf. **6**, 345 (2017)
19. Zhang, W., Yuan, H., Zhu, C., Chen, Q., Evans, R.: Does citizen engagement with government social media accounts differ during the different stages of public health crises? An empirical examination of the COVID-19 pandemic. Front Public Health **10**, 807459 (2022). https://doi.org/10.3389/fpubh.2022.807459
20. Russian language model for spacy library (2021). https://github.com/buriy/spacy-ru

Exploring the Anonymity of Social Media Users Using Micro-messages

Sarp Aykent(✉) and Cheryl Seals

Auburn University, Auburn, AL 36830, USA
{sarp,sealscd}@auburn.edu

Abstract. The widespread use of social media and social networking sites has transformed how people communicate. As a result, micro-messages exchanged daily by people increased drastically. The micro-messages, which limit the number of characters, are a unique way of communication. Social media users communicate publicly or privately using micro-messages. Also, social media users can use pseudo-identities to stay anonymous. The identity of the user can be revealed using author identification systems with their social media posts. The length limitation of the micro-messages introduces novel problems for author identification systems. In this work, we investigate the performance of author identification systems on micro-messages with extensive experiments. Our results demonstrate the capabilities of the author identifiers under various real-world scenarios.

Keywords: Author Identification · Social Media · Anonymity

1 Introduction

The Author Identification task identifies an author from their writing samples. The ability to automatically identify the authors has broad application areas in social networks, both by users and the platforms, thus attracting much interest. One of such usages is identifying undesirable actors such as cyber bullies, cybercriminals, and actors trying to spread fake news. Such actors can be flagged before committing a crime or any other adversarial effect by identifying potential actors in the early stage. To this extent, it is crucial to study the capability of the Author Identification systems to detect potential toxic actors.

While micro-messages are an effective way of communication, they introduce several new challenges for author identification: (1) The limited number of characters can affect the word choice with shorter ones, usage of emoji, or shortening the words by removing some characters. It is very challenging for machine learning models that use words to identify the author since those micro messages are not composed of ordinary words. (2) Unlike long texts such as news articles, the topics frequently change between posts. Using different topics makes it harder to track users based on the topics of the micro-messages [1]. (3) Multiple factors can

A. Coman and S. Vasilache (Eds.): HCII 2023, LNCS 14025, pp. 14–24, 2023.
https://doi.org/10.1007/978-3-031-35915-6_2

affect the author's writing style, including psychological and environmental factors. These factors cannot be directly observed since author identifiers can only observe the writing samples. Some of the psychological factors include the state of mind, happiness, and tiredness of the author at the time of writing. These signals can introduce a noise that will mislead the machine learning models to differentiate stylistic behaviors.

Social networks are hard to moderate because of their large size and unique properties. One such property is that one person can have multiple identities by creating multiple social media accounts under different handles. The same user with multiple handles introduces noise to the system because writing samples provided from different accounts are recognized as different users. The system will be penalized for predicting the wrong identity even though it might predict the correct identity that controls both accounts. Furthermore, some social media handles are controlled using automated software, also known as bots [2,3]. The bots can follow simple rules and phrases or can have more complex sets of rules for posting micro-messages. They introduce noise to author identifiers as detecting the writing style of bots does not generalize well to the rest of the users.

There are several works available on the Author Identification task of micro-messages [4–8]. However, none of those mentioned earlier works explore the performance of author identification systems under various conditions to fully understand their capabilities under real-world scenarios. In this work, we conducted experiments to answer the following question: "How confidently can we Identify an author on social media with X number of posts?". For this purpose, we perform a series of experiments under various conditions concerning the size of the system and the number of writing samples available from each user.

We use a real-world dataset from Twitter to test the model and compare how likely the identities can be identified under different conditions. Our experimental results show exciting findings that increasing the number of authors sometimes helps the author identifiers when the number of writing samples is limited. However, as expected, when we have more writing samples from the authors, the performance of the author identifiers increases, and we can make confident predictions when there are more than fifty writing samples from the same author. This work answers the question of how anonymous social media identities are and how likely these identities can be tracked under different handles. We believe these findings are essential foundations for understanding the applicability of the performant Author Identification systems we demonstrated in [6,7]. These insights are important for future research in how robust the author identification models are and directly impact topics such as identifying cybercriminals.

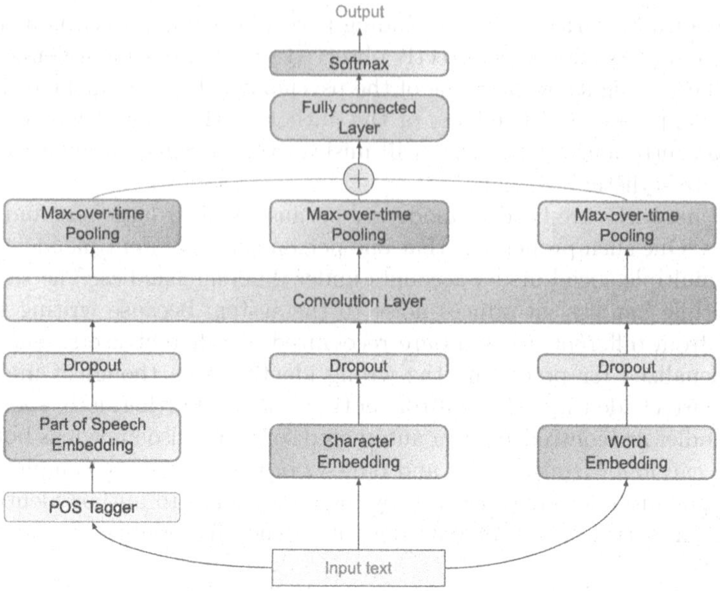

Fig. 1. AARef architecture diagram [6]. The input text are processed to three representations. The feature maps are calculated with shared convolutional layers and the salient features over the sequence are selected using max-over-time pooling operation. The output of the network predict the author using the final feature maps.

2 Method

To investigate the anonymity of social media users, we adapted the AARef framework [6]. The Fig. 1 illustrates the AARef framework. Various representations, including character, word, and part of speech tags, are processed through a convolutional neural network. The weights for convolutional layers are shared with all the representations. Therefore, the same weights are applied to different representations. By sharing the weights for different representations, the complexity increases are minimized. The most salient features are extracted per representation layer by max-over-time pooling. This pooling operation picks the highest value over the spatial dimension. Hence, the maximum score per writing sample is selected for each filter. The most salient features are fed to the prediction head. The prediction head is a multi-layer perceptron with a softmax activation function to predict the author of a given writing sample.

3 Experiments

In this section, experimental configurations are presented, which were designed to assess the impact of varying the number of authors and writing samples on the performance of our model. A series of experiments were conducted based on the results of the first experiment. We followed the preprocessing steps outlined in previous work [6] in all subsets. We replaced the numbers, username references, date, time, and website URLs with pre-defined meta tags. To maximize the ability to capture stylistic features from the tweets, we did not convert the text into lowercase to keep the case information. This is preferred to capture the way users capitalize certain words.

3.1 Experiment I: Varying Number of Authors and Writing Samples

In the first experiment, the parameters used in the experiments were the number of authors and the number of writing samples per author. We conducted experiments with the following parameters 10, 20, 50, 100, 200, 500, and 1,000 for all pairs of writing samples and authors. Each pair of the number of writing samples and the number of authors are evaluated with a 10-fold crossover. Therefore, each pair is trained ten times to be evaluated against a distinct test set. There are seven possible values for both parameters. Therefore, there are 49 configurations to experiment with. Hence, we experimented on 490 different subsets. The models are trained from scratch without any pretraining on the Author Identification task.

3.2 Experiment II: Varying Number of Authors and Writing Samples with AARef+

In the second experiment, we used the same range of combinations of the number of authors and writing samples as in the first experiment, but with the addition of a pretraining step using a pretraining dataset. The pretraining dataset was tested with two variations. The first variation has 1,000 authors with 1,000 writing samples per author and is denoted as AARef+_{1000}. The second variation has 2,000 authors with 1,000 writing samples per author and is denoted as AARef+_{2000}. The model was first trained on the pretraining dataset and then fine-tuned on the evaluation dataset.

3.3 Experiment III: Evaluation of AARef+

In the third experiment, the pretrained approaches, AARef+_{1000} and AARef+_{2000}, were evaluated on the varying number of authors and a varying number of writing samples from previous works [6, 7]. This experiment also compared the pretrained approaches with previous results and baselines.

3.4 Dataset

The Twitter dataset [4] is a collection of public tweets. This dataset is used in several micro-message research concerning author identification [4–7]. The dataset has two groups of subsets. These subsets include authors with at least 200 and

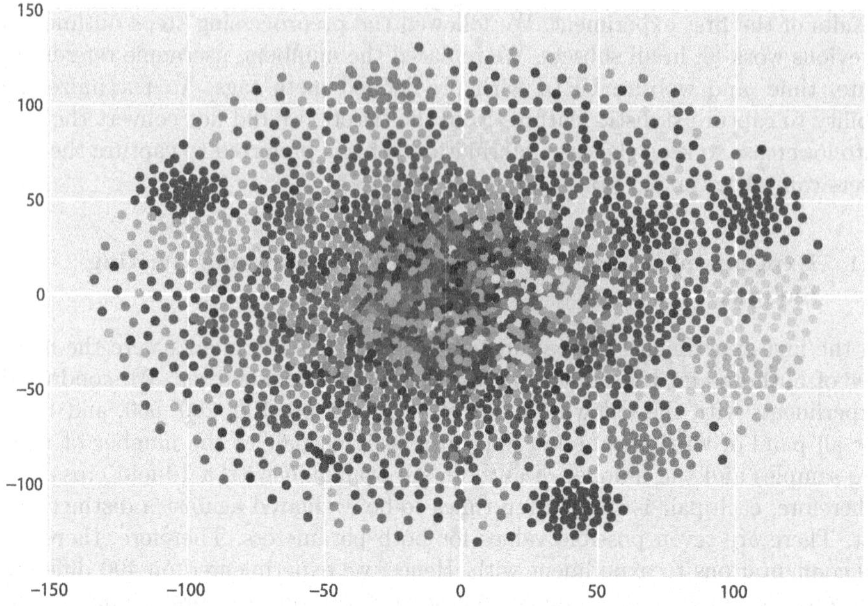

Fig. 2. t-SNE plot of 50 authors with 50 writing samples per author randomly sampled from the Twitter dataset. (Color figure online)

1,000 writing samples, respectively. Furthermore, The first subset contains a larger number of authors with fewer writing samples. It allows us to experiment on a dataset with a larger number of authors. Figure 2 shows the visualization of the dataset. As seen in the figure, some writing samples form clusters. For example, writing samples from authors on the right side of Fig. 2 with yellow, purple, dark green, and light blue are clustered together. This clustering is an indication of highly similar writing samples. The bots that post automated messages have similar properties since they tend to follow the same structure.

4 Results

4.1 Results of Experiment I: Varying Number of Authors and Writing Samples

Figure 3 displays the performance of AARef under different numbers of writing samples and authors. Table 3 provides further details. The first column lists the number of authors used in the experiment, and the remaining columns list the number of writing samples per author.

In the smallest setting of writing samples per author, AARef was unable to predict the authors confidently. However, accuracy increases with the number of authors when there are ten writing samples per author. This is not the case for the other writing sample per author conditions, where accuracy decreases

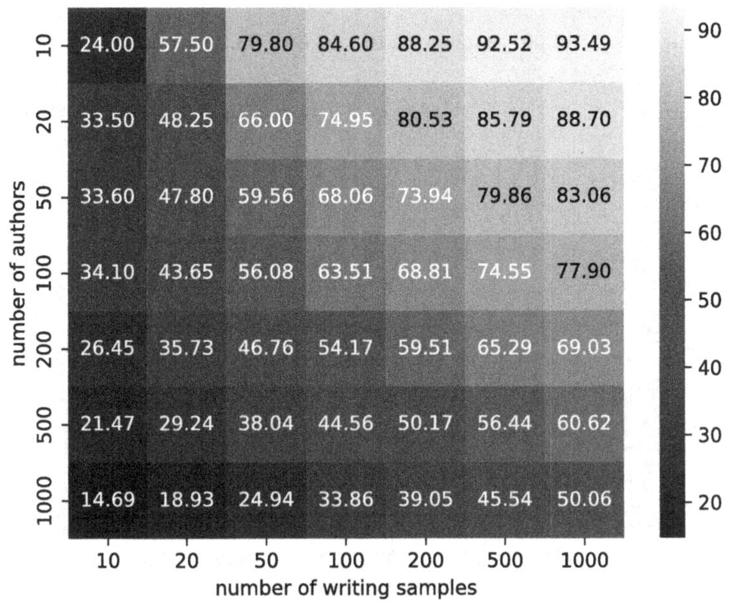

Fig. 3. Performance evaluation with varying authors and writing samples. The heatmap illustrates the performance of the author identification system with micro-messages. Each cell shows the average accuracy of ten distinct test sets. The performances are shown for Author Identification methods with varying pairs of several writing samples and the number of authors.

with the number of authors. This suggests that AARef cannot gather sufficient information about the environment in these conditions. Additionally, the performance of ten writing samples per author highly depends on the random sampling of authors and writing samples. Once the number of writing samples per author increases, AARef can achieve more than 90% accuracy. The performance improvement with large writing samples also indicates that AARef can scale with larger writing samples.

4.2 Results of Experiment II: Varying Number of Authors and Writing Samples with AARef+

In Fig. 4, the performance of $AARef+_{1000}$ is illustrated similarly to the performance illustration of AARef in Fig. 3. The heatmap plot shows the accuracy of the number of authors and the number of writing sample pairs. It is straightforward to see the performance of $AARef+_{1000}$ significantly improved on smaller subsets over AARef. For example, on the smallest subset with ten authors and ten writing samples per author accuracy of AARef increased from 24% to 71% with $AARef+_{1000}$, suggesting a 195% increase in performance. Although this is the extreme case with minimal training data, it shows how well AARef+ can perform in environments with low data availability.

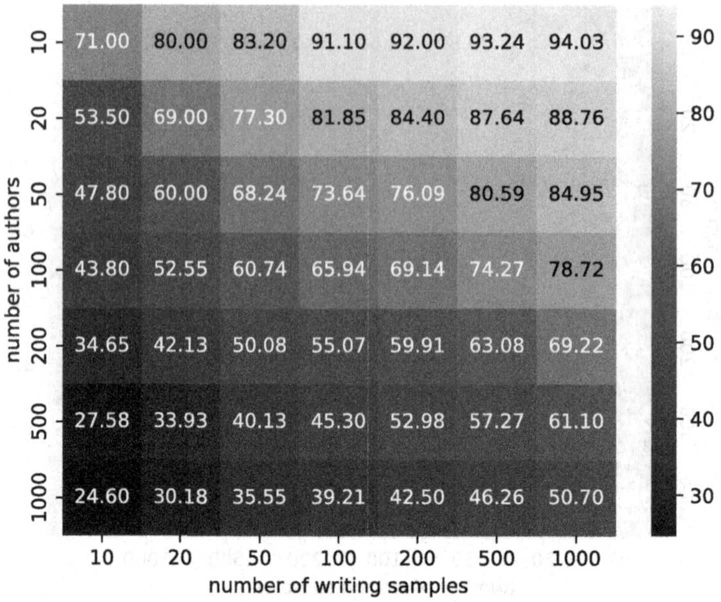

Fig. 4. Evaluation of AARef+$_{1000}$ with the varying number of authors and writing samples. The heatmap plot illustrates the performance of Author Identification methods with varying pairs of the number of writing samples and number of authors.

Table 1. Performance evaluation of AARef+$_{1000}$ with the varying number of authors and writing samples on the Twitter dataset. The table shows the average and standard deviation (±) of the accuracy. The columns represent the number of writing samples per author. The first values in the rows represent the number of authors.

a\w	10	20	50	100	200	500	1,000
10	71.00 ± 7.0	80.00 ± 8.4	83.20 ± 5.1	91.10 ± 2.0	92.00 ± 1.9	93.24 ± 0.6	94.03 ± 0.5
20	53.50 ± 9.9	69.00 ± 4.6	77.30 ± 4.7	81.85 ± 2.1	84.40 ± 1.5	87.64 ± 0.8	88.76 ± 0.8
50	47.80 ± 6.2	60.00 ± 4.7	68.24 ± 2.8	73.64 ± 1.3	76.09 ± 1.1	80.59 ± 0.7	84.95 ± 0.6
100	43.80 ± 3.3	52.55 ± 1.7	60.74 ± 1.2	65.94 ± 0.8	69.14 ± 1.1	74.27 ± 0.5	78.72 ± 0.4
200	34.65 ± 2.2	42.13 ± 2.7	50.08 ± 1.5	55.07 ± 0.8	58.73 ± 0.8	63.08 ± 0.5	69.22 ± 0.2
500	27.58 ± 1.3	33.93 ± 1.4	40.13 ± 0.7	45.30 ± 0.3	52.98 ± 0.3	57.27 ± 0.2	61.10 ± 0.2
1,000	24.60 ± 0.7	30.18 ± 0.5	35.55 ± 0.5	39.21 ± 0.4	42.50 ± 0.3	46.26 ± 0.3	50.70 ± 0.2

Since the performance improvement of AARef+$_{1000}$ is promising, we explored the performance of the larger pretraining sets. For this purpose, 1,000 more authors were sampled from the Twitter dataset. Therefore, AARef+$_{2000}$ trained with a total of 2,000 authors with 1,000 writing samples per author. Table 2 shows the average accuracy and standard deviation of AARef+$_{2000}$. For comparison Table 1 shows the average accuracy and standard deviation of AARef+$_{1000}$. The difference between the two models is marginal, especially on larger subsets. For

Table 2. Performance evaluation of AARef+$_{2000}$ with the varying number of authors and writing samples on the Twitter dataset. The table shows the average and standard deviation ($\pm$) of the accuracy. The columns represent the number of writing samples per author. The first values in the rows represent the number of authors.

a\w	10	20	50	100	200	500	1,000
10	68.00 ± 9.7	78.00 ± 9.3	86.60 ± 3.6	89.60 ± 2.5	91.95 ± 1.0	93.48 ± 0.6	94.16 ± 0.6
20	57.50 ± 6.8	69.00 ± 9.6	76.80 ± 4.2	81.65 ± 2.3	84.57 ± 1.2	88.02 ± 0.7	89.41 ± 0.7
50	47.60 ± 4.7	58.50 ± 4.2	69.00 ± 2.5	73.98 ± 1.0	76.74 ± 0.9	80.75 ± 0.6	82.36 ± 0.4
100	43.60 ± 4.5	52.05 ± 2.6	61.96 ± 2.0	66.71 ± 1.4	70.39 ± 1.3	74.17 ± 0.4	79.31 ± 0.3
200	34.50 ± 3.1	42.10 ± 2.4	52.05 ± 1.5	56.38 ± 0.7	59.57 ± 0.8	63.61 ± 0.4	68.14 ± 0.3
500	27.20 ± 1.3	34.36 ± 1.4	41.05 ± 0.9	45.08 ± 0.4	50.60 ± 0.3	57.53 ± 0.2	61.00 ± 0.2
1000	24.94 ± 0.8	30.76 ± 0.6	36.48 ± 0.6	39.92 ± 0.5	42.95 ± 0.4	46.52 ± 0.1	49.75 ± 0.2

example, on 1,000 authors with 1,000 writing samples per author AARef+$_{1000}$ outperforms AARef+$_{2000}$ by less than 2%. On the smaller subsets, the best performer change between experiments. The smallest subset with ten authors and ten writing samples AARef+$_{1000}$ outperforms AARef+$_{2000}$. However, with 20 authors and ten writing samples AARef+$_{2000}$ outperforms AARef+$_{1000}$. The comparable performance of AARef+$_{1000}$ and AARef+$_{2000}$ suggests that 1,000 are sufficient on these experimental configurations to pretrain the AARef+ with identical settings.

4.3 Results of Experiment III: Evaluation of AARef+

Table 3 shows the performance of approaches with varying the number of authors. In Table 3, the first column lists the algorithm used in the experiment, where the baseline methods are listed above the double lines, and our proposed method is listed below the double lines. The rest of the columns list the accuracies of the algorithms with 100, 200, 500, and 1,000 authors, respectively. The number in bold marks the highest accuracy in each column.

The variations of the pretrained model AARef+$_{1000}$ and AARef+$_{2000}$ outperformed AARef on the varying number of authors experiment. The best performing model was AARef+$_{2000}$ which improved the performance of AARef+$_{1000}$. The performance improvement is larger on smaller subsets, and this supports the argument that the model requires sufficient task-related data to perform its' best. For example, the improvement of AARef+$_{2000}$ on 100 authors over AARef is 5%, while an improvement on 200 authors is less than 3.1%. Furthermore, the improvement of AARef+$_{2000}$ on 500 authors over AARef is 1.8%, while an improvement on 1,000 authors is less than 1%.

Table 4 shows the performance comparison with varying the number of writing samples. In Table 4, the first column lists the algorithm used in the experiment, where the baseline methods are listed above the double lines, and our proposed method is listed below the double lines. The asterisk denotes the statistical significance between a given AARef+ variation and AARef. The rest of

Table 3. Performance of the algorithms with the varying number of authors.

Algorithms	Authors			
	100	200	500	1,000
CNN$_{Char1}$ [5]	49.24%	47.68%	41.37%	35.60%
CNN$_{Char2}$ [5]	49.96%	48.84%	42.92%	37.55%
CNN$_{W2V}$	47.21%	45.52%	39.85%	34.73%
CNN$_{FastText}$	51.83%	50.25%	44.18%	38.74%
CNN$_{WC}$ [7]	55.20%	53.14%	46.90%	41.28%
Rocha et al. [9]	43.99%	42.32%	36.63%	31.61%
k-signatures [4]	42.50%	41.10%	35.50%	30.30%
AARef [6]	57.18%	55.31%	47.99%	42.83%
AARef+$_{1000}$	59.92%	56.57%	48.52%	42.89
AARef+$_{2000}$	**60.32%**	**57.02%**	**48.89%**	**42.91**

Table 4. Performances of the algorithms with the varying number of writing samples.

Algorithms	Writing Samples			
	50	100	200	500
CNN$_{Char1}$ [5]	51.40%	58.20%	64.07%	70.30%
CNN$_{Char2}$ [5]	51.56%	58.25%	63.59%	69.80%
CNN$_{W2V}$	49.14%	56.68%	62.96%	69.70%
CNN$_{FastText}$	51.46%	59.14%	65.61%	72.46%
CNN$_{WC}$ [7]	54.36%	62.17%	68.34%	74.50%
Rocha et al. [9]	42.88%	49.90%	57.43%	66.71%
Theóphilo et al. [10]	30.20%	38.32%	45.53%	56.00%
AARef [6]	56.10%	63.51%	70.05%	76.04
AARef+$_{1000}$	61.87%*	67.37%*	71.45%	76.12
AARef+$_{2000}$	**62.19%***	**68.36%***	**72.31%***	**76.19**

the columns list the accuracies of the algorithms with 100, 200, 500, and 1,000 authors, respectively. The number in bold marks the highest accuracy in each column.

The variations of the pretrained model AARef+$_{1000}$ and AARef+$_{2000}$ outperformed AARef AARef on the varying number of writing samples experiment. The best performing model was AARef+$_{2000}$ which improved the performance of AARef+$_{1000}$. The performance improvement is larger on smaller subsets, and this supports the argument that the model requires sufficient task-related data to perform its' best. For example, the improvement of AARef+$_{2000}$ on 100 authors over AARef is 9.7%, while an improvement on 200 authors is around 7.6%. Furthermore, the improvement of AARef+$_{2000}$ on 500 authors over AARef is 3.2%, while an improvement on 1,000 authors is less than 1%.

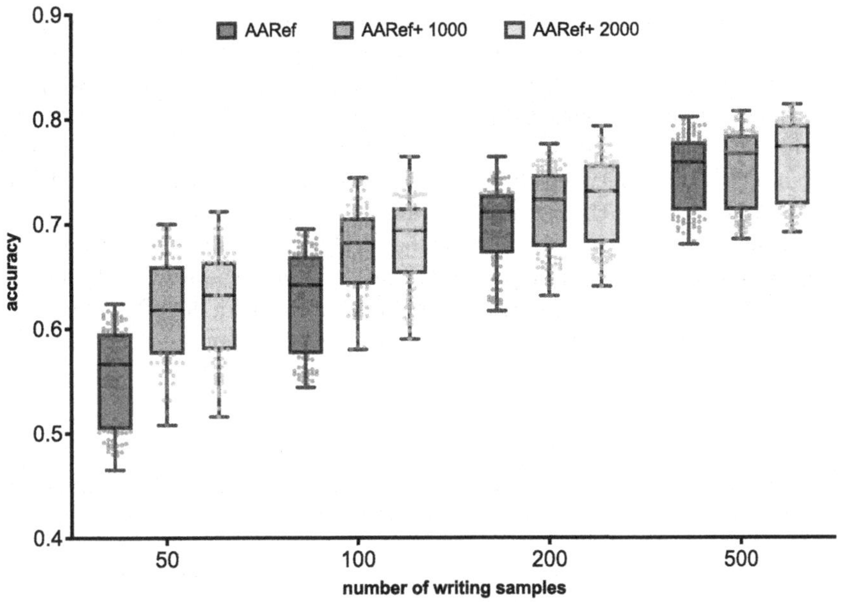

Fig. 5. Performance visualization of AARef variations on the varying number of writing authors experiment. Each box plot is visualized by aggregating the 100 runs. Each point denotes the accuracy of a single experiment. The bottom and top of the box represent the first and third quartiles, respectively, and the line within the box represents the median. The whiskers extending from the box indicate the range of the data.

In Fig. 5 the performances of the proposed approaches AARef, AARef+$_{1000}$, and AARef+$_{2000}$ are further compared. For each subset, and each variation, ten distinct groups with ten splits. Therefore, each box visualizes the accuracy of 100 runs.

To test the statistical significance of the performance improvement of AARef+$_{1000}$ and AARef+$_{2000}$ over AARef, two independent Student's t-test is conducted. AARef+$_{1000}$ significantly outperforms AARef on subsets with 50 and 100 writing samples. AARef+$_{1000}$ significantly outperforms AARef on subsets with 50, 100, and 200 writing samples.

5 Conclusion

In this work, we investigated the anonymity of social media users using their writing styles. Our results show the capability of existing author identification systems under various conditions. Based on our findings, social media users and social media networks can use adversarial users' identities to avoid undesirable behaviors. Our findings provide a guideline for the anonymity of users based on their social media usage. The identities of social media users with more than 1,000 writing samples can be predicted with more than 94% accuracy when the number of candidates is ten. The accuracy drops to 71.90% when the social media user posts ten micro-messages. Another important finding of our work suggests that Author Identifiers can be improved with training authorship data on a disjoint set prior to fine-tuning.

In future work, it would be interesting to analyze the ability to transfer authorship classifiers between different social media domains. This would allow larger datasets to train the authorship identification systems with more performant downstream datasets and less data availability. Another promising direction is incorporating various public information about the user and the post. For example, the time and the date of the post can provide helpful information about the characteristics and regular schedule of the author.

References

1. Manolache, A., Brad, F., Burceanu, E., Barbalau, A., Ionescu, R., Popescu, M.: Transferring BERT-like transformers' knowledge for authorship verification. arXiv preprint arXiv:2112.05125 (2021)
2. Heidari, M., Jones, J.H., Uzuner, O.: Deep contextualized word embedding for text-based online user profiling to detect social bots on Twitter. In: 2020 International Conference on Data Mining Workshops (ICDMW), pp. 480–487. IEEE (2020)
3. Knauth, J.: Language-agnostic Twitter-bot detection. In: Proceedings of the International Conference on Recent Advances in Natural Language Processing (RANLP 2019), Varna, Bulgaria, pp. 550–558. INCOMA Ltd., September 2019
4. Schwartz, R., Tsur, O., Rappoport, A., Koppel, M.: Authorship attribution of micro-messages. In: Proceedings of the 2013 Conference on Empirical Methods in Natural Language Processing, Seattle, Washington, USA, pp. 1880–1891. Association for Computational Linguistics, October 2013
5. Shrestha, P., Sierra, S., Gonzalez, F., Montes, M., Rosso, P., Solorio, T.: Convolutional neural networks for authorship attribution of short texts. In: Proceedings of the 15th Conference of the European Chapter of the Association for Computational Linguistics: Volume 2, Short Papers, pp. 669–674 (2017)
6. Aykent, S., Dozier, G.: AAREf: exploiting authorship identifiers of micro-messages with refinement blocks. In: 2020 19th IEEE International Conference on Machine Learning and Applications, pp. 1044–1050 (2020)
7. Aykent, S., Dozier, G.: Author identification of micro-messages via multi-channel convolutional neural networks. In: 2020 IEEE International Conference on Systems, Man and Cybernetics, pp. 675–681 (2020)
8. Aykent, S., Dozier, G.: Author Identification via a distributed neural-evolutionary hybrid (DiNEH). In: 2020 SoutheastCon, pp. 1–6 (2020)
9. Rocha, A., et al.: Authorship attribution for social media forensics. IEEE Trans. Inf. Forensics Secur. **12**(1), 5–33 (2016)
10. Theóphilo, A., Pereira, L.A., Rocha, A.: A needle in a haystack? Harnessing onomatopoeia and user-specific stylometrics for authorship attribution of micro-messages. In: IEEE International Conference on Acoustics, Speech and Signal Processing, pp. 2692–2696. IEEE (2019)

Mapping Opinion Cumulation: Topic Modeling-Based Dynamic Summarization of User Discussions on Social Networks

Ivan S. Blekanov(✉), Nikita Tarasov, Svetlana S. Bodrunova, and Sergei L. Sergeev

St. Petersburg State University, 199034 St. Petersburg, Russia
{i.blekanov,s.bodrunova,s.l.sergeev}@spbu.ru,
nkt.tarasov@yandex.ru

Abstract. In the recent years, a lot of methods have been proposed for detection of topicality of user discussions. Recently, the scholars have suggested approaches to tracing topicality evolution, including dynamic topic modeling. However, these approaches are overwhelmingly limited by representation of topics via lists of top words, which only hint to possible contents of topics and does not allow for real mapping of opinion cumulation [1]. We suggest a methodology for discussion mapping that combines neural-network-based encoding of user posts, HDBSCAN-based topic modeling, and abstractive summarization to map large-scale online discussions and trace bifurcation points in opinion cumulation. We test the proposed method on a mid-range dataset on climate change from Reddit and show how discussions may be summarized in a feasible and easily accessible way. Among the rest, we show that the bifurcation points in topicality are often followed by growth of a given topic, which may in future allow for predicting discussion outbursts.

Keywords: Cumulative deliberation · Opinion cumulation · Mapping discussions · Topic modeling · Abstractive summarization · Dynamic summarization

1 Introduction

As for today, topicality of online discussions, as well as opinion cumulation in them, has been a focus of scholarly attention for several decades. In the recent years, the scholars have moved to simple enough topic detection to more complicated and flexible models for dynamic assessment of discussion topicality. Finalized representations of topics may be misleading, as they create a feeling that topics start at the very beginning of discussions and stably last till its last moment, which is virtually never the case in real life. Moreover, opinion cumulation in time may play significant roles in public deliberation, especially when

A. Coman and S. Vasilache (Eds.): HCII 2023, LNCS 14025, pp. 25–40, 2023.
https://doi.org/10.1007/978-3-031-35915-6_3

it reaches spillover levels, and it is crucial to know when in time discussions split and diversify, as well as intensify or die out.

In response to this pressing need, many works have tried to trace discussion topicality in time. However, these attempts suffer from several significant research gaps. One is that the discovered topics are represented either by top words (that only hint on possible contents of a given topic) or by the most relevant full posts (which may be too long and/or too many and, thus, unfeasible to read within real-world time pressures). The second shortcoming is that topics are presented as evolving in time but not branching or ramifying. Third, the relations between topicality/opinion bifurcations and discussion intensity are obscure. Taken together, they so far prevent creation of a discussion mapping tool that would provide for easily readable and close-to-reality maps of user discussions that would adequately demonstrate accumulation or dissolution of opinion clusters, topics, or agendas.

To tackle this gap, we have tested a multi-step methodology that allows for producing a discussion map with feasible summaries of topics and subtopics, thus creating a tree-like representation of user-discussions. For that, we employ a combination of neural-network and probabilistic instruments, namely Transformer-based text encodings, HDBSCAN-based topic clustering, and LongT5-based abstractive summarization. We test the proposed method of discussion mapping on a middle-range dataset on climate change collected from Reddit in May to November 2022. As this is still work in progress, we test the necessary steps in their most feasible options; however, our method may be well refined and customized for other research goals.

The remainder of the paper is organized as follows. In Sect. 2, we describe the core of our approach and the research pipeline. Section 3 conveys our experiment and discusses the methodological steps in detail, including encoding, clustering, and summarization. In conclusion, we provide interpretation of the received results, including some non-expected ones.

2 Proposed Methodology

2.1 Core Principles

As it was stated before, the goal of this study lies in testing the methodology capable of representing topicality-based shifts in user discussions and, thus, of mapping the development of user discussions in time in a way that would allow for judging on topicality and/or opinion shifts and bifurcations. We propose two core components necessary for semantic opinion shift detection and presenting the results in a comprehensive and readable way.

First, to detect the initial points of discussion and possible opinion shifts, a topic modeling-based approach has been chosen. The general idea behind topic modeling lies in dividing the set of user messages into topical groups described via their corresponding top words. Traditional topic models such as LDA work as word-level bag-of-words-based representations. Newly developed methods of neural Transformer-based language models [2] in conjunction with robust clustering approaches have created a framework for novel topic models capable of deep understanding of text content. Initially proposed along with the Top2vec [3] model, this approach was later expanded in the BERTopic [4] model. It utilizes neural encoding, clustering methods, intermediate dimension reduction, and TF-IDF-based keyword selection. The latter can be used to obtain dynamic topic representations. Detailed description of the method will be presented in Sect. 3. Second, to present the results in a clearly readable format, we propose the use of an abstractive summarization model. This approach allows to generate concise representations of long user writings, describing the key points of a given text [5].

Altogether, this may provide the researchers and industry professionals with a tree-like map of any discussion, where discovered discussion segments of similar topicality get summarized for much quicker assessment. Bifurcation points inside the discussion may be detected via dynamic topics modeling, and individual discussion branches and sub-branches may get summarized in a way comfortable for the reader. Summarizations may comprise whole discussion segments from one bifurcation point to another ('sub-topics'), as we demonstrate below, or may be done more frequently or be customized depending on a researcher's final goal. Such an approach may allow for more cohesive and contextualized text representations, to become a viable alternative to the basic keyword/top-word representations of meaning found in topic models.

2.2 Model Description

Utilizing the previously described two-stage approach, we propose a method of dynamic mapping of topicality/opinion in online discussions. The method consists of the following steps:

1. Encoding of user posts using a Transformer-based model, in order to obtain more standardized text representations.
2. Dimension reduction of post encodings (from 384 to 50 vectors), in order to obtain contextualized encodings.
3. Topic modeling - that is, clustering the posts using the vectors from the previous step.
4. Obtaining topic representations for fixed-size small-time intervals. Here, we use a TF-IDF-based approach to obtain distributions of words for each topic with static IDF values and time-dependent TF values.
5. Timeline segmentation for each topic. We calculate the level of similarity of top words of each small time frame to the top-word list against the previous time interval. If, at some point, the vocabulary of a given time frame diverges significantly from the previous one, we consider the topic to have changed enough. By that, an isolated discussion branch is detected. Such a branch still relates to a particular 'big' topic discovered in step 3 but gemmates from the main discussion trunk, becoming one of the two or three major discussion sub-topics.

6. Abstractive summarization for each isolated discussion segment (sub-topic) in each topic. Again, here, we would like to underline that summarizations may be customized in accordance with the researcher's goals.

Figure 1 shows a graphic representation of the modeling process. In this pipeline, a clustering-based topic model is used for pooling the initial messages into time- and topic-specific groups. Abstractive summarization serves the role of an output layer, providing concise text snippets that include major foci of meaning for each message group. This dynamic summarization-based approach allows for a novel way of mapping the development of a user discussion via its easily readable and concise representation.

Besides the very idea of mapping discussions via combining detection of sub-topics and their summarization, the main advantage of our approach over earlier dynamic topic modeling approaches lies in the application of deep encodings for user texts. This allows the model to capture contextual meaning of words, providing message encodings with deeper semantic structure. This method allows for creating highly interpretive dynamic summarizations of the user discussions for further expert analysis.

3 Experimental Setup and Results

3.1 Dataset

The method was tested on a dataset collected from Reddit. The dataset focuses on climate change and comprises a period of seven months of active discussion (May to November 2022). For the purposes of testing, this particular topic was chosen due to a major climate change conference (CCC2022) being held during that time period. After technical pre-processing, the final dataset consisted of 54,565 user posts. Figure 2 shows the subreddits that contributed most to our dataset.

3.2 Encoding and Dimension Reduction

The sentence encoder all-MiniLM-L6-v2 was chosen as an encoding model [6]. The model was trained on a variety of different datasets, including a dataset of Reddit comments [7]. In this study, we use the model to obtain contextualized encodings for post content and headings. As such, each post is mapped to a 384-dimensional dense vector. The resulting vectors were reduced to 50 components using the UMAP library [8].

3.3 Clustering

HDBSCAN [9] was used to extract topics. This model has been used, as it is capable of quickly defining the number of clusters in a non-supervised way, without their pre-testing or multiple trials, as in classic topic modeling. For even more refined clustering, we advise to use the method of By using HDBSCAN,

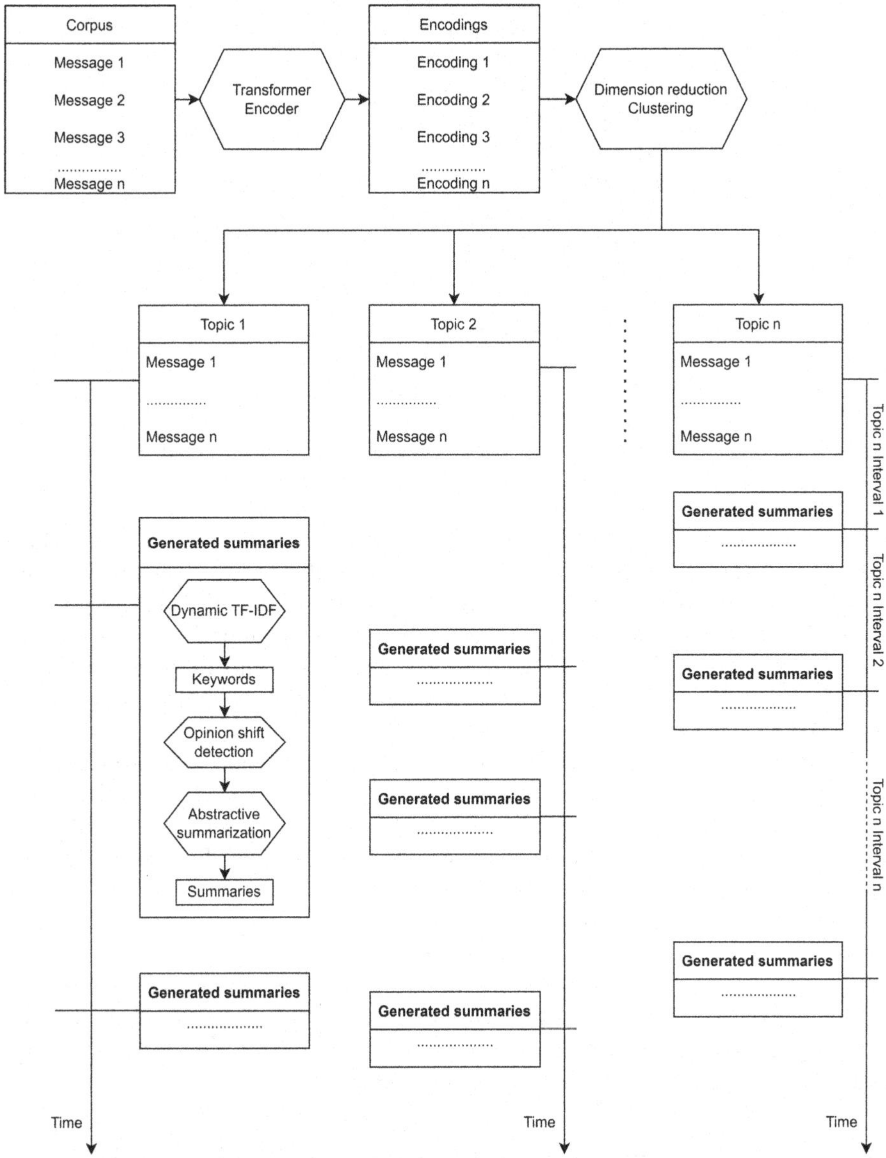

Fig. 1. The proposed method of dynamic discussion modeling

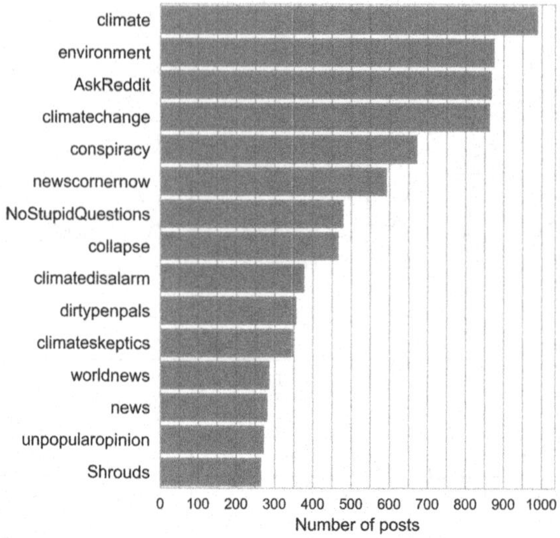

Fig. 2. The subreddits with the highest number of posts on climate change

50+ topics were discovered, but most of them were unstable and contained white noise. Using the methodology provided by the BERTopic implementation, the number of topics was reduced to 10 for a more streamlined visualization. For more precise analysis of real-world cases, this step can (and must) be omitted, thus allowing for a full-fledged HDBSCAN utilization and detection of small enough sub-topics throughout a given discussion. Multiple visualization methods were used to show varied aspects of each topic.

Figure 3 shows the accumulating number of posts per topic. The graph shows whether the number of posts within a given topic grows in time, week by week. For each weekly interval, the displayed value is not the number of posts within it but the number of all posts up to this interval (that is, the values of the current and all previous ones are summed).

Figure 4 is constructed similarly to Fig. 3, but with additional normalization of each topic by the total number of posts in it. If the graph line reaches above the median (black line, y = x), it means that the number of posts grows respective to previous days, while reaching below the media means the topic is dying out. The graph shows cumulation dynamics of individual topics. Figure 4 shows that some topics have grown in time, while some weakened.

3.4 Detection of Sub-topics and Their Summarization

Further on, we have detected the structure of topics in terms of possible sub-topics and revealed the timing of topic bifurcations. For detecting the bifurcation points, we needed to trace the changes in top words dynamically, throughout the duration of the topic. To do that, we have split all the posts in a given

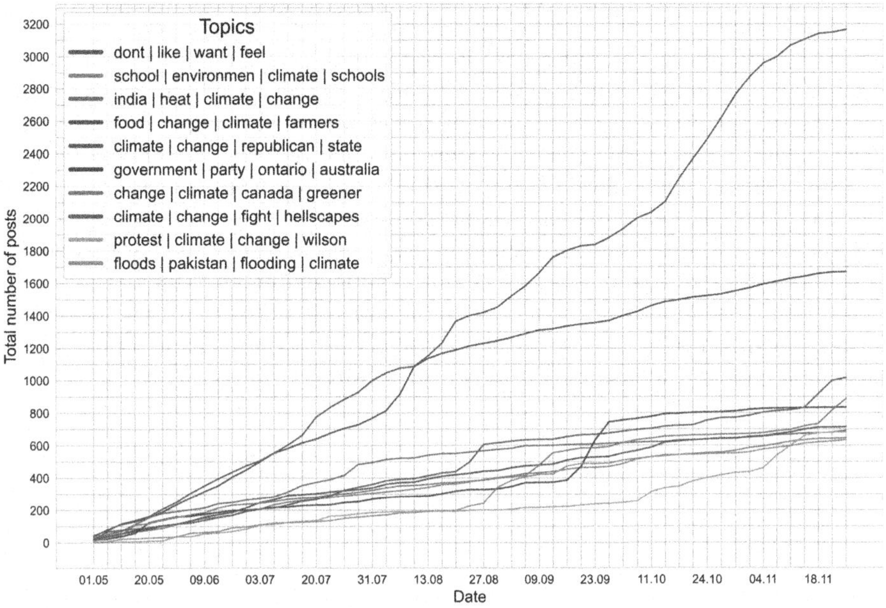

Fig. 3. Topic accumulation over time

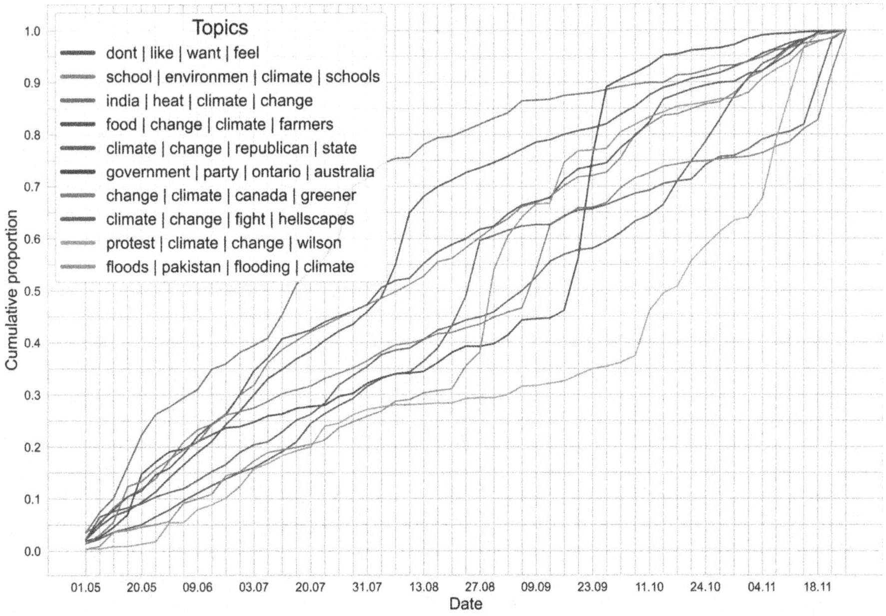

Fig. 4. Topic accumulation over time, normalised for each topic

topic into 50 time intervals of equal length. This number of intervals was pre-tested and empirically selected as optimal for our dataset, as it was enough to retrospectively assess the differences in top words, and growth of the number of intervals was much less feasible. For each interval, as stated in step 4 of our model description, a list of top words was obtained using a TF-IDF with time-dependent TF score. This procedure was realized the way offered by the BERTopic model. Thus, for each topic, 50 lists of 5 top words per interval were obtainted and then compared one to another in time. By that, we propose a way to automatically detect semantic shifts in user posts and pool the data based on these time intervals. A shift was detected if a significant enough number of words (more than 3) differed from the previous list of top words, with the changing words carrying onto the next segment to reduce the potential chance of detecting short term changes, focusing on a larger scale shifts.

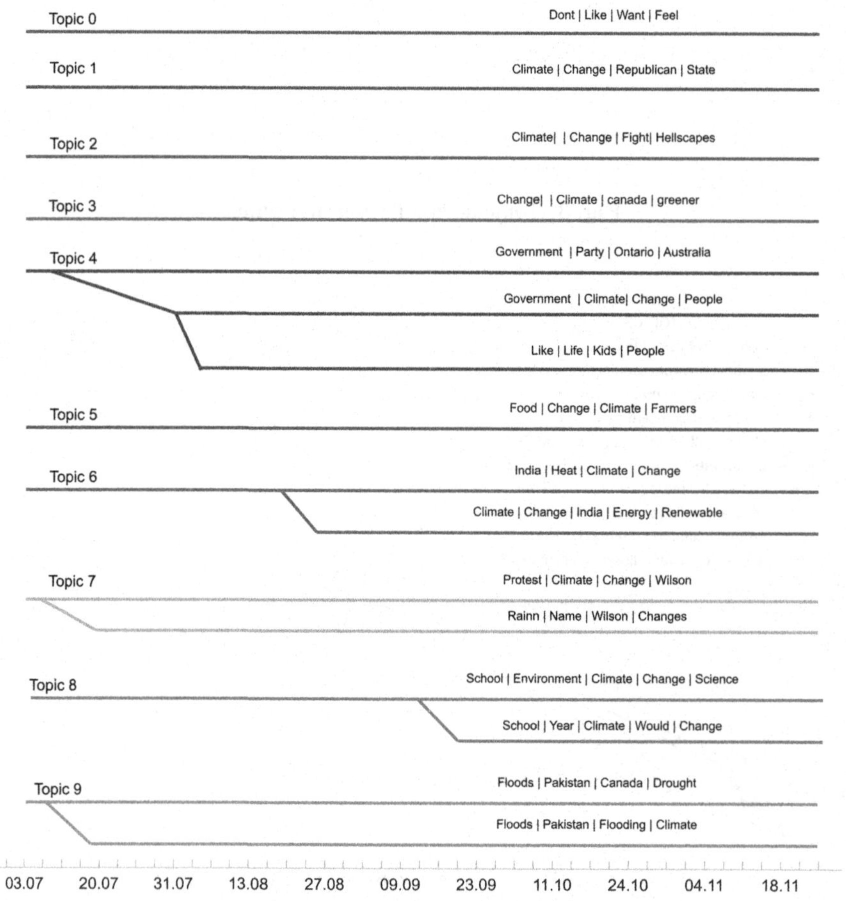

Fig. 5. Sub-topics in the dataset

A sub-topic, thus, lasted from one bifurcation point to the next one. However, as we were only testing the method, we did not detect many of such bifurcation points; in future, bigger detailisation is possible. The results of detection of sub-topics for all the 10 topics are presented on Fig. 5.

There are multiple ways of pooling posts for summarization. It can be done by splitting all posts by fixed-time intervals or accumulating groups of posts into chunks equal by the number of posts. However, this is not what could correspond to our task; we needed to summarize the discovered sub-topics, to demonstrate how the topicality transformed. Thus, we summarized all the posts in the discovered sub-topics - that is, the posts that accumulated between two semantic shifts and formed a separate branch within a bigger topic. Respective to this, the posts in each 'big' topic were split into groups conditioned by the bifurcation points. To summarize the posts, LongT5 model [10] tuned on a books dataset for the task of summarization [11] was used. LongT5 is a modification of a T5 [12] model capable of modeling on long sequences of texts, namely up to 16,384 tokens. In our case, this is a crucial advantage, as it provides a way to circumvent the common issue of non-feasibility of summarizing an entire set of long user posts. In previous research [13], we have tested several ways to pool the posts; however, each method caused notable information loss. This approach, however, allows for summarizing much larger amounts of user posts, with the main downside being a lack of training and tuning data for any given specific case. We have tested whether a model, pretrained on unrelated data (the booksum dataset) can provide an adequate result when applied to a set of posts obtained from a social network.

The examples of summaries for the sub-topics depicted on Fig. 5 are presented in Appendix 4. In the table in Appendix 4, Column 1 represents the topic number. Column 2 lists the top words of topic/sub-topic. Column 3 indicates the time intervals for each sub-topic. Column 4 states the number of posts that were summarized. Column 5 provides the sub-topic summarizations, with all the posts in a sub-topic summarized.

4 Discussion and Conclusion

In our paper, we have presented a method for mapping user discussions. It includes text encoding, topic clustering, and abstractive summarization, altogether allowing for detection of meaningful bifurcation points in a given discussion and summarize sub-topics situated between the bifurcation points. The obtained summarizations, as our preliminary assessment shows, are of good enough quality and allow for representing of the buzz in a given discussion, despite the machine trained on books still perceives the data from Reddit as books (or just one book). The summaries are easy and quick to read and allow for assessing how the shape of discussion changes.

In future, with more fine-grained summarization within sub-topics, one would easier detect opinion cumulation if multiple, more frequent summaries provide for short descriptions of users' agendas. Moreover, we have qualitatively assessed the graphs on Fig. 4 vs. the timing of bifurcation in topics on Fig. 5 and have come to a conclusion that the bifurcation points in topicality are often followed by growth of a given topic, which may in future allow for predicting discussion outbursts. As for now, the method proposed may be employed for detection of topicality shifts and detection of opinion cumulation.

Acknowledgements. This research has been supported in full by Russian Science Foundation, grant 21-18-00454 (2021–2023).

Appendix

Topic	Topic words	Subtopic time interval	Number of posts for summarization	Text
0	Climate Change Republican State	03.07 -24.11	300	The narrator continues his argument against climate change in this chapter, explaining that the evidence is overwhelming and that it would be impossible to deny it completely. He then discusses Bidenćampaign for President of the United States on climate change. On Day 4, the "reality TV challenge" comes up with new challenges for Biden: whether itś Poilieve or Jean Charrest, climate change can sink the next conservative leader. If someone does dont́ want to believe thereś definite proof, what irrefietable proof would they offer them to alter their opinion? In other words, no one will tell him about the climate change statistics. Even though Biden has already proposed a law making it illegal for rich men to set fires to add particulates to the air, people are still not willing to admit that they have been wrong all along. Finally, on Day 4, Gore announces that Congress must make peace with climate change before the midterm elections.
1	Dont Like Want Feel	03.07 -24.11	50	The narrator describes his life as Chaos, and the world is chaos. He has no passions or ambitions but wants to disappear. His brother probably will die soon because it's so badly treated. He hates everything. He doesn't know where to go from here. He can't find peace in anyone to love. He feels like he's already reached the end of his rope. He knows that society is going to get worse when climate change destroys civilization. He also realizes that people have been much better off than him since he started studying law. He thinks about suicide too. He does not want to be alone anymore. He just hates himself for being trapped in existence with all this bad news. He wishes he could live on a good note and on his own terms. He asks anyone else who is going through similar problems. They say that they are crippled with mental issues, lack of work, and one friend whom they talk to every month. She tells him that her best friend plans to have another child. She says that she would rather have four kids than five. She adds that there is only one problem: most families have two working mothers. She wants to speak to my friend more directly. She hopes that he regrets his behavior by coming across as means.

2	Climate Change Fight Hellsca-pes	03.07 -24.11	300	In this chapter, the narrator explains how people can come together and fight climate change better for less money. He also discusses some of the most important threats to humankind: penguins being threatened by climate change; giant cities becoming uninhabited; and so on. He asks what people can do to make it easier for them to stop climat-echange. Some of the best known examples are from the book "In which Carbon Emissions Threaten Methane" by Professor Carl-Octavius Otto Weiss. These include making methane more powerful in the atmosphere than expected, using burning it on fire as a way to slow climate change, cre-ating penguin colonies that are at risk of extinct because of climate changeś influence, and even forcing humans to use electricity to help control the climate. The worst sce-nario would be for people to delay action until they could no longer live in their own communities. People would start investing more into climate change immediately, leaving the mass of people hungry and thirsty. There would be political will and companies would invest more into fighting climate change. Finally, there would be an end to the worldś cur-rent cycle of heat and cooling. This is why we have to go underground and build a nuclear winter on the planet.
3	change climate canada greener	03.07 -24.11	700	In this chapter, Sebastian Vettel explains how climate change is making his life easier. He says that the Alberta Oil Sands are one of the most harmful places in the world because you can chop down trees and destroy them just to extract oils. Then he tells us that it's up to everyone in the Ontarian community to fight against climate change. They're all going to file lawsuits against the government for failing to reduce their greenhouse gas footprints by cutting back on energy-consuming businesses. We learn that five young people will sue the government over an international treaty that allows oil-industry companies to sue govern-ments for taking action toward climate change; they're also going to get some new statistics about how much each of these measures has saved Canada. It's clear that there's no way anyone could be more concerned about climate change than the seven young men who are suing the federal gov-ernment.
4	Governme Party Ontario Australia	03.07 -06.07	50	In this chapter, the author discusses the recent actions taken by the new government in Australia on climate change and how it will affect the country's economy. He also discusses Jaimie Macevoy's run for city council as well as other issues that are important to the community. The state government has slain many of its public board mem-bers, including returning to work with an executive named Greg McCarthy. A number of political parties have formed boards to advise governments on issues such as poverty, climate change, corruption, and violence against women. Some candidates have already been elected, but others have not yet been appointed. This list includes some of the most damaging decisions made by the current government.

	Governme Climate Change People	06.07 -30.07	50	The party launches its election campaign in North Shore with a crowd of supporters. Pacman, the partyś leader, delivers a long speech about how his party is committed to "unlocking New Zealandś potential economically and culturally." He says that the governmentś budget has failed to address many of the issues New Zealand faces, including housing, crime, and the environment. He also points out that the Prime Minister refused to answer many questions during his term as Minister for Mori or Pasifika affairs. He tells the crowd that he was proud of his record answering these questions but that this failed government had never given to the peopleś elected representatives on any occasion. He adds that it needs a road to net zero to secure the climate change authority and measures for proper national conversation.
	Like Life Kids People	30.07 -24.11	50	Australia's House of Parliament has passed a bill to reduce its greenhouse gas by 43 percent below the 2005 level by 2030. The Green Party supports the bill, but the conservatives are not ready to move from the Paris commitment to cut climate change by 28 percent to 35 percent. In addition to this new legislation, the government will introduce measures to improve the nation's transportation system and create new jobs. He will also make sure that Australia is able to thrive for all future generations. His government will invest in new roads, railways, air forces, and cybersecurity. He plans to build new national parks, oceanic parks, anti-piracy summits, and other measures to help slow and perhaps reverse the damage caused by climate change. He promises to replace the ban on gas cars by twenty-five with a better plan to phaseout gas cars. This will be an important step towards reducing climate change because it will save us from rising sea levels.
5	Food Change Climate Farmers	03.07 -24.11	150	The narrator discusses the latest developments in food production and politics. He uses examples from the Netherlands, India, and Africa to explain how climate change is affecting food supply chains. He also addresses concerns about food prices in the U. S. as well as issues of poverty and hunger in Africa. He suggests that farmers can use genetically modified plants to help combat climate change.
6	India Heat Climate Change	03.07 -21.08	100	In this chapter, the narrator explains how Indiaś actions toward the climate crisis have been misunderstood. He asks whether anyone can explain why India is making such a fuss over the topic of climate change and what it means to be an active citizen in the future. The narrators discuss several topics: 1) Heatwaves; 2) Climate Change; 3) India; and 4) Composting. They also discuss the role of Medha Patker, one of the pioneers of the "Narada BhaoAndolan" movement against the Sardar Saraovar Dam project in India.

	Climate Change India Energy Renew-able	21.08 -24.11	100	In this chapter, the author explains how India is planning to use deep sea cables to create a green electricity grid as well as reduce its energy consumption by up to 45%. He also discusses some of the latest developments in the Indian business community. For example, there are plans to build an underseal cable linking the Gujarat coast with the Middle East and creating a new renewable energy Grid as India and Arab Arabia. The article also mentions that Prince Abdul Aziz Bin Salman will be visiting New Delhi next month for a visit. Also, itś announced that India has already received invites from the Sultan of Salman to New Delhi. This makes the reader wonder whether climate change will hit much more often than it does now. According to one of the most recent reports on Indiaś economic loss due to heat waves, India lost about 159 Billion in key sectors because of extreme heat stress. If temperatures increase by a certain amount, labor hours will decline by 53%; snowfall will increase by 3 times that expected at a temperature of 1.4 deg. Heatwaves are increasing frequency and temperature across Europe. Meanwhile, India has set up a council on climate change called the "Climate Change Council" to discuss ways to combat climate change. There are many opportunities to attend the council: you can speak as a delegate or speaker; you can attend as part of a session; you may participate as if you were a speaker; etc.
7	Protest Climate Chnage Wilson	03.07 -06.07	100	In this short scene, the narrator explains how climate change protests are taking place in Sydney. He describes how an old lady dressed as an elderly woman throws a cake at Mona Lisaś painting and then throws roses at her. This is not a typical example of what happens when people try to raise awareness about a political issue. Itś more like "raising awareness" for money than for anything else. The man dressed up as an older woman yells that itś all about climate change. A bunch of people have been arrested for blocking roads or highways because theyŕe passionate about something. They dont́ want to get into trouble with big-time politicians who just want to make money. But thereś no way anyone can do anything about such a thing. So hereś some background on why: People tend to block roads when theyv́e got a passion for something. If youŕe going to advocate for something, you need to be willing to go against it. You know, things like voting for better urban planning, public transport, etc. And so forth. Thereś nothing wrong with these kinds of actions.
	Rainn Name Wilson Chnages	06.07 -24.11	150	Rainn Wilson has changed his name to Protest climate change, and heś been getting more and more public attention for the past few weeks. He changes his name from "Rainnahfall Heatwave Extreme Winter" to "Protestclimate Change." And then he announces that he is changing his name so that people can see him as an advocate for climate change. So what does this mean? Well, it doesnt́ seem like thereś much of a difference between throwing soup over Vangoghṕainting or throwing food at a famous paintings. The whole thing is just trying to get people to stop using oil in their lives. They are also spreading hate on reddit because they dont́ want to be seen as supporting the cause. In other words, theyŕe not helping anyone but themselves.

8	School Envi- ronmen Climate Change Science	03.07 -12.09	50	The top program for a student to study "climate change" requires a personal statement and an essay explaining how the degree will help him achieve his future goals. This is important because it allows students to tell their stories and explain what they have experienced in their lives. In this case, she has a background of studying "econ" and "math." She wants to be able to combine her passion for science with her desire to fight climate change. Sheś been working as a tech salesman since February 20, 2021 so she doesnt́ need a job but wants to do something meaningful. She knows that she can get into a graduate school where she can focus on helping people make better decisions about climate change while also getting a high paying job. Her biggest ambition is to become an economic analyst or consultant in any industry or local government. She needs experience in managing large scale projects like climate change and would like to work at a consulting company doing business research. She does not know how to write her personal statement; instead, she just wants to talk about why she wants to go to college. She had a hard time taking math classes due to lack of commitment. She wanted to pursue econ studies but didnt́ really want to finish them all. She was worried about having enough motivation to complete these courses when she got bad grades. Finally, she decided to try to apply to university after graduating from UW. She started looking for jobs outside of medicine and found some opportunities in finance. She tried to find career advice by asking other students who had taken a Geography or Earth Science degree. They were all very different. Some said that earth sciences and geography seemed more respected than other fields, but others said that law wasnt́ as respected as many other fields. Isnt́ there anything else you could do? If you are interested in finding out what kind of degree you should take, please feel free to ask.
	School Year Climate Would Change	12.09 -24.11	30	Engineering is the best career choice for high school students because itś about creating revolutionary inventions to benefit humanity. There are plenty of top engineering jobs available in India, including aerospace engineers, chemical engineers, and nuclear engineers. The fields of civil engineering, transportation engineering, and environmental engineering are also popular among those who love thinking outside the box - they can get international opportunities.

9	Floods Pakistan Flooding Climate	03.07 -10.07	100	The narrator discusses how climate change is making floods worse in the country. He says that there are more record-breaking records in the world because of it. A huge fire broke out at Islamabad on Tuesday, and the authorities rushed to rescue people from the affected area. The Prime Minister has instructed the capital development authority to forestall the fire immediately. In this chapter, the author describes some of the major disasters that have occurred since June 14, including an earthquake in India; a monoon storm in Bangladesh; and a series of floods in China. Sherry reports that many people have died due to the heavy rains. According to her, "This is one national disaster." As many as seven people have lost their lives in recent rain-retrieval incidents across the country," Rehman tells the nations chief minister, saying that this is a "national disaster." Since June 14, Monsoneon storms have killed about 77 people in Pakistan. This is not considered a big threat to the country but rather a challenge for its citizens. Climate change makes flooding worse.
	Floods Pakistan Flooding Climate	10.07 -24.11	150	The narrator discusses the recent heavy rains and floods in South Korea, Nigeria, Chad, and other countries. He says that climate change likely caused deadly floods because of its effects on the environment. A report finds that one third of Pakistans population is under water due to ancient flooding. Sherrie Rehman tells the AFP that she could make a "third of country underwater" by changing the climate. The government of Pakistan asks for help from the international donor community as it faces high inflation and an overconfident current account deficit. In response, the United States has pledged $139 million to help people affected by the disaster. As part of this commitment, the Azgartesy charity will donate more than $1 million to support relief efforts across the country through local, vetoed organizations.

References

1. Bodrunova, S.S.: Practices of cumulative deliberation: a meta-review of the recent research findings. In: Chugunov, A.V., Janssen, M., Khodachek, I., Misnikov, Y., Trutnev, D. (eds.) EGOSE 2021. CCIS, vol. 1529, pp. 89–104. Springer, Cham (2022). https://doi.org/10.1007/978-3-031-04238-6_8
2. Vaswani, A., et al.: Attention is All You Need. In: Advances in Neural Information Processing Systems, vol. 30 (2017)
3. Angelov, D.: Top2Vec: distributed representations of topics (2020). arXiv preprint arXiv:2008.09470
4. Grootendorst, M.: BERTopic: neural topic modeling with a class-based TF-IDF procedure (2022). arXiv preprint arXiv:2203.05794
5. Gupta, S., Gupta, S.K.: Abstractive summarization: an overview of the state of the art. Expert Syst. Appl. **121**, 49–65 (2019)
6. Reimers, N., Gurevych, I.: Making monolingual sentence embeddings multilingual using knowledge distillation (2020). arXiv preprint arXiv:2004.09813
7. Henderson, M., et al.: A repository of conversational datasets (2019). arXiv preprint arXiv:1904.06472
8. McInnes, L., Healy, J., Melville, J.: UMAP: uniform manifold approximation and projection for dimension reduction (2018). arXiv preprint arXiv:1802.03426

9. McInnes, L., Healy, J., Astels, S.: HDBSCAN: hierarchical density based clustering. J. Open Source Softw. **2**(11), 205 (2017)
10. Guo, M., et al.: LongT5: efficient text-to-text transformer for long sequences (2021). arXiv preprint arXiv:2112.07916
11. pszemraj/long-t5-tglobal-base-16384-book-summary · Hugging Face. https://huggingface.co/pszemraj/long-t5-tglobal-base-16384-book-summary. Accessed 4 Feb 2023
12. Raffel, C., et al.: Exploring the limits of transfer learning with a unified text-to-text transformer. J. Mach. Learn. Res. **21**(1), 5485–5551 (2020)
13. Blekanov, I.S., Tarasov, N., Bodrunova, S.S.: Transformer-based abstractive summarization for reddit and Twitter: single posts vs. comment pools in three languages. Future Internet **14**(3), 69 (2022)

Abstractive Summarization of Social Media Texts as a Tool for Representation of Discussion Dynamics: A Scoping Review

Svetlana S. Bodrunova(✉)

St. Petersburg State University, St. Petersburg 199004, Russia
s.bodrunova@spbu.ru

Abstract. Neural-network-based models of text analysis have been widely implemented for assessment of the dynamics and quality of online discussions, as well as for detection of individual opinions or opinion spectra. Techniques that allow for representing user opinions are being applied in studies of public deliberation, industry-and academe-based marketing studies, and a number of other areas in social research. One of the approaches used more and more in the recent 15 years is summarization, both extractive and abstractive. However, most studies of user opinions tend to treat opinions as finalized extracted/formulated targets, rather than parts of a discussion dynamics where opinions change each other and transform. In accordance with the concept of cumulative deliberation, we see opinion cumulation as a complex process, the dynamic features of which need to be accentuated in literature and more researched upon. In this paper, we review the works that employ abstractive summarization to detect opinions and discussion dynamics in social media data. We show that, despite the availability of already elaborated techniques and models, researchers do not apply them for detecting the dynamics of opinion cumulation and discussion mapping.

Keywords: abstractive summarization · topicality detection · opinion cumulation · cumulative deliberation · social media

1 Introduction

Today, automated text analysis is employed for resolution of multiple types of tasks relevant for political, social, communication, and marketing studies. Among the goals that the scholars try to achieve, there is prediction of people's various choices in social, political, and consumer lives via prediction of outcomes of user discussions. For that, assessment of dynamics and quality of public discussions, as well as detection of individual opinions or opinion spectra, is employed. Thus, the techniques that allow for aggregating large-scale textual data in order to detect and represent user opinions are being applied within the studies of public deliberation, industry- and academe-based marketing investigations, and a number of other areas in social research.

One of the approaches used more and more in the recent 15 years to represent aggregated user opinions is text summarization, extractive, abstractive, or hybrid [1]; fusion

A. Coman and S. Vasilache (Eds.): HCII 2023, LNCS 14025, pp. 41–54, 2023.
https://doi.org/10.1007/978-3-031-35915-6_4

and compression as summarization methods for social media are used less frequently. Extractive summarization focuses on finding the most representative text segments, while abstractive summarization implies a text rewriting step and uses new terms [2]. Both approaches have shown promising efficiency in representing long texts or text corpora, including data from social media, despite the reservations of the early 2010s [3]. However, both approaches, just as many other ones like topic modeling or sentiment analysis, tend to treat opinions as finalized extracted/formulated targets, rather than parts of a discussion dynamics where opinions influence each other and transform. By 2016, extractive summarization methods have, as some scholars have stated [4, 5], reached the peak of performance, while abstractive and hybrid approaches have been spurred by rapid development of neural networks (and deep learning models based on them) and encoder-decoder architectures. This is why we will mostly focus on abstractive summarization and especially on that done with the help of neural networks; to add more, deep-learning-based methods allow for eliminating the opposition between structure-oriented and semantics-oriented summarization techniques, as they capture both structural and semantic features of the texts in the dataset [5].

In 2020–2022, we have suggested the concept of cumulative deliberation and elaborated upon it [6, 7]. This concept implies that opinion formation in user discussions has non-deliberative character and can be better described by patterns that reconstruct opinion cumulation, rather than by any sort of round-robin rational opinion exchange. User opinions online exist in the form of tiny acts of participation (posts, comments, likes, or reposts) [8] which can also be seen as lowest-level communicative actions [9], see also [7]. Their gradual accumulation online is, in essence, how opinions, attitudes, and collective emotions grow [10]. Thus, opinion dynamics in the form of accumulation and dissipation of opinion clusters may be detected within discussions on social media. This, in its turn, implies that time-plus-opinion-bound segments within the discussions under scrutiny may be summarized, and the discussions can be mapped in terms of opinions / opinion shifts with the help of various summarization techniques.

Our earlier research [11, 12] shows that abstractive summarization allows for receiving successful summaries of textual data from several social media platforms. 'Successful' here means more than just adequate representing what people were posting about. Our summaries have allowed for judging upon how discussion agendas changed from news-oriented to issues-oriented ones within hours cross-culturally in case of internationally-relevant conflictual events. By this, they have also allowed for assessing on both opinion dynamics and discussion quality, as well as have shown how agendas spread in concentric nature from the conflict epicenter to other countries. Research similar to ours has been scattered around both social media studies and summarization research, and the role of summarizations for representation of discussion dynamics has not yet been in proper focus of automated research on user texts; we would like to emphasize it. In accordance with the concept of cumulative deliberation, we see opinion cumulation as a dynamic complex process, the dynamic features of which need to be accentuated in literature and more researched upon; and this is exactly what summarization can capture and help assess while opinions grow, that is, in real or nearly-real time. Moreover, discussion dynamics has political implications in several terms, starting from polarization and echo chambering [13] to social exclusion to the impact of explosive online events like cyberbullying, scandals, or mob attacks, including those on politicians and journalists [14].

In this paper, we review the works that either employ summarization techniques to detect and represent the dynamics of opinion cumulation or elaborate on particular methods that may be directly applied for depicting of opinion cumulation and assessment of temporal aspects of online discussions. In other words, such research techniques would allow for assessing the dynamics of opinions within user discussions, which would eventually allow for or help in mapping opinion/topicality streams. As this research area is emergent, the number of such works is still scarce; however, we see it important to underline the need for scholars to pay attention to dynamic aspects of opinion formation and to representing opinion development. Here, though, we need to note that the borders between summarization as a particular method of reworking original user data and summarization as a research goal that may be reached by other methods is blurred. For instance, there are reviews that see latent semantic analysis (LSA), topic modeling, or centroid-based (*k*-means) clustering as summarization methods [15, 16]. We, though, are stricter in methodological terms and will see summarization as a process that, first and foremost, aims at creating representational segments of texts; abstractive summarization implies text reformulation and creation of new, previously non-existent text, while extractive summarization finds and shows to the assessor the most characteristic and semantically saturated text fragment.

We have stated above that our goal is to look at the literature that deals with techniques of abstractive summarization for opinion/discussion mapping. As several comprehensive and systematic reviews of opinion summarization (including abstractive one) were published, *i.a.,* in 2019 [5, 6], 2020 [7, 8], 2021 [1, 18, 19], and 2022 [20, 21], we will predominantly focus on newer works published in 2020–2023, only mentioning older works where very necessary. However, there is a notable gap in more narrow-scope reviewing, e.g., of the application of abstractive summarization to mapping opinions and discussion dynamics, this is why we see our review as timely and necessary.

The explosive growth of summarization research allows for maximal narrowing down of our review even beyond this time frame. Thus, we limit it in the following way. First, we will focus on abstractive summarization only. This mean we incorporate the works that openly underline they use or develop abstractive-summarization-based methodologies; if a paper does not openly state this in the abstract and/or methods section, the paper is not reviewed. We will not review the papers focused on extractive summarization, however innovative and fitting to our goal they would be.

Second, we will only focus on abstractive summarization for social media. In practice, this implies that we will not review the method enhancements not dedicated specially to working with social media data. From our previous research on various methods of textual analysis we know that methods elaborated for structured data such as document archives or news pieces differ highly from the noisy, varying-length, and unstructured texts from social media. This is why methods elaborated for social media data deserve a separate review, and not one. This also means that we will not review the papers that test their methods on news datasets like XSum, CNN/DailyMail, or others; on biomedical data; on translation datasets; etc. We will even exclude Wikipedia-based papers, and we will only mention reviews-based research only where it directly relates to opinion representation.

Third, opinion dynamics and representation of temporal dynamics of user discussions is our special focus. Given all the stated above, we can trace three lines of research to be reviewed: 1) the works focused on method elaboration, with testing on real-world datasets from social media; 2) the works that perceive and use abstractive summarization as a tool in case studies to detect opinions, not as an ultimate methodological research goal; 3) the works that come the closest to the idea of opinion-based mapping of user discussion dynamics.

Fourth, ss social media datasets normally contain hundreds to millions of texts, we will orient our review more to techniques of abstractive summarization of multiple texts. For a recent enough review on single-document summarization, see [22].

Further on, the paper is organized as follows. Section 2, divided into three subchapters, will tell of today's abstractive summarization. It describes the method elaboration for Reddit and other social media platforms, as well as draws examples of case-study use of abstractive summarization in social science. Section 3 is dedicated to reviewing several only works on abstractive summarization vs. discussion dynamics. Section 4 concludes the paper by discussing its findings and setting prospects for future discussion mapping studies.

2 Abstractive Summarization and Its Application to Mining of Meanings from Social Media: Mapping Research Streams

The advent and spread of neural encoder-decoder architectures in the mid-2010s has opened doors for deep- and transfer-learning models suitable for high-level abstraction of text meaning similar enough to human summarization. With that, summarization studies have made a critical step forward, which deserves a separate piece of reviewing. Thus, e.g., authors [5] have singled out deep-learning abstractive summarization into a separate type in their typology, in addition to structure- and semantics-based summarization. Abstractive summarization may be performed with the help of many techniques. Moussa and co-authors [2] name template-based, graph-based, semantic-based, data-driven, machine-learning-based, and neural-networks-based types of abstractive summarization. Below, the latter type attracts our closest attention.

However, despite the evident need, abstractive summarization has been applied to social media data later than to more structured data. As stated above, for our goals, three functional streams of literature may be singled out: The works that elaborate on methodologies for social media suitable for mapping opinion dynamics; those that use summarization for social science goals relatively distant from opinion mapping; and those that approach opinion mapping in the closest way.

Below, we review the papers where researchers train and/or fine-tune the newest deep- and/or transfer-learning summarization models for social media research. 'Recent advances in the field of abstractive summarization leverage pre-trained language models rather than train a model from scratch' [23], though some authors still argue for initial training with the use of small number of real-world summaries [24].

Among those, the major focus of abstractive social media summarization studies has, till today, been on Reddit, due to a specific affordance of this platform called 'Too long; didn't read' (TL; DR). In essence, TL; DRs are short user summaries of their longer texts; that is, the platform allows for getting human summarizations for substantial amounts of data. These summarizations created by real people serve as baselines to compare with or marked-up datasets; we review them separately, due to their big number. The rest of the papers is for all other platforms, which Reddit easily outperforms in the number of research projects and papers.

2.1 Deep-Learning Abstractive Summarization for Datasets from Reddit: Methodologies of Meaning Extraction

In this sub-area of summarization studies, researchers may aim at several goals beyond the utmost goal of creating best-fit summaries. In particular, the authors test new neural-network models, participate in summarization challenges, and create large-scale marked-up datasets for common use. Below, we will show works that set one or several of these goals.

To our best knowledge, the first large-scale dataset from Reddit, namely the Webis-TLDR-17 one that contained nearly 4 million content-summary pairs, was yielded in 2017 [25]. Simultaneously, the Reddit data served for creating a method for collecting author summaries for long texts from social media. So far, three major Reddit-based datasets have been developed for testing summarization models, as well as several smaller ones that are not available for public use. In all of them, the TL;DR feature is crucial: The Reddit users provide their own summaries to longer posts, and their summaries are seen as benchmark human summarizations. Only very rare works on abstractive summarization (just as on extractive one, too) challenge the idea of the quality of human summarizations being benchmark; for Reddit, see [26]. In the early 2020s, Reddit remained the only social networking platform to provide large-scale data for text summarization in English, with Weibo and other Chinese-languages platforms gradually taking the lead. By 2018, a labeled dataset called 'Reddit TIFU' had been developed [27]. It contains 123,000 posts from Reddit with the same TL;DR summaries. For the so-called extreme summarization of very high levels of abstraction, the TLDR9 + dataset of 9 + million Reddit content-summary pairs was developed in 2021; from it, the authors [28] extracted high-quality summaries, to form a smaller TldrHQ sub-dataset. For several years, these datasets were the only reliable and publicly available datasets for social media summarization and could serve for fine-tuning new models.

In as late as 2019, the scholars were still sure that, 'as most recent models ha[d] been evaluated exclusively on news corpora, our knowledge of their full capabilities [was] still superficial' [29: 524]. Real tackling of the Reddit-based abstractive summarization has started in 2019, when Webis-TLDR-17 was used for the text summarization 'TL;DR challenge' [30] that showed that Reddit data were 'slightly noisier than the other datasets' of more structured nature [26].

The creators of the Reddit TIFU dataset suggested a multi-level memory-networks model [27] that performed better than basic seq2seq and extractive models available by 2019. Within the 2019 TL;DR challenge, authors [31] compared LSTM, LSTM + copy, Transformer, Transformer + copy, and Transformer + pretrained models for the n-gram abstractiveness performance evaluation in summarizations. Their pretrained Transformer model outperformed the ground truth for news summarizations; moreover, it worked best for the Reddit data. Thus, Transformer-based models were shown to be efficient for social media data without alterations to the core model architecture; pretraining and fine-tuning was shown to be enough. The authors, though, claimed that none of the models could 'learn true semantic natural language compression' (p. 520). In parallel, in 2019, authors [32] have tackled the problem of degenerated attention distribution and tested their proposed enhanced seq2seq model on six datasets, including two from Reddit.

Other works [33, 34] combined abstractive and extractive summarization (without a focus on application). By this, they assisted the challenge organizers in identifying influential summary aspects that affected summarization, including sufficiency and formal text quality [30].

The year of 2021 has seen novel neural-network models, mostly Transformed-based, like BART, T5, and LongFormer, applied to Reddit data – though, with the results being less promising than expected. Some works of 2020–2021 showed that BART-based models worked best for the Reddit datasets [35]. Among them, low-resource abstractive summarization methods based on combined transfer and meta learning [36] and perfection of pre-training by using extractive-type text masks [37] have been proposed. However, they have brought mixed results for news and social media datasets. The authors [35] have reached the best improvement levels exactly for the Reddit TIFU dataset in comparison with eight other datasets, which showed that social media data were well summarizable, despite their higher noise levels and diversity of lexicons and grammar. This corresponds to [35] showing that abstractive models worked better than extractive ones on the Reddit TIFU datasets. However, in contrast to these findings, the authors [37] have found that, on news datasets such as CNN/DailyMail and long-text XSum, their pre-training enhancer worked better than on Reddit TIFU. This may be explained by the fact that their model was more extractive and did not correspond to the abstractive nature of the Reddit summarizations.

In 2021, as stated above, joint efforts by IRLab and Adobe Research have resulted into preparation of two datasets recommended for wide use, namely TL;DR9 + and TL;DRHQ. Creation of these datasets aimed at fostering the so-called extreme summarization used to summarize large multi-text collections on high levels of abstraction and compression. However, the test results provided by the authors are discouraging: They train and test three deep-learning models of abstractive summarization (two BERT modifications and one BART) but Oracle-Ext, a model of extractive summarization, beats them all on the Reddit data [28].

In 2022, a Syntax-Enriched Abstractive Summarization (SEASum) framework was offered. It utilizes graph attention networks to introduce syntactic features of source texts, to tackle the issue of faithfulness of summaries [38]. The method has been tested on the CNN/Daily Mail and Reddit-TIFU datasets.

As our review shows, Reddit, despite being the leading platform for English-language abstractive summarization training and fine-tuning, is clearly lagging behind in real-world applications of the trained models. This opinion of ours is supported by the fact that, in the today's review papers, e.g., on transfer learning in summarization [19] and on seq2seq-based abstractive summarization [39], Reddit gains very low attention – the papers feature literally one paper on Reddit each. Most works use the Reddit datasets along with many others such as in [35], rather than focus on them. For the purposes of the current review, we need to state that the works that come close to using Reddit for opinion and/or discussion mapping are extremely rare (see Sect. 3).

2.2 Abstractive Summarization for Other Social Media Platforms

Platforms other than Reddit are used in abstractive summarization studies even more rarely than Reddit, as they need the amount of time for annotation and testing often simply unfeasible for researchers. However, many enough works have already tried elaborating on methodologies for social media summarization beyond Reddit. Some of such methodologies may be used for detection of dynamics; this is why we include them into our review. Some of such works, though, only aim at creating benchmark/gold-standard/silver-standard datasets for social media for further use. Twitter and YouTube are more popular in this respect, while Facebook is less researched upon, perhaps due to many obstacles for data collection it creates.

Another feature of today's abstractive summarization studies for social media is that most authors, including our own working group, prefer to leverage on the existing models via fine-tuning them; thus, transfer learning is gaining more and more space in abstractive summarization research. At the same time, most authors underline that the fine-tuning step is necessary and unavoidable [40].

Due to Twitter's platform affordances, mainly the short texts, abstractive summarization is rarely developed for this platform; most studies understandably prefer extraction of short texts from tweet corpora/pools rather than summarizing them (on our experiments on Twitter in three languages, see below). Recently, for Twitter, template-based abstractive summarization was offered; the summaries were created by trained journalists [40]. This team has also offered using the Wasserstein space for enhancing the summarization quality [41], testing it on Twitter, Reddit, and reviews.

The research on YouTube video transcripts varies highly in quality, from low-quality TF-IDF-based methodologies [42] to works that apply most up-to-date summarizers. In 2020–2022, Transformer-based models have started to be applied to YouTube video transcripts [43, 44] and YouTube video captioning [45–48], several works integrating text and video summarizations. Multimodal summarizations are being more and more developed [49], especially in the area of text-guided video summarization [50, 51]. However, not many research groups deal with real-world non-marked-up YouTube data, and, which is much more important, virtually no research summarizes the YouTube comments; thus, we still lack the method for YouTube discussion summarization that would be non-extractive.

For Chinese social media, existing training datasets like LCSTS serve extensively for testing the new models. Liang et al. [52] have recently suggested to improve the ROUGE scores directly via adding cross-entropy and reinforcement learning policy to the research pipeline, testing it on LCSTS and getting benchmark results. A similar work also based on the seq2seq approach and Chinese social media data suggests an enhanced technique which makes the model pay attention to the information in the previously generated summary [53]. A work on data of varying length, a truly significant problem for social media data, first trains the models on news datasets and then uses LCSTS to evaluate the model [54]. Another work on Chinese data falls into the recent trend of combining extractive and abstractive summarization for better performance [55]. Chinese authors have also proposed the method of topic-aware summarization, in line with many other works that unite topic modeling with abstractive summarization [56]. However, despite this technique is very promising in terms of discussion topicality and opinion mapping in time (see Sect. 3), we virtually do not see such research pipelines to be applied to discussion mapping.

Some Chinese working groups gather their own data, thus creating valuable datasets for future use. Huang et al. have created a dataset of what the authors call 'legal public opinion news' (whatever it could mean) taken from microblogs [57]. Gao et al. [58] have tackled the issue of main vs. secondary aspects and have tested the proposed method on a 10,000 + Weibo dataset.

Another stream of research here is elaboration and/or fine-tuning of the models for languages beyond English, Spanish, Arabic (for a recent review, see [59]), or Chinese which are the most frequent in summarization studies. Several research groups have worked with social media data on other languages like Bengali [60], German [61], Russian [12], Urdu [62], or Telugu [63].

2.3 Abstractive Summarization as a Method in Case Studies

The research reviewed above differs highly from what we review below, as the methodological orientation gives in here to the goals set up by social sciences. Here, we review for what purposes abstractive summarization is employed today for social media analysis; we do not touch works on detection of temporal dynamics of user discussions but first show that abstractive summarization is applied to several socially and politically relevant tasks. The methods developed in these works may also be applied for detection of opinion structure and dynamics. The streams of literature on social-science tasks for abstractive summarization (even if weak enough so far) may already be detected.

First, summarization serves for detecting democratic and deliberative quality of online communication, including spread of news, fact-checking, and user consensus. The work [64] focuses on capturing the consensus of opinions in user reviews; however, the proposed method, called OpineSum, may also be tested for political opinions and user consensus on public issues. Bhatnagar et al. [65] have proposed a workflow for partial automation of fact-checking on Twitter.

Second, another understandably big stream of applied research is about consumer opinion detection; here, we will only draw some examples, as reviewing this area would take another paper. For consumer opinions, abstractive summarization is considered to be way more efficient, but also way more complicated in realization [66]. Here, researchers, as a rule, deploy combinations of enhanced summarization and object-oriented sentiment analysis [67], as this allows for capturing both the popularity of goods/services and opinion polarity (for a recent literature overview, see [68]). For us, this is important that, in this research stream, the researchers seem to have come the closest to standardized opinion tagging [69].

Third, detection of malicious content is another popular focus of summarization studies, especially on Twitter. Here, an important work [70] proposes tweet stream summarization for spam detection; it is important for us, as it comes very close to the idea of dynamic representation of discussion/stream and opinion cumulation.

Detection of illness is another issue dealt with via abstractive summarization. In particular, mental health problem detection has been tested for Reddit [71], and depression detection – for Twitter [72].

However, again, we see that, within these streams (represented, though, by rare examples only), the authors do not relate the dynamics of opinion cumulation to the tasks they resolve; neither the methods they try to create have no focus on temporal or cumulative dynamics. Only several works of those that deal with abstractive summarization and social media data have been having these aspects in mind; we describe them in short below.

3 Abstractive Summarization as a Technique of Representing Discussion Dynamics

As it is evident from Sect. 2, representation of discussion dynamics has by no means been a priority for researchers who elaborated the abstractive summarization techniques for social media. However, there are several works that need to be highlighted in this respect.

Thus, Palma et al. [73] have proposed a mixed method of summarization of online discussions that incorporates social context. Previously, 'social context' understood as relations with other users exemplified by following, liking, commenting, and reposting had been used in extractive summarization studies [74], as part of the studies where social influence is employed for better summarization [75].

The paper by Gao et al. [58] mentioned above approach discussion/opinion mapping from another angle. Their work incorporates reader comments into the summarized data and detects what the authors call 'reader focused aspects', thus capturing the discussion on Weibo with better precision in terms of discussion structure.

A promising attempt to summarize Twitter for reputational assessment was made in [76], where the authors used both abstractive and extractive summaries. To our best knowledge, this method has not been further studied or widely applied neither for reputation management nor for discussion dynamics representation, as of 2023.

Our research group has been developing the methods for opinion cumulation assessment and representation of discussion dynamics for some time already. Thus, our first works [10, 11] has shown applicability of abstractive summarization to communication studies and their tasks, including mapping of micro-shifts in agendas of globally-relevant issues and cumulation of public emotions. We have trained our T5 and LongFormer models on Reddit data but applied them to Twitter real-world datasets on conflictual discussions like that on the *Charlie Hebdo* massacre. In our work of 2021 [12], we have continued to apply abstractive summarization to show how agendas spread cross-culturally, noting that the method was capable of capturing the differences between news-oriented and issue-oriented discussion segments. This work has allowed for mapping the micro-agendas in time, which has brought us to the idea of mapping online discussions with the help of abstractive summarization, a method that would differ from simple topic evolution research, as it would demonstrate the bifurcation points in the discussions and create trees of topicality. For this conference, we have suggested such a methodology [77], on which we will elaborate much more in the nearest future.

4 Discussion and Conclusion

Our review has not been systemic, as it had a certain scope of finding works close to the idea of applying abstractive summarization to tracing opinion dynamics on social media. Our research has shown that only a tiny handful of works have tried to do so, despite that, since 2017, social media, especially Reddit, have been in the focus of summarization researchers.

Till today, social media summarization of abstractive nature is an emergent area. Thus, Twitter is mostly summarized by extractive summarization, Facebook is next-to-unavailable for data collection, YouTube comments are overseen by researchers who only summarize the video content (via textual summaries or along with them), and Reddit mostly serves for elaboration of better methodologies. The Chinese part of abstractive summarization research has moved far enough in methods, too, but lags behind in applying the discovered methodologies for large-scale studies of Weibo or WeChat content just as well.

Given that abstractive summarization has already been applied to a range of social-science tasks like detection of user opinions on goods and services, fact-checking and news spread, or detection of illness and malicious content, we see promising perspectives in how abstractive summarization can serve in deliberation studies, especially for opinion cumulation research. We have offered a method of reconstructing user discussions and invite the scholars to elaborate more on today's online communication.

Acknowledgements. This research has been supported in full by Russian Science Foundation, grant 21-18-00454 (2021–2023).

References

1. Mridha, M.F., Lima, A.A., Nur, K., Das, S.C., Hasan, M., Kabir, M.M.: A survey of automatic text summarization: progress, process and challenges. IEEE Access **9**, 156043–156070 (2021)
2. Moussa, M.E., Mohamed, E.H., Haggag, M.H.: A survey on opinion summarization techniques for social media. Future Comput. Inf. J. **3**(1), 82–109 (2018)
3. Kim, H.D., Ganesan, K., Sondhi, P., Zhai, C.: Comprehensive review of opinion summarization (2011). https://www.ideals.illinois.edu/items/18805/bitstreams/67737/stream
4. Mehta, P.: From extractive to abstractive summarization: a journey. In: ACL (Student Research Workshop), pp. 100–106 (2016)
5. Gupta, S., Gupta, S.K.: Abstractive summarization: an overview of the state of the art. Expert Syst. Appl. **121**, 49–65 (2019)
6. Bodrunova, S.S., Blekanov, I.S., Maksimov, A.: Public opinion dynamics in online discussions: cumulative commenting and micro-level spirals of silence. In: Meiselwitz, G. (ed.) HCII 2021. LNCS, vol. 12774, pp. 205–220. Springer, Cham (2021). https://doi.org/10.1007/978-3-030-77626-8_14

7. Bodrunova, S.S.: Practices of cumulative deliberation: a meta-review of the recent research findings. In: Chugunov, A.V., Janssen, M., Khodachek, I., Misnikov, Y., Trutnev, D. (eds.) EGOSE 2021. CCIS, vol. 1529, pp. 89–104. Springer, Cham (2022). https://doi.org/10.1007/978-3-031-04238-6_8
8. Margetts, H., John, P., Hale, S., Yasseri, T.: Political Turbulence. Princeton University Press (2015)
9. Habermas, J.: Moral Consciousness and Communicative Action. MIT Press (1990)
10. Bodrunova, S.S., Nigmatullina, K., Blekanov, I.S., Smoliarova, A., Zhuravleva, N., Danilova, Y.: When emotions grow: cross-cultural differences in the role of emotions in the dynamics of conflictual discussions on social media. In: Meiselwitz, G. (ed.) HCII 2020. LNCS, vol. 12194, pp. 433–441. Springer, Cham (2020). https://doi.org/10.1007/978-3-030-49570-1_30
11. Bodrunova, S.S., Blekanov, I.S., Tarasov, N.: Global Agendas: detection of agenda shifts in cross-national discussions using neural-network text summarization for Twitter. In: Meiselwitz, G. (ed.) HCII 2021. LNCS, vol. 12774, pp. 221–239. Springer, Cham (2021). https://doi.org/10.1007/978-3-030-77626-8_15
12. Blekanov, I.S., Tarasov, N., Bodrunova, S.S.: Transformer-based abstractive summarization for Reddit and twitter: single posts vs. comment pools three languages. Future Internet **14**(3), 69 (2022)
13. Bodrunova, S.S., Blekanov, I., Smoliarova, A., Litvinenko, A.: Beyond left and right: real-world political polarization in Twitter discussions on inter-ethnic conflicts. Media Commun. **7**, 119–132 (2019)
14. Waisbord, S.: Mob censorship: online harassment of US journalists in times of digital hate and populism. Digit. J. **8**(8), 1030–1046 (2020)
15. Lin, H., Ng, V.: Abstractive summarization: a survey of the state of the art. In: Proceedings of the AAAI Conference on Artificial Intelligence, vol. 33, no. 01, pp. 9815–9822 (2019)
16. Widyassari, A.P., Rustad, S., Shidik, G.F., Noersasongko, E., Syukur, A., Affandy, A.: Review of automatic text summarization techniques & methods. J. King Saud University Comput. Inf. Sci. **34**(4), 1029–1046 (2020, 2022)
17. Wanjale, K., Marathe, P., Patil, V., Lokhande, S., Bhamare, H.: Comprehensive survey on abstractive text summarization. Int. J. Eng. Res. Technol. (IJERT) (2022). ISSN 2278-0181
18. Syed, A.A., Gaol, F.L., Matsuo, T.: A survey of the state-of-the-art models in neural abstractive text summarization. IEEE Access **9**, 13248–13265 (2021)
19. Alomari, A., Idris, N., Sabri, A.Q.M., Alsmadi, I.: Deep reinforcement and transfer learning for abstractive text summarization: a review. Comput. Speech Lang. **71**, 101276 (2022)
20. Zhang, M., Zhou, G., Yu, W., Huang, N., Liu, W.: A comprehensive survey of abstractive text summarization based on deep learning. Comput. Intell. Neurosci. (2022)
21. Ma, C., Zhang, W.E., Guo, M., Wang, H., Sheng, Q.Z.: Multi-document summarization via deep learning techniques: a survey. ACM Comput. Surv. **55**(5), 1–37 (2022)
22. Koh, H.Y., Ju, J., Liu, M., Pan, S.: An empirical survey on long document summarization: datasets, models, and metrics. ACM Comput. Surv. **55**(8), 1–35 (2022)
23. Zhao, Z., Chen, P.: To adapt or to fine-tune: a case study on abstractive summarization. In: Chinese Computational Linguistics: 21st China National Conference, CCL 2022, Nanchang, China, 14–16 October 2022, Proceedings, pp. 133–146. Springer, Cham (2022). https://doi.org/10.1007/978-3-031-18315-7_9
24. Bražinskas, A., Lapata, M., Titov, I.: Few-shot learning for opinion summarization. arXiv preprint arXiv:2004.14884 (2020)
25. Völske, M., Potthast, M., Syed, S., Stein, B.: TL;DR: mining Reddit to learn automatic summarization. In: Proceedings of the Workshop on New Frontiers in Summarization, pp. 59–63 (2017)

26. Bommasani, R., Cardie, C.: Intrinsic evaluation of summarization datasets. In: Proceedings of the 2020 Conference on Empirical Methods in Natural Language Processing (EMNLP), pp. 8075–8096 (2020)
27. Kim, B., Kim, H., Kim, G.: Abstractive summarization of Reddit posts with multi-level memory networks. arXiv preprint arXiv:1811.00783 (2018)
28. Sotudeh, S., Deilamsalehy, H., Dernoncourt, F., Goharian, N.: TLDR9+: a large scale resource for extreme summarization of social media posts. arXiv preprint arXiv:2110.01159 (2021)
29. Syed, S., Völske, M., Lipka, N., Stein, B., Schütze, H., Potthast, M.: Towards summarization for social media-results of the TL; DR challenge. In: Proceedings of the 12th International Conference on Natural Language Generation, pp. 523–528 (2019)
30. Syed, S., Yousef, T., Al-Khatib, K., Jänicke, S., Potthast, M.: Summary explorer: visualizing the state of the art in text summarization. arXiv preprint arXiv:2108.01879 (2021)
31. Gehrmann, S., Ziegler, Z., Rush, A.M.: Generating abstractive summaries with finetuned language models. In: Proceedings of the 12th International Conference on Natural Language Generation, pp. 516–522 (2019)
32. Li, L., Liu, W., Litvak, M., Vanetik, N., Huang, Z.: In conclusion not repetition: comprehensive abstractive summarization with diversified attention based on determinantal point processes. arXiv preprint arXiv:1909.10852 (2019)
33. Choi, H., et al.: VAE-PGN based abstractive model in multi-stage architecture for text summarization. In: Proceedings of the 12th International Conference on Natural Language Generation, pp. 510–515 (2019)
34. Liu, Y., Jia, Q., Zhu, K.: Keyword-aware abstractive summarization by extracting set-level intermediate summaries. In: Proceedings of the Web Conference 2021, pp. 3042–3054 (2021)
35. Chen, Y., et al.: CDEvalSumm: an empirical study of cross-dataset evaluation for neural summarization systems. arXiv preprint arXiv:2010.05139 (2020)
36. Chen, Y.S., Shuai, H.H.: Meta-transfer learning for low-resource abstractive summarization. In: Proceedings of the AAAI Conference on Artificial Intelligence, vol. 35, no. 14, pp. 12692–12700 (2021)
37. Zhang, J., Zhao, Y., Saleh, M., Liu, P.: PEGASUS: pre-training with extracted gap-sentences for abstractive summarization. In: International Conference on Machine Learning, pp. 11328–11339. PMLR (2020)
38. Liu, S., Yang, L., Cai, X.: SEASum: syntax-enriched abstractive summarization. Expert Syst. Appl. **199**, 116819 (2022)
39. Shi, T., Keneshloo, Y., Ramakrishnan, N., Reddy, C.K.: Neural abstractive text summarization with sequence-to-sequence models. ACM Trans. Data Sci. **2**(1), 1–37 (2021)
40. Bilal, I.M., Wang, B., Tsakalidis, A., Nguyen, D., Procter, R., Liakata, M.: Template-based abstractive microblog opinion summarization. Trans. Assoc. Comput. Linguist. **10**, 1229–1248 (2022)
41. Song, J., Bilal, I.M., Tsakalidis, A., Procter, R., Liakata, M.: Unsupervised opinion summarisation in the wasserstein space. arXiv preprint arXiv:2211.14923 (2022)
42. Albeer, R.A., Al-Shahad, H.F., Aleqabie, H.J., Al-shakarchy, N.D.: Automatic summarization of YouTube video transcription text using term frequency-inverse document frequency. Indonesian J. Electric. Eng. Comput. Sci. **26**(3), 1512–1519 (2022)
43. Latha, B., Nivedha, B., Ranjanaa, Y.: Visual audio summarization based on NLP models. In: 2022 1st International Conference on Computational Science and Technology (ICCST), pp. 63–66. IEEE (2022)
44. Vybhavi, A.N.S.S., Saroja, L.V., Duvvuru, J., Bayana, J.: Video transcript summarizer. In: 2022 International Mobile and Embedded Technology Conference (MECON), pp. 461–465. IEEE, March 2022

45. Xu, W., Miao, Z., Yu, J., Tian, Y., Wan, L., Ji, Q.: Bridging video and text: a two-step polishing transformer for video captioning. IEEE Trans. Circuits Syst. Video Technol. **32**(9), 6293–6307 (2022)
46. Amirian, S., Rasheed, K., Taha, T.R., Arabnia, H.R.: Automatic generation of descriptive titles for video clips using deep learning. In: Arabnia, H.R., Ferens, K., de la Fuente, D., Kozerenko, E.B., Olivas Varela, J.A., Tinetti, F.G. (eds.) Advances in Artificial Intelligence and Applied Cognitive Computing. TCSCI, pp. 17–28. Springer, Cham (2021). https://doi.org/10.1007/978-3-030-70296-0_2
47. Iashin, V., Rahtu, E.: Multi-modal dense video captioning. In: Proceedings of the IEEE/CVF Conference on Computer Vision and Pattern Recognition Workshops, pp. 958–959 (2020)
48. Lin, K., et al.: SwinBERT: end-to-end transformers with sparse attention for video captioning. In: Proceedings of the IEEE/CVF Conference on Computer Vision and Pattern Recognition, pp. 17949–17958 (2022)
49. Atri, Y.K., Pramanick, S., Goyal, V., Chakraborty, T.: See, hear, read: leveraging multimodality with guided attention for abstractive text summarization. Knowl.-Based Syst. **227**, 107152 (2021)
50. Narasimhan, M., Rohrbach, A., Darrell, T.: CLIP-it! language-guided video summarization. Adv. Neural. Inf. Process. Syst. **34**, 13988–14000 (2021)
51. Walia, P., Batra, T., Tiwari, S.N., Goel, R.: Abstractive-extractive combined text summarization of Youtube videos. In: International Conference on Innovative Computing and Communications: Proceedings of ICICC 2022, vol. 2, pp. 687–694. Springer, Singapore (2022). https://doi.org/10.1007/978-981-19-2535-1_55
52. Liang, Z., Du, J., Li, C.: Abstractive social media text summarization using selective reinforced Seq2Seq attention model. Neurocomputing **410**, 432–440 (2020)
53. Wang, Q., Ren, J.: Summary-aware attention for social media short text abstractive summarization. Neurocomputing **425**, 290–299 (2021)
54. Su, M.H., Wu, C.H., Cheng, H.T.: A two-stage transformer-based approach for variable-length abstractive summarization. IEEE/ACM Trans. Audio Speech Lang. Process. **28**, 2061–2072 (2020)
55. Zhang, Z., Liang, X., Zuo, Y., Li, Z.: Unsupervised abstractive summarization via sentence rewriting. Comput. Speech Lang. **78**, 101467 (2023)
56. Zheng, C., Zhang, K., Wang, H.J., Fan, L.: Topic-aware abstractive text summarization. arXiv preprint arXiv:2010.10323 (2020)
57. Huang, Y., Yu, Z., Guo, J., Xiang, Y., Xian, Y.: Element graph-augmented abstractive summarization for legal public opinion news with graph transformer. Neurocomputing **460**, 166–180 (2021)
58. Gao, S., et al.: Abstractive text summarization by incorporating reader comments. In: Proceedings of the AAAI Conference on Artificial Intelligence, vol. 33, no. 01, pp. 6399–6406 (2019)
59. Bani-Almarjeh, M., Kurdy, M.B.: Arabic abstractive text summarization using RNN-based and transformer-based architectures. Inf. Process. Manage. **60**(2), 103227 (2023)
60. Fouzia, F.A., Rahat, M.A., Alie-Al-Mahdi, Md.T., Masum, A.K.M., Abujar, S., Hossain, S.A.: A Bengali text summarization using encoder-decoder based on social media dataset. In: Hassanien, A.E., Bhattacharyya, S., Chakrabati, S., Bhattacharya, A., Dutta, S. (eds.) Emerging Technologies in Data Mining and Information Security. AISC, vol. 1300, pp. 539–549. Springer, Singapore (2021). https://doi.org/10.1007/978-981-33-4367-2_51
61. Aumiller, D., Fan, J., Gertz, M.: On the state of german (abstractive) text summarization. arXiv preprint arXiv:2301.07095 (2023)
62. Shafiq, N., Hamid, I., Asif, M., Nawaz, Q., Aljuaid, H., Ali, H.: Abstractive text summarization of low-resourced languages using deep learning. PeerJ Comput. Sci. **9**, e1176 (2023)

63. Babu, G.A., Badugu, S.: Deep learning based sequence to sequence model for abstractive Telugu text summarization. Multimedia Tools Appl., 1–22 (2022)
64. Louis, A., Maynez, J.: OpineSum: entailment-based self-training for abstractive opinion summarization. arXiv preprint arXiv:2212.10791 (2022)
65. Bhatnagar, V., Kanojia, D., Chebrolu, K.: Harnessing abstractive summarization for fact-checked claim detection. arXiv preprint arXiv:2209.04612 (2022)
66. Boorugu, R.; Ramesh, G.: A survey on NLP based text summarization for summarizing product reviews. In: 2020 Second International Conference on Inventive Research in Computing Applications (ICIRCA), pp. 352–356. IEEE (2020)
67. Zhang, M., Zhou, G., Huang, N., He, P., Yu, W., Liu, W.: AsU-OSum: aspect-augmented unsupervised opinion summarization. Inf. Process. Manage. **60**(1), 103138 (2023)
68. Han, Y., Nanda, G., Moghaddam, M.: Attribute-sentiment-guided summarization of user opinions from online reviews. J. Mech. Des. **145**(4), 041401 (2023)
69. Li, Q., Li, P., Li, X., Ren, Z., Chen, Z., de Rijke, M.: Abstractive opinion tagging. In: Proceedings of the 14th ACM International Conference on Web Search and Data Mining, pp. 337–345 (2021)
70. Mane, P., Sonekar, S., Kausar, S.: Development and implementation of tweet stream summarization technique for pernicious tweet detection. In: Iyer, B., Crick, T., Peng, S.L. (eds.) Applied Computational Technologies: Proceedings of ICCET 2022, pp. 477–485. Springer, Singapore (2022). https://doi.org/10.1007/978-981-19-2719-5_45
71. Sotudeh, S., Goharian, N., Deilamsalehy, H., Dernoncour, F.: Curriculum-guided abstractive summarization for mental health online posts. In: Lavelli, A., Holderness, E., Yepes, A.J., Minard, A.L., Pustejovsky, J., Rinaldi, F.: (eds.) Proceedings of the 13th International Workshop on Health Text Mining and Information Analysis (LOUHI), pp. 148–153 (2022). https://doi.org/10.48550/arXiv.2302.00954
72. Zogan, H., Razzak, I., Jameel, S., Xu, G.: DepressionNet: a novel summarization boosted deep framework for depression detection on social media. arXiv preprint arXiv:2105.10878 (2021)
73. Tampe, I., Mendoza, M., Milios, E.: Neural abstractive unsupervised summarization of online news discussions. In: Arai, K. (ed.) IntelliSys 2021. LNNS, vol. 295, pp. 822–841. Springer, Cham (2022). https://doi.org/10.1007/978-3-030-82196-8_60
74. Duan, Y., Chen, Z., Wei, F., Zhou, M., Shum, H.Y.: Twitter topic summarization by ranking tweets using social influence and content quality. In: Proceedings of COLING 2012, pp. 763–780 (2012)
75. He, R., Liu, Y., Yu, G., Tang, J., Hu, Q., Dang, J.: Twitter summarization with social-temporal context. World Wide Web **20**(2), 267–290 (2016). https://doi.org/10.1007/s11280-016-0386-0
76. Rodríguez-Vidal, J., Carrillo-de-Albornoz, J., Amigó, E., Plaza, L., Gonzalo, J., Verdejo, F.: Automatic generation of entity-oriented summaries for reputation management. J. Ambient. Intell. Humaniz. Comput. **11**(4), 1577–1591 (2019). https://doi.org/10.1007/s12652-019-01255-9
77. Blekanov, I.S., Tarasov, N., Bodrunova, S., Sergeev, S.L.: Mapping opinion cumulation: topic modeling-based dynamic summarization of user discussions on social networks. In: Meizelwitz, G. (ed.) Social Computing and Social Media: Experience Design and Social Network Analysis: 15th International Conference, SCSM 2023, Held as Part of the 25th HCI International Conference, HCII 2023, Copenhagen, Denmark, July 23–28, 2023, Proceedings, Part I. Springer International Publishing (Cham)

Analysis on the Language Use of L2 Japanese Speakers Regarding to Their Proficiency in Group Discussion Conversations

Hung-Hsuan Huang(✉)

Faculty of Informatics, University of Fukuchiyama, Fukuchiyama, Japan
hhhuang@acm.org

Abstract. This paper presents the analysis on the language use of non-native (L2) Japanese speakers with focus on their proficiency in group discussion conversations. Due to the demographic development the necessity to close the resulting gap with foreign employees/workers and thus, non-native speakers is increasing. This work is based on a corpus collected in an experiment which acquired multimodal sensory data in collaborative tasks with unbalanced mixed setup, composed of one none-native speaker and three native (L1) speakers. Each group was given the task to discuss two topics and find a joint decision. This work aims to find the insights how the proficiency of the speakers and the difference in being a native or non-native speakers changes the used vocabulary and decision-making process, which will later be a major issue to ensure an efficient work of such mixed groups. The analysis is based on findings of a total number of seven groups and thus seven L2 speakers. The analysis is on the activeness of the participants during the discussion, the variety of their vocabularies, and language familiarity on using modifier and oral-only expressions based on the results of POS (part of speech) analysis. The results show the characteristics which can be used in automatic assessment on proficiency level.

Keywords: Multiparty interaction · group discussion · multimodal interaction · L2 learner · conversation analysis

1 Introduction

In developed countries, the declining birthrate and aging population are progressing. Especially in Japan, the ratio of the population over 65 years old has been already as high as 28.1% and is expected to over 1/3 by 2036. On the other hand, the total population is expected to continuously decrease to be less than 100 million from current 126.4 million by 2053 [2]. In order to supplement the decreasing working population, Japanese government has started to relax the regulations on introducing foreign workers. The increase of foreigner workers in Japanese society can be expected in near future. In such a situation, foreigner

A. Coman and S. Vasilache (Eds.): HCII 2023, LNCS 14025, pp. 55–67, 2023.
https://doi.org/10.1007/978-3-031-35915-6_5

workers are the minority and have to collaboratively work with Japanese colleagues who are the majority. The working environment is optimized for the Japanese, the rules of the company were also established by the Japanese. Not only the language barrier, but the differences in habits, the way of thinking, common ground, and the communication styles oriented from cultural backgrounds may inhibit efficient team work.

Under an unbalanced environment where non-native (L2) speakers have to work with native (L1) speakers who are in majority, the L2 speakers may show degraded performance on the task due to the burden of language and unfamiliarity of the local culture. This may further decrease the team efficiency. Our project is aiming to understand the issues which may occur in an unbalanced teamwork, based on the results we would like to develop supportive technologies to close the gap and improve the team efficiency. This work is based on the corpus collected in an experiment which acquired multimodal sensory data in collaborative tasks with unbalanced group setup: each group is composed of one L2 speaker and three L1 speakers. Each group discussed two topics and made joint decisions on them. One topic is a free brainstorming one and the other one is the ranking problem on a list of candidates. There are less limits in the vocabulary of the former one and it is supposed to be more difficult for a L2 speaker to join. The discussion on the later one is supposed to be surrounding the candidates and thus should be easier for the L2 speakers to join. Each session for one topic is 15 min long. Experiments with such mixed groups as well as homogeneous groups (all L1 Japanese speakers speaking in Japanese, all L1 Chinese speakers speaking in Chinese) are conducted. From our knowledge, there is no such corpus available and we believe the data collected can provide valuable resources for developing tools in supporting unbalanced groups.

An example of such tools is a virtual reality environment where L2 speakers can practice how to work with L1 speaker virtual agents. In such cases, the system needs to automatically detect the language proficiency level of the L2 participant and adjust the behaviors of the virtual agents according to his/her level in runtime. In order to judge someone's proficiency level in a language, how he or she uses the language is supposed to provide a direct impact on the perception. We are then interested in the following research questions:

Q1: Is it possible to distinguish the proficiency level of Japanese language only from the L2 speaker's use of language (words)?

Q2: If the answer of the question above is "yes," what kind of characteristics of L2 speakers' language use can be potentially used as the features for detecting their proficiency level automatically?

Q3: Do the characteristics above vary depending on the topics of the discussions?

This paper reports the investigation of the research questions on a subset of the data corpus. Seven groups and thus seven L2 speakers are analyzed and are compared with 21 L1 speakers. The analysis is on the richness of their vocabularies, the use of oral-only expressions, and the use of suffix expressions that modify the meaning of the preceding words. We also compare the characteristics of such language use based on the proficiency level (low, middle, high) and native speakers.

2 Related Works

In the computer science field, there have been research works on machine learning based on nonverbal features, including such features as speaking turn, voice prosody, visual activity, and visual focus of attention on the interaction of small groups. Aran and Gatica-Perez [1] presented an analysis of participants' personality prediction in small groups. Okada et al. [8] developed a regression model to infer the score for communication skill using multimodal features, including linguistic and nonverbal features: voice prosody, speaking turn, and head activity. Schiavo et al. [9] presented a system that monitors the group members' nonverbal behaviors and acts as an automatic facilitator. It supports the flow of communication in a group conversation activity. There are works in exploring the barriers of L2 speakers in group discussion [10] or on their behavior changes between the group discussion in L1 and L2 languages [11]. But most of them are about using English as the L2 language. Although there are a number of research works on Japanese language learning in the fields of linguistics and language education [6], we found few works from the computer science field.

This work distinguishes previous one with the following settings:

- Unbalanced composition of L1/L2 speakers in the members of small groups.
- Comparable data of the sessions in Chinese-speaker/Chinese-speaker, Chinese-speaker/Japanese, and Japanese/Japanese combinations so that the behavior changes of both of Japanese and Chinese-speaker participants can be analyzed.
- Data corpus collection and analysis in Japanese as 2nd language in the computer science field where sensory data is recorded and meant for machine learning tasks.

3 Corpus Gathering Experiment

3.1 Experiment Design

In order to extract the characteristics of unbalanced groups, we conducted the experiment to compare unbalanced groups with homogeneous groups. Participants are formed to be groups in the following conditions:

Unbalanced groups: collaborative decision-making discussions were conducted by four participants, three native Japanese speakers and one native Chinese speaker who speaks Japanese as a second language. The language used is Japanese only. Chinese-speaking participants are required to be living in Japan for at least one year, pass Japanese Language Proficiency Test (JLPT) level N2, and be confident to talk in Japanese fluently.

Homogeneous groups: composed of native Japanese or Chinese speakers only. The languages used are the participants' native languages (Japanese or Mandarin Chinese).

Chinese speakers are chosen as the foreigner participant because they are the majority of foreigner students in Japan (Chinese and Taiwanese, 41% in 2018) [4]. All subjects are recruited in Kyoto University including students and office staff. Considering the potential wider range of foreign students and the ease for people in the same generation to talk, the range of the participants are limited to between 18 to 29. All groups are composed with equal numbers of male and female participants to prevent gender bias in the results.

In order to identify the causes of the differences of participants' behaviors, the following factors are considered in the selection of discussion topics: the categories and the knowledge level. For the categories of topics, we considered the factor of whether there are prior candidates to choose from in making the final decision. Following the previous work [7], two typical categories of topics were selected in investigating this factor, ranking style and brain-storming style of topics. Because each participant is invited to attend two experiments (unbalanced and homogeneous groups) if his/her schedule meets, two topics are prepared for each category.

Ranking Style Topics: participants are asked to collaboratively rank the items from a given list based on their importance or goodness. The discussion is supposed to surround the items in the list, and the participants are supposed to recall the vocabulary in a more limited space. The topic in this category should be easier for a L2 speaker. The topics for discussion in this category:

- Ranking of anime titles: participants are asked to predict the top-five rankings from a list of 15 Japanese anime titles based on their popularity. The correct answers are the scores of these titles on a Japanese SNS site where its members can discuss and score anime titles[1]. On this site, popular titles have at least several hundreds of evaluations and can be considered as a reliable source. Because it is possible that some participants do not know the titles of the anime, we prepare the preview video clips of each title which length around five minutes so the participants can prepare themselves before the discussion. There is no time limitation for the participants to watch the video clips, but they usually finish the preparation within 20 min.
- Winter survival exercise: this is a classic task in the research field of group dynamics [5]. The participants are asked to rank the top-five important ones from a list of 15 items with an assumption that they met an airplane crash in winter mountains. Item scores determined by experts are available for evaluating this task. Because the participants are not necessarily familiar with all of the items, the text descriptions of the functionalities of the items are provided to them.

[1] https://www.anikore.jp/pop_ranking/.

Brain-Storming Style Topics: participants are asked to collaboratively deliberate as many ideas as possible without prior candidates. In this work, the preparation of a debate is decided to be the brain-storming task. The participants are asked to discuss the supporting and defending points from a point of view where they are preparing to debate it with another team. Because reliable sources of the evaluation of group performance on this type of task are not available, the count of deliberated supporting/defending points can be used as an objective metric of group performance. Therefore, all experiment sessions have to be conducted with the same point of view on each topic. We set it to be the side of *positive* opinion of the topics. In such a task, the boundary of the vocabulary is supposed to be broader and should be more difficult for the L2 speakers to join.

- Deregulation for introducing foreign workers: the participants are instructed to discuss this issue from the view point of its effect on Japanese society.
- Justice of animal experiments: the participants discuss the trade-off between advances in medical technology and the rights of animals.

During the experiment, Chinese-speaking participants are expected to have some degree of handicaps in their communication with the Japanese language. We have a hypothesis: if there are manipulatable objects that can be used to convey the participants' ideas, the discussion may be facilitated to achieve better team performance.

The setup of the recording environment is shown in Fig. 1. The experiment participants sit around a 1.2 m $\times$ 1.2 m square table. Two video cameras are used to capture the overall scene. Everyone of them had a dedicated WebCam (Logitech Brio Ultra HD) to capture his or her face in large size in 1920 $\times$ 1080 resolution 60 Hz frame rate. Four additional WebCam (Logitech C920) are attached at diagonal direction of the table to compensate for the center ones in the case when the participants face to the sides. These cameras have 1920 $\times$ 1080 resolution and capture at 30 fps. For each trial the data set contains 15 min of four face camera recordings and four corner recordings. In addition to the eight WebCams, two high-resolution (4K) video cameras (Sony FDR AX-700) are used to capture.

The participants also wear motion capture suites (Noitom Perception Neuron 2.0), and their body movements including fingers are recorded. In five out of the 18 experiment sessions motion data was recorded at 60 fps with 33 sensors. The sensor data was interpreted with a human body model by the bundled Axis Neuron software and translated into a BVH file containing the 3D coordinates for 72 body parts 60 Hz. Each participant wore a headset microphone (Audio-Technica HYP-190H) which was connected to an audio digitizer (Roland Sonar X1 LE).

3.2 Experiment Procedures

All subjects were recruited in Kyoto University, nearly all of them are students with only one exception, an office staff. Nine native Chinese speakers (three males and six females, mean age: 25.1) and 33 Japanese participants (18 males and 15 females, mean age: 22.7) were recruited for the experiment. Considering the potential wider range of foreign students and the ease for people in the same generation to talk, the age range of the majority of the participants is from 18 to 29 with only two exceptions (one is 31 and one is 36). Chinese-speaking participants were required to have been living in Japan for at least one year, passed Japanese Language Proficiency Test (JLPT)[2] level N2 and above, and self-declared that they can communicate in Japanese fluently.

The experiment was conducted in an in-subject manner, that is, the participants participated in two experiments, in an unbalanced group and in a homogenous group (speak in Japanese or Chinese as their L1). These participants were formed into 17 groups: eight mixed ones, seven Japanese-only ones, and two Chinese speaker-only ones. All groups are composed of the participants in the same gender or equal number of male and female participants to prevent gender bias in the results. The differences of group dynamics may be caused by the balance of a member's cultural background and may be caused by the personal traits. After the introduction of the whole experiment, the big-five [3] personality test of each participant is conducted. They then discuss two assigned topics, one is a ranking style topic and the other one is in brainstorming style. Each discussion session is limited to 15 min. An alarm clock is placed in front of each participant to help them to conclude the discussion within the allowed time slot. After the experiment, they filled questionnaires which evaluate the performance of the group and the individual participants. As Fig. 1 shows, an alarm is placed in front of each participant so that they can be aware of how much time is remaining and try to finish their discussion within the allowed time slot. After each discussion session, the participants are asked to fill a questionnaire about the performance of the group, the other members, and themselves.

3.3 Analyzed Dataset

For the work reported in this paper, a subset of the collected corpus, seven mixed groups and thus seven L2 speakers are analyzed and are compared with 21 L1 speakers. Although the conditions in recruiting the L2 participants, they all at least hold the level N2 of JLPT and all claimed that they are fluent in speaking Japanese, their actual proficiency levels are diverse. For the analysis, the L2 participants are divided into three levels, low, middle, and high according to the following criteria by the experimenter. The experimenter is not a native speaker of Japanese language but has been living in Japan for more than 20 years since his 20's and holds professor positions for 13 years in Japanese universities. He teaches in Japanese and works in the field of communication science.

[2] https://www.jlpt.jp/e/.

High (H): the participant may have some foreign accent in his/her pronunciation and may have some non-native choices occasionally, but those are able to be compensated by L1 participants implicitly. The participant speaks Japanese fluently and has no difficulties in capturing L1 speakers' vocabularies and speed. The discussion is smooth and there are no observable issues occurring due to one of the participants being a foreigner.

Middle (M): the participant's proficiency level is perceived lower than the participants in the High group. The participant can speak Japanese fluently and can capture almost all of what the L1 speakers said. However, the participant's vocabulary is perceived to be limited. Sometimes the participant cannot figure out how to express his/her ideas and requires the assistance from the L1 speakers explicitly.

Low (L): the participant's proficiency level is perceived lower than the participants in the High and the Middle group. The participant does not speak Japanese fluently and the vocabulary is even more limited. The participant is perceived not to be not able to fully engage the discussion.

According to the criteria above, three of the L2 participants are rated as in the High group, two in the Middle group, and two in the Low group. The video data is then sent to a professional service for manual transcription. Since the L2 participants sometimes did not pronounce some words correctly or used wrong words, these *errors* are annotated with the correct words that the participants are supposed to say.

In Japanese, all words are connected and not separated by spaces. Also, the verbs are conjugated to show tenses. The words need to be extracted from the sentences, and the verbs need to convert to their original form to identify their meanings. The transcriptions are then processed with the Japanese morphological and part-of-speech (POS) analyzer MeCab[3]. MeCab is merely an engine and requires a dictionary to work. The dictionary, UniDic[4] which is developed by National Institute for Japanese Language and Linguistics is used in the task. After the POS analysis, 49 grammatical categories are found. These results include punctuations, symbols, and numbers which are not relevant to the purpose of this work. Also, we consider that some postpositional particles like *yori* (than), *de* (at), *kara* (from), *ni* (to), *no* (of) and so on are basic-level words and omit them from the targets of analysis. People's names are also omitted. As the results, 36 grammatical categories, 1,835 unique words, and totally 32,269 words are found in the dataset. The summary of the analyzed data set is shown in Table 1.

[3] https://taku910.github.io/mecab/.

[4] https://clrd.ninjal.ac.jp/unidic/.

Table 1. Summary of the corpus. The "B" block denotes the brain-storming task sessions, the "R" block denotes the ranking task sessions, and the "O" block denotes the overall data including both sessions. The columns show the data of individual L2 participants and are sorted in the order according to their proficiency groups. The items with (J) denote the average numbers of the three L1 participants in the groups.

		H1	H2	H3	M1	M2	L1	L2
B	unique word	270 (2.22)	201 (1.11)	131 (0.73)	144 (0.73)	81 (0.47)	64 (0.43)	20 (0.16)
	word count	996 (3.24)	889 (1.45)	386 (0.58)	405 (0.51)	217 (0.31)	155 (0.28)	44 (0.09)
	# of utterances	280 (2.74)	235 (1.34)	65 (0.43)	146 (0.74)	119 (0.62)	62 (0.36)	18 (0.12)
	word/utterance	**3.56 (1.24)**	**3.78 (1.12)**	**5.94 (1.21)**	**2.77 (0.70)**	**1.82 (0.52)**	**2.50 (0.71)**	**2.44 (0.84)**
	unique word (J)	122	180	181	198	171	150	124
	word count (J)	307	615	664	801	695	556	497
	# of utterances (J)	102	176	150	197	191	172	153
	word/utterance (J)	2.87	3.39	4.90	3.97	3.53	3.54	2.92
R	unique word	259 (2.31)	146 (0.83)	75 (0.38)	150 (0.77)	110 (0.58)	89 (0.61)	96 (0.57)
	word count	1,004 (2.88)	689 (1.25)	231 (0.29)	527 (0.67)	331 (0.40)	263 (0.49)	302 (0.50)
	# of utterances	270 (2.66)	210 (1.22)	91 (0.46)	178 (0.93)	170 (0.81)	117 (0.71)	167 (0.84)
	word/utterance	**3.72 (1.00)**	**3.28 (1.07)**	**2.54 (0.63)**	**2.96 (0.73)**	**1.95 (0.50)**	**2.25 (0.63)**	**1.81 (0.68)**
	unique word (J)	112	177	199	196	190	146	167
	word count (J)	349	550	807	791	832	541	605
	# of utterances (J)	101	172	200	191	211	165	198
	word/utterance (J)	3.72	3.08	4.04	4.04	3.92	3.57	2.68
O	unique word	428 (2.25)	278 (0.97)	167 (0.54)	246 (0.77)	150 (0.51)	126 (0.54)	107 (0.46)
	word count	2,000 (3.05)	1,578 (1.35)	617 (0.42)	932 (0.59)	548 (0.36)	418 (0.38)	346 (0.31)
	# of utterances	550 (2.70)	445 (1.28)	156 (0.45)	324 (0.84)	289 (0.72)	179 (0.53)	189 (0.53)
	word/utterance	**3.64 (1.10)**	**3.55 (1.09)**	**3.96 (0.92)**	**2.88 (0.72)**	**1.90 (0.52)**	**2.34 (0.66)**	**1.87 (0.68)**
	unique word (J)	190	287	308	318	292	234	232
	word count (J)	656	1,165	1,471	1,592	1,527	1,097	1,103
	# of utterances (J)	204	348	350	388	401	337	351
	word/utterance (J)	3.31	3.24	4.31	4.02	3.67	3.55	2.77

4 Analysis

4.1 Analysis on the Activeness

The first observation on the results of POS analysis is the activeness, or the amount of words they spoke and the length of their utterances. The intuitive hypotheses are:

- The higher the L2 participant's level is, he or she is more active in the discussion.
- If the L2 participant's level is near L1 level, then he or she is as active as the L1 speakers.
- If the L2 participant's level is near L1 level, then he or she can compose utterances as long as L1 speakers.

As shown in Table 1, generally the lower the proficiency level, the subjects were less active (spoke less words). It can also be found that while there are no obvious differences in the activities of High group subjects between the two categories of topics, the Middle and Low group subjects seem to be able to join the discussion easier in ranking topics. This coincides with the hypothesis that the subjects with lower proficiency should be able to recall words easier in a bounded space of discussion topics and provides partial answer to the research question Q3.

The participant H3 showed a tendency different to other participants, her activity in the ranking topic (Japanese anime) is less than in the brain-storming one (introduction of foreign workers). This is probably because she lacks knowledge about Japanese anime. Although overall her perceived proficiency level of Japanese language is high and her pronunciation is near native level, she was not so active in both categories of topics. This may be because her personality is more introverted. Therefore, it is not enough to assess someone's proficiency level merely on how much he or she speaks.

Then we investigated the length of the participants' utterances in the number of words. The assumption is if the L2 speakers speak broken Japanese, then their utterances should be shorter. Because the length of the utterance may depend on the topic, the ratio between the L2 speaker and the L1 speakers in the same group is compared. In the groups where the participant H1 and H2 belong, the L2 speakers actually spoke a lot more than the L1 speakers, but the ratio of word per utterance compared to L1 speakers is slightly larger than 1.0 while H3 is slightly smaller than 1.0. The ratios of Middle and Low level participants are less (around 0.5 to 0.7). The ratio of the word per utterance between L2 and L1 speakers seems to show a good characteristic of the L2 participant's proficiency level.

Fig. 1. Setup of the data corpus recording experiment. The female participant who is facing the camera is the L2 speaker who is perceived highest level of Japanese proficiency (H1)

4.2 Analysis on Word Use

The second analysis is on the distribution of the types of POS. We are interested in the richness of each subject's vocabulary and his/her skill in using the language. We approximate the richness of the participants' vocabulary as the ratio of unique words over the total number of the words spoken by a participant. The expectation is, if the participant has higher skill then this value should be higher because he or she knows more words and there is a larger variety in his or her word use. The measured results are shown in Table 2. Contrary to the expectation, lower rated L2 participants have higher variety of word use in their utterances. Compared to their L1 counterparts, participant H1 and H2 were lower than 1.0 while participant H3 to L2 were higher than 1.0. The results were probably caused by the absolute amount of uttered words of the participants. The fewer the less uttered words, the higher unique word/word count ratio is higher.

The MeCab POS analysis engine reported 49 types of POSs in the analyzed data corpus. After removing the POS types which are irrelevant in evaluating L2 speakers' proficiency level (Sect. 3.3), there are 36 types remaining. We then categorize them in the following three criteria:

Vocabulary: the regular words which can be considered as the speaker's vocabulary. These words are more knowledge oriented, that is, know the word or not. The higher the proficiency the speaker is, the more such words the speaker is supposed to know and use in the conversation. The words in 22 POS types are categorized in this category. These POS types are basically the variations of nouns, verbs, adjectives, and adverbs.

Modifiers: some Japanese words are not used independently but are attached in front of or behind other words to modify their meanings. For example, "mitai" is attached behind a noun to show that something is similar to that noun, "kaku" is attached in front of a noun to show mean each of the noun, "teki" is attached after a noun to make it possible to be used as an adjective, "garu" is attached after a verb to show that someone wants to do that action, and so on. These suffixes or prefixes are identified as 11 POS types by MeCab using UniDic. We consider these words themselves to be part of basic Japanese grammar and a L2 speaker who holds JLPT N2 should have the knowledge of almost all of them. However, they cannot be used to modify any word in the same POS type. There are idiomatic expressions, and there are implicit rules when they are used creatively (not an idiomatic expression but an original use by the speaker). A natural use of such expressions often requires a higher degree of linguistic sense or familiarity rather than the knowledge merely.

Oral-only expressions: like many other languages, there are some expressions which can only be used in casual oral conversation. They cannot be used in a written article or a formal conversation. Also, unlike a L1 speaker, who initially learns the language from the oral conversation conducted by family members, a L2 learner usually starts to learn the language for formal conversations. If the L2 learner does not have the chances to practice oral conversation with L1 speakers, they often cannot use those expressions well, even though they can understand the meanings. The POS analyzer identifies such oral-only expressions in three POS types: fillers, interjections, and the particles at the end of sentences. Examples of such expressions are: "jyan" is an informal expression used to request acknowledgement from the addressee of the utterances, "kke" is a request of a confirmation of an event in the past. The same as the category above, the knowledge itself of such expressions are basic, but a good use of the words in this category requires the familiarity of the language.

Table 2. Distribution of the L2 participants' uttered words regarding POS categories. The "O" block shows the overall state or the *richness* of the participants' utterances. "V" blocks show the distribution in the *vocabulary* categories and "F" blocks show the distribution in the *famalarity* categories. The "u" blocks show the numbers of unique instances and the "c" blocks show the numbers of total counts of the instances. The blocks with overlines show the numbers normalized with the number of utterances. The numbers in the parentheses are the ratio over the L1 speaker partners.

		H1	H2	H3	M1	M2	L1	L2
O	richness	0.214	0.176	0.271	0.264	0.274	0.301	0.309
	richness (J)	(0.751)	(0.658)	(1.252)	(1.268)	(1.316)	(1.379)	(1.192)
Vu	vocabulary	354 (2.52)	221 (0.97)	120 (0.49)	189 (0.75)	99 (0.44)	87 (0.51)	74 (0.42)
	noun	240 (2.62)	130 (0.98)	66 (0.45)	125 (0.79)	60 (0.45)	50 (0.52)	44 (0.42)
	verb	57 (1.99)	43 (0.78)	27 (0.54)	26 (0.49)	17 (0.37)	24 (0.64)	13 (0.34)
	adjective	19 (2.71)	20 (1.25)	5 (0.31)	15 (0.94)	7 (0.42)	2 (0.16)	4 (0.35)
	adverb	39 (3.00)	28 (1.14)	22 (.071)	24 (0.88)	15 (0.54)	11 (0.45)	13 (0.57)
$\overline{Vu}$	vocabulary	0.64 (0.92)	0.50 (0.77)	0.77 (1.04)	0.58 (0.90)	0.34 (0.61)	0.49 (0.83)	0.40 (0.87)
	noun	0.44 (0.95)	0.29 (0.78)	0.42 (0.97)	0.39 (0.95)	0.21 (0.62)	0.28 (0.82)	0.24 (0.87)
	verb	0.10 (0.74)	0.10 (0.62)	0.17 (1.11)	0.08 (0.59)	0.06 (0.51)	0.13 (1.06)	0.07 (0.65)
	adjective	0.03 (0.97)	0.04 (0.99)	0.03 (0.60)	0.05 (1.11)	0.02 (0.58)	0.01 (0.28)	0.02 (0.79)
	adverb	0.07 (1.10)	0.06 (0.90)	0.14 (1.48)	0.07 (1.04)	0.05 (0.77)	0.06 (0.79)	0.07 (1.27)
Vc	vocabulary	1,121 (4.19)	616 (1.19)	279 (0.41)	456 (0.62)	209 (0.30)	182 (0.48)	126 (0.27)
	noun	657 (4.41)	324 (1.25)	150 (0.45)	276 (0.70)	108 (0.28)	97 (0.54)	74 (0.30)
	verb	239 (3.43)	128 (0.83)	83 (0.48)	78 (0.42)	61 (0.31)	46 (0.48)	23 (0.20)
	adjective	41 (3.97)	29 (0.96)	11 (0.22)	26 (0.94)	10 (0.31)	2 (0.06)	6 (0.29)
	adverb	184 (4.76)	135 (1.81)	35 (0.29)	76 (0.60)	30 (0.36)	37 (0.57)	23 (0.28)
$\overline{Vc}$	vocabulary	2.04 (1.52)	1.38 (0.96)	1.79 (0.92)	1.41 (0.76)	0.72 (0.44)	1.02 (0.80)	0.68 (0.63)
	noun	1.19 (1.59)	0.73 (1.00)	0.96 (1.01)	0.85 (0.85)	0.37 (0.41)	0.54 (0.88)	0.40 (0.69)
	verb	0.43 (1.26)	0.29 (0.68)	0.53 (1.07)	0.24 (0.51)	0.21 (0.45)	0.26 (0.78)	0.12 (0.45)
	adjective	0.07 (1.48)	0.07 (0.79)	0.07 (0.45)	0.08 (1.10)	0.03 (0.45)	0.01 (0.12)	0.03 (0.65)
	adverb	0.33 (1.68)	0.30 (1.46)	0.22 (0.64)	0.23 (0.74)	0.10 (0.52)	0.21 (0.90)	0.12 (0.71)
Fu	modifier	53 (1.66)	40 (0.98)	28 (0.62)	35 (0.79)	25 (0.58)	26 (0.72)	17 (0.45)
	oral	194 (1.00)	359 (1.51)	135 (0.44)	245 (0.66)	194 (0.56)	125 (0.32)	160 (0.64)
$\overline{Fu}$	modifier	0.10 (0.60)	0.09 (0.77)	0.18 (1.27)	0.11 (0.93)	0.09 (0.80)	0.15 (1.19)	0.09 (0.75)
	oral	0.04 (0.46)	0.04 (0.71)	0.13 (1.92)	0.07 (1.18)	0.10 (1.49)	0.08 (0.91)	0.09 (1.28)
Fc	modifier	685 (3.52)	603 (1.47)	203 (0.42)	231 (0.48)	145 (0.30)	111 (0.33)	60 (0.15)
	oral	194 (1.00)	359 (1.51)	135 (0.44)	245 (0.66)	194 (0.56)	125 (0.32)	160 (0.64)
$\overline{Fc}$	modifier	1.25 (1.27)	1.36 (1.21)	1.30 (0.89)	0.71 (0.58)	0.50 (0.43)	0.62 (0.55)	0.32 (0.35)
	oral	0.35 (0.36)	0.81 (1.19)	0.87 (0.97)	0.76 (0.82)	0.67 (0.80)	0.70 (0.60)	0.86 (1.12)

Table 2 shows the analysis results according to the three categories above. In the vocabulary category, we further distinguish the variations of nouns, verbs, adjectives, and adverbs, respectively to see whether there are tendencies in different POS types. For all participants including both L1 and L2 speakers, nouns were the majority of all of the words analyzed. The ratio is from 1/2 to 2/3. The second are verbs while there were much less adjective and adverb instances. The ratio of nouns spoken by L2 speakers over L1 speakers is close to the total of all POS types in the vocabulary category. The intuitive expectation of vocabulary is, the more the unique words, the higher the proficiency level the speaker has. However, these values depend on the number of total words spoken by the participant and have no obvious tendency. On the other hand, the L2/L1 values normalized with the number of utterances more match the impression of the L2 participants' level. The participants in the High group have values close to 1.0 and the lower rated L2 participants have lower values. In addition, compared to the number of unique words ($\overline{Vu}$ values), the total counts of words ($\overline{Vc}$ values) fit the level better.

The results in language familiarity categories do not clearly meet the expectation where the higher the proficiency level the higher the values are. The normalized total counts ($\overline{Fc}$) of modifiers generally meet the order of the participant level while oral-only expressions have two exceptions. The H1 participant is low but the L2 participant is high. This probably imply that participant H1 has good knowledge of the Japanese language but may do not have so many chances in face-to-face conversations. This makes her utterances have less oral-only expressions and feel more formal.

5 Conclusions

This paper reports the investigation of the potential in using linguistic features of L2 speakers' language use to detect their proficiency level of Japanese language. We analyzed the L2 and L1 participants' distribution of their word use based on POS analysis in unbalanced group discussion. The results show that there are indeed characteristics for this purpose. The activeness of the participants, the richness of their vocabulary, the familiarity in using modifier expressions and oral-only expressions all show specific characteristics. Also, rather than raw values, values normalized with the total amount of utterance provide better information. The measurement depends on the topic of discussion and therefore multiple topics of conversation should be used for the assessment.

The results show that the proficiency level of a L2 speaker is not from low to high in one dimension. A L2 speaker may be able to pronounce the language with nearly no foreigner accent but may not have a large size of vocabulary. Or, a L2 speaker may have good knowledge of vocabulary but is not good in oral expressions. Therefore, we would like to explore more modalities such as the prosodic information of L2 speakers' pronunciation and develop a multi-dimensional assessment method.

Further direction of this work is to find the what kinds of computer aided support can be realized in what kind of situations during collaborative work of unbalanced group members. A short-term goal is to find the moments where non-native speakers have difficulty in expressing their thoughts and provide handily hints in runtime. In order to work on such detection task, the data corpus is still small, it is necessary for us to conduct more experiments to increase the number of groups for more generalized results.

References

1. Aran, O., Gatica-Perez, D.: One of a kind: inferring personality impressions in meetings. In: Proceedings of 15th ACM International Conference on Multimodal Interaction (ICMI 2013), Sydney, Australia, December 2013
2. The Cabinet Office: Annual report on the agening society: 2019. Technical report, July 2019
3. Claes, L., Vandereycken, W., Luyten, P., Soenens, B., Pieters, G., Vertommen, H.: Personality prototypes in eating disorders based on the big five model. J. Pers. Disord. **20**(4), 401–416 (2006)
4. Japan Student Services Organization: Survey results of enrollment status of foreign students in fy2018. Technical report, January 2019
5. Joshi, M.P., Davis, E.B., Kathuria, R.C., Ken Weidner, I.: Experiential learning process: exploring teaching and learning of strategic management framework through the winter survival exercise. J. Manag. Educ. **29**(5), 672–695 (2005)
6. Mori, Y., Hasegawa, A., Mori, J.: The trends and developments of L2 Japanese research in the 2010s. Lang. Training **54**(1), 90–127 (2020)
7. Nihei, F., Nakano, Y.I., Hayashi, Y., Huang, H.H., Okada, S.: Predicting influential statements in group discussions using speech and head motion information. In: 16th International Conference on Multimodal Interaction (ICMI 2014), pp. 136–143, Istanbul, November 2014
8. Okada, S., Nakano, Y., Hayashi, Y., Takase, Y., Nitta, K.: Estimating communication skills using dialogue acts and nonverbal features in multiple discussion datasets. In: 18th ACM International Conference on Multimodal Interaction (ICMI 2016), pp. 169–176, Tokyo, November 2016
9. Schiavo, G., Cappelletti, A., Mencarini, E., Stock, O., Zancanaro, M.: Overt or subtle? Supporting group conversations with automatically targeted directives. In: Proceedings of the 19th International Conference on Intelligent User Interfaces (IUI 2014), pp. 225–234 (2014)
10. Stroud, R.: Second language group discussion participation: a closer examination of 'barriers' and 'boosts'. In: Proceedings of the International Conference on Education and Learning (ICEL), Tokyo, January 2017
11. Yamamoto, S., Taguchi, K., Ijuin, K., Umata, I., Nishida, M.: Multimodal corpus of multiparty conversations in L1 and L2 languages and findings obtained from it. Lang. Resour. Eval. **49**, 857–882 (2015)

Identifying Influential Social Impact Websites with HITS Algorithms

Yang Ruei Jheng[1], Ping-Yu Hsu[1], Jiu Zhong Chen[1], Ming Shien Cheng[2](✉), and Yu-Chun Chen[1]

[1] Department of Business Administration, National Central University, No. 300, Jhongda Road, Jhongli, Taoyuan 32001, Taiwan (R.O.C.)

[2] Department of Industrial Engineering and Management, Ming Chi University of Technology, No. 84, Gongzhuan Road, Taishan, New Taipei 24301, Taiwan (R.O.C.)

mscheng@mail.mcut.edu.tw

Abstract. Advocators of ESG (Environment, Social, Governance) attempt to propose standards for business to report their sustainability measure to investors. The three aspects are corporate social responsibility in society. However, the indicators to reveal impact generated by social activities are still in the development. As an result, the Social Impact reported on websites and ESG reports are diversified and inconsistent. This research aimed at recommending model webpages to readers for the references of business world. This research implements variations of HITS algorithm to identify authority and hub pages excluding the influence of pages in the same website as self-references may seriously distort ranking result. Top 10 authority pages are recommended among 3 million webpages collected from the world wide web. The appropriateness of the pages is compared against first 10 links retrieved from Google search. Expert reviewers confirmed that the recommended pages were better than the links retrieved from Google.

Keywords: HITS Algorithm · ESG · Social Impact · CSR

1 Introduction

The concept of CSR was already mentioned in the book "Philosophy of Management" by British scholar Oliver Sheldon in 1923. In recent years, the concept of CSR has surfaced again due to the increasing exploitation of the environment and the rising awareness of environmental protection among the general public (Li Xiuying, Liu Junru, & Vol. 1 [1]). The importance of ESG as an action guideline for CSR is obvious. In a successful company, the "S(Social)" in ESG is about how to implement Social Impact. What kind of social impact do they have on society?

The HITS algorithm has been proven in previous studies to find opinion leaders in social networks (Sun, Bin, & Applications [2]) or to improve the accuracy of recommendation systems (Y.W. Liu & J.L. Huang. [3]). The above studies aim to find the most representative nodes in Internet graphs to find their hidden meaning. In short, the HITS algorithm coincides with this study to find the authority concept of "social impact" in

A. Coman and S. Vasilache (Eds.): HCII 2023, LNCS 14025, pp. 68–82, 2023.
https://doi.org/10.1007/978-3-031-35915-6_6

web pages. Therefore, this study used the HITS algorithm to analyze the social impact of each webpage and gave the ranking to find the best social impact criteria.

In this study, we collected many social impact-related web pages from the World Wide Web, modified the graphs, and then implemented the HITS algorithm to find the authority of social impact web pages.

This paper organized as follow: (1) Introduction: Research background, motivation and purpose. (2) Related work: Review of scholars' researches on HITS algorithm, CSR and ESG, social impact of ESG and Scopus. (3) Research methodology: Content of research process in this study. (4) Result analysis: Experimental results and the discussion of the test results. (5) Conclusion and future research: Contribution of the study, and possible future research direction is discussed.

2 Related Work

2.1 HITS Algorithm

Hyperlink-Induced Topic Search (HITS Algorithm, short for HITS) is a link-oriented graph theory algorithm that is well suited for use in Internet relationships. The HITS algorithm assigns an Authority Score and a Hub Score to each web page and ranks them (Fig. 1). The HITS algorithm has two basic assumptions.

1. A good Authority page will be pointed to by many good Hub pages.
2. A good Hub page will point to many good Authority pages.

These two assumptions give the relationship between the Authority page and the Hub page: mutual reinforcement, a recursive definition. (Gibson, Kleinberg, & Raghavan [4]).

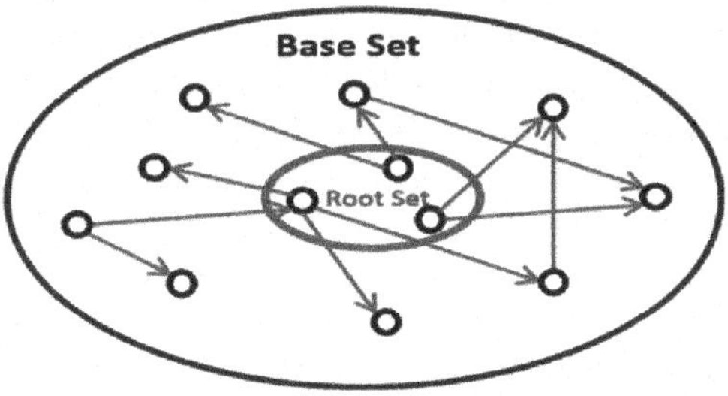

Fig. 1. Schematic diagram of Root Set and its derived Base Set

Based on the two points mentioned above, the HITS algorithm is good at extracting and finding better quality web pages in a web system for users' reference. Previous studies have also shown that HITS algorithms are commonly used in recommendation systems to find important topics in them (Y.W. Liu & J.L. Huang [3]). The HITS algorithm has been shown to coincide with this study's attempt to filter out unknown "social impact" authority from many web pages, and it is hoped that this will serve as a reference for future researchers.

The HITS algorithm gives each web page two scores, which are: 1. Authority Score and 2. Hub Score.

The HITS algorithm is as follows. Give the query term q in the search engine, take the first n pages (e.g., n = 200) from the total set of returned result pages as the root set (S), then S meets (Kleinberg [5]).

1. The pages in S are fewer in number.
2. The pages in S are related to query q.
3. The pages in S contain more authority pages.

So far, index-based Web search engines have been the main tool for users to search for information. However, these search engines are not suitable for many searches in the same domain, especially when the subject of any breadth contains thousands or millions of relevant pages (Chakrabarti et al. [6]). Therefore, how to present the correct and most valuable pages to users becomes an important issue. The HITS algorithm is a graphical algorithm to analyze the importance of web pages.

However, HITS also has obvious drawbacks, such as taking too long and being prone to Topic Drift (Nomura, Oyama, Hayamizu, Ishida, & Japan [7]). In this study, these problems were specially considered and improved, and the detailed experimental methods will be described in Sect. 4.

2.2 Social Impact of ESG

Previous studies have shown that investors consider ESG ratings an additional criterion in addition to a company's bond rating. However, bond ratings are similar for each company, while ESG ratings are significantly divergent (Dimson, Marsh, & Staunton [8]). At the same time, there is no significant return difference between ESG ratings and returns. Other studies have separated ESG into three separate factors and attempted to distinguish which factor is most strongly associated with financial performance (Ahlklo & Lind [9]). However, they both suggest that investors should no longer expect returns by judging by ESG ratings (Halbritter & Dorfleitner [10]). However, these studies suggest that when selecting two companies, choosing the one with the higher ESG rating is recommended.

These literature studies show that companies with higher ESG ratings mostly have better fundamentals, representing positive mutual feedback between the company and society. Therefore, ESG is not only an important issue that modern companies must pay attention to but also a key to the long-term operation of the company. However, there is no unified criterion for ESG (Dorfleitner, Halbritter, & Nguyen [11]). The literature above shows that there is no standardized standard for the "S" in ESG. What kind of social contribution is considered good? Is it possible to extract good social standards from some successful companies? In this study, we hope to find out the social impact of ESG by the HITS algorithm from the web pages of many successful companies and provide a reliable standard for subsequent researchers.

3 Research Methodology

This study is divided into three parts, as shown in Fig. 2. In the first stage, web crawlers will be used to collect as many Social Impact related web pages as possible and record all out-links of each web page to build a root collection. In the second stage, all web pages are stored in nodes and added to relationships according to the relationships accessed in the first stage to complete a directed graph containing all web pages. The third stage is to execute the HITS algorithm by this graph and modify the data or change the score weights to do the final result analysis.

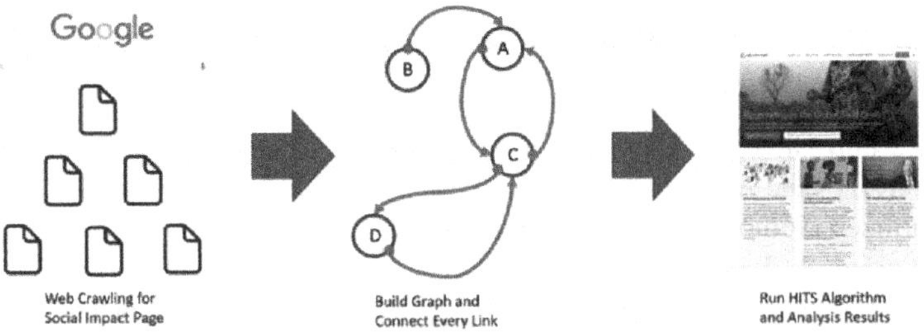

Fig. 2. The Research Architecture

3.1 Research Process

This study uses the HITS algorithm based on the query engine, so it is necessary to start the algorithm from the keyword query, and the keyword collection process is shown in the figure. The first part of this study is to search for papers in different fields using Scopus and retrieve the most repeated keywords as the set of keywords to start the algorithm. The idea of using the most repeated words is inspired by the association rule (Srikant & Agrawal [12]). We believe that the keywords satisfying a certain repetition can be used as the set of keywords to start the algorithm, just like the association rule satisfying the minimum support threshold and the minimum support confidence threshold.

The data collected above is stored in the graph with the data structure as in Fig. 3, so that G = (V, E) is a directed graph with vertex set V and edge set E, where E is a subset of V × V. For a given vertex Vi, In(Vi) is the set of vertices pointing to it (In-link set), and let Out(Vi) be the vertex pointing to Out-link.

3.2 Algorithms Processing

The algorithm first gives all the nodes in the graph a fixed Hub score, which is initially the same for each node, and the following are the weights of the nodes in the basic update algorithm (1).

1. Updated authority values of all nodes in the graph: for all nodes V, (v_i) the sum of all In-link(v_j) of the Hub values $v_j \in N_{in}(v_i)$.

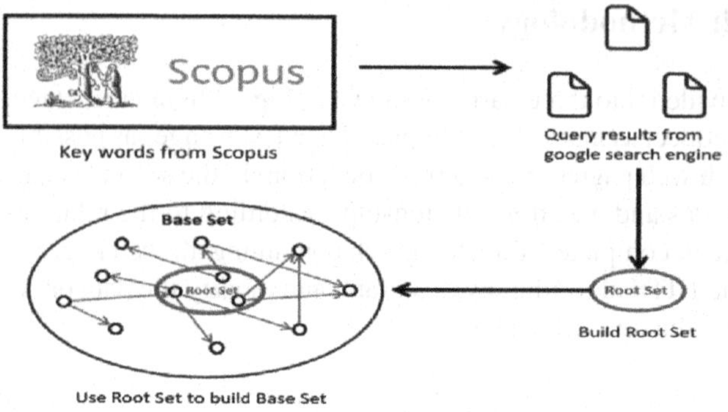

Fig. 3. Keyword search flow chart

2. Updated hub values of all nodes in the graph: for all nodes V, (v_i) the sum of all Out-link(v_i) of the Authority values $v_j \in N_{in}(v_i)$
3. Standardized Authority values and Hub values.
4. Repeat points 1, 2, and 3.
5. Terminate the iteration if the maximum number of iterations is reached or the error of change is less than the error tolerance.

$$
\begin{aligned}
Authority(v_i) &= \sum_{v_j \in N_{in}(vi)} hub(v_j) \\
hub(v_i) &= \sum_{v_j \in N_{in}(vi)} Authority(v_j)
\end{aligned}
\tag{1}
$$

This algorithm will be implemented using Python code, using two Dictionary containers to record the node's Authority score and Hub score, respectively, and update each individual node sequentially. The reasons for using Dictionary containers are (1) Python Dictionary is faster to find, and (2) Dictionary features can ensure that nodes will not be duplicated, and it is easier to add nodes dynamically afterward and to optimize the dynamic maintenance process if there is a follow-up.

4 Research Experiment

4.1 Data Collection

The first step is to create a set of keywords. Since this study is a new field of research, there are no keywords related to "social impact" for the root set to be implemented. Therefore, we first use the search engine built into the Scopus paper database and type in the keywords: 1. "Social Impact"; 2. "Social Value"; 3. "Value Impact".

A total of 352 papers were queried using the Scopus engine for the above three keywords, and the keywords mentioned in these papers were repeated more than 4 times (50 in total) as the starting query for the HITS algorithm. Each keyword query was processed through a brand new incognito browser to ensure query results are not altered by past query preferences, language, region, or private cookie results. After removing the first page of query results (about 9 results) for each keyword, including the abandoned results due to long response time and the duplicate results, we found that the total number of non-duplicate pages was 384. We used this as the Root Set of the program. Next, according to the web pages of the above root collection, requests were made in turn, and the hyperlinks in all HTML documents were obtained as many as possible from all responses. This section retrieved all < a > tags, and the HTML < a > elements create hyperlinks to external, other pages, files, email addresses, or other URLs.

In this study, a complete crawler and an indexing system were established to crawl tens of millions of data and store more than 3 million non-repetitive website data in total. In order to implement the HITS algorithm, the web crawler needs to crawl all the hyperlinks of the web pages. Although this is a simple task, the search time is huge, and the number of pages is very large. In addition, each link in the database needs to be compared, which is another huge amount of time spent (time complexity $O(N^3)$. And this does not include the various bugs web crawlers are bound to encounter. In summary, the whole crawling process is not an easy task. This study has proposed an effective solution, which will be described below.

This study is a hyperlink-oriented algorithm, so only the links starting with HTTP and HTTPS in the < a > tag in the HTML text of the web page were taken. The algorithm was suspended after the search of all websites in each layer, and the number of "non-duplicate pages" added in this layer was counted first. If the number of non-duplicate pages added in this layer is less than 10% of the total number of non-duplicate pages, then we consider that the Base Set is close to convergence. At each level, we have compared the pages in the database to see if there is any duplication. If there are duplicate pages, we delete them, otherwise, we put all non-duplicate sites into the next search level. This was repeated until the algorithm finally reached the convergence condition. In this study, we conducted 14 levels of search, and the rate of increase of non-duplicate new pages was 7.40318289134777%, and the total number of non-duplicate pages was 3031080 before the search was stopped (Fig. 4 and 5).

The following are the descriptive statistics of all the collected web data sets.

- The average number of Out-links per node = 71.69195092644324.
- Median Out-links per node = 29.
- Number of Out-links per node = 0.
- Maximum number of node out-links = 38400

However, the shortcomings of the HITS algorithm have been clearly pointed out in previous studies because it is an algorithm based on search engine query initiation, where the high time cost is the obvious shortcoming of the algorithm (Patel & Patel [13]). The crawling time of several days to weeks greatly reduces the smoothness of the study and is an insurmountable obstacle. This problem was also encountered in the implementation of this study, and because of the huge number of keywords searched in this study (50 in total), the hyperlinks extended from the root set were larger than those of other studies, and the total number of search sites was even close to hundreds of millions. Therefore, it is important to consider how to solve the significant time cost required to start this study.

In this study, the Python Selenium module was used to avoid the detection of the anti-crawler by using its human click simulation function. This is because the anti-crawler not only blocks the data collection in this study but also may cause the whole crawler to

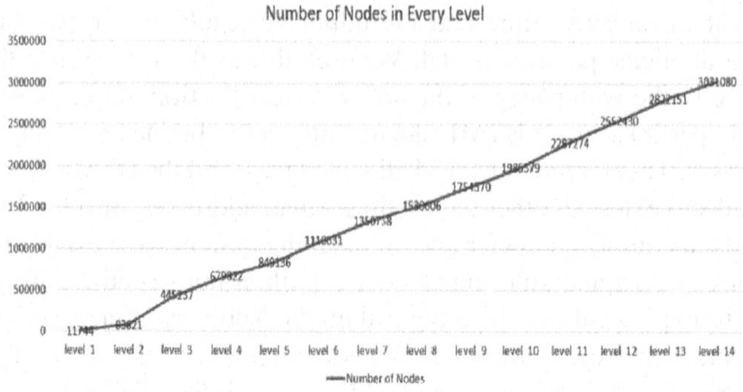

Fig. 4. The total number of pages in each layer (no duplicate pages)

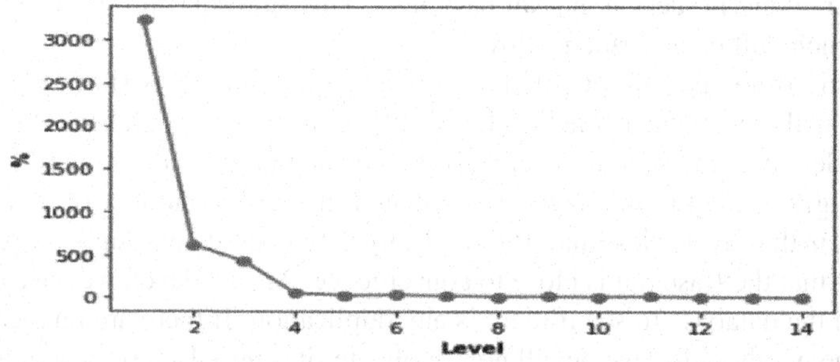

Fig. 5. Percentage increase of non-repeated web pages for each layer (conforms to power distribution)

stall or have no response. The detection of anti-reptiles by the Selenium module proved to be effective in this study, but the time cost was very high because it simulated human clicks. This study requires crawling tens of millions of data, so the Selenium module approach was not used in this study for the time being.

This section highlights the technique used in this study—Asyncio asynchronous programming for writing crawlers in Python. Python's asyncio module is a standard module for asynchronous frameworks introduced only in python 3.4. Previous research has used similar asynchronous programming logic and effectively optimized its code (Shettar & Shobha [14]).

In asynchronous programming, the programmer can execute a Coroutine by dropping it into the Event Loop (as shown in Fig. 6 below). Throughout the execution of the Event Loop, the Event Loop checks all the Coroutine tasks and classifies them into two categories, (1) the list of executable procedures and (2) the list of completed tasks. When a task has been completed, it will be classified as "Completed Tasks" until all tasks in the Event Loop have been completed (all are classified as Completed Task), then the Event Loop will be terminated.

The waiting time required for a typical linear crawler is very long. With such a large amount of crawling data as this study, it took days to tens of days just to crawl the hyperlinked information by waiting for each packet to be sent in turn. In addition, this

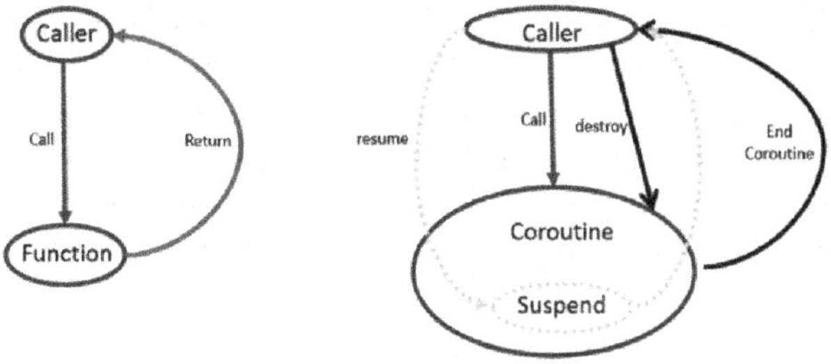

Fig. 6. Asynchronous programming Coroutine call principle and differences from general programs

crawler contains a lot of input/output operations. For such I/O-intensive operations, the linear crawler cannot effectively handle the errors often encountered by crawlers. Finally, this study was a program that encountered a lot of waiting (waiting for packets to come back) because the CPU processor spent a lot of time waiting for network I/O. However, if we directly use preemptive multitasking to split the crawlers in this study, most of the programs would still be waiting due to a large number of waiting for tasks (more than tens of millions of crawlers), and there may still be potential race conditions. Therefore, when executing a large amount of I/O code like this study, this study prefers to use asynchronous programming rather than linear crawlers and multi-execution sequential code programming.

After we wrote the program using Python Asyncio, we reduced the crawling time from tens of days to weeks to half a day (about 15 h), significantly reducing the crawling time.

4.2 Data Preprocessing

Split Info is often used to penalize nodes with too much branching (Harris [15]). We have speculated that this method is similar to the nodal-directed graph in this study. In the above-mentioned directed graph, if the node has many outward links, its Hub value may be better, affecting the subsequent Authority score. Therefore, this study tries to modify the algorithm by using Split Info (2).

$$-\sum_{i=1}^{k}\frac{N(v_i)}{N}log_2\frac{N(v_i)}{N} \tag{2}$$

The formula of Split Info is shown above. In this study, *N(vi)* is the number of instances assigned to node *vi,* and *k* is the total amount of splitting. Split Info splits the entropy of a partition into its sub-nodes and evaluates whether the split will produce a large number of sub-nodes of the same size. For example, if each partition has the same number of instances, then *vi:* $N(vi)/N = 1/k$, and the split information will equal *log2 k*. Therefore, if a node produces many splits, then its Split Info is also large, reducing the gain ratio.

In this study, Split Info was used as a penalty for nodes with too many outbound links, meaning that if a node (web page) has a large number of branches (outbound links), its hub value calculated from the original formula would keep adding up the weights of all outbound links in each iteration to update the weights. By dividing by the Split Info value, we try to restore the values of these nodes to a reasonable range.

Another problem was found in the data processing stage. The collected data mentioned above shows many web pages with the same hyperlinks as the original web pages. The following Fig. 7 shows the data of the duplicate domain.

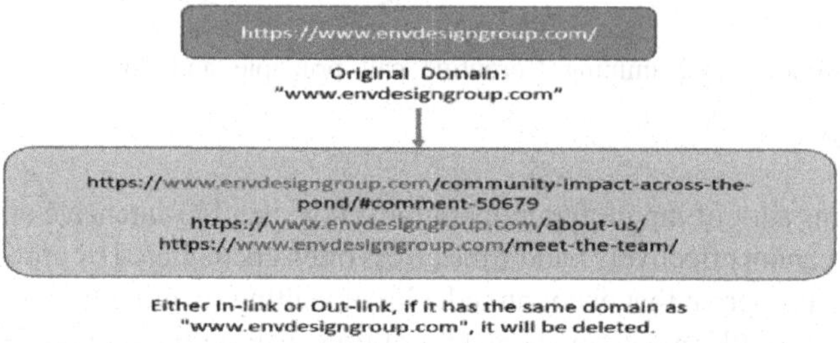

Fig. 7. It is found that in the collected data set, some webpages have subpages with the same domain.

This situation was not consistent with the previous assumptions. First, the search for the HITS algorithm was based on the hyperlink between different web pages. However, because the previous HITS algorithm implementation might not be able to focus on so many aspects (such as the 50 keywords in this paper), most of the searches and rankings were conducted in a single field. Most of the searches and rankings were conducted in a single field, so similar social networking sites such as "Amazon," "Facebook," "Tumblr," or the electronic commerce industry were not considered, and such sites usually have a large number of self-directed hyperlinks. Second, HITS pays much attention to the quality of the Root Set; otherwise, they found a set of websites could easily produce "Topic Drift," and the algorithm cannot determine the valid results from the low-quality data set.

Based on the above two points, this study attempted to leave only "outward" links in the relationship between websites, meaning that all hyperlinks leading to their own domains would be deleted, and the deleted data would be used to create graphs. In this study, we used Regular Expression to capture the domain part of each URL, sorted all the in-links and out-links of each URL in turn, and deleted the URLs with the same domain directly.

In this study, each URL was converted into a unique integer to implement the HITS algorithm, and these integers were used as IDs stored in the graph. After confirming that the nodes in the graph were non-duplicate, we assigned each node an initial Authority score and a Hub score. Usually, all nodes in the graph would start with the same weight, with additional changes described in the following methods.

4.3 Experimental Result and Analysis

A total of three experts were asked to evaluate the results of this study and rank the top 10 web pages analyzed by each of the four methods. Among them, "4" was the most agreed that it represents Social Impact Authority Page. "1" was the most disagreed. "0" was considered irrelevant. The results are shown in the table below.

In this study, four types of dispositions were performed on the previously collected datasets, (1) the original HITS algorithm, (2) Split-info was used to calculate the original data, (3) Same Domain Removal, and (4) used Same Domain Removal to process the data before using Split-info to compute. The result showed that the same domain collection was distributed into several regions due to the ranking relationship of the algorithm. In order to make the distribution of the top 10 authoritative web pages clearer, this study took the first web page of different domains as the representative and listed the top 10 authoritative web pages, respectively. The results are presented in Tables 1. The web pages were retrieved on May 20, 2022.

This study used Google Chrome as the browser to support the study results. In addition to being the first search engine to start the algorithm, it is also the most popular browser in the world today. Previous studies have shown that the Google Chrome search engine uses PageRank techniques to help it produce highly accurate results (Brin, Page, & systems [16]). The PageRank algorithm is described in detail in Page, Brin, Motwani, & Winograd [17].

This study verified that the keywords searched in the Scopus database: Social Impact, Value Impact, and Social Value were firstly typed in the untraceable google browser and compared the results of the keywords searched in the browser with the results of this study. We compared the search results of the keywords on the browser with the search results of this study to find out which was more representative in searching for Social Impact Authority. Figure 8 are the screenshots of the results of the above three keywords, respectively. The results of the Google browser search were used to determine whether the authoritative websites pointed out in this study were better than Google after expert discussion.

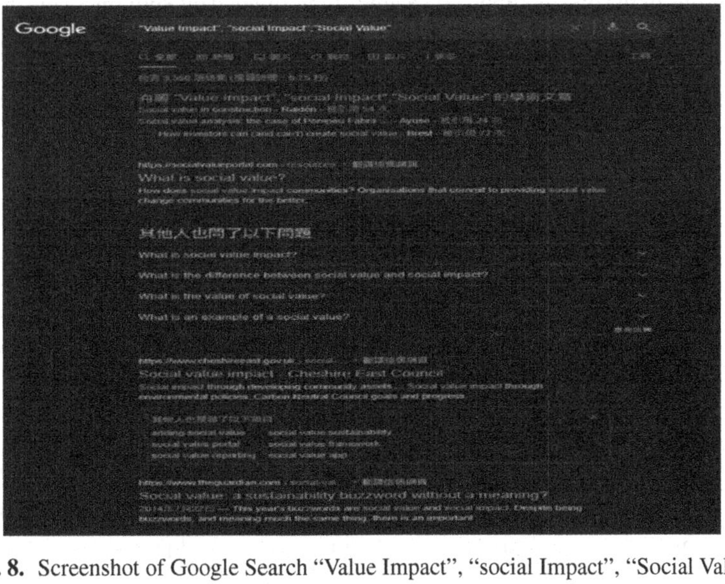

Fig. 8. Screenshot of Google Search "Value Impact", "social Impact", "Social Value"

First, experts agreed that the results of individual searches for Social Impact, Value Impact, and Social Value keywords did not represent the authority of Social Impact. Most noun explanations appeared first, and the results lacked a "global" character compared to this study.

Another expert suggested that the study was initiated by typing "Social Impact, Value Impact, and Social Value" into Scopus, and the 50 most frequent keywords were suggested. The search terms were then dropped into a blank Google browser. Therefore, when verifying the merits of authoritative websites, it is necessary to type in all three keywords together to have a fairer judgment. The first result is a link to a related paper, and then Social Value explains the definition of the term, which is not in line with the requirement to find an authoritative website.

The third search result was "Social value impact - Cheshire East Council (https://www.cheshireeast.gov.uk/council_and_democracy/your_council/social-value/social-value-impact.Aspx)." The experts believe that although it meets the definition of a Social Impact website, it has regional limitations. Compared to this study's results, the results have a more global perspective and are more representative of Social Impact's authoritative website.

In general, the first search result given by Google search is mostly "explanation of terms." Next, according to the keywords, links to discussion articles were given, or pages that were relatively local or might mention the keywords related to this study, but no authoritative websites with global representation were given. Compared to the results of this study, the web pages recommended by the Google search engine hardly matched the topics we were seeking.

Table 1 below shows the results of this study using four different methods. The results of the third authoritative website are already biased. "Twoje Drzwi do IT" means "Your Gateway to IT," a website that provides training and online consulting services, which is considered by experts to be very different from the objectives of this study.

The results of the two modified HITS algorithms divided by Split Info were discussed by experts and did not meet the objectives of this study, so they were not used.

However, Table 2 gives a fairer result. After expert discussion and comparison with the above Google results, the results of Table 2, "Same Domain Removal," best meet the criteria of "Global Social Impact Authority." Because the ranking results such as World Bank, MIGA, IFC, WHO, etc., have a global scope of business and do not focus on a single region or rank high because of relevant keywords, it is more authoritative and representative website compared to other results.

Table 1. Total of three experts

	Original HITS	Same Domain Removal HITS	Split Info HITS	Same Domain Removal and Split Info	google
Expert A	25	40	15	13	0
Expert B	27	39	21	10	0
Expert C	26	39	19	11	0

Table 2. HITS algorithm result after processing with Same Domain Removal method

1.	https://www.worldbank.org (World-Bank) The World Bank, this study identifies the pages considered to be the best social impact pages, through which experts unanimously agree to represent an authority on the organization's social impact, the World Bank is committed to eradicating poverty, and all its decisions must drive direct investment or international trade, laying the foundation for convenient capital investment. 
2.	https://www.miga.org/ (MIGA) The Multilateral Investment Guarantee Agency (MIGA) is a member of the World Bank Group. Its mission is to facilitate cross-border investment in developing countries by providing guarantees (political risk insurance and credit enhancement) to investors and lenders. 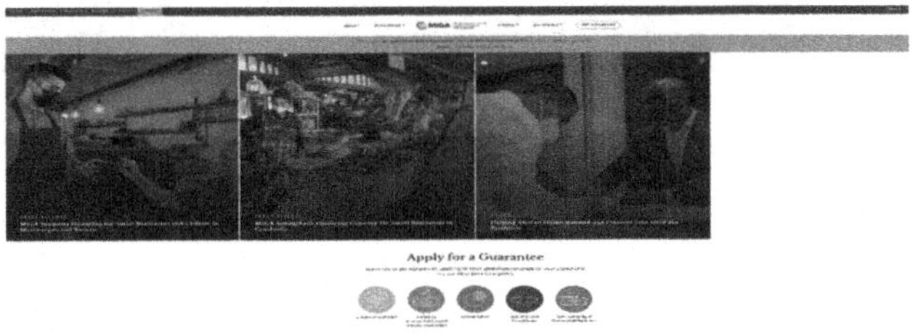
3.	https://www.ifc.org/ (IFC) IFC, a member of the World Bank Group, promotes economic development and improves people's lives by encouraging private sector growth in developing countries. 
4.	https://www.cao-ombudsman.org/ (CAO) The Office of the Compliance Advisor Ombudsman (CAO) is the independent accountability mechanism for projects supported by the International Finance Corporation (IFC) and the Multilateral Investment Guarantee Agency (MIGA), members of the World Bank Group. Act as an intermediary between the IFC and those affected by the program.

(continued)

Table 2. (*continued*)

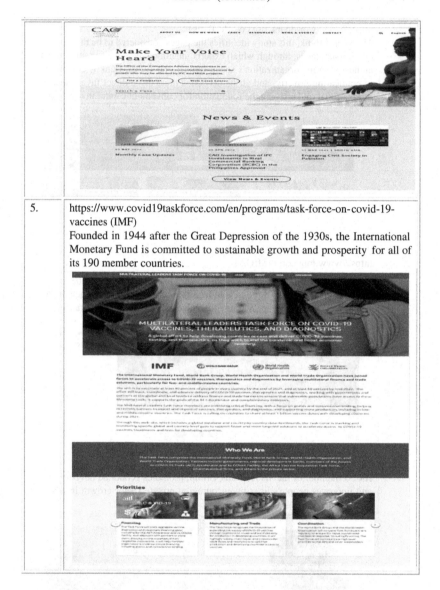

	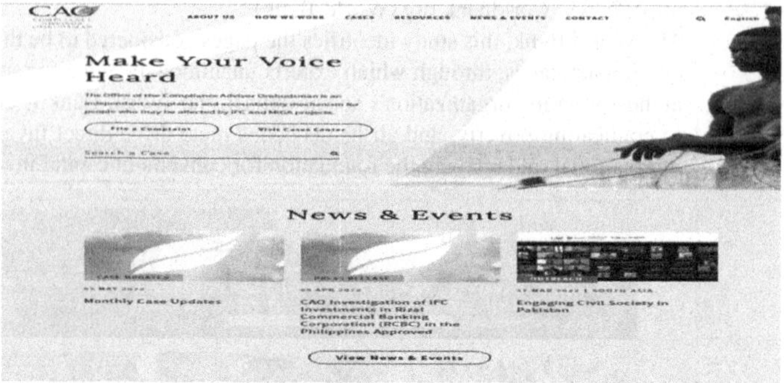
5.	https://www.covid19taskforce.com/en/programs/task-force-on-covid-19-vaccines (IMF) Founded in 1944 after the Great Depression of the 1930s, the International Monetary Fund is committed to sustainable growth and prosperity for all of its 190 member countries. 

5 Conclusion and Future Research

This study aims to determine the authority of social impact web pages by collecting a large number of social impact related web pages from the World Wide Web, modifying them with this graph, and then using the HITS algorithm to find out the authority of social impact web pages.

The contribution of this study can be summarized in two points.

1. The asynchronous crawler program adopted in this study can greatly reduce the crawler execution time compared to the original linear crawler, which saves a lot of time for the HITS algorithm to start.
2. Compared with the original algorithm, the HITS—Same Domain Removal method results in 10 web pages that can best represent the social impact.

This study used asynchronous programming to significantly shorten the crawler program time from tens of days to one day. We also found the top 10 social impact authority pages, which many experts and scholars confirmed, and have more global and oriented viewpoints than google search and more explanatory power.

In addition, this study also tried other additional methods to compare with each other. Compared with the previous study, this study can now search the keywords of the possible domain quickly, and the modified HITS algorithm is better than the original algorithm. The modified HITS algorithm can better search for the authority of the topic than the original algorithm.

The limitation of this study is that only English language web pages are extracted in principle, and the analysis ability of web pages in other languages may not be so comprehensive.

This study tried to reduce the score weight of web pages with many branches by using the Split Info method, which is well-intentioned but may be overly penalized by using Split Info, and it is suggested that subsequent researchers can work in this direction.

References

1. 李秀英, 劉俊儒,, 卷第一期, 楊., 東. 企業社會責任與公司績效之關聯性, 77–112 (2011)
2. Sun, G., Bin, S.J.: A new opinion leaders detecting algorithm in multi-relationship online social networks. Multimed Tools Appl. **77**(4), 4295–4307 (2018)
3. 劉宇雯, 黃俊龍: (2015). 實作HITS 演算法於實況串流頻道推薦系統
4. Gibson, D., Kleinberg, J., Raghavan, P.: Inferring web communities from link topology. Paper presented at the Proceedings of the Ninth ACM Conference on Hypertext and Hypermedia: Links, Objects, Time and Space—Structure in Hypermedia Systems: Links, Objects, Time and Space—Structure in Hypermedia Systems (1998)
5. Kleinberg, J.M.: Authoritative sources in a hyperlinked environment. Paper presented at the SODA (1998)
6. Chakrabarti, S., et al.: Mining the Web's link structure. Computer **32**(8), 60–67 (1999)
7. Nomura, S., Oyama, S., Hayamizu, T., Ishida, T.: Analysis and improvement of hits algorithm for detecting web communities. Syst. Comput. Japan **35**(13), 32–42 (2004)
8. Dimson, E., Marsh, P., Staunton, M.: Divergent ESG ratings. J. Portfolio Manag. **47**(1), 75–87 (2020)
9. Ahlklo, Y., Lind, C.: E, S or G? A study of ESG score and financial performance (2018)
10. Halbritter, G., Dorfleitner, G.: The wages of social responsibility—where are they? A critical review of ESG investing. Rev. Financ. Econ. **26**, 25–35 (2015)
11. Dorfleitner, G., Halbritter, G., Nguyen, M.: Measuring the level and risk of corporate responsibility–An empirical comparison of different ESG rating approaches. J. Asset Manag. **16**(7), 450–466 (2015)
12. Srikant, R., Agrawal, R.: (1995). Mining generalized association rules. In: IBM Research Division Zurich

13. Patel, P., Patel, K.: A review of PageRank and HITS algorithms. Int. J. Adv. Res. Eng. Sci. Technol., 2394–2444 (2015)
14. Shettar, R., Shobha, G.: Web crawler on client machine. Paper presented at the Proceedings of the International Multi Conference of Engineers and Computer Scientists (2008)
15. Harris, E.: Information gain versus gain ratio: a study of split method biases. Paper presented at the ISAIM (2002)
16. Brin, S., Page, L.: The anatomy of a large-scale hypertextual web search engine. Comput. Networks ISDN Syst. **30**(1–7), 107–117 (1998)
17. Page, L., Brin, S., Motwani, R., Winograd, T.: The PageRank citation ranking: bringing order to the web (1999)

Towards a Truly Collective Leadership: A Case for Symbiotic Relationships in Planetary Health and Artificial Intelligence

Wanda Krause(✉) and Alexandru Balasescu

Royal Roads University, Victoria, Canada
{wanda.1krause,Alexandru.Balasescu}@royalroads.ca

Abstract. To address the wicked issues perplexing the globe today that are ever more volatile, uncertain, complex, and ambiguous (VUCA), we need to be moving toward a truly collective leadership. We argue that a truly collective leadership is one that moves beyond the conceptualization of a singular leader to a collective that is highly engaged and relationship-centred, culturally attuned, and contextually informed. Such leadership recognizes that contexts are also global while local and we, human and non-human, alike, are all inextricably interconnected. We require such an approach for our ever-changing new realities of complexity. The paper, thus, discusses what this can look like with the issues of climate change, framed as such, if we focus instead on planetary health and artificial intelligence through the lens of symbiotic relationships. It discusses the importance of an overarching framework for supporting planetary health and understanding artificial intelligence from different wisdom traditions based on regenerative practices.

Keywords: Actor network theory · artificial intelligence · climate change · cognitive assemblages · collective leadership · planetary health · artificial intelligence · VUCA

1 Introduction

This paper inquires into what truly collective leadership must look like in order to address the wicked issues perplexing the globe today. Complex global challenges require collaborative solutions and innovative approaches that integrate worldwide values and views (Goryunova & Lehmann 2023). The paper investigates how we may take guidance from others beyond a singular conceptualization of a leader but rather a collective in non-static engagements allowing for emergent developments towards and as part of a change process. Both context and tasks are not static but rather impact the process and require changes to the process (Tolstikov-Mast & Aghajanian 2023). It investigates how, in fact, an engagement with all elements of being become necessary for sustainable change – that is, going beyond the mindset of quick fixes and solutions disconnected from reality of a highly complex, interdependent, and integrated world.

A. Coman and S. Vasilache (Eds.): HCII 2023, LNCS 14025, pp. 83–90, 2023.
https://doi.org/10.1007/978-3-031-35915-6_7

This approach requires a process of inquiry into how leading change must be from mental models, therefore, that are much more inclusive, dynamic, adaptable, and complex than the leadership paradigm widely understood and viewed as leadership. In this, the paper critically advances an approach that decenters our understanding of leadership as person-centered; as such, focusing on the engagement, and nature of relationships, rather than the person. To aid in this endeavor, it relies on systems thinking and offers two key global and wicked issues as examples for this inquiry. It argues for a shift in thinking from a person-centric mindset to a relation-centric mindset; that is, between people, as nodes, and people and other nodes of being and as self-in-systems to address wicked problems of our VUCA times. The term "wicked problems" was first described by Rittel and Webber (1973) as the inadequacy of traditional planning to address complex issues. We characterize wicked problems as being difficult to define and identify the leading cause of the problem are humans and, as such, are expected to find the solutions to the problems (Thatcher et al. 2020). Significantly, Tolstikov-Mast and Aghajanian (2023) argue that they also involve multiple actors, that they are socially and politically complex, as aligned to the context.

Two key barriers to reconceptualizing leadership are structures and binomials. It seems that it already became a truism to speak of 'wicked problems' in a VUCA world. But it also seems that, while we identify a VUCA world as a relatively new context and terrain generating new types of problems, we look for old-style solutions. We do this not merely in the way the solution is formulated on the surface, but certainly in the way in which we think of the structure of leadership. While we have expanded the concept of leadership to encompass different leadership styles, we still find ourselves conceptualizing leadership within the structure of the binomial of problem/solution. This paper, thus, further argues that structural changes in the context demand radical changes in the way leadership is conceived, and problems framed. To allow for the possibility to go beyond individual leadership to the embracing of collective leadership, we must a) move past seeing static structures that only allow for deterministic and singular directions, and b) the identification of problems and generation of solutions to understanding and adaptation to emergent contexts.

As attempts to address the barrier of static structures, recent and very recent leadership theories have introduced servant leadership, flat hierarchies, and awareness of human diversity. Each of these three approaches has done well to emphasize the recognition of the role of a multitude of inputs into the process of leadership. Arguably though, none of them questions the fact that the leadership position is occupied by an individual. While the very idea of the individual is a historic one and played a major role in the modern era colonization through the corollary of 'possessive individualism', we need to move beyond it in conceiving collective leadership. However, this paper, furthermore, argues that we need to conceptualize collective leadership not as a sum of individual leaders (as in Marvel studios). Rather, we must define collective leadership as an inclusive framework that allows for emergent inputs, including that from non-human actors. We need to turn the idea of leadership on its head and move it from leading toward the solutions to being led by the context and its constitutive elements. As such, we need to devise forms of collective leadership if we want to better respond and proactively adapt to the current challenges.

Our VUCA context today comprises two major defining elements and a derived corollary: climate change and artificial intelligence, giving way to energy transition. They both generate socio-environmental reshapings beyond our power of forecasting. Up to very recently, we defined our relationship to these challenges in a binomial, reactive manner: climate change/fight, mitigate, AI/counter negative effects of bias and nefarious use. We need to move towards giving more room to understand how our entire context changes driven by these elements, and how they might restructure everything we take for granted, from work and leisure to family and identity. To do this, we need to reframe from reacting for a while, and the framing of the problem/ solution is a reactive approach. We need to pause, integrate, understand, and adapt. This can only be done within a structure of leadership that de-emphasize the individual and integrates a multitude as a decisional (and not consultative) factor. The following inquires how we may do so with the two examples of climate change and AI.

2 An Integral Approach to Collective Leadership

Leadership, seen as a practice, has been one key approach that has been sensitive to difference, intersectionality, cultures, and context, rather than leadership residing in the traits or behaviours of particular individuals (Raelin 2016). For Raelin (2016), 'leadership-as-practice', as he calls it, centres the idea that people accomplish change together. Significantly, this approach seeks to move away from identifying valiant acts of leadership as initiated by a person at the top of a hierarchical formation and instead investigates how leadership emerges and unfolds through everyday life or day-to-day experience. Such understanding of leadership allows for the possibility of viewing engagement as the space in which leadership can be identified at many junctures of time rather than through some major act on part of an individual. From this standpoint, people do not reside outside of leadership but are rather embedded within it. We must look to the practice within which it is occurring, and from here we can enact the kind of leadership needed for our VUCA times (Krause & Balasescu 2022). Each of these dimensions are reciprocally shaped by the other, and they form a web of interactions that imply actors that are both human and non-human alike (Krause & Balasescu 2022). Accordingly, we conceptualize leadership as a social relationship whereby leadership is an influence relationship among leaders and collaborators (Rost 1997), which takes shape according to their own contexts and the nature of those actors as nodes or elements shaping and reshaping direction and at times even intent.

Such an adaptive, non-binomial approach draws from systems thinking and Integral theory. Wilber (2005) explores holistically how to integrate the interpersonal or subjective, the intercultural or organizational, and the macro-level social, political, and economical. We argue that it is imperative to first understand how leadership practice is an everyday event aligned to context and that it is imperative that awareness precedes practice as informed through multiple perspectives offered by actors (Krause & Balasescu 2022). Such a collective leadership is appreciative of and attunes to the different perspectives aligned to and informed by contexts to address wicked issues. Such an approach supports and embraces incremental shifts in thinking, being, and doing from a person-centric, leader-centric position to a relation-centric and context-aware position.

This is one that is integrative of the human and non-human alike as part of systems. Drawing on worldviews outside our largely western references, we rely on wisdom traditions that emphasize and seek systems as integrated wholes.

For example, Atleo (Umeek) speaks of *tsawalk*, which in the Nuu-chah-nulth language, means "one." Such a worldview sees all living things are part of an integrated whole, and these may be humans, plants, or animals. Harmony is made possible through their constant negotiation and mutual respect for the other, which rests on their relationships. While Western scientific inquiry might provide knowledge to what is visible, actors more typically within Indigenous ways of knowing and the Global South have knowledge about how to create change through what is invisible (Krause 2023). In fact, human-centric hierarchies are most often absent in Indigenous languages and lifeways with a profound and deep respect given for all human and non-human entities (Redvers et al. 2022). Through the following examples, we highlight how an inclusive and integral leadership approach is imperative for our fast-changing times.

3 Climate Change to Planetary Health

Despite the many organizations emerging around the globe addressing the climate crisis, climate change is premised on a singular conceptualization of a leader rather than a collective of engagements allowing for emergent developments towards and as part of a change process. Greta Thunberg, as an example, may well be an inspiration for especially youth. Ultimately, the thinking and leadership-in-practice that will carry us forward to sustainable change rest on the capacity for individuals to engage with one another, truly listen to Mother Earth's leadership and align practice to its guidance. As such, an engagement with all elements of being become necessary for sustainable change – that is, critically and urgently going beyond individual leaders and quick fixes and solutions disconnected from the reality of a highly complex, interdependent and integrated world. Shifting how we address climate change, as a key wicked issue of our VUCA world, will require shifting mindset around leadership, practice, how we engage, and how we connect the self/selves to the broader systems of which we are a part – currently on the trajectory of the climate crisis.

Nature-based solutions (NbS) aim to deliver simultaneous benefits for environmental and social well-being and contribute to the realization of the United Nations 2030 Agenda for Sustainable Development. The embracing of sustainability through the sustainability development goals is a step towards an integral approach in that through a broad range of actions, supporting and working with nature contributes to environmental and social goals (Dahdaleh Institute for Global Health Research 2021). The term, "planetary boundaries" has recently been introduced and defined as the safe "planetary playing field," or the "safe operating space for humanity" to stay within if we want to be sure to avoid major human-induced environmental change on a global scale (Couchere 2019). However, it has been argued that "[a]s humanity finds itself reaching the environmental limits of our planet, it is no longer radical to suggest a paradigmatic shift to embrace Indigenous worldviews that provide a philosophy for living centred on sustainable development" (Ratima, 2019, para. 12). An integrally or holistically oriented change process can serve to bring together knowledges and practices allowing leaders a better way to address climate issues that relate to our collective well-being as connected to the wider systems of planetary health.

To address complex wicked challenges for planetary health requires thinking and practices that are guided by systems principles, an understanding of globalization forces, insight into how to support vibrant civil societies, and, significantly, awareness of global mental models and worldviews that are diverse and anchored in wisdom (Krause 2023). Further to mindset, little understanding of the subject or, rather, the subjectification of climate change rather than seeing that we are part of the system remains a key barrier. Part of motivating a process for change at the individual level, or self in systems, significant to planetary health, includes decolonization of mindset. This means going beyond dominant western worldviews that continue to contribute a capitalist mindset, whether subtly or overtly as in one that extracts from the planet that which exclusively benefits "man and human communities" (Redvers et al. 2020). Such includes peeling back layers of bias and letting go of old ways of thinking that do not allow for new understanding, knowledge, and insight around our relations to non-human entities.

We also argue it is important to understand power and agency not within a finite form as 'power over' or controlling power but as power to, power with, power within, and power for (Krause 2012). By expanding perspectives and practices on power, we might be able to identify multiple forms of desire and goals, nuanced by context and inclusive of everyday concerns, needs, and actions (Krause 2012). One is both a leader and follower in a collective towards planetary health. To advance truly inclusive leadership around planetary health is to exercise power in its many forms and, thus, seek to influence change or impact. From these spaces, we can choose actions that are more ethical, empathic, or conscious in relation to those we have come to believe from which we are separate or are sovereign over. The argument is not for individual leadership from a liberal, individualistic, perspective. Rather, the argument is that self-leadership is anticipated as honed and developed in service of the whole, the planet, as an agent conscious of how its actions are impacted by and impact others in relationship also to the whole. Such, then, is an approach in mindset that includes but transcends a singular leader and a solution-binary through the appreciation of a multitude of agents as part of the planet.

A shift also involves shifting agency around the binomial to healing and regenerative practices. Here, too, the nexus of this shift is aligning practice with the shifted mindset around relationship. When we recognize that we are not separate from the climate changes but the source and inextricably linked to each other and the environment, essentially as one, we understand how our actions must then change with such consciousness. Such allows us to address the wicked issues of our VUCA times and be attuned to expanding the health of planetary systems based on. For this, we advocate delineating leadership and followership practice from a collectivist worldview of shared responsibility to support the health, well-being, and success of all. We advocate seeing and mapping the self in the wider systems to inquire into and strategize how we can foster and enhance the capacities for influence and transformation at all levels of systems. From the bottom up, that is, through individual development and transformation and sub-system development and transformation, we can then co-create new thinking and practices together. We believe these shifts are imperative if we hope to truly lead a regenerative process to healing ourselves and our planet as an inextricably linked collective.

Shifting thinking and practice is necessary to address how our current leadership conceptualizations feed current political and economic narratives. In the example of climate, it continues to deprive the land, water, and air of being in the world as equal rights-holders (Redvers et al. 2022). The denial of being is a deficit discourse and it perpetuates negativity, deficiency, and disempowerment (Ford et al. 2012; Redvers et al. 2022). Building on the decentering of the individual and the leader's hierarchization, Redvers (2022) calls for an orientation to planetary health and, more specifically, determinants to planetary health, to better "expand the call for the inclusion of equity rights to all of our relations, including Mother Earth and all of her inhabitants" (Redvers et al. 2022, para. 3). As such, we argue for a shift in mindset and practice around addressing climate change, as framed in binomial terms, to planetary health, through truly collective leadership.

4 Artificial Intelligence to Symbiotic Relationships

Another important element that needs to be considered is Artificial Intelligence. The recent and relentless exponential advancement in the domain challenges our understanding of the human experience in relationship with technology. We are way past the age of technology as a tool, and well into the era of technology as a subject of/in action. The Actor Network Theory (ANT) best expressed in Bruno Latour's work emphasizes the decentering of humans as subject and the diffusion of agency in the network of interlinked elements, human and non-human alike. Using the Hayles (2014) model of cognition, one can speak of cognitive assemblages, that is, complex interactions between human and nonhuman cognizers and their abilities to enlist material forces. In particular, a cognitive assemblage emphasizes the flow of information through a system and the choices and decisions that create, modify, and interpret the flow. While the ANT perspective postulates equal importance to the elements implied in a system of interaction, the cognitive assemblages introduce the idea of affordances. While a cognitive assemblage may include material agents and forces (and almost always does so), it is the cognizers within the assemblage that enlist these affordances and direct their powers to act in complex situations.

Regardless of the view we chose in order to understand our relationship with technology and AI, it is clear that the role of human agency changes dramatically. Decisions are no longer to be understood as the exclusive prerogative of human agency, but as an emergent state of interactions between networked cognizers that include non-human biological and non-biological agents. Thus, plants, animals, meteors and artificial intelligence are all part of the decision-making mechanisms, and the possibility of action is both circumscribed to and transcendent of specific agents. In this context and through these lenses leadership becomes a matter of symbiotic assemblages navigating complex systems, and understanding it may as well mean renouncing altogether at its prevalence. Simultaneity replaces succession and linear causality fades into the light of multiplicity of sources of action. Actionability within and through symbiosis offers the key to future leadership, and the meaning of collective is extended thus from individuals to assemblages and from human to non-humans of any kind.

5 Conclusions

We cannot afford approaching new problems with old tools, not more than we can afford relying on the centrality of individuality and humanness in leadership theories, if we are to remain in any way human. If we try to continue to minimize the role of collective, of symbiotic assemblages, and the non-human in the complex systems in which we exist, not only will we not be able to address the challenges that the transforming environment will subject us to, we will also lose our ability to be human. This is simply due to the fact that, while perceiving the necessity of complex and collective leadership, we would try to step into the roles that are not ours to begin with, and we would try to replicate ourselves as (the) non-humans with which we should in fact share the leadership role. Human leadership in this new context may as well mean knowing how to step down and not attempt to place human agency in all the nodes of the system, allowing the complexity, variance and diversity of agencies to manifest themselves and create the emergent collective and symbiotic leadership. The planetary health requires it.

References

Atleo, R., Umeek.: Principles of Tsawalk: An Indigenous Approach to Global Crisis. UBC Press (2011)

Couchere, D.: Indigenous values on climate change. Cultural Survival (23 September 2019). https://www.culturalsurvival.org/news/indigenous-values-climate-change

Dahdaleh Institute for Global Health Research. Synergies of planetary health research. (2020). https://www.yorku.ca/dighr/project/synergies-of-planetary-health-research-initiative/

Ford, J.D., Vanderbilt, W., Berrang-Ford, L.: Authorship in IPCC AR5 and its implications for content: climate change and Indigenous populations in WGII. Clim. Change **113**, 201–213 (2012)

Goryunova, E., Lehmann, R.: Achieving harmony. In: Dhiman, S.K., Marques, J., Schmieder-Ramirez, J., Malakyan, P.G. (eds.) Handbook of Global Leadership and Followership. Springer, Cham (2023). https://doi.org/10.1007/978-3-030-75831-8_23-1

Jones, W.A.: Artificial Intelligence and leadership: a few thoughts, a few questions. J. Leadersh. Stud. **12**(3), 60 (2018). https://doi.org/10.1002/jls.21597

Hayles, N.K.: Cognition everywhere: the rise of the cognitive nonconscious and the costs of consciousness. New Literary Hist. **45**(2), 199–220 (2014). http://www.jstor.org/stable/24542553

Krause, W.: Global leadership practices for planetary health. In: Dhiman, S.K., Marques, J., Schmieder-Ramirez, J., Malakyan, P.G. (eds.) Handbook of Global Leadership and Followership. Springer, Cham. (2023). https://doi.org/10.1007/978-3-030-75831-8_53-1

Krause, W., Balasescu, A.: Engagement as leadership-practice for today's global wicked problems: leadership learning for artificial intelligence. In: Meiselwitz, G. (eds) Social Computing and Social Media: Design, User Experience and Impact. HCII 2022. Lecture Notes in Computer Science, vol. 13315. Springer, Cham (2022). https://doi.org/10.1007/978-3-031-05061-9_41

Krause, W.: Civil Society and Women Activists in the Middle East. I.B. Tauris, London (2012)

Krause, W.: The role and example of Chilean and Argentinian mothers in democratisation. Dev. Pract. **14**(3), 366–380 (2004). https://doi.org/10.1080/0961452042000191204

Raelin, J. A.: (ed.) Leadership-as-Practice: Theory and Application, pp. 1-17. Routledge (2016)

Ratima, M.: Leadership for planetary health and sustainable development: health promotion community capacities for working with indigenous peoples in the application of indigenous knowledge. Glob. Health Promot. **26**(4), 3–5 (2019). https://doi.org/10.1177/1757975919889250

Redvers, N., et al.: The determinants of planetary health: an indigenous consensus perspective. Lancet Planet. Health **6**(2), e156–e163 (2022). https://doi.org/10.1016/S2542-5196(21)00354-5

Redvers, N., et al.: Indigenous natural and first law in planetary health. Challenges **11**(2), 29 (2020). https://doi.org/10.3390/challe11020029

Rost, J.: Leadership for the Twenty-First Century. Praeger (1997)

Rittel, H.W.J., Webber, M.M.: Dilemmas in a general theory of planning. Policy Sci. **4**, 155–169 (1973)

Thatcher, A. et al.: A future ethical stance for HFE toward sustainability. In: Thatcher, A., Zink, K., Fischer, K. (eds.) Human Factors for sustainability, pp. 51–74. CRC Press, Taylor & Francis Group (2020)

Tolstikov-Mast, Y., Aghajanian, C.: Intersectional approach to combatting human trafficking: applying an interdisciplinary global leader-follower collaboration paradigm. In: Dhiman, S.K., Marques, J., Schmieder-Ramirez, J., Malakyan, P.G. (eds.) Handbook of Global Leadership and Followership. Springer, Cham (2023). https://doi.org/10.1007/978-3-030-75831-8_38-1

Wilber, K.: A Theory of Everything: An Integral Vision for Business, Politics, Science and Spirituality. Shambhala (2001)

Inter-person Intra-modality Attention Based Model for Dyadic Interaction Engagement Prediction

Xiguang Li, Candy Olivia Mawalim, and Shogo Okada(✉)

Japan Advanced Institute of Science and Technology, Nomi, Japan
{s2020425,candylim,okada-s}@jaist.ac.jp

Abstract. With the rapid development of artificial agents, more researchers have explored the importance of user engagement level prediction. Real-time user engagement level prediction assists the agent in properly adjusting its policy for the interaction. However, the existing engagement modeling lacks the element of interpersonal synchrony, a temporal behavior alignment closely related to the engagement level. Part of this is because the synchrony phenomenon is complex and hard to delimit. With this background, we aim to develop a model suitable for temporal interpersonal features with the help of the modern data-driven machine learning method. Based on previous studies, we select multiple non-verbal modalities of dyadic interactions as predictive features and design a multi-stream attention model to capture the interpersonal temporal relationship of each modality. Furthermore, we experiment with two additional embedding schemas according to the synchrony definitions in psychology. Finally, we compare our model with a conventional structure that emphasizes the multimodal features within an individual. Our experiments showed the effectiveness of the intra-modal inter-person design in engagement prediction. However, the attempt to manipulate the embeddings failed to improve the performance. In the end, we discuss the experiment result and elaborate on the limitations of our work.

Keywords: Engagement Modeling · Interpersonal Synchrony · Attention Model

1 Introduction

Researchers have come to realize the importance of engagement prediction in the area of virtual communications and human-robot interaction. The engagement level has been a crucial factor in interaction diagrams. For example, an embodied conversational agent needs to adjust the interaction strategy based on the current engagement level of the subject. Many studies have been conducted based on various modalities via rule-based measurements or machine learning to predict engagement levels [21]. However, synchrony, a prosocial behavior phenomenon [3] which is closely related to high engagement, has not received enough attention in engagement modeling. Despite being a widely observed phenomenon, synchrony

A. Coman and S. Vasilache (Eds.): HCII 2023, LNCS 14025, pp. 91–105, 2023.
https://doi.org/10.1007/978-3-031-35915-6_8

is complex and challenging to define and delimit by rule-based methods. With the rapid development of data-driven deep learning, stunning progress has been made for numerous problems that are also hard to define and delimit with, such image classification tasks and content generation tasks. We believe that the modern deep learning model can capture the synchrony features and improve the prediction accuracy of engagement levels.

This paper introduces an intra-modality attention-based model for dyadic interaction real-time engagement level prediction. We first introduce the related concepts and the most influential works on engagement modeling. Then, we describe our model and evaluate its performance.

2 Related Works

2.1 Engagement and Synchrony

Nadine G. and Catherine P. have conducted an in-depth survey on the engagement for human-agent exchange [11]. There are many definitions in the literature focusing on various perspectives and targets. For example, Dan Bohus and Eric Horvitz describe engagement as "The process subsuming the joint, coordinated activities by which participants initiate, maintain, join, abandon, suspend, resume or terminate an interaction" [4]. In contrast, Poggi regarded engagement as "The value that a participant in an interaction attributes to the goal of being together with the other participant(s) and of continuing the interaction" [22]. Yu et al. [28] defined engagement in the voice communication system as "User engagement describes how much a participant is interested in and attentive to a conversation." Engagement can be observed multimodally from both verbal and non-verbal features. For example, engagement detection has been studied on prosodic features and emotions from speech [28], as well as facial expression, smile and gaze [10].

Synchrony is the temporal alignment among the participants during social interaction. Frank J. B and his colleagues defined synchrony as "The coordination of movement between individuals in social interactions" [2]. In loose terms, synchrony is similar to interpersonal coordination - "the degree to which the behaviors in an interaction are non-random, patterned, or synchronized in both timing and form" [3]. In later works, researchers viewed synchrony as a simultaneous synchronization of behaviors [15,23]. There are other similar concepts, such as the chameleon effects [6], co-occurrence [18], mimicry [7]. Synchrony has positively affected building rapport [25], smoothing social interactions [17], and promoting cooperation [27]. Emilie Delaherche et al. [9] have conducted an excellent survey on interpersonal synchrony for more insights.

2.2 Deep Learning Engagement Models

In the early stage of engagement prediction, researchers took a single image or frame from a video to predict the engagement level. For example, Omid Mohamad Nezami et al. [20] proposed a VGG-B [24] style deep neural network.

Their work was trained and evaluated on individual frames sampled from student study videos. Their model showed improved results over the histogram of oriented gradients and support vector machines [8]. Later, researchers included temporal information into consideration. For example, Hadfield et al. [12] studied child-robot attention tasks with long short-term memory (LSTM) models [14] and showed that temporal dynamics are crucial for engagement level prediction as LSTM models outperformed stationary classifiers.

Other approaches predicted engagement from modality features instead of video. In [1], a human-agent engagement prediction, employed a RESNet-18 [13] model as the backbone to extract attention signals from the gaze and head pose. Then they predicted the engagement level through rule-based policies on body postures and extracted attention signals. In [16], a student engagement prediction task over online lecture scenarios, the authors took face frames and facial landmarks for a fully connected neural network. In addition, they also used head pose and eye gaze features and fed them into a LSTM model. These works have studied the non-verbal features practical for engagement level prediction. Lastly, Soumia D. and Catherine P. [10] used gaze, head rotation, and facial action unit features and fed them into an LSTM model in a dyadic interaction engagement prediction task on NoXi dataset [5]. Their study consists of three models: target LSTM, partner LSTM, and dyadic LSTM. The result showed that additional information from the interaction partner boosted the prediction accuracy.

3 Methods

The task of our experiments is to predict the target participant's real-time engagement level from both interaction participants' modality features as input. We hypothesize that synchrony manifests as a form of feature similarity. The question becomes what kind of similarity and which time frame to compare the similarity. Different from refined features like the binary features of presence of smiling or other behaviors, measuring the similarity of sensor data such as face mesh is very challenging from the definition. We adopt a multi-stream deep neural network to let data speak for itself to extract similarity (Sect. 3.1 and 3.2). As for the time frame, we manually manipulate the embedding phrase of the network to control the feature grouping (Sect. 3.3) (Fig. 1).

3.1 Overall Structure

The overall model design follows multi-stream late-fusion scheme as shown in Fig. 2. The intuition is to allow the model to extract temporal synchrony features that reside within each modality between two participants. The multi-stream structure process the multi-modalities inputs in isolation. The intuition behind seeking temporal associations within the same modality is from the definitions of synchrony. Running in isolation avoids cross-modality learning that is not related

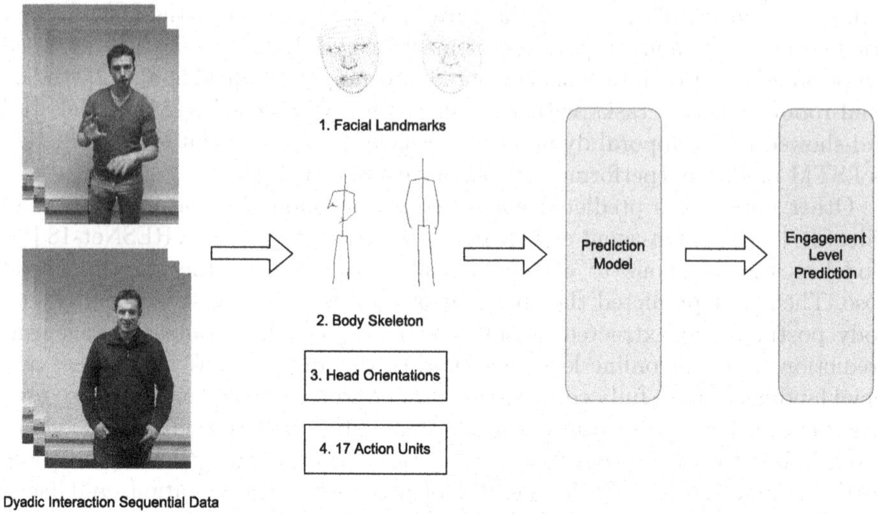

Fig. 1. Task Overview - We obtained facial landmarks, body skeletons, head orientations, and action units from the NoXi dataset as input features. The model will take four modalities sequence from present to past within a preset window length as input to predict the engagement level of the present sample.

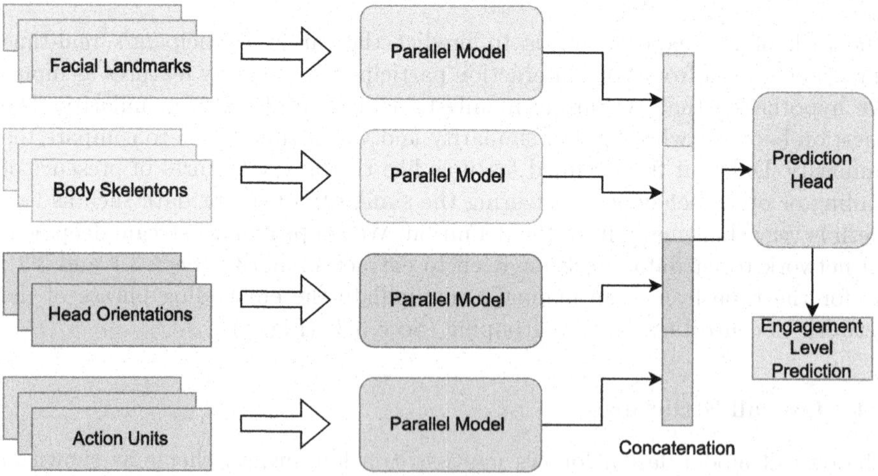

Fig. 2. Model Overview - Each modality sequence is fed into a separate parallel model, and the outputs are concatenated for the final prediction. All parallel models have identical structures (shown in Fig. 3) but with different layer dimensions adjusted for the input modality.

to synchrony. The main mechanism adopted for parallel models is the multi-head self-attention block. Attention models are incredibly flexible in learning temporal relationships. However, it also requires more training data to learn the attention matrix than models with built-in inductive bias. To tackle this issue, we designed two other embedding approaches to reduce the complexity of the attention matrix.

3.2 Multi-head Self Attention Backbone Model

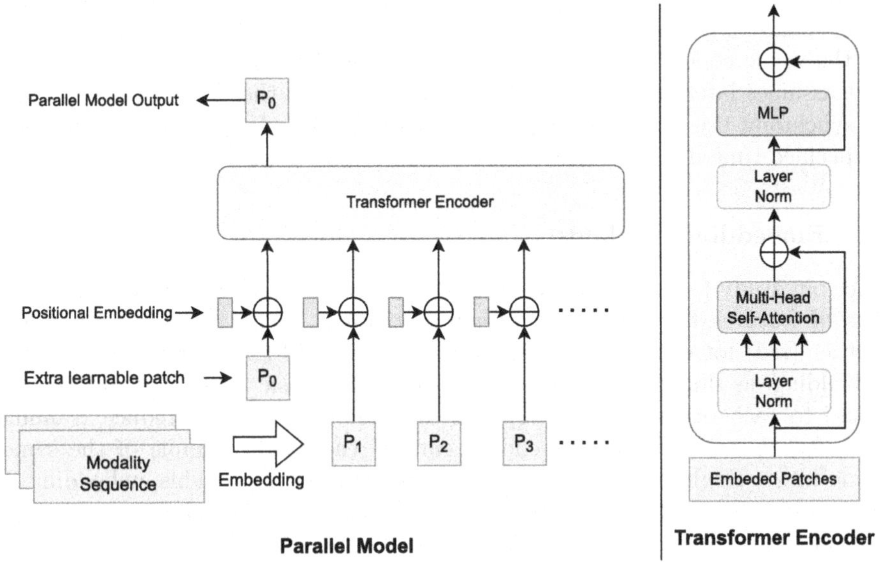

Fig. 3. Parallel Model Structure - The model takes the modality sequence as input, embeds them into patches (Embedding detail in Fig. 4), and processes the patches via a standard transformer block. A typical learnable "class token" patch is added to the sequence, serving as the parallel model fusion output.

Inspired by the fantastic work of ViT [19], we considered modality information as a series of "words" embedded and processed them with a transformer [26] encoder. Figure 2 illustrates the general structure of our parallel models. Modality sequences are first embedded into patches, applied positional embeddings, and processed by attention blocks. The flexibility of the attention mechanism comes from its learnable attention matrix. Embedded patches are first projected into matrices Q, K, and V with the exact dimensions P by L, where P the number of patches and L is the length of the embedding (Eq. 1). Then, the attention matrix is the matrix multiplication of Q and K with softmax and value scale (Eq. 2).

$$Q, K, V = linear(patches) \tag{1}$$

$$attentionMatrix = softmax(\frac{Q \times K^T}{\sqrt{P}}) \tag{2}$$

Each row of the attention matrix indicates the weight of all embedding patches to the corresponding patch. Softmax operation ensures the sum of each row equals 1. By performing matrix multiplication on the attention matrix and V, each row of the final output is the weighted sum of all embeddings.

$$attention = attentionMatix \times V \tag{3}$$

The uniqueness of the attention matrix is that it is learned from scratch without inductive bias. As a result, the nearby and faraway patches have an equal chance of gaining weight. This unbiasedness of the attention matrix is ideal for the vague concept of synchrony. For example, LSTM has an inductive bias that assumes later (newer) input contributes more to the prediction. However, for synchrony, the definitions are either behaviors aligned simultaneously or with unspecified time delay. Neither case fits perfectly with LSTM's bias.

3.3 Embedding Methods

Since our study focused on a dyadic interaction dataset, the input actually consists of features from both the target participant (blue) and the interaction partner (red) for every sample, shown at the top of Fig. 4. First, the separate embedding, as illustrated in Fig. 4 mid left, is the basic setup that all patches access to each other without imposed limitation. Second, to reduce training difficulty, the same frame embedding embeds the dyadic sample of the same frame into a single patch, shown at the mid right of Fig. 4. This embedding is based on strict case synchrony that defines the behavior aligned at exact timing. This method reduces the number of patches by half and simplifies the attention matrix.

If the separate embedding model is adequately trained, the embeddings will be fit towards the engagement task. In another sense, these embeddings are projections of the initial modality on a particular embedding domain. Furthermore, this domain is trained to represent necessary information for the engagement prediction task. We hypothesize that the cosine similarity of these projections is akin to the modality similarity for measuring synchrony. Therefore, the third method takes the embeddings from a trained separate embedding model and performs a dynamic warping algorithm (DTW) over the target and the partner sequence to obtain a matching table from the target to the partner. This matching represents the most synchronized partner sample of each target sample within the input sequence. Finally, the matching pair embedding embeds the matching pairs into patches. This method also reduced the number of patches by half.

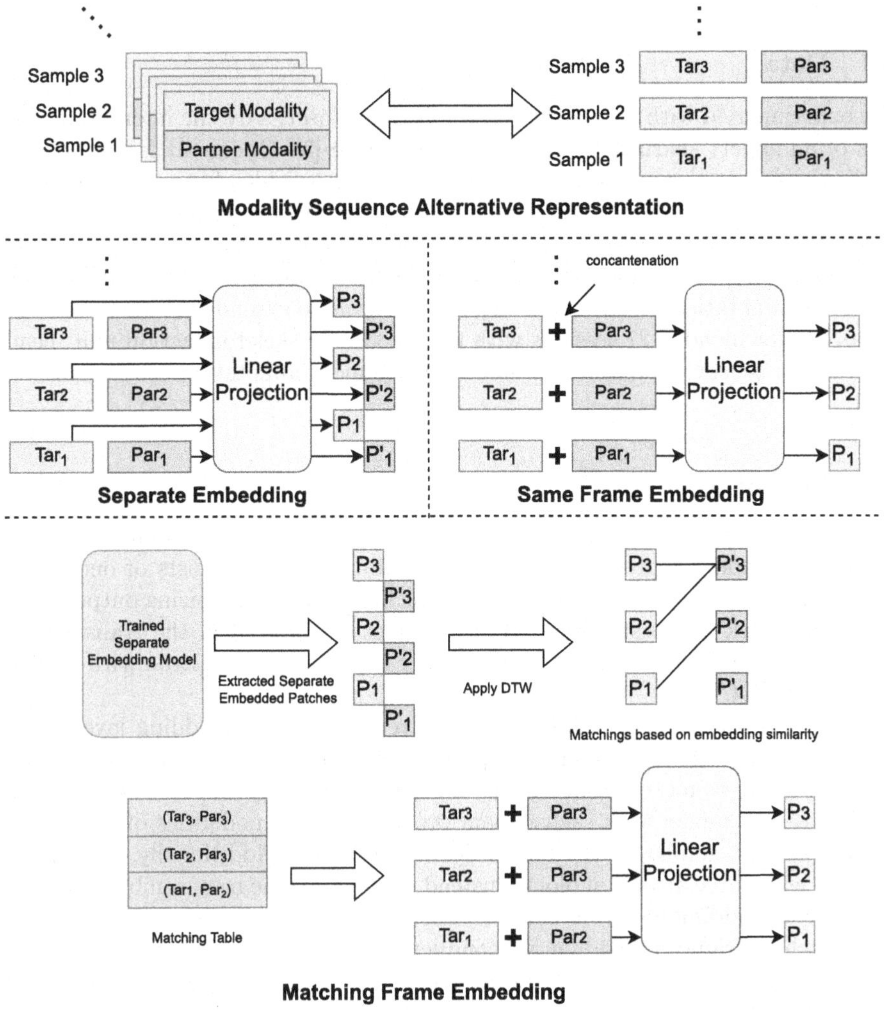

Fig. 4. Embedding Details - The topmost section describes an alternate representation of the dyadic modality input sequence. In this alternative representation, Tar_k stands for the kth input sample of the target participant. Similarly, Par_k stands for the kth input sample of the partner. In the mid-left section, Tar_k is embedded into P_k, where P represents embedded patches. Likewise, Par_k is embedded into P_k', which means each sample will be embedded into two separate patches. In the mid-right section, both the target participant and partner of the same sample k will be concatenated first, then embedded into one P_k, where the yellow color of P indicates a mix of both participants. Finally, in the bottom section, the trained separate embedding model serves as a feature extractor. The matching table contains matched pairs from the dynamic time-warping algorithm (marked as DTW in the figure). Dyadic samples are concatenated based on the matching table and embedded input patches. In this schema, P_k always contains Tar_k, but not necessarily Par_k. (Color figure online)

4 Experiments

4.1 Data

We experimented with our models on the NoXi dataset, a dyadic interaction corpus of an expert sharing knowledge with a novice [5]. One great feature of the NoXi dataset is the open-source database, which provides frame-level annotations and the original sensor data. We mainly used the engagement labels under the annotator gold standard, which annotated the data with continuous engagement values between 0 and 1. Additionally, we downloaded all other samples with available annotations of the same engagement scale to extend the sample size. In total, we downloaded 27 sessions with the face, body skeleton, action unit, head orientation sensor data, and continuous engagement annotation ranging from 0 to 1.

4.2 Models

All models consist of 4 parallel streams (face, skeleton, action unit, and head orientation) and a regression head. The backbone model consists of one linear embedding layer, an attention block, and one linear layer for resizing output. The attention block is the standard attention block introduced in the transformer. The late fusion prediction head is a two-layer multi-layer perceptron with hidden layer ratio of 4.

The differences across different models reside in the embedding layer. This part follows the three methods of separate embedding, same-frame embedding, and matching frame embedding. As a baseline, we experimented with a two stream LSTM model with each stream process all four modalities of the target or the partner, similar to the model described in [10]. Additionally, we experimented with three attention blocks instead of one for same frame embedding and separate embedding to test if a deeper and larger model improves the result. For the matching frame embedding, we conducted an extra experiment that directly embeds the extracted embeddings instead of embedding original modality The window constraint for time dynamic warping is set from the present to 3 s in the past. Additionally, the algorithm cannot skip the target participant, details shown in Algorithms 1 and 2. In Algorithm 1, X and Y are target patches and partner patches respectively, and W is the window constraint which is 75 samples (3 s). The output of Algorithm 1, the DTW cost table, is the input for Algorithm 2 to calculate the optimal path which consists of optimal matching pairs.

We used mean square error as loss function. The training adopted the leave-one-out strategy. The first session from Paris serves as the testing data, and the training utilized the remaining 26 sessions. We set the initial learning rate as 1e−4, the default attention blocks as 1, dropout rate as 0.3. To reduce the training time, the input is limited to 250 frames with a striding of 5 frames and we embed 5 frames as a single patch. All experiments ran for 50 epochs on GPU with a fixed random seed of 22718.

Algorithm 1. CostTable(X,Y,W)

```
Ensure: |X| = |Y|
  N ← |X| + 1
  dtw[] ← new[N × N]
  for i ← 0; i < N; i++ do
     for j ← 0; j < N; j++ do
        dtw[i, j] ← ∞                                ▷ Initialize costs to infinity
     end for
  end for
  dtw(0, 0) ← 0
  for i ← 1; i < N; i++ do
     for j ← max(1, i − W); j < i + 1; j++ do       ▷ loop with window constraint
        cost ← distance(X[i], Y[j])
        prev ← min(dtw[i − 1, j], dtw[i − 1, j − 1]  ▷ no skipping for target
        dtw[i, j] ← prev + cost
     end for
  end for
  return dtw
```

Algorithm 2. TracePath(dtw)

```
Ensure: rows(dtw) = columns(dtw)
  path ← new[]
  N ← rows(dtw)
  min ← ∞
  for j ← 0; j < N; j++ do
     if dtw[N − 1, j] < min then
        min ← dtw[N − 1, j]
        J ← j                          ▷ find the index of minimum total cost
     end if
  end for
  i ← N − 1
  j ← J
  while i ≠ 1 do
     prev ← min(dtw[i − 1, j], dtw[i − 1, j − 1])   ▷ no skipping for target
     if dtw[i − 1, j] = prev then
        i ← i − 1
     else if dtw[i − 1, j − 1] = prev then
        i ← i − 1
        j ← j − 1
     end if
     path add (i, j)
  end while
  return path
```

5 Results and Discussion

5.1 Experiment Results

Table 1. Experiment results - Mean Square Error and pseudo accuracy

Experiment Models	MSE	Pseudo Accuracy (±0.1)
Two stream LSTM (baseline)	0.0480	0.2750
Separate Embedding	**0.0278**	**0.3998**
Same Frame Embedding	0.0310	0.3228
Matching Frame Embedding	0.0361	0.3035
Separate Embedding with 3 Attention Blocks	0.0392	0.2754
Same Frame Embedding with 3 Attention Blocks	0.0303	0.3092
Matching Frame Embedding with Embedding as input	0.0389	0.2757

Since the annotations are continuous, we cannot simply calculate the accuracy of our results. Instead, we evaluate the performance by MSE and pseudo accuracy. First, MSE indicates the overall deviation of the prediction from the ground truth. Second, we set predictions within a ±0.1 tolerance range of the ground truth as positive predictions to calculate pseudo accuracy.

Table 1 lists each experiment's testing MSE and pseudo accuracy. The pseudo accuracy aligned with MSE, which showed no unexpected exceptions. This result indicated that the predictions from all models generally followed that lower MSE had higher pseudo accuracy. In other words, no particular model had most of its predictions accurate but had a small number of severely erroneous results that contributed to the majority of the MSE.

Our results showed that the intra-modality structure did improve the engagement level prediction accuracy. All models that adopted inter-person intra-modality structure outperformed the two-stream LSTM baseline model in MSE. However, except the separate embedding model, there is no significant improvement in pseudo accuracy.

The embedding methods also created distinct differences in the results. The separate embedding model, which had to learn the largest attention matrix, turned out to be the best-performed model. The same frame embedding model followed as the intermediate result. The worst result was the matching frame embedding models. Additionally, given our experiment setup, the deeper models with three attention blocks did not outperform their simpler counterparts. Finally, for matching-frame embedding, directly matching the extracted embedding patches resulted in an even worse result than matching the original modality features.

5.2 Discussions

In this section, we first discuss the reasons behind the experiment results. Then we highlight the limitations of this work.

Result Discussion

Modality Independent and Person Independent. The two-stream baseline processes each participant as an independent entity. In each stream, time series features of all modalities are processed in the sequential layers and contribute to the output. This structure properly utilizes the multi-modal features for each participant. However, the output of each stream contains mixed information about all input modalities. Once the information is intertwined, it would be improbable to learn the synchrony phenomenon as synchrony is observed within the same modality. A similar issue also applies to our multi-stream inter-person intra-modal model. Our models allow each modality stream to learn from two participants, which can also be considered treating each modality independently. The output of each stream contains mixed information from both participants, which can hinder the learning of cross-modality information of each person. In other words, the two-stream model prioritizes the cross-modal learning of each participant, while our model prioritizes the interpersonal synchrony of each modality. Our results showed that the inter-person intra-modality models all had better results than the two-stream baseline. That is interpersonal information outweighs cross-modal features in the dyadic scenarios. But different results may apply in different scenarios. Extensive experiments with different settings would be desired to validate our findings. Furthermore, these designs are not necessarily mutually exclusive. Developing models covering both structures as submodels with a weighted fusion can be promising.

Issues for Hand-Crafted Pair Embedding. Among our models, the two hand-crafted pair embedding models failed to outperform the baseline model by a considerable margin, especially for the pseudo accuracy. This is because no matter which hand-crafted method, we limited the possible cases of synchrony. Notably, we observed that the matching frame embedding model was harshly underperforming. There are two major reasons for this. First, the matching frame embedding depends on the matching algorithm which requires a reliable similarity function. In our hypothesis, a trained separate embedding model can serve as a feature extractor so that the cosine similarity of the extracted feature serves as the similarity function. However, our feature extractor was severely undertrained compared with commonly used feature extractors. As a result, the features could not be adequately projected into the new domain, and the cosine similarity of the extracted features could not appropriately reflect the modality similarity. Second, there is a missing sample problem created by the constraints for dynamic time warping. The constraints are that the target participant samples cannot be skipped or matched to future partner samples. As a result, the partner samples close to the present are discarded in nearly all cases. The only possible matching that uses the present partner sample is the same frame matching. Otherwise, the present partner sample will be the future sample for the rest of the target samples, which is prohibited by constraints. That is, the matching frame model can never obtain the newest features of the partner. Therefore, we need a better solution for the modality feature extraction and an improved matching algorithm.

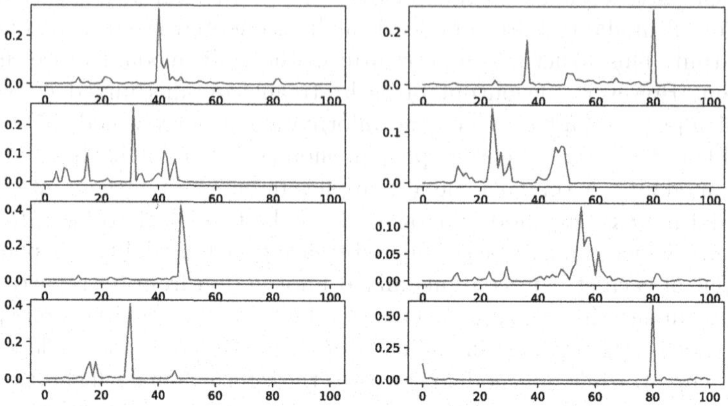

Fig. 5. A sample of attention weights for the extra patch from all 8 heads in the separate embedding model - Each figure represents an attention head. The x-axis indicates the index of the patches, where 0 is the extra patch, 1 to 50 are the target participant from past to present, and 51 to 100 are the partner from past to present. The y-axis shows the weights of which the sum equals 1.

Other Limitations

Explainability. We were unable to model synchrony directly. In the early stage of this work, we attempted to model the synchrony itself. For example, we used high-level features such as smiles and head nods and tried to define a successful case of synchrony. However, we found these high-level behaviors very individual-based. For example, some participants smile habitually, and some rarely smile. Eventually, we adopted a data-driven approach using base-level sensor data, which is less interpretable. Figure 5 shows a sample of attention weights for the extra patch, illustrated in Fig. 3, which is the only patch used for prediction. Therefore, in the case of one block of attention, we only need to examine the attention matrix's first row, i.e., the row for the extra patch. The figure indicates most heads are trained to get information from the target participant only, but some heads, three heads on the right side, partially get weights from the partner. As all heads in multi-head attention contribute to the output with learned weights, temporal information from both participants affected the prediction. This matches the our hypothesis that interpersonal information benefits the prediction, but getting any further explanation is challenging. We cannot be certain that these weights are a manifestation of synchrony.

Data and Annotation. We used continuous annotation because it was the most viable type of annotation across all sessions. However, for engagement level prediction, such precision is unnecessary. Moreover, training a regression task is significantly more problematic than a classification task. Another aspect of annotation limitation is the difficulty of obtaining frame-level annotations. In NoXi dataset, each session contains tens of thousands of frames. Annotating on such a scale is a daunting task for either crowd annotating or expert annotating.

Limited Optimization. Many machine learning techniques, such as hyperparameter grid search, can help improve the results. However, since our experiments are on the frame level, the training takes much longer than the conversation level tasks. As a result, our experiment could not optimize each model; instead adopted similar hyperparameters for all experiments. There is a possibility that some results can be significantly improved if supported by proper optimization techniques.

Individual Modality Effects. A common aspect of multi-modality research is to experiment with the contribution of each modality and different combinations of modalities. During our experiments, we encountered distinct attention distributions between parallel models. However, we considered this aspect beyond the scope of this paper. Which modality is better suited for the inter-person intra-modality structure remains an undiscussed topic.

6 Conclusion

This work explored the gap between engagement modeling and interpersonal synchrony. To enable models to capture the behavior synchrony between dyadic partners, we developed an inter-person intra-modality attention based model with different embedding schemas. Our experiments verified the positive impact of inter-person intra-modality features in engagement level prediction. We showed that time series feature processing grouped by each modality produced better results in the dyadic interaction scenario than those grouped by each participant. In future work, we plan to extend the model to cover both intra-modal inter-person and grouped-by-person submodels, explore different methods to assist training, and expand the training data to support more complex models.

Acknowledgement. This work was also partially supported by the Japan Society for the Promotion of Science (JSPS) KAKENHI (No. 22K21304, No. 22H04860 and 22H00536), JST AIP Trilateral AI Research, Japan (No. JPMJCR20G6) and JST Moonshot R&D program (JPMJMS2237-3).

References

1. Abdelrahman, A.A., Strazdas, D., Khalifa, A., Hintz, J., Hempel, T., Al-Hamadi, A.: Multimodal engagement prediction in multiperson human-robot interaction. IEEE Access **10**, 61980–61991 (2022). https://doi.org/10.1109/ACCESS.2022.3182469
2. Bernieri, F., Reznick, J., Rosenthal, R.: Synchrony, pseudosynchrony, and dissynchrony: measuring the entrainment process in mother-infant interactions. J. Pers. Soc. Psychol. **54**, 243–253 (1988). https://doi.org/10.1037/0022-3514.54.2.243
3. Bernieri, F., Rosenthal, R.: Interpersonal coordination: behavior matching and interactional synchrony. Fundamentals of Nonverbal Behavior. Studies in Emotion and Social Interaction, January 1991
4. Bohus, D., Horvitz, E.: Learning to predict engagement with a spoken dialog system in open-world settings. In: Proceedings of the SIGDIAL 2009 Conference: The 10th Annual Meeting of the Special Interest Group on Discourse and Dialogue, pp. 244–252. SIGDIAL 2009. Association for Computational Linguistics, USA (2009)
5. Cafaro, A., et al.: The NoXi database: multimodal recordings of mediated novice-expert interactions. In: Proceedings of the 19th ACM International Conference on Multimodal Interaction, ICMI 2017, pp. 350–359. Association for Computing Machinery, New York, NY, USA (2017). https://doi.org/10.1145/3136755.3136780
6. Chartrand, T.L., Bargh, J.A.: The chameleon effect: the perception-behavior link and social interaction. J. Pers. Soc. Psychol. **76**(6), 893–910 (1999)
7. Chartrand, T.L., Dalton, A.N.: Mimicry: its ubiquity, importance, and functionality (2009)
8. Cortes, C., Vapnik, V.: Support-vector networks. Mach. Learn. **20**(3), 273–297 (1995)
9. Delaherche, E., Chetouani, M., Mahdhaoui, A., Saint-Georges, C., Viaux, S., Cohen, D.: Interpersonal synchrony: a survey of evaluation methods across disciplines. IEEE Trans. Affect. Comput. **3**(3), 349–365 (2012). https://doi.org/10.1109/T-AFFC.2012.12
10. Dermouche, S., Pelachaud, C.: Engagement modeling in dyadic interaction. In: 2019 International Conference on Multimodal Interaction, ICMI 2019, pp. 440–445. Association for Computing Machinery, New York, NY, USA (2019). https://doi.org/10.1145/3340555.3353765
11. Glas, N., Pelachaud, C.: Definitions of engagement in human-agent interaction, pp. 944–949, September 2015. https://doi.org/10.1109/ACII.2015.7344688
12. Hadfield, J., Chalvatzaki, G., Koutras, P., Khamassi, M., Tzafestas, C.S., Maragos, P.: A deep learning approach for multi-view engagement estimation of children in a child-robot joint attention task. In: 2019 IEEE/RSJ International Conference on Intelligent Robots and Systems (IROS), pp. 1251–1256 (2019). https://doi.org/10.1109/IROS40897.2019.8968443
13. He, K., Zhang, X., Ren, S., Sun, J.: Deep residual learning for image recognition, pp. 770–778 (06 2016). https://doi.org/10.1109/CVPR.2016.90
14. Hochreiter, S., Schmidhuber, J.: Long short-term memory. Neural Comput. **9**(8), 1735–1780 (1997). https://doi.org/10.1162/neco.1997.9.8.1735
15. Hu, Y., Cheng, X., Pan, Y., Hu, Y.: The intrapersonal and interpersonal consequences of interpersonal synchrony. Acta Psychologica **224**, 103513 (2022). https://doi.org/10.1016/j.actpsy.2022.103513
16. Kaur, A., Mustafa, A., Mehta, L., Dhall, A.: Prediction and localization of student engagement in the wild. In: 2018 Digital Image Computing: Techniques and Applications (DICTA), pp. 1–8 (2018). https://doi.org/10.1109/DICTA.2018.8615851

17. Kendon, A.: Movement coordination in social interaction: some examples described. Acta Psychologica **32**, 101–125 (1970). https://doi.org/10.1016/0001-6918(70)90094-6
18. Kimura, R., Okada, S.: Personality trait classification based on co-occurrence pattern modeling with convolutional neural network. In: Stephanidis, C., et al. (eds.) HCII 2020. LNCS, vol. 12427, pp. 359–370. Springer, Cham (2020). https://doi.org/10.1007/978-3-030-60152-2_27
19. Kolesnikov, A., et al.: An image is worth 16 × 16 words: transformers for image recognition at scale (2021)
20. Nezami, O.M., Dras, M., Hamey, L., Richards, D., Wan, S., Paris, C.: Automatic recognition of student engagement using deep learning and facial expression (2018). https://doi.org/10.48550/ARXIV.1808.02324
21. Oertel, C., et al.: Engagement in human-agent interaction: an overview. Front. Robot. AI **7** (2020). https://doi.org/10.3389/frobt.2020.00092
22. Poggi, I.: Isabella Poggi Mind, Hands, Face and Body A Goal and Belief View of Multimodal Communication, March 2022. https://doi.org/10.1515/9783110261318.627
23. Reddish, P., Fischer, R., Bulbulia, J.: Let's dance together: synchrony, shared intentionality and cooperation. PLOS ONE **8**(8), 1–13 (2013). https://doi.org/10.1371/journal.pone.0071182
24. Simonyan, K., Zisserman, A.: Very deep convolutional networks for large-scale image recognition (2014). https://doi.org/10.48550/ARXIV.1409.1556
25. Sun, X., Nijholt, A.: Multimodal embodied mimicry in interaction. In: Esposito, A., Vinciarelli, A., Vicsi, K., Pelachaud, C., Nijholt, A. (eds.) Analysis of Verbal and Nonverbal Communication and Enactment. The Processing Issues. LNCS, vol. 6800, pp. 147–153. Springer, Heidelberg (2011). https://doi.org/10.1007/978-3-642-25775-9_14
26. Vaswani, A., et al.: Attention is all you need. In: Proceedings of the 31st International Conference on Neural Information Processing Systems, NIPS 2017, pp. 6000–6010. Curran Associates Inc., Red Hook, NY, USA (2017)
27. Wiltermuth, S., Heath, C.: Synchrony and cooperation. Psychol. Sci. **20**, 1–5 (2009). https://doi.org/10.1111/j.1467-9280.2008.02253.x
28. Yu, C., Aoki, P.M., Woodruff, A.: Detecting user engagement in everyday conversations (2004). https://doi.org/10.48550/ARXIV.CS/0410027

Learning User Embeddings with Generating Context of Posted Social Network Service Texts

Atsushi Otsuka[1(✉)], Kenta Hama[2], Narichika Nomoto[1], Ryo Ishii[1], Atsushi Fukayama[1], and Takao Nakamura[1]

[1] NTT Digital Twin Computing Research Center, Nippon Telegraph and Telephone Corp., 29F Shinagawa Season Terrace, 2-70 Konan 1-chome, Tokyo, Minato-ku 108-0075, Japan
atsushi.otsuka.vs@hco.ntt.co.jp

[2] Graduate School of Engineering Science, Osaka University, 1-3, Machikaneyama, Osaka, Toyonaka 560-8531, Japan

Abstract. Embedded representations that express the user's personality are essential for personalizing the output of machine learning. However, annotating training data to learn the embedding is difficult because one cannot directly observe a person's internal personality. This paper proposes a method for learning user embedding representations from social networking service data to make language models behave with personality. The method focuses on text posted by social networking service users and obtains the user's embedded representation by learning a model that predicts and generates sentences before and after the text input to the social networking service. Evaluation experiments showed that the proposed method could learn embedded expressions that reflected the user's attributes, such as location or personality.

Keywords: Deep learning · Embeddings · Text generation · Personality

1 Introduction

In natural language processing, the emergence of language models such as BERT [2] has produced significant results in various tasks. Several studies have been conducted to add individuality and diversity to these tasks rather than simply improving accuracy. For example, there is research on recommending products and information based on an individual's tastes and preferences [6], and dialogue processing reproduces an individual's behavior to ensure consistent utterances [23]. In particular, research to reproduce individuals has recently attracted attention as the Human Digital Twin[7, 15].

To reproduce the behavior of an individual itself, it is necessary to model the individual, including their attributes and personality. However, collecting data for training deep learning models with personalities is very difficult [22]. Furthermore, the task of annotating an individual's personality is a very costly operation. These are due to the difficulty of defining annotating because personality and individuality cannot be directly observed.

In this paper, we propose a learning method for individual user embeddings. Embedded representations represent a symbol, such as a word, as a high-dimensional real-valued vector. Our goal is to give machine learning models individuality by inputting the embeddings as to the deep learning model's initial value.

A. Coman and S. Vasilache (Eds.): HCII 2023, LNCS 14025, pp. 106–115, 2023.
https://doi.org/10.1007/978-3-031-35915-6_9

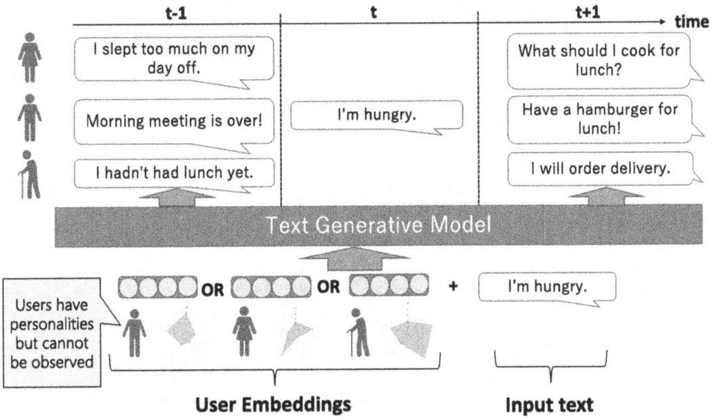

Fig. 1. Concept of our method. User's personalities are represented as an embedded vector from the generation of the preceding and following utterances.

Our proposed method uses text posted on social networking services (SNS) to learn embedded representations. Figure 1 shows an overview of the method. We assume that personal attributes and personality manifest themselves externally as a series of behaviors and statements of the individual, and some of them can be said to be expressed in the text posted on an SNS. Our method involves a learning the user's embedding layer and learning a generative model that predicts the text before and after the text that will be the context of the text posted on an SNS. Our main contributions are:

- We propose a novel unsupervised model-learning method for user embeddings that involves learning a generative model to predict the context of a user's posted text, and we train the model using publicly available tweet data.
- We compare the proposed embedding with that of Doc2Vec, a common document embedding, and find that the embedding representation of the proposed method reflects the user's personality characteristics.

2 Related Work

Prior work has been reported on user embeddings in research on recommendations. Pal [9] et al. proposed an embedded representation that reflects user preferences by incorporating embeddings of different content into a predictive user behavior model. Wang [21] et al. used RNNs to learn embeddings of a set of behaviors, such as click information and query logs. Shimei [10] et al. summarized a method for creating user embeddings using social media. Tagliabue [17] et al. proposed content-based embeddings for cold embedding. Plant [11] et al. reported a study that protects privacy in the case of language models with personality. Polignano [12] et al. proposed a method that combines two types of embedded representations of users and products for recommendations: graph-based and word-based. Christian [1] et al. proposed a model for personality prediction by feature extraction from multiple language models in SNS.

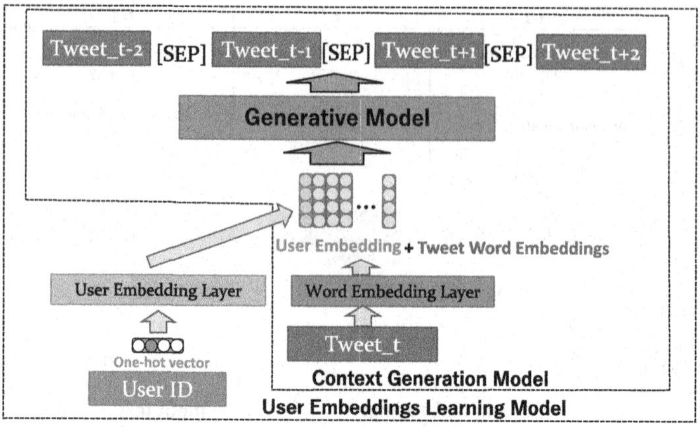

Fig. 2. Proposed Model.

Prior research also reported obtaining embedded expressions from the user-written text. Vu [20] et al. proposed a method for predicting responses to survey questionnaires from a user-posted text by combining embedding representations of SNS users encoded by BERT and psychological survey results. Song [16] et al. proposed a method for learning a user's embedding representation that considers the correspondent in addition to the e-mail message. Uban [18] et al. proposed a method to detect manifestations of anorexia by creating embedded expressions from the vocabulary of SNS texts. Huang [4] et al. propose a method for learning user embeddings that reflect interests and concerns by multitask-learning the interrelationships among three embedded representations: user, vocabulary, and product.

3 Method

In this section, we describe in detail the learning model and method for learning user embeddings. Our model consists of a user embedding layer and a context generation model, as shown in Fig. 2.

3.1 Context Generation Model

The context generation model is a model that generates predictions of tweets posted before and after the input tweet. Tweet $T_t = \{w_1, w_2, ..., w_l\}$ consisting of word pieces of length l, is input to the context generation model, where w_1 denotes a word piece of the tweet T_t. In this paper, we use a transformer-based language generative model [13, 19] for context generations. The training data for model learning is a series of tweets before and after the input tweet and is represented as,

$$\begin{aligned} S_t &= [T_{t-n}, w_{[SEP]}, T_{t-n+1}, w_{[SEP]}, \\ &\quad ..., w_{[SEP]}, T_{t+1}, w_{[SEP]}, ..., T_{t+m}] \end{aligned} \tag{1}$$

where $w_{[SEP]}$ is a one-hot vector corresponding to the special token [SEP] that indicates the tweet boundary. n and m are natural numbers, where T_{t-n} denotes the tweet n before and T_{t+m} denotes the tweet m after the input tweet T_t, and note that the output target data does not include T_t.

3.2 User Embedding Layer

The user embedding layer requires user IDs expressed as one-hot vectors. The number of dimensions of the one-hot vector is equal to the number of users u. The user embedding layer projects the one-hot vectors into a vector $E_\chi \in \mathbb{R}^d$ with a user word embedding matrix $W_e \in \mathbb{R}^{u \times d}$, where d denotes the number of dimensions of the vector. We regard a vector E_χ as a user embedding representation.

The vector E_χ of user embedding representations is concatenated to the input of the context generation model, and it is represented as,

$$U'_{T_{\chi_t}} = [E_\chi; U_{T_{\chi_t}}] \in \mathbb{R}^{d \times L+1} \tag{2}$$

where $U_{T_{\chi_t}}$ is a continuous value matrix projected by the embedding layer of the generative model from the input tweet T_t, and [;] denotes a vector concatenation across a row. The output S_{χ_t} for the input $U'_{T_{\chi_t}}$ is the same as in the context generation model.

4 Experiments

4.1 Model Training

For evaluation experiments, we created a dataset from a year's worth of 2015 tweet data. First, we randomly sampled 1,000 users from among all Twitter users, excluding BOTs and users with too few tweets per day. We created data pairs from each user's tweets and their contexts and prepared a dataset consisting of 1.2M data points. The Japanese T5 [13][1] model was used for the generation model, and the lengths of context n and m to be learned in context generation were set to 2. We used three GPUs (NVIDIA A6000) and trained the model with 10 epochs of all training data (42 h of training time).

4.2 Experiment with Context Generation

In this section, we will confirm that the context generation model is learning to take user information into account. A time series of loss function values during training of the generative model is shown in Fig. 3. The orange line represents the context generation model, and the blue line represents the user embedding representation model. The user embedding representation model has a smaller value of loss function at the end of learning than the context generation model without user embedding, indicating that learning with user embedding produces output closer to the teaching context.

To confirm that the context is generated based on the user, Table 1 shows the results of context generation for two users with different places of residence. User A lives in

[1] https://github.com/sonoisa/t5-japanese.

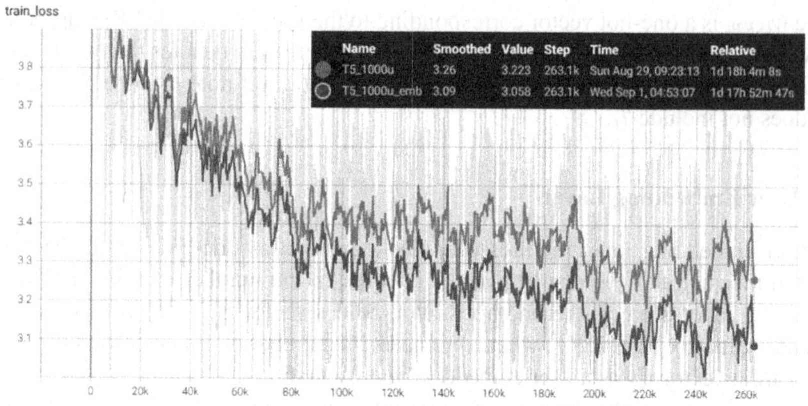

Fig. 3. Transition of loss functions while model training.

Tokyo, and User B lives in Yamanashi Prefecture, and this information was obtained from the Twitter location form. User A tweets that he is "*I will go to Yamanashi.*" which implies that he does not live in Yamanashi. On the other hand, user B is most likely living in Yamanashi, based on his tweet, "*I work in Kofu too.*". These results suggest that the user's information influences the context generation model.

To quantitatively evaluate that the proposed model generates a variety of user-specific contexts, 100 randomly selected tweets were input into the two models to generate ten contexts in each model. Table 2 shows the results of calculating the average value of the output context agreement by the F1 value of the BERTScore [24]. The user-embedded expression learning model has a lower BERTScore for each output, resulting in more diverse context generation. This result indicates that the proposed learning model can generate a variety of contexts according to user-specific features rather than general contexts.

4.3 Experiment with Down-Stream Task

We evaluated the performance of user embedding representations by performing the task of estimating the location of Twitter users. The purpose of this experiment was to test the hypothesis that context learning corresponds to learning user attribute information, which is the claim of this paper.

Setup. We first extracted users whose location information included "Hokkaido," "Tokyo," and "Aichi" from the 1000 users in the trained model. The number of obtained users was 100 for "Hokkaido," 68 for "Aichi" Prefecture, and 99 for "Tokyo," for a total of 267, divided 4:1:1 into training data, validation data, and test data. The evaluation scores were Precision, Recall, and F1.

The classification model was a neural network with two layers; the input dimension was 768 for the proposed method, the dimension of the hidden layer was 200, and ReLU [8] is used as the activation function. We trained the model with a stochastic gradient

Table 1. Output tweets from generated models. Note that each word is literal translation from Japanese.*Kofu* is the capital city of Yamanashi Prefecture. *Budokan* is the name of a stadium in Tokyo.

User	input tweet	output tweets			
	t	t-2	t-1	t+1	t+2
A	*Tokyo is the best place.*	*congratulations.*	*It is raining today in Tokyo.*	***It was snowing in Tokyo, too.***	*The weather is nice and pleasant today!*
	Yamanashi is the best place.	*Oh,i see*	***I met an uncle yesterday in Yamanashi.***	*I am at Budokan.*	***I will go to Yamanashi.***
B	*Tokyo is the best place.*	*congratulations.*	***Is it raining in Tokyo?***	*Glad it was sunny again today.*	***I went to Tokyo yesterday.***
	Yamanashi is the best place.	*Oh,i see*	***I work in Kofu too.***	***I still think Yamanashi is a wonderful place!***	Oh

Table 2. BERTScores of outputs for random inputs.

	w/o user embedding	w/ user embedding
BERTScore	0.923	0.753

descent, where the loss function was set to cross-entropy, and the dropout rate was set to 0.2.

The proposed method uses two different learning methods as:

all-training: The 232M parameters of the user embedding layer and the context generation layer are updated simultaneously.

fine-tuning: After training the context generation model, the 10M parameters of user embedding layer is trained for fine-tuning.

Comparison. We used Doc2Vec [5] as the method for comparison by considering each user's series of tweets as a document [3]. The number of dimensions of Doc2Vec was set to 200, and the learning algorithm was the Distributed Bag of Words version of Paragraph Vector. The classification model was the same as the proposed method, but the number of input dimensions was set to 200.

We used a concatenation of the Doc2Vec vector and the proposed embedding.

Result. The result of the location classification task is shown in Table 3. Since "fine-tune" had the highest scores, it was effective for the proposed method to learn user

Table 3. Results of location prediction: numbers are mean and standard deviation of 20 cross-validations. "concat" denotes result of inputting vector that is concatenation of fine-tuning and Doc2Vec vectors.

	Precision(%)	Recall(%)	F1-score
Doc2Vec	58.2 ± 4.4	56.4 ± 4.4	56.2 ± 4.7
all-training	43.4 ± 6.7	42.4 ± 5.7	41.9 ± 5.7
fine-tune	59.6 ± 4.1	58.9 ± 4.0	58.6 ± 4.0
concat	63.8 ± 3.9	60.7 ± 3.5	60.7 ± 3.6

Table 4. High-frequency words for each cluster. Note that each word is literal translation from Japanese.

	Doc2Vec	proposed
C1	*smile, study, laugh*	*Japan, work, nhk*
C2	*work, Japan, video*	*follow, please, work*
C3	*follow, laugh, fanny*	*follow, please, work*
C4	*picture, please, work*	*game, animation, work*
C5	*game, character, recently*	*work, game, picture*

embeddings after learning context generation. Furthermore, "concat", which is a concatenation of fine-tuning and Doc2Vec, was the highest. This result indicates that combining the conventional embedding representation and the embedding of the proposed method may improve the output reflecting individuality in deep learning models.

4.4 Evaluation Based on Similarity

We evaluated the embeddings in terms of similarity. We first performed clustering using the embeddings and investigated the similarity in terms of embeddings by observing the users belonging to each cluster.

Setup. The proposed model used in Sect. 4.3 and the embeddings of the 1000 users for Doc2Vec were classified into five clusters by k-means.

Word Based Similarity. We aggregated the calculation of the frequency of word occurrences in the tweets of users in each cluster. The top three high-frequency words in each cluster are shown in Table 4. With the proposed method, words such as "work" occur at a high frequency in all clusters. Row "word' in Table 5 shows the mean of the correlation coefficients for the frequency distribution of the top-20 words in each cluster with other clusters. The proposed method had a greater correlation between clusters than Doc2Vec. However, the test results showed no dominant difference in the mean values of the correlation coefficients.

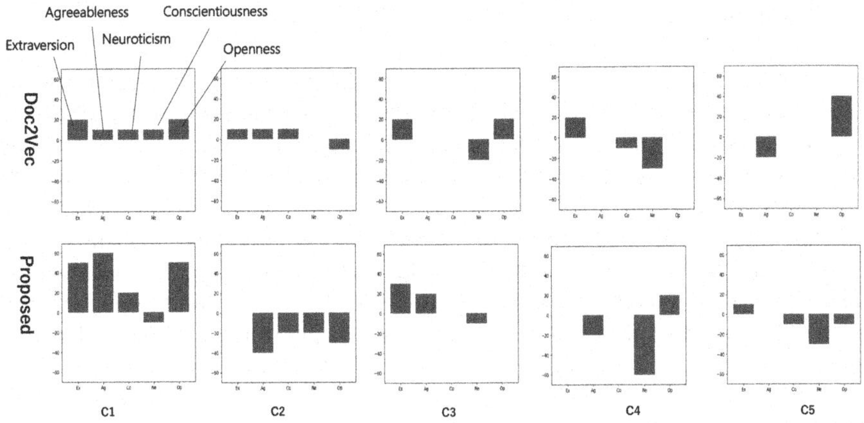

Fig. 4. User distribution for each cluster based on Big Five. C1-C5 denotes each cluster.Each graph represents distribution of users for each Big Five factor in each cluster.

Table 5. Mean correlation coefficient of word distribution between clusters."p-value" denotes result of performing Wilcoxon rank-sum test to test difference between the means of Doc2Vec and proposed method.

CC	Doc2Vec	Proposed	p-value
word	0.151	0.234	0.516
Big Five	0.787	0.156	$1.90\ e^{-5}$

Personality Based Similarity. We examined users' personalities in each cluster based on the Big Five [14]. We observed users' tweets in each cluster and judged them on the positives and negatives of each Big Five item of the user's personality as perceived by their tweets. Two raters viewed ten consecutive tweets at three random locations to determine the user's personality. The results of evaluating the impression of the tweets in the clusters are shown in Fig. 4. Doc2Vec had minor differences in distribution among clusters and a slight bias in the character of each cluster. In comparison, the proposed method had a highly skewed distribution of users in each cluster, e.g., C1 had a large number of positive users for each factor.

Row "Big Five" in Table 5 shows the mean of the correlation coefficients for the Big Five-based personality. Doc2Vec showed a strong correlation between the distributions of the clusters, while the proposed method showed no correlation. In other words, the proposed method was highly independent of each cluster from the point of view of the Big Five. The test results also showed a significant difference in the correlation coefficients between the proposed and comparison methods ($p < 0.05$), suggesting that the proposed embedding may include similarities based on the user's personality.

Proposed method aims to not limit to specific downstream tasks and does not require expensive human work such as dataset creation and labeling.

5 Conclusion

In this paper, we proposed an unsupervised method for learning user embeddings for acquiring personality in a deep learning model through a generation model for tweets. In an evaluation experiment, we obtained results suggesting that the user embeddings learned by the proposed method reflect the user's personality as well as attributes such as the user's location.

Future work is a detailed analysis of embedded user embeddings. Evaluation experiments revealed the possibility that the embedded vectors contain user personality information. Further analysis may lead to using the embedded vectors for dialogue and generation tasks that reflect the user's personality and thoughts. Since the proposed method applies to more than just SNS text, it should also be applied to other domains.

Limitations. The experiment of this paper used Japanese data. However, the proposed method can also be applied to multilingual data. The method creates embeddings from one-hot vectors. Thus, there are issues when adding new users. In this paper, the model was trained with a fixed window size for context generation. It is possible that better training could be achieved by dynamically setting the window size to account for the interval between text submissions.

References

1. Christian, H., Suhartono, D., Chowanda, A., Zamli, K.Z.: Text based personality prediction from multiple social media data sources using pre-trained language model and model averaging. J. Big Data **8**(1), 1–20 (2021). https://doi.org/10.1186/s40537-021-00459-1
2. Devlin, J., Chang, M., Lee, K., Toutanova, K.: BERT: pre-training of deep bidirectional transformers for language understanding. In: Burstein, J., Doran, C., Solorio, T. (eds.) Proceedings of the 2019 Conference of the North American Chapter of the Association for Computational Linguistics: Human Language Technologies NAACL-HLT, pp. 4171–4186. Association for Computational Linguistics (2019)
3. Ding, T., Bickel, W.K., Pan, S.: Multi-view unsupervised user feature embedding for social media-based substance use prediction. In: Proceedings of the 2017 Conference on Empirical Methods in Natural Language Processing (EMNLP 2017), pp. 2275–2284 (Sep 2017)
4. Huang, X., Paul, M.J., Dernoncourt, F., Burke, R., Dredze, M.: User factor adaptation for user embedding via multitask learning. In: Proceedings of the Second Workshop on Domain Adaptation for NLP, pp. 172–182 (Apr 2021)
5. Le, Q., Mikolov, T.: Distributed representations of sentences and documents. In: Proceedings of the 31st International Conference on Machine Learning, Proceedings of Machine Learning Research, vol. 32, pp. 1188–1196 (2014)
6. Li, L., Zhang, Y., Chen, L.: Personalized transformer for explainable recommendation. In: Proceedings of the 59th Annual Meeting of the Association for Computational Linguistics and the 11th International Joint Conference on Natural Language Processing (ACL 2021), pp. 4947–4957 (2021)
7. Miller, M.E., Spatz, E.: A unified view of a human digital twin. Hum.-Intell. Syst. Integration **4**, 23–33 (2022)
8. Nair, V., Hinton, G.E.: Rectified linear units improve restricted boltzmann machines. In: Proceedings of the 27th International Conference on Machine Learning (ICML 2010), p. 807–814 (2010)

9. Pal, A., Eksombatchai, C., Zhou, Y., Zhao, B., Rosenberg, C., Leskovec, J.: Pinnersage: Multi-modal user embedding framework for recommendations at pinterest. In: Proceedings of the 26th ACM SIGKDD International Conference on Knowledge Discovery & Data Mining (KDD 2020), pp. 2311–2320 (2020)
10. Pan, S., Ding, T.: Social media-based user embedding: A literature review. In: Proceedings of the Twenty-Eighth International Joint Conference on Artificial Intelligence (IJCAI 2019)
11. Plant, R., Gkatzia, D., Giuffrida, V.: CAPE: Context-aware private embeddings for private language learning. In: Proceedings of the 2021 Conference on Empirical Methods in Natural Language Processing(EMNLP 2021), pp. 7970–7978 (Nov 2021)
12. Polignano, M., Musto, C., de Gemmis, M., Lops, P., Semeraro, G.: Together is better: Hybrid recommendations combining graph embeddings and contextualized word representations. In: Fifteenth ACM Conference on Recommender Systems (RecSys 2021)
13. Exploring the limits of transfer learning with a unified text-to-text transformer. J. Mach. Learn. Res. **21**(140), 1–67 (2020)
14. Rothmann, S., Coetzer, E.: The big five personality dimensions and job performance. South African J. Indust. Psychol. **29**, 68–74 (10 2003)
15. Shengli, W.: Is human digital twin possible? Comput. Methods Programs Biomed. Update **1**, 100014 (2021)
16. Song, Y., Lee, C.J.: Learning user embeddings from emails. In: Proceedings of the 15th Conference of the European Chapter of the Association for Computational Linguistics: vol. 2, Short Papers (EACL 2017), pp. 733–738, Valencia, Spain (Apr 2017)
17. Tagliabue, J., Yu, B., Bianchi, F.: The embeddings that came in from the cold: Improving vectors for new and rare products with content-based inference. In: Fourteenth ACM Conference on Recommender Systems (RecSys 2020), pp. 577–578 (2020)
18. Uban, A.S., Chulvi, B., Rosso, P.: Understanding patterns of anorexia manifestations in social media data with deep learning. In: Proceedings of the Seventh Workshop on Computational Linguistics and Clinical Psychology: Improving Access, pp. 224–236 (Jun 2021)
19. Vaswani, A., et al.: Attention is all you need. In: Advances in Neural Information Processing Systems, vol. 30 (2017)
20. Vu, H., Abdurahman, S., Bhatia, S., Ungar, L.: Predicting responses to psychological questionnaires from participants' social media posts and question text embeddings. In: Findings of the Association for Computational Linguistics: EMNLP 2020, pp. 1512–1524 (2020)
21. Wang, T., Brovman, Y.M., Madhvanath, S.: Personalized embedding-based e-commerce recommendations at ebay. arXiv. vol. cs.IR (2021)
22. Welch, C., Gu, C., Kummerfeld, J., Perez-Rosas, V., Mihalcea, R.: Leveraging similar users for personalized language modeling with limited data. In: Proceedings of the 60th Annual Meeting of the Association for Computational Linguistics (ACL2022), pp. 1742–1752 (2022)
23. Zhang, S., Dinan, E., Urbanek, J., Szlam, A., Kiela, D., Weston, J.: Personalizing dialogue agents: I have a dog, do you have pets too? In: Proceedings of the 56th Annual Meeting of the Association for Computational Linguistics (ACL 2018), pp. 2204–2213 (2018)
24. Zhang, T., Kishore, V., Wu, F., Weinberger, K.Q., Artzi, Y.: Bertscore: Evaluating text generation with BERT. In: Proceedings of the 8th International Conference on Learning Representations (ICLR 2020) (2020)

Predicting Twitter Hate User Behavior Using Big Five Personality Traits and Ensemble Machine Learning

Suresha Perera, Supunmali Ahangama(✉), Indika Perera, and Sandunika Hathnapitiya

University of Moratuwa, Katubedda 10400, Sri Lanka
{sureshap,indika}@cse.mrt.ac.lk, {supunmali,164170g}@uom.lk

Abstract. Twitter has grown in popularity as a microblogging social media platform for people of all ages and locations to exchange and discuss important events, information, and news. Some Twitter users exhibit unique behaviors, and they use such platforms maliciously to spread hate content over social media platforms. These materials may be harmful to the mental health of people and cause suicide ideation, criminal behavior, or racism. On social media, hateful content spreads more quickly than other types of content by nature. Early detection of hate users can help to lessen its damaging effects. Different personality types exist among social media users, and these personality types influence how a person interacts with others, processes information, and makes decisions. This study determines whether personality is associated with the sharing of hate content by hate users, identifying the HIGH/LOW availability of Big Five personality traits. Meanwhile, three psychologists determine the personalities of Twitter users based on their profiles. With more than 80% accuracy for each personality trait, the ensemble approach (SVM, Random Forest, XGBoost) was used in this study to examine how the Big Five personality traits of Twitter users may be predicted using their Twitter user profiles' attributes and Twitter activity considering both English and Sinhala language Tweets in the Sri Lankan context. The findings of this study provide new empirical proof that there is a considerable relationship between people's personality traits and their harmful intentions, with neuroticism and extraversion being closely associated with hate users by raising anti-social traits in them.

Keywords: Big Five personality traits · Hate speech propagators · Hate user behaviour · Twitter

1 Introduction

There has been an exponential rise in internet communication over the past few years. Social media platforms like Facebook, Twitter, Instagram, Snapchat, and YouTube are some key platforms in communication. These social media platforms attract users from a variety of cultures and educational backgrounds, and the people who use them openly express their thoughts. Furthermore, the expansion of hate content on social media platforms is encouraged by the freedom of speech on the internet and the anonymity of

A. Coman and S. Vasilache (Eds.): HCII 2023, LNCS 14025, pp. 116–130, 2023.
https://doi.org/10.1007/978-3-031-35915-6_10

platform users. The lack of accountability by the platform owners also encourages the propagation of hate content over social media platforms. Further, hate speech propagators use some terms which cannot be directly identified as hate content and lack editorial oversight, which sometimes positively correlate with the engagement algorithms used by the platform owners. Additionally, hate speech is more likely to be heard on social media than it could be in traditional communication platforms since it grabs more attention than non-hate speech.

Hate content over social media platforms has adverse effects, such as causing psychological harm (Nielsen 2002). Those resulted in the violation of human dignity, build depression and even some situations, attempted suicide by being hate speech victims. It resulted in psychological effects on people such as low self-esteem, sleeping disorders, increased anxiety, and feelings of fear and insecurity (Chandra 2021). Therefore, it is important to reduce the propagation of hate content over social media platforms and reduce the adversarial effects on society.

It is essential to identify and regulate hate content on social media sites since there is a close connection between hate speech and actual hate crimes. Robert Bowers shot 18 people inside a Pittsburgh synagogue on October 27, 2018 (McIlroy-Young and Anderson 2019). He mentioned anti-Semitic remarks on the social media site Gab, mentioning the Tree of Life synagogue that he had targeted. A few countries have imposed bans on social media sites like Facebook and Twitter to stop the spread of hate speech.

Facebook, WhatsApp, Viber, and Instagram were recently totally taken down by the government of Sri Lanka as people used to spread messages of racial hatred following the Easter bombing (Wijeratne 2018). However, they do not have an effective impact on reducing hate content. Even though there are several laws and guidelines in place to protect the public, their inadequate execution compels the necessary deletion of such messages from users' timelines in all conceivable ways (Alshalan and Al-Khalifa 2020). Therefore, effective utilization of countermeasures to combat hate content is important to reduce the propagation of hate content over social media platforms.

The research on hate content online is not complete if user-generated content on social media platforms is only taken into account. It's critical to identify and study the user who posted hateful information on social media.

Social media has changed the way people interact with each other and represent themselves using their profiles. Further, they share their thoughts, feelings, insights, and emotions by writing, posting, reacting, and commenting. Therefore, they represent their actual personality from their profile. Those platform data can be used to predict their psychological characteristics. Personality is one of the most important psychological aspects which helps to identify the online behavior of the social media user. The automatic detection of personality traits has become important with the rapid development of social media platforms. Numerous studies have been conducted to identify personality traits with publicly available social media data (Xue et al. 2017).

This study used Twitter for the analysis of personality traits of the users online. The hateful people on social media platforms have a variety of personalities. A human language is developed through communication. The profile information presented on a Twitter profile are an indication of personality traits. In order to analyze the personalities of users, particularly those who propagate hatred, Twitter user profiles are examined in this study. Thus, the focus of this study is on Sri Lanka-specific hate user personality identification.

The study finds that the Twitter user profile attributes and the Twitter activities could be effectively used to predict the Big Five personality traits (extroversion, agreeableness, conscientiousness, neuroticism, and openness to experience) of Twitter users. For that, this study effectively uses the supervised machine learning method of ensemble approach (SVM, Random Forest, XGBoost using soft-voting classifier) with 80% accuracy to find the high/low availability of each personality traits among the Twitter users. This is more important when considering the hate users in finding their relationship between personalities and their behaviour on the Twitter social media platform. It is interesting to find that the extraversion and neuroticism traits are prominent among hate users.

Several theoretical and practical contributions have been made in this study. First, discover the link between a user's personality and the spreading of hate content over the Twitter social media platform. Second, it would also be helpful to pinpoint the hate users that might post hateful stuff on social media so that these users might be given low priority or visibility on their profiles. The Sinhala language has few/no personality predictions using only their Twitter profile extrinsic and intrinsic information, despite the fact that personality classifications are available for other languages like English. This study, therefore, helps Sinhala-speaking Twitter users identify their Big Five personality traits.

The remainder of this paper is organized as follows. The following section reviews the theoretical foundations of user personality in social media platforms. Following a discussion of the theoretical foundations of user personality, then explains the data collection, adapted methodology, and research design. Finally, the analysis and results are mentioned, followed by a discussion and conclusion.

2 Literature Review

In 1982, Goldberg developed the Big Five Model, which describes an individual's characteristics by considering patterns of thinking, feeling, and behavior, as well as how they are expressed in response to environmental changes in five ways, and it was reconfirmed in 1990 (Goldberg 1990). The Big Five Model is one of the most widely and frequently used personality models (Bachrach et al. 2012). It identifies five broad personality dimensions as (Stajner and Yenikent 2020) Openness, Conscientiousness, Extraversion, Agreeableness, and Neuroticism.

The personality detection was done manually by trained psychologists using a questionnaire. However, with the development of computational linguistics and Natural Language Processing (NLP), automatic identification of personality traits has become popular. Moreover, this has been boosted by social media usage by incorporating machine learning approaches for automatic personality prediction using Tweets, Facebook posts, etc. People communicate using words that reflect the human. Further, language aids to show humans' internal thoughts and their emotions. Therefore language and words play a major role in psychology and communication (Tausczik and Pennebaker 2010). In psychology, the most accepted model to describe the personality of a person is the Big Five model (Tadesse et al. 2018).

A survey paper identified various behavioral and linguistic implications of the Big Five model in the fields such as organizational behavior, advertising and marketing, and many other fields (Stajner and Yenikent 2020). The way social media users use the language and react on Facebook helps in identifying each dimension relevant to the Big Five model. There is a prevalence to use personality traits identification with hate instigators and targets where they experienced unique personality characteristics related to them such as anger, depression, and immoderation (ElSherief et al. 2018).

Personality prediction is observed based on a given set of data such as essays, social media posts, social media behaviour analysis, etc. Personality prediction based on linguistic feature analysis aided with several text analysis tools such as Linguistic Inquiry and Word Count (LIWC), Structured Programming for Linguistic Cue Extraction (SPLICE), and Medical Research Council (MRC) Psycholinguistic Database (Ong, Rahmanto and Suhartono 2017). LIWC is a text analysis program that counts words in psychologically significant categories. This has been used in a variety of experiments to demonstrate attentional focus, emotionality, social relationships, thinking styles, and individual differences (Tausczik and Pennebaker 2010). According to LIWC research, language style information is critical to understanding a person's state of mind. LIWC is used to automatically detect the personality from texts. SPLICE is a linguistic feature that has been used in several studies in this field of linguistic analysis. Upon input of text, the SPLICE gives various features such as negative and positive self-evaluation, part of speech features, and so on. The MRC Psycholinguistic Database computed features (Coltheart 1981) consists of linguistic and psycholinguistic features of each word.

A study (Bachrach et al. 2012) has used some Facebook features to find the personality traits using the Big Five model with the features such as number of Facebook friends, groups (number of associations with groups), number of Facebook "likes", number of photos uploaded by user, number of status updates by the user, and number of times others "tagged" user in photos. The likes and groups have a positive correlation with openness, highlighting users' increased involvement in seeking new things and ideas and sharing them with their friends. However, likes and groups have a negative correlation with conscientiousness while photos have a positive correlation. Conscientious people have a negative correlation with likes and groups while photos have a positive correlation where those people consider that using Facebook may waste their time hence resulting in fewer likes for objects as well as joining with fewer groups. However, those people upload more photos to show that they are more active than others. Extraverts tend to reach out and interact with other people on Facebook. Further, they share what's going on in their lives, and feelings via status updates. They engage with the objects by liking them to show their appreciation or sympathy. Moreover, there is a high chance of getting connected with groups where it provides the environment to interact with the wider community and exchange information. Furthermore, there is a positive correlation with the number of friends. People with low agreeableness are less concerned with what other people think and like different objects more freely. More agreeable people, on the other hand, are concerned that by liking, they will alienate themselves from their friends. Agreeableness is less correlated with those Facebook features. Users with neuroticism are positively correlated with Facebook likes where it is moderate for the lower levels of likes and stronger for the users with many likes and slightly positively correlated with several groups. Neuroticism users feel negative emotions such as anxiety, anger, or depression where they expect support from Facebook groups, like others' updates. Average neuroticism increases with the number of friends until reaching peak levels for roughly 200 friends. Beyond this peak level, neuroticism becomes negatively associated with the number of friends. Therefore, very neurotic people may tend to have fewer friends, but maintain closer relations, providing more support.

Another study (Xue et al. 2017) used three categories of features from users' profiles and what they have posted in the Big Five personality traits prediction model to recognize an individual's personality. They are profile-based static features (gender, address, nickname), profile-based dynamic features (number of followers or followings), and content-based micro-blogs features (raw data of users posted micro-blogs, including linguistic features, psychological features, and so on). All together 113 features have been used including 11 profile-based features such as length of the nickname, gender, province, city, language, length of self-description, number of friends, number of followers, number of followings, number of statuses, and number of favourites and 102 content-based features.

There are two disciplines observed in predicting personality in social media as computational linguistics and SNA. The Big Five model has been used to predict the personality of social media users and a study by (Tandera et al. 2017) used two data sets by using both linguistics and SNA. The first data set is myPersonality (Schwartz et al. 2013) and the second data set is manually collected where the personality labeling was done manually for the second data set using Apply Magic Sauce application (*Apply Magic Sauce - Prediction API*, no date) by Cambridge Psychometrics Centre to predict psychological traits from digital footprints of human behavior. They developed personality prediction using different machine learning and deep learning methods with LIWC, SPLICE, SNA features. Finally, they have identified that the deep learning methods perform well.

A study by (Schwartz et al. 2013) was conducted with personality, gender, and age in social media. They used R: Square-root of the coefficient of determination (for sequential/continuous outcomes), LIWC, topics, WordPhrases: words and phrases (n-grams of size 1 to 3 passing a collocation filter).

A study by (Farnadi et al. 2013) used LIWC, social network information (network size, betweenness, nbetweenness, density, brokerage, nbrokerage, and transitivity), time stamps (frequency of status updates per day, number of statuses posted between 6 am–11 am, number of statuses posted between 11 am–4 pm, number of statuses posted between 4 pm–9 pm, number of statuses posted between 9 pm–0 am, and number of statuses posted between 0 am–6 am.), and others (total number of statuses per user, number of capitalized words, number of capital letters, number of words that are used more than once, number of URLs, and number of occurrences of the string PROPNAME). They discovered some intriguing findings, such as the fact that Facebook status updates contain important cues about their authors' personality types, that there is no single type of feature that produces the best results for all personality traits, and that results for linguistic features improve when additional training examples from another domain are used (training examples from different social media platforms may build more accurate models).

Another study by (Tadesse et al. 2018) SNA features (network size, betweenness, density, brokerage, and transitivity measures), LIWC, and SPLICE based on the myPersonality dataset to predict personality traits using the Big Five model. LIWC features outperformed SPLICE features in the study. They discovered that using SNA features yielded better results than using linguistic features. They discovered that using XGBoost prevents overfitting and improves model performance and extraction speed.

Several research studies attempted to identify personality traits using the Big Five model with the Twitter social media platform (Golbeck et al. 2011; Sumner et al. 2012; Mathew and Kumar 2018). They have used some of the Twitter statistics such as the number of followers, followings, replies, hashtags, links, etc., and linguistic features to identify the personality traits using different classification algorithms.

Some studies have been conducted to identify the personality of Hate speakers. A study by (ElSherief et al. 2018) used original English tweets and replies for the personality analysis with IBM Watson Personality Insights API, which infers personality characteristics from textual information based on an open vocabulary approach. They have compared the personality traits of the hate users, general users, and hate target users whose Twitter account is targeted by a hate tweet and explicitly mentioned in the tweet using the mention. They indicated that hate users are more self-focused, contrary, proud, cautious of others, and can compromise morality. When considering openness, the hate users obtained lower scores for emotionality and adventurousness and higher imagination scores. For the emotional range, they have lower scores; however, the higher emotional range indicates that hate users are fierier, prone-to worry, melancholy, hedonistic, and susceptible to stress. Further, it shows that emotional range facets such as anxiety, depression, immoderation, and self-consciousness are embodied more in the tweets of hate users. Further, hate users have lower values for conscientiousness and extraversion with lower scores of activity levels, friendliness, and cheerfulness but higher scores for excitement seeking in comparison to general users.

According to (Mathew and Kumar 2018), hate users have higher extraversion, indicating that they are more energetic and talkative in nature. Moreover, they are more energetic, talkative, cheerful, excitement-seeking, outgoing, and sociable by nature.

The study of personality traits (ElSherief et al. 2018) is critical because it can be used to design next-generation counter-speech bots with greater effectiveness. Furthermore, the study discovered that the greater the openness, the more the counterspeech could be successfully used to decrease hate speech.

According to the previous studies, to the best of our knowledge, no analysis has been used on personality traits with social media hate speech propagators to rank them on SMPs. This study expected to use the Big Five personality model, which is identified as the most widely used in predicting the personality traits of social media users, to identify the level of influence and contribution to propagate hate speech over SMPs by hate speech propagators.

3 Methodology

There are various methods used to analyze the personality traits of people, and this study uses the Big Five model to identify the personality traits of hate users on Twitter. Each attribute has a few qualities that can be seen in user behaviour. Previous researchers have found that it is important to understand what characteristics need to score, whether a high/low score (Stidham, Summers and Shuffler 2018; Abdel-Khalek et al. 2022) for each personality.

This study concerns Twitter as the social media platform and Fig. 1 describes the overall flow of the entire process. They are obtaining the user data from Twitter (tweets and metadata), classifying tweets as hate or non-hate (Hathnapitiya, Ahangama and Adikari 2023; Rajapaksha, Ahangama and Adikari 2023), identifying hate and non-hate users based on the number of hate posts generated by users, classifying the personality traits of the hate and non-hate users as high/low by psychology experts, and use supervised machine learning algorithms to classify the users' personality traits as high/low. Finally, perform the relationship analysis between the Big Five personality traits with hate users.

We crawled the Twitter social media platform to get a diverse dataset for the study. In the beginning, Twitter used to browse a few random users' profiles and the last 200 tweets they had sent. The tweets were then divided into hate and non-hate categories using a specific Recurrent Neural Networks made up of FastText and Long-Short Term Memory (Dias, Welikala and Dias 2018). When labelling the tweets as hate or not, this study considered both Sinhala and English posts as the Users considered this study represents the Sri Lankan context. From that sample, this study considered 50 hate users who have tweeted more than five times and another 50 hate users who have tweeted fewer than five times or none.

The 100 Sri Lankan Twitter users from the above dataset (50 hate users and another 50 non-hate users) have been annotated into five classes to represent the Big Five personality traits. Each class has two labels: HIGH and LOW. The dataset was tagged by three psychology experts. Each user was given tweets and Twitter metadata. The standard indicator of inter-annotator agreement is the Cohen's kappa coefficient used as the inter-annotator agreement for categorical items (Cohen 2016). As a cutoff, the kappa value of 0.67 has been selected. The Cohen's Kappa for the inter-annotator agreement was 0.84.

Most of the time, users of the social media platform Twitter, use very informal language. To create a clean text, we removed slang words, emojis, stop words, punctuation, URLs, and other elements from the tweets using the steps in (Perera and Karunanayaka 2022). Preprocessing is done to make these datasets ready for experimentation by removing noisy, inconsistent, and incomplete data.

From the dataset, this study used the following features in Table 1 to predict the personality of Twitter users using supervised Machine Learning algorithms. Number of followers, Number of followings, Number of Favourites, Number of statuses are directly extracted from the twitter user's profile. Number of words in the user description, Number of mentions, Number of hashtags, Number of urls, Number of first person words, Number of second person words, Number of third person words are taken after processing the extracted tweets and metadata of each Twitter user. Number of hate tweets and Number of non-hate tweets were calculated after the tweets have been labelled as hate or non-hate with the existing methods used by the previous scholars. The sentiment analysis of the tweets was performed separately for the Sinhala and English tweets (Perera, Ahangama and Perera 2023). In order to identify negative, neutral, and positive tweets, this study

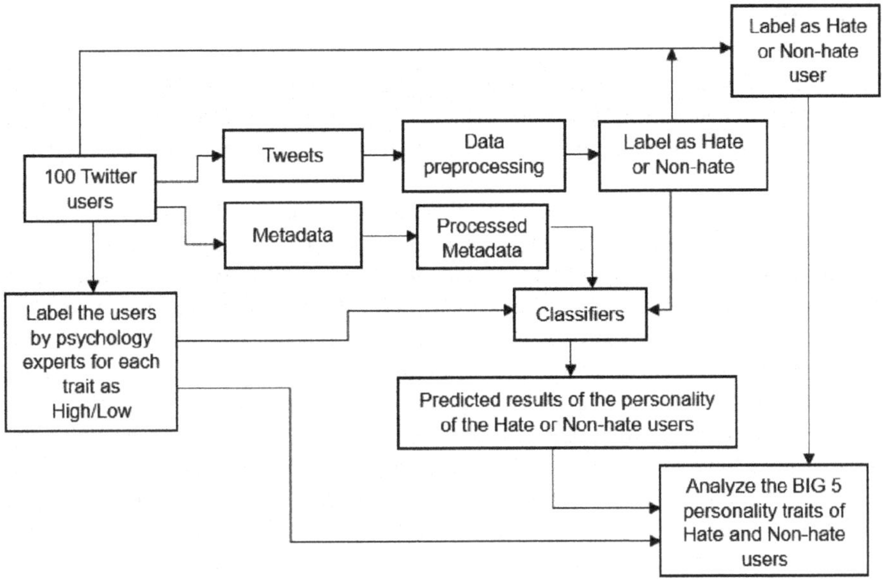

Fig. 1. The architecture of the identification of the relationship between hate user and their personality traits.

used the VADER sentiment analysis method. Then calculate the two features: Number of positive tweets and Number of negative tweets, Number of neutral tweets.

The four machine learning algorithms used in this study to predict personalities are SVM, Random Forest, XGBoost, and the ensemble method (SVM, Random Forest, XGBoost using a soft-voting classifier. There are three categories of features as the information directly crawled from the Twitter user profile (user profile information), the lexicon analysis and analysis of tweets by the hate and non-hate users (Tweet information), and the sentiment of the tweets expressed by the users (Sentiment).

Table 1. The features used to predict the personality of the hate and non-hate user

User profile information	Tweet information	Sentiment
Number of followers, Number of followings, Number of hate tweets, Number of non-hate tweets, Number of Favourites, Number of statuses, Number of words in the user description	Number of mentions, Number of hashtags, Number of URLs, Number of first person words, Number of second person words, Number of third person words	Number of positive tweets, Number of negative tweets, Number of neutral tweets

The evaluation of the classifiers was performed with accuracy, recall, F1 score, and precision. Then the hate and non-hate user personality traits would be analyzed.

4 Results

This study used four machine learning techniques to investigate the predictability of personality traits of hate and on-hate users, as mentioned in the methodology section. Table 2 depicts the classification algorithm outcomes in terms of precision, recall, accuracy, and F1 score.

From the results in Table 2, it is visible that the ensemble model achieved the highest accuracy among all models. The SVM model got the lowest accuracy compared to other models. Accuracies in SVM classifier lie between 63% to 77% for five traits. Both openness and neuroticism have 63% accuracy. It is the lowest accuracy level in SVM classifier for the given data. The extraversion trait has given 77%, the highest accuracy in the SVM classifier. RF classifiers offer improved accuracies than SVM for all five personalities. RF produced 91% accuracy for the neuroticism trait, the highest accuracy delivered by a single classifier. Agreeableness only achieved 74% accuracy, the lowest value in the RF classifier. XGB classifier produced accuracy values between 77% and 88%, where 77% for openness and 88% for agreeableness. The ensemble model has delivered the highest accuracy values for all five personality traits. It has given 93% accuracy for the openness trait. It is the highest accuracy value in the ensemble model. All accuracies in the ensemble model are higher than 80%. Results show that the ensemble model gives the highest accuracy, precision, and recall results among all tested models.

As depicted in the Fig. 2, openness, conscientiousness, and agreeableness are higher with non-hate users while extraversion and neuroticism are higher with hate users. However, twelve hate and 20 non-hate users fall in the high openness trait. High conscientiousness scores are available in 25 hate users, which is half of the hate user sample size and 27 non-hate users. Twenty-one hate and forty-nine non-hate users, which is almost all the non-hate users except one got high agreeableness. Thirty-six hate users fall in the high extraversion personality trait, while only twenty-seven non-hate users fall in the same category. Twenty-one hate and ten non-hate users have high neuroticism scores. There is a considerable difference between hate and non-hate users in agreeableness and neuroticism traits.

Low scores were calculated for the same high-five traits as depicted in Fig. 3. Out of fifty hate users, thirty-eight, and out of fifty non-hate users, thirty people have low openness scores. Twenty-five hate and twenty-three non-hate users have low conscientiousness. Low extraversion scores are available in fourteen hate users and twenty-three non-hate users. There is a big difference in low scores of the agreeableness trait. Only one non-hate user falls in low agreeableness, while twenty-nine hate users have low agreeableness. There are twenty-nine hate users who have low neuroticism scores, but forty non-hate users fall in the same category.

5 Discussion

The rapid development of information and communication technologies has transformed how people communicate various perspectives, beliefs, and motivations in society. One of the microblogging sites Sri Lankans utilize to communicate their information is Twitter. As individuals from various backgrounds also with various personalities communicate

Table 2. Comparison of the supervised machine learning algorithms on prediction of Big Five personality traits of Twitter hate and non-hate users

Personality Trait		O	C	E	A	N
SVM	Accuracy	0.63	0.67	0.77	0.73	0.63
	Precision	0.60	0.67	0.79	0.73	0.67
	Recall	0.63	0.67	0.77	0.73	0.63
	F1 Score	0.61	0.67	0.75	0.73	0.65
RF	Accuracy	0.87	0.88	0.84	0.74	0.91
	Precision	0.87	0.87	0.79	0.88	0.88
	Recall	0.87	0.88	0.78	0.80	0.88
	F1 Score	0.87	0.87	0.79	0.87	0.88
XGB	Accuracy	0.77	0.84	0.87	0.88	0.85
	Precision	0.80	0.85	0.87	0.87	0.88
	Recall	0.77	0.85	0.88	0.88	0.85
	F1 Score	0.76	0.85	0.87	0.88	0.84
Ensemble	Accuracy	0.93	0.90	0.90	0.90	0.90
	Precision	0.95	0.95	0.90	0.89	0.89
	Recall	0.95	0.91	0.95	0.80	0.94
	F1 Score	0.95	0.93	0.92	0.84	0.91

Note: O - Openness, C - Conscientiousness, E - Extraversion, A - Agreeableness, N - Neuroticism

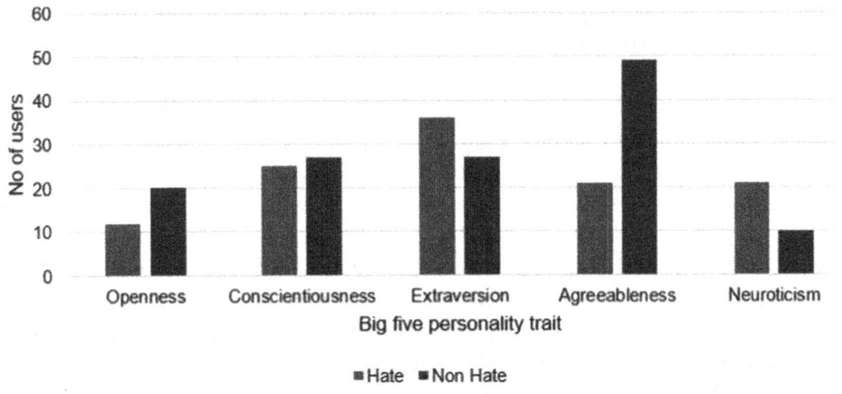

Fig. 2. High score comparison of Big Five personality traits between hate and non-hate users

with these platforms. As a result of that, hate speech propagation is a darker part of society that is felt by everyone. Therefore, it is necessary to identify the propagation of hate content over the Twitter social media platform as well as the users. A person's personality is more closely related to how they interact with others, processes information, and makes

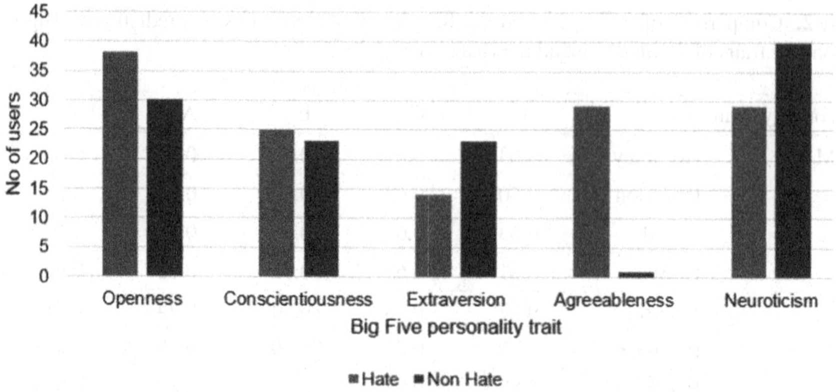

Fig. 3. Low score comparison of Big Five personality traits between hate and non-hate users

decisions. It is essential to consider whether there is a relationship between a person's personality and the spread of hate information on the Twitter social media platform. This research study analyses the relationship between Big Five personality traits and Twitter hate user profiles and activity. A comparison of the personality traits of hate and non-hate users was undertaken to distinguish their behaviors.

With the results of this study, it is evidenced that Twitter profile information and Tweet activities could be used to identify personality traits of people. We used four supervised machine learning models to implement the detection algorithms. They are SVM, RF, XGB, and Ensemble models. The ensemble model outperformed the results by achieving more than 80% accuracy for all five personality traits. The proposed system considered Sinhala language Tweets also. Analyzing Sinhala text with Big Five personality traits and Twitter data is a new approach in the text analysis research area. Hence, authors exploited that Big Five personality traits and Twitter data can use to analyze personality traits in low-resource languages like Sinhala. Future researchers can use these techniques to improve the detection results and introduce new approaches to identify hate speech to mitigate its negative impact on society.

Three psychologists were used in this study to classify Twitter users according to their personality qualities (Extroversion, Agreeableness, Conscientiousness, Neuroticism, and Openness). When we look at the results of the personality trait analysis, more hate users have high scores in extraversion personality trait factors. Extraversion trait represents sociability factors. Most hate users' Twitter profiles contain many tweets in different aspects. They seek social attention through their tweets. They want to engage with more people and convey their intentions to others and gather more people. Most of the identified hate users want to start conversations on different topics. Openness in hate users is low than non-hate users. Only twelve hate users have a high score in the openness trait. It depicts that hateful users resist new changes and new ideas. They do not want to deviate from their preferred routine. The Agreeableness trait is low among hate people. They are always suspicious and uncooperative with their environment. More hate users tend to spread their hate-related feelings among a broader audience. More hate users fall into the high neuroticism trait than non-hate users. Neuroticism trait depicts a tendency towards unstable emotions. Personalities with high score neuroticism trait have characteristics like worrying about many different things, being upset, and feeling sad. More hate users with high neuroticism factors seek more attention from society to feel safe and to overcome their emotional imbalance. We can say that with the attained values for each Twitter profile. Twenty-one hate users have high scores for neuroticism. Out of them, fourteen have high scores for the extraversion trait. With these results, we can say that when a hate user is emotionally unstable, that person tends to have a more companionable social media life. The Agreeableness score is low in more hate users. That means more hate users manipulate and do not care about others' needs and interests but want to achieve their intentions. The results show that neuroticism and extraversion positively associate with hateful profiles.

Out of the fifty forty-nine non-hate users have high scores for the agreeableness personality trait. People with a high score in agreeableness are generally optimistic and trusting of others. They want to keep peace and feel empathy for others. With the given results, we can find that most non-hate users need a calm and peaceful life and tend to offer a supporting hand to those in need. High openness factors are visible in more non-hate users than hate users. We can say that non-hate people are more creative and look for new opportunities than hate people. Out of fifty, forty non-hate people have low neuroticism scores. It shows that non-hate people are more mentally stable than hateful people. Non-hate people like to share new facts and spread knowledge and motivational content among their audience. The results show that neuroticism is negatively associated with non-hate people, while agreeableness is positively associated.

A study by (Mathew and Kumar 2018) defined two types of Twitter accounts. Some people comment on hateful tweets to mitigate the hate and reduce harmful outcomes. These accounts are called counter accounts (CA) (Mathew and Kumar 2018). Their findings proved that CAs score higher in agreeableness and conscientiousness. These results are also like our findings for non-hate profiles. With these results, our findings also depict that non-hate users are more thoughtful about social well-being in a peaceful world.

We are now limited to investigating only user profile information, tweet information, and sentiments. In addition to these features, we believe it is vital to take into account the NRC Word-Emotion Lexicon and social network analysis measures such as centrality in future.

6 Conclusion

In this paper, the authors attempt to predict the personality traits of hate and non-hate users using Twitter as the social media platform and the Big Five personality model, with an emphasis on the Sri Lankan context. A supervised learning approach using four machine learning algorithms is utilized to calculate personality traits based on what an individual publicly tweets as well as profile information. The ensemble method outperformed SVM, Random Forest, and XGBoost. This research has exploited that the Big Five personality can be predicted using public information data in the Twitter profile and tweets they share on Twitter. Three psychologists assign high/low values to each personality trait based on the Twitter user profile, and those data are used to train the classifiers. We extracted all the data from each user's Twitter profile needed to create the features listed in Table 1 to feed for the classifiers. The ensemble method outperformed the other three classification algorithms in terms of accuracy.

The study sheds light on how personality manifests itself on the Twitter social media platform, particularly with those who spread hate speech. When addressing the Sri Lankan context, the findings indicate that extraversion and neuroticism traits are prominent among hate users, while openness, conscientiousness, and agreeableness are higher among non-hate users on the Twitter social media platform. The ability to predict a user's personality traits, particularly hate users on social media platforms, enables policymakers, governments, and social media platform owners to make decisions to counter hate speech dissemination on social media platforms. A higher sample size would yield far better results. However, even with this 100 sample size, the results show these techniques used in this research study can be used to compute personality traits on Twitter hate and non-hate users. Furthermore, the study sheds light on how personality manifests itself in microblogs and provides an example of how social media can be used for personality research.

Acknowledgements. This research was supported by the Accelerating Higher Education Expansion and Development (AHEAD) Operation of the Ministry of Higher Education funded by the World Bank.

References

Abdel-Khalek, A.M., et al.: The big five personality traits as predictors of life satisfaction in Egyptian college students. Nordic Psychol., 1–18 (2022). https://doi.org/10.1080/19012276.2022.2065341

Alshalan, R., Al-Khalifa, H.: A deep learning approach for automatic hate speech detection in the Saudi Twittersphere. Appl. Sci. **10**(23), 8614 (2020). https://doi.org/10.3390/app10238614

Apply Magic Sauce - Prediction API (no date) Apply Magic Sauce. https://applymagicsauce.com. Accessed 19 Oct 2021

Bachrach, Y., et al.: Personality and patterns of Facebook usage, p. 9 (2012)

Chandra, M.: Towards a more holistic approach on online abuse and antisemitism. Ph.D. thesis. International Institute of Information Technology Hyderabad (2021). https://precog.iiitd.edu.in/Publications_files/mohit_chandra_masters_thesis_jan_2021.pdf

Cohen, J.: A coefficient of agreement for nominal scales. Educ. Psychol. Meas. **20**(1), 37–46 (2016). https://doi.org/10.1177/001316446002000104

Coltheart, M.: The MRC psycholinguistic database. Q. J. Exp. Psychol. Sect. A **33**(4), 497–505 (1981). https://doi.org/10.1080/14640748108400805

Dias, S.D., Welikala, M.D., Dias, N.G.J.: Identifying racist social media comments in Sinhala language using text analytics models with machine learning. In: 2018 18th International Conference on Advances in ICT for Emerging Regions (ICTer), Colombo, Sri Lanka, pp. 1–6. IEEE (2018). https://doi.org/10.1109/ICTER.2018.8615492

ElSherief, M., et al.: Peer to peer hate: hate speech instigators and their targets. In: Proceedings of the Twelfth International AAAI Conference on Web and Social Media (ICWSM 2018), p. 10 (2018)

Farnadi, G., et al.: Recognising personality traits using Facebook status updates. In: Proceedings of the International AAAI Conference on Web and Social Media, vol. 7, p. 6 (2013)

Golbeck, J., et al.: Predicting personality from Twitter. In: 2011 IEEE Third International Conference on Privacy, Security, Risk and Trust and 2011 IEEE Third International Conference on Social Computing. 2011 IEEE Third International Conference on Privacy, Security, Risk and Trust (PASSAT)/2011 IEEE Third International Conference on Social Computing (SocialCom), Boston, MA, USA, pp. 149–156. IEEE (2011). https://doi.org/10.1109/PASSAT/SocialCom.2011.33

Goldberg, L.R.: An alternative "description of personality": the big-five factor structure (23), 14 (1990)

Hathnapitiya, S., Ahangama, S., Adikari, S.: Early detection of sinhala fake news in social media. In: International Conference on Advanced Research in Computing – ICARC (2023a)

Mathew, B., Kumar, N.: Analyzing the hate and counter speech accounts on Twitter, p. 11 (2018)

McIlroy-Young, R., Anderson, A.: From "Welcome new gabbers" to the Pittsburgh synagogue shooting: the evolution of gab. In: Proceedings of the International AAAI Conference on Web and Social Media, vol. 13, pp. 651–654 (2019). https://doi.org/10.1609/icwsm.v13i01.3264

Nielsen, L.B.: Subtle, pervasive, harmful: racist and sexist remarks in public as hate speech. J. Soc. Issues (2002, Preprint)

Ong, V., Rahmanto, A.D.S., Suhartono, D.: Exploring personality prediction from text on social media: a literature review **9**(1), 7 (2017)

Perera, S., Ahangama, S., Perera, I.: Influence rank of hate users in Twitter: an analysis during Sri Lanka's political and economic crisis. In: International Conference on Advanced Research in Computing – ICARC (2023)

Perera, S., Karunanayaka, K.: Sentiment analysis of social media data using fuzzy-rough set classifier for the prediction of the presidential election. In: 2022 2nd International Conference on Advanced Research in Computing (ICARC), Belihuloya, Sri Lanka, pp. 188–193 (2022). https://doi.org/10.1109/ICARC54489.2022.9754173

Rajapaksha, N., Ahangama, S., Adikari, S.: Fine-tuning XLM-R for the detection of Sinhala hate speech content on Twitter and Youtube. In: International Conference on Advanced Research in Computing – ICARC (2023b)

Schwartz, H.A., et al.: Personality, gender, and age in the language of social media: the open-vocabulary approach. PLoS ONE **8**(9), e73791 (2013). Edited by T. Preis. https://doi.org/10.1371/journal.pone.0073791

Stajner, S., Yenikent, S.: A survey of automatic personality detection from texts. In: Proceedings of the 28th International Conference on Computational Linguistics, Barcelona, Spain, pp. 6284–6295 (2020)

Stidham, H., Summers, J., Shuffler, M.: Using the five factor model to study personality convergence on student engineering design teams. In: 15th International Design Conference, pp. 2145–2154 (2018). https://doi.org/10.21278/idc.2018.0508

Sumner, C., et al.: Predicting dark triad personality traits from Twitter usage and a linguistic analysis of tweets. In: 2012 11th International Conference on Machine Learning and Applications (ICMLA), Boca Raton, FL, USA, pp. 386–393. IEEE (2012). https://doi.org/10.1109/ICMLA.2012.218

Tadesse, M.M., et al.: Personality predictions based on user behavior on the Facebook social media platform. IEEE Access **6**, 61959–61969 (2018). https://doi.org/10.1109/ACCESS.2018.2876502

Tandera, T., et al.: Personality prediction system from Facebook users. Procedia Comput. Sci. **116**, 604–611 (2017). https://doi.org/10.1016/j.procs.2017.10.016

Tausczik, Y.R., Pennebaker, J.W.: The psychological meaning of words: LIWC and computerized text analysis methods. J. Lang. Soc. Psychol., 24–54 (2010). https://doi.org/10.1177/0261927X09351676

Wijeratne, Y.: The control of hate speech on social media: lessons from Sri Lanka. SSRN Electron. J. (2018, Preprint). https://doi.org/10.2139/ssrn.3275106.
Xue, D., et al.: Personality recognition on social media with label distribution learning. IEEE Access **5**, 13478–13488 (2017). https://doi.org/10.1109/ACCESS.2017.2719018

A Machine Learning Approach to Prediction of Online Reviews Reliability

Giuseppe Sansonetti(✉), Fabio Gasparetti, and Alessandro Micarelli

Department of Engineering, Roma Tre University, Via della Vasca Navale, 79, 00146 Rome, Italy
{gsansone,ailab}@dia.uniroma3.it

Abstract. The Internet accompanies us in every moment of our lives, supporting us in many ways. Among these, it helps us when we want to choose the best services and products. So when it comes to picking a movie to watch, a restaurant to eat in, a hotel to stay in, or a product to buy, we grab our smartphone and visit one of the countless sites where users can report their experiences and read those of others. However, as often happens, even in this case there are possible scams of which we must beware. In this paper, we propose a machine learning system for predicting the reliability of online reviews. Specifically, our system collects reviews from Amazon, extracts various features, and gives them as input to an ensemble learning system based on three anomaly detection algorithms. To demonstrate the benefits of our approach, we report the results of a comparative analysis with some state-of-the-art systems using the data collected by ReviewMeta. These results have allowed us to realize how widespread the phenomenon of online fake reviews is.

Keywords: Machine learning · Fake reviews · Anomaly detection

1 Introduction

The Internet represents one of the major achievements of Computer Science. Every day it accompanies us in our lives [9,29]. It allows us everywhere and every time to satisfy our information needs [10,17], as well as to communicate with whomever we want [51]. Intelligent systems such as recommender systems [7,18] suggest items to buy [5], music songs to listen to [42], movies to watch [3], news articles to read [6,19], research papers to study [20,21] and people to get in touch with [13]. They recommend new points of interest [44,48] (e.g., cultural or artistic resources [11,46] such as museums [15,35] or restaurants [4,49]), multimedia applications for enhancing their fruition [36,47,54], and the best itineraries among them [8,16]. However, in the face of all these extraordinary benefits, there are still threats to avoid such as fake news and fake reviews. By *fake news*, we mean misinformation spread specifically for malicious

A. Coman and S. Vasilache (Eds.): HCII 2023, LNCS 14025, pp. 131–145, 2023.
https://doi.org/10.1007/978-3-031-35915-6_11

purposes [45]. By *fake reviews*, we mean all reviews that do not represent a real evaluation of the experience the user had with the product [1,56]. The problem addressed in this paper concerns precisely the detection of fake reviews posted on online markets. To solve this problem, we propose a system that rely on machine learning [52] techniques to predict the reliability of online reviews. It retrieves data from the popular e-commerce site Amazon[1] through a scraping module and then processes it by extracting the information of interest. From this information, the system identifies several features, some related to the reviews and others related to their authors. These features are then given as input to an ensemble learning module of three different anomaly detection techniques. To evaluate the performance of the review reliability prediction system, our system includes an additional scraping module. This module extracts data from ReviewMeta[2], a site that predicts the reliability of reviews based on a proprietary algorithm. Thus, we could compare the values predicted by our system with those collected by ReviewMeta. A comparative analysis between our system and others proposed in the literature for the same purpose has shown the remarkable performance provided by our approach. The results of our study have allowed us to realize that the phenomenon of fake reviews is much more widespread than one might imagine.

2 Related Work

In this section, we review some approaches proposed in the research literature for the detection of online fake reviews.

Jindal and Liu were among the first researchers to study the reliability of online reviews [24]. They focused on evaluating the text of the reviews, looking for potentially fake ones based on purely linguistic aspects. The authors carried out their studies on a dataset retrieved from Amazon. Their aim was to find reviews that turned out to be total or partial copies of others. The rationale behind this is that companies interested in advertising their products contact customers or train specialized bots based on a original text that can vary little between the different users who work on it. Their goal is indeed to adapt the reviews to the given product and avoid that they are too generic. In later work, the authors extended the meaning of duplicate. While previously they limited themselves to checking reviews in the single context of a product, in [23] possible duplicates have become of three different types:

- Duplicate reviews of the same product with a different user ID;
- Duplicate reviews from the same user ID but on different products;
- Duplicate reviews from different user IDs on different products.

In [25], exploiting the duplicate reviews detected in the past, the authors propose a classifier that leverages the latter as positive training data (therefore, considering them as false reviews) and the remaining reviews as negative training data. Starting from those first research activities carried out mainly based

[1] https://www.amazon.com/.
[2] https://reviewmeta.com/.

on the text of the reviews, there have been many developments concerning the additional analyzes that can be carried out and the possible further considerations on the textual characteristics of a review. However, all the approaches proposed from then on can be classified into two main categories: the one based on review analysis and the one based on reviewer analysis.

2.1 Methods Based on Review Analysis

In [26], the authors resume the approach proposed by Jindal and Liu in their previous research, once again tackling the problem of identifying fake reviews through text analysis. In particular, they propose to search review copies using the Kullback-Leibler divergence as a rating measure associated with an SVM classifier.

In [27], further analyses based on the syntactic text characteristics (in particular of the unigrams) are introduced, realizing an unsupervised probabilistic language model to evaluate the diffusion of fake reviews. In [28], the authors propose a new type of analysis for online reviews that, for the first time, also exploits the semantics of the review to search for misleading ones. The rationale is that a copy can be evaluated not only textually but also for its semantics. However, this approach proves useful in analyzing online reviews in general but less useful in evaluating reviews related to an individual product. The reason is that, on a significant number of reviews belonging to the same product, there is necessarily a minimum quantity of them that are semantically similar but which are not to be considered fake, being evaluations expressed on the same product and having a high probability of being similar between them.

In [14], the authors hypothesize that companies interested in advertising their product through misleading reviews contact users for increasing the average rating of the given product. They, therefore, focus on analyzing the review distribution over time. Indeed, to promote the object, unexpected spikes in reviews are produced in a short time, considering this behavior as anomalous. Thus, the authors first investigated the distribution anomaly of fake reviews on Amazon and TripAdvisor, and then proposed statistically-driven strategies that consider the distribution of these anomalies to detect fake reviews.

In [38], the authors propose a Bayesian classifier built using the reviews filtered by Yelp[3]. This site, unlike others, uses an algorithm for filtering reviews, not publishing those that do not meet evaluation criteria. This algorithm is not public but the reviews that are considered negative are.

In [30], the authors propose an approach developed in collaboration with Dianping[4], the largest Chinese review hosting site, by exploiting the algorithm site filtering. Dianping's algorithm has high precision, however, it is not possible to accurately evaluate its accuracy, as all fake reviews detected by the system are almost certainly fake, but the remaining reviews may not all be true. Several classifiers have been created that rely on the Learning from Positive and Unlabeled Data (PU Learning) approach. This approach is semi-supervised with

[3] https://www.yelp.com.
[4] https://www.dianping.com/.

labeled data (i.e., the fake reviews identified by the algorithm) and unlabeled data (i.e., reviews that the algorithm does not identify as fake and on which the label is uncertain).

In [43], the authors present an approach, named *SpEagle*, which performs the analysis based on all metadata (text, creation time, rating, etc.) and relational data, and groups them into a unified framework for identifying suspicious users and reviews, and products likely to be targeted by spam. The approach is unsupervised learning, however providing for the possibility of integrating the model with labeled reviews to adopt a semi-supervised *SpEagle+* approach.

2.2 Methods Based on Reviewer Analysis

Unlike the previous ones, the approach discussed in [31] relies on the reviewer analysis rather than on the characteristics of the review itself. The authors argue that it is better to study reviewers because the information obtained from their behavior is much more indicative than the information that can be obtained from the text of a review. Hence, they proposed a method of analysis based on assigning a score to each reviewer, through which the review was evaluated to identify those deemed fake.

In [41], the authors focused on identifying groups of authors who write fake reviews, who are referred to as *spammers*. In particular, this approach focuses on authors writing their reviews on several products rather than on a single product. The research relies on the rationale that companies interested in advertising their product, and devaluing a competing product, hire people to publish reviews. These reviews are, therefore, made by the same user on several products, evaluating one of them positively and those of its competitors negatively. By searching for the presence of groups of users with similar behavior, reviews deemed fake can thus be identified. Each reviewer was evaluated based on eight criteria that express her behavior in the group considered. This aspect was also addressed in [40], where the author introduced four further evaluation criteria for evaluating the reviewer, which in this case do not refer to her behavior in the group, but represent individual values. Both approaches rely on a Support Vector Machine for Ranking (SVM-Rank) to classify the reviewers and, therefore, their reviews evaluated based on the criteria considered.

In [39], the authors present an unsupervised model, called *Author Spamicity Model*, which, taking into consideration the behavioral characteristics of a user, defined as *fingerprints*, uses them on a clustering algorithm to identify if she is to be considered spammer or not. So the intuition of their research is that users can be classified into only two different groups, spammers and non-spammers. Based on this classification, their reviews are identified as fake or not.

In [55], the authors tackle the problem of identifying spammers by evaluating the behavioral characteristics of the authors, who have been grouped through clustering algorithms, in different communities, which have then been labeled as *spammer community* or *non-spammer community*.

In [33], the authors follow a different approach that aims to detect review spam and spammers at the same time. To this aim, a graph model was developed based on criteria relating to the review, which consist of the analysis of its specific characteristics (e.g., the length of the review, the date it was published, etc.) and criteria related to the author (e.g., percentage of helpful votes received on written reviews, deviation of ratings from average product ratings, etc.).

In [32], a hybrid method based on the evaluation of both reviews and authors is proposed. A series of evaluation functions are used for reviews based on similarity values, which are calculated at the textual level and, therefore, based on the content of the review as follows:

- Similarity with other reviews written by the same author;
- Similarity with other reviews on the same product;
- Similarity with the reviews on other products.

In the same way, evaluation functions are used for authors as follows:

- Frequency of user reviews;
- Frequency of reviews on a product;
- Frequency with which a user writes about the same product.

In [12], the goal is to recognize online campaigns placed on crowdsourcing sites that require the massive publication of fake reviews. To this aim, the authors analyze crowdsourcing sites and social networks, exploiting graph methods for identifying relationships between reviewers, which make it possible to identify groups of authors with deceptive purposes and, consequently, to identify fake reviews that correspond to them.

In [50], authors focus on manipulating the average rating of a product by spammer authors. The assumption is that when a product, subject to fake reviews, is devalued due to the average rating of the reviews it has obtained, spammers take action to raise this average. The behavior of the authors was then observed based on this criterion, evaluating whether in specific time windows there was a peak of reviews on a specific product capable of raising its average rating. A further consideration was to identify as suspect authors who express a rating percentage that deviate from the majority opinion and, therefore, from the average rating.

3 The Proposed Approach

In this section, we present the overall architecture of our system. In particular, we describe the modules that allowed us to collect training and testing datasets, as well as the machine learning module.

The problem addressed in this paper concerns the detection of fake reviews posted on online markets. To this aim, we have designed and developed a system that leverages machine learning techniques to predict the reliability of online reviews. Figure 1 shows the overall architecture of our system, where it is possible to notice two scraping systems for data retrieval, and a central component for training the model for reviews classification.

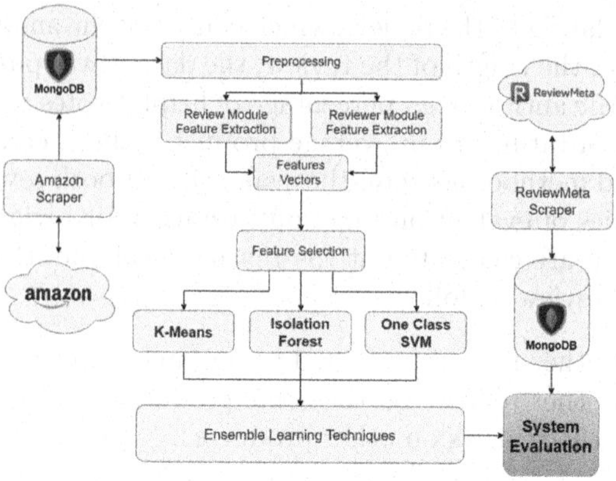

Fig. 1. The overall system architecture.

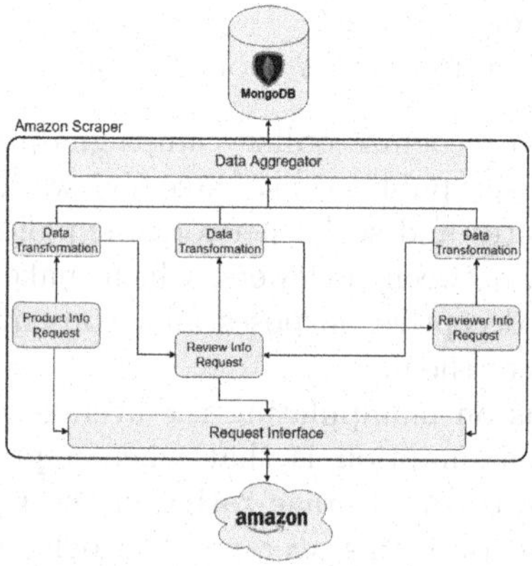

Fig. 2. The architecture of the Amazon scraper.

The first scraping system (see Fig. 2) enabled us to extract information from the popular e-commerce site Amazon. More specifically, starting with a given product, we collected all its data (average rating, producer, seller, etc.) and all the reviews posted on it. From the latter, we extracted all the details such as the text, the creation time, the rating, and possible tags. Furthermore, for each review, we also extracted information about the author who wrote it, retrieving from Amazon all the details related to her profile and all the other reviews she posted. Indeed, in our study we want to analyze the reviews relating to a product and the behavior of the user who is the author of the reviews. In this way, we want to have more observation points on a single review to better define its reliability and classify it as *fake* or *trust*. Our aim, therefore, is to find not only the information and reviews of a specific product, but also all those related to the user who wrote a review for the product at hand. Furthermore, we want to obtain information on all products that are the subject of reviews from that user.

At the end of this scraping operation, we collected the dataset whose statistics are shown in Table 1.

Table 1. Statistics of the dataset retrieved through scraping on the Amazon site.

Reviews	Products	Users
1,464,202	625,952	54,604

From this data, we then identified the different features of the reviews. To this aim, we realized two different modules, one for reviews and one for the user. In this way, we extracted 17 total features, 9 related to the review and 8 to its author. Such features rely on linguistic and statistical analyzes, thus evaluating both the texts of the reviews and their metadata such as the creation time, the rating, and the length of the text. We then performed the feature selection phase. Using the feature vectors created during the extraction phase, we used the all-subsets algorithm to select the features suitable for each machine learning technique. This algorithm relies on the evaluation of each possible subset made up of 17 features, for a total of 2^{17} subsets (i.e., $131,072$ subsets). This approach is time expensive but allows the best subsets to be detected with high accuracy. After selecting the different features that proved best for each different approach, we trained the final model for prediction through the use of three different technologies that were then combined using the ensemble learning technique known as bagging (Fig. 3).

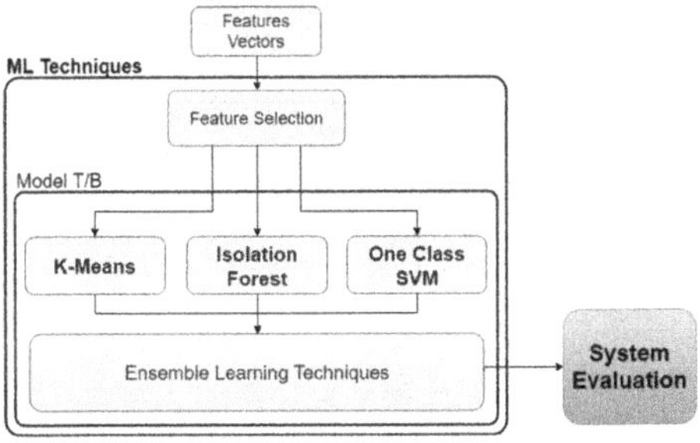

Fig. 3. The architecture of the machine learning module.

For the prediction phase, we then employed three anomaly detection techniques: the first one based on clustering, the second one based on local density distribution, and the last one based on Support Vector Machines (SVMs). As a clustering technique, we used the well-known K-Means algorithm that divides the data into two separate groups: *anomalous* data and *normal* data. As an algorithm based on the local distribution density, we used Isolation Forest, which aims to isolate the data. The easier it is to isolate one data from the others, the more likely it represents an anomaly. Finally, we used One-Class SVM (OCSVM) as a classification technique. OCSVM aims at dividing the data arranged on a multidimensional plane into two different regions: a positive region, which corresponds to a high concentration of points and identifies normal data, and a negative region, which has a lower concentration of data and identifies anomalous data (see Fig. 4).

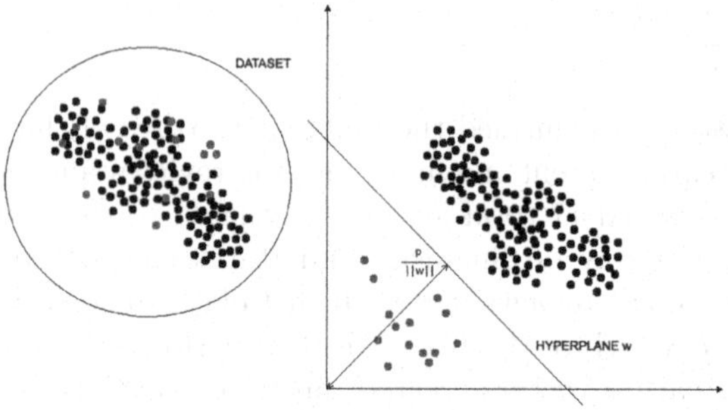

Fig. 4. One-Class Support Vector Machine (OCSVM).

In the dataset we collected, the reviews are not tagged. We have, therefore, implemented an additional scraping system (see Fig. 5) to extract new data from ReviewMeta.

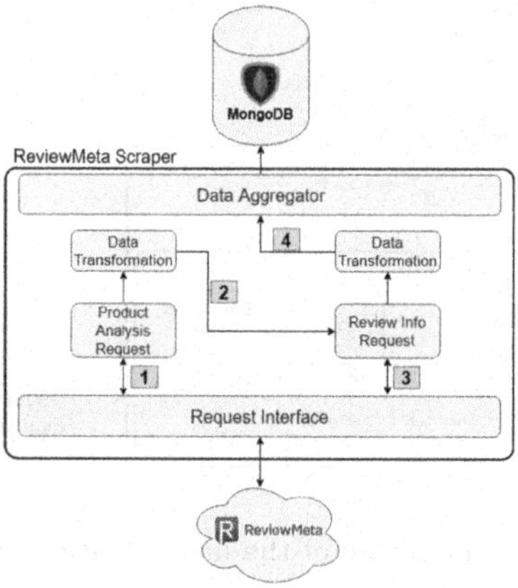

Fig. 5. The architecture of the ReviewMeta scraper.

This site offers a service based on a proprietary algorithm that performs various statistical analyzes on the reviews of a product and categorizes them by dividing them into three classes: *fake*, *warm*, and *true*. In detail, the scraper provides for a specific request to the ReviewMeta site for product analysis (1). If the analysis has already been carried out previously, this is updated by evaluating all the new information deriving from the new reviews. Following this request, some information relating to the reliability percentage of negatively evaluated reviews (i.e., those identified as fake) is extracted from the site (2) by requesting specific information on them (3). The data is processed (4) by extracting information about their reliability percentage and saving the information in the non-relational database. Thereby, we obtained about 61,000 reviews classified as shown in Table 2.

Table 2. Statistics of the dataset retrieved through scraping on the ReviewMeta site.

Reviews	Amount
Reviews with reliability percentage 0%–35%	28,925
Reviews with reliability percentage 36%–70%	3,519
Reviews with reliability percentage 71%–100%	28,537
Total reviews	60,981

4 Experimental Evaluation

In this section, we report the experimental results obtained by evaluating the performance of our system. We also report the results of a comparative analysis between our system and others proposed in the literature [34,37].

Thanks to the information obtained from ReviewMeta, we could proceed with the system evaluation by measuring the *Cohen's kappa* metric. The kappa coefficient represents the degree of accuracy and reliability of a classification. It is an index that represents how consistent the result obtained is in relation to how much the maximum obtainable result is. It compares the values on which "prediction" and "reality" agree with those in which there is instead disagreement. In our case, this evaluation metric enabled us to evaluate the agreement between the values predicted by the system and those obtained by ReviewMeta. Cohen's kappa can assume values ranging from −1 to 1. The higher the value, the higher the agreement between the values predicted by the system and those by ReviewMeta. For the calculation of Cohen's kappa, the predicted results (i.e., the results obtained from the classification carried out by the implemented system) are compared with the values obtained from reliable sources, which can be human judges, who manually carried out the classification operation of data, rather than information obtained from other systems whose reliability is proven and verified. In our study, the data was retrieved, as mentioned, from ReviewMeta. Contextualizing such considerations in our scenario, we derived Table 3

where

- G1 represents our model, namely, what we predict;
- G2 represents the information taken from ReviewMeta;
- A represents the amount of reviews that G1 detects as *normal* and G2 detects as *true* (the true positives, i.e., the reviews rated as real by both judges);

Table 3. Computation of Cohen's kappa.

	G1			
G2		Normal	Anomalous	
	True	A	B	$ST = A + B$
	Fake	C	D	$SF = C + D$
		$SN = A + C$	$SA = B + D$	$TOT = SN + SA = ST + SF$

- B represents the amount of reviews that G1 detects as *anomalous* and G2 detects as *true* (the false negatives, i.e., reviews rated as false but really positive);
- C represents the amount of reviews that G1 detects as *normal* and G2 detects as *fake* (the false positives, i.e., reviews rated as real but really fake);
- D represents the amount of reviews that G1 detects as *anomalous* and G2 detects as *fake* (the true negatives, i.e., reviews rated as false by both judges);

From this, it follows that Cohen's kappa is computed as follows:

$$K = \frac{P_0 + P_E}{1 - P_E} \tag{1}$$

where P_0 and P_E are calculated as follows:

$$P_0 = \frac{A + D}{TOT} \tag{2}$$

$$P_E = \frac{SN}{TOT} * \frac{ST}{TOT} + \frac{SA}{TOT} * \frac{SF}{TOT} \tag{3}$$

As already mentioned, the values that the Cohen's kappa can take are between −1 and +1. Specifically, the model is evaluated as follows:

- If k has values less than 0, then there is no match;
- If k assumes values between 0 and 0.4, then the agreement is poor;
- If k assumes values between 0.4 and 0.6, then the agreement is discrete;
- If k assumes values between 0.6 and 0.8, the agreement is good;
- If k assumes values between 0.8 and 1, the agreement is excellent.

The results obtained through our system are shown in Table 4.

Table 4. Experimental results.

Metric	KMeans	Isolation Forest	One-Class SVM	Ensemble Learning
Kappa Score	0.64	0.62	0.67	0.83

As we can note, the system evaluation allowed us to achieve a value higher than 0.8. Table 5 shows the results obtained from similar approaches to fake review detection.

Table 5. Results of a comparative analysis between our system and some unsupervised learning systems proposed in the research literature.

Ref.	Target	ML Technique	Result	Notes
[31]	Product review spammer	Unsupervised approach	Cohen's kappa $k = 0.48$	Manual labeling of reviewers
[28]	Fake reviews	Unsupervised approach based on language models	Cohen's kappa $k = 0.81$	Reviews labeled as fake and non-fake by four human judges
[40]	Opinion spammer groups	Unsupervised approach based on relational models	Cohen's kappa $k = 0.79$	Reviews labeled as fake and non-fake by eight human judges
[38]	Product review spammers	Unsupervised approach based on Bayesian classifiers	Cohen's kappa $k = 0.73$	Reviewer labeling based on behavioral features
[53]	Store review spammers	Unsupervised approach based on graph models	Cohen's kappa $k = 0.61$	A small set of stores labeled by human judges
Our approach	Fake reviews	Unsupervised approach based on ensemble learning	Cohen's kappa $k = 0.83$	Labels retrieved through scraping on ReviewMeta

Note how for such studies human judges were paid to manually label the reviews. Differently, we used ReviewMeta as ground truth given the difficulties in producing an equally numerous labeled dataset. Generally speaking, those findings let us realize how widespread the fake reviews phenomenon is, certainly more than one could imagine.

5 Conclusions and Future Works

In this article, we have presented a system for predicting the reliability of online reviews related to different products. This system exploits an ensemble learning approach based on three anomaly detection algorithms. Scraping techniques allowed us to collect data to train and test our system. A comparative evaluation with similar state-of-the-art systems has shown the benefits of our approach.

The possible future developments of our approach are manifold. Among these, the first undoubtedly concerns the nature of the data used. In our system, we used the data collected by the ReviewMeta site as a ground truth, which relies on a proprietary algorithm to evaluate the reliability of product reviews on e-commerce sites. It represents a limitation of our approach. Ideally, you could hire human judges to label reviews or re-evaluate the data retrieved by ReviewMeta. Another possible future development could concern the consideration of new features that take into consideration the semantics of the text or the relationship between users and businesses or between groups of users who act together on the same products to raise the average rating, thus making the most attractive product in the eyes of possible future buyers. Finally, in this article we have presented a comparative analysis between our approach and others which, like ours, rely on classic machine learning algorithms. In the future, we would also like to compare our approach with online review prediction systems that rely on deep neural networks (e.g., see [2,22,57]). However, as is known, deep learning approaches require large amounts of data to be truly effective, which represents a significant hurdle in the online review scenario.

References

1. Abhinandan, V., Aishwarya, C., Sultana, A.: Fake review detection using machine learning techniques. Int. J. Fog Comput. (IJFC) **3**(2), 46–54 (2020)
2. Bathla, G., Singh, P., Singh, R.K., Cambria, E., Tiwari, R.: Intelligent fake reviews detection based on aspect extraction and analysis using deep learning. Neural Comput. Appl. **34**(22), 20213–20229 (2022)
3. Biancalana, C., Gasparetti, F., Micarelli, A., Miola, A., Sansonetti, G.: Context-aware movie recommendation based on signal processing and machine learning. In: Proceedings of the 2nd Challenge on Context-Aware Movie Recommendation, CAMRa 2011, pp. 5–10. ACM, New York, NY, USA (2011)
4. Biancalana, C., Gasparetti, F., Micarelli, A., Sansonetti, G.: An approach to social recommendation for context-aware mobile services. ACM Trans. Intell. Syst. Technol. **4**(1), 10:1–10:31 (2013)
5. Bologna, C., De Rosa, A.C., De Vivo, A., Gaeta, M., Sansonetti, G., Viserta, V.: Personality-based recommendation in e-commerce. In: CEUR Workshop Proceedings, vol. 997. CEUR-WS.org, Aachen, Germany (2013)
6. Caldarelli, S., Gurini, D.F., Micarelli, A., Sansonetti, G.: A signal-based approach to news recommendation. In: CEUR Workshop Proceedings, vol. 1618, pp. 1–4. CEUR-WS.org, Aachen, Germany (2016)
7. Cena, F., Gena, C., Grillo, P., Kuflik, T., Vernero, F., Wecker, A.J.: How scales influence user rating behaviour in recommender systems. Behav. Inf. Technol. **36**(10), 985–1004 (2017)
8. D'Agostino, D., Gasparetti, F., Micarelli, A., Sansonetti, G.: A social context-aware recommender of itineraries between relevant points of interest. In: Stephanidis, C. (ed.) HCI 2016. CCIS, vol. 618, pp. 354–359. Springer, Cham (2016). https://doi.org/10.1007/978-3-319-40542-1_58
9. D'Aniello, G.: Fuzzy logic for situation awareness: a systematic review. J. Ambient Intell. Humanized Comput. 1–20 (2023)
10. D'Aniello, G., Gaeta, M., La Rocca, I.: KnowMIS-ABSA: an overview and a reference model for applications of sentiment analysis and aspect-based sentiment analysis. Artif. Intell. Rev. **55**(7), 5543–5574 (2022)
11. De Angelis, A., Gasparetti, F., Micarelli, A., Sansonetti, G.: A social cultural recommender based on linked open data. In: Adjunct Publication of the 25th Conference on User Modeling, Adaptation and Personalization, UMAP 2017, pp. 329–332. ACM, New York, NY, USA (2017)

12. Fayazi, A., Lee, K., Caverlee, J., Squicciarini, A.: Uncovering crowdsourced manipulation of online reviews. In: Proceedings of the 38th International ACM SIGIR Conference on Research and Development in Information Retrieval, SIGIR 2015, pp. 233–242. ACM, New York, NY, USA (2015)
13. Feltoni Gurini, D., Gasparetti, F., Micarelli, A., Sansonetti, G.: Temporal people-to-people recommendation on social networks with sentiment-based matrix factorization. Future Gener. Comput. Syst. **78**, 430–439 (2018)
14. Feng, S., Banerjee, R., Choi, Y.: Syntactic stylometry for deception detection. In: Proceedings of the 50th Annual Meeting of the Association for Computational Linguistics: Short Papers, ACL 2012, vol. 2, p. 171. Association for Computational Linguistics, Stroudsburg, PA, USA (2012)
15. Ferrato, A., Limongelli, C., Mezzini, M., Sansonetti, G.: Using deep learning for collecting data about museum visitor behavior. Appl. Sci. **12**(2) (2022)
16. Fogli, A., Sansonetti, G.: Exploiting semantics for context-aware itinerary recommendation. Pers. Ubiquit. Comput. **23**(2), 215–231 (2019)
17. Gasparetti, F., Micarelli, A., Sansonetti, G.: Exploiting web browsing activities for user needs identification. In: Proc. of the 2014 CSCI. vol. 2 (March 2014)
18. Gasparetti, F., Sansonetti, G., Micarelli, A.: Community detection in social recommender systems: a survey. Appl. Intell. **51**(6), 3975–3995 (2021)
19. Gena, C., Grillo, P., Lieto, A., Mattutino, C., Vernero, F.: When personalization is not an option: an in-the-wild study on persuasive news recommendation. Information **10**(10) (2019)
20. Hassan, H.A.M., Sansonetti, G., Gasparetti, F., Micarelli, A.: Semantic-based tag recommendation in scientific bookmarking systems. In: Proceedings of the 12th ACM Conference on Recommender Systems, pp. 465–469. ACM, New York, NY, USA (2018)
21. Hassan, H.A.M., Sansonetti, G., Gasparetti, F., Micarelli, A., Beel, J.: BERT, ELMo, USE and InferSent sentence encoders: the panacea for research-paper recommendation? In: Tkalcic, M., Pera, S. (eds.) Proceedings of ACM RecSys 2019 Late-Breaking Results, vol. 2431, pp. 6–10. CEUR-WS.org (2019)
22. Javed, M.S., Majeed, H., Mujtaba, H., Beg, M.O.: Fake reviews classification using deep learning ensemble of shallow convolutions. J. Comput. Soc. Sci. 1–20 (2021)
23. Jindal, N., Liu, B.: Analyzing and detecting review spam. In: Proceedings of the 2007 Seventh IEEE International Conference on Data Mining, ICDM 2007, pp. 547–552. IEEE Computer Society, Washington, DC, USA (2007)
24. Jindal, N., Liu, B.: Review spam detection. In: Proceedings of the 16th International Conference on World Wide Web, WWW 2007, pp. 1189–1190. ACM, New York, NY, USA (2007)
25. Jindal, N., Liu, B.: Opinion spam and analysis. In: Proceedings of the 2008 International Conference on Web Search and Data Mining, WSDM 2008, pp. 219–230. ACM, New York, NY, USA (2008)
26. Lai, C.L., Xu, K.Q., Lau, R.Y.K., Li, Y., Song, D.: High-order concept associations mining and inferential language modeling for online review spam detection. In: Proceedings of the 2010 IEEE International Conference on Data Mining Workshops, ICDMW 2010, pp. 1120–1127. IEEE Computer Society, Washington, DC, USA (2010)
27. Lai, C.C.L., Xu, K., Lau, R.Y.K., Li, Y., Jing, L.: Toward a language modeling approach for consumer review spam detection. In: ICEBE, pp. 1–8. IEEE Computer Society (2010)

28. Lau, R.Y.K., Liao, S.Y., Kwok, R.C.W., Xu, K., Xia, Y., Li, Y.: Text mining and probabilistic language modeling for online review spam detection. ACM Trans. Manage. Inf. Syst. **2**(4), 25:1–25:30 (2012)
29. Leung, L.W.: Embedding into Our Lives: New Opportunities and Challenges of the Internet. Chinese University Press, Beijing (2009)
30. Li, H., Chen, Z., Liu, B., Wei, X., Shao, J.: Spotting fake reviews via collective positive-unlabeled learning. In: Proceedings of the 2014 IEEE International Conference on Data Mining, ICDM 2014, pp. 899–904. IEEE Computer Society, Washington, DC, USA (2014)
31. Lim, E.P., Nguyen, V.A., Jindal, N., Liu, B., Lauw, H.W.: Detecting product review spammers using rating behaviors. In: Proceedings of the 19th ACM International Conference on Information and Knowledge Management, CIKM 2010, pp. 939–948. ACM, New York, NY, USA (2010)
32. Lin, Y., Zhu, T., Wu, H., Zhang, J., Wang, X., Zhou, A.: Towards online anti-opinion spam: spotting fake reviews from the review sequence. In: Proceedings of the 2014 IEEE/ACM International Conference on Advances in Social Networks Analysis and Mining, ASONAM 2014, pp. 261–264. IEEE Press, Piscataway, NJ, USA (2014)
33. Lu, Y., Zhang, L., Xiao, Y., Li, Y.: Simultaneously detecting fake reviews and review spammers using factor graph model. In: Proceedings of the 5th Annual ACM Web Science Conference, WebSci 2013, pp. 225–233. ACM, New York, NY, USA (2013)
34. Mewada, A., Dewang, R.K.: Research on false review detection methods: a state-of-the-art review. J. K. S. Univ. Comput. Inf. Sci. **34**(9), 7530–7546 (2022)
35. Mezzini, M., Limongelli, C., Sansonetti, G., De Medio, C.: Tracking museum visitors through convolutional object detectors. In: Adjunct Publication of the 28th ACM Conference on User Modeling, Adaptation and Personalization, UMAP 2020 Adjunct, pp. 352–355. ACM, New York, NY, USA (2020)
36. Micarelli, A., Neri, A., Sansonetti, G.: A case-based approach to image recognition. In: Blanzieri, E., Portinale, L. (eds.) EWCBR 2000. LNCS, vol. 1898, pp. 443–454. Springer, Heidelberg (2000). https://doi.org/10.1007/3-540-44527-7_38
37. Mohawesh, R., et al.: Fake reviews detection: a survey. IEEE Access **9**, 65771–65802 (2021)
38. Mukherjee, A., Venkataraman, V., Liu, B., Glance, N.: What yelp fake review filter might be doing? In: Proceedings of the 7th International Conference on Weblogs and Social Media, ICWSM 2013, pp. 409–418, January 2013
39. Mukherjee, A., et al.: Spotting opinion spammers using behavioral footprints. In: Proceedings of the 19th ACM SIGKDD International Conference on Knowledge Discovery and Data Mining, KDD 2013, pp. 632–640. ACM, New York, NY, USA (2013)
40. Mukherjee, A., Liu, B., Glance, N.: Spotting fake reviewer groups in consumer reviews. In: Proceedings of the 21st International Conference on World Wide Web, WWW 2012, pp. 191–200. ACM, New York, NY, USA (2012)
41. Mukherjee, A., Liu, B., Wang, J., Glance, N., Jindal, N.: Detecting group review spam. In: Proceedings of the 20th International Conference Companion on World Wide Web, WWW 2011, pp. 93–94. ACM, New York, NY, USA (2011)
42. Onori, M., Micarelli, A., Sansonetti, G.: A comparative analysis of personality-based music recommender systems. In: CEUR Workshop Proceedings, vol. 1680, pp. 55–59. CEUR-WS.org, Aachen, Germany (2016)

43. Rayana, S., Akoglu, L.: Collective opinion spam detection: bridging review networks and metadata. In: Proceedings of the 21th ACM SIGKDD International Conference on Knowledge Discovery and Data Mining, KDD 2015, pp. 985–994. ACM, New York, NY, USA (2015)
44. Sansonetti, G.: Point of interest recommendation based on social and linked open data. Pers. Ubiquit. Comput. **23**(2), 199–214 (2019)
45. Sansonetti, G., Gasparetti, F., D'Aniello, G., Micarelli, A.: Unreliable users detection in social media: deep learning techniques for automatic detection. IEEE Access **8**, 213154–213167 (2020)
46. Sansonetti, G., Gasparetti, F., Micarelli, A.: Cross-domain recommendation for enhancing cultural heritage experience. In: Adjunct Publication of the 27th Conference on User Modeling. Adaptation and Personalization, pp. 413–415. Association for Computing Machinery, New York, NY, USA (2019)
47. Sansonetti, G., Gasparetti, F., Micarelli, A.: Using social media for personalizing the cultural heritage experience. In: Adjunct Proceedings of the 29th ACM Conference on User Modeling, Adaptation and Personalization, UMAP 2021, pp. 189–193. Association for Computing Machinery, New York, NY, USA (2021)
48. Sansonetti, G., Gasparetti, F., Micarelli, A., Cena, F., Gena, C.: Enhancing cultural recommendations through social and linked open data. User Model. User-Adapt. Interact. **29**(1), 121–159 (2019)
49. Sardella, N., Biancalana, C., Micarelli, A., Sansonetti, G.: An approach to conversational recommendation of restaurants. In: Stephanidis, C. (ed.) HCII 2019. CCIS, vol. 1034, pp. 123–130. Springer, Cham (2019). https://doi.org/10.1007/978-3-030-23525-3_16
50. Savage, D., Zhang, X., Yu, X., Chou, P., Wang, Q.: Detection of opinion spam based on anomalous rating deviation. Expert Syst. Appl. **42**(22), 8650–8657 (2015)
51. Singh, C., Pavithra, N., Joshi, R.: Internet an integral part of human life in 21st century: a review. Curr. J. Appl. Sci. Technol. **41**(36), 12–18 (2022)
52. Vaccaro, L., Sansonetti, G., Micarelli, A.: An empirical review of automated machine learning. Computers **10**(1) (2021)
53. Wang, Z., Hou, T., Li, Z., Song, D.: Spotting fake reviewers using product review graph. J. Comput. Inf. Syst. **11**(16), 5759–5767 (2015)
54. Xie, L., Deng, Z., Cox, S.: Multimodal joint information processing in human machine interaction: recent advances. Multimedia Tools Appl. **73**(1), 267–271 (2014)
55. Xu, C.: Detecting collusive spammers in online review communities. In: Proceedings of the Sixth Workshop on Ph.D. Students in Information and Knowledge Management, PIKM 2013, pp. 33–40. ACM, New York, NY, USA (2013)
56. Yu, S., Ren, J., Li, S., Naseriparsa, M., Xia, F.: Graph learning for fake review detection. Front. Artif. Intell. **5** (2022)
57. Zhang, D., Li, W., Niu, B., Wu, C.: A deep learning approach for detecting fake reviewers: exploiting reviewing behavior and textual information. Decis. Support Syst. **166**, 113911 (2023)

Automated Detection of Different Publication Patterns of Online Deliberation as a Research Domain

Daniil Volkovskii[1,2,3], Olga Filatova[1,2](✉), and Radomir Bolgov[1,2]

[1] ITMO University, 49 Kronverksky Prospekt, 197101 St. Petersburg, Russia
dvolkovskiy@hse.ru, {o.filatova,r.bolgov}@spbu.ru

[2] Saint Petersburg State University, 7 Universitetskaya Embankment, 199004 St. Petersburg, Russia

[3] Russia National Research University Higher School of Economics, 20 Myasnitskaya, 101000 Moscow, Russia

Abstract. The paper intends to contribute to a better comprehension of literature on online deliberation and demonstrate possibilities of using software provided for automated processing of information arrays downloaded from bibliographic databases for scientometric analysis of a complex interdisciplinary research domain. We present a descriptive analysis of sources and authors in order to detect what meanings (networked) deliberation may have, comprising a short review on basic directions of research domain. Also, the conceptual structure of research field is analyzed using bibliometric analysis which allows to generate a map of main and highly relevant themes studied. As a result, we suggest future research directions for deliberative studies. In total, 1946 publications from databases of Scopus during the period 1968–2022 are analyzed. The outcomes indicate on an opportunity of effective using the functionality of Biblioshiny and VOSviewer to investigate trends in science. Qualitative interpretation of results assists to propose a few valuable directions for deliberative studies which should be developed further. The first prominent observance is a lack of studies exploring e-deliberation and its quality in the conditions of exogenous shocks (war, pandemics, natural disasters). One more less discovered venue correlates with studying citizens' motivations and purposes to participate in political conversation via online platforms. The third research idea is devoted to understanding what online deliberation represents and what effects it may have on citizenry and government.

Keywords: Deliberation · Online Deliberation · Bibliometric Analysis · Research Domain

1 Introduction

Today, the current state of deliberative democratic theory is extremely hard to evaluate unambiguously (Savin, 2019) as it has quite different tendencies and directions of elaboration. The state of political theory in 1990s was described by John Dryzek as a

A. Coman and S. Vasilache (Eds.): HCII 2023, LNCS 14025, pp. 146–163, 2023.
https://doi.org/10.1007/978-3-031-35915-6_12

deliberative turn, then the theory of deliberative democracy became a mainstream in political science in 2000s, even going beyond a political theory. Two decades later after deliberative turn, Dryzek distinguished a few more turns in the deliberative democracy such as institutional, systemic, practical and empirical ones which were outlined in a clear manner in his work "Foundations and Frontiers of Deliberative Governance" (Dryzek, 2010). A number of theoretical, methodological and empirical studies devoted to deliberative democracy, democratic deliberation and online deliberation has increased exponentially in the last decade covering new aspects and directions of research thought. However, despite a constantly growing quantity of studies in this field and improvement of their quality, there is a crisis of democracy which is interpreted as an "overload" of opportunities for citizens to have their voices heard "accompanied by marked decline in civility and argumentative complexity" (Dryzek et al., 2019). These days, the real world of politics is far from a deliberative ideal due to huge polarization and incivility that have a negative impact on civic participation (Buchanan et al., 2022), precariousness and inefficiency of simple arguments and solutions for ambiguous and complex issues that lead to "susceptibility by citizens to ill-reasoned, populist, and increasingly authoritarian appeals from political elites" (Buchanan et al., 2022). Nevertheless, there is accruing empirical evidence that deliberative practices, programs, and structures have potential and offer some ways to mitigate the recessionary political situation.

Online deliberation can be considered as one of effective instruments allowing to raise the deliberative quality of politics. However, there are some problems correlating with conceptualization of deliberation, including online deliberation as well, due to a growing body of literature on deliberation that has stretched the concept (Bächtiger et al. 2010; Friess & Eilders, 2015). As a result, it may be confusing to understand what conditions are needed for deliberation to occur and how to define it exactly.

The present research is aimed at contributing to a better understanding of literature in the field of online deliberation in three ways. Firstly, to develop a descriptive analysis of papers and authors in order to determine what (online) deliberation does mean and what directions this research domain has. Secondly, to analyze the conceptual structure of research field employing bibliometric analysis. It helps create a map of main and highly important topics studies which may be grouped. Databases of Scopus publications were investigated to solve these problems. Third, to suggest future research directions. Totally, we analyzed 1946 publications during the period 1968–2022. The main purpose of this article is to demonstrate possibilities of using software provided for automated processing of information arrays downloaded from bibliographic databases for scientometric analysis of such a complex interdisciplinary research domain as online deliberation.

2 Online Deliberation as a Research Domain

2.1 What Does Deliberation Mean? Conceptualizing and Proposing Own Definition

The term of (public) deliberation is a central category to deliberative democracy theory. In recent decades, the idea of deliberation has been considered in public and scholarly discourse as "a cornerstone of democracy" (Delli Carpini, 2002) and as "a remedy for the imperfections of the democratic system" (Witkowska 2012). Public deliberation

Table 1. Conceptualization of deliberation

Authors & years	Meaning	Basic set of attributes
Cohen, 1997	Public argument and reasoning among equal citizens prior to a decision	Public argument, reasoning, equal, decision
Bohman & Rehg, 1996	Deliberation is a participatory form of politically, morally, and ethically justified discourse when citizens voluntarily discuss politics in a casual manner to present competing perspectives through public reasoning instead of bargaining	A participatory form of justified discourse, public reasoning instead of bargaining
Dryzek, 2010	Deliberation should be associated with discussions that are (unnaturally) calm, reasoned, argumentative, whereas the genuine communication in democracy should include the real-life discursive processes that are intrinsically social, intersubjective invoking all kinds of 'unruly and contentious communications from the margin'	Reasoned, argumentative discussions, discursive processes
Chambers, 1996	Debate and discussion aimed at producing reasonable, well-informed opinions in which participants are willing to revise preferences in light of discussion, new information, and claims made by fellow participants. Although consensus need not be the ultimate aim of deliberation, and participants are expected to pursue their interests, an overarching interest in the legitimacy of outcomes (understood as justification to all affected) ideally characterizes deliberation	Reasonable, well-informed opinions, consensus, legitimacy of outcomes

(*continued*)

Table 1. *(continued)*

Authors & years	Meaning	Basic set of attributes
Gastil, Black & Lawra, 2008	The process of getting people together to examine problems carefully and find out solutions for the existed problem based on the reasons where differences and views highly respected	To examine problems, find out solutions, based on the reasons, respected views
Bächtiger, Dryzek, Mansbridge, & Warren, 2018	Mutual communication that involves weighing and reflecting on preferences, values, and interests regarding matters of common concern	Mutual communication, weighing, reflecting on preferences, matters of common concern

is a multi-dimensional theory studied in political philosophy (Gutmann & Thompson, 1996; Cohen, 1997), political communications (Carcasson, Black, & Sink, 2010; Gastil, 1993; Pearce & Littlejohn, 1997), public opinion research (Gastil, 2008; Page, 1996), citizen's juries (Crosby, 1995). We pay attention to two significant things which should be known about definition of deliberation. First, there is a plethora of definitions of (public) deliberation as "deliberation is a rather complex concept, and it should be used with care" (Steiner, 2008). Secondly, there is no unified term which can be tested empirically by all scholars in a standard way due to various techniques of conceptualization and operationalization of the concept.

In order to propose our own definition of deliberation, first, we present some definitions which are highly relevant to deliberative studies. Then, we highlight main and common components of deliberation which should be comprised when giving a description on what deliberation is (see Table 1). Our definition of deliberation is predominantly based on works of Cohen (1997), Bohman (1996), Dryzek (2010), Chambers (1996), Gastil, Black & Lawra (2008), Bächtiger, Dryzek, Mansbridge, & Warren (2018). Thus, we perceive deliberation as a process of inclusive reasoned, respected discussion of citizens with the prevalence of dialogical form of communication, aiming at solving common problems and reaching consensus, or legitimacy of outcomes.

2.2 What is e-deliberation? Main Directions of Research on Online Deliberation

Since 1990s, researchers have begun to study in more detail the role of the Internet, ICT in discussing political problems and making decisions on certain political issues (Chadwick, 2006; Davis, 1999; Davis & Owen, 1998; Römmele, 2003). Today, one of the most discussed forms of political Internet communication is online deliberation on issues of common interest to all participants. The modern political science demonstrates a growing number of communication practices of justification between citizens, civil institutions, media and authorities (Chambers, 1996; Habermas, 1996, 2006; Wessler, 2018) in relation to socio-political problems in the public sphere that occur online (Coleman, 2018; Coleman & Shane, 2012; Kersting, 2013; Warren, 2009). Internet-based deliberation can be understood as "the interest in the capacity for information and communications technology (ICT) to support political debate and decision making" (King, 2018). A more recent definition of e-deliberation is described as "an online deliberation process that uses Internet to sense public opinion on one or more specific issues, to enable and enhance discussion among citizens, and to shape consent among citizens" (Fitsilis, 2022). According to V. Tsakanikas, G. Rokkou, and V. Triantafyllou (2022), e-deliberation presents different categories of systems which are dependent on the subject of deliberation, its goals, participants' and moderators'/coordinators' experience of e-participation, general characteristics of platforms: online forums, deliberative polls, votes, discussions, e-surveys, e-petitions (Tsakanikas, Rokkou, & Triantafyllou, 2022). In our understanding, online (Internet, web, digital, electronic, networked, Internet-based) deliberation is a deliberation conducted in online environment with usage of electronic means of communication. The main point in any term of e-deliberation is the usage of ICT and Internet.

Internet-based deliberation is a relatively new field that currently comprises a lot of changes and developments in subject of scholarly attention and variety of approaches to studying it (Davies & Chandler, 2011). S. Gangadharan (2009) observes online deliberation's "multiple histories", while Davies (2009) describes the field of networked deliberation as fragmented. In addition to this, according to Davies, an academic community formed around digital deliberation agenda seems to be fragmented as well, since many scholars and practitioners work separately from each other (Davies, 2009). As a consequence, it leads to duplicated efforts and lost opportunities that could benefit to a more comprehensive and unified understanding of online deliberation and research approaches to it. Instead, there are many conflicting and inconsistent assumptions about nature of digital deliberation, its operationalization and measurement which may be noticed in the literature (Coleman & Moss 2012).

D. Friess and C. Eliders (2015) observed that research on online deliberative practices gained tremendous scholarly attention in the first decade of the 21st century. The great amount of theoretical and empirical literature has become available (Black, Welser, Cosley, & DeGroot, 2011; Davies & Gangadharan, 2009; Gerhards & Schafer, 2010; Price & Cappella, 2002; Stromer-Galley & Martinson, 2009). Nonetheless, there are still many open questions regarding the relation between such relevant components of online deliberation as design, communication processes and outcomes that are needed to be clarified in normative (finding an ideal), descriptive (investigating empirical nature) and prescriptive ways (how things can be altered in order to achieve progress) (Davies & Gangadharan, 2009). The scholars distinguished three main directions of research on online deliberative practices (Friess & Eliders, 2015; Jonsson & Åström, 2014; Strandberg & Grönlund, 2018).

a) Institutional input ("design") – the institutional design that sheds light on the preconditions of deliberation, enables and fosters it. For example, it may include institutional arrangements (e.g., participatory budgeting), platforms (e.g., government-run platform), and socio-political elements (e.g., internet access rate and social strata).
b) Productive outcome ("results") – the expected results of deliberation, their internal (e.g., new knowledge and experience, change of positions and preferences) and external effects (e.g., policy metamorphoses).

c) Communicative throughput ("process") – the communication processes through which individuals participate and its quality, ways how consensus can be democratically built and reached.

The early 2000s revealed an enormous academic interest in empirical studies on online deliberation (Davies, 2009). There was a lot of optimism towards benefits of ICT in overcoming practical issues of web deliberative process. However, online deliberation research had gradually moved from early enthusiasm to pessimism and, most recently, to a more qualified and balanced exploration of the relationship between technology and democracy. Although technologies may facilitate greater availability of data and information, it is not enough for strengthening democracy. For example, Price and Cappella (2002) indicated that the increased accessibility of information did not expand the usage of such information. Scheufele and Nisbet (2002), Davis (2009), and Lusoli and others (2006) observed that citizens' usage of ICT reinforced a gap between engaged and unengaged citizens. Sunstein's (2001) observations of polarization and previously mentioned works showed that while ICT managed to remove barriers of time, geography and cost to deliberative processes, there were still challenges and negative consequences for Internet-based deliberation.

Social media and ICT have become more significant in the last two decades (Davis 2009, Boyd, & Ellison, 2008). According to Daniel Halpern and Jennifer Gibbs (2013), social media may perform as a catalyst for online deliberation, since it provides a deliberative space to discuss and encourage political participation, both directly and indirectly. However, as an opposing effect, social media promotes unintentional access to heterogeneous information which can lead to political disagreements (Barnidge, 2018; Maia et al., 2018) and spread of incivility, hate speech (Herbst, 2010; Rowe, 2015; Sobieraj & Berry, 2011; Coe, Kenski, & Rains, 2014) that diminishes the quality of deliberation and participant's desire to be engaged in it. We suppose this is one of the reasons why scholars currently focus more on intensive research of institutional settings, platforms, its design, tools and software, but not on communication process and its quality.

Our study helped understand what research direction currently dominates in the field of online deliberation and what gaps are needed to be filled by future studies.

3 Workflow of Conducted Bibliometric Analysis

The bibliometric study aimed at detecting various publication patterns of online deliberation as a research domain and was driven by the following research questions:

RQ1: What is the state-of-the-art of online deliberation reflected by the most cited papers, most important authors, sources (journals), countries, etc.?

RQ2: What are the key themes/concepts in the literature of online deliberation?

The process of bibliometric analysis includes several stages and methods.

Study design included selecting a bibliographic database for data collection (in this case, Scopus); developing a search strategy.

Totally, we found 1946 publications during the period 1968–2022 with the following search:

KEY ("online deliberation" OR "electronic deliberation" OR "e-deliberation" OR "e-deliberation" OR "computer-mediated deliberation" OR "web-deliberation" OR "digital deliberation" OR "virtual deliberation" OR "Internet deliberation" OR "deliberation online" OR "social media deliberation" OR "networked deliberation") OR TITLE-ABS-KEY ("electronic participation" OR "e-participation").

Data collection included:

- searching Scopus based on the chosen search strategy;
- exporting the retrieved bibliographic records to Plain Text and bib formats;
- uploading the collection (Plain Text) on Biblioshiny (2017);
- exporting the collection from Biblioshiny as an Excel file;
- importing the same collection in bib format in Mendeley for screening.
- Data analysis included:
- automatic checking for duplicates (both in the Mendeley library and the Excel file exported from Biblioshiny);
- screening titles, abstracts, and keywords of each record in Mendeley, deleting irrelevant records in Mendeley and Excel as described below. Following Lan & Anders (2000), we excluded the analysis of reviews, editorials, prefaces and forewords because they presented a limited view of the subject addressed. We included only the items in English. Yet, English is internationally accepted and widely used for publishing research.

Following Dekker and Bekkers (2015), we have selected a set of criteria for including articles in the review:

1. English language, Peer-review process
2. Original research (empirical and theoretical studies; excluding editorials, reviews, previews, forewords, etc.)
3. Relevance to the research questions, we excluded the articles:

a) not specifically addressing online deliberation;
b) addressing non-political online deliberation topics (arts, culture, etc.);
c) addressing another context (e.g., health or education or private sector).

- cleaning Authors' keywords of the final collection in Excel:

After cleaning the keywords in Mendeley, we took 285 items, namely 126 ("deliberat(ion/ive)"), 37 ("discours(e/ive)"), 110 ("discussion"), 12 ("argumentat(ion/ive)"). After deleting duplications, we took 212 publications.

After cleaning the keywords in Biblioshiny, we took 174 publications. After deleting duplications, we took 148 publications.

- uploading the final collection (Excel) on Biblioshiny and performing different bibliometric analyses (e.g., calculation of main bibliometric measures, such as most productive authors;
- keyword co-occurrence network analysis, country collaboration network analysis).

Data visualization was performed using the functionality of Biblioshiny and VOSviewer for visualizations, using Excel graphs (e.g., for visualization of annual scientific production and frequency distribution of Research Areas).

Qualitative interpretation of results aims at defining key areas of research, themes, and relations between authors in online deliberation studies. It will allow to detect the meaningful lacunas in this research area and parallelism in various research locations and provide suggestions for future collaborations.

4 Interpretation of Results

4.1 What is the State-of-the-Art of Online Deliberation Reflected by the Most Cited Papers, Most Important Authors, Sources (Journals)?

The bibliometric analysis enabled to identify the most cited sources which are presented on Fig. 1. The most cited document was «Social media as a catalyst for online deliberation? Exploring the affordances of Facebook and YouTube for political expression» by Halpern and Gibbs (2013). Their paper was devoted to the potential of social networks as a catalyst for e-deliberation. The scholars assessed such social media channels as Facebook and YouTube to understand whether these platforms meet the necessary conditions for deliberative democracy. They evaluated two traditional predictors of e-deliberation: the affordances of identifiability and networked information access. Based on discourse analysis of networked messages, Halpern and Gibbs concluded that Facebook expanded the flow of information to other networks and allowed to conduct more symmetrical conversations among participants, while YouTube showed lower figures for politeness in the more anonymous and deindividuated environments.

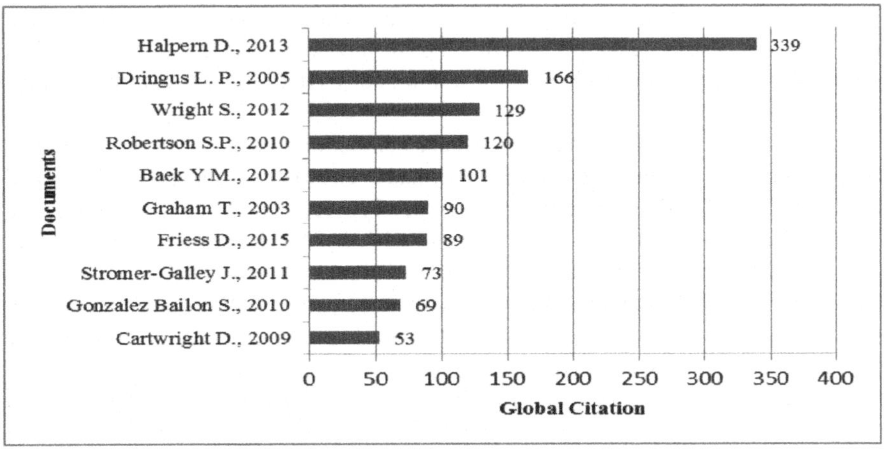

Fig. 1. Most global cited documents and authors

«Using data mining as a strategy for assessing asynchronous discussion forums» by L. P. Dringus and T. Ellis (2005) was the second most cited source. Their work aimed at demonstrating how data mining may offer promise as a strategy for exploring and building alternative representations for the data underlying asynchronous discussion forums. The authors took attempt to sort out the question, "what is data from an online forum?" among other key questions. Using temporal participation indicators, Dringus and Ellis managed to reveal how employing data and text mining techniques in the query process could improve the instructor's ability to estimate the progress of a threaded conversation.

After articles of D. Halpern and L.P. Dringus, our analysis showed a paper of S. Wright (2012) named «Politics as usual? Revolution, normalization and a new agenda for online deliberation» as the most cited document in Scopus database. The article argued that the split between revolution and normalization schools (these discourses are about the role of new media in shaping politics) had a negative impact on further empirical analyses of political Internet-based talk. This paper had three main conclusions: 1) the majority of investigators failed to consider the nature of revolutionary change in any detail, tending to frame and interpret their research results with the very technologically determinist accounts of revolutionary change; 2) the revolution/normalization frame led scholars to disproportionately analyze current political institutions and practices, using narrow definitions of politics which are irrelevant and often inappropriate in the context of new media; 3) the revolution/normalization frame led researchers to construe their empirical data in an excessively negative way. As a result, Wright proposed a few suggestions on how scholars could refine online deliberation research and make it more optimistic.

In the Sect. 2, we mentioned some mostly cited works by D. Halpern and J. Gibbs (2013), D. Friess and C. Eliders (2015) and the directions of research proposed by them. However, we could not track this tendency among other most cited works. Considering the most cited documents and scholars represented in the Fig. 1, we investigated that the majority of papers were about institutional input (Halpern (2013); Dringus (2005); Gonzalez-Bailon (2010); Cartwright (2009); several studies contained communication throughput (Robertson (2008); Graham (2003)), theory and review (Wright (2012); Friess (2015)), and combination of three directions (Baek (2012); Stromer-Galley (2009)).

According to Fig. 2, it may be noticed that a number of sources had been rising since 2005. As for types of sources, we see that they had been gradually appearing: Policy and Internet in 2003, ACM International Conference Proceedings Series in 2005, Lecture Notes in Computer Science in 2006, International Journal of Electronic Governance in 2007. The last one was Journal of Information Technology and Policy since 2011. A quantity of Policy and Internet publications started increasing only since 2014, however, as mentioned before, it was formed in 2003. The impressive results of growth were illustrated by Lecture Notes in Computer Science since 2009. It saw a sharp increase since 2012 till 2017. As a result of accumulation, currently, it is the dominating source in comparison to others. ACM International Conference Proceedings Series, International Journal of Electronic Governance, and Journal of Information Technology and Policy had constantly growing patterns alternating with periods of stable indicators. In 2022, Policy and Internet and International Journal of Electronic Governance obtained the lowest figures for cumulate occurrences among others, although Policy and Internet emerged much earlier than other sources. Interestingly, a common trend among all sources, except Policy and Internet, was observed: the first year of appearance was characterized by growth and then there were some periods without changes (ACM International Conference Proceedings Series 2005–2006 and 2006–2010 respectively, Lecture Notes in Computer Science 2006–2007 and 2007–2009 respectively, International Journal of Electronic Governance 2007–2008 and 2008–2011 respectively, Journal of Information Technology and Policy 2011–2012 and 2012–2017 respectively); after those periods of stability, we could discover the growth of sources again.

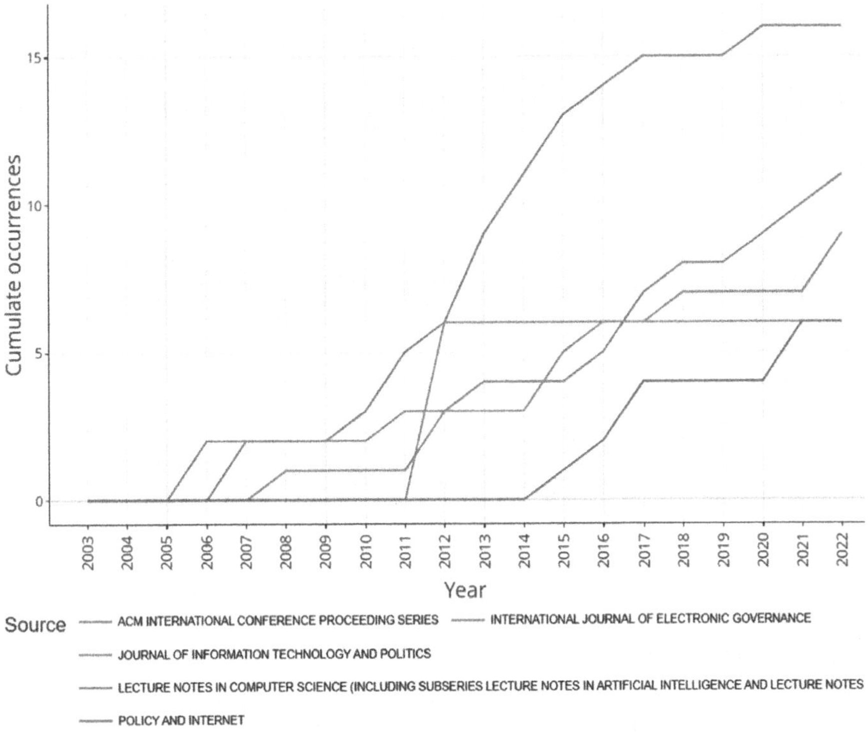

Fig. 2. Source Dynamics

4.2 What Are the Key Themes/concepts in the Literature of Online Deliberation?

Figure 3 shows trend topics from 2008 to 2022. The most widespread themes were forums (2008–2020), political (2010–2020), electronic (2012–2022), discussion (2010–2019), e-participation (2010–2019), design (2011–2019), social (2013–2021), deliberation (2012–2020), deliberative (2012–2020), and online (2012–2015). The most frequent terms engaged were online (in 2015), deliberation (in 2016), deliberative (in 2017), discussions and social (in 2016), political (in 2013), discussion (in 2012). We noticed that scholars focused predominantly on online deliberation, political discussion, deliberative discussions, deliberative forums, social media, online participation, online discourse, digital platforms and their design. It means that an institutional input venue currently dominates in deliberative studies.

Figure 4 demonstrates co-occurrence network of keywords that summarizes the research content. We found "deliberation" and "online" as the largest nodes in the network, followed by "discussion", "discourse" and "social media". We can see several segments of the network. For instance, a "red" segment shows a co-occurrence of the words "deliberative", "discussions", "democracy" and "citizens" which indicates that the main purpose of deliberation is to strengthen the democracy and citizens. A "green" segment shows a co-occurrence of the words "social media", "discourse", "citizens"

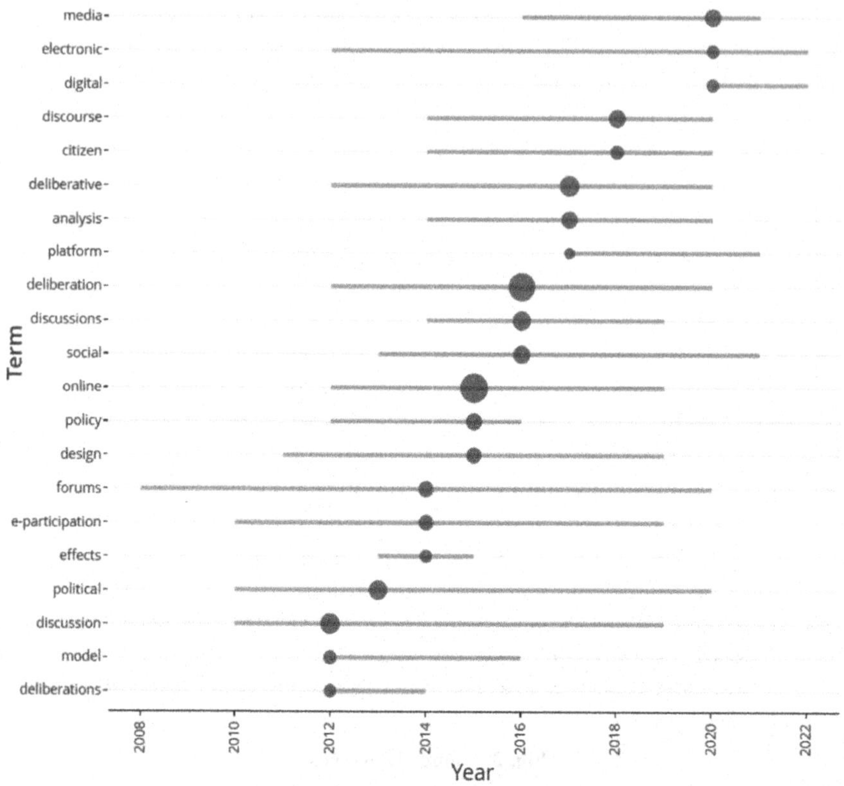

Fig. 3. Trend topics

and "dialogue", which we can interpret as many authors adhere to the approach according to which social media generate a discourse, empower the citizens and promote the dialogue between citizens and government. At the same time, we can see the absence (or week representativeness) of such topics as "deliberation effects" and "deliberation assessment". It means that these topics are still emerging, taking a low development and increasing (but still low) relevance. We can see that online deliberation remains a field which includes a "variety of arenas" and "wide range of methods", comparing to the previous study of 2014 (Jonsson & Åström, 2014). Meanwhile, more and more attention is paid to democratic aspects of online deliberation, comparing to the findings of 2014.

In the last two decades, the body of literature on e-deliberation has grown rapidly, but the majority of empirical studies have focused predominantly on communication processes. These investigations aimed at measuring the quality of deliberation in Internet discussions based on values and dimensions of deliberation (Filatova, Kabanov, & Misnikov, 2019; Volkovskii & Filatova, 2021; Volkovskii, Filatova, & Bolgov, 2022). Other studies have concentrated on the results of e-deliberation (Han et al., 2015; Price & Cappella, 2002; Strandberg, Berg, Karv, & Backström, 2021). There has been still a problem earlier noticed by Price, Stromer-Galley and Muhlberger in 2009 that input-output models currently dominate in research agenda whereas a lack of throughput research remains

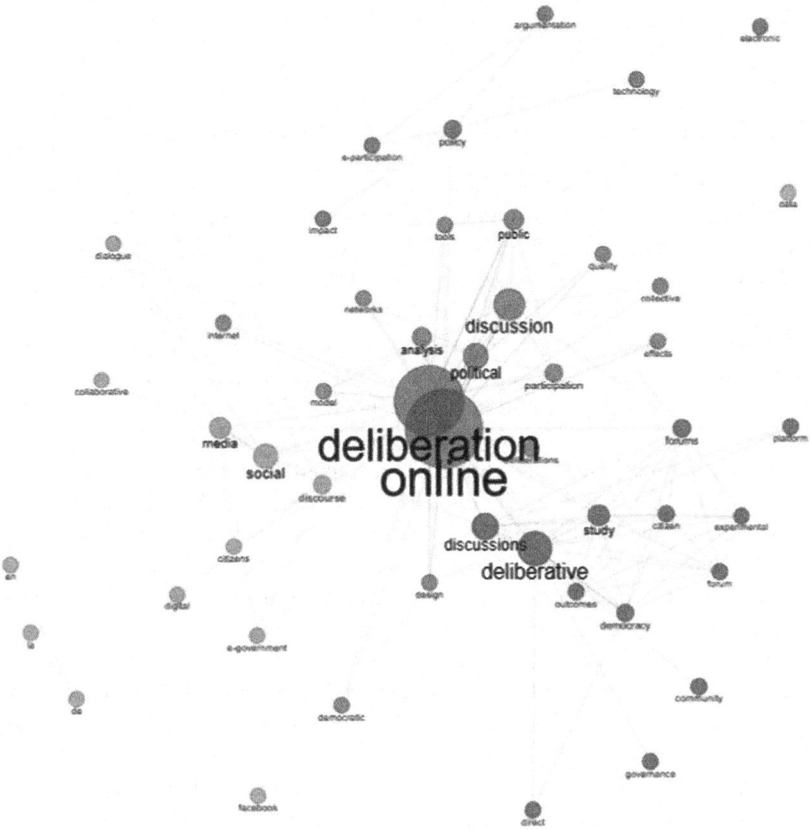

Fig. 4. Co-Occurrence Maps of Keywords in the International Agenda. Source: Biblioshiny

and gets neglected. Their criticism was that deliberation is treated as a black box, adding that analysis is often limited to "observing change from before to after the deliberation without considering what has happened during the discussion" (Stromer-Galley & Muhlberger, 2009).

5 Discussion

5.1 Study Limitations

It should be noted that the choice of keywords for the search is determined by initial knowledge of the author on this topic. This fact determined the findings (see Fig. 4). We searched for data in Scopus, traditionally used for these purposes. We can distinguish "Authors", "Keywords", "Titles", "Source" and "Year of publication" as fields of research interest. Web of Science (WoS) has better and more diverse data than Scopus. However, the advantage of Scopus is the indexing of conference proceedings, not only journal articles, as well as more publications on social sciences and humanities than WoS. At the same time, the books are not included in the sample. This fact may significantly affect the findings.

5.2 What Are the Gaps and Future Research Opportunities in the Field?

Little has changed during the last decade as our analysis confirmed the same pattern mentioned by us earlier. We tracked the articles mostly devoted to institutional input or combination of it with productive outcome/communicative throughput. However, there were almost no studies investigating all three aspects of deliberation and their causal links (design-process-results). The empirical studies still concentrate more on a deliberative communication as a dependent variable and effects of design (input) on its process (Alnemr, 2020; Gonçalves, Cecília, & Baranauskas, 2022) rather than on effects of the communication process on the outcomes of deliberation (Price, Nir, & Capella, 2006). However, only in the last 5–7 years a number of works dedicated to studying communicative throughput (Del Valle, Sijtsma, Stegeman, & Borge, 2020; Esau, Fleu, & Nienhaus, 2020; Esau, Friess, & Eilders, 2017; Volkovskii, 2021), especially with integrating automated and machine methods (Fournier-Tombs, & Di Marzo, 2020; Shin & Rask, 2021), has begun to grow. The sharp increase can be explained by the fact that "deliberation is a key element of governance, and assessing its quality is crucial to the development of better governance practices" (Shin & Rask, 2021). Indeed, it is now commonly acknowledged that governments can no longer address and solve social problems by themselves, they should tend to cooperation with citizenry and civil society in order to make well-balanced collective decisions and share responsibility together (Torfing, Sørensen, & Røiseland, 2019).

A review on literature assisted us to propose a few directions for deliberative studies which should be developed in the future. The first prominent observance is a lack of studies exploring e-deliberation and its quality in the conditions of exogeneous shocks (pandemic, war, natural or technogenic catastrophes, ecological crisis). Online deliberation is traditionally studied during the periods of social certainty, but our bibliometric analysis showed the shortage of theoretical findings and empirical studies of deliberation in crises. One more less explored venue correlates with citizens' motivation and intentions to participate in political conversation and online deliberation. The focus should be shifted on participants' behavior, engagement and motives to discuss politics. The are some studies examining motivations. However, there is little known about the motivations of people who take part in formal deliberation venues (Stromer-Galley, Bryant, & Bimber, 2009). The third research idea is about understanding what online deliberation represents and what effects it has. Only a few studies proposed a definition of networked deliberation and described its process in terms of contributions and advantages. However, online deliberation is not always good as it may have negative effects on participants. This influence should be deeply studied not only by scholars of political communications, but also by psychologists and sociologists.

6 Conclusion

The conducted research demonstrated the capabilities of automated detection of different publication patterns of online deliberation. The concept of online deliberation is interdisciplinary and, along with related concepts, is studied from positions of different fields. The interdisciplinary nature of this scientific direction, intersection of different approaches makes the case particularly interesting for usage in bibliometric research. The results indicated on a possibility of effective using the functionality of Biblioshiny and VOSviewer to analyze interdisciplinary trends in world science. Using a sample that is not completely representative, we identified many features that can serve as the subject of further, more detailed analysis. The methodology of bibliometric analysis presented in this article can be used and further developed in the analysis of more extensive academic fields—E-Participation and E-Governance. As a part of the project "Institutional Transformation of e-Participation Governance in Russia: A Study of Regional Specifics", it is planned to analyze the conceptual structure of the research field using bibliometric analysis, which will allow to create a map of basically studied themes.

Acknowledgements. The study was supported by the Russian Science Foundation, project No. 22-18-00364 "Institutional Transformation of E-Participation Governance in Russia: a Study of Regional Peculiarities" (https://rscf.ru/project/22-18-00364/) and project No. 21-18-00454 «Mediatized Communication and Modern Deliberative Process» (https://www.rscf.ru/project/21-18-00454/). The bibliometric analysis with usage of automated method was employed in terms of the project No. 22-18-00364, the theoretical review on deliberation and e-deliberation – the project No. 21-18-00454.

References

Alnemr, N.: Emancipation cannot be programmed: blind spots of algorithmic facilitation in online deliberation. Contemp. Polit. **26**(5), 531–552 (2020)

Bächtiger, A., Niemeyer, S., Neblo, M., Steenbergen, M.R., Steiner, J.: Disentangling diversity in deliberative democracy: competing theories, their blind spots and complementarities. J. Polit. Philos. **18**, 32–63 (2010). https://doi.org/10.1111/j.1467-9760.2009.00342.x

Baek, Y.M., Wojcieszak, M., Delli Carpini, M.X.: Online versus face-to-face deliberation: Who? Why? What? With what effects? New Media Soc. **14**(3), 363–383 (2012). https://doi.org/10.1177/1461444811413191

Barnidge, M.: Social affect and political disagreement on social media. Soc. Media + Soc. **4**(3) (2018). https://doi.org/10.1177/2056305118797721

Black, L.W., Welser, H.T., Cosley, D., DeGroot, J.M.: Self-governance through group discussion in Wikipedia: measuring deliberation in online groups. Small Group Res. **42**(5), 595–634 (2011)

Bohman, J.F.: Public Deliberation: Pluralism, Complexity, and Democracy (1996)

Boyd, D., Ellison, N.: Social network sites: definition, history, and scholarship. J. Comput. Mediated Commun. **13**, 210–230 (2008). https://doi.org/10.1111/j.1083-6101.2007.00393.x

Buchanan, C.M., et al.: Deliberation, cognitive complexity, and political engagement: a longitudinal study of the impact of deliberative training during emerging adulthood. J. Deliberative Democracy **18**(1), 1–13 (2022)

Carcasson, M., Black, L.W., Sink, E.S.: Communication studies and deliberative democracy: current contributions and future possibilities. J. Public Deliberation **6**(1), 1–42 (2010)

Cartwright, D., Atkinson, K.: Using computational argumentation to support e-participation. IEEE Intell. Syst. **24**(5), 42–52 (2009). https://doi.org/10.1109/MIS.2009.104

Chadwick, A.: Internet Politics: States, Citizens, and New Communications Technologies. Oxford University Press, New York (2006)

Chambers, S.: Reasonable Democracy. Cornell Univ. Press, Ithaca (1996)

Coe, K., Kenski, K., Rains, S.A.: Online and uncivil? Patterns and determinants of incivility in newspaper website comments. J. Commun. **64**, 658–679 (2014)

Cohen, J.: Deliberation and democratic legitimacy. deliberative democracy: essays on reason and politics. In: Bohman, J., Rehg, W. (eds.). The MIT Press. Massachusetts (1997)

Coleman, S., Moss, G.: Under construction: the field of online deliberation research. J. Inform. Tech. Polit. **9**(1), 1–15 (2012)

Coleman, S.: Can the internet strengthen democracy? Eur. J. Commun. **33**(4), 461 (2018)

Crosby, N.: Citizen juries: one solution for difficult environmental questions. In: Renn, O., Webler, T., Wiedemann, P. (eds.) Fairness and Competence in Citizen Participation: Evaluating Models for Environmental Discourse, pp. 157–174. Kluwer, Boston (1995)

Davies, T., Chandler, R.: Online deliberation design: choices, criteria and evidence. In: Nabatachi, T., Weiksner, M., Gastil, J., Leighninger, M. (eds.) Democracy in Motion: Evaluating the Practice and Impact of Deliberative Civic Engagement. Oxford University Press, Oxford (2011)

Davies, T.: The blossoming field of Online Deliberation. In: Davies, T., Gangadharan, S.P. (eds.) Online Deliberation: Design, Research and Practice. CSLI Publications, San Rancisco (2009)

Davis, R., Owen, D.: New Media and American Politics. Oxford University Press, New York (1998)

Davis, R.: The Web of Politics: The Internet's Impact on the American Political System. Oxford University Press, New York (1999)

Dekker, R., Bekkers, V.: The contingency of governments' responsiveness to the virtual public sphere: a systematic literature review and meta-synthesis. Gov. Inf. Q. **32**(4), 496–505 (2015). https://doi.org/10.1016/j.giq.2015.09.007

Del Valle, M.E., Sijtsma, R., Stegeman, H., Borge, R.: Online deliberation and the public sphere: developing a coding manual to assess deliberation in Twitter political networks. Javnost Public **27**(3), 211–229 (2020). https://doi.org/10.1080/13183222.2020.1794408

Delli Carpini, M.X.: Political Decision-Making, Deliberation and Participation, 1st edn. JAI, Asterdam (2002)

Dringus, L.P., Ellis, T.: Using data mining as a strategy for assessing asynchronous discussion forums. Comput. Educ. **45**(1), 141–160 (2005). https://doi.org/10.1016/j.compedu.2004.05.003

Dryzek, J.S., Bachtiger, A., Chambers, S., Cohen, J., Druckman, J.N., Felicetti, A., et al.: The crisis of democracy and the science of deliberation. Science **363**(6432), 1144–1446 (2019)

Dryzek, J.S.: Foundations and Frontiers of Deliberative Governance, pp. 6–9. Cambridge University Press, Cambridge (2010)

Esau, K., Fleu, D., Nienhaus, S.: Different arenas, different deliberative quality? Using a systemic framework to evaluate online deliberation on immigration policy in Germany. Policy Internet, 1–27 (2020)

Esau, K., Friess, D., Eilders, C.: Design matters! An empirical analysis of online deliberation on different news platforms. Policy Internet **9**, 321–342 (2017)

Filatova, O., Kabanov, Y., Misnikov, Y.: Public deliberation in Russia: deliberative quality, rationality and interactivity of the online media discussions. Media Commun. **7**(3), 133–144 (2019)

Fitsilis, P.: Building on Smart Cities Skills and Competences. Human factors affecting smart cities development (2022). https://doi.org/10.1007/978-3-030-97818-1

Fournier-Tombs, E., Di Marzo Serugendo, G.: DelibAnalysis: understanding the quality of online political discourse with machine learning. J. Inf. Sci. **46**, 810–922 (2020)

Friess, D., Eilders, C.: A systematic review of online deliberation research. Policy Internet **7**(3), 319–339 (2015). https://doi.org/10.1002/poi3.95

Gangadharan, S.P.: Understanding diversity in the field of online deliberation. In: Davies, T., Gangadharan, S.P. (eds.) Online Deliberation: Design, Research, and Practice, pp. 329–347. CSLI Publications, Stanford (2009)

Gastil, J.: Democracy in Small Groups: Participation, Decision Making, and Communication. New Society, Philadelphia (1993)

Gastil, J.: Political Communication and Deliberation. Sage, Thousand Oaks (2008)

Gerhards, J., Schafer, M.S.: Is the internet a better public sphere? Comparing old and new media in the USA and Germany. New Media Soc. **12**(1), 143–160 (2010)

Gonçalves, F.M., Cecflia, M., Baranauskas, C.: Designing in pandemic context: scientific collaboration through the opendesign platform. Interact. Comput. (2022). https://doi.org/10.1093/iwc/iwac030

Gonzalez-Bailon, S., Kaltenbrunner, A., Banchs, R.E.: The structure of political discussion networks: a model for the analysis of online deliberation. J. Inf. Technol. **25**(2), 230–243. https://doi.org/10.1057/jit.2010.2

Graham, T., Witschge, T.: In search of online deliberation: towards a new method for examining the quality of online discussions. Communications **28**(2), 173–204 (2003). https://doi.org/10.1515/comm.2003.012

Gutmann, A., Thompson, D.: Democracy and Disagreement. Harvard University Press, Cambridge (1996)

Habermas, J.: Between Facts and Norms. Contributions to a Discourse Theory of Law and Democracy. MIT Press, Cambridge (1996)

Habermas, J.: Political communication in media society: does democracy still enjoy an epistemic dimension? The impact of normative theory on empirical research. Commun. Theor. **16**(4) (2006)

Halpern, D., Gibbs, J.: Social media as a catalyst for online deliberation? Exploring the affordances of Facebook and YouTube for political expression. Comput. Hum. Behav. **29**(3), 1159–1168 (2013). https://doi.org/10.1016/j.chb.2012.10.008

Han, S.-H., Schenck-Hamlin, W., Schenck-Hamlin, D.: Inclusion, equality, and discourse quality in citizen deliberations on broadband. J. Public Deliberation **11**(1) (2015). Article 3

Herbst, S.: Rude Democracy: Civility and Incivility in American Politics. Temple University Press, Philadelphia (2010)

Jonsson, M., Åström, J.: The challenges for online deliberation research: a literature review. Int. J. E-Politics **5**(1), 1–15 (2014)

Kersting, N.: Online participation: from 'Invited' to 'Invented' spaces. Int. J. Electron. Gov. **6**(4) (2013)

King, M.: Deliberation and decision making online: evaluating platform design. Ph.D. thesis, University of Westminster Social Sciences (2018)

Lan, Z., Anders, K.: A paradigmatic view of contemporary public administration research: an empirical test. Adm. Soc. **32**(2), 138–165 (2000)

Lusoli, W., Ward, S., Gibson, R.: (Re)Connecting politics? Parliament, the public and the internet. Parliam. Aff. **59**(1), 24–42 (2006)

Maia, R.C.M.: Deliberative media. In: Bächtiger, A., Dryzek, J.S., Mansbridge, J. (eds.) The Oxford Handbook of Deliberative Democracy (2018)

Page, B.I.: Who Deliberate? Mass Media in Modern Democracy. University of Chicago Press, Chicago (1996)

Pearce, W.B., Littlejohn, S.: Moral Conflict: When Social Worlds Collide. Sage, Thousand Oaks (1997)

Price, V., Cappella, J.N.: Online deliberation and its influence: the electronic dialogue project in campaign 2002. IT Soc. **1**(1), 303–329 (2002)

Price, V., Nir, L., Capella, J.N.: Normative and informational influences in online political discussions. Commun. Theory **16**(1), 47–74 (2006)
Price, V.: Citizens deliberating online: theory and some evidence. In: Davies, T., Gangadharan, S.P. (eds.) Online Deliberation: Design, Research and Practice, pp. 37–58. CSLI Publications, Stanford (2009)
Robertson, S.P., Vatrapu, R.K., Medina, R.: Off the wall political discourse: Facebook use in the 2008 U.S. presidential election. Inf. Polity **15**(1–2), 11–31 (2010). https://doi.org/10.3233/IP-2010-0196
Römmele, A.: Political parties, party communication and new information and communication technologies. Party Politics, 7–20 (2003)
Rowe, I.: Deliberation 2.0: comparing the deliberative quality of online news user comments across platforms. J. Broadcast. Electron. Media **59**, 539–555 (2015). 10.1080/08838151.2015.1093482
Savin, N.: The concept of the political in deliberative democratic theory. Ph.D. thesis, Moscow (2019)
Scheufele, D.A, Nisbet, M.C.: Being a citizen online: new opportunities and dead ends. Harvard Int. J. Press Politics **7**(3), 55–75 (2002)
Shin, B., Rask, M.: Assessment of online deliberative quality: new indicators using network analysis and time-series analysis. Sustainability 13 (2021)
Sobieraj, S., Berry, J.M.: From incivility to outrage: political discourse in blogs, talk radio, and cable news. Polit. Commun. **28**, 19–41 (2011)
Steiner, J.: Concept stretching: the case of deliberation. Eur. Polit. Sci. **7**(2), 186–190 (2008)
Strandberg, K., Berg, J., Karv, T., Backström, K.: When citizens met politicians – the process and outcomes of mixed deliberation according to participant status and gender, innovation. Eur. J. Soc. Sci. Res. **34**(5), 638–655 (2021)
Stromer-Galley, J., Martinson, A.M.: Coherence in political computer-mediated communication: analyzing topic relevance and drift in chat. Discourse Commun. **3**(2), 195–216 (2009)
Stromer-Galley, J., Muhlberger, P.: Agreement and disagreement in group deliberation: effects on deliberation satisfaction, future engagement, and decision legitimacy. Political Commun. **26**(2) (2009)
Torfing, J., Sørensen, E., Røiseland, A.: Transforming the public sector into an arena for co-creation: barriers, drivers, benefits, and ways forward. Adm. Soc. **51**, 795–825 (2019)
Tsakanikas, V., Rokkou, G., Triantafyllou, V.: Toward E-deliberation 2.0. In: Fitsilis, P. (ed.) Building on Smart Cities Skills and Competences. Human Factors Affecting Smart Cities Development (2022). https://doi.org/10.1007/978-3-030-97818-1
Volkovskii, D., Filatova, O., Bolgov, R.: Social media deliberation: civil or uncivil, reasoned or unreasoned? In: Proceedings of Central and Eastern European eDem and eGov Days 2022 (CEEEGOV 2022), Budapest, Hungary, pp. 21–26 (2022)
Volkovskii, D., Filatova, O.: Online deliberation on social media as a form of public dialogue in Russia. In: IMS 2021 – International Conference "Internet and Modern Society", pp. 146–156. CEUR Workshop Proceedings, St. Petersburg (2021)
Volkovskii, D.: Experience of applied research in online deliberation: an analysis of civility in American online discussions. In: IMS 2021 – International Conference "Internet and Modern Society", pp. 199–205. CEUR Workshop Proceedings, St. Petersburg (2021)
Warren, E. (ed.): The Oxford Handbook of Deliberative Democracy, pp. 348–364. Oxford University Press (2018). https://doi.org/10.1093/oxfordhb/9780198747369.013.11
Warren, M.E.: Governance-Driven Democratization. Critical Policy Stud. **3**(1) (2009)
Coleman, S., Shane, P.M.: Connecting Democracy: Online Consultation and the Flow of Political Communication. MIT Press, Cambridge (2012)
Wessler, H.: Habermas and the Media. Theory and the Media. Cambridge, Medford, MA: Polity (2018)

Witkowska, M.: Deliberation as a tool to find solutions to overcome the crisis in the Wright, S.: Politics as usual? Revolution, normalization and a new agenda for online deliberation. New Soc. **14**(2), 244–261 (2012). https://doi.org/10.1177/1461444811410679

Social Computing and Social Media in Multi-cultural Contexts

Cumulative Polarization: Patterns of Accumulation of Neutral and Politicized Echo Chambers on Russian Twitter

Svetlana S. Bodrunova(✉), Ivan S. Blekanov, and Nikita Tarasov

St. Petersburg State University, St. Petersburg 199004, Russia
s.bodrunova@spbu.ru

Abstract. Opinion cumulation on social networks has been widely researched upon; however, we still lack knowledge on its dynamics. In particular, political polarization that leads to echo chambering with democratically inefficient homophily of views is mostly studied in terms of resulting echo chambers and factors shaping it, but not in terms of formation dynamics; this may misinform understandings of the nature of echo chambers. The concept of cumulative deliberation [1] implies opinion divergence and growth of clusters of posts/comments that may contain differing opinions in online discussions, where a 'tug-of-war' model of winning the dispute may be traced. However, in our earlier work [2], we have shown that user discourse may diverge into neutral vs. politically opinionated clusters, rather than, e.g., left vs. right or loyal vs. oppositional. Our other research [3] shows that, in case of global or nationwide events, news content spreads first, and then, with a time lag, issues of public importance raise in the discussions. Combining this knowledge, we use Twitter data from Russia to reveal the dynamics of echo chambering as cumulation of neutral vs. polarized content in time. For that, we use a multi-step research pipeline that includes, i.a., web graph analytics, k-means clustering, creation of frequency vocabularies, Granger testing, and visual mapping. We show that echo chambers of news-based and opinion-based nature form in different time and depend upon the lifestyle of their actors. We detect cumulative patterns in formation of echo chambers, including one where the spread of news leads to discourse radicalization and one called 'the spiral of influence' in interdependence of clusters.

Keywords: cumulative deliberation · dynamic polarization · echo chambers · opinions · social media · clustering

1 Introduction

Political and social polarization has become a fundamental feature of today's political systems, both in democracies and countries with no stable democratic traditions. The growth of polarization has coincided with digitalization of social communication, and especially with the rise of social networking platforms. Complex relations between socially-mediated online discussions and political polarization have been studied practically since social networks have appeared on stage; however, evidence on whether social media truly foster polarization varies from full belief to full rejection.

A. Coman and S. Vasilache (Eds.): HCII 2023, LNCS 14025, pp. 167–182, 2023.
https://doi.org/10.1007/978-3-031-35915-6_13

A significant gap in online political polarization studies is that, in the overwhelming majority of cases studied, polarization is seen as a structural feature of discussions that leads to echo chambering, and echo chambers, in their turn, are viewed as stable elements of discussion structure consisting of users with particular stable positions. Several years ago, we have offered another view on discussion polarization [2], showing that echo chambers have a discursive, rather than structural, nature. This may imply that echo chambering is not divergence of users according to their ties in discussions, but divergence and co-development of certain discourses within online talk.

Another gap in online polarization studies is that echo chambers are assessed as finalized structures, rather than dynamic and flexible ones. Dynamics of echo chambering is assessed extremely rarely, partly because there is lack of conceptual thinking on how opinions accumulate online and how exactly they may cast impact upon offline deliberation. We have offered the concept of cumulative deliberation [1] that allows for seeing opinion cumulation as a neutral and dynamic process with systemic features that are yet to be discovered. Thus, we would like to unite both gaps in our current research and assess echo chambers as dynamic discursive features.

In our work [2], we have also shown that discursive echo chambers may be divided into those based on more or less neutral news and those politicized or even radicalized. Also, we have shown elsewhere [3] that news content tends to appear first in discussions, and then issues around the discussion topic arise, both nationally and cross-culturally. Having in mind all the abovementioned, we pose several research questions on whether news-based or politicized echo chambers appear first and how they shape the overall discussion dynamics.

For that, we use a previously marked-up Twitter dataset from 2013 where we had detected echo chambers; for a number of reasons discussed below, this dataset is more suitable for our studies than today's ones. We assess the dynamics of echo chambering discourses, including how participants changing positions affect them. The remainder of the paper describes our conceptualization (Sect. 2), research questions (Sect. 3), the research pipeline, pre-processing, and new methods applied (Sect. 4), results (Sect. 5), and their discussion (Sect. 6).

2 Cumulative Dynamics vs. Opinion Polarization in Online Talk

2.1 Dynamic Polarization as a Scientific Problem

Over the past 20 years, research on user polarization has become a major line within the studies of online communication in general and its deliberative quality in particular. There are many works dedicated to the dynamics of polarization (for example, see the review of works before 2011 on the simulation of opinion formation in [4], and modern reviews in [5, 6]), but not all aspects have been studied yet.

So far, the polarization process was investigated in three ways: by evaluating empirical data and modeling [7], via user surveys (including panel surveys) and experiments [8]. In early polarization studies, there were at least as many works that modelled polarization and growth of echo chambers online as the empirical papers, and they appeared no later than 2000, i.e., even earlier than most social networking platforms. By modeling polarization (mainly via system modeling), researchers have been investigating what states a polarized online discussion can come if seen as a closed system.

Back in 2000, by applying spin-Ising model and Monte Carlo simulation, a conclusion was made about two possible outcomes of forming opinions within a closed group. Simple communication rules, as the simulation showed, lead to complex dynamics and power law in how decisions are distributed over time. As a result, a closed community evolves either towards dictatorship or into a stalemate in which it is impossible to make any common decision [9]. Thus, the authors conclude that only an open society can make decisions democratically without evolving into either of the extremes.

Törnberg and colleagues [10] have shown that the polarization process obeys the logic of systems theory, as it has phase states and points of no return. Namely, they have documented the hysteresis effect, which means that the transition to a fragmented state cannot be reversed, even if the costs of returning to the previous state may increase. '[D]ue to systemic feedback effects, if polarization passes certain tipping points, we may experience run-away political polarization that is highly difficult to reverse' [10: Abstract]. Let us add to this that, as shown in an influential work by Sobkowicz and colleagues [4: 472], polarization consists of two components, namely a change in the opinions of users and the development of communication networks running parallel to each other and influencing each other over time.

Empirical research of online polarization studies real cases of polarization based on data from social networks (and many scientists still complain that there is little connection between modeling and empirical research – for example, models are not tested on real cases). Empirical studies discover the relations between polarization, on one hand, and exogenous and endogenous factors shaping discussions, on the other. Of exogenous factors, most often, cognitive (cross-cultural perspective) and technological (platform perspective) contexts are tested. Thus, Yarchi and colleagues [11] showed that polarization patterns differed significantly on three platforms – Twitter, Facebook, and WhatsApp – in three aspects: interactional (user interaction and their heterophile or homophile position preferences), positional (what political positions were voiced), and affective (what emotions and attitudes were expressed). It was shown that Twitter demonstrates the expected polarization (the discrepancy and mutual dislike of the echo chambers grew), whereas Facebook was the least polarized and even resembled a crossroads of opinions, and WhatsApp showed de-polarization over time, which contradicts the expectations formed by research based on modeling. Our own work [2] (referred to by Yarchi and colleagues as an example of contextual conditionality of polarization) showed differences in the patterns of fragmentation in Russia, Germany and the USA easily explained by the structure of political field and how it is mirrored on the platform.

However, in general, very few works specifically focus upon the temporal dynamics of polarization – e.g., on which type of content is the first to start forming the echo chambers. This is important, as, given the institutional nature of users, it immediately leads to another question – that on the roles of media on platforms as primary distributors of many potentially viral (and potentially one-sided) content pieces. It would also allow us to see whether the dissemination of verified and politically unbiased news can resist the formation of radical discussion clusters by hindering consensus and reducing aggression in discussions – or whether, on the contrary, the growth in the volume of news content leads to an increase in the volume of problematized content, in the intensity of the discussion as a whole, and in the speed of polarization.

Some research related to understanding how time works in discussions has also been done since the late 2000s. For example, by 2010, it became clear that conflictual discussions on certain issues (which we had designated as ad hoc conflictual discussions [12]) developed mainly in the first few days. Some studies pay attention to the first days in the discussion, as, in online communication, the dynamics of opinion formation is much more intense than in the daily news cycle. In a well-known work on dynamic debates [13], the first day of the discussion was used for evaluation. The authors showed that, in their case, the aspects of polarization could be divided into structural (interactive), positional, and affective, and affective parameters of polarization were those subjected to intense dynamics. More recent work on Israel also revealed that the polarization of positions and their deeper interpretations varied only minimally over time [14]. However, this is not always the case: In our work of 2021–2022, it is shown that users switch from sharing news content to discussing the agenda literally in the second hour of active discussion, and by the end of the day the agendas can even transcend to other language segments if its subject matter is global in nature [3]. Another interesting aspect of the understanding of time in cumulative deliberation is the 'time to reach consensus' that the researchers model, and the degree of polarization is measured just by the time needed to form a consensus [15]. However, such works do not answer the question on deliberation without consensus [16] – how do we assess the degree of polarization if consensus has not developed?

Experimental works have also inquired how we define what polarization is and what the role of social networks in shaping polarization could be. Is this a real discrepancy between users that would grow in time due to being in social networks – or is it about just identifying the existing user positions through the content of social media? Based on the results of an experimental survey, authors [8] showed that polarization detected via measuring of vector distances between US presidential candidates and between their respective parties depended on the content of tweets, in particular on their tonality: It increased in time if users saw more negative tweets. This effect does not coincide with simple choice of like-minded people and is produced by content-embedded frames. This proves that endogenous (discursive) factors in discussions may influence political preferences of their participants, and the strength of this effect may increase over time.

2.2 News Media Consumption and Political Polarization

Many studies have pointed out that the dynamics of polarization is related to the consumption of news. Thus, authors [7] found that high probability of the formation of echo chambers is associated precisely with polarized media consumption, but also (to a lesser extent) with (non-)tolerance to the opposite opinion and the speed of updating individual opinions. These dependencies stayed regardless of the size and structure of the Twitter segments on which the simulation was carried out. In another study [17], users were conditionally divided into 'mass market' and 'niche' (radical), as based upon consumption of certain media. The authors demonstrated that 'niche' users tended to form echo chambers and contributed more to polarization than the readers of mainstream media. Beam et al. [18] showed that Facebook, just like in the works mentioned above, created an opinion crossroads, and news consumption on this platform led to a slight de-polarization. Interestingly, in different working groups, news content is perceived either as either neutral (as opposed to political, issue-based, opinionated, or emotional one) or politically biased and containing different positions on a particular issue. So, the authors claimed that the de-polarization effects they found arose primarily due to communication between users who consumed news with opposing attitudes (counter-attitude news), especially if such communication happened accidentally.

However, very few studies examine how news (neutral) and issue-based (most often opinion-laden) content interacts throughout the entire time and space of a discussion. Here we will build on our earlier case studies. In 2019, we showed that, in very different contexts (in Russia, Germany, and the USA), in conflictual discussions on Twitter, it was not the left/right opposition but echo chambering based on the extent of content neutrality. In particular, news-spreading clusters separated from more politicized clusters [2]. However, our reconstruction was static, and whether news content shaped the development of the discussions as wholes or individual echo chambers was not asked. In 2021, via abstractive summarization, we showed (using the #jesuischarlie case), as indicated above, that conflictual discussions on inter-ethnic topics begin with news content, but very quickly move to bringing in background issues related to religion, human rights, professional journalism etc., and such a discussion becomes cross-border.

Taken together, our findings have raised questions about how the news discourse interacts with discussing political issues in time and how individual discursive echo chambers influence each other and the development of the discussion as a whole. As already shown above, interaction with news content by reading can lead to de-polarization, but if the content is shifted to radical positions, then, on the contrary, we can expect growth of polarization. But so far there are no works that would assess the mutual influence of news content and politicized content within one discussion.

The 2019 paper shows that discursive fractures are contextual (i.e., they do not repeat cross-nationally and partially correspond to the structure of the national political field in its fragmentation, but not the party structure). Therefore, to assess the interaction of news and politicized content, we will be looking at two discussions from those previously studied, where news vs. politicized clusters clearly formed. Operationally, this meant that, in each case, there had to be at least five clusters: a news-based one, at least two politicized/issue-based one, a group with mixed discursive belonging, and a group of users who did not belong to any of the previous cluster (the 'neutral' group which may not form any visible cluster). This condition was met by the cases of Russia (the conflict in Biryulevo, 2013, the dataset collected in 2014) and Germany (the conflict in Cologne, 2015–2016, the dataset collected in 2016).

3 Research Questions

For the current study stemming from the abovementioned ones, we have formulated the following research questions (RQs) aimed at detecting temporal cumulative patterns in online conflictual discussions and the roles of news content in the dynamics of the whole discussions and individual echo chambers in them.

RQ1. Which echo chambers arise first? Are they news-based or issue-based/politicized/radical?

RQ2. What are the temporal relationships between news-based and non-news-based echo chambers? Are they independent from each other, spur each other, or slow down the unfolding of each other?

RQ3. What is the relationship between the unfolding of echo chambers and the dynamics of the discussion in general? Is it independent of their growth, spurred on by one or more of them, or slowed down by them?

4 The Research Method

4.1 The Markup Procedures for Clustering Users

The study uses marked-up datasets prepared earlier by the working group to study discursive echo chambers in conflict discussions about immigrants/ethnic groups on Twitter in Russia, Germany and the USA. The markup was prepared as follows:

1. Web discussion graphs have been restored.
2. Within the graphs, influencers were identified by analyzing nine metrics – four absolute ones (number of tweets, comments, likes, and retweets) and five graph-based ones (betweenness, PageRank, degree, in-degree, and out-degree centralities). The lists of users ranged by metrics meanings were prepared; they were cut at approx. #100, depending on the exact metrics meanings; thus, 900 usernames were identified in 9 lists, one list per metric. Then repeating usernames were eliminated; the final lists included both the most active tweeters and commentators and the most influential ones.
3. The tweets of each influencer were pooled. The pools were coded from −2 to 2 for four variables marking the attitude to four political actors, namely the leader of the country, the ethnic minority, the radical majority, and the police/local authorities.
4. Using the Statistica package, *k*-means clustering users was carried out, groups of influencers were obtained based on combinations of their attitudes to four political actors. For each of the cases, three or four clusters of influencers were obtained, which showed the non-binary nature of the polarization of influential users.
5. Frequency vocabularies were obtained for each cluster of influencers within each country case. The vocabularies were cleaned with the help of expert reading of words common for different clusters. Thus, the vocabularies were made unique; they characterized the discourse of each cluster in a unique way.

Then, for the 2019 study, the vocabularies were applied to the polled tweets of the rest of the users (beyond influencers), in order to mark each user in each dataset as belonging to this or that discursive cluster. This helped identify the volume of discourse that would belong a particular cluster. A user was recognized as belonging to one or another cluster if at least two words from the unique cluster vocabulary were found in his/her tweet pool. The number of words needed to characterize belonging to a cluster was pre-tested; the two-lemma combination has demonstrated the optimal efficiency in detecting cluster belonging, which meant that many users would be clustered (that is, cluster reduction was avoided). As a result, five or six user clusters were obtained for each case: Three to four of them contained either news-based or politicized content, clusters, and there were also a mixed cluster (which meant that its users used lexicons from more than one vocabulary) and a group of non-clustered ('neutral') users.

Then, all the users were colored according to their clusters, and the discussion web graphs containing coloring were restored, in a version with the neutral cluster and in a version without it; the latter was needed in order to demonstrate the configuration of the polar and mixed clusters more clearly. The graphs were restored taking into account comments and reposts received by the users of the polar and mixed clusters. The resulting representations may be found in [2].

This research of ours has shown that user polarization did not follow the same pattern in the three countries. For our present study, we have chosen the Russian case, as it had distinct clusters which, however, overlapped significantly (unlike in the German case), which allows for suggesting that the clusters might be inter-penetrable, as previously argued by Bruns [19]. In Russia, we have seen a low degree of user homophily, although it was noticeable that the news-based and nationalist clusters did not mix and could be visually distinguished. The cluster of non-nationalist but anyway aggressive discourse of 'angry citizens' was also noticeable. The role of mixed discourse was virtually invisible in the discussion core; it did not have a distinct position in the graph that would allow for determining its role.

4.2 The Research Pipeline

Such representations of the discussions suggest that polarization (in terms of formation of clusters) may unfold in time; we assumed that it could be possible to trace the accumulation of clusters and their mutual influence over time. To answer RQ1 – RQ3, we used mapping based on the vocabulary application, but conducted it not only for users (more precisely, for their pooled tweets), but also for individual tweets. This time, due to very short individual tweets as units of analysis, belonging to a cluster was assigned by one word only from a particular vocabulary. We also tested the relationship between clusters through the Granger test, as well as the relationship between cluster and general dynamics of the discussion. We also point out that the datasets of the 2010s are used in the current study for two reasons: 1) they have low percentage of bots and trolls; 2) today, data collection from Western platforms is extremely difficult from the territory of the Russian Federation.

For the current study, the processing pipeline for the marked-up data includes data uploading, lemmatization and tokenization, user clustering and random double-checks, representation of tweets with metadata, including the user's mane, date, and class; aggregation of messages based on cluster-detection by user, by time, or as a combination of the two; and visualization. The datasets were lemmatized and tokenized using the nlp library, with the model adapted for Russian (ru_core_news_sm). Similarly, sets of words for each corpus were lemmatized.

Further, each tweet was assigned a cluster – based on the occurrence of one or more words from frequency vocabularies. If words from different clusters were detected in one tweet, the tweet was assigned a 'mixed' status; tweets without the words from the vocabularies were designated as neutral. One-word markup sufficed for short texts.

5 Results

To answer the RQs, we assessed the appearance of the marked-up tweets in time and conducted visual assessment and Granger causality tests, both throughout the discussion and for the first days. We also assessed user activity in changing their positions in relation to the volume of clusters and the whole discussion dynamics.

As stated in Sect. 4, we have visualized the accumulation of tweets and users in time in all the clusters of the discussion. The visualization is presented on Fig. 1 (three weeks) and Fig. 2 (its first two days).

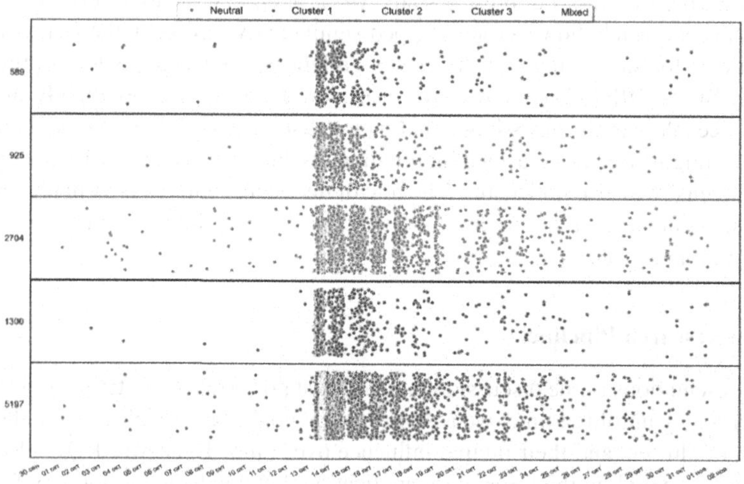

Fig. 1. Cluster dynamics in the Biryulevo case, Russia, three weeks (Color figure online)

Note for Fig. 1 and 2. Red: the mixed cluster; blue: 'angry citizens'; orange: the news-based cluster; green: anti-establishment nationalists; gray: the neutral cluster.

We have also assessed whether the dynamics of clusters affects each other and the overall intensity of the discussion.

We see that the start of cluster formation clearly depends upon the nature and lifecycle of the actors who form clusters. Thus, on the day after the alleged murder of young Muscovite Egor Sviridov by an Azerbaijani, ordinary citizens were the first to wake up (at circa 5 to 6 am). Then, by 8 to 9 am, the media and journalists who started work joined the discussion, and later, by 11 am to 12 pm, nationalist-minded users began to seize the talk (see Fig. 2). Thus, the first few hours of the discussion became key for unfolding of the echo chambers, which then did not change over time (see Fig. 1). This supports the results of previous studies on the rapid unfolding of echo chambers.

Note for Fig. 3 and 4. Red: the mixed cluster; blue: 'angry citizens'; orange: the news-based cluster; green: anti-Putin nationalists.

We do not see any serious radicalization of the discussion over time in general (see Fig. 3), but we see three bursts of radicalism within 2–4 h on different days (see Fig. 4), spurred mostly by the appearance of media information. We also see (Fig. 4) that the

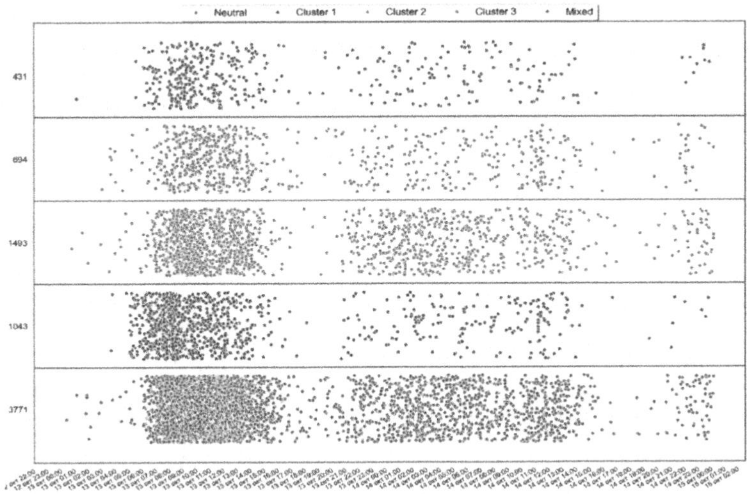

Fig. 2. Dynamics of clusters in the Biryulevo case, Russia, two days (Color figure online)

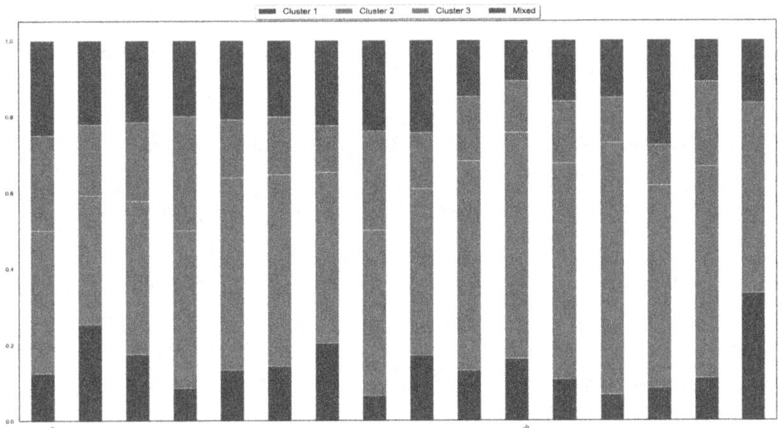

Fig. 3. Cluster dynamics in the Biryulevo case, Russia, the first three days, six-hour steps (Color figure online)

discussion intensity, partly shaped by nationalist influencers starting from the first hours, nevertheless decreased, as the percentage of two negative clusters did not grow but even decreased, while the news-based discourse increased, due to both media's active posting and reposts. The pattern of 'spreading news - > discussion radicalization' that within 3 to 4 h is also obvious (see curly brackets on Fig. 4).

The mutual influence of clusters, calculated via the Granger test, allows for identifying a 'spiral of influence' in how clusters depend on each other (see Table 1).

From Table 1 we see that the media and nationalists develop in the first discussion outburst as generally independent clusters that affect only each other, and the influence

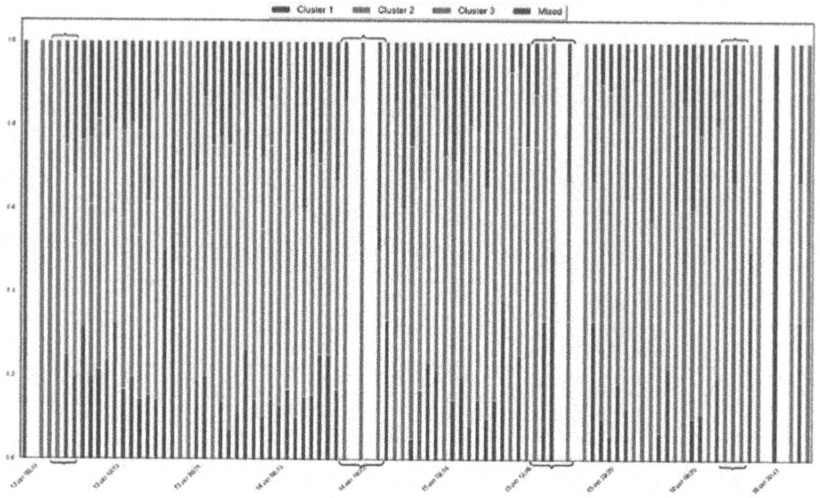

Fig. 4. Cluster dynamics in the Biryulevo case, Russia, the first three days, hourly steps (Color figure online)

Table 1. Mutual influence of clusters in the Biryulevo case, the first three days of the discussion, hourly steps

	Neutral	'Angry citizens'	News-based	Nationalist	Mixed	TOTAL
Neutral		Λ 12,75***	Λ n/s	Λ n/s	Λ 12,53***	Λ n/s
'Angry citizens'	Λ n/s		Λ n/s	Λ n/s	Λ 14,48***	Λ 10,07**
News-based	Λ n/s	Λ 4,37*		Λ 12,64***	Λ n/s	Λ 7,08**
Nationalist	Λ 5,22*	Λ 12,77***	Λ 5,26*		Λ n/s	Λ n/s
Mixed	Λ 6,16*	Λ n/s	Λ n/s	Λ n/s		Λ 5,45*
TOTAL	Λ 6,70*	Λ 16,33***	Λ n/s	Λ n/s	Λ 10,96**	

of the news on nationalists is more pronounced than the opposite. Taking into account the pattern of 'spreading news – > discussion radicalization' revealed on hourly steps, it can be argued that the 'spiral of influence' in the Biryulevo case developed as follows: news discourse spurred the nationalist one, then both of them spurred 'angry citizens', and then the 'angry citizens' spurred the mixed cluster and the total volume of the discussion. However, activity of 'angry citizens' also depended upon the total volume of the discussion and the volume of neutral tweets. Our conclusion of 2017 about the leading role of the network of nationalist users in directing this discussion, made via the analysis of the links between influencers without taking into account the temporal aspects of the discussion, has been confirmed in dynamics. Nationalists influenced individual clusters within the discussion (media, 'angry citizens', and the neutral cluster), and the volume of media discourse influenced the volume of discussion both directly (by reposting) and through other clusters that grew after reposting (nationalists and 'angry citizens'). However, in the Biryulevo case, while nationalists boosted the talk, it was news that played the role of regulating the volume of other clusters in the chain 'media – nationalists – 'angry'/neutral/mixed – the total intensity of the discussion.'

We also, as stated in RQ1, wondered why clusters are formed and remain stable. Is it users who choose a position once and for the entire discussion – or do clusters remain more or less stable or increase/decrease due to the influx/outflow of users who have joined them? To assess this, we have reconstructed the appearance of users in clusters (Fig. 5) and the change of user positions (the arrival of new users in clusters) (Fig. 6).

Figure 5 shows the presence of users with a certain position during the first days of the discussion; the position, as mentioned above, was assigned if at least two words from the cluster's unique dictionary were present in the user's message pool. The first appearances of users are shown. In Fig. 6, the picture is more complicated: The moments of the users' changes of position in a given cluster are shown, i.e., the moments of a user's transition to a particular discursive cluster.

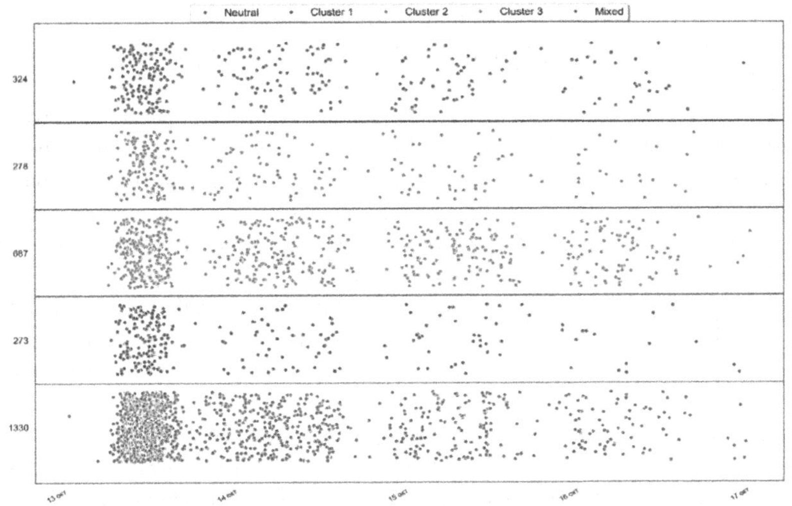

Fig. 5. Carriers of cluster discourse, Biryulevo case (Color figure online)

Note for Fig. 5 and 6. Red: the mixed cluster; blue: 'angry citizens'; orange: the news-based cluster; green: anti-Putin nationalists; gray: the neutral cluster.

On Figs. 5 and 6, we see that stability of clusters is maintained in two ways: It is the arrival of new users to the cluster who do not change their position later, and that of the users who have changed their position. The news cluster, as we see, grows due to the change of discourse more than the clusters of 'angry citizens' and nationalists. Due to this, there is a slight displacement of more radical discourses.

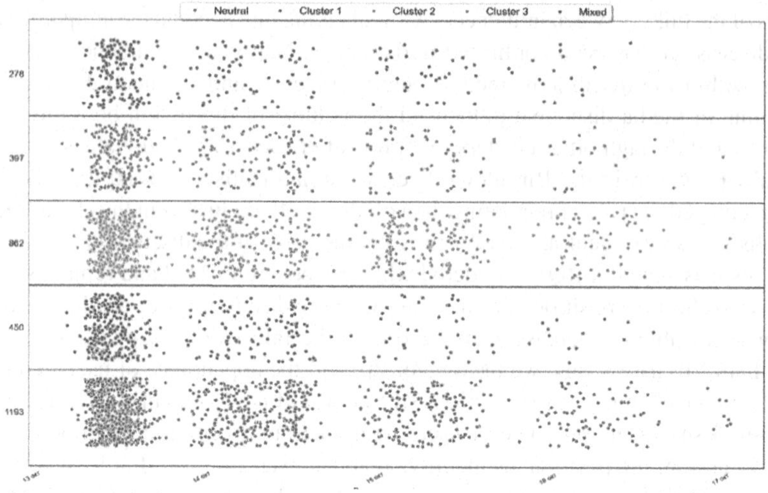

Fig. 6. Users who have changed the cluster, Biryulevo case (Color figure online)

We can interpret the data as follows. The first hours of the discussion are key when there is an outburst of negative sentiments and rifts in the discourse; echo chambers form on their basis in connection with the daily life cycle of participants. At the same time, a large number of users do not immediately identify with the cluster, but change it in the first hours. This may be due to the retweeting of news about the events and needs additional verification. But then consolidation of discourses takes place, when the clusters grow both by new participants in the discussion and by the change of positions of many users. Having thrown away the main critical energy in the first hours and not expecting any pronounced reaction from political institutions, as well as constantly reading news about the situation, users begin to repost news more than publish radical statements, and gradually radicalism comes to naught. There is 'learning of the news language' either by reposting or by interiorizing media vocabulary about the trigger event, and this process is somewhat more intense than it is for the nationalist discourse.

To test whether the clusters influence the dynamics of the discussion, we conducted another Granger. Here we assessed if the number of users who changed the discourse in each cluster and in general affects the dynamics of clusters and discussions in general (Table 2) – and vice versa, whether the dynamics of clusters affects the change of position by users (Table 3). The line 'unstable [users]' in the tables marks the users who change positions several times within one Granger test step (that is, within one hour).

Tables 2 and 3 confirm the independent nature of the media and nationalist discourses and additionally highlight the dependence of the dynamics of the cluster of 'angry citizens upon discourse dynamics in other clusters (news-based, nationalist, and unstable), as well as on the entire volume of changing positions in the discussion. Thus, it can be assumed that the cluster of 'angry citizens' has a reactive nature: As soon as news or nationalist tweets begin to spread (i.e., a number of users change the discourse through retweets), 'angry citizens' pick them up and discuss, and their discourse begins to grow in volume. The same happens with the neutral cluster, but under the influence of the mixed and

Table 2. The impact of changing user positions upon cluster dynamics, Biryulevo case, the first three days, hourly steps

	Neutral	'Angry'	News-based	Nationalist	Mixed	Total
Neutral	Λ n/s	Λ n/s	Λ n/s	Λ n/s	Λ n/s	Λ 4,71*
'Angry'	Λ n/s	Λ n/s	Λ n/s	Λ n/s	Λ n/s	Λ n/s
News-based	Λ n/s	Λ 7,42*	Λ n/s	Λ n/s	Λ n/s	Λ n/s
Nationalist	Λ n/s	Λ 6,04*	Λ n/s	Λ n/s	Λ n/s	Λ n/s
Mixed	Λ 7,89**	Λ n/s	Λ n/s	Λ n/s	Λ n/s	Λ n/s
Unstable	Λ 6,10*	Λ 15,89***	Λ n/s	Λ n/s	Λ 3,33†	Λ n/s
TOTAL	Λ n/s	Λ 12,05***	Λ n/s	Λ n/s	Λ n/s	Λ 10,08**

Table 3. Influence of cluster dynamics on the change of user positions, Biryulevo case, the first three days, hourly steps

	Neutral	'Angry'	News-based	Nationalist	Mixed	Total
Neutral	Λ n/s	Λ n/s	Λ n/s	Λ n/s	Λ n/s	Λ n/s
'Angry'	Λ n/s	Λ n/s	< 6,37*	< 6,27*	Λ n/s	Λ n/s
News-based	Λ n/s	Λ n/s	Λ n/s	Λ n/s	Λ n/s	Λ n/s
Nationalist	Λ n/s	Λ n/s	Λ n/s	Λ n/s	Λ n/s	Λ n/s
Mixed	Λ n/s	Λ n/s	Λ n/s	Λ n/s	Λ n/s	Λ n/s
Unstable	< 7,23**	< 6,99*	Λ n/s	Λ n/s	< 12,04***	< 6,21*
TOTAL	Λ n/s	Λ n/s	Λ n/s	Λ n/s	Λ n/s	Λ n/s

unstable clusters. This result is also confirmed by the opposite effect: The dynamics of news and nationalists affect how many users become 'angry citizens.' And the dynamics of an unstable cluster quite logically depends upon larger clusters of neutral, 'angry', and 'mixed' users, as well as upon the discussion volume, as, with the growth of large clusters, the number of those who retweet many different positions or discuss with different people inevitably grows. This conclusion about the distinction in the nature (independent vs. reactive) of clusters is new in the theory of political polarization in online discussions.

Thus, the research questions may be answered as follows.

RQ1. The echo chamber that appeared first was that of angry citizens, but then, within two hours, media took over, and after that, the nationalist cluster started to form. Thus, the growth of echo chambers is clearly linked to life cycles of the users who form them, especially media and local dwellers. Politicized clusters may appear first but they do not clearly form before media-based information spreads. It is legitimate to suggest that radicalization (and growth of the respective echo chamber) takes place after new portions of news content virally spread within the discussion. Thus, echo chambers influence each other's dynamics. Also, the clusters are permeable, and users change positions often enough to make the clusters truly fuzzy; the view on echo chambers as stable structures within discussions needs to be corrected.

RQ2. We have discovered that, within the Biryulevo discussion, there were autonomous and reactive clusters. News-based and nationalist clusters could be called autonomous, as they only spurred each other and were not heated by any other cluster. In contrast, the cluster of 'angry citizens' was highly reactive, being dependent in its development upon nearly all the other clusters, except for the mixed one. The latter, in its turn, grew if the overall volume of the discussion started to grow, which also included the neutral and 'angry citizens' clusters. Thus, the bigger the discussion was, the more space was occupied by an 'opinion crossroads', which may seem logical but is still unexpected as a result if one considers unavoidable cluster dynamics described by Conover and colleagues [20]. We have discovered a 'spiral of influence' in the chain of cluster growth: 'Media – nationalists – 'angry'/neutral/mixed – the total intensity of the discussion.' Thus, news-based clusters, despite not being the first to blow a whistle, could shape the volumes of other clusters and, via that, affect the intensity of the discussion, both directly and indirectly. These results are clearly supported as well in the assessment of cluster dynamics, as 'angry citizens' is the only cluster that is affected by other politicized and news-based clusters.

RQ3. We have shown (see Table 1) that the overall discussion growth is affected by how intensely news disseminate and by the number of 'angry citizens' as the biggest politicized cluster. Interestingly, the discussion growth did not depend on nationalist speakers whose leaders formed an internal chain of influential accounts inside the discussion [21]. Vice versa, the general dynamics of the discussion affects bigger clusters, those of mostly neutral and mixed character. As to the shifts of users and opinions between echo chambers, they do not affect the discussion growth.

6 Discussion and Conclusion

In this paper, we have shown that polarization and echo chambering in Twitter-based discussions looks different if assessed in dynamics. In particular, the echo chambers, indeed, form at the very first stages of discussing, but do not continue as stable discussion structures uniting certain users but more as discursive lines within user talk, with users coming and going. The dynamics of discursive clusters depends on both 'discourse carriers' and people who join the cluster temporarily by using particular lexicons characteristic for specific political attitudes. Seen that way, echo chambers look permeable, fuzzy, overlapping, and flexible, closer to the conceptualization by Bruns [19].

Our research shows that polarization dynamics may be subordinate in its beginning to the nature of the discussants and their life cycles; this is another contribution to echo chambering studies. For some reason, this commonsensical conclusion was not recorded in previous studies. And based on it, we can conclude that the life cycles of actors represented on the platform and in the discussion should be added to the number of exogenous factors of cumulative deliberation [1].

Our findings support what we have found in the *Charlie Hebdo* case via abstractive summarization, where the news discourse dominated for about an hour, and then issues like journalistic ethics, opposition to radicalism, religion, current politics, etc. began to penetrate into it [3]. We see this pattern in Fig. 2. Thus, the 'zero' stage in the development of polarization is appearance of conflicting news; 'one' is an explosion of concern and the first emotions; 'two' is the growth of a three-cluster confrontation (two politicized clusters opposing each other and the media discourse); 'three' is the relative extinction of radicalism due to its partial displacement by news and interiorization of news vocabulary by the discussion participants; 'four' is a general decrease in the discussion activity, if none of the clusters explodes again and there is no new trigger event. Interestingly, the distribution of news content provides for a tactical loss, but a strategic gain in terms of the deliberative quality of the discussion: The incoming news perceived negatively induces short outbreaks of nationalism but, in general, media content gradually displaces the radical one. Therefore, we can still recommend publishing news on social media as soon as they arrive, without waiting for a politically 'convenient' moment: even if this is followed by a small surge of radical commenting, the very presence of news for reposts can eventually drive the discussion tone closer to neutrality.

We have also detected that clusters in discussions may be independent, where dynamics is determined by internal logic and the actors' nature, or reactive, where dynamics is influenced by other clusters. Whether news-based and radical clusters tend to be more independent than the 'general public' ones needs further research.

The surprise was that the total volume of the position change does not affect the dynamics within the clusters, as in the case of Biryulyovo. Thus, the volume of changing positions is not a significant deliberative factor in our case. However, this as well deserves further investigation.

Based on our results, we can preliminarily claim that we have identified an actor-time pattern for the first (often key) days of ad hoc discussions on social media. It includes an explosion of citizens' concern, the reaction of the media and the opposite political cluster, the gradual vaporing out of dissent and substitution of radicalized speech by news content.

Acknowledgements. This research has been supported in full by Russian Science Foundation, grant 21-18-00454 (2021–2023).

References

1. Bodrunova, S.S.: Practices of cumulative deliberation: a meta-review of the recent research findings. In: Chugunov, A.V., Janssen, M., Khodachek, I., Misnikov, Y., Trutnev, D. (eds.) EGOSE 2021. CCIS, vol. 1529, pp. 89–104. Springer, Cham (2022). https://doi.org/10.1007/978-3-031-04238-6_8
2. Bodrunova, S.S., Blekanov, I., Smoliarova, A., Litvinenko, A.: Beyond left and right: real-world political polarization in Twitter discussions on inter-ethnic conflicts. Media Commun. **7**, 119–132 (2019)
3. Blekanov, I.S., Tarasov, N., Bodrunova, S.S.: Transformer-based abstractive summarization for Reddit and Twitter: single posts vs. comment pools in three languages. Future Internet **14**(3), 69 (2022)
4. Sobkowicz, P., Kaschesky, M., Bouchard, G.: Opinion mining in social media: modeling, simulating, and forecasting political opinions in the web. Gov. Inf. Q. **29**(4), 470–479 (2012)

5. Dong, Y., et al.: Consensus reaching in social network group decision making: research paradigms and challenges. Knowl.-Based Syst. **162**, 3–13 (2018)
6. Iandoli, L., Primario, S., Zollo, G.: The impact of group polarization on the quality of online debate in social media: a systematic literature review. Technol. Forecast. Soc. Chang. **170**, 120924 (2021)
7. Prasetya, H.A., Murata, T.: A model of opinion and propagation structure polarization in social media. Comput. Soc. Networks **7**(1), 1–35 (2020). https://doi.org/10.1186/s40649-019-0076-z
8. Banks, A., Calvo, E., Karol, D., Telhami, S.: #polarizedfeeds: three experiments on polarization, framing, and social media. Int. J. Press/Politics **26**(3), 609–634 (2021)
9. Sznajd-Weron, K., Sznajd, J.: Opinion evolution in closed community. Int. J. Mod. Phys. C **11**(06), 1157–1165 (2000)
10. Törnberg, P., Andersson, C., Lindgren, K., Banisch, S.: Modeling the emergence of affective polarization in the social media society. PLoS ONE **16**(10), e0258259 (2021)
11. Yarchi, M., Baden, C., Kligler-Vilenchik, N.: Political polarization on the digital sphere: a cross-platform, over-time analysis of interactional, positional, and affective polarization on social media. Polit. Commun. **38**(1–2), 98–139 (2021)
12. Bodrunova, S.S., Litvinenko, A.A., Blekanov, I.S.: Comparing influencers: activity vs. connectivity measures in defining key actors in Twitter ad hoc discussions on migrants in Germany and Russia. In: Social Informatics: 9th International Conference SocInfo 2017, Oxford, UK, 13–15 September 2017, Proceedings, Part I, pp. 360–376. Springer, Cham (2017). https://doi.org/10.1007/978-3-319-67217-5_22
13. Yardi, S., Boyd, D.: Dynamic debates: an analysis of group polarization over time on twitter. Bull. Sci. Technol. Soc. **30**(5), 316–327 (2010)
14. Kligler-Vilenchik, N., Baden, C., Yarchi, M.: Interpretative polarization across platforms: how political disagreement develops over time on Facebook, Twitter, and WhatsApp. Soc. Media + Soc. **6**(3), 2056305120944393 (2020)
15. Jain, G., Sreenivas, A.B., Gupta, S., Tiwari, A.A.: The dynamics of online opinion formation: polarization around the vaccine development for COVID-19. In: Qureshi, I., Bhatt, B., Gupta, S., Tiwari, A.A. (eds.) Causes and Symptoms of Socio-Cultural Polarization, pp. 51–72. Springer, Singapore (2022). https://doi.org/10.1007/978-981-16-5268-4_3
16. Jezierska, K.: With Habermas against Habermas: deliberation without consensus. J. Deliberative Democracy **15**(1) (2020). Art.13
17. Campbell, A., Leister, C.M., Zenou, Y.: Social media and polarization (2019). https://economics.uq.edu.au/files/15694/Zenou-Y-Social-Media-and-Polarization.pdf. Assessed 15 Jan 2023
18. Beam, M.A., Hutchens, M.J., Hmielowski, J.D.: Facebook news and (de)polarization: reinforcing spirals in the 2016 US election. Inf. Commun. Soc. **21**(7), 940–958 (2018)
19. Bruns, A.: Echo chambers? Filter bubbles? The misleading metaphors that obscure the real problem. In: Hate Speech and Polarization in Participatory Society, pp. 33–48. Routledge, London (2021)
20. Conover, M., Ratkiewicz, J., Francisco, M., Gonçalves, B., Menczer, F., Flammini, A.: Political polarization on Twitter. In: Proceedings of the International AAAI Conference on Web and Social Media, vol. 5, no. 1, pp. 89–96 (2011)
21. Bodrunova, S.S., Blekanov, I.S., Maksimov, A.: Measuring influencers in Twitter ad-hoc discussions: active users vs. internal networks in the discourse on Biryuliovo bashings in 2013. In: 2016 IEEE Artificial Intelligence and Natural Language Conference (AINL), pp. 1–10. IEEE (2016)

Management of Cultural Institutions. Case Study: Management of Performing Arts in Romania

Adela Coman(✉), Ana-Maria Grigore, and Andreea Ardelean

The University of Bucharest, Bucharest, Romania
{adela.coman,andreea.ardelean}@faa.unibuc.ro

Abstract. Cultural institutions are a part of any human community. The way these institutions are managed to leave their mark on our individual and collective evolution. Therefore, the managers of cultural institutions can play a role as a catalyst of change. As much as the external environment challenges increase and multiply (e.g. the COVID-19 pandemic; technological progress; changes of taste and preferences of consumers), cultural managers face a triple mission: to adapt their organizations to this new context, to find new ways of managing the relationship with the audience while creating an external framework flexible enough so as to allow artists to express their own visions and manifest their creativity.

The objectives of our study are the following: (1) to identify what the management styles are that cultural managers use as a consequence of recent evolutions in technology, health (the COVID-19 pandemic) and lifestyle (remote work, online learning, etc.); (2) to identify what the management strategies that they have adopted are in order to attract (new and old) audiences into the theaters while increasing financial sustainability and preserving the status of relevance of these institutions in their respective communities.

The research method is the sociological survey. In order to collect data, we asked managers of cultural institutions (theater, opera, operetta) – located in Bucharest, Cluj-Napoca, Timişoara, Arad and some other smaller towns in Romania – to answer our questionnaire and where possible, we interviewed some of them. As such, our research has a quantitative dimension, as well as a qualitative one. Descriptive statistics and correlational analysis are used for testing our hypotheses. Our case study addresses both public and private funded institutions.

This paper is organized in 3 sections: in the first part, we explain the conceptual framework of the performing arts and its management. In the second section, we discuss in detail the recent changes in the external environment and the way these challenges (profoundly) impact the performing arts. In the third section, we analyzed these evolutions from the cultural managers' perspective with an emphasis on their management styles and strategies they have adopted in order to survive and thrive in the future. A number of concluding remarks are presented at the end of the paper.

Keywords: cultural institutions · performing arts · management styles · management strategies

A. Coman and S. Vasilache (Eds.): HCII 2023, LNCS 14025, pp. 183–199, 2023.
https://doi.org/10.1007/978-3-031-35915-6_14

1 Introduction

One of the most distinctive outcomes of the crises of the kind provoked by COVID-19 pandemic did change convictions, alter perspectives and reinforced contradictions at the societal level. The cultural sector faces the challenges of technology while struggling to identify new ways of surviving (Bradbury et al. 2021).

The rapid pace of digitalization reduces the dependence on physical space and presence (Amankwah-Amoah et al. 2021). Cultural institutions are forced to reorganize, to adapt their operational models to the new reality and to look for alternative sources of funding.

The loss of proximity to their audiences is heavily experienced by the artists of the performing arts institutions in particular. In the last two years, consumers experienced less social interactions and less real emotions in the digital space. Digital communities of consumers are now connected with digital communities of performing artists.

As a result, patterns of cultural consumption and production are emerging and evolving. The way these cultural institutions are managed to leave their mark on our individual and collective evolution. Therefore, the managers of cultural institutions can play a role as a catalyst of change. Managers of performing arts institutions will need to find new ways to face risks and to reduce uncertainty over demand by developing new ways of facing a triple mission: to adapt their organizations to this new context, to find new ways of managing the relationship with the audience while creating an external framework flexible enough so as to allow artists to express their own visions and manifest their creativity.

This paper is organized in 3 sections: in the first part, we explain the conceptual framework of the performing arts and its management. In the second section, we discuss in detail the recent changes in the external environment and the way these challenges (profoundly) impact the performing arts. In the third section, we analyzed these evolutions from the cultural managers' perspective with an emphasis on their management styles and strategies they have adopted in order to survive and thrive in the future. A number of concluding remarks are presented at the end of the paper.

2 Literature Review

As far as concepts are concerned, culture is approached from the following perspectives: as an expression of human nature; an organizational factor of the society; a result of creative activity, as well as a set of norms that regulates the life of both society and human beings. It is through culture that knowledge, beliefs, traditions, attitudes, symbols, images, values, norms and artefacts are conveyed (Breban 1992). On the other hand, management is perceived as the science of organization and leadership of various institutions in order to provide high-quality goods and services. At first glance, culture and management may seem to be two contradictory terms. The former is commonly associated with self-expression and creativity while the latter represents regulated processes and hierarchies. However, if culture is to be institutionalized and possibly even financially lucrative, it has to be organized professionally. Cultural management emerges at exactly this intersection.

According to John P. Kotter (1990), cultural management is the art of planning, organizing, supervising and monitoring activities within the not-for-profit and for-profit arts and the cultural sector. These activities include management and administration. Cultural institutions were severely hit by the crises provoked by COVID-19 pandemic because so many of them had to close their gates and to cancel or postpone shows and events. The independent cultural sector lost its most important sources of funding: their audiences.

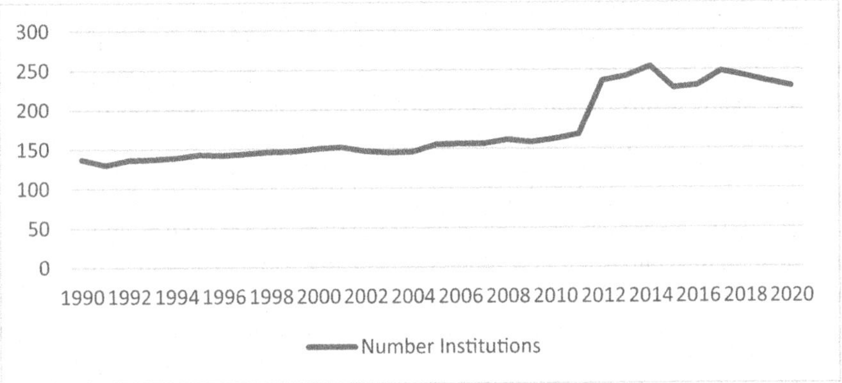

Fig. 1. Evolution of Performing Arts and Concert Institutions between 1990–202 Source: Romanian National Institute for Statistics

As we can see on the graph, the general trend of the emergence of performing arts and concert institutions had constantly been increasing in Romania until 2019. However, the unstable period caused by the COVID phenomenon led to the gradual closure of some of these institutions in 2020 and 2021 respectively, with a slight decrease observed (Fig. 1).

According to *Encyclopaedia* Britannica (2010), culture represents an "assembly of human knowledge, beliefs and behaviours" that transmits the accumulated lore to future generations and consists of "language, ideas, beliefs, customs, taboos, codes, institutions, tools, technologies, artworks, rituals, ceremonies and symbols". UNESCO confirms this definition: in a broad sense, culture may be appreciated as an assembly of spiritual, material, intellectual and emotional features that characterizes the society or the social group. Culture includes art, literature, lifestyle, cohabitation, as well as systems of values, traditions and beliefs.

The rapport between *management* and *culture* has known an ascending evolution starting with the 1970s when the beneficial influence of economic institutions on the cultural sphere was confirmed.

Cultural management is based on the premise of building a system which could extend the cultural industry from an economic point of view and, thus, increase the cultural level of society. According to contemporary specialists, management represents, before anything, an economic subject. However, going beyond the limits imposed by economy, this science may direct the institutions with cultural and artistic profiles towards a final product, a source of aesthetic and ethical values. Therefore, cultural management represents a major interdisciplinary activity which directly contributes to the development of cultural and artistic areas, thus becoming an educational, moral and aesthetic element – that is, an influential factor of the spiritual life for both society and individual (Dvoracic 2013).

Cultural management imposes listening and becoming aware of the changing process of reality, its in-depth analysis and adequate decision making to contribute to the growth of the sector, as well as reference social and artistic communitites. By definition, all changing processes generate opposition and discomfort within institutions of performing arts, as well as in its staff and traditional audiences. Decision-making, responsibility-division and result evaluation processes depend on values, procedures and their organizational culture as far as the performing arts are concerned (Bonnet and Schargorodsky 2017). A "discretionary" note within decision-making processes and a particular bohemian spirit may cause difficulty in reaching established objectives. Beyond dominant management styles within the public and private sectors of each country, institutions of performing arts encounter difficulties in building management models that are transparent, effective and efficient (Vasiliu 2004).

Dominated by new forms of communication and by the myriad of information means, postmodern culture imposes a new relativist mentality while manifesting in all social contexts, as well as artistic, stylistic, literary, philosophical and scientific orientations. The new relation between culture and society expresses the character of postmodern culture by representing a derivative of global changes. The author Mario Vargas Llosa, a Nobel Prize laureate, characterizes the contemporary civilization as a sick world in constant search of entertainment. This "civilization of performance" places entertainment at the top of the hierarchy of values. Well-being, freedom, laicism, the disappearance of the intellectual, culture democratization and entertainment promotion are placed at its basis by these aesthetic and moral declines. Communication techniques create various avant-garde ideologies and transform culture into a "contemporary supermarket" that offers the possibility to create a cultural similitude specific to personal preference.

Within the contemporary cultural context and, at the same time, under the influence of postmodernist ideology, performing arts suffer the metamorphoses of a new identity, different from their classic appearance – similar to the ones suffered by the entire society. Social, cultural and political factors of the century of speed become significantly imprinted on perfoming arts while modifying the audience's preferences and values. Digital technology and non-valuable mediatization carry out a powerful influence while generating dissonant hybrid artistic styles. Traditional cultural forms suffer radical experiments and metamorphoses, reinterpretations of meaning, decontextualization, as well as complete redefinitions. As proof, there are thousands of drama, lyrical and contemporary choreography shows intensely organized and promoted by the majority of managers of culture institutions. In his study entitled "Postmodernismul și identitățile culturale. Conflicte și coexistență [Postmodernism and cultural identities. Conflicts and Coexistence]", the philosopher, Virgil Nemoianu (2012), suggests the necessity of an immediate reconstruction of an equilibrium between the technical and economic progress, on the one hand, and the spiritual progress, on the other hand. Within these contexts, cultural management becomes an essential factor and an active participant in the value correction process of the postmodern society. In any organization, the manager is the responsible person for the performance of all the employees that are subordinated to him or her.

The manager's main role is to organize material and human resources that are at his or her disposal in order to help the organization to reach its goals and objectives (Croitoru, 2017).

According to legislation, the selection of the manager position in Romania (general executive) is carried out on the basis of a job competition on management projects concluded with the winner signing a contract with the respective institution (alin.2,3). Afterwards, the general executive is obliged to establish a board of directors with a deliberative role consisting of: deputy directors, a legal adviser, the union delegate and a representative of the central or local administration to which the institution is subordinated (cap.4 art.19, alin.1B). At the same time, the general executive has the responsibility to establish a board for the Arts. This has a consultative role and it consists of scholars coming from within, as well as from the outside of the institution (alin.2).

With regards to the funding of institutions of performing arts, these receive subsidies from the state or local budget depending on the case, from the budget of local or central authorities to which they are subordinated, but they also use their own income or the revenue from various sources (cap.5, art.20).

According to Byrnes (2009), the cultural manager's roles are as follows: planning and development; marketing and public relations; maintenance of relations with each head of department; human resource management; financial resources management, as well as maintaining the relations with the local and national authorities. In addition, one key-role of the cultural manager is represented by formal and informal communication – necessary for the good management of the relationship with his or her employees. According to the same author, the cultural manager is the person who controls classic management tools with the touch of an artist while using particularly needed creativity. The cultural manager needs to be intelligent, disciplined, responsible, committed and quick in decision making and conflict resolution he or she has the power to influence the community, its values and mindset the cultural manager is responsible of defining their own objectives on a social, educational and economic level and, last but not least, of harnessing all resources at his or her disposal, including the transmission of joy, connection and the sense of belonging" (p. 55).

3 Recent Changes in the External Environment: The Impact on Arts and Culture

One of the roles that culture has in a democratic society is to create diversified horizons of expectation, to convey experiences, to stir the interest for the myriad of ways in which life may be lived and understood. Briefly, it has to offer the social being the sensible needed tools for a complex and critical sense of reality (Vasiliu 2006).

To subsidize culture is a necessity – we are all aware of this fact. However, when culture is conditioned by political, financial and ideologic interests, it can become a powerful means of manipulating the audience's preference (Nita 2004).

We already know that, when compared to commercial marketing, cultural marketing proposes citizens a "truly special" kind of product and, consequently, it initiates an offer that ends up in demand in the spirit of the "truly special" kind of product. Thus, as mass culture has gained more ground, art has become a consumer product like any other under the pressure of globalization and, as a result, lost its sacred and emotional character. Therefore, culture may be sacred and inspirational, as well as a (purely) economic and entertaining product. Given this reason, the public subsidy for culture implies responsibility towards society and citizens; responsibility that equally belongs to the one who allots the resources, just like it belongs to the one that manages them (the cultural manager) (Suteu 2006).

Cultural consumption tremendously increased during the COVID-19 pandemic. Institutions of performing arts worldwide answered this by providing free access to shows in order to help people cope with the situation; to help them find meaning; to offer stories; to help people stay together given the absence of physical contact. Thus, we might have distanced from each other physically, but culture brought us back together.

However, performance shows are created by artists, intellectuals, thinkers and those people whose roles are crucial – organizers and technicians. In Romania, the Ministry of Culture has been quite slow with regards to the support provided to artists and staff from performance institutions. As a result, given the closing of show halls (most of them during a time period of one to five months), part of these people gifted with creative, intellectual and technical abilities set to serve to the configuration of a symbolic identity of communities, either reoriented themselves towards fields that were more productive financially (TV) or permanently left the artistic field.

National policy models that are in favour of culture – practiced by the French that generously finance it – have lost ground in favour of the planned Anglo-Saxon approach that is strict and "poor". The Anglo-Saxon model is more inclined towards the idea of culture perceived as a form of entertainment. This distorts the identity of communities and orients it (through an abundance of images and "recreational" manifestations) towards an effortless show that lacks depth (Croitoru and Craciun 2015).

Communication technologies geometrically multiplied this effect: cultural production, distribution and consumption have started to be confused. Immediate and total access to information, creation and "cultural product" created a sense of saturation at the level of selection: nowadays, we consume everything online without taking quality into consideration.

The consumer has become both producer and distributor. Thus, we moved from a society of "art connoisseurs" to one in which everyone is entitled to their opinion – as opinions are all equally considered. Rigorous cultural selection has been replaced by "I like it". As a result, "I like it", therefore, I consume it (Munteanu 2015).

Under the pressure of disruptive events, such as the pandemic, war, recession or climate changes, the Ministries of Culture from European countries have lost their symbolic power. Cultural administrations no longer match the evolutions of the cultural system; artist communities have started to fall apart; creations are "flowing" whereas subsidies allotted to culture and performance institutions, as well as their national methods of allocation can no longer keep up with European and global evolution of cultural practices.

In the absence of flexible management tools, cultural managers have tried to find their own solutions for redesigning and reconsidering the managerial act in such a way that it brings back into focus the intellectual and creative qualities of shows: an entirely risky and delicate mission as far as economy is concerned.

Our case study refers to the types of changes that occurred in the field of performing arts and to the way in which the managers of institutions of performing arts adapted to these changes (regarding practised management styles, as well as specific actions carried out within organizations).

4 Methodology

The research carried out is of an exploratory nature, having both a qualitative and a quantitative approach. In making the questionnaire, the basic principles were taken into account when constructing and designing the survey (Bolton and Brace 2022). Also, random sampling (Thompson 2012) was used when emails were sent to the managers of performing arts institutions from Romania. The data collection took place in May-June and November of 2022 and the sample consists of 23 persons, from which:

- 26% women, 74% men;
- 18% with musical studies, 55% - theater studies, 9% - foreign language studies, 9% - socio-human studies, 9% - technical studies;
- 73% from Bucharest and 27% not from Bucharest
- 18% - between 1–5 years of experience at work, 30% - between 5–10 years of experience, 30% - between 10–15 years of experience, 18% - between 15–20 years of experience, 4% - more than 20 years of experience at work
- age: 9% - between 21 – 29 years, 9% - between 30–39 years, 30% - between 40–49 years, 22% between 50–59 years, 30% - more than 60 years
- 48% - public funding, 52% - private funding

The data were processed in SPSS Statistics and the main method used in this study involves hypothesis testing, necessary in the process of determining whether there is a significant statistical difference to validate the above hypotheses. Because most of the variables included in the questionnaire are categorical then the following statistical tests will be applied: Pearson Chi-Square Test, the Linear-by-linear Association test - when there is at least one ordinal variable, the Fisher's exact test of independence and the Likelihood Ratio test - the most used ones in this research, being most accurate in the case of a small sample (Lehmann and Romano 2022). These tests take the form of two hypotheses to be verified (Taff 2018):

- *the null hypothesis*: No association between the two variables;
- *the alternative hypothesis:* Association between the two variables; in which situation the null hypothesis should be rejected whenever a p-value is less than 0.05.

The results can be guaranteed at a significance level of 90% with a margin of error of $\pm 15\%$.

In order to gain a more in-depth understanding of the subject, qualitative analysis was also applied, where the basic research method was the interview (Dawson 2019). The use of this method is recommended to be applied to small samples and it created the opportunity to identify patterns or repeated ideas that might emerge.

To test our conceptual framework, we performed nine in-depth interviews. We developed and collected primary data using the online survey of cultural institutional managers in Romania. We were also interested to check if there were differences and similarities between the Romanian art managers' approach and the art managers' from other countries in Europe.

The interviews provided useful data and nuances complementary to the survey. The interviews were based on open-ended questions prompting the respondents to engage in a storytelling approach to describe their experiences as art manager in a turbulent and volatile environment, along with their perceptions. In the end, meanings found from participants' experiences are described in a meaningful text organized in themes. (Sundler et al. 2019).

The interviewees' profile is presented in the following table (Table 1):

Table 1. The socio-demographic data of the respondents

Respondent Code	Title, Public/ private sector	Country	Gender, Age	Educational level
Interviewee 1	General manager, private sector	Romania	Male, +50	PhD
Interviewee 2	General manager, public sector	Romania	Female, + 40	Postgraduate University
Interviewee 3	General manager, owner, private sector	Romania	Male, +55	PhD
Interviewee 4	General manager, public sector	Romania	Female, +40	Bachelor degree
Interviewee 5	General manager, public sector	Romania	Female, +40	Bachelor degree
Interviewee 6	General manager, public sector	Romania	Female, + 40	Bachelor degree
Interviewee 7	Artistic Director, owner, private sector	UK	Male, +55	Postgraduate University
Interviewee 8	Manager, public sector	Czech Republic	Male, +45	Postgraduate university
Interviewee 9	Art manager, private sector	Norway	Male, +60	Bachelor degree

This qualitative research aimed to capture the art managers' perspective/opinions regarding the last years' "events" worldwide and how all the subsequent changes have affected their organizations. Questions were crafted in such a way in order to extract information about respondents' views of what happened (what the major challenges they faced were) and how they intend to proceed in the future - what type of strategy they have in mind in general, specifying human resources politics in particular; and, last but not least, if and how the relation with the public has changed.

In the process of completing our panel of interviewees, we tried as much as it had been possible to cover different types of people from both sectors: public and private. The interviews lasted about one hour and were transcribed to enable the use of direct quotations in this article. The sample of interviewees comprised 4 females and 5 males. All the respondents have a high level of education.

Hypotheses of the Research:

H1: Participatory management is practiced by the majority of managers of performing arts institutions.

H2: For the managers of private institutions, the main mission is to create their own aesthetic vision/options, while the managers of state-funded performing arts institutions - pursue the constant attraction of new audiences.

H3: More than 70% of managers of performing arts institutions have adopted the hybrid format as an effect of the COVID-19 pandemic (face-to-face shows, but also online shows).

H4: Over 90% of cultural institutions use social media as the main tool for communication and cultivating the relationship with the public.

H5: Identifying the factors that can influence the management style of managers of performing arts institutions among socio-demographic data: graduate profile, gender, age, seniority at work, location of the institution, financing method.

H6: There are differences in approaches between managers from Romania and managers from other European countries.

5 Findings and Discussions

When referring to the postmodernist ideology, respondents' opinions are divided: 5% totally agree, 26% partially agree, 26% partially disagree, 5% totally disagree and 39% are neutral.

The most important function considered by the managers so that the institution performs within society is the socio-cultural function with the lowest score of 1.7. This follows the political function with a score of 2.26, the educational function with 2.58, and last, but very close to the previous one, the economic function with 2.6.

The scores were much tighter in aspects related to the choice of the most important function that a manager performs within the institution, but the lowest score (2.26) belongs to planning and development, being closely followed by human resources management, with a score of 2.3 and the management of financial resources, with a score of 2.34. Next comes the relationship with the public (2.56), and then the relationship with local and national authorities (2.82).

52% of the respondents consider that the central objective of a manager should be on focusing how to constantly attract new audiences while 26% consider that it should consist in creating and following an aesthetic option of their own. Only 5% chose approaching aspects of social interest and 5% - inclusion of disadvantaged groups, while 12% considered other factors as being important, such as cultivating the emotional intelligence through performances. Contrary to expectations, most managers of private institutions just as most managers of state-funded performing arts institutions considered as essential the pursue of constant attraction to new audiences. Both categories considered as less important – creating their own aesthetic vision/options.

When it comes to the strategy that managers want to use to achieve the proposed goals, opinions are also divided: 30% focus on the pursuit of artistic excellence, 30% on the transformation of the institution into a territorial cultural standard, 13% on providing opportunities to artists at the beginning of their careers, 9% on facilitating the access of citizens from all social categories to the act of culture and 9% on valuing the national cultural heritage.

The most preferred managerial style is the participative management with 57%, followed by management based on objectives with 30.4% and, at a great distance, management through budgets with 5%.

Within the organization that they lead, 52% never call for delegation, 30% - rarely and 18% - often and, when making important decisions in their organization, most of them consult with their subordinates. 45% consider that the formal hierarchy is precisely respected while the rest consider that it is not.

36% feel like the focus falls on achievement of tasks and objectives while the rest choose the relative balance between tasks and people. No one considered human aspects (people's social problems and human contacts) as important.

The actions that the managers have in mind to achieve the proposed objective have the following order:

- Capturing attention and attracting new audience (community orientation) with a score of 1.7;
- Exploring the aesthetic side (artistic orientation) with a score of 2.13;
- Constant satisfaction of the public's direct requests (customer orientation) with a score of 2.3;
- Increasing/maximizing profit through a better management of financial resources (orientation towards profitability) with a score of 2.5;
- Obtaining awards and, in this way, a very good reputation from critics (orientation towards social prestige) with a score of 3.13.

Most managers during the COVID-19 pandemic organized and offered online shows and 67% of the total respondents continued to offer online shows even after the end of the COVID-19 pandemic. To a great extent, 27% considered that the preservation of online shows was and is still influenced by the changing lifestyle of the audience-spectator while 27% considered that to a small or to a very small extent and 45% of the respondents still do not have clear opinions about this aspect.

The main traditional and classic means of communication used in managing the relationship with the spectators were ordered by the respondents, as follows:

- Facebook with a score of 1.63
- Instagram with a score of 2.09
- the radio with a score of 2.27
- newsletters with a score of 2.54
- advertising campaigns with a score of 2.9
- the television with a score of 3.09
- Twitter with a score of 4.8

Table 2. Analysis of potential influencing factors

Factor	Associated variables
Age	–
Gender	central goal; strategies in achieving the goal; actions to achieve the proposed objective
Graduate Profile	agree/disagree with postmodernist ideology; appeal to delegation; the emphasis falls on the achievement of tasks and objectives or on the relative balance between tasks and people; organize or not online shows during and after the COVID crisis; compliance or not with the formal hierarchy
Seniority at work	appeal to delegation
Location of the institution (Bucharest or others)	the main traditional and classical means of communication: Twitter; organizing and offering online shows during and after the COVID crisis; the emphasis falls on the achievement of tasks and objectives or on the relative balance between tasks and people
Financing method (public or private funding)	the main traditional and classical means of communication: television, Twitter, Instagram; orientation towards social prestige; agree/disagree postmodernist ideology

Source: Our elaboration using SPSS Statistics based on questionnaire answers

Age does not influence managers' decisions, strategies or options and there is a connection between seniority at work and appealing to delegation. Women, as managers of institutions, generally consider that the central objective of their mission is the creation and pursuit of their own aesthetic option, while men emphasize the constant reaching to new audiences. The strategy used by the majority of women includes the transformation of the institution into a territorial cultural standard, while the majority of men choose the search for artistic excellence. At the same time, women also consider it very important to explore the aesthetic side (artistic orientation) compared to men in order to achieve the proposed objective. The performing arts institutions in Bucharest, compared to those in the country, do not use Twitter as one of their main means of communication; they emphasize the balance between tasks and people, and they offered online shows during and after the COVID crisis. The profile of the completed studies plays an important role regarding topics as to agree/disagree to the postmodernist ideology; whether to appeal to delegation; whether to choose the achievement of tasks and objectives or a balance between tasks and people; to organize or not online shows during and after the COVID crisis; compliance or not with the formal hierarchy. Managers of institutions that receive public funding compared to those that receive private funds are more inclined to agree with the postmodernist ideology, to be focused on social prestige and to use television, Twitter and Instagram as the main means of communication (Table 2).

In the remaining part of this section, we selected quotations from the art managers' responses to illustrate the main traits of organizational management of last years.

Inevitably, the social crisis generated by this prolonged pandemic episode, with its sudden and explosive occurrence, forced management at all levels – social and economic – to make decisions and take actions on the spot, a reactive behavior. The first priorities were directed to "reasonable functionality" or often mere survival in harsh economical conditions and serious challenges of social and medical nature. Among others, the cultural organizations were badly hit.

Cultural organizations not only needed to adapt to society's new ways of working, but they also needed to become 'fit for the future'.

In such a context, the management actors and instruments proved their creative capacity; they delivered new managerial approaches and new models that were appropriate and effective. Among these, we should mention the outbreak of a new managerial concept: *the management of atypical crises*, which, through innovative solutions could reduce negative effects and build new basis to restart and revive the mechanisms of resilience and growth (Nicolescu 2022).

Yet, another tendency should be observed: the capacity of top-leaders and managers to *pivot* in real time, to change the decisions and directions of action, to adjust to turbulent and atypical contexts. As the following art manager explained:

"We tried to reinvent ourselves and the most important step we had to take was to leave the theatre hall (which the audience could not enter for quite a long period of time) and to create an outdoor season in which, beside the paying audience, we also had many random spectators – the majority of whom were probably attending a show for the first time in their lives." (I3).

The *agility* and *resilience* of an organization imposed new lines of coordination in many companies. These ad-hoc politics helped firms to go on, to retain the human resource and preserve an otherwise fragile financial balance. As one art manager explained:

"Fortunately, we managed to find solutions in order to continue our activity in such a way that our staff were not affected. Technical and artistic teams worked tremendously, and, as a result, we managed not to cancel the projects we had proposed before the pandemic except for one. Not to work for a long period of time could have meant catastrophic effects on each of us and, moreover, on the dynamics of the entire group." (I3).

Also, another tendency in managerial decisions in these times has been observed: to design and implement agile, flexible strategies, capable to face complex, sinuous evolutions, more than often unforeseeable. One of the interviewed managers underlined that he is preoccupied by:

"Constant adaptation to the changes that are taking place, flexibility, strategies to increase the number of events, as well as national and international collaborations, the approach of current and acute topics for humanity – attention towards the environment, global warming, etc." (I5).

Many of the cultural organizations reset their approach, developing new ways of working – and new approaches to creating and distributing art (creating shows with smaller casts, outdoor theater, performances filmed, making attractive ticket offers) – and showing ambitions to embrace further changes that will allow them to flourish in the future.

Analyzing the received responses, we identified several types of strategies born in the pandemic:

The *"replicating"* strategy which – through a set of well-based decisions directed mainly to reduce costs and the number of material assets – stops the downturn of income, provides financial stability and redeems the profitability, generating resources for future growth (Nicolescu 2022). As managers comment:

"We have created shows with small casts; we signed partnerships with theatres from Bucharest that had shows in Ploiești; during the summer of 2021, we built a stage in the courtyard of the theatre and seat rows for 80 spectators; Despair makes you come up with new ideas! You do not want to lose the contact with your audience." (I.4).

"It was a challenge to completely wake up one day entirely isolated. We tried the online option as well, but this implied a different approach, additional technical requirements for recording, specialist teams and equipment that would contribute to the implementation of the show and, obviously, additional marketing costs. With the definite advantage that this would keep us together, we enjoyed the interaction and the fact that we had the possibility to have a particular continuity in our connection with our loyal audience. Moreover, in this way, we managed to reach another type of audience that would not have been reachable otherwise, that is, the Romanian diaspore. At the same time, it was a challenge to handle the costs that had continued to flow – we managed to renegotiate the rent of the building, but it was still a mandatory monthly expense." (I1).

The *"opportunistic" strategy*, that takes advantage in a rapid and effective way of all the occasions that the new context offers, has eventually changed the trajectory of the firm, sometimes temporarily, sometimes permanently (Nicolescu 2022).

"The pandemic "inspired" us: we had 3 outdoor shows, as well as shows in the city. We projected on the façade of the theatre while the spectators attended the show and posted pictures on social media. We had recorded shows to archive before the pandemic had started, but they were of poor quality (we did not have the necessary digital infrastructure). However, we ended up recording better shows on VIMEO due to the pandemic – therefore, if there are similar situations in the future, we will have high-quality recordings in the archives." (I5).

For the post-pandemic era, we detect other patterns:

The *"recovery" strategy* aimed to reach the quantitative and qualitative levels of organizational performance in a few years, as in previous periods before the crisis, through revamping production, human resources, networks-in innovative ways (Verboncu 2018).

We selected the following reactions:

"This is a re-setting phase. We are looking at new producing and marketing models that can re-energize our work. It will soon be back at the original pre-Covid levels – but we need to re-ignite audiences further"(I7).

"I would describe it as the big inhale phase before a new exciting adventure". (I8).

"Financially, we are still in a rehab period". (I1).

Oriented growth strategy aimed to reach better overall performances compared to previous results, to strengthen the capacity and competitiveness of the organization in its environment (Verboncu 2018).

We selected the following answers:

"Due to definite and reasonable objectives, as well as a rather linear increase, we managed to establish the foundation of a new building." (I6).

"Development strategy, 1–2 big shows per year, the increase of the number of cultural soirees with 20–30% every year." (I2).

Although the pandemic has caused significant economic and psychological hardship, particularly for those working in the arts and cultural sector, many people turned to the arts as a vital means of coping with the challenges of the pandemic (Bradbury et al. 2021). In addition, some of the art managers also appreciated that the *public* were nearby them:

"Fortunately, the relationship with the audience does not seem to have been affected as the attitude is the same with a part of the audience being loyal to shows and returning to attend all our shows. We have kept in touch with them via means of mass media as my colleagues were responsible of this aspect during the pandemic. Somehow, we managed to encourage one another." (I1).

"No, the relationship with the audience has not been affected – we tried to keep them close to us." (I6).

"As manager, you do not only take over an institution and manage a few salaries. You take over something that is more important, meaning the audience. We have tried to reduce or even revoke the distance between us and the spectators in the last years regardless of the conditions imposed by the restrictions." (I3).

An idea, as brilliant as they come and a manager as competent as they come-will not be carried out without *resources.* Some of the managers interviewed reported difficulties with both human and financial resources:

"It was difficult to get the actors back together after the pandemic. It was even more difficult to get them back independently. They rushed towards television or job positions that provided a stable income." (I2).

"We found that there is a growth in people leaving theatre to work in the TV and Film - the technical part - sound and lighting. Trade fairs are all back post-covid and so, a lot of staff have moved into these areas – so we are really struggling to find good technical people." (I9).

"In management terms, it is very hard to get good marketing and digital content employees because they can earn much better money elsewhere. So we run a number of internship schemes to try and get graduates to work with us – even if it is for a short period of time."(I7).

It is well-known that essential for a cultural institution manager is the ability of "public relation" and "team building" (Verboncu and Nicolescu 2011).

So, as we discussed above, in Romania, the relationship with the audience does not seem to have been affected, the attitude is the same, part of the audience is a loyal one who returns to all the shows; in the Czech Republic (another post-communist country): first, the percentage drop in attendance, but with the beginning of winter, there came an unexpected increase that may have eclipsed the best seasons before COVID crisis, and so far, the trend has continued; in the UK and Norway: digital world/ Netflix has definitely had an impact on how people want to spend their time and hard work is needed to get the public away from the TV and direct it into live space again.

Regarding the relation with the employees: everyone was looked after and financially supported during COVID, but after this, the following phenomena were recorded in some places: a growth in people leaving theatre to work in TV and Film and struggling to find good technical people because a lot of them moved in other fields.

It is clearly outlined that managers and leaders need new ways of approaching risks in order to truly confront the economic changes and challenges that will come. Leadership has become more practical and more pragmatic, top-down and bottom-up. Problems are too big and too many to be solved only by the leader – "lone hero" – in the role of the saviour (Cornea 2023). This tendency of leadership to be more open, more empathic and more collaborative is reflected within the results of our inquiry as well. Thus, the dominant style is the participative one: people's involvement and accountability are employed, and we may observe a tendency towards the balance between the focus on results and the focus on people."

Another tendency in management – driven by the pandemic – may be recognized, and that is the intensification of humanistic management. This greatly focuses on people, their personalities, necessities, aspirations, expectations, emotions, their relationship with others, emotional intelligence, social climate, the ambience of the workplace, as well as individual and organizational resilience (Nicolescu 2022).

As a conclusion, the biggest challenge in Romania concerned the transition to an online platform, because this involves a different approach, additional technical requirements for recording, teams of specialists and equipment to do this, and additional marketing costs. UK deals with problems like Brexit – that has impacted the ability to produce work with international partners, to tour in Europe and reduced access to funding; or the Ukrainian war that has removed many international partnerships both in Russia – where they are not allowed to work –, and Ukraine – where they cannot work; or with young writers not being interested in writing for the stage and more interested in YouTube videos, social media etc. A big change in Norway nowadays seems to be a focus on family and children; more exactly, a high focus on work for youth could mean new funding will be allotted.

In the Czech Republic, within the social sphere, the gap between the poor and the rich is becoming wider, experiencing also a general rise in prices, which is affecting the social sphere that causes a decrease in the audience.

Overall, in Romania, the public is relatively constant, the social part being still an essential component and the performing arts institutions were not being affected by the fact that they had been facing problems in the field of digitalization. Economically developed countries, such as the UK or Norway, are facing decreases in the number of audiences caused by much more accessible options, such as Netflix or TV. Here, a feature of citizens' convenience is observed. In the Czech Republic, a fluctuation in the number of spectators was observed, from very few to more and more, all against a backdrop of panic related to resources and energy. Surprisingly, Romanians are rather faced with political games and complicated laws which constrain the cultural sector. Unlike Romania, the minimum wage of the staff from performing arts institutions and the increase in the cost of living are considered to be the biggest challenges in other European countries.

As common elements, in all countries during the COVID crisis, performing arts institutions received funds to survive and there were problems in reestablishing their technical teams almost everywhere.

6 Conclusions

The statistical test results support H1, H3, H4. H2 are partially supported because there are no significant statistical differences between the two types of managers (of public and private institutions), both choosing to pursue the constant attraction of new audiences. For H5, the only irrelevant factor is age. All the other socio-demographic data correlate with different characteristics that define management style. H6 was supported as well, but a few similarities were also identified.

As shown in our study, participative management is practiced by the majority of managers of performing arts institutions. The cultural managers' behaviour is a reactive one while their strategies have put on a variety of forms specific to the management of atypical crises: the reduction of negative effects generated by the crisis, as well as the construction of a new beginning through the call made for innovative solutions have all been stressed.

Several types of the strategies we have identified are the following: the replicating strategy (oriented towards cost reduction); opportunism as a strategy of harnessing the advantages of the crisis; recovery strategy (returning to the pre-pandemic levels of performance); growth-oriented strategy (reinforcement of the institutional capacity and competitiveness).

Cultural managers have acutely experienced the need to invest in technology. Recorded and high-quality online shows are requested by a larger audience and they are absolutely necessary under crisis situations. With the possibility of using artificial intelligence and virtual reality, will cultural managers manage to create the feeling of connection between artists and spectators that we can only experience within show halls filled with an audience nowadays? How may the performance institutions contribute to the contouring of community identities and to the generation of a constant creative flow that may support values, preferences, customs and manifestations specifc to a democratic society?

The limits of the present paper are mainly linked to the limited number of respondents from Romania and abroad who answered our questions (questionnaire and interviews).

As future research directions, we believe that it may be useful to explore and research the following: the chains responsible with the creation of values of the business-to-client type applied to the perfoming arts field; the consumer's satisfaction used as a measuring indicator of the show within performing arts institutions that provide the classic format, as well as the online show; last but not least, strategies specific to atypical crises with which we are faced more often nowadays.

References

Amankwah-Amoah, J., Khan, Z., Wood, G., Knight, G.: COVID-19 and digitalization: the great acceleration. J. Bus. Res. **136**, 602–611 (2021)

Bolton, K., Brace, I.: Questionnaire Design: How to Plan, Structure and Write Survey Material for Effective Market Research, 5 edn. Kogan Page (2022.) ISBN-13: 9781398604148

Bonnet, L., Schargorodsky, H.: Managementul teatrelor. Modele si strategii pentru organizatii si institutii de spectacol, Ed. Pro Universitaria, Bucurest, (2017)

Bradbury, A., Warran, K., Mak, H.W., Fancourt, D.: The Role of the Arts during the COVID-19 Pandemic, London (2021)

Breban, V.: Dictionar general al limbii romane [General Dictionary of the Romanian Language], vol. 1, p. 235. Enciclopedica Publishing House, Bucharest (1992)

Byrnes, W.: Management and the Arts, 4th edn. Taylor & Francis, Focal Press (2009)

Cornea, R.: Portretul liderului in criza, Business Magazine (2023). https://www.businessmagazin.ro/actualitate/afaceri/portretul-liderului-in-criza-ce-caracteristici-trebuie-sa-aiba-seful-21598329

Croitoru, C., Craciun, A.: Managementul cultural. In Barometrul de consum cultural 2015. Preferinte, practici si tendinte, INCFC, Bucuresti (2015)

Croitoru, C.: Particularitati ale marketingului cultural, Ed. Pro Universitaria, Craiova (2017)

Dawson, C.: Introduction to research methods, 5th edn. Robinson (2019)

Dvoracic, A.: Managementul cultural in contextual actual, ASACHIANA – Revista trimestriala de Biblioteconomie si Cercetari Interdisciplinare, 2nd year, vol. 1, oct-dec (2013)

Encyclopaedia Britannica, vol. 4, Bucharest, Litera Publishing House, p. 319 (2010)

Kotter, J.P.: A Force for Change: How Leadership Differs From Management. The Free Press, New York (1990)

Lehmann, E.L., Romano, J.: Testing Statistical Hypotheses. Springer, Cham (2022). ISBN 9783030705770

Munteanu, A. M.: Noile media, Ed. Universitara, Bucuresti (2015)

Nemoianu, V.: Postmodernismul şi identităţile culturale. Conflicte şi coexistenţă, Editura Universitatii. Alexandru Ioan Cuza, Iasi (2012)

Nicolescu, O.: Chapter 1 - Provocari si abordari innovative manageriale in contextul pandemiei de COVID-19. In : Nicolescu, O., Popa, I., Dumitrascu, D. (eds.) Abordari si studii de caz relevante privind managementul organizatiilor din Romania, Editura Pro Universitaria, pp. 11–30 (2022)

Nita, A.M.: Strategii de marketing in teatru. Oscar Print, Bucuresti (2004)

Ordonanța nr. 21 din 31 ianuarie 2007 privind instituțiile si companiile de spectacole sau concerte, precum si desfăşurarea activității de impresariat artistic. Emitent: Guvernul României, Monitorul Oficial nr. 82/2 februarie 2007 (2017). https://legislatie.just.ro/Public/DetaliiDocument/79172

Sundler, A.J., Lindberg, E., Nilsson, C., Palmér, L.: Qualitative thematic analysis based on descriptive phenomenology. Nurs **6**, 733–739 (2019)

Suteu, C.: Another Brick in the Wall. Brockman Studies, Amsterdam (2006)

Taff, A.: Hypothesis Testing: The Ultimate Beginner's Guide to Statistical Significance, Createspace Independent Publishing Platform (2018). ISBN: 1718665032

Thompson, S.: Sampling, 3 edn. Wiley, Hoboken (2012). ISBN-13: 9780470402313

Vasiliu, D.: Politici culturale. Secvente majore. UNATC, Bucuresti (2004)

Vasiliu, D.: Repertoriu de politici culturale. UNATC, Bucuresti (2006)

Verboncu I.: Cum conducem? Editura Universitara (2018)

Verboncu I., Nicolescu O.: Managerial re-projection in cultural institutions, In: International Conference Modern Approaches in Organisational Management and Economy, Faculty of Management, Academy of Economic Studies, Bucharest, Romania, vol. 5, no. 1, pp. 640–646 (2011)

Twitter as a Communication Tool for Flood Disaster Mitigation in Jakarta

Muhammad Hazim Khabir[1(✉)], Achmad Nurmandi[1,2], and Misran[1]

[1] Department of Government Affairs and Administration, Universitas Muhammadiyah, Yogyakarta, Indonesia
{muhammad.hazim.psc22,misran.psc20}@mail.umy.ac.id, nurmandiahmad@umy.ac.id

[2] Department of Government Affairs and Administration, Jusuf Kalla School of Government, Universitas Muhammadiyah Yogyakarta, Yogyakarta, Indonesia

Abstract. This study aims to analyze disaster mitigation communications and communication patterns between the people of Jakarta and the government in handling floods via Twitter. This type of research will use a descriptive qualitative approach. This paper will use Nvivo12. The primary data source for this research is the activity records of Twitter users using the hashtag #tinggimukaair #peringatandinijkt. The findings in this article are digital communication via Twitter with hashtags including #tinggimukaair #peringatandinijkt. The hashtag #tinggimukaair is used to find information on the height of the flood level, and the location of the flood. Meanwhile, the #peringatandinijkt hashtag is used by the DKI Jakarta Provincial Government to share information related to disaster mitigation, such as rainfall, and center number assistance. With digital communications interconnected with point-to-multipoint (PMP) channels, one of the features frequently used on Twitter is the use of hashtags used on government and public Twitter accounts. The use of hashtags on Twitter is of course to build awareness of the disasters that have occurred in Jakarta, especially in dealing with floods that occur every year.

Keywords: Twitter · Hashtag · Digital Native · Mitigation

1 Introduction

Providing emergency information to population living in the vulnerable areas, therefore, has become a measure of disaster resilience and a policy priority (Feldman et al. 2016). Given the increasing presence of social media in everyday life, it can be a major platform for sharing emergency information such as warnings, disaster relief efforts, crisis mapping for escape routes, search and rescue, and connecting community members following a disaster (Houston et al. 2015). Twitter is one of the prime social media platforms, which has been used not only during emergency situations, but it also changed the way people create, disseminate, and share emergency information (Li et al. 2018). The real-time characteristic of Twitter makes it a suitable crowdsourcing platform for dissemination and collection of information including texts and pictures during disasters and crisis events (Yuan and Liu 2018). As twitter generates a large of amount of

A. Coman and S. Vasilache (Eds.): HCII 2023, LNCS 14025, pp. 200–211, 2023.
https://doi.org/10.1007/978-3-031-35915-6_15

data, the researchers have attracted to analyse this data. The data can reveal different aspects of user behaviour which is useful for companies to provide online services, create awareness among people and use people network to make decisions for government institutions. As twitter is one of the most prominent social networking site used by people to express their views in the form of a tweet (Sujay et al. 2018). In the digital era, many actors can use social media. Apart from individuals, the government uses social media to interact with the community virtually to increase participation and accountability. New media such as the internet, applications, and social media create a new interaction style between the government and society (Nurmandi et al. 2020).

Social media is defined as websites and applications that enable users to create and share content or to participate in social networking. These sites provide a platform for discussion on issues that has been unnoticed in today's world. It is one of the most modern and favourite form of social media including many features and social characteristics in it. It has many advantages on same channel like as communicating, texting, images sharing, audio and video sharing, fast publishing, linking with all over world, direct connecting. It is also a cheapest fast access to the world so it is very essential for all age group of peoples. Information and communications technology (ICT) refers to all the technology used to handle telecommunications, broadcast media, intelligent building management systems, audio visual processing and transmission systems, and network-based control and monitoring functions (Kumari 2020).

Information Communication Technology (ICT) defines and revolutionizes the way we live and work. By providing impact and prospects in the digital world that offers ease of communication offered accelerates connectivity. The use of technology today is important by not having boundaries globally with the current internet diversity, and this is certainly a means of communication that brings a new paradigm in interacting between people. The internet brings the transformation of conventional communication users into a digital platform, one of which is Twitter being a communication tool that makes it easier for people to find information with the use of hashtag signs on Twitter.

Twitter is not only a platform for human interaction in the digital world, but with the presence of Twitter is able to change the pattern of political communication, in Indonesia political communication is related to communication by the government and society, Information Communication Technology (ICT) defines and revolutionizes the way we live and work. By providing impact and prospects in the digital world that offers ease of communication offered accelerates connectivity.

The use of technology today is important by not having boundaries globally with the current internet diversity, and this is certainly a means of communication that brings a new paradigm in interacting between people. The internet brings the transformation of conventional communication users into a digital platform, one of which is Twitter being a communication tool that makes it easier for people to find information with the use of hashtag signs on Twitter. Twitter is not only a platform for human interaction in the digital world, but with the presence of twitter able to change the pattern of political communication (Setiawan 2022).

In Indonesia, social media as a strategy for public communication related to information on the Flood Disaster Mitigation. Flooding is one of the natural disasters that often occurs every year in Indonesia, especially in Jakarta. The floods that hit the capital city of Jakarta almost every year are a challenge for the government. Climate change is projected as the cause of rising water and river levels resulting in increased rainfall in some areas. Flooding and inundation are common in the capital and buffer areas. The existence of social media is easy in responding to disasters, especially floods throughout Jakarta and its surroundings.

Through the Regional Disaster Management Agency (BPBD) DKI Jakarta utilizes social media as a communication tool based on applications to convey disaster preparedness information, such as floods in the rainy season. By using @BPBDJakarta Twitter account, information related to floods and weather uses this application to the fullest. Activity on Twitter accounts mitigates information through status or tweets, for example for @BPBDJakarta accounts that use #tinggimukaair #peringatandinijkt hashtags. The social media had to listen to various aspect messages to spread information about flood mitigation in Jakarta, government communication through social media and the public on Twitter. This two-way communication model uses the retweets and comments feature available (Trajkova et al. 2020).

The government must provide correct information regarding disaster management mitigation related to floods that occur every year. by activating information technology through Twitter media as a means of public communication and disaster information mitigation. From the explanation above, this study aims to find out the comparison of information about floods, with digital citizenship with social media activities, the community and the government can exchange information through Twitter which can effectively provide information and socialization through interactions that are quite helpful in handling flood mitigation in Jakarta.

2 Literature Review

2.1 Technology for Government

The literature on the use of technology for disaster management shows a growing interest in the field. However, it also shows that the main focus of contemporary literature is on the technology-specific opportunities and challenges of enhancing disaster management by investigating technology-specific, phase-specific and task-specific aspects of the use of technology for disaster management (AlHinai 2020). With current developments, the use of technology is increasingly needed, especially in handling disasters that can provide information using digital media as a tool that can provide information quickly. The concept of E-government can be interpreted as using data and telecommunications technology for efficient and effective governance and providing transparent and satisfying services to the public (Twizeyimana and Andersson 2019). ICT or information technology and information have become part of the government's work to improve performance, including leadership effectiveness, public participation, and information disclosure (Harguem 2021). Information Communication Technology (ICT) refers to all the technology used to handle telecommunications, broadcast media, intelligent building management systems, audio visual processing and transmission systems, and network-based control and monitoring functions.

ICT refers to technologies that provide access to information through telecommunications. It is similar to Information Technology (IT), but focuses primarily on communication technologies. This includes the Internet, wireless networks, cell phones, and other communication mediums (Kumari 2020). ICT is technology that supports activities involving information. Such activities include gathering, processing, storing and presenting data. Increasingly these activities also involve collaboration and communication. Practicality enjoys using ICTs which fulfil a need and help them complete tasks in their everyday lives. They see the ICTs they use as being function specific and highly tied to a single aspect of their lives, be it for use in their work, family, leisure, or community. These technologies are viewed as for their own personal use and they place a high value on those with proven functionality. They have no interest in exploring how to use a single ICT in every facet of their lives. Practicality place ICTs in function-specific rooms, often placing computers in home offices and televisions in entertainment rooms. Practicality see ICTs as tools (Birkland 2019).

2.2 Digital Native and Disaster Mitigation

The use of digital technologies has become a central cultural technique that increasingly determines educational opportunities, the possibility of upward social mobility, participation in social life and good job prospects. Thus, as a technological and social phenomenon, digitalization affects virtually all areas of life. (Janschitz and Penker 2022). The information society has found ease abounding since entering the internet age. People are also easier to connect to interact with each other. They communicate, behave, work, and think as digital natives (Pujasari Supratman 2018). Digital communication is the main way to communicate with each other connected through social media. Social media is a tool for government communicators to communicate with the community. Using social media, the government can connect with the community at any time, both of which have been integrated as an adaptation and innovation for government work progress (Mergel 2016).

The existence of social media is now an alternative medium for institutions or companies to explore to help them fulfil the vision, mission and goals of their own organizations, and information about innovative values in the e-government system as a whole (Fajriyah, Antoni, and Akbar 2020). Collaboration between government and social media in e-government practices in social scientist studies can positively impact public responsibility and trust in the government (Song and Lee 2016).

However, with virtual or e-government communication channels, social media is not the primary communication tool to reach public participation because virtual communication still has shortcomings. For example, Santander Smart city in Spain conducts direct meetings to continue programs communicated through social media (Díaz-Díaz and Pérez-González 2016). The important role of the government in providing responsibility in overcoming the dialectic between the government and society. The critical role of social media for the government is as a medium for disaster communication and to provide disaster preparedness messages as public information (Eko et al. 2022). Information about disaster mitigation by the government can officially become valid data for the community in dealing with disasters (Palen and Hughes 2018).

In an emergency, social media is not only a coordination and communication tool used by the government but has become part of a tool towards humanity as a preparedness measure for disaster. Looking at Takashi's explanation by categorizing the function of social media as a means of disaster communication, as shown in Table 1 below.

Table 1. Category and description of social media use Takhsi 2015

No	Category social media usage	Descriptions
1	Situational report	Information regarding disaster emergencies, mitigation, handling or preparedness used by individuals and organizations
2	Government critics	Information from official government social media to provide public information during a disaster emergency
3	Relief effort coordination	Use of social media for philanthropic activities or volunteering in cases of disaster emergencies

3 Research Methodology

This study used a qualitative, defines descriptive qualitative (QD) as a research method that moves on a simple qualitative approach with an inductive flow. This inductive flow means qualitative descriptive research (QD) begins with an explanatory process or event which can finally be drawn as a generalization which is a conclusion from the process or event. This study uses qualitative description by analyzing political communication activities and Ridwan's branding on Twitter social media (Nurmalasari and Erdiantoro 2020). Data collect through (@BPBDJakarta) Twitter account. Furthermore, the data were coded using the NVivo 12 plus research application to determine each coding Twitter account's metadata classification. The NVivo software is one of the qualitative data analysis tools used by many qualitative researchers around the world (Sotiriadou, Brouwers, and Le 2014). Researchers would describe the NVivo process results to determine a comparison or difference regarding the two accounts' mitigation information.

The data was taken using the NVivo 12 plus Capture feature in Chrome web browsing to view content in the form of content from social media. The NVivo 12 plus visualization in this study uses the coding feature manually to find data, analysis is used to study data processing and answer analysis. With the word cloud, we are able to analyze and find words that often arise from findings that are commonly used and discussed. This study also looks at cluster distribution to visualize and collect dominant data/words that have similarities and differences.

4 Analysis, Finding and Discussion

4.1 Information Topic Intensity on Official Twitter Government

Figure 1 shows the number of word frequencies used by Twitter in the DKI Jakarta government through the @BPBDJakarta Twitter account. In this account, the word "Rain" dominates information sharing during the floods in Jakarta. The word "peringatandini-JKt" is often used to refer to the frequency of information about flood data widely on the account @BPBDJakarta.

Fig. 1. Word Frequency @BPBDJakarta

Netizens' tweets that have been collected are often uploaded by following #peringatandinijkt. Analysis related to #peringatandinijkt aims to find out from the words that most often appear in a tweet or post followed by a #peringatandinijkt. There are some words that are quite dominant, the dominant word is mostly in line with the hashtag they attached, namely #peringatandinijkt. There is a dominant word appearing in the upload that attaches #peringatandinijkt, the dominant words are Rain, Wind, Potential, and Flood.

4.2 Domination Information Massage on @BPBDJakarta

The results of the search using NVivo 12 plus, are based on a number of frequently appearing accounts that use hashtags to communicate such as the #perigantandinijkt hashtag which is continuously updated on the Twitter timeline. In Fig. 2, there are five accounts that are used the most. If you look at the pie chart, the BPBDJKT account uses

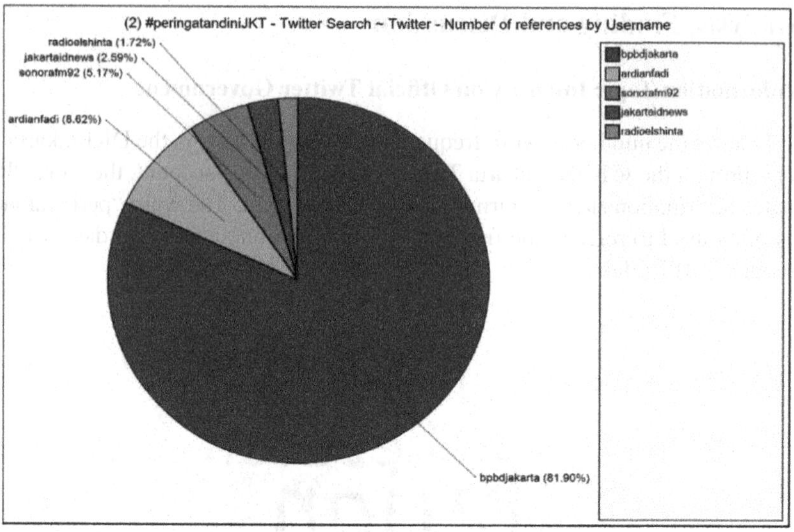

Fig. 2. The Number of Reference by username

this hashtag more often, other accounts quite often and the other three rarely use this hashtag.

The use of hashtags is generally often used by Twitter users for conversations related to issues or news that are demographically present in Jakarta. This is to create a conversation network about the problem of flooding, especially areas that are often the worst affected among others. Civil society will of course be facilitated by using hashtags to make complaints digitally through the features on Twitter. Apart from that, of course, for flood prevention mitigation which can be immediately updated related to flood information quickly. Information related to flooding in Jakarta has a distribution of mentions that are often used in providing information. Figure 3 shows the account @infobmkg often mentions the hashtag #peringatandiniJKT. The other 3 accounts that use mention the most are @BPBDJakarta 2 others quite often but not so intently.

The distribution of mentions in Fig. 3 is a utilization of the existing features on Twitter, with the convenience of these features, of course, it will be very easy when providing information that can connect one to another, the convenience of these features can be immediate and fast when there is new information. This is possible because of the reply feature on Twitter which can be immediately received by the account concerned which is mentioned in the form of a notification, new interactive media allows for direct feedback and there is a transformation of the boundaries between audiences and information producers. This means that in new media the audience is not merely placed as an object which is the target of the message. The audience and changes in media technology and the meaning of the medium (news distribution) have renewed the role of the audience to be more interactive with the message (Nasrullah 2016) (Fig. 4).

Based on Fig. 3, the number of tweets is more than re-tweets, this shows that the intensity of news/tweets made on Twitter is very active and varied. Twitter has its own traits and characteristics, which may be simpler than other social media tools. Many

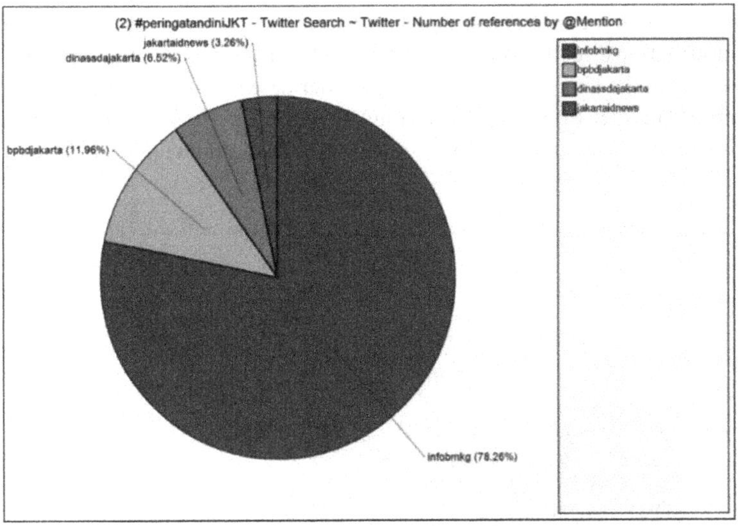

Fig. 3. The number of references by @mention

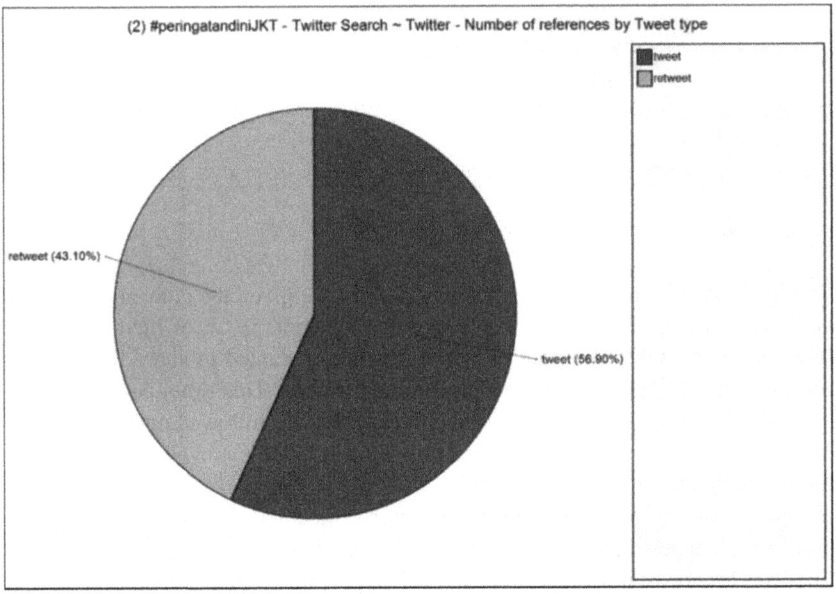

Fig. 4. The Number of Reference by Tweet type

terms exist only on this bird symbol site. First, Twitter operates a digital information service that enables users to send and track micro-messages known as (tweets) of no more than 140 characters. The tweet facility is designed for use on mobile devices and PCs. Twitter is used to post any status, repost other users' statuses (retweet), respond to other users' posts (replays), and share links. Users may also have links to their blog posts sent via Twitter, either post-by-post or automatically. This feature certainly helps provide information directly, as a noun, is a tweet from another account that is forwarded to followers with the aim of spreading it to a wider network. As an adjective, the action of forwarding a tweet from another account for followers to see. (Quote retweets are retweets that are written in quote form so they look like replies) (Rezeki 2020).

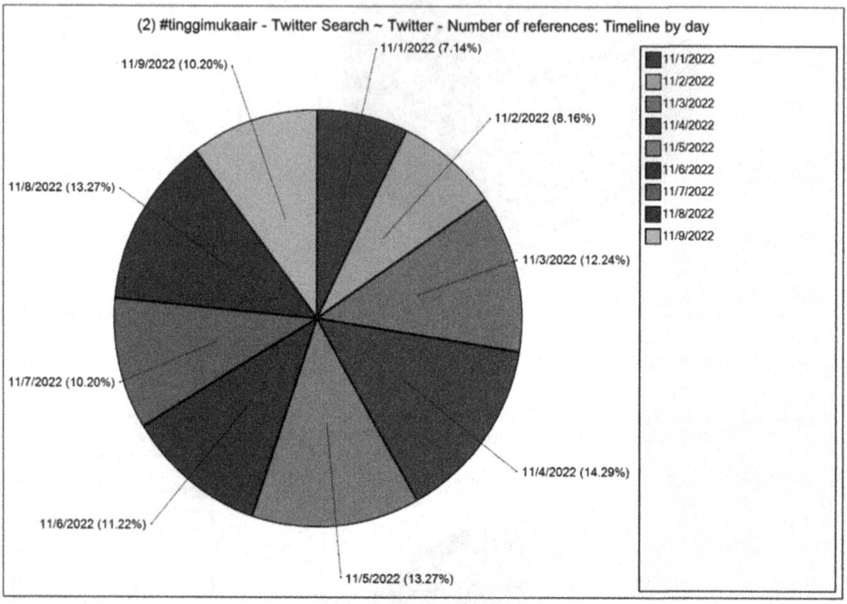

Fig. 5. Timeline by Day

In Fig. 5, by presenting the tweet feature, users are given the convenience to share a tweet both individually and tweets from other accounts to all of their followers by finding one or several tweets that they like. Even just wanted to share the tweet with followers in the @BPBDJakarta account on the timeline. This timeline within Twitter works to display a stream of tweets from accounts that are followed on Twitter viewing constant supportive content from various recommendations as well as Retweeting or liking Tweets made within the homepage.

To update the information held by any user or account owner, people can follow (subscribe to) that person's Twitter account. When a Twitter user has followed someone's account, any broadcast information (posts) will appear in an updated feed which is called the timeline. The number of followers (total number of people followed) and followers (total number of people following) is always updated in a specific box on the Twitter profile page (Emeraldien, Sunarsono, and Alit 2019).

Figure 6 shows the distribution of clusters connected to the actors in presenting flood-related information. The most visible interaction is on the accounts @infoBMKG and @BPBDJakartam, the two accounts provide a fairly wide distribution in distributing related information, in this case the use of hashtags for each actor. This is the distribution and reception of information that is dominated by the general public, these two actors

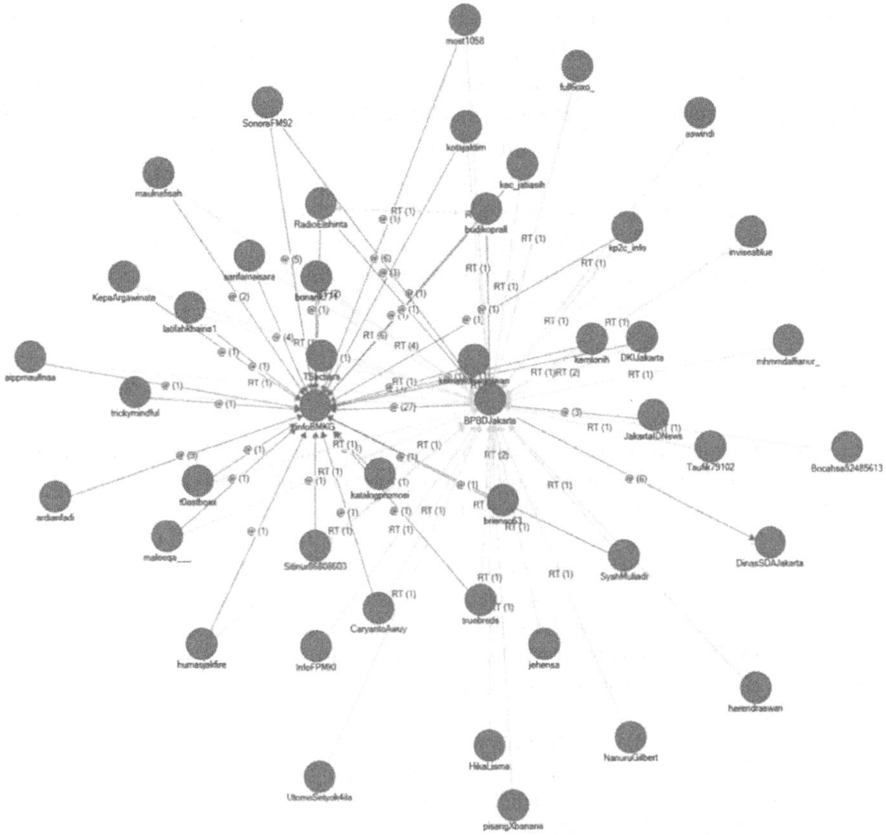

Fig. 6. Cluster search pada Twitter

are a link and source for the public to obtain information related to flooding in Jakarta, especially when an alert occurs and water overflows to the surface.

Referring to the explanation above, the author sees that Twitter users during the flood in Jakarta aka the tone of official information by the government through @BPBDJakarta accounts consistently and periodically. Media activity increased during floods, messages sent by the government and the public in the form of photos, videos during reports that appeared in the community. Thus, the social media accounts owned by the Jakarta Disaster Management Agency (BPBD) consistently provide periodic information both before and when there has been a flood.

5 Conclusion

The digital era has made the government adapt to using communication technology through the mass media to carry out information on mitigating Flood in Jakarta. Unlimitedness of communication through wireless channels helps the effectiveness and efficiency of government work in public services. In the midst of a flood situation, the province of Jakarta actively communicates virtually via official Twitter account @BPB-DJakarta. The results concluded in this study include information on mitigating floods Jakarta's Twitter account. Significant results in this study include information on digital media, especially through Twitter, which can be used to influence the Jakarta government to make a serious commitment in dealing with flood prevention. There needs to be good disaster management, so that the response can be maximized, especially by providing education to the public, both through socialization through social media and directly to the community. Suggestions for further research development with the government's mass media activity is to analyze tweets, retweets, and hashtags on communication activity on Twitter to expand the analysis.

References

AlHinai, Y.S.: Disaster management digitally transformed: exploring the impact and key determinants from the UK national disaster management experience. Int. J. Disaster Risk Reduct. **51**, 101851 (2020). https://doi.org/10.1016/j.ijdrr.2020.101851

Birkland, J.L.H.: Understanding the ICT user typology and the user types. Gerontechnology **95–106** (2019). https://doi.org/10.1108/978-1-78743-291-820191009

Díaz-Díaz, R., Pérez-González, D.: Implementation of social media concepts for e-government: case study of a social media tool for value co-creation and citizen participation. J. Organ. End User Comput. **28**(3), 104–121 (2016). https://doi.org/10.4018/JOEUC.2016070107

Setiawan, R.E.B.: Analysis of the governor's communication model on Twitter 209 (Iconpo 2021), pp. 215–19 (2022)

Setiawan, R.E.B., Nurmandi, A., Muallidin, I., Kurniawan, D., Salahudin, D.: Technology for governance: comparison of disaster information mitigation of COVID-19 in Jakarta and West Java. In: Ahram, T., Taiar, R. (eds.) IHIET 2021. LNNS, vol. 319, pp. 130–137 (2022). Springer, Cham. https://doi.org/10.1007/978-3-030-85540-6_17

Emeraldien, F.Z., Sunarsono, R.J., Alit, R.: Twitter sebagai platform komunikasi politik di Indonesia. SCAN Jurnal Teknologi Informasi Dan Komunikasi **14**(1), 21–30 (2019). http://ejournal.upnjatim.ac.id/index.php/scan/article/view/1457/1207

Fajriyah, F., Antoni, D., Akbar, M.: Faktor - Faktor peranan penggunaan social media e-government: studi kasus pemerintah kota prabumulih. Jurnal Nasional Ilmu Komputer **1**(1), 1–11 (2020). https://doi.org/10.47747/jurnalnik.v1i1.55

Feldman, D., et al.: Communicating flood risk: looking back and forward at traditional and social media outlets. Int. J. Disaster Risk Reduct. **15**, 43–51 (2016). https://doi.org/10.1016/j.ijdrr.2015.12.004

Harguem, S.: A conceptual framework on IT governance impact on organizational performance: a dynamic capability perspective. Acad. J. Interdiscip. Stud. **10**(1), 136–51 (2021). https://doi.org/10.36941/ajis-2021-0012

Houston, J.B., et al.: Social media and disasters: a functional framework for social media use in disaster planning, response, and research. Disasters **39**(1), 1–22 (2015). https://doi.org/10.1111/disa.12092

Janschitz, G., Penker, M.: How digital are 'digital natives' actually? Developing an instrument to measure the degree of digitalisation of university students – the DDS-index. BMS Bull. Sociol. Methodol. Bulletin de Methodologie Sociologique **153**(1), 127–159 (2022). https://doi.org/10.1177/07591063211061760

Kumari, S.: Social media and ICT. JAC J. Compos. Theory **XIII**(II), 921–25 (2020)

Li, L., Zhang, Q., Tian, J., Wang, H.: Characterizing information propagation patterns in emergencies: a case study with Yiliang earthquake. Int. J. Inf. Manag. **38**(1), 34–41 (2018). https://doi.org/10.1016/j.ijinfomgt.2017.08.008

Mergel, I.: Social media institutionalization in the U.S. federal government. Gov. Inf. Q. **33**(1), 142–148 (2016). https://doi.org/10.1016/j.giq.2015.09.002

Nasrullah, R.: Teori Dan Riset Media Siber (Cybermedia). Kencana, Jakarta (2016)

Nurmalasari, Y., Erdiantoro, R.: Perencanaan dan keputusan karier: konsep krusial dalam layanan BK karier. Quanta **4**(1), 44–51 (2020). https://doi.org/10.22460/q.v1i1p1-10.497

Nurmandi, A., Dewi Kurniasih, S., Kasiwi, A.N.: Teknologi Informasi Pemerintahan. UMY Press, Yogyakarta (2020)

Palen, L., Hughes, A.L.: Social media in disaster communication. In: Rodríguez, H., Donner, W., Trainor, J.E. (eds.) Handbook of Disaster Research. HSSR, pp. 497–518. Springer, Cham (2018). https://doi.org/10.1007/978-3-319-63254-4_24

Pujasari Supratman, L.: Penggunaan media sosial oleh digital native. Jurnal Ilmu Komunikasi **15**(1), 1–14 (2018)

Rezeki, S., Irwansyah, R.: Penggunaan sosial media Twitter dalam komunikasi organisasi (Studi kasus pemerintah provinsi Dki Jakarta dalam penanganan COVID-19). J. Islam. Law Stud. **04**(02), 63–78 (2020)

Song, C., Lee, J.: Citizens' use of social media in government, perceived transparency, and trust in government. Public Perform. Manag. Rev. **39**(2), 430–453 (2016). https://doi.org/10.1080/15309576.2015.1108798

Sotiriadou, P., Brouwers, J., Le, T.-A.: Choosing a qualitative data analysis tool: a comparison of NVivo and Leximancer. Ann. Leisure Res. **17**(2), 218–234 (2014). https://doi.org/10.1080/11745398.2014.902292

Sujay, R., Pujari, J., Bhat, V.S., Dixit, A.: Timeline analysis of Twitter user. Procedia Comput. Sci. **132**, 157–166 (2018). https://doi.org/10.1016/j.procs.2018.05.179

Trajkova, M., Alhakamy, A., Cafaro, F., Vedak, S., Mallappa, R., Kankara, S.R.: Exploring casual COVID-19 data visualizations on Twitter: topics and challenges. Informatics **7**(3), 1–22 (2020). https://doi.org/10.3390/INFORMATICS7030035

Twizeyimana, J.D., Andersson, A.: The public value of e-government – a literature review. Gov. Inf. Q. **36**(2), 167–178 (2019). https://doi.org/10.1016/j.giq.2019.01.001

Yuan, F., Liu, R.: Feasibility study of using crowdsourcing to identify critical affected areas for rapid damage assessment: Hurricane Matthew case study. Int. J. Disaster Risk Reduct. **28**, 758–767 (2018). https://doi.org/10.1016/j.ijdrr.2018.02.003

West Java Government Branding Using Social Media: A Case of Ridwan Kamil Personal Branding

Mifahul Khairiyah[1(✉)], Achmad Nurmandi[2], Misran[1], and Dimas Subekti[1]

[1] Department of Government Affairs and Administration, Universitas Muhammadiyah Yogyakarta, Yogyakarta, Indonesia
{m.khairiyah.psc22,misran.psc20}@mail.umy.ac.id

[2] Department of Government Affairs and Administration, Jusuf Kalla School of Government, Universitas Muhammadiyah Yogyakarta, Yogyakarta, Indonesia
nurmandi_achmad@umy.ac.id

Abstract. This study aims to analyze Ridwan Kamil's Twitter social media in building personal branding ahead of the 2024 general election. This study uses a qualitative method. The data source in this study is the Twitter social media account @ridwankamil. The research data collection period was carried out from January 2022 to December 2022. The data analysis technique was through the Nvivo 12 Plus application. The results of this study indicate that the content of Ridwan Kamil's political communications through the Twitter social media account @ridwankamil can build personal branding through the hashtag #indonesiajuara. Ridwan Kamil's branding often displays his daily activities on his Twitter account to show consistency in what he does every day and what he displays to the public. Ridwan Kamil in building positive perceptions of the public using personal Twitter is reflected through the content of images, videos, and tweets that describe himself as an egalitarian, humorous, open, credible, and responsible person. The contributions in this research form the basis for building political image and branding through social media.

Keywords: social media · Political Communications · Branding · Ridwan Kamil

1 Introduction

Along with the very rapid development of technology, humanity has shifted to devoting its time to communication technology which is disseminated as new media which then gave rise to the existence of social media. The existence of social media then also plays a role in influencing matters in the political field in the cyber sphere globally. With this, social media can be used as a form of political actor branding, through social media, political actor branding is formed through a digital political campaign process (cyber realm). Social media and political practice have an intensity relationship, and both play an important role in political communication [1]. In addition, it is believed to provide an opportunity to demonstrate their abilities in political branding which can be seen from

A. Coman and S. Vasilache (Eds.): HCII 2023, LNCS 14025, pp. 212–222, 2023.
https://doi.org/10.1007/978-3-031-35915-6_16

polls and social interactions with the public through social media [2], moreover this supports the importance of achieving professional values of integrity and credibility, and the objectivity of spreading information [3]. Based on [4] Twitter has developed into a social media platform that is able to bridge political communication channels more quickly, Twitter then over time becomes a platform used by politicians to push an agenda, Twitter is also used to start discussions, express opinions, and views in the form of a tweet which is of course used to influence people's mindset towards the political situation or potential political candidates for the community. The use of social media Twitter for public interest and political communication is increasingly being used by political elites, regional leaders, and state officials [5].

Ridwan Kamil utilizes Twitter social media to form self-image, Ridwan Kamil's Twitter content is in the form of events or campaign activities that are followed daily. This choice is not without reason, from the contents of Twitter to attract the attention of followers to form Personal Branding [6]. Ridwan Kamil is a political figure who has the potential to become a presidential candidate in 2024 Ridwan Kamil often enters the figure exchange ahead of the 2024 election, driven by his activity and popularity on social media. Ridwan Kamil is also often a newsmaker who uses social media as a source of news from the mainstream media. Ridwan Kamil is a figure who often enters the radar of figures who deserve to be reckoned with in the 2024 presidential election. This is one of the reasons for making Ridwan Kamil both the subject and object of this research. Social media activity is a factor in Ridwan Kamil's popularity as a regional head, compared to other regional heads. Even Ridwan Kamil has made a statement stating that he is ready to fight as a presidential candidate in the 2024 elections [7].

There have been many previous studies related to personal branding by candidates or political parties ahead of general elections. Research from [8], during the 2014 presidential election, Jokowi Widodo used online media to build self-image, the results of his research showed that the figure of Jokowi was highly highlighted and branded in such a way as an honest, simple person and close to the community. Personal Branding is now a trend ahead of the general election. The results show that Jokowi Widodo won the 2014 presidential election with the branding he did through online media. Republican political figure Donald Trump has a background as a businessman, during the 2016 presidential election he also used Twitter to carry out personal branding. One of the issues that was displayed or highlighted was nationalism that protected the native peoples of the United States or the campaign phrase "America is Great Again" which was popular during the presidential election at that time. As a result, even though his image has become a figure of controversy and many are not happy with his political opponents who consider his campaign style to be very amateurish and unprofessional, Donald Trump has proved that he is still accepted by the people of the United States and won the presidential election [9].

Other research has also observed personal branding from the 2018 West Java gubernatorial election on social media. [10] explained that the candidate for governor of West Java Province used Twitter as a tool to form personal branding during the campaign. United States politicians in the era of social media make great use of the internet as a media campaign tool [11]. The next research is how Sandiaga Uno uses his personal Twitter to carry out branding during the campaign process which depicts themselves as someone close to the community so that they can create sympathy or admiration from the public [12]. During the 2019 elections KH. Ma'ruf Amin also succeeded in using Twitter social media as a tool to seek support, especially for Muslim voters. The branding strategy and campaign model he built were about religious activities, events supporting/voter meetings, and visiting several strategic places such as Islamic boarding schools [13]. Political communication is considered successful and right on target, this reflects closeness to the community.

Previous research has shown the importance of personal branding strategies in elections. The purpose of this research is to strengthen previous research that has never existed. This article is expected to be able to complement the deficiencies of existing previous studies related to branding in politics in the era of digital political communication by utilizing social media, but also able to contribute knowledge for political leaders, political practitioner and consultant, social media specialist in recognizing the concept of branding in politics. This article will answer two questions:

RQ1: How is Twitter used as a medium for political communication?
RQ2: How is Ridwan Kamil's personal branding on Twitter social media?

2 Literature Review

2.1 Use Social Media in Political Communication

This political communication is defined as a complex communication activity using language and symbols, which is used by leaders, media, citizens, citizen groups, experts to give effect and to the results imposed on the public policy of the nation, state., or society, there are seven main dimensions of political communication, namely communication activities that bridge between political institutions and the media; emphasizing symbols and language, mediation and mediatization; media technology; diverse, multifaceted media, and decline of gatekeeping; interactions among leaders, media, and citizens, as well as the functioning of economic and political structures [14], Social media is often seen as a platform that allows for more direct relations between political leaders and their citizens. Social media functions to support the campaigns of politicians [15]. In the end, political leaders are starting to realize the importance of social media for conducting political communication, rather than just making use of the mainstream mass media.

Twitter has gradually become one of the social media tools influencing how online political communication practices are now impacting the way political actors interact with citizens in Nigeria [3]. Social media is often seen as a platform that allows more direct links between political leaders and their citizens. Social media functions to support the campaigns of politicians [16] In the end, political leaders began to realize the importance of social media for political communication, rather than just utilizing the mainstream mass media, then also how Trump also managed to engage Twitter users for 100 The first day of his presidency to gain Public Support for Trump has been confirmed by the number of "likes", retweets and comments, the latter with more positive than negative connotations. Thinking about the role of politicians' social media, traditional media innovation with new communication paradigms and, above all, citizen action-reactions that reproduce spectacle discourse, thus empowering a new political influencer strategist [17]. [18] against the tweets of five political leaders in Italy, namely Matteo Salvini,

Beppe Grillo, Giorgia Meloni, Matteo Renzi, and Nichi Vendola revealed that among the types of social media, Twitter plays a central role in hybridizing and redefining political communication. Tweets have become the digital version of soundbites, and politicians are using them to reach a wider audience thanks to the features available. It is stated that Twitter is the perfect medium for the formation of a populist brand in implementing public communication in the digital era.

2.2 Personal Branding

One important factor for a political leader to be able to gain popularity on social media is to have a good brand so that the goals of political communication can be achieved effectively. Brand, image, or credibility has been proven to play a role in explaining the effect of support for political leaders on social media [19]. Branding is increasingly being used in politics to incorporate symbolism, ideology, values, and policy promises onto political parties/candidates. Therefore, this branding is not only used by political actors but also by political parties through a series of values, beliefs and promises [20]. Previous research related to elections in Indonesia also shows that young voters build their understanding of politics and political parties through "stories" and symbolic representations of political candidates [21]. [22], politicians, political leaders, and parties are busy building brands based on ability, character, and trustworthiness to gain public trust and support. Democracy requires credible candidates and parties. Other research has also observed personal branding from the 2018 West Java gubernatorial election on social media. [10] explained that the candidate for governor of West Java Province used Twitter as a tool to form personal branding during the campaign. This is done to introduce, sharpen self-image and increase popularity. The characteristics of Twitter which prioritize dialogue can also build interactive communication and influence the perceptions of prospective voters towards the image displayed. Furthermore, other studies to assess identity, image, reputation, or position which will ultimately support the development of strategy and management of branding in politics [23].

3 Method

This study uses a qualitative research approach. [24] defines descriptive qualitative (QD) as a research method that moves on a simple qualitative approach with an inductive flow. This inductive flow means qualitative descriptive research (QD) begins with an explanatory process or event which can finally be drawn a generalization which is a conclusion from the process or event. In this study using qualitative descriptive by analyzing political communication activities and Ridwan's personal branding in Twitter social media.

Data collection through Ridwan Kamil's Twitter account can be in the form of tweets, retweets, hashtags, images, videos, and others, which allows registrars to document and analyze data systematically. Furthermore, it is supported by various types of literature reviews that reinforce the truth of previous research, to cover up how social media users of Ridwan Kamil's Twitter account view Twitter media activity in the run-up to the 2024 Election, starting from January 2022 to December 2022. This research focuses on

Ridwan's Personal Branding Kamil and how Twitter is used as a political communication without having to meet directly with the intended target. Selection of this account as part of viewing political communication activities.

The analysis in this study uses the Nvivo 12 Plus software on the NCapture feature. The NVivo software is one of the qualitative data analysis tools used by many qualitative researchers around the world [25]. This feature can retrieve data from Twitter social media in a systematic and in-depth manner, then an analysis is carried out using the NVivo 12 Plus software with several tools. Such as cluster analysis used to determine the relationship of communication actors in this study Word similarity is used to see the communication delivered by communication actors using pear-son correlation. Pearson Correlation is a correlation measure used to measure the strength and direction of a linear relationship between two variables.

4 Result and Discussion

4.1 Ridwan Kamil's Twitter Post

Social media is included as one of the tools to communicate with the audience and potential voters, so the communication side must always be intertwined in it. In this case, the required variable is the message to be conveyed which must be in accordance with the target to be achieved [28]. It was stated that political actors, including political leaders or prospective political leaders, found effective and efficient political communication strategies to communicate and interact with the public through social media. However, not just conveying information, political leaders deliberately form branding as part of their political communication strategy to gain support and influence the public. That the presence of new media has a significant impact on political activity, especially the process of political communication [29] (Fig. 1).

Fig. 1. Ridwan Kamil's Twitter post. Source: Processed from Ridwan Kamil's Twitter

Showing the uploaded tweets are activities that aim to form Personal Branding accompanied by supporting photos and videos, the @ridwankamil account uploads tweets about his daily activities starting from family life to the activities he carries out as Governor of West Java, directly showing his leadership da public is something that is important that as a leader, he always updates information on regional development so that the general public can easily control and participate in monitoring development developments in his area. So that this open and informative figure stuck with Ridwan Kamil. Not only information about development, Ridwan Kamil also gave messages about his development plans for West Java Province through visits he made to areas and potential middleclass businesses.

4.2 A Twitter Account that is Often @Mantions Ridwan Kamil

Mention, which is offensive to other users in the photo title and in the photo comments section, aims to communicate with the offended user (Fig. 2).

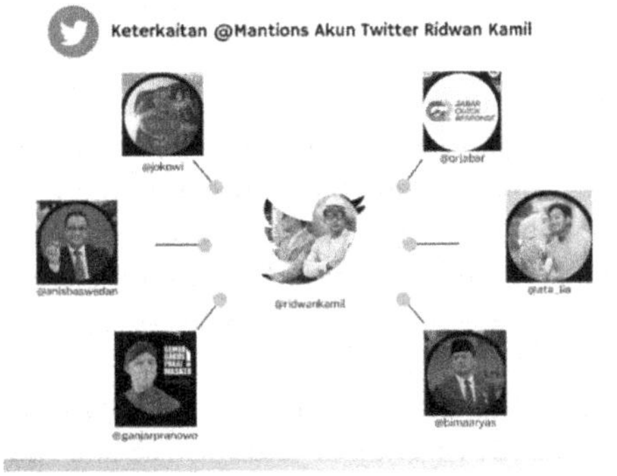

Akun	Persentase
Jokowi	16,59%
Atalia	12,44%
Qrjabar	8,29%
Anis Baswedan	5,07%
Bimaaryas	4,61%
Ganjar Pranowo	3,23%

Fig. 2. Mention made by @Ridwan Kamil Source: Processed by researchers using Nvivo12plus (2022)

Based on Nvivo12 Plus analysis, @ridwankamil has been very active in presenting work programs, public services to political communications. If you look at the picture above, you can see that most of Ridwan Kamil's political communications or interactions through his Twitter account @ridwankamil are more focused on political matters. Apart from that, he also interacted with the Twitter account of the West Java government which is engaged in public services and humanity. The communication interactions carried out by Ridwan Kamil on Twitter social media seemed to tend towards politics and were quite participatory with the president, other provincial governors, as well as deputy governors. West Java, his wife, and the community. The relationship shows the intensity of Ridwan Kamil's two-way communication with the public.

4.3 Hashtags Often Used by Ridwan Kamil

A hashtag is a label (tag) in the form of a word prefixed with the symbol #. The hashtag feature is important because it makes it very easy for users to find photos spread across Instagram with a specific label (Fig. 3).

In the picture above you can see the intensity of using #Jabarjuara as an idea that aims to present West Java which is able to liberate independence with unity, justice, justice,

Word	Persentase
Jabarjuara	51,52%
Indonesiajuara	32,80%
Jabarjuaralahirbatin	2,76%
G20	0,80%

Fig. 3. Intensity of Use of Ridwan Kamil's Twitter #Hashtag Source: Processed by researchers using Nvivo12plus (2022)

and prosperity. The word "Jabar Champion" was originally intended so that anyone who diligently interpreted and shouted it, his subconscious would make "champion" or "Excellence" the spirit of his life's work ethic. "Jabar Champion" is also a simple word that when spoken is like a prayer. The more it is shouted, the more real it becomes. What we keep thinking, we will get. The strength of the mind besides #Jabarjuara there is also #Jabarjuaralahirbatin. This means that West Java does not only focus on building physical infrastructure, but spiritual infrastructure must also be considered.

In addition to the hashtags #Jabarjuara and #Jabarjuarahirbatin, the hashtags that are often used are #IndonesiaJuara because the 2024 Election is getting close and Ridwan Kamil uses #IndonesiaJuara as a national level personal branding, no longer using hashtags only limited to the coverage area of West Java, we can observe this in when he ran for mayor of Bandung he often used #bandungjuara on Twitter then to follow the political contestation to become governor of West Java he often used the Hashtag #Jabarjuara this is proof that when he wanted to take part in a political contest he used Hashtag as part of his personal branding in Indonesia.

Then the use of #G20 or Group of Twenty is a major forum for international economic cooperation which consists of countries with the largest economies in the world consisting of 19 countries and 1 European Union institution. G20 members consist of South Africa, the United States, Saudi Arabia, Argentina, Australia, Brazil, India, India, Britain, Italy, Japan, Germany, Canada, Mexico, Republic of Korea, Russia, France, China, Turkey, and the European Union. The current G20 Indonesia Presidency 2022 takes the theme "Recover Together, Recover Stronger". Through this theme, Indonesia wants to invite the whole world to work hand in hand, support each other to recover together and grow stronger and more sustainable [30]. The use of #G20 is Ridwan Kamil's support for this activity. Furthermore, it can be seen between the correlations of #jabarjuara as follows (Table 1).

The correlation between the #hashtags of Jabarjuara and Indonesiajuara is most often compared, it can be seen from the data above that the correlation is 0.984974, then the correlation between #hashtags Jabarjuara and Jabarjuaralahitbatin is 0.462152 and the correlation between #hashtag Jabarjura and G20 is only 0.061334.

Table 1. Cluster analysis of Twitter hashtag

Code A	Code B	Pearson correlation coefficient
Jabarjuara	Indonesiajuara	0,984978
	Jabarjuaralahirbatin	0,462152
	G20	0,061334

Source: Processed by researchers using Nvivo12plus.

Furthermore, #jabarjuara was used as personal branding by Ridwan Kamil. According to McNally and Speak [27], it is stated that a strong personal brand always has three basic things that unite. 1. Distinctiveness A strong personal brand describes something that is very specific or distinctive so that it is different from most people. Kkhasan here can be represented by personal qualities, physical appearance, or expertise. 2. Relevance A strong personal brand usually describes something that is considered important by society and has relevance to the character of the person. If there is no relevance, it will be difficult to strengthen the people's mind. 3. Consistency of a strong Personal Brand is usually the fruit of consistent branding efforts in various ways to form what is commonly referred to as brand equity (brand excellence). Based on the findings on Ridwan Kamil's Twitter, the post fulfills the characteristics of the personal branding process from McNally and Speak to these 3 characteristics.

Personal brand peculiarities that Ridwan Kamil also often shares portraits of his personality, starting from uploading playing with his children and wife to portraits of his hobby as an architect on a Twitter account, the most distinguishing thing is, in each of his posts he always pins unique netizen comments with funny answers. This is what characterizes Ridwan Kamil in social media which he uses as a means of building personal branding. Ridwan Kamil, who appears in each of his Twitter content, shows his personal side, which is humorous and down-to-earth. Of all the features that are used as a whole, the range of activating the use of language that is humorous and up to date is also classified as quite intensive by Ridwan Kamil. Ridwan Kamil's closeness to his followers has made him much liked, his communicative figure has made him sit in many influencer podcast programs, so that his life which is not widely known ends up being an inspirational story for many people. Not only that, the success of Ridwan Kamil's positive personal branding is also supported by his other family, such as his wife and children who are active in social and community activities, this is also an attraction for netizens who think that Ridwan Kamil's family is support main system for his success in leading.

Relevance of Personal Brand Ridwan Kamil often displays his daily life on his Twitter account to show that there is unity and what is shown to the public with what he does in daily life, without anything being engineered. Not only the figure as the Governor is displayed on his Twitter, but also the figure of himself as an ordinary person and as a father is also shown. It is this relevance that indicates Ridwan Kamil's balanced figure both in cyberspace and in the real world. Like other social media users, who also want to share their little happiness with the public in cyberspace.

Consistency Personal Brand behavior that is displayed daily is very consistent, especially on Twitter so that a positive perception will be built in the public. The behavior and character that is formed here must be continuously carried out to maintain the continuity of personal branding, of course by continuing to carry out routine activities as usual on the Twitter account @ridwankamil. High consistency will maintain and strengthen the value or image that has been or will be formed. Apart from that, in strengthening the brand that is being built, Ridwan Kamil regularly and actively uploads videos or photos of his activities as a governor in West Java through the social media Twitter. Thus, distinctiveness, relevance, and consistency in building Personal Branding are still being carried out. Currently, Ridwan Kamil is still a politician who is idolized by most society, besides being considered to represent young people who will one day become president and vice president in the future, personal branding does not guarantee victory but will become a provision or capital in the next general election.

5 Conclusions

On the social media Twitter, Ridwan Kamil is able to build his image, as a leader he is a pioneer in how to use virtual world timelines to open a real space for communication without borders and barriers between Ridwan Kamil and his staff as the government. In social media, Political branding refers to the distinction of a Ridwan Kamil as a politician who wants to portray himself as a different person from politicians in general. Like he is egalitarian, close to the people, open, credible, and accountable. The main emphasis of the Ridwan Kamil brand on differentiation strengthens Ridwan Kamil's branding through branding Indonesia as a champion because this hashtag is an effort to compare we not only for political contestation in West Java but rather want to brand ourselves through #indonesiajuara to participate in political contestation at the national level. It is this difference that makes a political brand stronger and makes Ridwan Kamil's brand easier to recognize and announce to the public. Ridwan Kamil's political branding as a product of political communication in Indonesia in contemporary times is formed by using messages summarized on Ridwan Kamil's Twitter social media.

References

1. Kahne, J., Bowyer, B.: The political significance of social media activity and social networks. Polit. Commun. **35**(3), 470–493 (2018). https://doi.org/10.1080/10584609.2018.1426662
2. Lin, J.S., Himelboim, I.: Political brand communities as social network clusters: winning and trailing candidates in the GOP 2016 primary elections. J. Polit. Mark. **18**(1–2), 119–147 (2019). https://doi.org/10.1080/15377857.2018.1478661
3. Opeibi, T.: The twittersphere as political engagement space: a study of social media usage in election campaigns in Nigeria. Digit. Stud. Le Champ Numer. **9**(1), 1–32 (2019). https://doi.org/10.16995/dscn.292
4. Emeraldien, F.Z., Sunarsono, R.J., Alit, R.: Twitter sebagai platform komunikasi politik di Indonesia. SCAN J. Teknol. Inf. dan Komun. **14**(1), 21–30 (2019). http://ejournal.upnjatim.ac.id/index.php/scan/article/view/1457/1207
5. Stieglitz, S., Dang-Xuan, L.: Social media and political communication: a social media analytics framework. Soc. Netw. Anal. Min. **3**(4), 1277–1291 (2012). https://doi.org/10.1007/s13278-012-0079-3

6. Widiastuti, T.W.: Analisis elaboration likelihood model dalam pembentukan personal branding di Twitter. J. ASPIKOM **3**(3), 588 (2017). https://doi.org/10.24329/aspikom.v3i3.107
7. CNN Indonesia: Ridwan Kamil Masih Tunggu Waktu yang Tepat Putuskan Gabung ke Partai. CNN Indonesia (2022). https://www.cnnindonesia.com/nasional/20221114191254-32-873664/ridwan-kamil-masih-tunggu-waktu-yang-tepat-putuskan-gabung-ke-partai
8. Fatayati, S.: Branding politikjokowidodo dalam pilpres 2014 di media online **27**, 25–39 (2016)
9. Enli, G.: Twitter as arena for the authentic outsider: exploring the social media campaigns of Trump and Clinton in the 2016 US presidential election. Eur. J. Commun. **32**(1), 50–61 (2017). https://doi.org/10.1177/0267323116682802
10. Srisadono, W.: Komunikasi Publik Calon Gubernur Provinsi Jawa Barat 2018 dalam membangun Personal Branding Menggunakan Twitter. J. Pustaka Komun. **1**(2), 213–227 (2018)
11. Smith, K.N.: TRACE: Tennessee research and creative exchange social media and political campaigns Kristian Smith chancellor's honors program May 2011 (2011)
12. Setiawan, D., Nurmandi, A.: Sandiaga Uno: personal branding di Twitter. J. Public Policy **6**(1), 19 (2020). https://doi.org/10.35308/jpp.v6i1.1657
13. Rahmat, A.F.: Twitter media platform to set-up political branding: analyzing @Kiyai_Marufamin in 2019 presidential election campaign, vol. 4, no. 1 (2020). http://jurnal.umt.ac.id/index.php/nyimak
14. Perlof, R.M.: The Dynamics of Political Communication: Media and Politics in a Digital Age. Routledge, Amerika Serikat (2021)
15. Schwanholz, J., Graham, T., Stoll, P.T.: Managing democracy in the digital age: internet regulation, social media use, and online civic engagement (2017)
16. Verdegem, P., D'heer, E.: Social media logic and its impact on political communication during election times. In: Schwanholz, J., Graham, T., Stoll, P.T. (eds.) Managing Democracy in the Digital Age, pp. 119–135. Springer, Cham (2018). https://doi.org/10.1007/978-3-319-61708-4_7
17. Pérez-Curiel, C., Naharro, P.L.: Political influencers. A study of Donald Trump's personal brand on Twitter and its impact on the media and users. Commun. Soc. **32**(1), 57–75 (2019). https://doi.org/10.15581/003.32.1.57-75
18. Bracciale, R., Martella, A.: Define the populist political communication style: the case of Italian political leaders on Twitter. Inf. Commun. Soc. **20**(9), 1310–1329 (2017). https://doi.org/10.1080/1369118X.2017.1328522
19. Hidayati, F.R.: Komunikasi Politik dan Branding Pemimpin Politik Melalui media Sosial: A Conceptual Paper. J. Lensa Mutiara Komun. **5**(2), 145–161 (2021). https://doi.org/10.51544/jlmk.v5i2.2385
20. Susila, I., Dean, D., Yusof, R.N.R., Setyawan, A.A., Wajdi, F.: Symbolic political communication, and trust: a young voters' perspective of the Indonesian presidential election. J. Polit. Mark. **19**(1–2), 153–175 (2020). https://doi.org/10.1080/15377857.2019.1652224
21. Susila, I., Dean, D., Harness, D.: Intergenerational spaces: citizens, political marketing and conceptualising trust in a transitional democracy. J. Mark. Manag. **31**(9), 970–995 (2015). https://doi.org/10.1080/0267257X.2015.1036768
22. Pich, C., Dean, D.: Political branding: sense of identity or identity crisis? An investigation of the transfer potential of the brand identity prism to the UK conservative party. J. Mark. Manag. **31**(11–12), 1353–1378 (2015). https://doi.org/10.1080/0267257X.2015.1018307
23. Nai, A., Martínez i Coma, F.: The personality of populists: provocateurs, charismatic leaders, or drunken dinner guests?, West Eur. Polit. **42**(7), 1337–1367 (2019). https://doi.org/10.1080/01402382.2019.1599570

24. Nurmalasari, Y., Erdiantoro, R.: Metode penelitian deskriptif kualitatif dalam perspektif bimbingan dan konseling. Quanta **4**(1), 44–51 (2020). https://doi.org/10.22460/q.v1i1p1-10.497
25. Sotiriadou, P., Brouwers, J., Le, T.A.: Choosing a qualitative data analysis tool: a comparison of NVivo and Leximancer. Ann. Leis. Res. **17**(2), 218–234 (2014). https://doi.org/10.1080/11745398.2014.902292
26. Montoya, P.: The Personal Branding Phenomenon, pp. 1–6. Pers. Brand. Press (2002)
27. McNally, D., Speak, K.D.: Be your own brand. Danc. Times **109**(1307), 26–27 (2003)
28. Barniat, Z.: Political communications in the social media of industrial revolution 4.0, pp. 59–67
29. Indrawan, J., Ilmar, A.: Kehadiran media baru (new media) dalam proses komunikasi politik. Medium **8**(1), 11–17 (2018)
30. Indah, R.N.: Apa itu G20 dan Manfaatnya untuk Indonesia (2022). https://www.djkn.kemenkeu.go.id/kpknl-singkawang/baca-artikel/14747/Apa-itu-G20-dan-Manfaatnya-untuk-Indonesia.html

Social Media Activism in South Africa

Kyle Kretschmer, Rebecca Njuguna, and Adheesh Budree(✉)

University of Cape Town, Cape Town 7700, South Africa
{krtkyl004,njgreb001}@myuct.ac.za, adheesh.budree@uct.ac.za

Abstract. This research focuses on the perception of South African online activists of intrinsic benefits and limitations associated with social media. The number of social media users has more than doubled in the last decade due to the medium creating an open public space where one can share their opinions and voice with minimal restrictions. Having an open public space with few rules and restrictions proves ideal for online activism with the potential to reach a larger audience. The ability to spread information faster by using social media provides for greater reach and awareness. A qualitative study interrogating social activism in South Africa was undertaken. Responses indicated that the digital divide together with inherent financial limitations inhibited the access to social media activism. These include the high cost of mobile data and ICT devices which limited many groups' access to digital devices, which in turn limits their capability to participate in social media activism. The findings also demonstrate that South African activists often concentrate more on Western issues than local ones due to the Western platform challenge. There are also typically fewer social media users in locations where poverty is prevalent because of the several financial limitations influencing access to social media and many South African activists found it difficult to infiltrate affected audiences because they weren't active on social media. These challenges have an impact on social media activism as they restrict its use in South Africa. Additional research can now be conducted to identify solutions for these shortcomings.

Keywords: Social media activism · South Africa · digital divide · usage constraints

1 Introduction

The usage of social media has increased dramatically over time; this phenomenon has not only impacted first world countries [6] but developing countries have also adopted social media in digital networks in conjunction with social movements and activism [7]. Digital networks [8] refer to the social network built using digital technologies to create communication from one point to another. The phenomenon in discussion is social media activism which involves modern forms of media that encompass interactive participation where individuals can share how they feel and increase awareness to their online social presence [9]. The amount of people who use social media worldwide in 2022 is estimated to be 4.62 billion people who are 58.4% of the world population [10].

A. Coman and S. Vasilache (Eds.): HCII 2023, LNCS 14025, pp. 223–233, 2023.
https://doi.org/10.1007/978-3-031-35915-6_17

The percentage of social media users being just over half the population is considered an impressive accomplishment when comparing it with the number of social media users in 2015 which was 2.07 billion [10, 11]. One of the reasons why the percentage of social media users doubled in usage was a result of social media creating an open public space where one could share their opinions and voice without any restrictions [12]. Having an open public space with no rules and restrictions was ideal for online activism since it allowed people to share local issues with the potential to reach a larger audience [13, 14].

The benefit of social media compared to previous methods of spreading awareness is that users can swiftly communicate information and mobilize supporters thanks to the interactive elements and widespread usage [7]. Facebook and Twitter, for example, may reach a considerably broader audience compared to traditional media such as posters and news [13]. The ability to spread information faster by using social media provides for a greater reach and recognition of difficulties that get spread to create awareness [13] The use of social media activism has facilitated transparency and the dissemination of awareness across countries [15], but there are still unresolved issues that limit its potential in developing nations [16, 17].

1.1 Problem Statement

While social media activism has made it easier to educate a broader audience about a variety of issues, it has also left many people who lack access to social media unaware of the problems raised by online activism or unable to participate in said activism [13, 16, 17]. Such a barrier for those who don't have access to online activism can be viewed as a digital divide [19]. In South Africa where there is unequal access to technological resources and education, the digital divide is even more pronounced [19]. In terms of online activism, the digital divide separates those citizens with internet access who can engage in activism and have a high level of familiarity with local issues from those who do not [16]. As a result, there is a disconnect between offline and online activism, and some even veered in separate directions [18]. As a result of this disconnect and existing digital divide, it is important to investigate the factors that influence people's participation in social media activism as well as their perceptions of it.

2 Related Literature

There exists a gap in literature related to research around the factors that influence social media activism in South Africa [12, 16, 17]. The objective of this study is to further investigate this gap by identifying the factors that influence social media activism in South Africa. Theoretical notions and patterns were developed to understand factors influencing social media activism in South Africa by analysing the perspectives of South African activists.

2.1 Social Media Activism

Social media activism is an online coordinated form of protest without any physical presence or pre-existing offline campaign [7, 20, 21]. Social media platforms are modern forms of media that encompass interactive participation. Individuals can observe responses to their online social presence and receive attention, which makes them feel more comfortable sharing their views, opinions, and enquiries [9]. In addition to enabling people to express their opinions, social media also offers three other advantages: it enables people to build public or semi-public profiles within regulated systems like Facebook, Instagram, or Twitter. Finally, social media enables users to browse and explore their list of connections as well as those formed by others inside the system. Users can also build a digital connection with a list of other users that they know or just wish to follow on the platform [22]. Given the capability to connect to the system digitally, users can engage in conversations with friends or anonymous users outside of their immediate geographic area [13, 14].

The creation of such an environment has allowed social media activism to flourish in usage [13]. Social media activism has gained a lot of attention to movements all around the world, where numerous issues have spread in awareness, thanks to the rising usage of social media [23]. Social media activism has the advantage of enabling minority groups to easily communicate and be heard [24]. Online and offline activism are increasingly becoming intertwined and complementary social-psychological tools for politicization, discussion, mobilization, and conflict resolution [24]. This adds to the diversity and liveliness of social media, but it also has the potential to divide and polarize civilizations.

The importance of social media activism was presented in the Black Lives Matter movement (BLM) where it proved to be an indispensable tool for BLM leaders and supporters alike [26]. The BLM movement was in protest of the murder of black individuals by the police force in the United States. Even though the movement started its online activism in 2013, it exploded in 2020 where Covid-19 pandemic was a big part of that explosion [26]. The Covid-19 pandemic prompted many individuals to lose their jobs, work from home, and cease traveling, resulting in a higher number of people participating in the social movement than ever before [27].

The use of social media activism wasn't only popular for the BLM movement. It has been popular for the past decade where the first considerable level of activism in social media can be traced to what is often referred to as the "Twitter Revolution". In June 2009, there was a movement in Iran where activists used Twitter to broadcast the crimes the regime was committing [28]. Twitter and other similar websites were successful in spreading the news and letting people around the world know what was happening in Iran [28, 29]. However, some scholars also doubt the significance of social media's role in the political upheaval [28, 30].

South Africa is a country historically plagued by slavery and colonial rule [31], which delayed the countries educational renewal, cut boundaries arbitrarily, ignored social and natural divisions of geography, and fuelled disputes in many situations [31]. Several communities still live in the segregated areas forced upon during the colonial rule, and this historical reality is still present today in areas where there is a widening digital divide and a high percentage of illiteracy [31]. Sebeelo [32], theorizes that, despite the continent of Africa still lagging behind other parts of the world in terms of smartphone ownership and internet availability, there is enough evidence to demonstrate that online movements have profoundly changed political activity in Africa. The presence of social media activism in South Africa may be seen by looking at campaigns like #RhodesMustFall, but the reach of these movements is still in question because of the factors that influence social media activism in South Africa. The existence of a digital divide can be seen in many movements involving internet activism where the digital divide could impact the reach of the movement [25]. This, amongst a number of other challenges around social media activism in South Africa still exist.

2.2 Social Media Activism Challenges

The following table describes the challenges that influence social media activism in South Africa (Table 1).

Table 1. Challenges influencing social media activism.

Factors	Proposition	References
Financial limitations	The cost of ICT devices and the cost of mobile broadband data are two major factors that influence social media usage. With the financial constraints in developing nations, lower percentages of people have access to ICT devices.	[23,37]
Computer Illiteracy	Although the problem of computer literacy is significant, it is an expensive process to address because many people in developing townships lack access to education and cannot afford the high costs of instruction.	[41,29]
Lack of Awareness	The groups involved in social media activism use a variety of techniques to bring behaviours and consequences to light to create large levels of retaliation and awareness. In developing countries with the lack of awareness-raising capabilities due to the digital divide or language barriers, socioeconomic issues fail to propagate.	[32]
Lack of Importance	The level of public awareness about the topic has an impact on its importance. Employment, education, money, and neighbourhood safety issues all have an impact on whether the problem will expand. The importance of the socioeconomic issues plays a significant role because if the topic is not of major concern, many people will disregard it.	[22,15]
Western Platform	The situation in sub-Saharan Africa does not always ensure that activists around the world will have access to content and issues found in Africa. Activists may be using similar methods, approaches, and goals but with the separation of content by country, sub-Saharan Africa is left in the dark. With majority users on social media having western backgrounds the content that is shared has a more western focus on culture and issues.	[5,24]
Digital Divide	The existence of the digital divide in different groups related to social media activism such as among activists who post socioeconomic issues but can't reach certain audience due to them lacking access to the internet.	[3,39]
Misinformation	Misinformation used in social media activism protests has the ability to alter perceptions of the real issue and spread false information increasing different beliefs of an issue. It could cause repulsion like it was identified with the Covid-19 vaccine.	[45]

As more societal and economic issues are publicized on social media, the challenges of social media activism have also increased [33]. A significant number of these challenges are rooted in perceptions.

2.3 Perceptions of Social Media Activism

There are still a range of perceptions of social media activism, and not all of them are favourable, even though it has increased and improved the opportunities for social communication. Cortés-Ramos et al., [34] performed focus groups discussions with youth in Spain regarding their online experience of social activism movements. The youth perceived social media activism as plagued with unreliable internet sources, online bullying, mistrust in the government, and privacy-related issues.

Participation in social activism is not always beneficial to mental health and can occasionally even worsen it [34, 35]. One can suffer from fatigue brought on by long-term activism's overwhelming psychological and emotional demands. Being politically active can make one more visible, which makes them more likely to be mistreated and shunned by the public and political opponents. It can also occasionally cause relationships with friends and family to fall apart due to ideological differences. It was further identified that social activism may worsen mental health after being exposed to media coverage of certain movements, like police brutality in USA, because the activist may encounter more difficulties as they work to change the status quo, such as being hurt during a protest or being stigmatized by close friends or family [35].

Wilkins et al. [36] argues that if increasingly over-used, social media activism leads to 'slacktivism'. Slacktivism involves low-impact action that derails future engagement and social change [36]. Consistent with the slacktivism hypothesis, Schumann and Klein [37] discovered that participating online hinders offline engagement for the same reason because of the satisfaction of contributing to the group.

The optimistic perspective of social media activism was that technological advances would further advance social change [36]. The social change can be created by the spread of viral videos that explain what a movement is about and why it then starts mass mobilisation [36]. The usage of social media activism has created a method to spread awareness on issues in a faster, more global process as compared to traditional methods [7]. South Africa offers many opportunities for social media activism and it can give many people a voice.

3 Approach to Theory

The primary research objective of this study was to investigate the factors that influence social media activism in South Africa. To develop theoretical concepts, it is necessary to identify such factors by identifying the perceptions of social media activism from South African citizens. By utilizing the perspectives of the public, the themes found in literature were supported and new, pertinent ideas emerged. With an interpretivist research philosophy, the inductive approach to theory was most followed as it built on the participants' insights.

The sample population for the research paper was social media activists and participants in social media activism. Social media activists are identified as those who are at the forefront of most online activism issues and spread awareness using multiple methods. Participants in social media activism, however, tend to be those who spread awareness through posting on their social media platforms with little additional effort, which is referred to as armchair activism [38].

Data was collected using semi-structured interviews. On completion of each interview, they were transcribed and saved to a secure cloud storage. After transcription, they were loaded into Nvivo qualitative research software where they were coded. The data analysis method followed was thematic analysis where a complete understanding of the data by coding and categorizing was conducted.

4 Findings

The use of social media activism by South African activists was identified to be most significantly influenced by four main factors. These factors are:

- Financial limitations
- Illiteracy
- Western vs Local
- Disinformation

Each of the factors identified are associated with specific challenges as shown in Table 2.

Table 2. Factors influencing social media activism in South Africa

Factor	*Challenge(s) to SMA*
Financial Limitations	□ Poverty in developing countries Challenge □ Unequal opportunities Challenge □ Skills gap Challenge □ Lack of education Challenge □ Language barriers Challenge
Illiteracy	□ Poverty Challenge □ Language barriers Challenge □ Media Illiteracy Challenge □ Digital Divide Challenge
Western vs Local	□ Lack of content creators □ Social media users □ Echo Chambers Challenge □ Development levels □ Western Platform Challenge □ Specific audiences
Disinformation	□ Malicious Gain Challenge □ Fake News Challenge

4.1 Financial Limitations

A significant challenge identified was access to technology due to the digital divide which exists in the South African socio-economic environment [23, 38, 39]. The findings indicated that with the existence of the digital divide and financial limitations, access to social media activism was inhibited. The high cost of mobile data and ICT devices limits many groups' access to digital devices, which in turn limits their capability to participate in social media activism [1, 2].

There is a rapid development of new technologies that arises with features that supplant those of earlier technologies, where disadvantaged people are commonly unable to catch up to the innovators and are thus excluded from enjoying the advantages of new technological opportunities and run the risk of falling even further behind [3, 40]. Falling behind has the effect of creating *unequal opportunities* and a *skills gap* where restricted citizens lack the resources to upgrade their skills by use of digital devices [40]. Until the accessibility issues with mobile devices and the high cost of data are resolved, the digital divide will likely continue to hinder social media activism.

The findings also indicated how a *language* and *educational barrier* was produced because of financial constraints. Saleh [31] demonstrated how almost all African countries with very low internet access are among the least developed countries in the world in terms of health, education, and income. The connection between internet and poverty is established, demonstrating how a lack of internet access typically translates into lower rates of income and education [31].

4.2 Illiteracy

Findings also suggested that illiteracy was a large impending factor that influences social media activism in South Africa. Cammaerts [7] describes social media activism as the integration of media and communication tools into activists' daily life, as well as how their efforts achieve both practical and symbolic goals. Integration of media and communication tools necessitates a certain level of literacy, whether computer or media literacy.

Several communities in South Africa still live in segregated areas forced upon during apartheid, and this historical reality persists today leading to a widening digital divide and a high percentage of illiteracy [31]. As identified in the financial limitations section, those areas in Africa with low internet access are among the least developed areas in terms of health, education, and income [31]. Coupled with illiteracy, there was also media and technology illiteracy since individuals who couldn't afford education typically couldn't afford technological devices [41].

Additionally, according to the findings, the challenges of the digital divide and media literacy arise in the absence of access to technological devices. This results in the residents of developing townships being unable to participate in social media activism. The problem of computer literacy is significant and it will cost a lot of money to address because many people in developing townships don't have access to *education* and can't pay the high costs associated with training [42].

4.3 Western vs. Local

Many popular social media platforms are of western origin, hence there is a greater emphasis on western issues compared to local issues [43]. Moazzam [43] argues that social media is a source of penetration of cultures from dominant countries to developing countries. Peters et al., [44] argue that despite over 80 percent of Facebook users, now known as Meta, being outside of the US and Canada not much is implied about how people from non-western cultures use Facebook. Both the articles echo the challenge of social media platforms having a western focus and go as far as to identify the existence of culture colonization through social media. Developing nations are socially more conservative than western nations because of their high rates of poverty and illiteracy [43]. Western nations, on the other hand, have modern societies with alluring social values that interest those in developing nations [43].

South Africa tends to be more conservative in its use of social media activism because of illiteracy and poverty. The findings also showed how South African activists often concentrated more on Western issues than local ones due to the *Western platform* challenge. There are *fewer social media users* in locations where poverty is prevalent because of the several financial limitations that have been identified as influencing access to social media [24]. With the existence of the financial limitations there is a divide between people who have access to social media and those who don't. Lower participation rates in South Africa's social media activism are a result of this divide.

The findings showed that because of this digital divide, certain South African activists found it difficult to contact specific audiences because they weren't active on social media. The *Echo Chamber* challenge also included elements of the digital divide [45]. When using social media for activism, echo chambers occur when a person follows other activists and assumes that because there are many posts on a particular problem, it is well-known. Because they are confined to their own echo chamber, they fail to inform people who are not their followers about the problems.

4.4 Disinformation

The challenges around disinformation involved the spread of fake news and associated malicious gain. Fake news can intentionally or unintentionally misinform or deceive audiences. These reports are typically produced to either sway people's opinions, further a political agenda, or create confusion, and they can frequently bring in money for web publications [4]. In social media activism, malicious action refers to when someone uses words or acts to damage the reputation of another person or movement. Actions against the movement are taken by those opposed to it or who stand to gain from its demise to detract from its goal. The findings for both fake news and malicious gain highlighted how both adversely affect social media activism movements.

5 Conclusion

This study explored the factors influencing social media activism in South Africa and explained how these factors influence the spread of social media activism. Each of the factors presents unique challenges that impact the use of social media activism.

Financial limitations involve challenges associated with poverty in developing countries, unequal opportunities, skills gap, lack of education and language barriers. Illiteracy challenges involve poverty, language barrier, media illiteracy and the digital divide. Challenges around western vs local influences involve the lack of local content creators, social media users, echo chambers, development levels, western platform, and specific audiences. The final factor of disinformation has the two challenges of malicious gain and fake news. South African activists acknowledged that social media activism has many opportunities in South Africa to give people a voice. It is recommended that South African organizations and government should support the use of social media to build the awareness of online activism. Successful efforts can ensure that fewer residents in South Africa are left in the dark. Future studies could build on the findings of this research by utilizing a larger sample size and multimodal data collection techniques to increase the precision of their conclusions.

References

1. Marler, W.: Mobile phones and inequality: findings, trends, and future directions. New Media Soc. **20**(9), 3498–3520 (2018). https://doi.org/10.1177/1461444818765154
2. Correa, T., Pavez, I., Contreras, J.: Digital inclusion through mobile phones?: A comparison between mobile-only and computer users in internet access, skills and use. Inf. Commun. Soc., 11–23 (2020)
3. Roessler, P.: The mobile phone revolution and digital inequality: scope, determinants and consequences. Pathw. Prosper. Comm. **15**, 1–10 (2018)
4. Brennen, B.: Making sense of lies, deceptive propaganda, and fake news. J. Media Ethics **32**, 179–181 (2017)
5. Al-Haidari, N., Kabanda, S., Almukhaylid, M.: The challenges of implementing social media marketing in the tourism industry, pp. 3–11 (2021)
6. Cammaerts, B.: Social media and activism. In: The International Encyclopaedia of Digital Communication and Society, pp. 1027–1034 (2015)
7. GeeksforGeeks post. https://www.geeksforgeeks.org/what-is-digital-networking/. Accessed 22 July 2022
8. Manning, J.: Social media, definition and classes of. In: Harvey, K. (ed.) Encyclopedia of Social Media and Politics, pp. 1158–1162 (2014)
9. Smart Insights post. https://www.smartinsights.com/social-media-marketing/social-media-strategy/new-global-social-media-research/#:~:text=More%20than%20half%20of%20the,social%20media%20is%202h%2027m. Accessed 22 July 2022
10. Back linko blog. https://backlinko.com/social-media-users. Accessed 10 Apr 2022
11. Ferrara, E.: #COVID-19 on Twitter: bots, conspiracies and social media activism, pp: 1–21 (2020)
12. Stone, L.B., Veksler, A.E.: Stop talking about it already! Co-ruminating and social media focused on COVID-19 was associated with heightened state anxiety, depressive symptoms, and perceived changes in health anxiety during Spring 2020. BMC Psychol. **10**(1), 7–15 (2022). https://doi.org/10.1186/s40359-022-00734-7
13. Longest, K., Kang, J.-A.: Social media, social support, and mental health of young adults during COVID-19. Front. Commun. **7**, 1–10 (2022). https://doi.org/10.3389/fcomm.2022.828135
14. Zunes, S.: Sudan's 2019 revolution. The Power of Civil Resistance, pp. 7–29 (2021)

15. Suthar, S., et al.: Epidemiology and diagnosis, environmental resources quality and socio-economic perspectives for COVID-19 pandemic. J. Environ. Manag. 6–10 (2021)
16. Shaw, J.: Citizenship and COVID-19: syndemic effects. Ger. Law J. **22**(8), 1635–1660 (2021)
17. Ng, L.H.X., Cruickshank, I.J., Carley, K.M.: Cross-platform information spread during the January 6th capitol riots. Soc. Netw. Anal. Min. **12**(1), 1–5 (2022). https://doi.org/10.1007/s13278-022-00937-1
18. Krönke, M.: Africa's digital divide and the promise of e-learning. Afrobarometer Policy Pap. **66**, 1–19 (2020)
19. Li, Y., Bernard, J.-G., Luczak-Roesch, M.: Beyond clicktivism: what makes digitally native activism effective? An exploration of the sleeping giants movement. Soc. Media Soc. **7**(3), 5 (2021). https://doi.org/10.1177/20563051211035357
20. Foster, M.D., Rathlin, J.: #MeToo as an 'angry mob' or in search of meaning? Using language to assess the focus of #MeToo tweets across four events. Comput. Hum. Behav. Rep. **5**, 1 (2022). https://doi.org/10.1016/j.chbr.2022.100173
21. Collin, P., Rahilly, K., Richardson, I., Third, A.: The benefits of social networking services. cooperative research centre for young people. Technol. Wellbeing, 7–18 (2011)
22. Online optimism blog. https://www.onlineoptimism.com/blog/social-media-activism/. Accessed 20 Aug 2022
23. Greijdanus, H., et al.: The psychology of online activism and social movements: relations between online and offline collective action **35**, 49–54 (2020). https://doi.org/10.1016/j.copsyc.2020.03.003
24. Elliott, T., Earl, J.: Online protest participation and the digital divide: modeling the effect of the digital divide on online petition-signing. New Media Soc. **20**(2), 698–719 (2018). https://doi.org/10.1177/1461444816669159
25. Gerbaudo, P.: The pandemic crowd: protest in the time of Covid-19. J. Int. Aff. **73**(2), 61–75 (2020)
26. Olson, R.E.: Roles of social media in the black lives matter movement, pp. 10–17 (2021)
27. Rahimi, B.: The agonistic social media: cyberspace in the formation of dissent and consolidation of state power in postelection Iran. Commun. Rev. **14**(3), 158–178 (2011). https://doi.org/10.1080/10714421.2011.597240
28. Hoskins, A., Shchelin, P.: The war feed: digital war in plain sight. Am. Behav. Sci. **67**(3), 449–463 (2023). https://doi.org/10.1177/00027642221144848
29. Robertson, B., Marchant, J.: A safe refuge? Minorities and the state in Iranian. Online J. Virtual Middle East **9**(2), 70–110 (2015)
30. Ibrahim, S.: Media and information literacy in South Africa: goals and tools. Sci. J. Media Educ. **39**, 35–43 (2012). https://doi.org/10.3916/C39-2012-02-03
31. Sebeelo, T.B.: Hashtag activism, politics and resistance in Africa: examining #ThisFlag and #RhodesMustFall online movements. Insight Afr. **13**(1), 95–109 (2021). https://doi.org/10.1177/0975087820971514
32. Uldam, J.: Social media visibility: challenges to activism. Media Cult. Soc. **40**(1), 41–58 (2017). https://doi.org/10.1177/0163443717704997
33. Cortés-Ramos, A., Torrecilla García, J.A., Landa-Blanco, M., Poleo Gutiérrez, F.J., Castilla Mesa, M.T.: Activism and social media: youth participation and communication. Sustainability **13**(18), 10485 (2021). https://doi.org/10.3390/su131810485
34. Alexander, A., et al.: Perceptions of mental health and exploring the role of social activism among African Americans exposed to media coverage of police brutality and protests. J. Racial Ethn. Health Disparities, 1–10 (2022)
35. Wilkins, D., Livingstone, A., Levine, M.: All click, no action? Online action, efficacy perceptions, and prior experience combine to affect future collective action. Comput. Hum. Behav. **91**, 97–105 (2019)

36. Schumann, S., Klein, O.: Substitute or stepping stone? Assessing the impact of low-threshold online collective actions on offline participation. Eur. J. Soc. Psychol. **45**(3), 308–322 (2015)
37. Digital 2021: global overview report. https://datareportal.com/reports/digital-2021-global-overview-report. Accessed 21 Aug 2022
38. Public Health: Social determinants of health. How social and economic factors affect health, pp. 6–8 (2013)
39. Cochrane, J.: Factors affecting access to digital technologies and the resulting impact for students in a P-12 context, vol. 35, 1, pp. 1–14 (2020)
40. Lechman, E., Popowska, M.: Harnessing digital technologies for poverty reduction. Evidence for low-income and lower-middle income countries. Telecommun. Policy **46**(6) (2022)
41. Aker, J.C., Mbiti, I.M.: Mobile phones and economic development in Africa, vol. 24, pp 207–232 (2010)
42. Naseer, M., Latif, M., Ahmed, M.: Cultural imperialism through social media influence of western dressing through Facebook in Urban areas of Pakistan. Media Sci., 160–171 (2021)
43. Peters, A.N., Winschiers-Theophilus, H., Mennecke, B.E.: Cultural influences on Facebook practices. Comput. Hum. Behav. **49**, 259–271 (2015)
44. Enjolras, B., & Salway, A.: Homophily and polarization on political twitter during the 2017 Norwegian election. Soc. Netw. Anal. Min., 13–15 (2023)
45. Pennycook, G., Rand, G.: Accuracy prompts are a replicable and generalizable approach for reducing the spread of misinformation. Nat. Commun., 1–13 (2022). https://doi.org/10.1038/s41467-022-30073-5

Designing a Robot as an Interaction Frontend for Elderly People Living in Aging Mountainous District in Japan

Itaru Kuramoto[1](✉), Jun Baba[2,3], and Junya Nakanishi[2]

[1] The University of Fukuchiyama, Kyoto, Japan
Kuramoto-itaru@fukuchiyama.ac.jp
[2] Osaka University, Suita, Japan
[3] CyberAgent Inc., Tokyo, Japan

Abstract. There are many elderly people living in mountainous area in Japan. Health care, welfare, and disaster prevention support to them becomes difficult due to the decrement of population, especially special skilled medical and/or welfare staffs. Robot-based support can reduce such problematic situations, so we proposed the design of a semi-autonomous communication robot for the elderly people living in aging mountainous district. The robot has 1) daily communication function, 2) announcement for disaster prevention, and 3) telecommunication between the elderly people and medical/welfare staffs in remote via the robot. In the implementation of the former two functions, the robot communicates the people autonomously with keyword-base message selection method. The latter one is based on audible telecommunication system. Considering the design, the first function is important to make the elderly people talk to the robot naturally in their daily lives.

Keywords: human-robot interaction · elderly people · mountainous district · aging · health care · welfare · disaster prevention

1 Introduction

In Japan, about 67% of homeland is mountainous forest area (in 2017, measured by Ministry of Agriculture, Forestry and Fisheries, Japan [1]). There still are many people living in this kind of areas, and a large part of them are elderly people because the areas are their birthplaces. In such a place, health care including medical and welfare support, and sharing disaster prevention information for the elderly people are quite important. In the past, special skilled medical/welfare staffs or workers in local government, who were younger than the living people, had carried out such support works by face-to-face manners. In most of cases, the staffs went to the elderly people's home, communicated to them, and gathered their medical/welfare needs from the conversation, because they were hardly to move to the place where the staffs worked.

A. Coman and S. Vasilache (Eds.): HCII 2023, LNCS 14025, pp. 234–242, 2023.
https://doi.org/10.1007/978-3-031-35915-6_18

However, in recent years, such face-to-face-based care works become difficult due to lowering population, which leads higher rate of elderly population. The rate in mountainous district is higher than city area, so the needs to such supports also becomes higher. In spite of the situation, the load of support works in the area tends to be much higher, and needs larger costs to give the same style of medical/welfare supports to the elderly people living in the area. Another problem is the decrement of the number of medical and welfare staffs. Currently, when the elderly people in the area want to receive such cares by the skilled staffs, they must go to the staff's offices far from their living mountainous places. The movement tends to be a tough work for them. In Japan, some researches reported that the care supports in mountainous area are covered mainly by their families [2], because gathering support staffs in such areas becomes more difficult [3]. This tendency would become more serious.

To tackle with the problematic situation, we plan to introduce a semi-autonomous communication robot as a giver of the health care, welfare support and disaster prevention information in the aging mountainous area (Fig. 1). In this paper, we propose the design of the robot, including features which are needed to support elderly people.

Fig. 1. The proposed communication robot system.

2 Supporting Elderly People in Aging Mountainous District

There are two purposes for supporting elderly people;

- medical and welfare support: daily survey of the people's health, and
- disaster prevention information support: announcing forecast/disaster alert directly to the people.

Commonly, the medical and welfare support have been done by some special skilled medical and/or welfare staff. The first step of care supports was making conversation to the elderly people. The staffs went to the home of the elderly people in mountainous area, and made interviews with them for their health and daily life. In such conversation, there were many hints about their health and quality of life, which were not able to be gathered only by medical consultations. Recently, the less medical/welfare workers were, the heavier the work became. There are many kinds of devices gathering medical parameter (i.e. blood pressure, body temperature, and so on) automatically, but direct interviews to the people are still important to check and understand their health and welfare conditions precisely.

The disaster alert and its prevention information, including shelter operation status in the district where the elder people live, are normally prepared by the local government, and announced through TV news and/or websites. However, in TV announcement is too sparse for them living in mountainous area, since the population in the area is small. Local and precise information could be informed via a website maintained by the local government of their living area, but the elderly people with less skills for digital devices are hardly to access websites with them.

3 Design of the Robot for Supporting Elderly People

We propose an interaction robot to solve the problems mentioned in Sect. 2. The robot has three functions:

1. **autonomous verbal daily communication**: for them to use the robot daily in order to make the robot fit in their daily life,
2. **autonomous verbal informing**: to inform important information including disaster alert and its prevention information, and
3. **audio-based remote communication channel**: for elderly people to communicate with medical and/or welfare staffs directly.

To prevent the confusion of the usage of the robot, all these functions should be produced single interaction style. In addition, the elderly people who are the main user of the robot has little skill for digital devices, so these functions should be implemented by speech-based interaction. Whenever the user, an elderly person, talks to the robot in verbal, the robot replies audible messages based on one of these functions. For visually-suited, complex, or large information such as a map to the disaster prevention shelter, a small information display is complementally used.

As usual, the user asks the robot about something daily such as weather forecast, recent news, and so on. The robot autonomously replies the user about what they asking based on function 1. Not only replying, but the robot informs directly to the user about the information of disaster prevention, when he/she is by the robot, or when he/she comes around the robot, based on the function 2.

To perform medical and/or welfare support, interviews by the medical/welfare staffs are valuable, because a small change of their daily activities and their mental conditions, commonly gathered from a communication in both verbal and non-verbal, are informative about their health and quality of life, as mentioned before. It is however difficult for a current autonomous communication mechanism to make an interview suited for each elderly person. To cover such a case, the robots at first simply asks the users about their daily situations and impressions. The answers from the users are recorded and sent to the staffs. When the staffs listen to the recorded answers, and considered that they need more detail of the users' daily situations, the staffs can communicate with the users directly through the robots by the function 3. The function also solves the problem about the difficulties for the small number of staffs visiting to the users. The staffs also avoid to move to the mountainous area where the users live in.

The first function is not directly supported the aims described in Sect. 2, but this is quite important to make the latter two functions effective. Because the robot has the first function, the user will use the robot anytime they want. Based on the daily use, they can communicate the staffs smoothly through the robot, and they can quickly notice disaster alert and its prevention information announced by the robot.

4 Implementation

The system overview of the interaction robot is described in Fig. 2. As shown in Fig. 1, the system hardware in an user's home consists of a table-size communication robot[1], a speaker microphone with a noise canceller, a wide angle camera, a tablet-size display, and a small desktop PC. For voice recognition and synthesis, some WebAPIs are used through the Internet. To avoid the misrecognition of the voice of the robot itself, all the audio is output by the speaker microphone. The robot's controls including state transition management, body movement, and construction of the messages are processed by the small PC. The camera is used both of body recognition of the user and remote communication to a medical/welfare staff.

4.1 Autonomous Talk with a Robot

The robot changes its state based on triggers including recognizing the user's existence and a keyword in verbal. Figure 3 shows a part of the state transition diagram of the robot. At the beginning, the robot's state is the initial state. A trigger is indicated on each arrow. When the trigger comes, the state is changed to the next one along the arrow with the trigger. At the same time, an action command will be operated, whose name is shown in square brackets in the figure. The command name is dispatched to actions including verbal messages, robot's actions, and an image for the display at the side of

[1] Communication Robot Sota™, Vstone Co., Ltd., https://www.vstone.co.jp/products/sota/index.html (in Japanese).

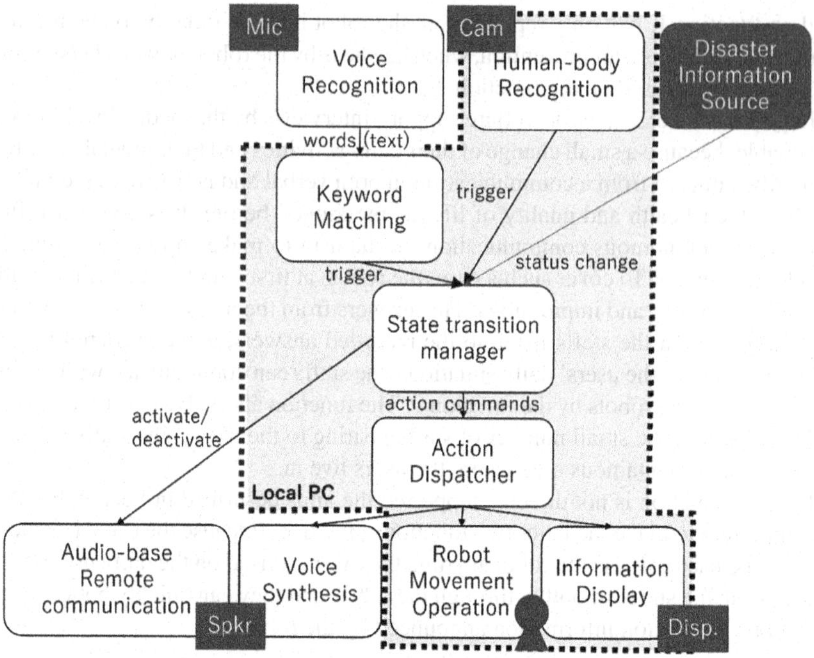

Fig. 2. An overview of the proposed interaction robot system.

the robot. Voice synthesis system then performs to make audible replies of the robot with the movement of the robot, and the robot shows the image on the display.

We implement three types of triggers: 1) voice recognition, 2) human body recognition, and 3) noticing the change of information sources. For the first trigger type, the single-word recognition is used. When the robot receives the users' utterances, the STT (speech-to-text) system transforms the utterance to a sequence of the words. The robot checks whether there are pre-defined keywords (for example, "hello", "forecast", etc.) in the words. When one of the keywords is matched, the robot replies a corresponding prepared message in verbal. The triggers of this type are indicated in Fig. 3 as "keyword: *word*." A part of keywords is shown in Table 1.

Human body recognition system is in operation all through the time the robot is executing. From the view of a camera attached on the system, the human-body recognition system calculates whether the human exists or not, and if exists, the distance from the robot to the recognized human. The distance is shorter than a pre-configured value, the trigger "user appeared" is sent to the state transition manager.

As the third type of triggers, which corresponds to the function 2, the robot constantly polls the disaster prevention information website by local government. If the website changes to show the disaster prevention information of the users' living area, the robot constructs the message base on the information. At the same time, the trigger "disaster info. raised" is occurred so that the robot can announce the information when the user comes around the robot.

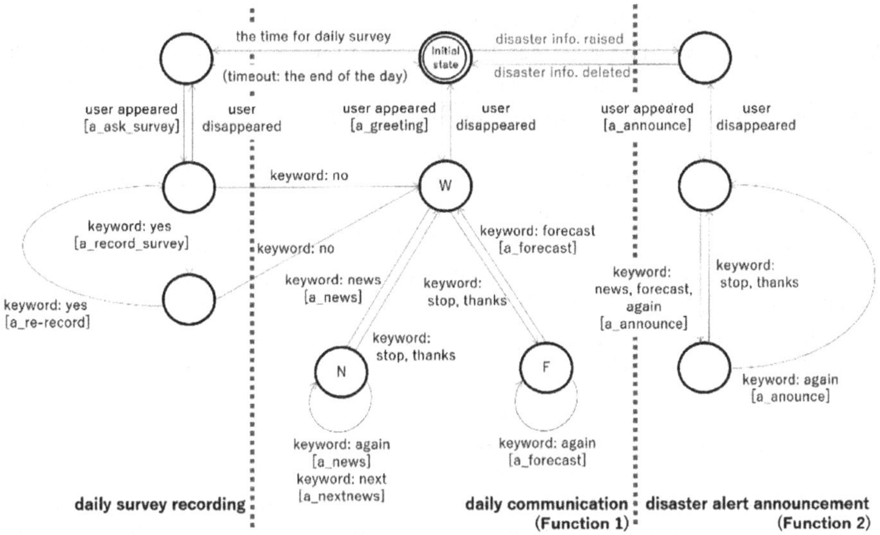

Fig. 3. State transition diagram of the robot (a part).

Table 1. Trigger keywords (a part).

Trigger keyword	Recognized words from utterances[a]
yes	yes, sure, go ahead
no	no, no thanks
thanks	thank, appreciate, good job
stop	stop, finish
greeting	hello, good morning, good evening, good afternoon
news	news, interesting
forecast	weather, sunny, rainy, cloudy, snowy, windy, rain, snow
again	repeat, pardon, again, one more

[a]The original language is Japanese, and these are the translation. They might not precisely match the exact nuance of recognized words.

Some replying messages should be changed based on the current situation, such as a weather forecast. In such a case, the robot produces the message based on the information scraped from the suited information source, in this situation, a weather forecast website.

Here is an example of the state transition of the robot and its actions: In normal daily communication situation (shown in the center of Fig. 3), at first the robot's state is initial. When the robot recognizes the user coming, the robot's status is changed to the state indicated "W" in Fig. 3 along the arrow indicating "user appeared." At that time, a command "a_greeting" starts, so the robot then says a greeting to the user based on the dispatched action, and wait for his/her speech. After that, when he/she says "How is the weather today?" to the robot, the word "weather" hits the keyword "forecast" as mentioned in Table 1. The state therefore changes to the next state indicated "F", the robot automatically replies today's weather forecast information to him/her. When the user disappears, the robot stops talking and waits the user come back again, in the initial state.

These techniques used in the proposed system is rather simple, and some sophisticated autonomous communication method like AI can be utilized. However, the system is introduced in an usual home where elderly people lives. In many cases, they do not have a wide internet connection in a mountainous distinct. They mean that they cannot use any expensive hardware with a system with large computation resources, so our research aims to support the elderly people's health and welfare with a low-cost and simple devices and systems.

4.2 Remote Communication with Staffs

A medical and/or welfare staff is available to use a remote communication system. When the staff needs to communicate to the elderly person as an user, the staff starts the system. Then the robot announces the user that the staff wants to communicate with you directly. After acceptance by the user, the audio-based communication channel is established, and they can communicate directly each other. At the time, only the staff can capture the user's appearance visually, because the non-verbal information of the user should be transferred to the staff. When the communication ends, the staff closes the communication channel by the remote communication system.

Fig. 4. The operator's screen of remote communication via the robot.

The operator's screen is shown in Fig. 4. In common, one staff has several people to support, so the operator, a medical and/or welfare staff in this situation, can watch several people's situation simultaneously in the interface (at the blue box in Fig. 4). The operator can start and end communication verbally by clicking a certain view of an elderly people at the place. There is a case that the elderly people want to talk to the operator, and ask the robot to start communication with the operator. In such a case, the robot does nothing, but the operator can reply them via the function. To avoid mishearing them, especially when two (or more) people talk simultaneously, each view shows the last speech of each elderly person in text via STT system. The system can only one sentence in the views, but the sentence might be enough to judge whose talk is important.

5 Related Works

Utilizing embodied robot in social environment becomes popular. Okafuji et al. [4] introduced small robots to a shopping mall for attracting pedestrians. Such a research indicates that robots are able to have a power to communicate people emotionally. Emotional communication is important to make a rapport between a robot and an user, especially when the robot stands in the user's daily life immersively. In the proposed system, we use a table-top size, in the other word, a "cute" robot with a child-like voice synthesis system. The robot seems more familiar to the elderly people than serious adult appearance and voice, especially in their home.

In a closer situation of the research, the care support robot in a hotel is proposed [5]. The system is similar to the proposed system, which do not have a remote communication function. They are same that the robot implements for talking with one person, and the importance of friendly and trustworthy interaction to make rapport for continuing communication with the robot. However, the design of the robot in a hotel is different from that in a house of elderly people in the view of, for example, privacy invasion, information personalization, and so on.

In the view of care for elderly people, there are many researches about designing robots and their usage, for instance, participatory design [6], using telepresence robot [7], and so on. The main part of health care robot supports detection of falls and calling for help, lifting, and monitoring location [8]. Comprehensive robot technologies for elderly people in the view of caretaker [9], but the scale of such technologies tends to be large so that it is difficult to introduce them to people living mountainous district. In another view, not social factors are needed to build relationships between robots and elderly people, but more small, personal things such as using verbal/non-verbal communication, the place where the robot is, and naming the robot is important to establish relationships between robots and users [10].

In all cases, the design is deeply related to the elderly people's social and living environment, so the robot design should include consideration of such user-specific environments.

6 Conclusion and Future Work

In this article, we described the design of a semi-autonomous communication robot for supporting medical care, welfare and disaster prevention to elderly people living in aging mountainous district. It includes autonomous daily communication, announcement of disaster prevention information, and remote communication to medical/welfare staffs via the robot. The users, the elderly people, only talk to the robot to receive the support functionalities.

Experimental evaluation is needed to measure the effectiveness of the system. We are planning a month-long experimentation at least to clarify whether the target elderly people use the robot in every day.

Acknowledgement. This research is a part of the project "Rules and regulations of using AI as an alternative to the administration of long-term care insurance - from the viewpoint of community management and social capital (project leader: Prof. Kawashima, N.)", on Area Cultivation, Topic-Setting Program to Advance Cutting-Edge Humanities and Social Sciences Research, granted by Japan Society for the Promotion of Science.

References

1. MAFF Japan: The rate of forest based on prefecture. (in Japanese). https://www.rinya.maff.go.jp/j/keikaku/genkyou/h29/1.html. Accessed 31 Dec 2022
2. Nomoto, H.: A comparative study of family caregiving in mountainous areas: a case study of Nakajima-cho district and Matsuyama City, Ehime, Japan. J. For. Econ. **51**(2), 30–38 (2005). (in Japanese). https://doi.org/10.20818/jfe.51.2_30
3. Suzuku, Y.: Current state of care for the elderly people in mountainous areas. Agric. Hortic. **93**(6), 497–501 (2018). (in Japanese)
4. Okafuji, Y., et al.: Behavioral assessment of a humanoid robot when attracting pedestrians in a mall. Int. Jo. Soc. Robot. **14**, 1731–1747 (2022). https://doi.org/10.1007/s12369-022-00907-9
5. Nakanishi, J., Kuramoto, I., Baba, J., Ogawa, K., Yoshikawa, Y., Ishiguro, H.: Continuous hospitality with social robots at a hotel. SN Appl. Sci. **2**(452) (2020). https://doi.org/10.1007/s42452-020-2192-7
6. Rogers, W.A., Kadylak, T., Bayles, M.A.: Maximizing the benefits of participatory design for human–robot interaction research with older adults. Hum. Factors **64**(3), 441–450 (2022). https://doi.org/10.1177/00187208211037465
7. Fiorini, L., Sorrentino, A., Pistolesi, M., Becchimanzi, C., Tosi, F., Cavallo, F.: Living with a telepresence robot: results from a field-trial. IEEE Robot. Autom. Lett. **7**(2), 5405–5412 (2022). https://doi.org/10.1109/LRA.2022.3155237
8. Broadbent, E., et al.: Attitudes towards health-care robots in a retirement village. Australas J. Ageing **31**(2), 115–120 (2012)
9. Ezer, N., Fisk, A.D., Rogers, W.A.: More than a servant: self-reported willingness of younger and older adults to having a robot perform interactive and critical tasks in the home. In: Proceedings of the Human Factors and Ergonomics Society Annual Meeting **53**(2), 136–140 (2009)
10. Klamer, T., Allouch, S.B.: Acceptance and use of a social robot by elderly users in a domestic environment. In: IEEE 2010 4th International Conference on Pervasive Computing Technologies for Healthcare, pp. 1–8 (2010). https://doi.org/10.4108/ICST.PERVASIVEHEALTH2010.8892

Considerations on FinTech Models in Romania – Specific Aspects Regarding Communication with Customers and the Recognition of Financial Flows Generated by These Models in the Accounting of Privately Owned Companies

Cristina Nicolaescu(✉), Lucia Risti, and Monica Bija

"Aurel Vlaicu" University of Arad, Bd. Revoluţiei, Nr. 77, Arad, Romania
cris.nicolaescu2@gmail.com

Abstract. This article aims to fulfill several objectives related to the specific aspects of FinTech models in Romania.

The first objective consists in making a synthesis of the field literature related to FinTech models in Romania. Another objective is the analysis of the appropriate tools used the analysis of how FinTechs influence company-client relationships in Romania, given that the appearance and expansion of FinTech has generated changes on a social level as well as in the user's profile of FinTech models, is another objective of this research. We also analyzed the influence of FinTech models on the interaction between the public and private financial sectors. Another objective of the research is to identify new methods and accounting tools for the quantification and the recognition of these financial operations in Romania, in order to respond to the need for speed and financial-accounting credibility and we made a prediction of the evolution of FinTech in Romania.

The conclusions at the end of the article refer to all these objectives, most of them being based on the survey conducted on the basis of questionnaire that we applied to both companies and individuals to see the extent to which they use digital services, what kind of services, if they prefer specialized companies or traditional ones, what are the reasons why they use/do not use or think about using/not using these services in the future.

Keywords: FinTech operations · communication · accounting

1 Introduction

If today the payment of a plane ticket or a consumption with the smartphone is a natural thing, we must be aware that they are possible through financial technological innovation. These simple operations described above, if we look at things in their entirety, are just tiny sequences of the electronic payment system created to provide and support

A. Coman and S. Vasilache (Eds.): HCII 2023, LNCS 14025, pp. 243–270, 2023.
https://doi.org/10.1007/978-3-031-35915-6_19

settlement operations and integrated globally. FinTech generates another paradigm of financial culture manifested through new models of applications, financial products and new types of businesses at the heart of which is the innovation of financial technology. Thus, settlements made between financial or non-financial entities, be they private or public, specific to the capital market or public credit, based on FinTech models will be customized by the importance of technology both in terms of improving internal processes and in the field of communication and interaction with customers.

FinTech technologies will make it possible to meet the two actors, the payer and the payee in the virtual environment. The areas where FinTech innovation can be applied relate in particular to payment services, creditworthiness assessment and automated investment advice using artificial intelligence for this purpose. Financial institutions in this context can completely change their appearance by working only in the online environment. The relations with the beneficiaries of the services, the interaction and communication with them will be carried out exclusively through social networks in conditions of optimizing the supply of products and services.

So, our research will have as its object the study of another financial business model, the analysis of the processes and techniques specific to a business in the virtual environment and its tools appropriate to the online environment and obviously the new types of services as well as the innovative ways to communicate and interact with customers, obviously with the specific opportunities and risks. How will account adapt to these amazing, through its originality and the rapidity with which it unfolds, facets of heritage, because from an accounting point of view this is their representation, remains a challenge for the study of this science. If the principle of accounting involves the recognition of transactions when they take place, it is interesting to investigate what will be the accounting instruments that will allow this to happen and how all these operations will be quantified responding to the need for financial and accounting speed and credibility.

First let's answer the question of what is FinTech? There are a multitude of definitions of FinTech, between them, we mention: FinTech "new financial industry that applies technology to improve financial activities" (Schueffel 2016), FinTech are "technology-based businesses that compete against, enable and/or collaborate with financial institutions" (Pollari 2016 FinTech are "financial services delivered by technology" (Swan 2017), FinTech is "the use of technology to deliver financial solutions" (Arner, Barberis, and Buckley 2017), FinTech refers to the application of new technology in providing financial solutions to individuals and firms (Imerman and Fabozzi 2020). FinTech is an acronym resembling an amalgamation of finance and technology, comprising the combination disruptive technologies (Artificial Intelligence, Big Data, Internet of Things, Distributed LedgerTechnology, etc.) with established business activities (e.g. payments, investments, financing), resulting in new products, services, and business processes (Woroch, Strobel, Wulfert 2022), etc. Analyzing the literature, we found that many of the definitions are repeated or the articles cite the same sources for defining the concept of FinTech and related ones [36].

A pertinent conclusion to these definitions seems to me to be that offered by Prashant Subhash Chougule, Dipti Tulpule and Aparajita Dasgupta Amist, namely that "FinTech is about provision of Financial Services by harnessing the improved affordability, high speed, enhanced reach & last level customization made possible by the ongoing innovations in technology, so as to provide a personalised, positive, hassle-free & seamless experience to the financial services consumer, of course, for a reasonable profit" [36].

On the other hand, we would conclude that a generic answer would be that FinTech is nothing more than a start-up, a new company, the result of a new business, new in terms of concept, means, methods and tools, which addresses a new type of customer-consumer, another generation that want more comfort and discretion and that has less patience when it comes to solve its financial problems, regardless of their nature (payments, investments, searching for sources of financing, etc.) and who likes to "play" with digital money (Perhaps because of their appetence for everything that is virtual…).

Regarding this article, from the beginning it should be noted that the purpose of the article is to analyze some of the aspects of the FinTech phenomenon in Romania, therefore the international phenomenon will be used only as a frame of reference. Thus, although the starting point in the analysis of each objective of the article will be the international experience, the novelty element will be brought by the presentation of the peculiarities of the phenomenon in Romania.

In this idea, although the presentation of international literature on this subject is part of the article, more emphasis will be placed on Romanian literature and its peculiarities.

Because we cannot talk about FinTech without talking about technology, the analysis of the tools used will also be part of this article, but thanks to train in the economic and not technical field of the authors, it will not have a large weight within the article.

Once we know the capabilities and attributes of the digital instruments used, a new logical question arises, that of the conditions and safety of the initiated payments, of the necessary authorizations, the execution of the compensation operation and the confirmation of the transfer. In these circumstances, the consumer's trust in the payment service provider must be justified by the provision of the regulatory framework but also by the transparency of the management of the interface between the two of them.

Obviously, the emergence and expansion of FinTech has generated some mutations, including on a social level, because it strongly influences the relationships of companies-customers, the speed with which the profits of the premiums are marked and the speed with which the customer has access to a service. So one topic that our study wants to address is represented by how FinTechs influence company-client relationships in Romania.

As it mentioned in policy research paper entitled Consumer Risks in Fintech, New Manifestations of Consumer Risks and Emerging Regulatory Approaches prepared by the staff of the World Bank with external contributions in April 2021, "FinTech is increasingly recognized as a key enabler for financial sectors worldwide, enabling more efficient and competitive financial markets while expanding access to finance for traditionally underserved consumers" [55]. But this new model of human interaction, in addition to the obvious benefits, comes with certain risks for the users/consumers of these services. As a result, in order to enjoy the benefits offered by these revolutionary services, consumers need to be aware of the potential risks they take when using these services.

The lack of detailed knowledge of these services by customers and often the capacity related to their development can generate the risk of fraud or misconduct by FinTech entities or third parties.

Certain features of FinTech operations can lead to conflicts of interest between service providers and consumers of those services.

In some situations, increases in the risk of cyber fraud may be observed, in the case of these platforms, by exploiting the vulnerability and lack of knowledge in the field of users.

Some companies that base their funding or investments on these platforms may face liquidity problems or even go bankrupt. Financial problems can generate transactions based on these platforms and individuals with a certain profile and consumer personality.

With these aspects in mind in this article, we have developed and analyzed a questionnaire to determine how consumers, current or potential, of services affected by FinTech platforms see these risks and to what extent they are willing to accept them.

The state through public institutions is also part of the economic ecosystem, as a result of which it must adapt to the changes imposed by technological progress and the use of modern technologies in daily transactions. In this idea, in the article we presented some of the measures that ensure the digitisation of public services in Romania and not only.

Many of the private companies in Romania have used the opportunities offered by FinTech platforms or banks to optimize their activity, be it online payments, financing, investments or the use of digital money. These operations will involve specific arrangements for entry in the accounts. Proposals on these modalities that will be made in this article.

2 Literature Review

The general academic research on the topic of FinTechs followed the development of Webster J, Watson RT (2002) phased in specific technologies and followed and tried to systematize conceptually the field and then explain the evolution and connections specific to the level of sophistication of these operations at a given time [47].

Thus, in the early 2000s, the term e-finance was imposed, defined in the works of Barber BM, Odean T (2001), Greiner ME, Wang H (2010) that in the specialized literature refers to the entire range of operations and digital financial communication interfaces Allen F, McAndrews J, Strahan P (2002), Antweiler W, Frank MZ (2004), Petzel E (2005) [2, 5, 7, 21]. The initiators of the domain have tried to define in this context the two words "electronic" respectively "finance". Several authors have highlighted the relationship between the two terms, eventually concluding that e-finance is nothing more than the perimeter of interaction of the financial interest of different players in a specific financial market. Obviously this place is regarded as an interface, an electronic one according to the predictions of Teschner F, Kranz TT, Weinhardt C (2015), both technical and communicational between two participants [42].

Starting from the e-finance concept stated in the work of Greiner ME, Wang H (2010), which was used especially to express electronic operations from the beginning of financial digitization, in the following years another Digital-Finance concept was imposed, which already had an operating area, both technical and conceptual, which related to the entire financial system, through the massive introduction of digital technology [21]

Karlan, D., Kendall, K., Mann, R., Pande, R. (2016) encompassing virtually all specific operational, institutional and financial communication segments [23]. Obviously, the academic literature has become much richer, the studies trying to highlight, starting from the realities of the financial market Lee M. (2009), concepts, roles, functions, methods Devine P. (2015), new financial instruments and models [17, 25]. What would the FinTech concept bring in addition as illustrated in Zavolokina L.'s article, Dolata M. Schwabe G. (2016) to Digital-Finance? Perhaps additional importance given to IT-type technological innovation. It seems that the innovations in the area of hard, software, electronic money (cryptocurrency) and gadgets related to Jones H (2016) are going in parallel.

The concept of Digital-Finance has crystallized in the literature a set of functions, namely the Business Function, the Investment Function, the Digital-Money Function, the Payment Instrument Function, the Insurance Function and last but not least the Digital Advisory Function.

Regarding the research of the Business Function, we have identified in the literature studies that approach the subfunction of financing through the works of Liu C., as the opener of the new financial paradigm then Dapp T. (2014), Doering P. Neumann S., Paul S. (2015) but also the subfunction of digital technology analyzed in the work of Gattenio C.A. (2002) [16, 27].

Between the specialized works on digital financing on factoring system we mention Klapper's work (2006) with its reverse factoring form highlighted by Penttinen andTuunainen's work (2011) which provides a nuanced picture of the economic benefits of the electronic invoice.

Along with these in the last decade, financing operations on "crowdfounding" platforms have been increasingly imposed, a phenomenon analyzed through a series of academic papers that study it such as Burtch G, Ghose A, Wattal S. (2013), Thies F., Wessel M., Benlian A. (2014), Kim Y. Park Y.J., Choi J., Yeon J. (2015), Maier E. (2016), Bessière V., Stéphany E. (2017), Lee, I., Shin, Y.J. (2018), Omarova, S. T. (2019), CSR Chan, A Parhankangas (2017), Motilska A.&Kuzma (2018), Wilson M.A. (2019), Babich V., Allon G. (2020), Chandler J.A., Short J.C. (2021), Abdeldayem M., Aldulaimi S. (2022) and others.

The topic of digital investment refers to all types of investments made through smart technology, whether they refer to smartphones, PCs, tablets or other gadgets used for the purpose of online transactions in the capital market, the banking market or specialised P2P platforms. Studies in this regard have been conducted by Greiner M.E., Wang H. (2009), Duarte J., Siegel S., Young L. (2012), Lin M., Prabhala N.R., Viswanathan S. (2013), Gao L., Waechter K.A. (2015) [18, 21].

Regarding the study of the functions of Digital Money respectively digital means of payment, the segment of electronic money as a means of exchange, from account money, virtual or digital money respectively cryptocurrency, all perform the traditional functions of money, that is, those of currency, means of payment, means of saving (investing) only that the instrument is electronic and has no material form. Many of the characteristics and peculiarities of this phenomenon have been analyzed through the academic papers dedicated to Grinberg R (2012), Glaser F, Zimmermann K., Haferkorn M, Weber MC,

Siering M. (2014), Brie're M., Kim Oosterlinck, Szafarz A. (2015) or Dyhrberg A.H. (2015) [10].

For the field of digital insurance, the literature is poor for this field, identifying so far only the work of Arumugam M and Cusick K (2008), which, however, does not come up with a study based on the realities of today's digital-insurances but only makes predictions from the perspective of 2008, which does not meet the relevant needs of knowledge. So it remains an unexplored area from an academic point of view.

And last but not least, the academic literature on digital-advice is covered with relatively recent papers that address research in an autarchic way, either from the perspective of user behavior, mentioning some of them namely Marot E., Fernandez G., Carrick J., Hsi J. (2017), Chan-Lau, Chuang D.&Sun (2018), Andersen, Jonas V., Bogusz C.I. (2019), Lund J. (2020), Luo Sumai, Yongkun Sun, Rui Zhou (2022) either from the perspective of banking, equity or online platform managers Douglas W. A., BarberisJ., Ross P. B. (2017),Chen G. Faz X. (2019), Mutton T. (2020) addressing FintTechs under the influence of covid-19, Nathan, Robert J., Budi Setiawan, Mac N. Quynh. 2022, Rabbani, Mustafa R. (2022).

In the Romanian academic literature on FinTech we have identified a recent paper Barbu C.M., Florea D.L., Dabija D.C., Barbu M.C.R. (2021) that addresses issues related to the behavior of FinTech consumers [8].

The analysis of the players on the FinTech market and of the relationships that are created between them in Romania were highlighted by Hadad and Bratianu (2019) and Moraru and Duhnea (2018) [22, 32].

Then the works of Bălţoi I.C.M. (2020) and Mihail L.G. (2018) which can represent a landmark in our research because they address most of the topics proposed by us.

The specific FinTech tools and mechanisms in Romania are studied in the work Manta, O. (2018).

An interesting paper proposes Duma F. and Gligor R. (2018) which analyzes the response of students in Romania regarding the behavior versus–versus online settlements and investments in cryptocurrencies [19].

The work Micu and Micu (2016) proposes innovative elements for the service providers on the Romanian capital market, respectively on the Bucharest Stock Exchange, but also in the area of interaction with customers of this institution. In order to be implemented they must be agreed by the players on the exchange and obviously regulated [29].

We can also include in the specialized literature the Deloitte Report (FinTech in CEE) for 2022 for Romania and Poland where, following the research carried out by this specialized company, a real advice for entrepreneurs from the two countries in the FinTech area is carried out through their conclusions.

Concluding, the academic literature was written as FinTech technology developed. It is obvious that at a global level both the technology and its theoretical expression through specialized works represent a phenomenon of greater amplitude than the Romanian one, where only in recent years there is a concern for the study of the phenomenon.

3 Research Methodology

Regarding the research methodology, we will try to achieve the proposed objectives by analyzing the field literature on this subject, as well as the normative acts that regulate FinTech and its activity in Romania.

We will also compare the quality and quantity of works in Romania and the normative acts that regulate FinTech activity with those in other countries. The research will also make use of the empirical analysis of concrete but revealing cases of the phenomenon in Romania, in order to establish the current situation.

To achieve the objective related to the adjustment of accounting, we will use the scenario, proposing models of accounting records of FinTech operations in the accounting of private companies. We will use the same research method to forecast a possible evolution of this sector in Romania and its relationship with the traditional forms of financial transactions.

In order to determine the profile of users of FinTech platforms in Romania, we will develop a questionnaire which will be applied on a relevant sample of respondents.

A case study is a design that allows the researcher to develop a deep analysis of a case (Saunders et al. 2016). With a case study, it is possible to collect a full amount of information related to the case. This makes the case studies appropriate when the study aims to explain a question "how" or "why" (Saunders et al. 2016). Because this study aims to explain how digitization has affected the relationship of financial institutions with customers, we have conducted a research in this field, especially due to the fact that in Romania such studies are almost non-existent [38].

There are two main methods of data collection, the quantitative method and the qualitative method. The quantitative method is usually an exact method, and its advantage is that it can be achieved at any time; in addition, the quantitative method is associated with the positivist paradigm, which usually results in findings that are very reliable (Collis & Hussey 2014, p. 130) [12].

We are taking a quantitative approach to collect empirical data and draw some statistical conclusions that may be the basis for generalizing findings for further applications (Creswell 2014; Williams 2011) [13]. The quantitative method uses numerical data (Saunders, et al. 2009, p. 151) [38]. In our study, we chose the interpretive paradigm.

Our study is considered an exploratory study because the topic of FinTech is quite new, and the authors have very little information about the impact of FinTech platforms on individuals, but also on companies. We relied on the knowledge of participants who have experienced in the financial sector, even though their knowledge of FinTech is limited due to the new and the lack of specialized literature, which makes us limit ourselves to such exploratory studies rather than explanatory studies.

We used a structured, self-administered online questionnaire to collect data from consumers of financial products.

The questionnaire was designed based on items and scales already used in previous studies, adapted and adjusted to fit the context of this study (Oliveira et al. 2014, Xie, J.; Ye, L.; Huang, W. 2021) [34].

In addition, the questionnaire was divided into two distinct sections, the first analyzing the current behavior adapted by respondents versus-digital platforms, and the second, targeting the future scenario of evolution of these platforms. In the first part, we analyzed constructs such as perceived value, perceived risk, usage facilities. Other aspects analyzed were the behavior of respondents towards prudence and expectations when it comes to investments and capital raising and also towards digital counselling. Another component of the survey focused on the behavior of companies towards FinTech platforms.

Based on the premise that companies and individuals in their capacity as FinTech users have totally different behaviors, we have developed two sets of questionnaires: one set that addresses companies and one for individuals.

4 Analysis, Interpretation of Data and Discussion

4.1 Definitions and FinTech History in Romania

Next, we will ensure the achievement of the objectives set as they were previously presented, but before, in order to understand the phenomenon and the presented aspects, we will make a brief review of some significant historical landmarks in the evolution of the FinTech phenomenon marking the points that this article tries to achieve in this evolution, regarding the situation in Romania.

Thus, if we were to establish a definite moment of the appearance on the financial market of FinTech, we cannot fail to mark the moment of inflection generated by the financial crisis with a peak moment of 2007–2008. This was a challenge for all individuals in the financial market and beyond, as it also involved artificial intelligence creators. Let everyone question the fairness and morality of banks if we can say so, and artificial innovation has tried to come up with new technologies and occupy a segment of the services offered until then, generally by banks.

This is how we see between 2013 and 2014 a tripling of investments in FinTech technologies and on both sides of the Atlantic, with the approach to how to do business moving from mass management to one targeted by person. If by the end of the first decade of the 2000s the client knew that in order to perform a financial operation he had to go to an ATM or even to the bank, the younger generation solved the same thing with the help of the laptop or even easier with the help of the smartphone. Here's how a new category of investors has emerged alongside classic players that are more flexible in terms of finding quick and simpler solutions from the customer's perspective.

It makes sense to say that based on the attraction of the younger generation to these technologies, FinTechs are primarily addressed to them and therefore become an increasingly important segment of the financial market in countries with young, educated and emerging populations that can afford their acquisition or in those cities around the globe with a strong and sophisticated capital market where it is essential that financial information circulates with great speed. This aspect represents another point of interest in the research that we want to address here, to find out what is the real impact between the young population in Romania of FinTechs in the conditions in which Romania has registered in recent years one of the best GDP growth rates, which leads us to the conclusion that Romania had a growth rate of the average income of the good active population and therefore we want to know how much of the additional income unit has influenced the growth of investment in FinTechs. It's interesting how the FinTech market will settle because about 60% of the world's young population is found in Asia.

Starting from the joining of the two technology and financial ends, the term FinTech (Suryono R.R., Budi I., Purvandari B. 2020) has developed over time, both as a concept and in scale of the activities it describes. Thus, the dimensions of the concept were structured on three main lines, namely the business function, the technologies and the supply institutions [40].

Analyzing the business function (Popova Y.2021; Tepe G., Geykci U.B., Sancack F.M. 2021) we can say that FinTechs have imposed themselves on the one hand as a result of technological innovation materialized in software for the management of financial operations of financial services providers or digital platforms for making payments with the help of more or less sophisticated electronic tools (mail, smartphones) [37]. On the other hand, they represent the failure of the traditional financial market (Mention Al. 2019), as we know it, with an identifiable moment by the financial crisis of 2007–2008 [28]. That was the moment when the new digital technology was able to propose a new financial paradigm and an impulse in the market grabbing given by the COVID-19 crisis (Alber N. and Dabour M. 2020) that forced social distancing and thus an exponential increase in remote transactions through online platforms and tools [1].

The perspectives looked good, that is, digital platforms (Yingying Z.Z., Rohlfer S. and Rajasekera J. 2020) were to replace the classic system of financing, without costs, without fees, without multiple approvals for access to finance and with a non-human specialist who proposed a scheme of financing or placement of availability based on electronically collected and processed data on the efficiency of the resources placed, reducing transaction costs by staggering percent.

The second identified function of FinTechs respectively technologies (Varma P., Nijjer S., Sood K., Grima S. and Apoga R.R. 2022) we can say that they already existed quite in time before we talked about FinTechs [43]. The technology existed separately, only it took a little while for IT technology providers to seize the opportunity to expand their range of customers on financial operations as well. Obviously, it was again about necessity, given that the traditional banking institutions showed resistance to the technological attack that was indeed coming with a series of facilities such as speed, more efficient management but at the same time the bankers had to give up some of their traditional income, consisting of the various commissions collected. It is true that once digital technology is accepted, banks have also considerably reduced their specific costs, referring only to those with labour force, if we were to specify a considerable category. Tages of up to 90% [45].

Then the third function we can assign to FinTech is that of financial agent (Morana, S., Gnewuch, U., Jung, D., Granig, C. 2020), (D'Acunto F., Rossi A.G. 2022) institutional in this market, a new leading digital financial services provider that is able to create and manage the interface between provider-client, between demand supply in the financial market, financial agent who is able to provide diversified and sophisticated financial services such as crowdfounding its APIs in which costs tend to zero [15, 31].

Coincidentally or not, after the financial crisis from 2007–2008, in the period 2008–2018, FinTech start-up companies (Micu I., Micu A. 2016) appeared on the Romanian financial market. Although almost 50 companies operate, the investments attracted are modest, only 8 million euros, excluding from them the funds from the transactions, respectively, the operations on the capital market [29]. About 50% of the financing went to the insurance segment, the rest being divided between SMEs by 23%, corporate banking by 20% and retail banking by 10%. From the point of view of the segment of the economy in which these 49 FinTech companies operate, they are dispersed on retail banking-18, technology-9, banking for SMEs-8, support services-6, fuses-3 and so on corporate banking. As a comparison term having the Poland standard, which in the centre-eastern area of Europe is the leader, there are FinTechS with local funding of 64 million euros in the same period of the last decade (2008–2018). The other central and eastern European countries have an equally small number (excluding Poland with more than 170) of active FinTech companies but with higher investments, generally over 100 million euros, according to the study above.

The same RBI study lists the Romanian FinTechs that have established themselves on the market, namely Argentum, Fintech OS, Minutizer, Confidas, SymphoPay, Think-Out, Instant Factoring, Smart Bill respectively Revolut, Orange Money, Monese, N26, TransferWise, Monzo, PayPal. Beside these in the area of investments are active venture capital funds such as Early Game Ventures, Gapminder, Gecad Ventures, the accelerators naming between them Techcelerator, Spherik Accelerator, Innovation Labs, Risky Business but also business angels (techangels.ro).

Identifying, these financial service providers in Romania are primarily start-ups, e.g. companies that have designed a new type of business consisting of digital financial services, IT companies that have diversified their activity by also specializing in providing this type of services and not least the commercial banks operating in Romania and which have restructured and digitized in large part their services. All these three institutional types are today specialized in factoring activities, money lending through banks or through leasing companies, electronic invoicing services, investment management, savings, portfolio management on the capital market, foreign exchange, insurance of all types including private pension funds for the time being.

In the following table are summarized the main "players on the FinTech market" in Romania at the level of 2022, grouped on the services offered, according to Future Bank [55] (Table 1).

4.2 Tools and Technologies Used

In the following part we will review the main technologies that ensure the operation of digital businesses. As it has already been mentioned in the article due to the economic expertise of the authors, we will not go into detail regarding the technical characteristics of these technologies, but we only list, define and specify which of the digital businesses benefit from the support of the respective technology.

The first technology we refer to is blockchain technology. Blockchain is a type of Distributed Ledger Technology (DLT) that occupies a permanent spot in finance industry by enhancing cryptocurrency technology and other technologies with essential implementation in financial services [4].

Another tool used in the spread of Fintech are social networks. Boyd and Ellison define "social network sites as web-based services that allow individuals to (1) construct a public or semi-public profile within a bounded system, (2) articulate a list of other users with whom they share a connection, and (3) view and traverse their list of connections and those made by others within the system" [9]. According to Zhou (2022) the main

Table 1. Romania's FinTech map 2022

Types of services offered	Companies
LENDING & CROWDFUNDING	BankSpot, Credify, Factor, Instant Factoring, Fagura, Filbo, Stock Estate
INVESTMENT & WEALTH MANAGEMENT	Seedblink, Ronin, Vestinda
SAAS & ENABLERS	Allevo, Druid, Ebriza, FinboardX, Fin light, fintechOS, Keez, Paid, Pluridio, Prime dash, Qoobiz, Solo, Symphopay, Tailent, ThinkOut, Traderion, Cloud Software Development
OPEN BANKING	Banki, Finqware, Smart System, Smart FinTech
PERSONAL FINANCE	Cashcontrol, Lendrise, Salarium
PAYMENT & WALLETS	24 pay, Besz, Enfineo, Figo.Pay, Kids Finance, Minutizer, mobilePay, Mone POS, ovelt, Pago, paybyface, PO online payments, twispay, volt
INSURTECH	24, Paypact
BLOCKCHAIN &CRYPTO	Modex, Coreto, FilmChain, XOXNO, SWAZM, Morfin, Multivers, Tailpath
SPECIAL ENTRIES	Confidas, Monitor, Doctor business, payment, smartbill, Deadlines,
CHALLENGERS	iBanFirst, Mokka, money, OrangeMoney, peysera, tbi bank, Revolut

Fintech operation which benefits from this facility is Fintech mortgage lending across social networks [50].

P2P (peer to peer) technology is another technology that facilitates the use of FinTech. Peer-to-Peer (P2P) networking emerged as a disruptive business model displacing the server based networks within a point in time [24]. The P2P file sharing applications can be categorized into two types: centralized/hybrid or decentralize/pure architectures. The P2P file sharing applications can be categorized into two types: centralized/hybrid or decentralize/pure architectures [14]. In the centralized model there is the presence of a central server to index contents and peers. This model is easy to manage and gives a competent search. However, it has a limited scalability and a single point of failure. Decentralize P2P systems eliminate a central server, thus enhancing the reliability [11].

The most widespread FinTech application of this tool is P2P (Peer-to-Peer) Lending. P2P (Peer-to-Peer) Lending is described as a money lending service practiced through online platforms that helps in matching lenders directly to borrowers [4].

Another technology used by FinTech applications is NFC. Vibhor Sharma, Preeti Gusain and Prashant Kumar define NFC (near field communication) as wireless technology which provides communication between two mobile phones which contain NFC tags, using short range radio waves [39].

Regarding Mohamed Mostafa Abd Allah Near Field Communication (NFC) is a technology for high frequency wireless short-distance point-to-point communication [30].

This tool is used in FinTech operations for payment processing. Broadly speaking, the mechanism involves the communication between two devices, one of the payer and the second of the person receiving the amount. After starting the transaction, the money is transferred from the payer's account to that of the cashier.

4.3 Perception of Romanian Consumers for the Products and Services Offered by FinTech

In the last decade, 49 FinTech companies have entered on the Romanian market, positioning themselves in the "emerging market" category according to a study conducted in 2021 by Raiffeisen Bank International (RBI) about the FinTech sector in Central and Eastern Europe. At the institutional level, the FinTech field is represented in Romania since 2020 by the Romanian FinTech Association (RoFin.tech) which has a stated purpose of "increasing the image and relevance of the association, both internally and externally, but also transforming it into a true advisory forum for the financial authorities in Romania in the process of developing the FinTech ecosystem," according to its press release. It has 18 members representing FinTech start-up companies that target first SMEs and then pay-day-loans. At the same time, the association is a founding member of the European Digital Finance Association (EDFA), observing the step taken for the intention to institutionalize the Romanian FinTech segment. It has baked as members in Romania Online Payments and Salarium and partners of Raiffesen Bank Romania, FintechOS, Deloitte, EY Law or Transilvania Bank.

Clarifying in the above lines which are the institutions providing services let's continue to see who is the target customer and which are the Romanian companies that use the product.

On the one hand, we are talking about the traditional client of banks, e.g. micro-enterprises, SMEs or start-ups or financial institutions together with authorized individuals or simple individuals. Given the fact that banking companies have digitized a large part of their activity, many of these Romanian clients choose to continue to finance themselves through commercial banks, in Romania over the last 30 years a type of attachment behavior based on customs has developed.

From the questionnaire applied to 70 companies in the Western part of Romania (63% services, 16% production, 21% trade) we can find that 43% of the respondents make digital settlements (online payments, PayPal, Apple Pay, etc.) a relatively modest score we appreciate and only 27% of them resort to financing on digital platforms. Our explanation would be that the banks' activity in Romania is heavily regulated, which gives a plus of trust to the customer. As well as the big-data systems for storing and managing the data of banks' customers offer a comfort with which the Romanian client is familiar.

Unfortunately, this score highlights once again the fact that the Romanian entrepreneur does not act sufficiently in order to identify new ways of financing the activity, that is, it would be necessary to identify educational and advertising channels in order to increase the level of financial culture of the company in Romania. At the same time, we are witnessing a phenomenon of financial eviction in which companies suffer from underfunding, having in the Romanian state a serious competitor, as they have to look for new financing opportunities, manifesting in this area an impermissible sufficiency, also confirmed by the low score in terms of resorting to digital consulting (9%) as an alternative, in order to obtain information on new services such as digital investment platforms, a robo-advisor providing this processed data, e.g. evaluated, scored, ranked and compared.

Also, only 9% of them place their capital using technologies or mobile trading devices to make a profit. Given that the Romanian state borrows heavily from banks, month by month. But what in Romania we believe that will make the difference and will guide customers towards choosing FinTechs are the high costs involved in the collaboration of Romanian companies with banks, the interest rates charged on the Romanian banking market being between the highest in the EU (for example, Romania borrowed with interest rates 4 times higher in 2022 compared to 2020 taking into account long-term loans according to the BCE).

This can be a reasonable reason for Romanian customers to choose something else. This is also apparent from the responses of respondents to the question of willingness to move to the provision of digital financial services. 82.9% of the respondents responded favourably, the reasons being first of all the lower costs or not at all and the speed of operations increased (on a scale from 1 to 5 the score was 4.29) then another agreed reason was their opinion on the increase in the financial stability of the company (4.26 on a scale from 1 to 5).

However, a favourable intention of the Romanian companies regarding the digitization of financial activities resulted from the respondents' questionnaire regarding the traditional-FinTech coexistence where they said 42.9% that they would coexist, and 37% appreciated that in the future FinTech will swallow traditional financial services.

As far as individuals are concerned, after collecting the data, we obtained 394 quality responses for analysis. In terms of age, 15.4% of respondents were between 18–25 years, 60.4%, between 25–35 years, 14.7% between 35–50 21.3%, and over 50 years, 3.6%. In terms of sex, 74.1% of respondents were women, 25.4% were men and 0.5% were identified as being of a different gender. Regarding the highest level of education, 58.4% of respondents have a high school diploma, 25.4% have a college degree, and 8.1% have a graduated postgraduate degree. 6.6% have doctoral studies.

Following the research, the ranking of the use of financial services on FinTech platforms shows that digital payments are on the first place (76.6% of respondents use them), followed by digital financing (17.6%), digital insurance (17.25%), digital investments (10.65%), digital money (8.12%), and finally, digital financial advisory (8.62%). Along with use, interest in digital funding grows in the rankings. It goes to the second position, which means that retail clients are attracted to new digital modes of financing, such as peer-to-peer loans and crowdfunding.

We notice that the most affected variable is age; the older the customers are, the less interest and use of digital banking services. Information about respondents' gender shows that men are more prone to change than women, and that despite their high interest, use remains lower, given the higher adverse risk of women than men. Finally, digital services, such as digital investments, are used more widely by higher-income customers.

The latest trend mentioned is confirmed by the high correlation between revenue and digital investment use.

The investigation of the clients' appetence towards the future scenarios reveals that in a very large proportion (76.8%) they are ready to switch to a digital supply of financial services, to the detriment of the classic ones. Again, the most substantial variable is age; the older the age, the less confidence in the sharing of financial information, regardless of the nature of the entity providing the services. Another significant variable is the level of education; the higher the education, the greater the trust in sharing financial information.

We find that on a Likert scale of 5, we have a median of 3.83 representing the interest in digital financing means. To the same extent, the interest for digital investment means is at 3.68, the interest in digital money, 3.34, digital insurance, 3.4, financial advice 3.56. Digital payments lead in this ranking with 4.08. We conclude that there is a real interest in this field between individuals, consumers of financial products.

The advantages that those questioned are in terms of the appropriateness of financial inclusion, which ensures better access to financial services to disadvantage groups, median 3.74, the opportunity to have better and more personalized banking services, 3.94, the opportunity to have lower transaction costs and faster services, 4.07, the opportunity for a potential positive impact on financial stability 3.93, the opportunity for easier access to capital 3.75. In general, the more attractive benefit is offering low-cost transactions and faster service. At the same time, the one that poses a minor threat is the risk of discontinuity of banking services.

Age is clearly a factor that differentiates the answer to the question. New generations are being born in the digital age and, based on the data collected, younger clusters are ready to embrace technological progress in the financial field.

The propensity towards declining the use of digital financial services in favour of traditional ones, taking into account factors such as the risk of confidentiality and data security (2.98 on the Likert scale), the risk of discontinuity of services (2.99) and the risk of inappropriate marketing practices (2.97), is, as we can see, lower than the intention to adopt these services.

Finally, the results regarding the future of Fintech platforms in the view of the respondents questioned show us that they are optimistic about their survival, in one way or another, (26.8% believe that they will fully seize the financial services market, 47% consider that they will coexist together with the classical financial institutions). A percentage of 21.7% predict that they will be acquired by traditional banks/insurance companies, while 4.5% believe that they will fail.

Like all research, this study has some limitations but, in our opinion, it provides avenues for future research in the field. Given the relative experience of consumers in the current financial context in the market, we have focused on consumers' perceptions of the concept of FinTech rather than necessarily on their real experience in using services of this nature.

4.4 The Role of the State in the Existence of FinTech in Romania and the Interaction of the Public Financial Sector - Private Financial Sector

First of all, we must note that the FinTech sector in Romania is insufficiently regulated. This is an obstacle to the development of a partnership from the outset because public financial services are highly regulated. However, since 2005, the State Treasury has implemented the electronic payment system, a digital interface through which settlements between the taxpayer and the state are made in seconds, and only the printed format of the operation will be transmitted in a few days. At the same time, the introduction of the Electronic Multiple Payment Order (OPME), introduced from 2020 by Order of Minister, represented for public institutions, economic operators and other entities a step forward in the digitization of payment operations from and to the accounts opened at the State Treasury units through which they carry out their own activity.

The condition for activating the on-line settlements of the public/ private actors, whether we refer to the taxable subjects paying taxes and fees or those from the private sector who provide works and services to the public sector, is that the public institutions are registered in the Register of public entities as well as the economic operators and other entities than public institutions, who are correspondents of the State Treasury, for making payments from the accounts opened at the State Treasury units through which they carry out their own activity. Also, the person who makes the digital payment as a representative of the private company must be enrolled in the Virtual Private Space (SPV). The F1129 form is submitted online through the Forexebug National Reporting System by public institutions and, respectively, through the e-guvernare.ro portal by economic operators and other entities than public institutions.

Starting with the end of 2022, the State Treasury initiated the digitization of the public loan through the TEZAUR and FIDELIS programs of issues of government securities denominated in lei and euros, very liquid, in the short and medium term, the procedure being digitized if the individual investor makes the purchase through the banking system or through the Bucharest Stock Exchange.

As regards the public procurement of goods and services, the SEAP (Electronic System of Public Procurement) system has been implemented in Romania, which is an electronic platform used for the purpose of transparency of the public procurement process and procedures. Using this interface, public authorities acquire by electronic means the goods and services approved in the institution's own budgets and operate its capital expenditure. The use of SEAP ensures simplification and streamlining of the procedures for participation in the licity of suppliers, increased transparency, simplified and fast auditing.

Public investments in Romania are made by the State Treasury through the BNR, which acts as an agent of the state by placing the temporary availability of the BGC (general consolidated budget). The state treasury, through the general account opened at the central bank of the National Bank of Romania, places the funds available from the receipts of budgetary revenues of a fiscal nature, peaks that coincide with tax payment due dates.

4.5 FinTech Recognition Aspects in Private Company Accounting

Another objective that we aim to achieve in this article is to find new accounting methods and instruments for the quantification and recognition of financial operations carried out through FinTech technologies, while applying the principle of accrual accounting, in order to meet the need for speed and financial-accounting credibility.

For this purpose, we will start from three defining elements, namely:

- the business functions that FinTech technologies cover;
- FinTech technology providers;
- beneficiaries/customers of FinTech technologies.

In terms of business functions, we will consider the functions proposed by Gomber, Koch and Siering (2017) within the first dimension of the Digital Finance Cube. According to this concept, the digital finance business functions are: Digital Financing, Digital Investments, Digital Money, Digital Payment, Digital Insurances and Digital Financial Advice [20].

The accounting flows generated by these operations will be analyzed at the level of both poles of the economic operation, therefore it is important to know what these poles are.

Thus, a first pole is FinTech service providers. In a first, more general classification, it can be said that these suppliers are commercial banks and FinTech companies. In a more detailed classification the later category can be divided into:

- large technology companies that also operate in the field of financial services, but not exclusively (Apple, Google, Twitter, Facebook, etc.);
- companies that provide infrastructure or technology that facilitates transactions with financial services, various financial market utilities and stock exchanges (MasterCard, Fiserv, First Data, NASDAQ, etc.);
- smaller companies, often start-ups, very flexible and mobile, that focus on a specific technology or innovative process, such as Stripe for mobile payments, Betterment for automatic investments, Prosper for peer-to-peer loans, Moven for retail banking or Lemonade for insurance.

As for the clients of FinTech services, they can be individuals, private companies, public institutions or even financial institutions.

In this article we will focus on the registration of FinTech operations in the accounting of private companies, given that individuals do not conduct double-entry accounting and public and financial institutions have their own accounting regulations. As a result, we will consider both suppliers and users of these services as private companies their specific legislation regulated whose accounting (in Romania, for example, OMFP 1802/2014, in other states the international IAS/IFRS regulations complemented by specific national regulations, etc.).

The first business function, namely digital financing, involves obtaining the necessary funds to finance businesses using various digital platforms. As forms of financing can be used: crowdfunding, borrowing, leasing, etc.

Three individuals will be involved in this process: the applicant for the amount, the bidder and the company that makes available the platform through which the operation will be carried out.

For the applicant, from an accounting point of view, we will have to record a liquidity inflow, and, depending on the nature of the financing, the appearance of a liability to the offeror (if the financing is assimilated to a loan) or a capital increase (if the financing represents an investment that turns the bidder of the amount into a shareholder of the requesting entity).

For the one who makes the amounts available, the operation will generate a liquidity outflow materialized either by the appearance of a claim against the entity receiving the amounts or by obtaining shares and, implicitly, the capacity of shareholder, in this entity.

In the case of loan financing, interest will also be involved, which will be recognized as accounting expenses and at the offerer as income.

Usually in the case of using platforms, the platform manager will receive, either from each party involved or only from the applicant, a certain amount of money in the form of commission. For this entity the commission will be recognized, from an accounting point of view, as an income and will generate a liquidity inflow.

Digital investment is another function that FinTech technologies can cover. In this case, that function supposes placing the liquidity of an entity in such a way as to obtain as much of the added value as possible. For this, FinTech technologies provide portfolio management services, solutions and algorithms for the beneficiary to make their own placements, mobile devices that provide real-time access to information from the financial markets and the possibility to trade independently of the location and human advisors or brokers (Tai and Ku 2013; Zhang and Teo 2014), or access to platforms that combine social media networks with investment strategies (social trading described by Doering et al. 2015; Pan et al. 2012). In Romania, an example of such a platform is the one offered by Seedblink.

From an accounting point of view for the company that makes the trades the fact that the investments are made through real, virtual or direct brokers does not influence the way of recognizing these transactions. As a result, the placements will be accompanied by liquidity outflows and increases in the securities portfolio. Depending on the buyer's intention to keep these securities for the short or long term, they will be recognised in the buyer's accounts as a cash equivalent (quasi-liquidities/short-term investments) or as financial fixed assets.

If the transaction takes place through a broker, either physically or virtually/online, usually there is also a commission paid to it that will be recognized as an expense.

Digital money (digital currency, virtual currency, electronic money or cryptocurrency) describes a type of currency that performs (more or less) all the typical functions of money, but exists only electronically and is used mainly on the Internet. Such digital money serves as a means of exchange, unit of account and deposit of value, but unlike traditional money, it only exists digitally.

From an accounting point of view, the record of transactions with virtual currencies is a great challenge because most accounting systems do not have structures and procedures in place for these situations.

Since 2008, with the appearance of Bitcoin, the most famous virtual currency at the moment, virtual currencies (or cryptocurrencies) have been in a continuous development, from the existing types to the way in which they can be used. Until recently, a series of uncertainties hovered over these currencies, such as those related to their nature, the legality of their use as a means of payment, reflection in financial statements or taxation, reported not only in Romania, but also at international level. According to the definition given by the European Banking Authority (ABE) in the Virtual Currency Warning to Consumers, a virtual currency is an unregulated form of money in digital form, which is not issued or guaranteed by a central bank and which can serve as a means of payment.

Internationally, one of the first exhaustive studies of the nature of virtual currencies was conducted by Venter (2016). It looked at the possible classification of virtual currency in asset classes already existing in IFRS-based international regulations and concluded that, contrary to popular opinion, virtual currencies are neither currency within the meaning of IAS 7 Statement of Cash Flows nor financial instruments within the meaning of IAS 32 Financial Instruments: presentation or IFRS 9 Financial Instruments.

In 2019, at the request of the International Accounting Standards Board (IASFB), the Committee for the Interpretation of International Reporting Standards (IFRIC) issued a point of view related to the accounting of virtual currencies, namely those that meet three specified conditions:

a) are digital or virtual currencies registered on the basis of distributed ledger technology that uses cryptography for security;
b) they are not issued by a judicial authority or by another third party;
c) do not give rise to a contract between the holder and another party.

As a result, two solutions are proposed: due to the non-physical nature of these struts, their records should be kept with the help of intangible assets/intangible assets structures in which case they fall under the scope of IAS 38 Intangible Assets or as inventories, due to their high degree of liquidity and the possibility of being traded (bought/sold) like stocks, in which case they fall under the scope of IAS 2 Inventories.

So we can see the concern of accounting systems to provide solutions for accounting for the operations in which these currencies are involved. In the following we will also present such solutions, in the case of the most common situations, namely:

- companies that use cryptocurrencies in their current activity (as a means of payment or collection);
- companies that purchase cryptocurrencies to place their availabilities (for investment purposes);
- companies that mediate transactions with cryptocurrencies;
- companies that "create" cryptocurrency, basically by validating blockchain processes based on validation protocols.

From an accounting point of view, the problem arises both in terms of the value at which these assets are valued at various times (entry, inventory, end of the financial year and at the exit) and the recording of transactions with them in the accounting.

At the first problem, the solution would be to measure these currencies at fair value, while also taking into account their fluctuations in value which, like exchange rate differences, will also be able to be recognised in expense accounts, unfavourable ones, respectively of income, favourable ones.

Regarding the accounting flows in the case of the entities that are in the first situation, the transactions to which we will refer will be the use of cryptocurrencies as a means of collection for the services rendered/works performed/goods delivered and the use of cryptocurrencies as a means of payment for various debts (towards suppliers, employees, etc.).

Due to the fact that in this situation virtual assets exist in the entity's assets for a longer period of time, in my view they should be classified as intangible assets.

According to the transactions presented, the cryptocurrency operations that we will analyze from an accounting point of view will be: the collection of receivables and the payment of debts.

In case of collection of a debt in virtual currency in addition to the settlement of the debt against the clients, which is treated as a separate operation, the entry of the intangible asset of the nature of the virtual currencies will be recorded, also separately. In both cases apart from the corresponding receivables and cryptocurrency accounts, an intermediary debt account will be used, for example various creditors.

In the case of debt payment transactions in addition to debt settlement and cryptocurrency outflow operations, it should also be borne in mind that these coins at the entrance had a value and now, at the exit of the patrimony, their value may be different. As a result, in addition to the intermediate account this time of receivables (such as various debtors), we will also use an expense account (where we will record the entry value, accounting, of the currencies used in the payment of debts) respectively an income account (in which we will record the current value of these coins).

In terms of accounting in the second situation, it is about companies that purchase cryptocurrencies with the help of intermediary companies that act on various trading platforms. Cryptocurrencies are then kept in an e-wallet until the entities decide to exchange them for real currency, thus obtaining a gain.

As a result, the operations that will be recorded in the company's accounting will be: the purchase of coins, the update of the value of coins in the entity's portfolio at the end of each financial year and the sale of coins.

The acquisition will involve increasing the value of the entity's virtual assets, either inventories, if the purchase is made for speculative purposes, in the short term, or intangible assets (non-marketable assets) if the investment is made over the long term (more than one year) and the decrease in liquidity when paying those assets.

The discounting, as we have specified, will generate, as the case may be, expenses, in case of unfavourable differences (the current value of currencies lower than the accounting value, at the entrance), respectively revenues, in the case of favorable differences (the present value of the currencies higher than the book value, at the entrance).

The sale will be recorded as an outflow of virtual assets, while recognising an expense equal to the cost of their acquisition and a liquidity inflow equal to the sale price of these currencies, which represents the income from this transaction. Depending on the ratio of expenses for the purchase of currencies to the revenues earned through their sale, the transaction will generate profit for the entity, if the revenues will be greater than the expenses or loss, in the reverse situation.

In the case of companies that mediate cryptocurrency transactions, these are entities that generally carry out the following transactions through virtual or real ATMs: cash collection (real currency) in exchange for cryptocurrencies, applying a commission to the amount received; collection of cryptocurrencies in exchange for real currencies, applying a commission to the amount received.

In this situation, the companies, in the case of each transaction, will recognize their income from the commissioning of the transaction. The sale of cryptocurrencies on real currencies will cause the value of these assets to decrease in the company's patrimony and increase its liquidity, usually in bank accounts. As with any cryptocurrency outflow due to differences in value at the time of entry and exit, this will be taken into account by recognizing an expense at the level of the carrying amount of the cryptocurrencies exited and an income at the level of the current value of these cryptocurrencies.

If a cryptocurrency is received for which real currencies are paid, we will register the increase of these non-material assets simultaneously with the decrease in liquidity, usually in the bank.

For companies that generate cryptocurrency in the first place, it must be determined whether those who obtain new virtual currencies by validating blockchain processes (also called "miners" in practice, a term also taken up in the specialized literature (Eigelshoven et al. 2020; Sedlmeir et al. 2020, Jorgensen and Beck 2022), provide a service (validating certain information/processes for the benefit of the network) or not. An additional difficulty arises from the fact that the "miners" do not have contracts concluded with any counterparty for the services they bring to the network [35].

Secondly, it is worth pointing out that in order to make mining the "miners" bear significant costs, among which the most important are those with the computing technology, with the necessary applications and with the electricity consumed. Some of the accounting problems that arise in connection with the virtual currency mining activity are:

- the initial cost of recording in accounting one of the difficulties appeared is the distribution of production costs on the virtual currencies obtained. In these companies, the question may arise of the impossibility of using the standard cost of production. In addition, virtual currencies can be obtained over time, not at a single time during the month, and it is necessary to allocate the costs incurred (for example, if the monthly costs are distributed over the currencies obtained in that month or the quarterly costs can be distributed by the number of currencies obtained in that quarter). Another problem may be related to the notion of production in progress, which in the case of cryptocurrencies cannot be identified (concretely, the costs incurred in May also partially refer to currencies obtained in June, the mining process being continuous).
- the classification of the currency obtained by mining. If the currency obtained is intended for sale later (which is very likely), it will be classified as a stock. If the currency obtained is used (in whole or in part) for the company's needs in terms of payments (such as the payment of wages, suppliers or other purposes), it will be classified as an intangible asset [35].

Taking into account these aspects the obtaining of virtual currencies, if they are sold to third parties, it will be possible to assimilate the obtaining of finished products, with the corresponding accounting records. The sale of these "products" will take into account both the common aspects regarding the sale of any finished products and the specific aspects of cryptocurrency transactions, as presented in the previous expositions.

If obtaining cryptocurrencies is the counterparty for a service provided to the blockchain network, it additionally appears, in addition to the actual cryptocurrency transactions, the recording of the changes in the service provided.

Digital payments represent another function of the FinTech technologies. Hartmann (2006) defines the electronic payment as „being all the payments that are initiated, processed and received electronically". The process of electronic payments covers the transfer of certain sums of money from the payer to the beneficiary through an electronic payment mechanism, independent from the location (Lim 2008; Weir et al. 2006) [35].

Today, one can differentiate among three peer-to-peer payment methods (Bradford and Keeton, 2012). Firstly, a non-banking model in which "a person instructs a non-banking intermediate, such as PayPal, to send funds towards another consumer" [35].

Secondly, a model centred on the bank in which "the individual interacts directly with a bank to ask for a transfer from the person's bank account in the receiver's bank account". In this case, the users do not have to enlist at other services providers, but they can use the services of their bank, so that the concerns related to safety to be rather low.

Thirdly, a model cantered on the card in which "the payment is entirely processed through a network of credit or debit card". A disadvantage of this model is that both parties involved in a transaction must have a card which functions with the network on which the service is based.

In Romania, a provider of such services is Finqware which, in addition to collection and payment operations, also offers services to manage the companies' liquidities.

Characteristic to these digital payments is the fact that the moment the payment was initiated, the service provider validates the payment so the receiver can be assured that the money will be received even though it has not been added yet in the bank account.

This feature requires, in accounting terms, a specific analysis because according to the time span between payment validation or in accounting terms, from the moment the debt is fully paid, and the moment when the sums actually enter the provider's account, either a new bond with a higher degree of liquidity or an amount about to be settled can be registered.

Arumugam and Cusick (2008) had already assumes in 2008 that the peer-to-peer concept might spread on the insurance market, allowing digital insurances. They consider that is probable that people who look for insurances to make an alliance with family members and friends instead of using the services of insurance companies. Moenninghoff and Wieandt (2012) claim that such alliances reduce the information asymmetry and moral hazard. One of the established suppliers on the global market is friedsurance.com, founded in 2010. On this platform, individuals can form alliances to reduce the costs of insurances at the same level of protection [35].

In Romania, a modified alternative of these services is offered by PayPact which insures for a commission the declaration of damages and their online evaluation, road and juridical assistance for both the culprit and the injured party, as well as the unfolding of the procedures with the insurance companies.

In this situation, from an accounting perspective, there are no notable aspects. Thus, the company that assures this service will register its income from the charged commission and the company which benefits from this service will register this expense as a service.

The last category of FinTech services which we will analyse is represented by digital financial consultancy. These services are available on several review websites and portal for comparing services and products such as informatic equipment, touristic stores and medical services. On these platforms, the products and services are evaluated, graded, classified, assessed and compared. The research has already pointed out that these kinds of assessments have a real influence on the customers' behaviour (Hu et al. 2008).

In the financial domain, the platforms which offer these kinds of services can be differentiated on the basis of two characteristics: first of all, the providers which offer mainly reviews on financial products (for example, seekingalpha.com) and second of all, the providers which focus on comparing financial products (for example, comparethemarket.com) on the basis of figures and characteristics. Some suppliers apply a mixture of both elements (for example, creditkarma.com).

The terms trading community, investment community and shares community describe communities which discuss and share information about shares and investments. Often, these kinds of discussion and information exchange take place on well-known internet forums such as Yahoo Finance, Google Finance, ragingbull.com or aktienboard.com (Lu et al. 2010). The studies have pointed out that the exchange of information among investors can have an influence on the investment behaviour. Wysocki (1998) identified an influence of the online exchange of information on the next day's trading volumes. Antweiler and Frank (2004) pointed out that investors are influenced by other people's opinions [35].

A new development in the domain of financial counselling are the algorithms which offer investment proposals without any or minimum human intervention, based on predefined parameters concerning the investment objectives, the financial fund and risk aversion. These robo-counsellor are focusing at present on portfolio management and investment strategies based on established theories, such as the modern theory of portfolio and the limited classes of assets, such as the shares and the funds traded at the stock exchange. Mostly, they are not conceived to take into consideration the more personal aspects of financial investment, such as real estate or individual fiscal situations.

From an accounting perspective, these services as well do not stand out due to some notable aspects. Thus, the company which assures this service will register the income as charged commission, if there is one as such, and the company which benefits from the service will register its expense with this service.

5 Conclusions

In accordance with the objectives which we set for this study, we proceed by presenting the conclusion which we reached, by pointing out that for each of the studied directions we tried to highlight the situation in Romania by comparing it with the international one on the basis of the literature in the domain.

Thus, by analysing the domain literature which makes reference to FinTech we observed that at a global level both the technology and its theoretical expression through specialised studies represents a phenomenon with a greater amplitude than the Romanian one, where only in the past few years, it can be observed a certain preoccupation for the study of the phenomenon.

Regarding the given definitions and the approaches that were carried out we concluded that a generic answer would be that FinTech is nothing more than a start-up, a new company, the result of a new business, new as concept, means, methods and tools, which addresses to a new type of customer-consumer, a new generation that wants more comfort and discretion and which has less patience when it comes to solving its financial problems, regardless their nature (payments, investment, searching for new financing sources, and others) and that likes "to play" with digital money (maybe because of their appetite for everything virtual…).

Another finding was that, although at the beginning, the FinTech phenomenon in Romania had a special dynamic, it increased in magnitude over the years. One reason could be the fact that from the point of view of the Internet, an essential element for the best functioning of these services, Romania occupies the 10 the place in the rank of the fastest countries for fixed broadband internet, according to the study carried out between November 2021 and November 2022 by Ookla [56].

Regarding FinTech service providers in Romania, we concluded that they are primarily start-ups, companies that have designed a new type of business consisting of digital financial services, IT companies which have diversified their activity by specializing in the provision of this type of service as well and commercial banks which operate in Romania and have largely restructured and digitized their services.

As for the impact of FinTech on young Romanians, the Romanian academic system already had in its 2022 offer a master's degree program exclusively addressed to FinTech. From this point of view, there is a good informational start-up, because it allows access to knowledge in an institutionalized and structured way.

Regarding the role of the state and the public sector in Romania, it can be observed that although FinTech services and the operation of companies in this field are not sufficiently regulated for the time being, the Romanian state, through its specialized institutions, has kept up with the banking institutions in terms of its digitization effort. From our point of view, it is possible that sometime in the future, the FinTech platforms will become a partner of the state, competing with banks in terms of procuring the necessary funds, or in any case the state will remain a partner of a digitized financial system regardless of the formula in which the FinTechs will partner with the banks. The state will remain a faithful partner in any formula due to the permanent needs of financing public activities and against the background of the expansion of the public financial sector in the last century, a trend difficult to stop on the background of a state, which generically speaking, is becoming increasingly social.

There is no doubt that there will be regulations which will ensure financial discipline and transparency because public money must be protected because it is the society's money, but if there is interest from both sides, the partnership with FinTech will work, as it has been profitable for banks to have a special client to manage, the state, under minimal risk conditions and which has turned out to be extremely profitable.

However, the study pointed out that, from an accounting point of view, in Romania, the current accounting legislation provides the necessary framework for the accounting of digital operations at the level of private companies. However, in this case as well, there is room for improvement, meaning that in order to better highlight the impact of these operations in the company patrimony and results, it would be necessary to introduce new accounting accounts.

By studying the academic literature on the issue of FinTech in Romania, the research hypothesis from which we started our study was that the emergence and expansion of

FinTech generated by mutations on a social level, thus strongly influencing company-client relationships. We decided to study the validation of this prediction by developing two sets of questionnaires, of 22 questions each, one applied to companies from the western part of Romania and the other to individuals in the same area. In our study, we analysed the following digital services: payments, financing, investments, insurance, cryptocurrencies and financial consulting. Another monitored aspect referred to whether consumers resort to specialized or banking platforms for these services. Next, we tried to find out the respondents' opinion regarding the reasons why they would use/would not use one of the mentioned platform categories. For the last question, the respondents were asked their opinion on the future scenario they imagine in terms of the relationship between specialized FinTech companies and traditional banking/insurance institutions.

The testing was an empirical one and it was carried out in the months of December 2022 and January 2023, thus offering extremely recent information. Based on the answers received from the two categories of respondents, we processed these results using the non-parametric descriptive statistics method.

From the questionnaire applied to the companies, we found out that on the first place in the ranking of the services used in the Western region of Romania, the most used service is the one of digital payments. A relatively more modest score was achieved by financing on digital platforms. Our explanation is that the activity of banks in Romania is strongly regulated, which gives the client more confidence. However, what will make the difference in Romania and guide customers towards choosing FinTechs are the high costs involved in the collaboration of Romanian companies with banks, the interest rates charged on the Romanian banking market being among the highest in the EU. This can be a reasonable reason for Romanian customers to choose something else, as it resulted from the responses of company-respondents to the question regarding the willingness to switch to the provision of digital financial services. Most of the respondents answered favourably, the reasons being primarily lower or no costs and increased speed of operations. Another reason was their opinion regarding the increase in the financial stability of the company.

According to our study, there are few companies that invest their capital using mobile trading technologies or devices to gain profit. However, a favourable intention of Romanian companies regarding the digitization of financial activities resulted from the questioning of respondents on their opinion on the future of FinTech companies. To this question, the majority expressed their confidence in the future existence of FinTech companies, over a third even stating that in the future specialized FinTech companies will absorb traditional financial services.

In conclusion, Romanian companies are interested in accessing FinTech technology, but there is a slowdown in the pace of their development, on one hand generated by insufficient investments in this area, but also by the insufficient financial education of administrators, a polarization of digital financial technologies being observed, especially in urban areas and among the young, educated or well-off population, which means young populations and the middle and upper classes for now. One of the impediments seems to have a psychological nature, the respondents showing some reluctance regarding the risks associated with data confidentiality, security of transacted funds, the possible discontinuity of services (frequent internet outages in rural areas) or even some inappropriate marketing practices.

Regarding the individuals, after data collection, we obtained 394 quality answers for the analysis.

Following the research, the ranking of the use of financial services on Fin Tech platforms shows that digital payments are on the first place, followed by digital financing, digital insurance, digital investments, digital money while digital financial consulting is at the end of the ranking. The second position occupied by digital financing services reflects the fact that retail customers are attracted to new digital ways of financing, such as peer-to-peer lending and crowdfunding, generally due to lower costs.

Another conclusion of the study was that the most affected variable is age; the older customers are, the less interest they have in using digital services. Moreover, the information regarding the respondents' gender points out that men are more prone to change than women, and that, despite their high interest, the use remains lower, considering that women have the higher level of adverse risk than men. Finally, digital services such as digital investments are more widely used by customers with higher incomes. This trend is confirmed by the high correlation between income and digital in the use of investments.

Investigating the customers' opinion on future scenarios, reveals the fact that in a very large proportion they are prepared to switch to a digital provision of financial services, to the detriment of the classic ones. Again, the most substantial variable is age; the older the age, the lower the trust in sharing financial information is, regardless the nature of the service provider. Another significant variable is the level of education; the higher the education is, the greater is the trust to share financial information.

By globally analysing the results of the questionnaires applied to individuals we can conclude that there is a real interest among the consumer in these digital financial services. The advantages that those surveyed perceive are the opportunity for financial inclusion, the opportunity to have better and more personalized banking services, the opportunity to have lower transaction costs and faster services, the opportunity of a potential positive impact on financial stability and, the opportunity of an easier access to capital. Generally, the more attractive benefit is the promise of lower transaction costs and faster service. At the same time, the one that represents a minor threat is the discontinuity risk of banking services.

The study demonstrated that the propensity to decline the use of digital financial services in favour of the traditional ones, by taking into account factors such as the confidentiality and data security risks, the risk of service discontinuity and the risk of inappropriate marketing practices, is much lower than the intention to adopt these services.

The results regarding the future of Fintech platforms, in the view of the individual respondents point out that they are optimistic about their survival, in one way or another, alone or together with the traditional financial service providers. Only a small percentage considers that financial digital services will fail.

As any research, this study has certain limitations but, in our opinion, it offers possibilities and investigation paths for future research in the field.

Undoubtedly the world of the future will be a digital world where the Internet will be everywhere, a world to which we will have to adapt, a world that will offer benefits that we would do well to take advantage of. We will be able to do this only by changing ourselves, by evolving together with the world we live in. That is why we believe that studies that take a look into this future are welcomed, allowing both people and companies to prepare for the times to come, including resorting to new financial methods which will allow them the financial optimization that the future offers them.

References

1. Alber, N., Dabour, M.: The Dynamic relationship between FinTech and social distancing under COVID-19 pandemic: digital payments evidence. Int. J. Econ. Finance **12**(11), 1 (2020). ISSN 1916-971X E-ISSN, pp.1916–9728
2. Allen, F., McAndrews, J., Strahan, F.: E-finance: an introduction. J. Financial Serv. Res. **22**, 5–27 (2002)
3. Alt, R., Beck, R., Smits, M.T.: FinTech and the transformation of the financial industry. Electron. Mark. **28**(3), 235–243 (2018). https://doi.org/10.1007/s12525-018-0310-9
4. Anifa, M., Ramakrishnan, S., Joghee, S., Kabiraj, S., Bishnoi, M.M.: Fintech innovations in the financial service industry. J. Risk Financial Manag. **15**, 287 (2022). https://doi.org/10.3390/jrfm15070287
5. Antweiler, W., Frank, M.Z.: Is all that talk just noise? The information content of internet stock message boards (2004). https://doi.org/10.1111/j.1540-6261.2004.00662.x
6. Babich, V., Allon, G.: Crowdsourcing and crowdfunding in the manufacturing and services sectors (2020). https://doi.org/10.1287/msom.2019.0825
7. Barber, B.M., Odean T.,Greiner, M.E., Wang, H.: Digital finance and FinTech: current research and future research directions. J. Econ. Perspect. **15**(1), 41–54 (2001)
8. Barbu, C.M., Florea, D.L., Dabija D.C., Barbu M.C.R.: Customer experience in FinTech. J. Theor. Appl. Electron. Commer. Res. **16**(5), 1415–1433 (2021)
9. Boyd, D.M., Ellison, N.B.: Social network sites: definition, history, and scholarship. J. Comput. Mediat. Commun. **13**(1), 210–230 (2008)
10. Brière, M., Kim Oosterlinck, K., Szafarz, A.: Virtual currency, tangible return: portfolio diversification with bitcoin. J. Asset Manag. **16**(6). SSRN Electron. J. **16**(6), 365–373 (2015). https://doi.org/10.2139/ssrn.2324780
11. Clarke, I., Sandberg, O., Wiley, B., Hong, T.W.: Freenet: a distributed anonymous information storage and retrieval system. In: Federrath, H. (eds.) Designing Privacy Enhancing Technologies. LNCS, vol. 2009, pp. 46–66. Springer, Heidelberg (2001). https://doi.org/10.1007/3-540-44702-4_4
12. Collis, J., Hussey, R.: Business Research – A Practical Guide for Undergraduate & Postgraduate Students. Palgrave MacMillan Higher Education, Hampshire (2014)
13. Creswell, J.W.: Research Design: Qualitative, Quantitative and Mixed Methods Approaches, 4th edn. Sage, Thousand Oaks (2014)
14. Dan G., Carlsson N., Chatzidrosso I.: Effective and highly available peer discovery: a case for independent trackers and gossiping. In: 2011 IEEE International conference on Peer-to-Peer (P2P) Computing, pp. 290—299 (2011)
15. D'Acunto, F., Rossi, A.G.: IT Meets Finance: Financial Decision Making in the Digital Era. https://ssrn.com/abstract=4100784. Accessed 12 Jan 2023
16. Dapp, T., Fintech – Die digitale (R)evolution im Finanzsektor, Deutsche Bank AG Deutsche Bank Research Frankfurt am Main Deutschland (2014)

17. Devine, P.: Blockchain learning: can crypto-currency methods be appropriated to enhance online learning? (2015). https://oro.open.ac.uk/44966/8/Devine2015-altc-blockchainlearning-transcript.pdf
18. Duarte, J., Siegel, S., Young, L.: Trust and credit: the role of appearance in peer-to-peer lending. Rev. Financial Stud. **25**(8), 2455–2484 (2012)
19. Duma, F., Gligor, R.: Study regarding Romanian student's perception and behavior concerning the FinTech area with a focus on criptocurrencies and online payments. On-line J. Model. New Eur. **27**(2018), 86–106 (2018)
20. Gomber, P., Koch, J.A., Siering, M.: Digital finance and FinTech: current research and future research directions. J. Bus Econ. **87**, 537–580 (2017). https://doi.org/10.1007/s11573-017-0852-x
21. Greiner, M.E., Wang, H.: Building consumer-to-consumer trust in e-finance marketplaces: an empirical analysis. Int. J. Electron. Commer. **15**(2), 105–136 (2010)
22. Hadad, S., Bratianu, C.: Dematerialization of banking products and services in the digital era. Manag. Mark. Chall. Knowl. Soc. **14**(3), 318–337 (2019). ISSN 2069-8887
23. Karlan, D., Kendall, K., Mann, R., Pande, R., Suri, T., Zinman, J.: Research and Impacts of Digital Financiarl Services (2016). http://www.nber.org/papers/w22633
24. Kisembe, P., Jeberson, W.: Future of Peer-To-Peer Technology with the Rise of Cloud Computing (2017). https://doi.org/10.5121/ijp2p.2017.8304. https://www.researchgate.net/publication/319579735_Future_of_Peer-ToPeer_Technology_with_the_Rise_of_Cloud_Computing
25. Lee, M.C.: Factors influencing the adoption of internet banking: an integration of TAM and TPB with perceived risk and perceived benefit. Electron. Commer. Res. Appl. **8**(3), 130–141 (2009)
26. Lestari, D., Rahmanto, B.T.: Fintech and its challenge for banking sector. Manag. J. Binaniaga **06**(01), 55–69, p-ISSN: 2527 – 4317, e-ISSN: 2580 – 149 6th Accreditation Rating, June 2021
27. Liu, C.: FinTech and Its disruption to financial institutions, research anthology on blockchain technology in business. Healthc. Educ. Gov., 1679–1699 (2021). https://doi.org/10.4018/978-1-7998-5351-0.ch090
28. Mention, A.L.: The future of fintech. Res. Technol. Manag. **62**(4), 59–63 (2019). https://doi.org/10.1080/08956308.2019.1613123pp.59-63
29. Micu, I., Micu, A.: Financial technology (fintech) and its implementation on the romanian non-banking capital market. SEA Pract. Appl. Sci. **2**(11), 379–384 (2016)
30. Allah, M.M.A.: Strengths and weaknesses of near field communication (NFC) technology. Glob. J. Comput. Sci. Technol. **11** (2011). Type: Double Blind Peer Reviewed International Research Journal Publisher: Global Journals Inc. (USA). ISSN: 0975-4172 & Print ISSN: 0975-4350
31. Morana, S., Gnewuch, U., Jung, D., Granig, C.: The effect of anthropomorphism on investment decision-making with robo-advisor chatbots. In: Proceedings of European Conference on Information Systems (ECIS), pp. 1–18 (2020)
32. Moraru, A.D., Duhnea, C.: E-banking and customer satisfaction with banking services. Strateg. Manag. **23**(3), 003–009 (2018)
33. Negrea, C.I., Scarlat, E.I.: The digital Leu challenges and possible areas of implementation. In: "Ovidius" University Annals, Economic Sciences Series, vol. XXII, no. 1, pp. 377–385 (2022)
34. Oliveira, T.: Understanding the internet banking adoption: a unified theory of acceptance and use of technology and perceived risk application. Int. J. Inf. Manag. **34**, 1–13 (2014)
35. Păunescu, M., Popa, A.F, Ciobanu, R.: Propuneri privind înregistrarea în contabilitate a criptomonedelor potrivit reglementărilor contabile românești disponibil la (2022). http://CBR-Proposals-regarding-accounting-for-cryptocurrencies-in-accordance-with-romanian-accounting-a65.pdf

36. Chougule, P.S., Tulpule, D., Amist, A.D.: FinTech a conceptual review. Int. J.Innov. Sci. Res. Rev. **03**(07), 1494–1498 (2021). http://www.journalijisr.com. Review Article ISSN: 2582-6131
37. Popova, Y.: Economic basis of digital banking services produced by FinTech company in smart city. J. Tour. Serv. **23**(12), 6–104 (2021). ISSN 1804-5650
38. Saunders, M., Lewis, P., Thornhill, A.: Research Methods for Business Students. Pearson, New York (2009)
39. Sharma, V., Gusain, P., Umar, P.: Near Field Communication, Conference on Advances in Communication and Control Systems 2013 (CAC2S 2013), pp. 342–345 (2013). Atlantis Press
40. Suryono, R.R., Budi, I., Purwandari, B.: Challenges and trends of financial technology (fintech): a systematic literature review (2020). http://www.mdpi.com/journal/information. https://doi.org/10.3390/info11120590
41. Renduchintala, T., Alfauri, H., Yang, Z.: Roberto Di Pietro and Raj Jain a survey of blockchain applications in the FinTech sector. J. Open Innov. Technol. Mark. Complex. **8**(4), 185 (2022). https://doi.org/10.3390/joitmc8040185
42. Teschner, F., Kranz, T.T., Weinhardt, C.: The impact of customizable market interfaces on trading performance, electronic markets. Int. J. Netw. Bus. **25**, 325–334 (2015)
43. Varma, P., Nijjer, S., Sood, K., Grima, S., Rupeika-Apoga, R.: Thematic analysis of financial technology (fintech) influence on the banking industry. Risks (2022). https://doi.org/10.3390/risks10100186
44. Venter, H.: Digital Currency – A Case for Standard Setting Activity (2016). https://www.ifrs.org/-/media/feature/meetings/2016/december/asaf/digital-currency/asaf-05-aasb-digitalcurrency.pdf.
45. Vijai, C.: Fintech in India – opportunities and challenges. SAARJ J. Bank. Insur. Res. (SJBIR) **8**(1), 42–54 (2019)
46. Zhang-Zhang, Y., Rohlfer, S., Rajasekera, J.: An Eco-Systematic View of Cross-Sector Fintech: The Case of Alibaba and Tencent (2020). http://www.mdpi.com/journal/sustainability. https://doi.org/10.3390/su12218907
47. Webster, J., Watson, R.T.: Analyzing the past to prepare for the future writing a literature review. MIS Q. **26**(2), 13–23 (2022)
48. Williams, C.: Research methods. J. Bus. Econ. Res. (JBER) **5**(3) (2011)
49. Xie, J., Ye, L., Huang, W., Ye, M.: Understanding FinTech platform adoption: impacts of perceived value and perceived risk. J. Theor. Appl. Electron. Commer. Res. **16**, 1893–1911 (2021)
50. Zhou, X.: FinTech lending, social networks, and the transmission of monetary policy research department. Working papers from the Federal Reserve Bank of Dallas (2022). https://doi.org/10.24149/wp2203
51. FinTech: Market Analysis Q3/2022 Trends (2022). https://ukfinancialservicesinsights.deloitte.com/post/102i0t8/fintech-market-analysis-q3-2022-trends
52. https://m.facebook.com/RaiffeisenBankRomania/photos/afla-mai-multe-despre-piata-fintech-din-europa-centrala-si-de-est-ece-raiffeisen/3266685003357130/
53. First edition of Romania FinTech Report 2022 (2022). https://www.rofin.tech/reports/
54. https://futurebanking.ro/raport/romania-s-fintech-map-2022
55. https://documents1.worldbank.org/curated/en/515771621921739154/pdf/Consumer-Risks-in-Fintech-New-Manifestations-of-Consumer-Risks-and-Emerging-Regulatory-Approaches-Policy-Research-Paper.pdf
56. https://www.ookla.com/s/media/2023/01/ookla_fastest-countries_fixed_1222.png

Narrative Communities on Social Networks and the Roles of Legacy Media in Them: The Case of User Complaints in Russian Regions

Kamilla Nigmatullina(✉), Svetlana S. Bodrunova, Alexander Polyakov, and Renat Kasymov

St. Petersburg State University, 7/9 Universitetskaya nab., St. Petersburg 199034, Russia
k.nigmatulina@spbu.ru, renat_rbc@mail.ru

Abstract. On social networks, user complaints and comments they drive form a special type of hybrid discourse of user posts/comments, media publications, and various (re)actions by authorities, from monitoring procedures to response posts on official portals and social media to real action [1]. As our previous research suggests [2], user complaints form stable cross-regional thematic domains based on continuous 'complaint – response' narratives and, thus, may gather discussion communities of yet unknown permanence. Even if such communities are 'discontinued' [3] in terms of stable participation of both ordinary users and institutions, they still accumulate substantial amounts of popular discontent and foster cumulative formation [4] of moods towards authorities, social issues, and quality of life on the regional level. We interpret such detectable complaints-based groups as narrative communities and qualitatively assess the roles played by legacy media in these communities of opinion. We also show that decentering of local journalism takes place in the socially-mediated ecosystems affected by both preferential treatment by the state and the rise of informal newsgroups that attract massive audiences. However, in times of rising uncertainty re-centering of journalism may happen.

Keywords: social media · cumulative deliberation · narrative communities · user engagement · news media · newsgroups · complaints · russia

1 Introduction

Social media of today host mass-scale public discussions. Users tend to discuss issues of public importance that continue in time. Social media have become an important milieu within public sphere where social dissent and discontent accumulates [2, 4]. We argue that discussions on issues form narrative communities and/or communities of opinion in which issues gain public recognition and get continuously discussed.

Such narrative communities form around gatekeeper accounts of varying provenance. We detect three major types of gatekeepers, namely the accounts of local authorities, local legacy media, and local informal newsgroups. The context for formation of narrative issue-based communities in Russian regions comprises subordination of most local

A. Coman and S. Vasilache (Eds.): HCII 2023, LNCS 14025, pp. 271–286, 2023.
https://doi.org/10.1007/978-3-031-35915-6_20

media to regional administrations, growing presence of local governing bodies on social media, restrictive legal environment that has led to elimination of most oppositional news outlets, and destruction of public discussion on 'undesired' Western social media platforms. Such an environment fosters media decentering from opinion formation processes and allows for non-mediated decision-making.

In this paper, we ask whether legacy media may preserve their democratic functions within such environments. For that, we collect data from the Russia-based platform *Vkontakte* (VK) for 22 regions and map dominant gatekeepers; then we qualitatively assess the roles of media in formation of narrative communities, using statistics of user engagement, interpretive reading, and discussion tracing.

The remainder of the paper is organized as follows. Section 2 describes the theoretical and empirical context of opinion formation on Russian social media and poses the research questions and hypotheses. Section 3 describes sampling and data analysis. Section 4 reveals the research results, and Sect. 5 generalizes on our conclusions.

2 Complaints-Based Narrative Communities in Russian Regions

2.1 Narrative Communities and Community Narratives: The Forces that Shape Online Community Building

Narrative community as a concept has been developing since the 1990s. Narrative communities are defined as 'consist[ing] of closely interacting participants who frequently discuss their views of the world' [5]. The concept has been utilized for detection and conceptualization of offline communities of practice (like Israeli backpackers [6] or tourists who use recreational vehicles [5]). However, today, most research is focused upon online communities, as they may be tracked by various methods, including narrative analysis and community detection.

Interestingly, research on narrative communities overlaps with that on community narratives [7] and that on community as narrative. In most of the literature of pre-Internet era, narratives serve as community markers/detectors and are seen as either a way of communal expression of will/attitude, a method to reveal the community borders [8], or a way to debunk the relationship between a certain social process and individual experience [9]. Research from the 1990s suggests that social cognition may also take narrative forms [10], thus helping in reshaping the shared understandings of social problems. Moreover, narratives were shown to play a role – or, rather, multiple roles – in community building, both offline and online. In the 1990s, narrative-based networking was described by clinical psychologists as having capacities of affecting both personal narratives/self-concepts [11] and social behavior, including socialization [7, 12]. Narratives are also believed to shape communal life [13]. Some communication philosophers even insist that communities, at all, exist only when a 'we-narrative' of and about a given community exists [14: 22], seeing communities as being constituted by and dependent upon particular forms of narration [15].

In online realms, networked narratives arise [16]. Narratives identify 'online community space [that] provides emotional support and a space for social interaction in an interpersonal relational context between geographically dispersed individuals', especially for social groups of activist or politically vulnerable nature. Narratives add to community growth, as 'shared narratives provide context for each additional narrative, allowing for the development of interpersonal relationships,' and the community itself [17]. Albrechtslund [18] underlines two other major functions of narratives in online communities (of gamers, in this case), namely sensemaking for an online co-practice and building of a shared identity.

Some research has focused on political roles of narrative communities. MacIntyre has critically influenced community psychology studies by stating that communities were groups of people who argued together in a constructive way, which was later developed into communities seen 'as overlapping groupings capable of engaging in meaningful dialogue' – that is, as communities of political practice [19: 56] relevant for public spheres and decision-making. Works by Rappaport, including [20], link community narratives to community empowerment. Moreover, narratives may complement or challenge the status quo in national and local public spheres. E.g., in antivaxxer discussions, shared common narrative strategies build a competing consensus based on personal expertise [21]. It was stated, i.a., that narrative communities utilize technology for resistance and resilience [17].

Our previous research [2] suggests that certain types of persistent discussion communities may form via practice of policy criticism and/or critique of local authorities. They may form despite the pressure of platform affordances which may not support negative emotions, while platforms still become places where collective grievances on agendas are expressed [22]. However, we see virtually no research on narrative communities formed via policy criticism. There is a conceptualization of critical publics by Toepfl [23], among which he distinguishes leadership-critical, policy-critical, and uncritical publics. However, such publics are non-defined in his theory in terms of their structure and discursive belonging. We suggest that such publics may take shape of discursive or narrative communities that gradually grow in time and space, having a chance for relatively long and stable existence. As our concept of cumulative deliberation implies [4], policy-critical publics may have cumulative character and, thus, grow or diminish in time, as well as continue in time via forming detectable stable structures. So far, publics were assessed in their final state relevant to policymaking; however, their dynamics is also important, as we can detect the moment in time when they become relevant, as well as whether they dissipate and how exactly. Moreover, via assessing the policy-critical communities in their growth, we could also assess the roles of various actors in their formation and public pressure upon decision-makers, as well as the public reaction of the authorities within these narrative communities. In particular, the roles of journalists are assessed in literature within either publics or discussions online, but very rarely in terms of their impact upon formation of critical online communities.

Such communities have, in the recent years, received a push in formation due to growth of alternative socially-mediated forms of city media – namely, local/regional newsgroups, accounts of 'overheard' city talk, and online media represented on social networks. Such media have been called 'new gatekeepers in town' [24]. In them, as our previous works demonstrate, the bulk of user complaints concentrates, and around these complaints commenting unfolds. We would like to inquire whether narrative communities form within the user talk that discusses complaints.

2.2 Communities of Opinion and Gatekeepers of Discontent on Social Media

In media and democracy studies, the roles of legacy media accounts in public dialogue are under scrutiny [25], as we need to know whether, in online communities of opinion [26], they preserve their normative roles of information disseminators, discussion organizers, and bridges between authorities and publics that would convey public dissent and demands to the powerful. However, mediatization of politics has also led to the growing possibilities for authorities to be present online and react directly to user dissent, including complaints. Moreover, new players that change the landscapes of online public spheres, especially in (semi-)autocracies like Russia, are amateur news accounts and local newsgroups [24]. Absence of political accounts in major online discussions [27] allows new local media to accumulate and lead the regional narratives of dissent. Thus, we see the three potential types of social media accounts that would allow for formation of the narrative communities in the Russian regions. These are:

- traditional gatekeepers of social dissent, that is, accounts of local media;
- new gatekeepers of social dissent, that is, local amateur newsgroups;
- mediatized addressees of social dissent, that is, accounts of local authorities.

Posts and comments on user complaints in them take part in maintaining the narrative communities on certain themes of popular discontent, but the three of them are expected to differ in origin and nature of active deliberators, discussion length, and the role of legacy media in the discussion.

The three types of gatekeepers differ in their normative roles in the online deliberation on local issues. Thus, local legacy media operate today in hybrid environments, reaching their audiences physically, on web 1.0, and via social media, forming their own ecosystem [28] and taking part in accumulation of opinions [4]. They are expected to perform democratic functions, including informing and political newsmaking [29], community integration [30], and linking local governments to local publics. However, with the growing mediatization of local governance and rise of alternative news sources like newsgroups, under pressures of excessive information flows and emotionalization of media content, the process of decentering journalism has been taking place, both in democracies [31] and in countries with no long democratic traditions [2]. Decentering refers to the diminishing role of local media in deliberation of local issues. Interestingly, mediatization of local governance appears to be both similar in various countries and highly contextual. On one hand, direct communication with voters via social media has been growing worldwide. On the other hand, presence of government representatives in online discussions varies highly across contexts; in Russia, e.g., we had detected an institutional vacuum in both conflictual and complaints-based discussions [2; 28].

All this poses questions on the roles of the three gatekeepers in creation of narrative communities of opinion. Legacy media and authorities that might be expected to create such communities do not always take part in this process, while amateur local newsgroups are rarely equipped with professionalism, including media ethics, for creation of rational and balanced public dialogue.

2.3 Mapping Complaints-Based Narrative Communities in Russian Regions

Given what is stated in 2.2, at this stage of research, we aim at two goals. First, mapping of Russian regions is necessary, in order to see what types of gatekeepers dominate. Second, we will assess what roles the three gatekeepers play in the formation of narrative communities around user complaints.

Complaints were selected for the assessment of narrative community formation, as they accumulate both emotional peaks and conglomerates of rational suggestions. However, on social media, comments rarely reach the form of well-shaped and well-organized discussions, which makes their patterns hard to detect. Moreover, on Russian social networking platforms such as *Vkontakte* (VK.com, or VK), the ecosystems are adjusted to fostering emotional reactions more than to growing chains of topical messages. However, despite this and other limiting factors such as, e.g., botization, VK has been recognized as key for official state communication, along with Telegram as a nearly-official messenger. Over 150,000 organizations have been obliged to establish at least one account on a social network (most of them preferred VK). On the contrary, Facebook, Twitter, and Instagram have been called undesired and claimed to spread extremist and anti-Russian views, which prevents them being used for official communication today. This is why we will focus on VK and will configure our research questions the way that helps detect the varying features of discussions in the narrative communities within the three types of local gatekeepers of social dissent.

The active struggle in the Russian media space was also shaped by a range of laws on foreign agency that treated both individuals and organizations, including oppositional media. By September 2022, most of them ceased to exist, moved to foreign jurisdictions, or continued on Telegram (not on VK). Thus, local legacy media on VK were mostly regional newspapers or TV channels that received some sort of support or (at least) tolerance from local authorities. Audience consolidation in terms of opinion building was also taking place, as circa 3.8 mln people who opposed the official Russian position, by various estimates, left Russia during the first months of the military conflict. The conflict has influenced the state information policy, accelerating the process of digitalization of bureaucracy and local decision-making institutions. After 2017, the state has sharply intensified Internet regulation, which has led, i.a., to withdrawal or banning of many titles from the media space. With these trends taken together, relative etatization and depoliticization of the socially-mediated public discussion on VK may be noted. Discussions on this social network have even previously been recognized by scholars as de-politicized and trivial [32]; as for now, oppositional media have been next-to-absent in Russian regions. However, 'new gatekeepers' could to some extent be viewed as an alternative, as they provided space for satirical treatment of current events, social critique, and user-generated content that contained complaints and described shortcomings of local life, while legacy media remained linked to either authorities or big regional businesses.

2.4 The Research Questions

In our research, we focus on how types of narrative communities affect discussion efficiency and media roles, including those most studied within the research on media decentering [31]. In accordance with the research goals stated above, we have formulated the following research questions and hypotheses:

RQ1. What is the shape of complaints-based narrative communities in Russia? How do narrative communities distribute in Russian regions? Are there regions where media-based narrative communities dominate?

RQ2. What is the role of media accounts as discussion organizers within the narrative communities, in comparison with those of local authorities and local newsgroups?

H2a. Discussion length on media accounts will be significantly shorter than on those of local authorities (longer) and newsgroups (the longest), as the two latter allow for either direct communication with authorities or freer expression of discontent.

H2b. The number of user comments on media accounts is much smaller than on those of authorities and newsgroups.

RQ3. What is the role of media accounts as discussion participants within the narrative communities, in comparison with that of local authorities and local newsgroups?

H3. Media accounts themselves are rarely involved in commenting, which is also true for local newsgroups who see themselves more as news providers, unlike the authorities' accounts who comment on user complaints more often.

3 Data Collection and Analysis

Selection of Time Span. We have selected September and October 2022 as the period of an outburst of societal anxiety and complaining due to the first wave of military mobilization that took place in all Russian regions. It has led to both a significant news outbreak and to growth of online discussions. On September 21, 2022, President of Russia Vladimir Putin announced partial mobilization of citizens in reserve liable for military service. Putin's decree has become the main newsbreak of the end of 2022 for the entire Russian society, and many media outlets have begun to cover events in accordance with the interests of their owners or the elites influencing them. E.g., oppositional media focused on the emigration of Russians following the mobilization decree, as well as on events related to the blocking of some online media and the implementation of the law on foreign agents in relation to individuals and legal entities. Heated discussions on social media and messengers like Telegram have, to some extent, spurred authorities' communication activities in response to public anxiety and the incoming news from the army. In addition, local recruitment points have seen a lot of incidents related to mess within the recruitment system and conscripts' lists, many of which were reported via new gatekeepers on VK and Telegram, rather than on legacy media. Thus, we have selected September and October 2022 as the time span when all three types of gatekeepers were critically affected by the incoming agendas and audience behavior.

Data Collection. Was performed via manual selection of 66 most popular accounts of the three types (one per type, that is, three accounts per region) in 22 Russian regions and automated parsing of posts and comments on VK. All posts for September and October 2022 were collected and the top 3 most comprehensive ones (by views, comments, and reposts) were selected along with comments to them. The list of regions included Astrakhan, Bashkortostan, Chelyabinsk, Irkutsk, Kaliningrad, Karelia,

Khabarovsk, Krasnodar, Krasnoyarsk, Leningrad Region, Lipetsk, Murmansk, Nizhniy Novgorod, Novosibirsk, Omsk, Perm, Rostov-on-Don, Samara, Tatarstan, Tyumen, Voronezh, YUGRA (Khanty-Mansi Autonomous Region).

In each region, the top 3 media outlets were detected via the 'Medialogia' web portal ranking list, as for the 3rd quarter of 2022. The media that had VK accounts with the largest number of subscribers were selected for the sample. The official pages of the heads of regions (verified by a special VK check mark) were chosen as the accounts of the authorities; if there was no account of the governor or the number of subscribers was relatively small, we opted for the pages of the regional governments. In addition, the heads of the regions were checked for popularity measured by mentions by the same 'Medialogia' for the 3rd quarter of 2022, to make sure they were among the popular accounts. For the third type of gatekeepers, the most popular news groups were selected, which names contained the names of the respective regions. Most often, these were the groups with the names 'Typical [city]' or '[city] online.' Some of these groups allegedly belonged to local authorities, but it was impossible to find public confirmation of this.

Within the collected data, we have chosen the posts where comments contained complaints and/or discussions around them – in fact, over 90% of posts in each case.

Two legacy media accounts (*Kuban' News* and *74.ru*) were eliminated due to absence of comments switched off by moderators. Under some posts, comments were also missing: E.g., in *Ircity*, they disappeared in October. In Tyumen, a post on mobilization had 155,000 views in the media account, 1,221 reposts, 1,800 likes/dislikes, and not a single comment; presumably, they were deleted manually. For posts with less than 5 comments registered, the duration of the discussion was assigned 0.

Thus, a total of 64 accounts were closely examined in VK, with a total of 8,946,230 subscribers, 1,738,857 of them saw posts in two months (see Table 1).

Data Analysis All accounts were assessed by the following parameters: average VRpost (audience coverage by post, %), number of subscribers, entries, views, comments, likes, reposts, average views, average comments, average likes, average reposts, most viewed

Table 1. Sample description

Parameter	Authorities	Legacy media	New gatekeepers
VR (audience coverage / subscriber reach), on average per post (% of subscribers seeing a post)	**74.3%*** (10.3% to 179.5%)	8.4% (1.5% to 31.3%)	11.7% (1.9% to 27.8%)
Average size of the public, thousand subscribers	61.2 (7.9 to 211.5)	98.9 (5.9 to 349.8)	**246.6** (24.2 to 582.7)
Average size of audience seeing the post, thousand subscribers	**45.4** (4.3 to 190.1)	6.5 (0.1 to 20.6)	25.9 (1.1 to 57.7)

(continued)

Table 1. (*continued*)

Parameter	Authorities	Legacy media	New gatekeepers
Average number of published posts per month (September / October)	56 (5 to 359)	**838** (302 to 1586)	391 (38 to 989)
Dynamics of N posts (September to October)	**+ 7.9%** (-42.9% to + 54.3%)	+ 1.8% (-22.1% to + 31.6%)	-0.6% (-22.1% to + 34.1%)
Dynamics of N views (September to October)	+ 15.7% (-56.3% to + 77.9%)	**+ 19%** (-27.6% to + 191.1%)	+ 4% (-20.6% to + 28.9%)
Dynamics of N comments (September to October)	+ 11% (-83.7% to + 143.7%)	**+ 13.5%** (-100% (closed) to + 137%)	-11.7% (-60% to + 55%)
Dynamics of N reposts (September to October)	**+ 20.6%** (-75.9% to + 132.1%)	-7.3% (-49.2% to + 34.8%)	-16.3% (-53.6% to + 36.7%)
Dynamics of the average N comments per post (September to October)	+ 5%	**+ 12.1%**	-8.9%
Average N comments in the top 3 posts	397	206	**605**
The average length of the discussion in top 3 posts	16.3 **days**	6.4 days	9.5 days
Dynamics of the average N comments in top 3 posts (September to October)	+ 1.3%	**+ 64.6%**	-9.2%
Dynamics of the average discussion duration in the top 3 posts (September to October)	+ 61.4%	**+ 86.1%**	+ 82.8%

Note. * - the highest meaning is highlighted for each row

posts, number of views on the top 3 posts, the most commented posts, the number of comments on the top 3 posts, and duration of the discussion.

We have employed frequency analysis for assessment of the number of comments and user activity, manual account assessment for detection of user types, and interpretive reading for detection of cumulative patterns in user discussions.

4 Results

RQ1. Mapping of the narrative communities via simple account statistics has revealed quite unexpected misbalances is how complaints-based discussion structures today in Russian regions (see Table 2).

Table 2. Dominance of gatekeepers in 22 Russian regions by three parameters

Type	N comments in top 3 posts	N comments on average	VR post
Governor / authorities	**27%** Irkutsk, Kaliningrad, Leningrad region, Perm, Tatarstan, YUGRA	**77%** Krasnoyarsk, Omsk, Rostov-on-Don, Nizhny Novgorod, Novosibirsk, Chelyabinsk, Perm, Samara, Kaliningrad, Irkutsk, Tatarstan, YUGRA, Karelia, Voronezh, Murmansk, Leningrad region, Khabarovsk	**100%** All regions
Mass media	**18%** Chelyabinsk, Khabarovsk, Krasnoyarsk, Lipetsk	**9%** Bashkortostan, Lipetsk	-
Media-like accounts	**55%** Astrakhan, Bashkortostan, Karelia, Krasnodar, Murmansk, Nizhniy Novgorod, Novosibirsk, Omsk, Rostov-on-Don, Samara, Tyumen, Voronezh	**14%** Astrakhan, Krasnodar, Tyumen	-

First of all, we need to underline that our previous results [2] which told of the zero presence of governmental and media accounts within VK-based discussions on complaints that unfold on legacy and new media accounts needs to be complemented by the current results. While authorities are not present as discussion participants on media accounts, they seem to be quite successful in building their own narrative communities on their accounts. The accounts of the authorities are leading in terms of the coverage of views per post, the average size of the audience per post, the dynamics of the number of posts and reposts, and the average length of the discussion in the comments in the top 3 posts over a period of two months. Despite the much smaller number of posts during the two months, public attention to these posts grew, and the major deliberative parameters such as audience coverage and duration of discussion were better than those for both types of media. Stratified, they, again, show that, in over ¾ of regions, government accounts attracted more comments on average than media, and were outperforming media for VR in 100%(!) of regions.

Professional media have also experienced a relative return of user attention. In general, they show low efficiency, posting over two times more frequently than media-like accounts and nearly 15 times more often than authorities, but having much lower audience reach. The length of discussions under their posts in top posts varies from 3 to 6 days, 1,5 times and 2,5 times shorter than for new media and authorities, respectively, though normatively it is the legacy media that are expected to organize discussions and support the narrative communities while they are elaborating decisions. However, during the mobilization which was perceived by many as a crisis, audiences partly returned to viewing and commenting, especially the most popular posts (+64.6%), and the length of discussions grew nearly twice, forming more stable communities of opinion. Discussions became longer on all three types of gatekeepers, but legacy media experienced the biggest growth followed by new media-like accounts, while the discussions at the authorities' accounts grew less intensely. This shows that there is still room left for the audiences to form communities of opinion around media accounts in crisis times, despite regular low attention to their content.

Newsgroups and media-like non-editorial accounts entered the time of mobilization as the most popular sources, but have demonstrated drops in user attention, as the audiences turned to more politicized and urgent information that only the authorities and legacy media could provide. However, in over 50% of regions, their most popular posts still kept them as important gatekeepers. Newsgroups, in general, tended to create longer discussions than legacy media, but during the.

Despite our results for RQ1 draw a picture of partial re-centering of local media and growth of audiences' direct communication with authorities throughout the 22 regions, this may be a bit misleading, as regional differences are high, and the results need to be contextualized in further studies. Given the results in Table 2, we, in future, will cluster the regions in terms of dominance of certain types of gatekeepers.

Second, we show in both this and previous works that the shift of media roles implies both deprivation of the role of discussion organizers and non-development of the role of discussion participants. The remaining role is discussion watchers, which implies echoing user discontent and subordination to local authorities in disseminating information on their replies to people's complaints. This may be explained by the fact that most local media are owned by either local authorities or state-affiliated businesses, which deprives media of their watchdog roles.

An important observation can be made about user reactions and the discourse of complaint within the communities of opinion. Thus, topics that evoke complaining comprise many posts; the topics less popular if judged by the number of posts dedicated to them and the views in these posts turn out to be the most commented upon. Moreover, the focus of comments does not always relate to the news topic. There were often cases when users, having seen the reaction of the local authorities to complaints, continued to ask questions beyond the topic of the post, in the hope of getting an answer – and they received it. Thus, the topic of the news might not be the most interesting (as, e.g., in the case of the news on the governor's visit somewhere), but the discussion in the comments turned into a 'hotline' for a governor or a government, with certain 'complaint themes' being more persistent than news topics. This supports our view of user commenting under posts in the three gatekeeper account types as narrative communities / communities of opinion. This also clearly corresponds to the idea of cumulative deliberation [4], which needs to be further explored.

We should also report atypical patterns in comment samples of several regions. The first non-standard pattern of discussion development is that, after a certain time, messages (or stickers) non-related to the post topic appear on the already exhausted comment thread, thus artificially prolonging the comment period, with an unclear goal. The second pattern describes the activity of individual complainants who simultaneously publish the same question in all the gatekeepers' accounts using the same text. Third, there is also content that is repeated in different regions (mainly videos with nationwide news), also published at about the same time. One can associate this with the pro-government content produced by the information management centers of regional governments. Thus, we see attempts of strategic interference to the discussions and influencing the narratives featuring complaints, which demands attention.

RQ2. It is on social networks where Russian local media turn out to be secondary to government accounts, in both the speed of reaction to user complaints and user attention. Often posts and comments from the accounts of heads of regions or governments become the basis for journalistic publications, and not vice versa. Journalists remain voiceless within user discussions, as well as lose their chances for creating a deeper discussion on local issues if the authorities answer individual user complaints quicker than journalists can pick them and introduce to the news cycle. Thus, the logic of news production today plays against journalism professionals and against the public sphere itself, depriving regions of user complaints becoming a source for generalization in journalistic enquiry and a spur for deeper discussion. Neither narrative nor cumulative character of opinion formation help local journalists engage into efficient issue-based reporting and discussion organization, which leaves them the roles of discussion watchers only, deprived of the watchdog and agora roles.

H2a. The hypothesis was partly confirmed. In general, media accounts turned out to be the least engaging the audiences in lengthy discussions. However, authorities, not newsgroups, were the most engaging. Unlike the authorities' accounts which follow an unspoken recommendation to respond to all complaints and requests of citizens on social networks quite quickly and correctly, and unlike the accounts of newsgroups which do not respond to comments but use provocative style and do not limit comments, media accounts are not engaged in any activity dedicated to community or narrative formation, and also limit commenting. The latter is primarily due to legally binding responsibility for potential dissemination of fakes and/or extremist statements (account holders being also responsible for commenters!). Observing an increase in aggression, user discontent, and botization, in October, the media preferred either to limit commenting or to reduce interaction with subscribers. However, the users still addressed them more in October than previously, which hints to the potential of local legacy media for community building and support of the narratives based on complaints, if not for the restrictive regulation.

H2b. The hypothesis was fully confirmed (see Table 2). In terms of the number of comments in general, the government accounts are leading, and in terms of the number of comments on top 3 engaging posts, newsgroups are ahead. At the same time, legacy media are leading in the dynamics of the increase in comments in October (see Table 1). However, this conclusion has several limitations. Firstly, hiding and 'cleaning up' comments on such a sensitive topic as partial mobilization affects the overall dynamics. Secondly, the most popular posts often include sweepstakes, contests, or reportage videos non-related to the post topic. Finally, the fact that the agendas of all three gatekeeper types differs also distorts the results. Government accounts publish only information important for regional management; the media focus on socially relevant agendas; and newsgroups are a mix of local social agendas, national and even world news, and entertainment content in substantial quantities. Thus, being cautious about direct comparisons, we can only state that we see signs of re-centering of media in user attention during the period of anxiety, and that, even given the re-centering, legacy media were losing to other gatekeepers in terms of user engagement.

RQ3. If the role of the discussion organizer is, at least partly, fulfilled by legacy media, their role as discussion participant is minimized. As it can be seen from Table 1, legacy media increased the volume of publications within the crisis period, but lost momentum in the number of reposts. A lot of information is produced, but it does not make people react. For emotional satisfaction of information needs, subscribers turn to informal communities, and for solving local problems they directly address the accounts of the authorities. Crisis times engage audiences more and make re-address legacy media, but this is definitely not enough to bring media back to the center of narrative communities.

H3a. The hypothesis is confirmed – i.a., by observations on the course of discussions under specific posts in the sample. As stated above, the topic of user complaints to the authorities does not always correspond to the post topic. Prompt response by government representatives to citizens provokes an increase in comments, but at the same time they cannot be considered a full-fledged deliberative discussion. Solving an individual problem often does not imply public dialogue on the issue. Moreover, sometimes fellow commenters may not support the complainer and react negatively to his/her complaint; this, though, does not create an opinion crossroads but, rather, helps silencing complaints and allows for letting them down by both authorities and media. This practice clearly needs additional research in terms of deliberative quality of user disagreement and institutional reactions to such disagreements.

5 Discussion and Conclusion

Narrative communities that form on social networks generally reflect the moods and problematic issues of citizens in real life. Along with that, discussion flows in semi-autocracies are shaped both political and commercial factors, such as by fairly intensive information policies of the state authorities, market competition, informal news communities acting as an aggregator of local agendas, and the production of content by local media that still see social networks as an additional channel for news dissemination of information, not an autonomous space where local communities reside.

A fairly large amount of social discontent accumulates on social networks, monitored by local authorities and media, as well as provoking engaging comments in informal newsgroups, which provide a platform for open expression of discontent via publication of user complaints. As our previous studies have shown, in which we interviewed newsgroups moderators, the professional community of journalists is divided in opinion whether working with complaints is the direct responsibility of journalists, while the authorities clearly see their role in reducing social discontent in the space of social networks and increasing the volume of published 'constructive' content in order to demonstrate efficient problem solving and prompt response to citizens' requests. However, such reshaping of institutional response to social discontent decenters journalists via competition pressures of two sorts, of which one is the competition with authorities for quicker pickup of user complaints, and the second is the one from informal newsgroups that attract much bigger audiences and allow for freer discussion of local agendas.

An important role in the restructuring of information flows in social networks is assigned to state public pages and, in particular, the personal pages of governors and heads of regions. Posts on the pages of local politicians become a source of information for both citizens and journalists, mostly in a top-down way. However, the bottom-up chain of articulation of social discontent via media is broken. Even the top-down communication between politics and media, in which important governmental input was provided via press secretaries to influential media, is substituted by direct broadcasting through the accounts of government officials on social networks. Users have a chance to react, but further engagement of authorities into socially-mediated dialogue does not happen, leaving public discussion the function of vaporing out dissent. Depending on the charisma and political position of politicians, popularity of their accounts may be several times higher than that of local public affairs media.

The processes of decentering journalism are vivid on VK if we examine such classic media roles as informing, providing feedback, information verification, social orientation, gatekeeping, and watchdog. At the same time, we cannot state that media accounts do not affect opinion formation. Moreover, in times of crisis, such as pandemic or military mobilization, media accounts become more visible as foci of public attention. In journalists' reportages, the public is looking for confirmation or refutation of facts and rumors, important additions to known information and, of course, interpretation of events. In the accounts of the authorities, people are interested in solving momentary problems and operational comments on important events in the region. Newsgroups shift to more marginal positioning in times of crisis, as they do not directly deal with public needs, but primarily respond to demand for higher quality of life, lifestyle orientation, and leisure.

User complaints are the most indicative on narrative communities formed around public affairs issues, as they accumulate various facets of complaints-based discourse, namely substantial, emotional, and behavioral ones. User complaints create peaks of formation of narrative communities, attracting the entire range of opinions, emotions, and in all the three major socially-mediated gatekeepers.

State policies towards certain platforms critically influence the formation of narrative communities, as the latter are shaped by platform affordances, state presence, and moderation practices bound by the legal and political environment. In Russia, with the de-facto destruction of a large segment of socially-mediated discussion in the 'undesired' Western platforms and obligation of local authorities to be present on VK has directed user discontent more towards direct VK-based communication with authorities. VK not only forms certain patterns of interaction between community members, but also receives support and preferential treatment on the part of the authorities. The bulk of the public affairs discourse has moved to VK, and the struggle between different types of narrative communities is unfolding there.

All in all, on social networks, professional media have partly lost their positions in formation of narrative communities to the accounts of the authorities and informal news groups. Decentering of journalism on social networks shows up via its diminished roles in collecting discontent and failing to find those responsible for problem solving. Nevertheless, in times of crises, media remain anchors and providers of guidance and orientation, which leaves room for a return to basic democratic functions.

Acknowledgements. This research has been supported in full by Center for International Media Research of St. Petersburg State University, project #94033584.

References

1. Nigmatullina, K., Rodossky, N.: Pandemic Discussions in VKontakte: Hopes and Fears. In: Meiselwitz, G. (ed.) HCII 2021. LNCS, vol. 12775, pp. 407–423. Springer, Cham (2021). https://doi.org/10.1007/978-3-030-77685-5_30
2. Nigmatullina, K., Bodrunova, S.S., Rodossky, N., Nepiyushchikh, D.: Discourse of complaining on social networks in Russia: Cumulative opinions vs. decentering of institutions. In: Antonyuk, A., Basov, N. (eds), Proceedings of 6th conference 'Networks in the Global World – 2022' (in print)
3. Smoliarova, A.S., Bodrunova, S.S., Blekanov, I.S., Maksimov, A.: Discontinued public spheres? Reproducibility of user structure in Twitter discussions on interethnic conflicts. In: HCI International 2020 – Late Breaking Posters: 22nd International Conference, HCII 2020, Copenhagen, Denmark, July 19–24, 2020, Proceedings, Part I 22 (pp. 262–269). Springer, Cham (2020)
4. Bodrunova, S.S.: Practices of Cumulative Deliberation: A Meta-review of the Recent Research Findings. In: Chugunov, A.V., Janssen, M., Khodachek, I., Misnikov, Y., Trutnev, D. (eds.) EGOSE 2021. CCIS, vol. 1529, pp. 89–104. Springer, Cham (2022). https://doi.org/10.1007/978-3-031-04238-6_8
5. Pearce, P.L., Wu, M.Y.: A mobile narrative community: communication among senior recreational vehicle travellers. Tour. Stud. **18**(2), 194–212 (2018)
6. Noy, C.: A narrative community: Voices of Israeli backpackers. Wayne State University Press (2007)
7. Rappaport, J.: Community narratives: tales of terror and joy. Am. J. Commun. Psychol. **28**, 1–24 (2000)
8. Mankowski, E.S., Rappaport, J.: Narrative concepts and analysis in spiritually-based communities. J. Commun. Psychol. **28**(5), 479–493 (2000)

9. Maton, K.I.: Narrative concepts, spiritually based communities: strengths and future development. J. Commun. Psychol. **28**(5), 529–533 (2000)
10. Wyer Jr, R.S.: Knowledge and Memory: The Real Story: Advances in Social Cognition, Volume VIII. Psychology Press (2014)
11. Russell, R.L., Van den Broek, P.: Changing narrative schemas in psychotherapy. Psychother. Theor. Res., Pract., Training, **29**(3), 344 (1992)
12. Miller, P.J., Moore, B.B.: Narrative conjunctions of caregiver and child: a comparative perspective on socialization through stories. Ethos **17**(4), 428–449 (1989)
13. Rappaport, J., Simkins, R.: Healing and empowering through community narrative. Prev. Hum. Serv. **10**(1), 29–50 (1991)
14. Carr, D.: An Argument for Continuity. Memory, Identity, Community: The Idea of Narrative in the Human Sciences, **7** (1997)
15. Fisher, W.R.: Narration, reason, and community. In Writing the social text (pp. 199–217). Routledge, London (2017)
16. Kozinets, R.V., De Valck, K., Wojnicki, A.C., Wilner, S.J.: Networked narratives: understanding word-of-mouth marketing in online communities. J. Mark. **74**(2), 71–89 (2010)
17. Rodriguez, M. C. G.: 'The stories we tell each other': Using technology for resistance and resilience through online narrative communities. In: Emotions, technology, and health, (pp. 125–147). Academic Press (2016)
18. Albrechtslund, A.M.: Gamers telling stories: understanding narrative practices in an online community. Convergence **16**(1), 112–124 (2010)
19. Lewis, T.A.: On the limits of narrative: Communities in pluralistic society. J. Relig. **86**(1), 55–80 (2006)
20. Rappaport, J.: Empowerment meets narrative: listening to stories and creating settings. Am. J. Community Psychol. **23**(5), 795–807 (1995)
21. Duchsherer, A., Jason, M., Platt, C.A., Majdik, Z.P.: Immunized against science: narrative community building among vaccine refusing/hesitant parents. Public Underst. Sci. **29**(4), 419–435 (2020)
22. Wahl-Jorgensen, K.: Emotions, media and politics. John Wiley & Sons (2019)
23. Toepfl, F.: Comparing authoritarian publics: the benefits and risks of three types of publics for autocrats. Commun. Theor. **30**(2), 105–125 (2020)
24. Dovbysh, O.: New gatekeepers in town: How groups in social networking sites influence information flows in Russia's provinces. Social Media + Society, 7(2), 20563051211013253 (2021)
25. Mellado, C.: Digital journalistic cultures on social media. In: The Routledge Companion to News and Journalism, (pp. 487–496). Routledge, London (2022)
26. Wahl-Jorgensen, K.: From letters to tweeters: Media communities of opinion. In: The Routledge Companion to British Media History (pp. 589–599). Routledge, London (2014)
27. Smoliarova, A.S., Bodrunova, S.S., Blekanov, I.S.: Politicians driving online discussions: Are institutionalized influencers top twitter users? In: Kompatsiaris, I., Cave, J., Satsiou, A., Carle, G., Passani, A., Kontopoulos, E., Diplaris, S., McMillan, D. (eds.) INSCI 2017. LNCS, vol. 10673, pp. 132–147. Springer, Cham (2017). https://doi.org/10.1007/978-3-319-70284-1_11
28. Herhausen, D., Grewal, L. Cummings, K.H., Roggeveen, A.L., Villarroel Ordenes, F., Grewal, D.: Complaint de-escalation strategies on social media. J. Market. **87**(2), 210–231 (2023)
29. Blair, H.: Participation and accountability at the periphery: democratic local governance in six countries. World Dev. **28**(1), 21–39 (2000)
30. McLeod, J.M., et al.: Community integration, local media use, and democratic processes. Commun. Res. **23**(2), 179–209 (1996)

31. Wahl-Jorgensen, K.: News production, ethnography, and power: On the challenges of newsroom-centricity. In: Bird, S. Elizabeth (ed.) The Anthropology of News and Journalism: Global Perspectives. Indiana University Press, Bloomington (2009)
32. Bodrunova, S.S., Litvinenko, A.A.: New media and political protest: the formation of a public counter-sphere in Russia, 2008–12. In: Russia's changing economic and political regimes: The Putin years and afterwards, pp. 29–65. Routledge, London (2013)

How Does the Online News Portal Framing the Phenomenon of Street Fashion in Indonesia

Resti Ryhanisa(✉) and Filosa Gita Sukmono

Department of Communication Studies, Faculty of Social and Politics, Universitas Muhammadiyah Yogyakarta, Kasihan, Indonesia
resti.r.isip19@mail.umy.ac.id, filosa@umy.ac.id

Abstract. The purpose of this study is to explain the framing of online news portals Kompasiana and Harian Terbit about the Citayam Fashion Week (CFW) phenomenon as street fashion in Indonesia. The study uses Nvivo as qualitative tool in qualitative approach a qualitative method to analyse the data. The findings shows that online media framing plays an important role in forming public opinion about the CFW street fashion phenomenon. The Kompasiana news portal displays framing content with the most dominant content being New Media Effects, while Harian Terbit is Public Response. The intensity of reporting on the CFW phenomenon was highest when this phenomenon was going viral. Besides that, The framing narrative spread by the two news portals focuses on a new phenomenon in Indonesia which is known as street fashion and also the behavior of teenagers in following social media trends.

Keywords: Street Fashion · Online News · Framing · Media

1 Introduction

Citayam Fashion Week is a street fashion phenomenon in Indonesia [1]. Citayam Fashion Week can be equated and compared to the 1980s-established 'Harajuku' style of street fashion in Japan [2]. Citayam Fashion Week is a trending phenomenon among young Indonesians, especially in the capital city of Jakarta. Young people from outside the Jakarta area, especially those from the Citayam area, gather in the Central Jakarta area of the National Bank of Indonesia (BNI) to showcase models and fashion styles to the public [3]. These young people come wearing clothes that are attractive to the general public (eccentric) [4]. At first, the activities of Citayam teenagers gathered on the side of the road (sidewalk) to chat and take pictures. Still, since the emergence of a viral video in cyberspace containing interviews with several teenagers, namely Bonge, Jeje, and Kurma, at that location, it has become one of the things that animated the area where this phenomenon occurs. The viral video, which contains interviews with these teenagers, visualizes the joy when they gather at that location. Not only that, but this viral video also showcased their unique dress style and was eventually ogled by various parties [5].

The fashion trend at Citayam Fashion Week (CFW) eventually became a fashion taste among teenagers in that location [5]. These teenagers create their fashion style to

A. Coman and S. Vasilache (Eds.): HCII 2023, LNCS 14025, pp. 287–295, 2023.
https://doi.org/10.1007/978-3-031-35915-6_21

be introduced to the general public [6]. This phenomenon has been widely discussed for some time because there has been much news in Indonesia's mainstream online media. The online news portal that contains the Ciyatam Fashion Week phenomenon has its point of view on each of its reports. Online news portals are one of the mass media that has an essential power in disseminating information [7]. To attract the public's attention, information must be seasoned with perspectives depending on the political policies of the media. The purpose of framing itself is to communicate information so that an image, impression, or specific meaning is desired by the media, which the public will capture [1].

Several previous studies related to street fashion and framing analysis. Research from [8] which explains media framing of online news platforms, as well as research by [9] which explains framing analysis using the Zhong Dang Pan Gerald M. Kosicki method with the object of the online news platform Citayam Fashion Week phenomenon. In the research written by [10] explained how media framing affects the emergence of anti-China sentiment and COVID-19. Research was written by [9] talk about framing model analysis Zhongdang Pan Gerald M Koscki with the object of a Youtube social media account. Further research described by [11] Discusses the importance of a medium representing the information you want to convey. While research is written by [12] explained about the framing of a news story on an online platform that contains the flood disaster in the Indonesian capital, Jakarta.

Based on the explanation of relevant previous research, which only focuses on media framing, studies need to comprehensively explain the aspects or elements that support framing in each news story. Therefore, the novelty of this research is focused on how the media frames an account of the street fashion case in Indonesia. So the purpose of this study is to explain the framing of online news portals about the Citayam Fashion Week phenomenon as street fashion in Indonesia.

2 Overview of Literature

2.1 Framing Analysis Concept

Framing an event as a message and spreading it to the public [13, 14] Framing is the process of emphasizing a message or making it more visible rather than providing information about reality, with the audience focusing on the informative message [9]. Gitlin states that framing is an informative and formative strategy that simplifies reality by selecting, repeating, and highlighting certain aspects so that an event or topic gets the reader's attention [15]. Media coverage, media agenda, and emerging theories are theories from framing analysis [16]. Framing analysis is the arrangement of message body ideas that provide context and issue suggestions through selecting, pushing, deactivating, and refining what needs special attention [17]. Framing is based on the assumption that how an issue is described in a news report can influence how the public perceives the problem [7].

Then, as a tool that bridges the existence of framing. The media will play a central role in shaping the understanding of events and public opinion so that reporting on disasters in national newspapers provides direct explanations [18]. Social construction is constructed through the media and uses the theory of Vincent S. Sacco (1995) to examine how social structure is formed and expressed in a medium [19].

2.2 Street Fashion

Street fashion refers to the style of clothing created by the general public. They put their style together using various existing fashion elements to stand out. Street fashion can come from anyone, regardless of class status. However, it should be noted that in Japan, street fashion is dominated by women and girls who own fashion trends [20]. The characteristics of street fashion that make it different are reflected in the style of dress of the people who go there [21]. Street fashion is an important area that can address the consumer experience associated with the tourism industry [22]. The consumer experience can directly lead to fashion retail's key competitiveness, which must be overcome to overcome the limitations of offline conditions and revitalize the sector [23].

Over the last decades, the term "street fashion" has been commonly used worldwide to represent youth fashion. It is widely accepted that street fashion emerged from the youth subculture rather than from fashion professionals. As a result, fashion is used as a means of group identity to differentiate groups from the culture at large and other groups [24]. Subcultural styles became a source of fashion that extended from the streets to designers. Experts see subcultural styles as innovations that result in new fashion diffusion processes [24].

3 Research Method

This study uses a qualitative method with a framing analysis approach. The data source for this research is online media on the Kompasiana news platform and the Harian Terbit. Three selected trending news from each online platform, Kompasiana, and Harian Terbit, are then used as research objects. This research is a literature study period data collection technique in this study, starting from June 2022 to September 2022, because the news was viral then. This study uses NVIVO 12 plus software as a data analysis tool. Figure 1 shows the flow in data analysis using NVIVO 12 plus.

Figure 1 shows the flow of conducting this research. The first step is to collect news data on Kompasiana and Harian Terbit publications, with three news stories each using NCapture. In the second stage, the data that has been obtained is then uploaded to the NVIVO 12 Plus software for analysis—the third stage uses the crosstab query feature in analyzing and visualizing research data. Then the fourth stage, the data results are displayed in the discussion for later analysis based on theory and other supporting data. The fifth stage is drawing conclusions based on the debate that has been done.

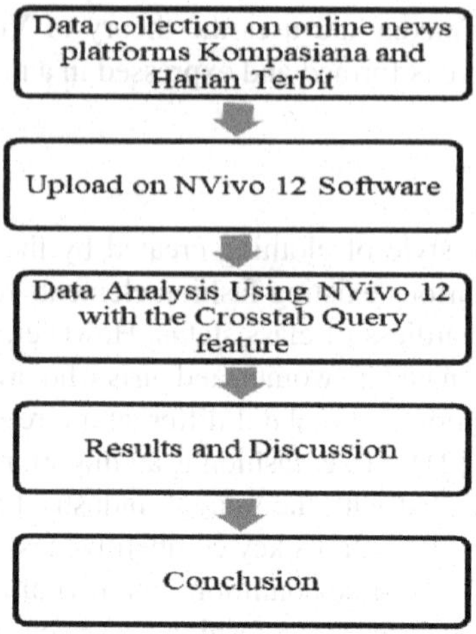

Fig. 1. Research Stage

4 Result and Discussion

4.1 Framing Content Analysis

Ervin Goffman's (1974) framework analysis suggests that we all actively classify, organize, and interpret our life experiences to make sense of them [25]. Framing determines how events are defined. The structure also determines whether the event is considered a social problem. Therefore, a frame is always related to public opinion. How viewers react and react to events depends, among other things, on how those events are viewed and interpreted. When an incident is seen as a social problem and defined as a public problem, public attention increases [8]. In Indonesia's context of the Citayam fashion week phenomenon, online news portals package news with their perspectives. Figure 2 shows the results of the NVIVO 12 Plus analysis showing framing content from Kompasiana and Terbit Daily media. More details can be seen in Fig. 2.

The results of this study indicate that Kompasiana's online media framing focuses more on new media effects, namely as much as 50%. The rest is seen in youth behavior of as much as 40% and public response of as much as 10%. From the chart above, it is found on the Kompasiana online news platform that the New Media Effect outperforms two other factors on the online news platform. The phenomenon of street fashion (Citayam Fashion Week) occurs amidst the onslaught of new media widely used by the public, so many people are aware of this phenomenon through their social media accounts. That is why the Kompasiana online news platform dominates with new media effects.

Meanwhile, Harian Terbit's online media publications focus more on public response, namely 66%, rather than adolescent behavior, only 25%. New media affects as much as 8%. The general answer on the online news platform Terbit is superior to the other two aspects. The online news platform Terbit is more concerned with the public's response to its news as public opinion and then returns it to the community.

This illustrates that Kompasiana sees the Citayam Fashion Week phenomenon as a result of the massive use of new media, such as social media, among the general public.

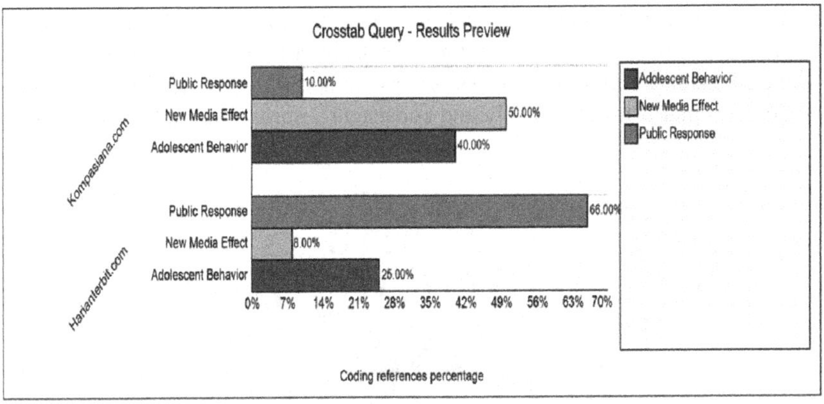

Fig. 2. Data results using Crosstab Query

So that the unique Citayam Fashion Week phenomenon can become the primary trend on all social media platforms. The emergence of virtual reality, virtual communities, and virtual identities are phenomena often seen together with the presence of new media. This phenomenon arises because new media provide opportunities for users to use the most expansive possible space in new media, expand the broadest possible network and show an identity that is different from the real world [26]. It is undeniable that social media has a significant impact on one's life. Small startups can become big on social media and vice versa [27]. The rapid development of social media is also because everyone has their media. Social media is different if traditional media such as television, radio, or newspapers require a lot of capital and labor. Social media users can access the internet without much cost and quickly do it themselves [28]. With the state of social media, especially online news platforms that the wider community can access, it makes it easier for online news platforms to frame news and ultimately lead opinion to the broader community for a phenomenon.

Unlike the online media Kompasiana, which sees it from the perspective of community response. The Citayam Fashion Week phenomenon has yet to escape the discussion of many people, both in terms of support and cons. As one of the residents commented, many people positively see this activity or sensation. "My opinion about this activity is as long as it has a positive impact, not rioting and littering, it is okay to be fashion *trends*, my opinion, "Alfia said. Quoted from an article on the online news platform Poskota.co.id, one of the governments who expressed opposition to Citayam Fashion Week street fashion. Said the Deputy Mayor of Central Jakarta, Irwandi, to journalists. However, apart from that, Kompasiana has a role in constructing news narratives about Citayem Fashion Week for the public as readers. So the public response that supports or opposes it can be calculated from the news published by Kompasiana online media.

4.2 Media Framing Narrative on Citayam Fashion Week

Framing narratives in reporting on the street fashion phenomenon Citayam Fashion Week on online news platforms Kompasiana and Harian Terbit were obtained from analysis on NVIVO 12 Plus with word characteristic frequencies. Figure 3 explains the word narrative representing the Citayam Fashion Week street fashion phenomenon spread on the Kompasiana and Terbit Daily news portals. In addition, Fig. 3 shows that framing on online news platforms intensively and consistently spreads narratives in word form.

Fig. 3. Narrative framing of online news platforms Kompasiana and Harian Terbit

Based on Fig. 3, online news platforms Kompasiana, and Harian Terbit spread framing narratives about the Citayam Fashion Week street fashion phenomenon. The two news platforms gave rise to reports about the Citayam Fashion Week phenomenon as street fashion in Indonesia marked with the words "Week," "Fashion," and "Citayam." Then, the two news portals also gave rise to framing narratives about the behavior of Indonesian youth and the massive use of social media marked with the words "Anak" (Kid), "Remaja" (Teenage), "sosial" (Social), and "media" (media).

These findings confirm the theory [29], Framing frames an incident or event into a message and spreads it to the public. Framing analysis is defined as the construction of video messages that provide context and topic suggestions through selection, prompting, deactivation, and refinement, which require special attention [17]. Framing is based on the assumption that how an issue is described in a story can affect

4.3 Reporting Intensity of Online News Platform

Reporting intensity, namely regular uploading to online news platforms on an online news platform, is carried out repeatedly by online media, with varying frequencies and consisting of quantitative and qualitative aspects. Figure 4 shows the intensity of the spread of news about the Citayam Fashion Week street fashion phenomenon, which was uploaded to online news platforms in Indonesia from June to September 2022. The data in Fig. 4 was taken using NVIVO 12 plus using the chart analysis feature.

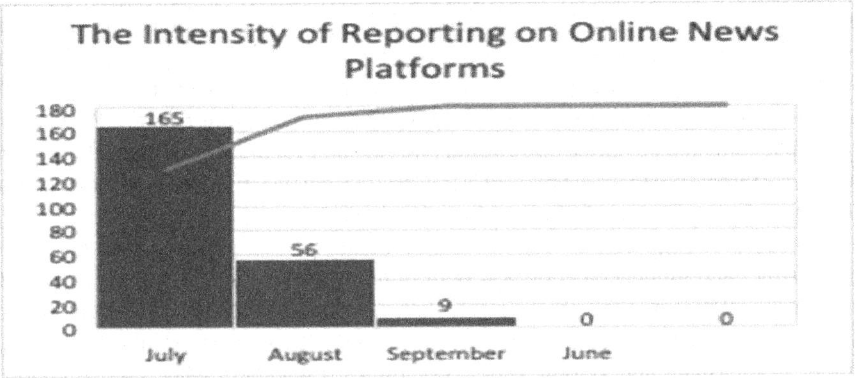

Fig. 4. Reporting intensity data on Citayam Fashion Week

It can be seen in Fig. 4 that the news about Citayam Fashion Week street fashion on online news platforms in Indonesia started in early July 2022 and immediately soared from mid-July to the end of July. The lively Citayam Fashion Week street fashion phenomenon on social media makes people excited to find out what the Citayam Fashion Week street fashion phenomenon is and what happens to this phenomenon. With this in mind, people finally flocked to find out what was going on through online news platforms, and the media eventually published more news about this phenomenon. That way, July became the month when the information on the Citayam Fashion Week street fashion phenomenon on online news platforms became very high.

The potential impact of iterative framing is significant to a broad audience. There is evidence that the fragmentation of the media and its wider audience, both online and offline, increase unilateral news exposure [30]. Closely related to the world of fashion, news on online news platforms regarding the Citayam Fashion Week street fashion phenomenon provides space for discussion and criticism from the public. This is because, for some people, the unique and different clothes they wear are not just clothes they want to display as a form of self-expression. Many people describe this phenomenon as a negative thing because many young people with deviant behavior participate in the Citayam Fashion Week street fashion phenomenon.

Compared to mid-2022, the Citayam Fashion Week street fashion phenomenon started to fade from June to September. As a result, people are no longer touting this phenomenon. Even online media has stopped reporting on this phenomenon as time passes. An observer from the University of Indonesia, Devie Rahmawati, said, "The name of the digital world is the period of virality, the period of fame, and so on; the period is very fast, very volatile because the social algorithm is indeed fast," said Devie. "Usually popularity is also very short because there will always be new interesting content which attracts the public's attention again" [31].

5 Conclusions

The conclusion of this study shows that online media framing plays a vital role in forming public opinion about the Citayem Fashion Week street fashion phenomenon. The Kompasiana online news portal displays framing content, with the most dominant news element being New Media Effects. Meanwhile, the online news portal Harian Terbit raises the point of view of framing content with a more dominant factor, namely Public Response. Then, the intensity of reporting on the Citayam Fashion Week street fashion phenomenon on online news portals was the highest in July 2022. In addition, the framing narrative spread by the two news portals focused on CFW as a new phenomenon in Indonesia known as street fashion and youth behavior. In following social media trends.

This research implies that news in online media has a significant role because it can construct and influence people's way of thinking about something that is reported. Online news platforms have great power; they can persuade readers. The limitation of this research is that the research object only focuses on two online news platforms, namely Kompasiana and Harian Terbit. For future researchers who want to conduct similar research, it is recommended to increase the time used. So the results obtained are better and more accurate. In addition, the following researchers can research other sources of online news platforms outside this research to compare the results.

References

1. Shabana, A., Harmonis, H., Indira, Z., Andini, M.: Post-reform cinema public space on Detik.com news portal. Komunikator **14**(1), 30–41 (2022)
2. Rudianto, R., Anshori, A.: News Framing on Malay Deli Culture in medan.tribunnews.com Online Media. Komunikator **12**(2) (2020)
3. Tirto Id, Citayam Fashion Week: Mendobrak Bias Kelas, Ciptakan Subkultur Baru (2022)
4. Prestianta, A.M.: Mobile journalism practice in the Kompas.com newsroom. Komunikator **14**(2), 137–147 (2022)
5. Fauzan, A.: Citayam fashion week Bentuk Artikulasi Kultural dan Identitas fashion Anak Muda. Univ. Airlangga **3**, 111–118 (2022)
6. WHO, "העינימ, לנגד שבאמת מה את לראות קשה הכי" *הארץ*, vol. 7, no. 8.5.2017, pp. 2003–2005 (2022)
7. Kencana, W.H., Meisyanti, M.: The implementation of mass media digital platform in Indonesia. Komunikator, vol. 12, no. 2 (2020)
8. Santosa, R.: Analisis framing Pemberitaan Etnis Tionghoa dalam Media Online Republika di Bulan Februari 2016. J. E-Komunikasi **4**(1), 1–12 (2016)
9. Ahdi, M.W.: Analisis framing Zhongdang Pan dan Gerlad M. Koscki tentang Deradikalisasi Akun 164 Channel, p. 100 (2022)
10. Lyu, Z., Takikawa, H.: Media framing and expression of anti-China sentiment in COVID-19-related news discourse: an analysis using deep learning methods. Heliyon **8**(8), e10419 (2022)
11. Klein, C., Reimann, R., Quintana, I.O., Cheong, M., Ferreira, M., Alfano, M.: Attention and counter-framing in the Black Lives Matter movement on Twitter. Humanit. Soc. Sci. Commun. **9**(1), 1–12 (2022)
12. Pinontoan, N.A., Wahid, U.: Analisis framing Pemberitaan Banjir Jakarta Januari 2020 Di Harian Kompas.Com Dan Jawapos.Com. Komuniti J. Komun. dan Teknol. Inf. **12**(1), 11–24 (2020)

13. Van Hulst, M., Yanow, D.: From policy 'frames' to 'framing' theorizing a more dynamic, political approach. Am. Rev. Public Adm. **46**(1), 92–112 (2016)
14. Subekti, D., Nurmandi, A., Mutiarin, D.: Mapping publication trend of political parties campaign in Social Media: a bibliometric analysis. J. Polit. Mark. 1–18 (2022)
15. Jagadeesh, V., Piramuthu, R., Bhardwaj, A., Di, W., Sundaresan, N.: Large scale visual recommendations from street fashion images. In: Proceedings of ACM SIGKDD International Conference on Knowledge Discovery and Data Mining, pp. 1925–1934 (2014)
16. Labonté, R., Mohindra, K.S., Lencucha, R.: Framing international trade and chronic disease. Global. Health **7**, 1–15 (2011)
17. Yusof, S.H., Hassan, F., Hassan, S., Osman, M.N.: The framing of international media on Islam and Terrorism. Eur. Sci. J. **9**(8), 104–121 (2013)
18. Prasetya, N.M.: Analisis framing terhadap Pernyataan Resmi Kemenpora RI dan PSSI dalam Kasus Sanksi FIFA terhadap Indonesia. Komunikator **10**(November 2017), 10–23 (2019)
19. Hanifa Madina, I., Sukmono, F.G., Junaedi, F.: Micro-influencer marketing beauty brand on Social Media. In: Stephanidis, C., Antona, M., Ntoa, S., Salvendy, G. (eds.) BT - HCI International 2022 – Late Breaking Posters. HCII 2022, CCIS, vol. 1655, pp. 40–47. Springer, Cham (2022). BT - HCI International 2022 – Late Breaking Posters, pp. 40–47 (2022). https://doi.org/10.1007/978-3-031-19682-9_6
20. Jiratanatiteenun, A., Mizutani, C., Kitaguchi, S., Sato, T., Kajiwara, K.: The Transformation of Japanese Street Fashion between 2006 and 2011. Adv. Appl. Sociol. **02**(04), 292–302 (2012)
21. Hao, Y., Shin, E.: A study on fashion street in Beijing-through street fashion and its images. J. Adv. Res. Soc. Sci. Humanit. **5**(5), 172–184 (2020)
22. Robinson, E., Aveyard, P.: Emaciated mannequins: a study of mannequin body size in high street fashion stores. J. Eat. Disord. **5**(1), 1–6 (2017)
23. Choi, Y.J., Kim, H.: Fashion Street competitiveness in a downtown area of small and medium-sized cities: a case study on Mokpo. Int. J. Costume Fash. **21**(2), 19–30 (2021)
24. Maharani, A.P., Junaedi, F., Sukmono, F.G.: Online trusts; how media shaping student trust towards vaccination news. In: Stephanidis, C., Antona, M., Ntoa, S., Salvendy, G. (eds.) HCI International 2022 – Late Breaking Posters. HCII 2022. Communications in Computer and Information Science, vol. 1655, pp. 48–55. Springer, Cham (2022). https://doi.org/10.1007/978-3-031-19682-9_7
25. Pan, Z., Kosicki, G.M.: Framing analysis: an approach to news discourse. Polit. Commun. **10**(1), 55–75 (2012)
26. Watie, E.D.S.: Komunikasi dan media sosial (communications and social media). J. Messenger **3**(2), 69–74 (2016)
27. Subekti, D., Nurmandi, A., Mutiarin, D., Suswanta, Salahudin: Analysis of Twitter's election official as tools for communication and interaction with Indonesian public during the 2019 presidential election in Indonesia. In: Antipova, T. (ed.) Advances in Digital Science. ICADS 2021. Advances in Intelligent Systems and Computing, vol. 1352, pp. 309–323. Springer, Cham (2021). https://doi.org/10.1007/978-3-030-71782-7_28
28. Anang: Fikih Media Sosial Di Indonesia. Asy Syar'Iyyah J. Ilmu Syari'Ah Dan Perbank. Islam **5**(2), 202–225 (2020)
29. Ardyarama, R., Junaedi, F., Sukmono, F.G.: The cross-cultural acceptance of Japanese animation, analysis of Social Media. In: Stephanidis, C., Antona, M., Ntoa, S., Salvendy, G. (eds.) HCI International 2022 – Late Breaking Posters. HCII 2022. CCIS, vol. 1654, pp. 249–256. Springer, Cham (2022). https://doi.org/10.1007/978-3-031-19679-9_31
30. Lecheler, S., Keer, M., Schuck, A.R.T., Hänggli, R.: The effects of repetitive news framing on political opinions over time. Commun. Monogr. **82**(3), 339–358 (2015)
31. Journoliberta: Pro Kontra Citayam Fashion Week (2022)

Temporal Dynamic of a Global Networked Public: A Case Study of Russian-Speaking Instagram Bloggers with Migration Background

Anna Smoliarova(✉)

St. Petersburg State University, St. Petersburg, Russia
anna.smolyarova@gmail.com

Abstract. Instagram provides users with several affordances, including enough space for bloggers to mention each other to stress the collaborative nature of the content creation. These affordances have led to the development of a new type of user structure: shared mediated discussion based on collaborative efforts of social media influencers. During the first months of the COVID outbreak, Russian speaking social media influencers across the world initiated a global information exchange. I identified six cases in March-April 2020 when bloggers from different countries participated in collaborative posting and published posts on the same day on a given topic containing a unique hashtag and direct links to authors from other countries bloggers. The authors participated in the series of collaborative posting with varying degrees of involvement. The geography of ties between authors changes for each case of collaborative posting but remains global at scale.

Keywords: Social network analysis · User generated content · Visualizing social interaction

1 Introduction

During COVID-19 pandemic, non-native speakers experienced more difficulties in accessing and understanding government messaging and were also more likely to endorse misinformation about coronavirus in general and vaccination in particular [15; 23; review in 11]. Besides language barriers, 'lack of information reflecting the lived experience of individuals and/or consideration of their specific circumstances or vulnerability' also led to the inequality in access to information [11]. Nonsurprisingly that social networks were in most cases the primary source of information about COVID-19 among transnational migrants, being almost one and a half times more popular than online media [see review in 8], as social media platforms help to generate rich situational information that reflects special experience and needs of the population with migration background. Social media influencers with migration background perform a significant role in development of migrants' communicative connectivity [10, 12]. Within parasocial relations with the SMIs who are perceived "authentic and 'people like us'" [1], social media users perform 'micro-practices of political and deliberative participation' contributing to the 'process of accumulation, redistribution, and dissipation of public opinion' [2].

A. Coman and S. Vasilache (Eds.): HCII 2023, LNCS 14025, pp. 296–307, 2023.
https://doi.org/10.1007/978-3-031-35915-6_22

Unlike media for migrants, whose audience usually resides only in the country where this media is published, the audience of Instagram bloggers is often wider and includes at least three groups of subscribers: Russian-speaking residents in the country of the blogger, Russian-speaking migrants in other countries and residents of Russia or other former post-Soviet republics. Earlier, I showed that even in the non-news agenda, bloggers with migration experience create a critical audience [20] and participate in shaping the image of states for a foreign audience and for migrants living in this state [22]. Moreover, migrant bloggers cooperate and organize collaborative posting aimed at audiences that reside in different countries. Within such collaboration several bloggers publish posts on the same day on a given topic with a unique hashtag and include mentions of other bloggers participating in such an organized publication in the text of the post. I explore those cases of collaborative posting, when the authors of the posts invite subscribers to get acquainted with the experience of life in other countries. To do this, the text of the post includes direct links to bloggers from other countries indicating the country and an offer to get acquainted with the entire selection of posts using a unique hashtag.

A previous study [21] showed how Instagram bloggers with migration background residing in China and Italy acted as journalists when they started covering COVID-19 in the first four months of 2020. They preferred an informing tone, and even criticized the news media for spreading panic. The purpose of this study is to find out whether bloggers acted as journalists when they took part in the so-called collaborative posting about the pandemic, targeting global audiences.

2 Theoretical framework

2.1 Pandemic, Infodemic, and Instagram

Very first publications about COVID-19 discourse on Twitter demonstrated "the severe impact of misleading people and spreading unreliable information" [16: 9]. Li et al. [13] found out that in January 2020 posts refuting rumors were almost 20 times less widespread on Weibo than posts about virus in general and statistical data. Dewhurst et al. [6] studied a random sample of tweets posted in 24 languages between 9th January and 25th of March and found a semantical difference between initial reports and later worldwide pandemic. This tendency in general supported the previous findings suggesting that users of social networks, microblogging services, and photo- and video-sharing platforms generate rich situational information in response emergency situations of different kind: civil unrest incidents, natural disasters, food contamination [4; e.g. review in 13]. Among other emergency situations, previous virus-related outbreaks, such as Ebola or Zika, were widely researched. However, Instagram, a worldwide famous photo- and video-sharing social networking service owned by Facebook, has received little research attention in comparison with Twitter [14, first dataset for COVID-19 by 24]. Platform affordances and peculiarity of its audience significantly influence information and misinformation spreading during COVID-19 [5]. Thus, for this paper I summarized the findings from rare Instagram-related research of communication during public health emergencies.

Seltzer et al. [18] investigated public sentiment and discourse about Zika virus on Instagram in May – August 2016. They found that a significant share of posts was misleading or included unclear information about the virus. Many users expressed fear and negative sentiment through the images they posted. Another study about presence of Zika virus in mass self-communication demonstrated that users' activities on Instagram and Pinterest were similar in terms of virus prevention communication [7].

A study of Ebola-related communication evaluated the level of noise as 78% of the entire sample downloaded by hashtag #ebola [19]: 36% posts were unrelated to the topic at all, 42% contained jokes. Hashtag-oriented research on Instagram has some restrictions because hashtags on Instagram are used to raise the general visibility of the posts or for personally developed folksonomy. To avoid these restrictions, I turned to the research method that allows to gather data from Instagram through the sample of social media influencers.

Guidry et al. [9] compared Ebola-related activities of three world health organizations on Instagram and Twitter: all three organizations were not highly active in combatting misleading information on both platforms. They conclude that "Instagram may be a particularly useful platform for establishing meaningful, interactive communication with the publics in times of global health crises, as evidenced by significantly greater levels of engagement on the part of health organizations and the publics".

2.2 Targeting Vulnerable Social Groups via Social Media

Long before the pandemic, it was known that "messages are more effective when they strategically match audience needs, values, background, culture and experience" [17: 45]. After the outbreak of COVID-19, several publications focused on the quality of communication between different population groups and authorities of all levels. Their conclusions are mostly pessimistic: "Merely translating public health information is not likely to be sufficient; information needs to be tailored and targeted so it is conveyed in ways that resonate with the target population" [8]. Migrants as a social group that is marginalized in terms of national languages are even more vulnerable due to the lack of trustworthy information during disasters or epidemics.

The lack of rapidly updated information in a native language and of a social environment that helps people to estimate the trustworthiness of information is crucial. Inequalities in access to information among population with migration background were related to language barriers and lack of information reflecting the lived experience of individuals and/or consideration of their specific circumstances or vulnerability [11]. The actors potentially capable to disseminate trustworthy information through social media platforms, are social media influencers that possess unique position due to their parasocial relations with the followers. As Zhang and Zhao [25] put it, they are capable to construe "authentic" personal COVID-19 experience from the vlogger's perspective and in relation to their transnational audience. However, in comparison to the number of studies dedicated to the role of social media influencers in spreading trustworthy information during the pandemic, the activities of the SMI with migration background remain understudied. This paper aims to contribute to this gap with a case study of Russian-speaking Instagram bloggers with migration background and their global cooperation during Spring 2020.

3 Methodology

My previous study was focused on Russian-speaking Instagram bloggers with migration background in China and Italy covering information about COVID-19 during the first months of the pandemic. One of the Italian bloggers involved social media influencers form other countries in collaborative posting. This type of collaboration between social media influencers assumes that they simultaneously publish posts on a common topic marked by a unique hashtag and mention each other in the posts. In the case of COVID-19, this mechanism of collaboration has been used by social media influencers to create a global exchange of factual information about the measures taken by the governments in the countries where they are residing (see Fig. 1).

Fig. 1. An example of the post typical for the collaborative posting

Following the first unique hashtag, I revealed a chain of six hashtags used by 58 Russian-speaking Instagram bloggers with migration background from 37 countries worldwide during March – April 2022. Information about the data sample is represented in the following Table 1.

Table 1. Unique hashtags used by the social media influencers.

#hashtag	N of posts	Date
Corona_situation_in_my_country	20	14.03.2020
Corona_situation_in_my_country_2	18	21.03.2020
Corona_situation_in_my_country_3	16	30.03.2020
value_life	30	04.04.2020
Corona_situation_in_my_country_new	14	08.04.2020
Corona_situation_update	15	22.04.2020

The texts of the posts were saved manually, including the following metadata: a unique hashtag, a unique post code, the author of the post, the country of residence of the author of the post, the date of publication. With a web crawler written in Python with the library 'instaloader', I also gathered the comments left to the posts (up to 10000 for the whole sample) with metadata considering the type of the comment (stand-alone comment or comment in response).

4 Findings

4.1 RQ1. How was the Collaborative Posting Organized?

Within the sample the involvement of the authors was not equal in terms of frequency and contribution to the collaborative posting. Two thirds of the social media influencers participated just once, followed by the group of bloggers who joined from two to four times (see Fig. 2). The group of bloggers who participated in almost every unique hashtag forms a quazi-editorial core that initiates the posting and is responsible for the continuity of the networked arena.

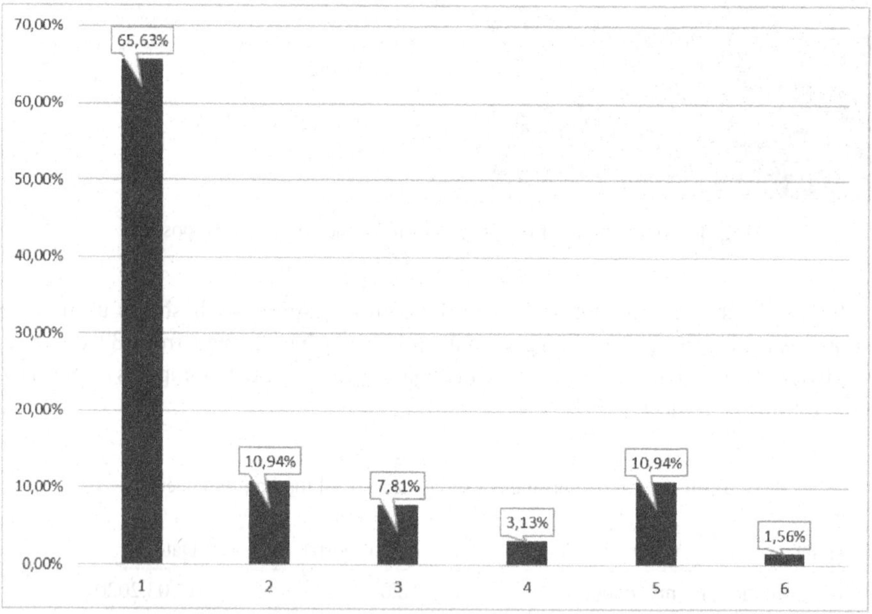

Fig. 2. The spread of involvement of social media influencers.

Those who joined from hashtag to hashtag one might call 'freelancers', they contribute to the heterogeneity of the networked public representing different world regions and providing audience with an opportunity to follow the updates of the situation and even to face some criticism absent in the first posts. Finally, the biggest group of 'one-time-collaborators' multiply the reach of the networked public because they contribute to connecting their follower-followee networks through the direct mentions of other bloggers in their posts written for the collaborative posting.

Despite the fact that collaborative posting is first of all described with the direct mentions included in the text of the posts, not all the authors include direct link to other social media influencers (see Table 2).

Table 2. The share of posts without direct mentions per hashtag.

#hashtag	N of posts	% of posts without direct mentions
Corona_situation_in_my_country	20	35
Corona_situation_in_my_country_2	18	27
Corona_situation_in_my_country_3	16	31
value_life	30	46
Corona_situation_in_my_country_new	14	35
Corona_situation_update	15	40
		MD = 35

Still, due to the character of the gathering data, each post contains a unique hashtag and a call to read about what is happening in other countries through this hashtag. In their posts published within the collaborative posting, social media influencers include the hashtag into a standardized text that describes the collective character of the initiative:

- "Today, bloggers from different countries talk about what is really happening in their countries in connection with the coronavirus and what measures the states are taking - by tag #…" (14.03.2020).
- "Read about what is happening in other countries now from my fellow bloggers by tag #…" (30.03.2020).
- "What is happening in other countries, find out first-hand from the coolest bloggers by the tag…" (04.04.2020).
- "Read about what is happening in other countries in connection with the spread of coronavirus by tag #… And from my fellow bloggers…" (08.04.2020).
- "Read reliable information about other countries by tag #…" (22.04.2020).

Social media influencers also were visible among the commenting users. The whole dataset includes 4542 commenting users, two thirds of them commented just once – 3047 out of 4542 users. There is a small group, 3,6% of all commenting users, who commented 7 times and more, either responding to different posts or participating in a dialogue under one post. A significant share –35% of actively commenting users – were social media influencers participating in the collaborative posting. However, taking into consideration that Instagram as a platform might be characterized as more difficult for the social media influencers to involve their followers into a discussion, I admit that still the posts about COVID-19 attracted users' attention and some followers left digital traces of this attention (see Fig. 3).

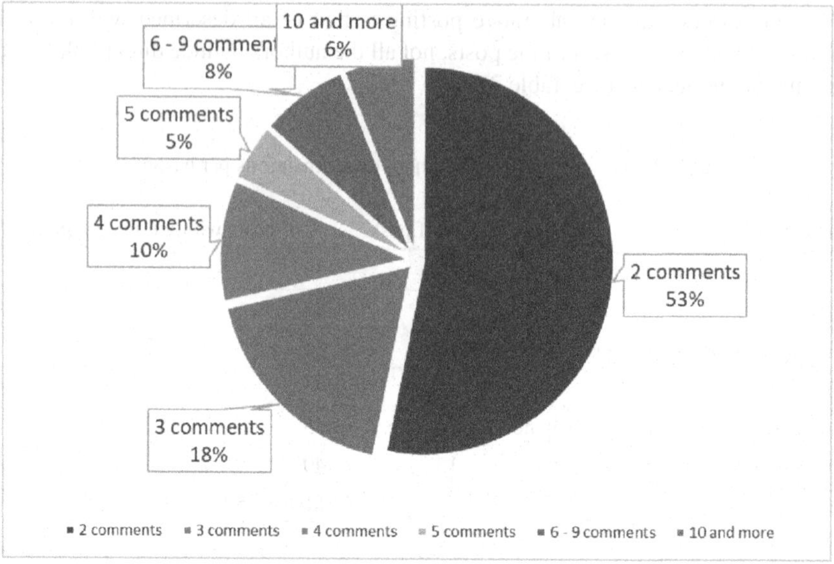

Fig. 3. The spread of involvement of the commenting users.

Thus, the collaborative posting includes the following forms of collaboration between social media influencers:

1) joint publication (on the same day, marked with a unique hashtag and including a standardized text describing the goals of the collaborative posting);
2) a call to read other posts that can be found with the unique hashtag;
3) a call to read posts written by particular bloggers from other countries that can be found through direct mentions included into the post;
4) comments under the posts published by other participants of the collaborative posting.

Taking in a whole, these forms of collaboration allow to develop shared mediated discussion milieus being created by networked micro-publics that are based on collaborative efforts of content creators who aim at gaining attention of limited groups of users.

4.2 RQ2. How Does the Network Between Follower-Followee Networks of the Separate Social Media Influencers DiffeDdepending on Hashtags?

To answer this research question, I reconstructed graphs for six hashtags in the sample with Gephi. The graph reflects the dataset of posts and comments to them, thus, each node is a user (author of the post or a commenting user), while each edge is a directed link from the commenting user to the post, or a response from the author or another commenting user. The layout of the graphs is based on the combination of OpenOrd and ForceAtlas. OpenOrd algorithm is useful to detect clusters, while ForceAtlas was used as a spatial algorithm that helps to prevent overlap of the nodes for the final visualization

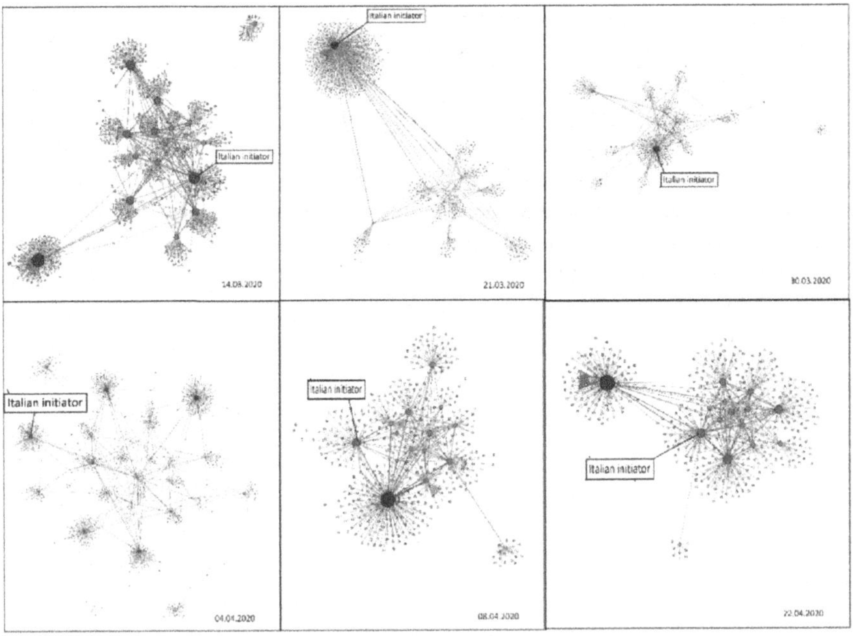

Fig. 4. The networks of the follower-followee networks for each hashtag.

(Fig. 4). The size and the color brightness of the node correspond to the pagerank of each user participating in the public.

As shown on the graphs, most members of the hashtag network are still concentrated around the social media influencers. They act as nodes for crystallization of a cumulative discussion. The ties connecting social media influencers expand their reach and bridge different follower-followee networks. According to the cumulative approach, tiny bridges formed by the comments the social media influencer left to the post of another social media influencer contribute to the continued reproduction of networked publics as arenas and (dis)continued imagined collectives [3] and form “the very fabric of online discussions” [2].

4.3 RQ3. Did the More Involved Social Media Influencers Increase Influence During two Months of Collaborative Posting?

As I described above, a significant share of social media influencers participated in the collaborative posting at least twice per two months. To answer this question, I selected 14 bloggers among which three bloggers joined the collaborative posting three times, six joined four times, and five represent the ‘quazi-editorial team’ who participated every time. For each of them the pagerank was measured separately for every hashtag, and then the median and the standard deviation were measured.

Surprisingly, I did not reveal a clear pattern that distinguish between bloggers depending on their level of involvement. An expected exclusion is an Italian blogger who initiated the collaborative posting had the highest median pagerank, hence, in April she moved to the second place by the absolute numbers. She took twice the extremum position with the pagerank 0,229 for the network that emerged on 21st of March 2020 (MD = 0,012) and with the pagerank 0,097 for the network from the 30th of March (MD = 0, 017). The standard deviation for her pagerank within two months of collaborative posting reaches 0,08 (MD = 0,021). The second outliner is a Russian blogger who became significantly visible on the 8th of April with the pagerank 0,102 (MD = 0,025). The standard deviation measured for her pagerank is almost twice high than the median and reaches 0,038. Besides these two outline bloggers, the pagerank of other bloggers doesn't deviate significantly; The median of the standard deviation for the whole sample is 0,021, while without outliners it decreases up to 0,003.

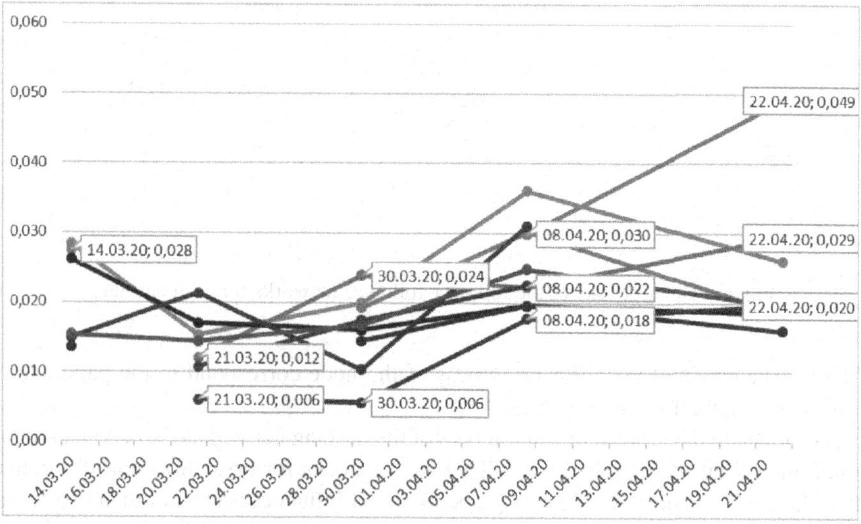

Fig. 5. The dynamics of the influence of the influencers within the networks around hashtags

However, as shown on the Fig. 5, the dominant majority of the often posting social media influencers have increased their pageranks from the beginning of the collaborative posting. Six of them the pagerank within the network on the last time the blogger participated in the collaborative posting was twice higher than within the network on the first time.

5 Conclusion

Instagram provides users with several affordances, including enough space for bloggers to mention each other to stress the collaborative nature of the content creation. These affordances have led to the development of a new type of user structure: shared mediated discussion milieus emerge being created by networked micro-publics. They are based on collaborative efforts of content creators who aim at gaining attention of limited groups of users. My previous research has shown that female bloggers perform cross-national grassroots critique beyond news agenda. While studying how bloggers in China and Italy covered the first months of the pandemic, I found that one of the Italian Russian-speaking social media influencers organized content creators around the world and invited them to share information about what is happening with the coronavirus and what measures are being taken by governments of different countries. In this paper, I explore how female Russian-speaking Instagram bloggers formed a global 'weak' public and created an alternative arena where people from different countries shared information and perceptions of pandemic, including judgements of governmental efforts and care about migrants.

In an effort to expand the audience, Russian–speaking bloggers with migration experience began to launch contribution publications - a coordinated output of posts at about the same time on the same topic, united by a common unique hashtag. This hashtag marks the topic of the publication, and in addition to the opportunity to view all posts by hashtag, contributing bloggers include direct links to bloggers from other countries in the text of the post. These contribution publications are addressed to an international audience and are created taking into account the potential of blog promotion, which is a welcome result of cooperation.

Thus, these networks are being formed-arenas of a global level, where native speakers of the Russian language living in different countries, both with and without migration experience, can get acquainted with the experience of Russian–speaking residents of other countries (in this case, "learn first-hand" how this or that country copes with the pandemic). Since Instagram blogs with more than several thousand subscribers are highly likely to be considered as commercial media projects, posts for participation in a contribution publication are prepared taking into account the appeal to an international audience and represent analytics that allows a blogger to position himself as an expert and author worthy of the attention of Instagram users. The question arises where the border lies between international journalism and this kind of blogging.

At the same time, we are not talking about creating a global media project with a brand, editorial policy and regular release of content on Instagram. Participants in the contribution publication are personal media projects that are simultaneously related individuals. For each unique hashtag, the membership is reassembled, and the stable core includes only 12% of all bloggers who have participated in publications for almost two months. By analogy with ad hoc groups of the public, this method of organization can be called ad hoc media. They become the basis for the existence of a parallel structure of public communication, as they simultaneously initiate a discussion and create an arena for participation, expression and exchange of experience.

Acknowledgements. This research has been supported in full by Russian Science Foundation, grant 21–18-00454 (2021–2023).

References

1. Abidin, C., Ots, M.: Influencers tell all. Unravelling Authenticity and Credibility in a Brand Scandal. In: Edström, M., Kenyon, A.T. Svensson, E.M. Blurring the lines: market-driven and democracy-driven freedom of expression, pp.153–161. Nordicom (2016)

2. Bodrunova, S.S.: Influencing Theory: From Opinion Leaders to Points of Crystallization of Public Opinion. Sociodigger **2** (5(10)), 30–35 (2021)
3. boyd, d.: Social network sites as networked publics: Affordances, dynamics, and implications. In: Z. Papacharissi (ed.), A networked self: Identity, community and culture on social network sites, pp. 39–58. New York: Routledge (2010)
4. Bruns, A., Liang, Y.E.: Tools and methods for capturing Twitter data during natural disasters. First Monday. **17**(4), 1–8 (2012)
5. Cinelli, M., et al.: The COVID-19 social media infodemic. Sci. Rep. **10**(1), 1–10 (2020)
6. Dewhurst, D.R., Alshaabi, T., Arnold, M.V., Minot, J.R., Danforth, C.M. Dodds, P.S. Divergent modes of online collective attention to the COVID-19 pandemic are associated with future caseload variance. arXiv preprint arXiv:2004.03516 (2020)
7. Fung, I.C.H., et al.: Zika-virus-related photo sharing on Pinterest and Instagram. Disaster Med. Public Health Prep. **11**(6), 656–659 (2017)
8. Goldsmith, L.P.: The use of social media platforms by migrant and ethnic minority populations during the COVID-19 pandemic: a systematic review. medRxiv (2022)
9. Guidry, J.P., Jin, Y., Orr, C.A., Messner, M., Meganck, S.: Ebola on Instagram and Twitter: how health organizations address the health crisis in their social media engagement. Public Relations Review **43**(3), 477–486 (2017)
10. Hepp, A., Bozdag, C., Suna, L.: Diasporic media as the 'focus' of communicative networking among migrants. In: Mediating cultural diversity in a globalized public space, pp. 96–115. Palgrave Macmillan, London (2012)
11. Kalocsányiová, E., Essex, R., Fortune, V. Inequalities in Covid-19 messaging: a systematic scoping review. Health Communication, pp. 1–10 (2022)
12. Leurs, K., and Smets, K. Five questions for digital migration studies: Learning from digital connectivity and forced migration in (to) Europe. Social Media+ Society, 4(1), 2056305118764425 (2018)
13. Li, L., et al.: Characterizing the propagation of situational information in social media during covid-19 epidemic: a case study on weibo. IEEE Trans. Comput. Soc. Syst. **7**(2), 556–562 (2020)
14. Maares, P., Hanusch, F.: Exploring the boundaries of journalism: Instagram micro-bloggers in the twilight zone of lifestyle journalism. Journalism **21**(2), 262–278 (2020)
15. McCaffery, K.J., et al.: Health literacy and disparities in Covid-19–related knowledge, attitudes, beliefs and behaviours in Australia. Public Health Res. Pract., **30**(4), Article e30342012. https://doi.org/10.17061/PHRP30342012 (2020)
16. Mourad, A., Srour, A., Harmanani, H., Jenainati, C., Arafeh, M.: Critical impact of social networks infodemic on defeating coronavirus COVID-19 pandemic: Twitter-based study and research directions. IEEE Trans. Netw. Serv. Manage. **17**(4), 2145–2155 (2020)
17. Reynolds, B., Seeger, M.: Crisis and emergency risk communication as an integrative model. J. Health Commun. **10**(1), 43–55 (2005)
18. Seltzer, E.K., Horst-Martz, E., Lu, M., Merchant, R.M.: Public sentiment and discourse about Zika virus on Instagram. Public Health **150**, 170–175 (2017)
19. Seltzer, E.K., Jean, N.S., Kramer-Golinkoff, E., Asch, D.A., Merchant, R.M.: The content of social media's shared images about Ebola: a retrospective study. Public Health **129**(9), 1273–1277 (2015)
20. Smoliarova, A., Bodrunova, S.S.: InstaMigrants: Global ties and mundane publics of Russian-speaking bloggers with migration background. Social Media+ Society, 7(3), p.20563051211033809 (2021)
21. Smoliarova, A., Gromova, T. Sharkova, E.: Bloggers against panic: Russian-speaking Instagram bloggers in China and Italy reporting about COVID-19. In: Pollock, J.C., Vakoch, D.A. (eds) COVID-19 in n International media: Global pandemic perspectives, pp. 162–171. Routledge (2021)

22. Smoliarova, A., Taranova, Y., Vagaitceva, M.: Participation of Transnational Migrants in the Formation of the Host Country Image Through Mass Self-communication. In: Alexandrov, D.A., et al. (eds.) DTGS 2021. CCIS, vol. 1503, pp. 389–402. Springer, Cham (2022). https://doi.org/10.1007/978-3-030-93715-7_28
23. Tjaden, J., Haarmann, E., Savaskan, N.: Experimental evidence on improving COVID-19 vaccine outreach among migrant communities on social media. Sci. Rep. **12**(1), 1–10 (2022)
24. Zarei, K., Farahbakhsh, R., Crespi, N., Tyson, G. A first instagram dataset on covid-19. arXiv preprint arXiv:2004.12226 (2020)
25. Zhang, L.T., Zhao, S.: Diaspora micro-influencers and COVID-19 communication on social media: the case of Chinese-speaking YouTube vloggers. Multilingua **39**(5), 553–563 (2020)

Digital Transformation in Business and Industry 4.0 Through Social Computing

Archetypes of Blockchain-Based Business Models

Simon Behrendt[1(✉)] and Christian W. Scheiner[2,3]

[1] Institute for Entrepreneurship and Business Development, Universität zu Lübeck, Lübeck, Germany
s.behrendt@uni-luebeck.de

[2] Institute for Entrepreneurship and Business Development, Universität zu Lübeck, Lübeck, Germany
christian.scheiner@uni-luebeck.de

[3] Christian-Albrechts-Universität zu Kiel, Kiel, Germany

Abstract. Blockchain technology has the potential to significantly impact both existing and new business models. In existing business models, the use of blockchain can improve efficiency and security by providing a decentralized and tamper-proof way for conducting transactions and storing data. This can streamline processes, increase transparency, and increase trust as well as accountability among all involved parties. In terms of new business models, blockchain technology allows for creating entirely new types of businesses that were previously not possible due to the limitations of traditional centralized systems. As the blockchain technology has the potential to disrupt existing industries and create new ones, examining its impact on business models is highly relevant. Therefore, a framework for blockchain technology business models and archetypes for blockchain technology is developed based on various established ventures and literature about business models as well as blockchain technology. The results contribute to the blockchain literature by introducing a new framework for blockchain technology business models and new archetypes for blockchain technology.

Keywords: Blockchain Technology · Business model · Framework · Archetypes · Distributed ledger

1 Introduction

Blockchain technology has the potential to significantly impact both existing and new business models. In existing business models, the use of blockchain can improve efficiency and security by providing a decentralized and tamper-proof way for conducting transactions and storing data [1]. This can streamline processes, increase transparency, and increase trust as well as accountability among all involved parties. In terms of new business models, blockchain technology allows for creating entirely new types of businesses that were previously not possible due to the limitations of traditional centralized systems. At this, new forms of digital markets and online communities are possible, where users can directly buy and sell goods and services, or share and collaborate on

A. Coman and S. Vasilache (Eds.): HCII 2023, LNCS 14025, pp. 311–322, 2023.
https://doi.org/10.1007/978-3-031-35915-6_23

projects, without the need for intermediaries or centralized authorities. This could lead to the emergence of new types of organizations and business models that were previously impossible. For example, the use of smart contracts on blockchain technology allows for the creation of decentralized autonomous organizations, which are essentially organizations that are run entirely by code [2]. Blockchain technology could disrupt and transform entire industries, such as social media, content creation, and e-commerce, by enabling more decentralized and peer-to-peer forms of collaboration and exchange. Given the disruptive potential of blockchain technology to both existing and new industries, it is highly relevant to explore its effect on business models. Given the disruptive potential of blockchain technology to impact both current industries and the development of new ones, exploring its effect on business models is of great interest. Therefore, a framework for blockchain technology business models is developed and archetypes for blockchain technology are identified based on various established ventures and literature about business models as well as blockchain technology. These might be valuable for researchers looking to understand the potential applications and impact of this technology on the business world. In addition, they could be useful for companies looking to harness the power of blockchain technology and for those looking to create new ventures in this space.

2 Theoretical Background

2.1 Business Models

The concept of a business model has been widely discussed in both academic and corporate communities due to its significance in providing a comprehensive framework for comprehending and evaluating a company's operations and strategies [3, 4]. In academic circles, business model research has been the subject of numerous studies, with articles and papers published in leading management and business journals [3, 5]. In recent years, there has been a growing consensus among scholars and practitioners regarding the definition of a business model. This definition encompasses a comprehensive representation of the mechanisms a firm employs to conceive, dispense, and reap the benefits from its offerings [4, 6, 7].

A business model describes the rationale of how a company intends to generate revenue and make a profit [3]. It encompasses the product or service that a company offers, the target customer segments, the distribution channels, and the revenue streams. The business model also outlines the resources and capabilities that are required to deliver the offering and how the company intends to acquire and manage them.

Alexander Osterwalder's business model framework is widely regarded as the dominant framework. This framework provides a comprehensive and structured approach for analysing and designing business models. It outlines nine elements that are essential for a successful business model, including customer segments, value propositions, channels, customer relationships, revenue streams, key resources, key activities, key partnerships, and cost structure. This framework has been adopted by organizations of all sizes and industries, and it has become a widely recognized tool for business model innovation and strategy formulation. Osterwalder's framework has been further developed and refined over the years, but its core elements have remained unchanged, demonstrating its relevance and utility in the fast-paced and ever-evolving business world. He describes the business model canvas is his book "Business Model Generation: A Handbook for Visionaries, Game Changers, and Challengers" which he co-authored with Yves Pigneur in 2010 [8]. The book is widely considered as a standard of business modelling and has been translated in over 30 languages. This paper builds upon the previously mentioned business model elements proposed in the book of Osterwalder and Pigneur. The elements prove to be reasonable for the research as they are used in similar ways by other business model frameworks [9, 10].

Business model archetypes are frameworks that serve as a tool for describing and analysing the fundamental structure of a business [10–12]. They provide a common language and set of categories that can be used to compare and evaluate various business models, making it easier to understand the key elements that define a particular business model. By using archetypes, companies can more easily identify the strengths and weaknesses of their existing business models and explore alternative models that may be better suited to their needs. Additionally, by providing a standardized way of describing business models, archetypes can facilitate communication and collaboration between different stakeholders, such as executives, investors, and customers, enabling them to have a shared understanding of a company's business strategy.

2.2 Blockchain Technology

Blockchains are decentralized and distributed ledger system used to record transactions securely and transparently [13]. The decentralized nature of blockchains makes them inherently resistant to modification of the data, providing a secure and reliable method of record-keeping [14]. Blockchain technology has a wide range of potential applications, including in finance [15], supply chain management [16], digital identity [17, 18], and more.

Technical Foundation. The technical foundation of blockchain technology is based on cryptography and consensus algorithms [19]. Cryptography is used to secure the transactions and to ensure that the information recorded on the blockchain is tamper-proof [20]. This is achieved using digital signatures and hash functions [21]. Digital signatures are used to authenticate the identity of the parties involved in a transaction, while hash functions are used to create a unique digital fingerprint of the transaction. This fingerprint is then added to the blockchain, creating an immutable record of the transaction. Blockchains are comprised of blocks, which contain a batch of transactions. Each block is linked to the previous block, forming a chain of blocks that cannot be tampered with. The data stored on the blockchain is maintained by a decentralized network of nodes. This creates a system that is both transparent and secure, as every node has a complete copy of the blockchain and can validate transactions independently.

Consensus algorithms are used to ensure that all participants in the network agree on the state of the blockchain [22]. They are a crucial component inf blockchain technology as they ensure secure and reliable validation of transactions. This brief overview will examine five common consensus algorithms:

- Proof of Work (PoW): PoW requires miners to solve mathematical problems to validate transactions and secure the network [21, 22]. It allows for a decentralized network where anyone can participate as a miner, helping to prevent centralization. PoW is used in the Bitcoin blockchain and widely used, but energy-intensive and slow.
- Proof of Stake (PoS): PoS requires validators to hold a portion of coins as stake to validate blocks [22, 23]. It is energy-efficient and faster but can lead to centralization if a small group holds a large portion of stake.
- Delegated Proof of Stake (DPoS): DPoS is a variation of PoS where participants vote for representatives to validate blocks [22, 23]. It is efficient but can lead to centralization if a small group holds a large amount of voting power.
- Proof of Authority (PoA): PoA is used for closed networks with trustworthy participants [24]. It uses a fixed group of validators but can lead to centralization if a small group holds a large amount of authority.
- Byzantine Fault Tolerance (BFT): BFT requires a majority of validators to reach consensus for secure validation [25]. It is fast and efficient but can lead to centralization if a small group holds a large amount of voting power.

Each algorithm has its own benefits and trade-offs, and the choice depends on the specific requirements of the blockchain network.

Types of Blockchains. Blockchains come in various forms, with at least four main types: Public blockchains, Private blockchains, Hybrid blockchains, and Sidechains.

- Public blockchains are the most well-known type of blockchain and open to anyone and accessible to anyone with an internet connection [26]. They are decentralized and allow for transparent, secure, and tamper-proof transactions. The most famous example of a public blockchain is the Bitcoin blockchain. Public blockchains are considered to be the most secure type of blockchain because they are decentralized and use cryptographic algorithms to secure transactions. However, they also have the drawback of being slower and more expensive than other types of blockchains.
- Private blockchains, on the other hand, are closed networks that are only accessible to a select group of participants [26]. They are often used in business and financial contexts where the participants want to keep the transactions private. Private blockchains are faster and more efficient than public blockchains because they are not subject to the same security requirements as public blockchains. However, they are also considered to be less secure because they are centralized and can be subject to manipulation.
- Hybrid blockchains are a combination of both public and private blockchains [26]. They allow for a certain level of transparency and security, while still allowing for the privacy of certain transactions. Hybrid blockchains can be useful for businesses and organizations that need to maintain the privacy of certain transactions while still providing a certain level of transparency.

- Sidechains are a type of blockchain that runs parallel to a main blockchain [26]. They enable the secure transfer of assets and information between the main blockchain and the sidechain.

Application of Blockchain Technology. Blockchain technology has several potential applications. One of the most well-known is in the financial services industry, where it is being used to create new types of financial instruments and to improve the efficiency of existing ones [15]. For example, blockchain technology is being used to create digital assets such as tokens, which can be used to represent ownership of an asset or a unit of value. This has the potential to democratize access to capital and to create new opportunities for investment. Blockchain technology is also being used in supply chain management to improve transparency and traceability [16]. This allows for real-time tracking of goods as they move through the supply chain, making it easier to detect and prevent fraud. In addition, it is being used in other industries such as healthcare, real estate, and voting systems. Blockchain technology has a wide range of potential applications, including:

- Cryptocurrencies: One of the most well-known applications of blockchain technology is the creation of cryptocurrencies, such as Bitcoin. This has the potential to disrupt traditional monetary systems and create new opportunities for businesses and consumers [27].
- Financial services: Blockchain technology can be used to create decentralized financial systems, such as peer-to-peer lending platforms, decentralized exchanges, and remittance services [15].
- Supply chain management: Blockchain technology can be used to track the origin, movement, and ownership of goods and products, ensuring that the supply chain is transparent, secure, and efficient [16, 28].
- Healthcare: Blockchain technology has the potential to revolutionize the healthcare industry by improving the security, privacy, and efficiency of healthcare data management [29].
- Real Estate: Blockchain technology can be used to create a secure and transparent record of real estate transactions, making the process faster, cheaper, and more efficient. This has the potential to disrupt traditional real estate practices and create new opportunities for businesses and consumers [30, 31].
- Digital identity: Blockchain technology can be used to create digital identities that are secure and cannot be tampered with [17, 18], providing a foundation for secure digital services such as e-voting and digital signatures [31].

These are just a few examples of the many areas where blockchain technology is being used or has the potential to be used. As the technology continues to evolve and mature, it is likely that new applications and use cases will emerge, further disrupting traditional systems and creating new opportunities for businesses and consumers.

Implications for Business Models. The implementation of blockchain technology has significant implications for business models [1]. By removing intermediaries and creating a decentralized system, businesses can save money and increase efficiency [32].

Additionally, the secure and transparent nature of blockchain technology can help to increase trust in the system, and in turn, increase adoption.

One of the key implications for business models is the potential for new business models to emerge [1]. For example, decentralized financial services can disrupt traditional banking models, and peer-to-peer platforms can provide new opportunities for businesses and consumers. A Decentralized Autonomous Organization (DAO) is a type of organization that operates on the blockchain using smart contracts [2]. It is designed to be decentralized, meaning that decision-making and execution is done by the collective efforts of its members, rather than by a central authority. DAOs offer benefits such as transparency, security, and cost-effectiveness, and have the potential to revolutionize the way organizations operate in the digital age. DAOs are well-suited for applications in decentralized governance, community management, and decentralized finance. As blockchain technology continues to evolve, DAOs are poised to play an increasingly important role in shaping the future of decentralized systems.

Another important implication is the potential for existing business models to be disrupted [1]. For example, the transparency and security provided by blockchain technology can disrupt traditional supply chain management systems, and digital identities built on blockchain can disrupt traditional identity verification methods.

3 Propositions and Conceptual Model Development

In today's business world, technology plays a crucial role in shaping and altering business models. To fully grasp the impact of technology on business, an initial step is to evaluate the technology's characteristics and identify suitable business models for its commercialization. In this context, blockchain technology is analysed in this paper. This technology has the potential to disrupt existing industries and create new ones. In the past it has triggered a lot of hype [33]. Now that the technology has been around for a few years, a closer look at its impact on the market is taken. The literature on business models is studied and a data set drawn from companies using blockchain technology around the world is used. A business model framework and archetypes for blockchain technology are therefore defined based on literature and several existing ventures.

To investigate the impact of blockchain technology on business models, a business model framework was first developed. The elements and specifications commonly used in business model research are used for this purpose [8]. For the business model framework, three meta-characteristics value propositions, front-end and back-end were applied.

Value proposition, defined as the unique value a company offers to its customers, has been identified as a crucial element of a successful business model [6, 7]. In fact, a robust value proposition can serve as a catalyst for the development and implementation of other components within a business model, such as customer segments, revenue streams, and key activities [4]. Therefore, incorporating value proposition as a meta-characteristic within a business model framework can provide several benefits.

Including value proposition as a meta-characteristic emphasizes its importance and central role in shaping a firm's overall strategy. A well-defined value proposition can differentiate a firm from its competitors and position it for long-term success. Moreover, it can help a firm understand its customers' needs and design its offerings, accordingly, thereby improving customer satisfaction.

Additionally, incorporating value proposition as a meta-characteristic can improve the overall clarity and consistency of a business model framework.

The terms "front-end" and "back-end" are commonly used in software development to describe the different components of a system. Similarly, in a business context, the front-end elements can be thought of as the components that are visible to the customer, while the back-end elements represent the hidden infrastructure that supports the customer-facing operations.

The front-end elements, or customer-facing elements, of a business model are the components that define how a company interacts with its customers. These elements include customer segments, channels, customer relationships, and revenue streams. These elements are the face of the business, and they determine how the company presents itself and the value it offers to its customers. Hence, the term "front-end" accurately captures the customer-facing nature of these elements.

A brief description of the front-end elements is as follows:

1. Customer Segments: This refers to the specific group of customers that a business targets [8]. It is important to identify the characteristics of these segments, such as demographics, behaviour, and needs, to tailor the company's value proposition and customer relationships accordingly.
2. Channels: This refers to the ways in which a company reaches and communicates with its customers [8]. It could be through a physical retail location, an e-commerce website, a sales team, or a combination of these and other channels.
3. Customer Relationships: This refers to the nature of the relationship that a company has with its customers [8]. This can range from a transactional relationship where the customer makes a one-time purchase, to a more ongoing relationship, such as a subscription-based service.
4. Revenue Streams: This refers to the ways in which a company generates revenue from its customers [8]. It could be through the sale of a product, a recurring subscription fee, or advertising revenue.

The back-end elements, or customer-hidden elements, of a business model are the components that define the company's operating model. These elements include key resources, key activities, key partners, and cost structure. These elements are the behind-the-scenes components that support the customer-facing operations, and they determine how the company will deliver its value proposition to customers. Hence, the term "back-end" accurately captures the hidden nature of these elements.

A brief description of the back-end elements is as follows:

1. Key Resources: This refers to the physical, intellectual, and human resources that a company needs to deliver its value proposition to customers [8]. Examples of key resources include a manufacturing facility, a patent portfolio, and a skilled workforce.
2. Key Activities: This refers to the critical activities that a company needs to perform to deliver its value proposition to customers [8]. Examples of key activities include research and development, production, and marketing.

3. Key Partners: This refers to the third-party organizations that a company works with to deliver its value proposition to customers [8]. Examples of key partners include suppliers, distribution partners, and technology providers.
4. Cost Structure: This refers to the expenses associated with delivering a company's value proposition to customers [8]. It includes both variable costs (such as raw materials) and fixed costs (such as rent).

The previously developed business model framework was expanded by incorporating a blockchain dimension. For this expansion CB Insights [34] was used to compile a database of firms that use blockchain technology as a part of their business model. CB Insights is a well-known and respected market intelligence platform that provides valuable data and insights on emerging technologies, including blockchain. As a source for a database of firms that use blockchain technology as part of their business model, CB Insights is highly recommended due to its extensive and constantly updated database of companies. CB Insights uses a combination of artificial intelligence and expert analysis to gather and present data in a clear and easy-to-use format, making it a valuable resource for research and analysis in the field of blockchain technology. Companies that contained the word "Blockchain" in their description as of February 2023 were the starting point. 5758 companies were found as a possible sample. To ensure the relevance and success of the companies in the used sample, only those that are still active and have secured a minimum of $100K in funding were included. The final set of relevant companies covered 1685 companies with total funding of $33.97B. Upon examining the final set of companies, it was discovered that the companies can be divided into two clusters. Each company can only be associated with one of the two clusters. In the first cluster, blockchain technology is used to enhance an existing business model, while in the second cluster, the business model is enabled by the blockchain technology. This means that the use of blockchain technology is integral to the success of the business, providing value and solving problems in a way that would not be possible without it. The final framework is shown in Table 1.

Table 1. Blockchain Technology Business Model Framework.

			Blockchain Technology Dimension	
			Blockchain Technology is enhancing an existing business model	Blockchain Technology is enabling a business model
Business Model Dimension	Value Propositions			
	Front-end	Customer Segments		
		Channels		
		Customer Relationships		
		Revenue Strems		
	Back-end	Key Ressources		
		Key Activities		
		Key Partners		
		Cost Structure		

Based on this defined framework, the blockchain business model archetypes are examined. Business model archetypes serve as a structure for describing and analysing the fundamental makeup of a business. They provide a uniform terminology and set of categories to compare various business models, enabling the identification of the defining elements of a specific business model. As the business model environment continually evolves, the analysis showcases three business model archetypes that are prevalent among companies utilizing blockchain technology. They emerged as salient and similar configurations of the blockchain technology business model framework. The three archetypes of blockchain technology business models emerged as prominent and distinct configurations within the blockchain technology framework. These archetypes offering a comprehensive representation of the diverse ways in which the technology is being utilized in the business world.

The three blockchain technology business model archetypes are:

1. Blockchain Technology for Front-End Enhancement: The first archetype involves businesses that leverage blockchain technology to enhance their customer-facing operations. For instance, blockchain-based solutions can be used to improve the user experience by making transactions faster and more secure. This can lead to increased customer satisfaction and, in turn, higher revenue. The archetype is located in the Blockchain Technology Business Model Framework on the business model dimension in the front-end and on the blockchain technology dimension in enhancing an existing business model.
2. Blockchain Technology for Back-End Enhancement: The second archetype involves businesses that use blockchain technology to streamline their internal operations. By using blockchain-based solutions, businesses can automate manual processes, reduce errors, and improve the efficiency of their operations. This can result in reduced costs and improved margins. The archetype is located in the Blockchain Technology Business Model Framework on the business model dimension in the back-end and on the Blockchain Technology Dimension in enhancing an existing business model.
3. Blockchain Technology-Enabled Business Models: The third archetype involves businesses that have built their operations entirely around blockchain technology. For example, businesses that operate decentralized exchanges or provide decentralized finance solutions are examples of this archetype. These businesses are at the forefront of the blockchain revolution and are poised to capture significant value as the technology continues to mature. The archetype is located in the Blockchain Technology Business Model Framework on the blockchain technology dimension in enabling a business model and includes both front-end and back-end on the business model dimension.

Blockchain technology enabled business models can further be divided into two sub-archetypes:

1. Infrastructure Providers: These are companies that focus on providing the underlying technology and infrastructure for the deployment and use of blockchain applications. They often offer blockchain platforms, development tools, and security solutions for enterprise clients.
2. Blockchain-Based Application Providers: These are companies that leverage blockchain technology to build specific applications, such as digital wallets, payment

systems, and decentralized exchanges. They aim to solve specific business problems and provide a better user experience for end-users.

These two clusters represent different approaches to using blockchain technology and offer a broad overview of the diverse ways that blockchain is being applied in the business world.

4 Conclusion

The study has provided insights into the impact of blockchain technology on business models. The framework in this study highlights the crucial role of value proposition in shaping a company's overall strategy, as well as the importance of front-end and back-end elements in defining a company's operating model. The expanded framework, which incorporates a blockchain dimension, offers a comprehensive approach for evaluating the impact of blockchain technology on business models.

The analysis of the data set of companies using blockchain technology around the world revealed archetypes of business models that are being employed in the market.

The Blockchain Technology Business Model Framework and the archetypes is valuable for researchers and practitioners alike who are interested in understanding the potential areas for application and the impact of this technology on organizations and industries. In addition, they are useful for companies and start-ups seeking to leverage the capabilities of blockchain technology.

References

1. Nowiński, W., Kozma, M.: How Can Blockchain Technology Disrupt the Existing Business Models? EBER. **5**, 173–188 (2017). https://doi.org/10.15678/EBER.2017.050309
2. Wang, S., Ding, W., Li, J., Yuan, Y., Ouyang, L., Wang, F.-Y.: Decentralized autonomous organizations: concept, model, and applications. IEEE Trans. Comput. Soc. Syst. **6**, 870–878 (2019). https://doi.org/10.1109/TCSS.2019.2938190
3. Zott, C., Amit, R., Massa, L.: The business model: recent developments and future research. J. Manag. **37**, 1019–1042 (2011). https://doi.org/10.1177/0149206311406265
4. Teece, D.J.: business models, business strategy and innovation. Long Range Plan. **43**, 172–194 (2010). https://doi.org/10.1016/j.lrp.2009.07.003
5. Nielsen, C., Lund, M., Montemari, M., Paolone, F., Massaro, M., Dumay, J.: Business Models: A Research Overview. Routledge (2018). https://doi.org/10.4324/9781351232272
6. Osterwalder, A., Pigneur, Y., Tucci, C.L.: Clarifying Business Models: Origins, Present, and Future of the Concept. CAIS. 16, (2005). https://doi.org/10.17705/1CAIS.01601
7. Shafer, S.M., Smith, H.J., Linder, J.C.: The power of business models. Bus. Horiz. **48**, 199–207 (2005). https://doi.org/10.1016/j.bushor.2004.10.014
8. Osterwalder, A., Pigneur, Y.: Business Model Generation: A Handbook for Visionaries, Game Changers, and Challengers. (2010)
9. Wirtz, B.W., Pistoia, A., Ullrich, S., Göttel, V.: Business models: origin, development and future research perspectives. Long Range Plan. **49**, 36–54 (2016). https://doi.org/10.1016/j.lrp.2015.04.001
10. Bocken, N.M.P., Short, S.W., Rana, P., Evans, S.: A literature and practice review to develop sustainable business model archetypes. J. Clean. Prod. **65**, 42–56 (2014). https://doi.org/10.1016/j.jclepro.2013.11.039

11. Stubbs, W., Cocklin, C.: Conceptualizing a "sustainability business model." Organ. Environ. **21**, 103–127 (2008). https://doi.org/10.1177/1086026608318042
12. Bocken, N., Short, S., Rana, P., Evans, S.: A value mapping tool for sustainable business modelling. Corp. Gov. **13**, 482–497 (2013). https://doi.org/10.1108/CG-06-2013-0078
13. Narayanan, A.: Bitcoin and cryptocurrency technologies: a comprehensive introduction. Princeton University Press, Princeton (2016)
14. Bakos, Y., Halaburda, H., Mueller-Bloch, C.: When permissioned blockchains deliver more decentralization than permissionless. Commun. ACM. **64**, 20–22 (2021). https://doi.org/10.1145/3442371
15. Gomber, P., Kauffman, R.J., Parker, C., Weber, B.W.: On the fintech revolution: interpreting the forces of innovation, disruption, and transformation in financial services. J. Manag. Inf. Syst. **35**, 220–265 (2018). https://doi.org/10.1080/07421222.2018.1440766
16. Wang, Y., Singgih, M., Wang, J., Rit, M.: Making sense of blockchain technology: how will it transform supply chains? Int. J. Prod. Econ. **211**, 221–236 (2019). https://doi.org/10.1016/j.ijpe.2019.02.002
17. Grassi, P.A., et al.: Digital identity guidelines: authentication and lifecycle management. National Institute of Standards and Technology, Gaithersburg, MD (2017). https://doi.org/10.6028/NIST.SP.800-63b
18. Camp, L.J.: Digital identity. IEEE Technol. Soc. Mag. **23**, 34–41 (2004). https://doi.org/10.1109/MTAS.2004.1337889
19. Hao, W., et al.: Towards a trust-enhanced blockchain P2P topology for enabling fast and reliable broadcast. IEEE Trans. Netw. Serv. Manage. **17**, 904–917 (2020). https://doi.org/10.1109/TNSM.2020.2980303
20. Yang, J., Wen, J., Jiang, B., Wang, H.: Blockchain-based sharing and tamper-proof framework of big data networking. IEEE Netw. **34**, 62–67 (2020). https://doi.org/10.1109/MNET.011.1900374
21. Nakamoto, S.: Bitcoin: A Peer-to-Peer Electronic Cash System. (2008)
22. Zheng, Z., Xie, S., Dai, H., Chen, X., Wang, H.: An Overview of Blockchain Technology: Architecture, Consensus, and Future Trends. In: 2017 IEEE International Congress on Big Data (BigData Congress), pp. 557–564. IEEE, Honolulu, HI, USA (2017). https://doi.org/10.1109/BigDataCongress.2017.85
23. Li, W., Andreina, S., Bohli, J.-M., Karame, G.: Securing Proof-of-Stake Blockchain Protocols. In: Garcia-Alfaro, J., Navarro-Arribas, G., Hartenstein, H., Herrera-Joancomartí, J. (eds.) ESORICS/DPM/CBT -2017. LNCS, vol. 10436, pp. 297–315. Springer, Cham (2017). https://doi.org/10.1007/978-3-319-67816-0_17
24. Singh, P.K., Singh, R., Nandi, S.K., Nandi, S.: Managing Smart Home Appliances with Proof of Authority and Blockchain. In: Lüke, K.-H., Eichler, G., Erfurth, C., Fahrnberger, G. (eds.) I4CS 2019. CCIS, vol. 1041, pp. 221–232. Springer, Cham (2019). https://doi.org/10.1007/978-3-030-22482-0_16
25. Sankar, L.S., Sindhu, M., Sethumadhavan, M.: Survey of consensus protocols on blockchain applications. In: 2017 4th International Conference on Advanced Computing and Communication Systems (ICACCS), pp. 1–5. IEEE, Coimbatore, India (2017). https://doi.org/10.1109/ICACCS.2017.8014672
26. Kim, H.M., Turesson, H., Laskowski, M., Bahreini, A.F.: Permissionless and permissioned, technology-focused and business needs-driven: understanding the hybrid opportunity in blockchain through a case study of insolar. IEEE Trans. Eng. Manage. **69**, 776–791 (2022). https://doi.org/10.1109/TEM.2020.3003565
27. Lansky, J.: Possible State Approaches to Cryptocurrencies. JoSI. **9**, 19–31 (2018). https://doi.org/10.20470/jsi.v9i1.335

28. Gonczol, P., Katsikouli, P., Herskind, L., Dragoni, N.: Blockchain implementations and use cases for supply chains-a survey. IEEE Access. **8**, 11856–11871 (2020). https://doi.org/10.1109/ACCESS.2020.2964880
29. Mettler, M.: Blockchain technology in healthcare: The revolution starts here. In: 2016 IEEE 18th International Conference on e-Health Networking, Applications and Services (Healthcom), pp. 1–3. IEEE, Munich, Germany (2016). https://doi.org/10.1109/HealthCom.2016.7749510
30. Ullah, F., Al-Turjman, F.: A conceptual framework for blockchain smart contract adoption to manage real estate deals in smart cities. Neural Comput. Appl. **35**. 5033–5034 (2021). https://doi.org/10.1007/s00521-021-05800-6
31. Saari, A., Vimpari, J., Junnila, S.: Blockchain in real estate: recent developments and empirical applications. Land Use Policy **121**, 106334 (2022). https://doi.org/10.1016/j.landusepol.2022.106334
32. Curran, K.: E-Voting on the Blockchain. The JBBA. **1**, 1–6 (2018). https://doi.org/10.31585/jbba-1-2-(3)2018
33. Subramanian, H.: Decentralized blockchain-based electronic marketplaces. Commun. ACM. **61**, 78–84 (2017). https://doi.org/10.1145/3158333
34. Urban, N.T.: Blockchain for Business. Presented at the (2020). https://doi.org/10.34156/9783791046082-61
35. CB Insights - Technology Market Intelligence, https://www.cbinsights.com/, Accessed 6 Feb 2023

Implementing Digital Transformation Processes in Industry 4.0

Héctor Cornide-Reyes[1(✉)], Jenny Morales[2], Fabián Silva-Aravena[2], Alfredo Ocqueteau[3], Nahur Melendez[1], and Rodolfo Villarroel[3]

[1] Facultad de Ingeniería, Departamento de Ingeniería Informática y Ciencias de la Computación, Universidad de Atacama, Copiapó, Chile
{hector.cornide,nahur.melendez}@uda.cl

[2] Facultad de Ciencias Sociales y Económicas, Departamento de Economía y Administración, and Universidad Católica del Maule, Talca, Chile
{jmoralesb,fasilva}@ucm.cl

[3] Escuela de Ingeniería Informática, Pontificia Universidad Católica de Valparaíso, Valparaíso, Chile
{alfredo.ocqueteau,rodolfo.villarroel}@pucv.cl

Abstract. Today, companies are subject to the absolute digitization of consumer behavior and their internal stakeholders. To successfully meet this challenge, companies need to define a digital transformation strategy. Unfortunately, most companies do not have a methodology to guide this transformation. As a result, the conduction of the process is complex, and there is no adequate diagnosis or route consistent with the company's objectives. All this leads to disordered and inefficient technological implementations, which generate a high level of uncertainty. In this article, we present the results of a literature review analysis that compiles evidence regarding how companies are addressing the challenge of digitally transforming themselves for Industry 4.0. The findings have allowed us to formulate new research questions and hypotheses based on the results reported in the selected primary studies. We recovered a total of 21 primary studies, which we classified according to three criteria: guidelines, assessments, and agile method. The increase in the number of publications in recent years shows the attractiveness of the subject. The results obtained allow us to draw important conclusions that will help to conduct future research on this topic. In future work, we plan to extend this work further and propose usability principles based on Lean. Another line of work is to explore the artificial intelligence techniques that Industry 4.0 uses in its digital transformation processes.

Keywords: Digital Transformation · Industry 4.0 · Agile Methods · Change Management · Literature Review

1 Introduction

Currently, technological advances and the need to make changes driven by Industry 4.0 represent the most significant challenges faced by organizations seeking

---

The original version of the chapter has been revised. A correction to this chapter can be found at
https://doi.org/10.1007/978-3-031-35915-6_46

A. Coman and S. Vasilache (Eds.): HCII 2023, LNCS 14025, pp. 323–335, 2023.
https://doi.org/10.1007/978-3-030-87872-6_24

to improve their competitive conditions. To address this, organizations seek to digitally transform themselves so that their organizational culture and the incorporation of new technologies allow them to be more competitive and provide a better service to their users. Digital transformation processes guide companies to restructure their work strategies to improve their competitiveness. [15,18]. These processes use agile methods and practices to improve internal performance levels to enhance business strategy. In recent years, organizations have undertaken several initiatives to explore new digital technologies and how they can benefit from them. As a result, organizations have found it necessary to establish new management practices to govern this complex transformation. Although some methodological proposals guide the digital transformation processes, there are still problems in driving the process, in the associated organizational cultural changes, and in obtaining the results that organizations expect [14]. One of the reasons for these problems is that, as transformation processes progress, organizations tend to lose focus, become somewhat disorganized and activities become more technology-driven than people-driven.

The focus of digital transformation processes must always be the people, i.e., the users who belong to the company and the customers who receive the product or service they provide. For many organizations, cultural transformation is the biggest challenge due to the complexity involved in adopting principles and values shared by all members of the organization. Therefore, to increase the probability of success in achieving the objectives defined in the digital transformation processes, it is essential to have as much knowledge as possible about the existing implementation experiences, the implementation guidelines that organizations have used, and the most appropriate evaluation methods to facilitate the implementation of new digital transformation processes. Currently, the people who make up the different industries, whether they are part of the supply or demand, are mostly considered Digital Natives, whose human and consumer behavior is influenced mainly by technology. Some studies indicate that the cognitive structure of the new generations has been influenced by the new technological and cultural tools that impact how young people perceive the world, which turns out to be very different from the way adults of previous generations learn since the preferential visual, auditory and kinesthetic sensory channels, the speed to grasp the peculiarities of reality, the handling of the abstract and the concrete, as well as the type of thinking used, are all modified. [19]. Prensky [24] further developed the idea of the digital native in his book, where he stated that the digital native likes to receive information quickly, multitask, prefers graphics to text, randomly accesses information as needed, is networked, and prefers instant gratification and rewards. There are even studies that led to the creation of the Digital Native Assessment Scale (DNAS), which was developed and validated to measure digital nativity [34].

Motivated to explore the development of these processes, we conducted a literature review to analyze and discuss the scientific evidence describing the results of the implementation of digital transformation processes. To perform this review, a search string was defined using the PICOC method. The databases considered in this review were Web of Science, Scopus, IEEE Xplore, and ACM Digital Library. Fifty-one primary studies were selected and analyzed, obtaining quite encouraging results. A set of good practices was identified for new organizations to organize transformation processes with a higher probability of success. Likewise, it was possible to identify methods to evaluate the impact on users, with Lean UX being the agile method most used by organizations. The digital transformation of Industry 4.0 already uses Artificial Intelligence [33] to improve the understanding of its internal processes and, in this way, define the objectives to be achieved more clearly.

This article is organized as follows: Section 2 describes the research method used. Section 3 shows the results obtained in the literature review, and the evidence found to answer the research questions, and finally, in Sect. 4, the conclusions.

2 Methodology

The main goal of this work is to collect evidence on how companies are approaching digital transformation processes for Industry 4.0. To achieve this objective, a literature review was conducted based on the guidelines proposed by [21,27]. The process was conducted through the following steps: 1) statement of research questions; 2) search process; 3) selection of studies; and 4) analysis of results. All these steps are described below.

2.1 Research Questions

We have defined three specific research questions to obtain more detailed knowledge and a comprehensive view of the subject. The research questions to be answered in this study are as follows:

- RQ1. What are the guidelines for implementing digital transformation processes for Industry 4.0 used?
- RQ2. How is the impact of digital transformation on the company's users/customers or services evaluated?
- RQ3. How are agile methods integrated into digital transformation processes in Industry 4.0?

2.2 Search Process

The citation databases used were SCOPUS and Web of Science (WoS), while the scientific publication databases used were ACM Digital Library and IEEE Xplore. This selection is mainly due to the reputation of these databases in the discipline, as well as the fact that we have full access to the published material. Table 1 details the method used to construct the search string. For this purpose we use the method *PICOC* [22] whose acronyms represent the criteria that drive the process. The analysis criteria are: **P** de Population; **I** de Intervention; **C** de Comparison; **O** de Outcomes y **C** de Context.

Based on the PICOC method, the following search string was developed: *(organization OR company OR institution) AND (beggining OR starting OR novel) AND ("digital transformation" OR "Industry 4.0" OR "management 4.0") AND (guidelines OR (implementation AND (successful OR assessment*

Table 1. Construction of the search string using the PICOC method

Population	Intervention	Comparision	Outcomes	Context
organizations and companies starting to implement digital transformation	Use of formal or agile methods for change management	Not applicable	Digital transformation implementation guidelines Implementation methods Implementation success stories Implementation assessment	Industry 4.0
organization/company/Institution/begining/ starting digital transformation/Industry 4.0/ Managment4.0	Guidelines Agile	Not applicable		Industry 4.0
(organization or company or institution) AND (beginning or starting or novel) AND (digital transformation OR Industry 4.0 OR management 4.0)	Guidelines Agile	Not applicable	guidelines OR ((successful OR assessment OR evaluation) AND implementation)	Industry 4.0

OR evaluation))). This search string was validated with a set of articles that we identified and used as a control group. The investigation was initially carried out in November, and its last update was carried out in mid-December 2022.

The inclusion/exclusion criteria were as follows:

- Articles since 2012 were considered.
- It must state experiences of digital transformation processes.
- Must be in the English language.

2.3 Selection of Primary Studies

The data extraction form was developed with the following fields: Article title, Year, DOI; Type (Journal, Conference); Goal; Main results; Scope of the study; Used implementation guidelines (Yes/No); Used agile practices (Yes/No); Evaluation method; Conclusions; Evidence RQ1; Evidence RQ3; Evidence RQ3. The search behavior was defined as follows:

- As a first filter (1F), we proceeded to review all the titles and keywords of the articles returned by each database. We then proceeded to eliminate repeated articles.
- As a second filter (2F), we proceeded to read the abstracts of all the articles that passed the first filter.
- Finally, the selected articles were downloaded from the web, read completely and added to the data entry form created in Microsoft Excel according to the defined protocol.

After running the search string in each query database, the results were obtained: 94 WoS articles, 68 articles in SCOPUS, 21 papers in IEEE Xplore, and 145 articles in ACM Digital Library. Subsequently, filters (1F and 2F) were applied as described in the previous paragraph. The results were obtained: 26 WoS articles, 23 articles in SCOPUS, 0 articles in IEEE Xplore, and 2 articles in ACM Digital Library. Finally, we have selected 21 primary studies to be analyzed and discussed (see Table 2).

Table 2. Selected primary studies, goals and results.

Year	Ref.	Goals	Main results
2016	[26]	It aimed to develop a maturity model and its related tool to assess the Industry 4.0 maturity of manufacturing companies.	A conceptual maturity model for Industry 4.0 was developed. This conceptual model makes it possible to collect data on the development status of companies in different industries and to identify additional success factors for effective Industry 4.0 strategies.
2018	[3]	It aims to discuss the challenges faced by companies in relation to digital transformation and propose a model to overcome them	The challenges related to digital transformation are systematized, and it is emphasized that digital transformation must be implemented following established steps
	[17]	To describe the change that a company must make in order to move from a traditional production system to a digitalized one within the Industry 4.0 approach.	The results show that the implementation of the Industry 4.0 strategy affects the financial results of a PYME by increasing profits and total revenues
	[8]	To provide guidelines to support organizations in their shift towards digitization.	It proposes a guideline that considers organizational culture, change management, and sense-making as important concepts when defining a starting point
	[20]	To provide an idea of the extent to which participatory practices and mindsets are leveraged in the early stage digital transformation process.	The findings indicate that participatory design practices have limited implementation, and there is an apparent disparity between customer-centric organizational culture and company development practices
	[5]	To present a methodology developed to design self-assessment tools for Industry 4.0 readiness	Creation of a new self-assessment guideline for Digital Transformation.
2019	[30]	This study aims to present the digital transformation design to improve energy and product efficiency in a tire production plant	After completing the processing of the data collected on the digital transformation, it is possible to evidence that it has provided an effective use of the structure, increased productivity reduced waste and facilitated maintenance operations
	[9]	Propose an ontology for modeling Digital Transformation initiatives.	It proposes a new model to extend and improve the ArchiMate model.
2020	[29]	The objective is to provide a new holistic framework for implementing Lean.	The findings show that the most influential factor in the cause the group is "technology and product design," indicating the need for companies to focus on Industry 4.0 during their operations
	[25]	The objective is to identify models that meet the needs of companies and enable top management to use this information in strategic planning for Industry 4.0 implementation.	The professionals considered the Readiness I4.0 model the most attractive because it uses objective questions to facilitate the understanding of the proposal
	[35]	Develop a digital transformation framework based on current strategic technological guidelines.	Through a case study, it is observed that technology has enabled progress for the company but the recommended approach is to position the transformation in an agile way.
2021	[33]	The objective is to define the ethical principles that are key to success, resource efficiency, cost and time, and sustainability using digital technologies and artificial intelligence to enhance digital transformation.	This study concludes that innovative corporate organizations that initiate new business models are more likely to succeed than those dominated by a more traditional and conservative attitude
	[4]	Examines the barriers to implementing digitalized work in an administrative court and highlights COVID-19 as a trigger in the transformation of work practices	It is identified that the changes in digital transformation must consider the context of the organization and the participation of people as key within the process to successful
	[31]	The objective is to review ways to implement high performance Lean automation.	They found three sets of practices: start-up, transition, and advanced. The companies with the greatest improvement in performance were those in start-up and transition
	[12]	This article seeks to redefine the main drivers of digital transformation in parliament.	A digital parliament transformation framework is proposed
	[28]	Propose an evaluation model adapted to the capacity, characteristics, technological and organizational capabilities of PYME in developing countries	The main result is the proposal of an Industry 4.0 Maturity Model for PYMEs, considering 05 dimensions: strategy, digitization of human capital, smart factory, smart processes, smart products & services.
2022	[13]	The objective is to identify the approach to building an agile culture as a basic prerequisite for its effective implementation of digital transformation	Respondents across the research sample agreed most strongly with the statements: team performance is more important than individual performance; employees are encouraged to look for the best ways to get the job done and information is shared openly and regularly in the organization
	[16]	The objective is to study how Design Thinking can help to assist small and medium-sized companies to face the digital transformation	User-centered design thinking was identified as crucial in selecting technologies for implementation that prioritized usability and provided value to all stakeholders
	[6]	Develop a model to assess manufacturing capacity, integrating relevant improvement strategies and new technologies to realize a digital transformation aligned to organizational objectives.	Development of a GUVEI (Get, Use, Virtual, Expand, Improve) sequence model for the application of Industry 4.0 technologies
	[7]	Describe the implementation of a dynamic process of social impact assessment of an organization, following the UNEP guidelines for SO - LCA, and with the participation of experts from different businesses and other stakeholders	The main result is the methodology designed since it provides an instrument validated by experts and supported by digital transformation tools, which are capable of quantifying the social impact of the activities generated by organizations on their environment
	[2]	Develop a Digital Code of Ethics for the Merck KGaA Company, which is rigorous and suitable for implementing the digital ethics challenges arising in the Company.	The methodology is based on an exhaustive review of the available literature and of the various principles, guidelines, and recommendations

2.4 Analysis of Results

Figure 1 shows the distribution of the primary studies selected for each year, while Fig. 2 shows the distribution by type of contribution. According to the above, there is a balance between the number of articles from conferences and journals. It is also possible to observe how in recent years, the current interest in the scientific community has increased in reflecting topics related to digital transformation and Industry 4.0.

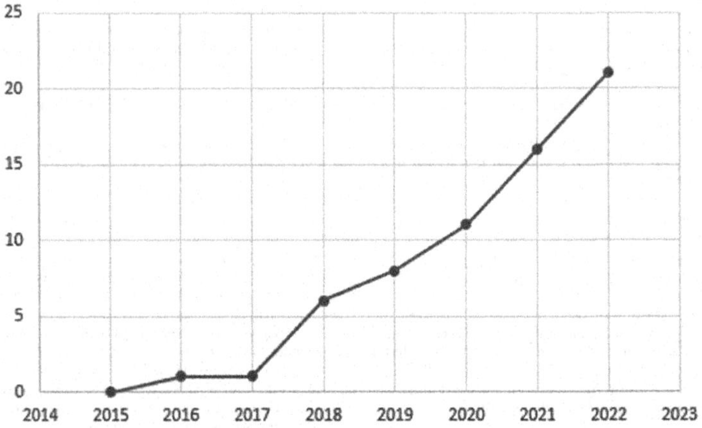

Fig. 1. Selected primary studies accumulated by year.

Table 3, shows the correspondence between the defined research questions and the selected primary studies.

Table 3. Matching research questions and primary studies

Research Questions	References to primary studies
RQ1. What are the guidelines for implementing digital transformation processes for Industry 4.0 used?	[26]; [3]; [17]; [8]; [29]; [25]; [33]; [31]; [28]; [16]; [6]; [7]; [2]; [35]; [30]; [5]; [9]
RQ2. How is the impact of digital transformation on the company's users/customers or services evaluated?	[26]; [3]; [17]; [8]; [4]; [31]; [12]; [28]; [16]; [6]; [7]; [2]; [35]; [5]; [9]
RQ3. How are agile methods integrated into digital transformation processes in Industry 4.0?	[3]; [20]; [29]; [13]; [2]

The Sect. 3 will describe the different works described in Table 2, according to the research questions defined.

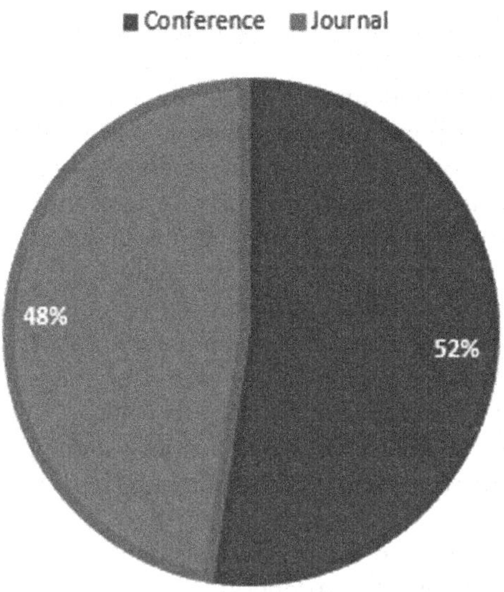

Fig. 2. Distribution of selected primary studies according to type.

2.5 Limitations

For this research we have focused on the main scientific article databases, WoS and Scopus, excluding others such as SciELO or Latindex. To include conference proceedings, we have included the IEEE and ACM publishers, which have a significant presence of publications in Computer Engineering and Computer Science. Proceedings books from other publishers and that are not indexed in WoS or Scopus are excluded from our search. Therefore, it is very likely that the works that have been left out of this study are a minority, and have a lower impact on scientific dissemination (in terms of impact factor and number of citations) than the articles considered.

3 Discussion of Results

The analysis of the information to discuss the results was carried out by analyzing the selected primary studies, according to the research questions that gave rise to the present study.

3.1 RQ1. What Are the Guidelines for Implementing Digital Transformation Processes for Industry 4.0 Used?

After reviewing the selected primary studies, the large number of experiences in leading digital transformation processes is remarkable. Most of the studies highlight the importance of people in this process. The role played by people in these processes is key to increase the probability of success in the goals defined by the company [7,20,25,33,35].

Regarding the use of guidelines or frameworks to drive the digital transformation process, we can point out that there is still a need for a formal mechanism to guide this process. Some of the studies seek to create their framework [6,9,29,35],maturity models [25,26,28] or guidelines [7,8,30] customized according to the country and industry being developed.

In [9], the authors propose an ontology to define a specific language to model digital transformation initiatives. This work is very interesting as it addresses one of the difficulties that most of the companies that try to carry out these processes have to face [3]. The definition of an ontology helps to establish a single language that will undoubtedly help to achieve a better understanding of the process by the people who belong to the companies. This work can be considered a good starting point for the construction of conceptual models of digital transformation.

In [8], present a guideline for conducting digital transformation processes based on a literature review. This proposal is quite generic, which could help its application in companies of different industries. The proposed guideline considers organizational culture, change management, and identity creation essential concepts.

In [25], the authors present the results obtained by experimenting with 9 companies of different sizes and types of activity. The applied model defines 8 fundamental pillars, these are Innovation Culture, Strategy and Leadership, Smart Factory, Agile Management, Governance and Processes, Digital Infrastructure, Logistics, and, finally, Smart Products and Services. The results indicate that the professionals consider the Readiness model I4.0 [32] as the most attractive because it uses objective questions to facilitate understanding of the proposal.

In [12] describes a successful digital transformation process from the user's perspective. It describes a framework for transformation based on the evaluation of empirical data from an expert survey of parliamentarians and administrators. The survey was answered by a total of 32 respondents from 25 countries. In terms of priorities, it was found that data, people, and information systems are within the expectations of the digital parliament. On the other hand, it also mentions that social barriers, culture, and resistance to change, together with the lack of plans or strategy, can hinder implementation. It also indicates that applicability, maturity, and usability point to technology such as legal informatics, integrated tools, and services.

In [30], the results of a digital transformation design to improve energy and product efficiency in a tire production plant are presented. The study concludes that after completing automation, MES, and ERP system integration, continuous data flow has been ensured from the bottom of the pyramid to the top. After processing collected data and digital transformation, end-to-end traceability has been provided, as well as effective use of structure, increased productivity, reduced waste, and facilitated maintenance operations.

3.2 RQ2. How Is the Impact of Digital Transformation on the Company's Users/customers or Services Evaluated?

Regarding the evaluation of the impact of a digital transformation process, it was possible to identify the following approaches:

- **Self-assessment questionnaires or guidelines:** Undoubtedly, the application of questionnaires to measure the degree of satisfaction of users/customers with the digital transformation process is the most widely used method. Interviews were conducted to measure the process and assess whether stakeholders' resistance to change had decreased after the process adjustments. Through this evaluation, it was possible to adjust the activities so that the level of acceptance of the judges changed and became positive. In [12] For example, a questionnaire with 15 questions divided into five sections was used:
  1. Demographic data (country, sector, scientific background).
  2. Digitization process (level, transformation, priorities, relevance).
  3. Barriers and drivers of transformation (organizational, digital).
  4. e-Parliament trends (significance and importance).
  5. Emerging digital technologies (applicability, maturity, usefulness, and sustainability).

  In [5] used self-assessment guidelines to measure the readiness of SMEs to face the challenges imposed by Industry 4.0. The data collected were complemented with the analysis of different maturity models. This research generates a product of a new self-assessment guideline to evaluate the impact of digital transformation processes.
- **Ethnography**: This qualitative social science research method [10] is widely used to systematically describe and interpret a social phenomenon. It is based on observation by a group of experts to evaluate the digital transformation process. The method can be used *Before* to gather information about the organizational culture, *During* to receive instant feedback about the process and make the necessary adjustments, and can be used *After* to make a retrospective evaluation of everything that happened during the process. In [16], Ethnography was used to reflect on the project and to provide a detailed description of the logistics and decision-making in the activities carried out.
- **Measurement of Indicators:** In [6] developed a model to evaluate manufacturing capacity with the purpose of carrying out a digital transformation aligned with organizational goals. By applying this model, it was possible to obtain the following results: (1) The level of inventory is reduced by more than seven times; (2) production per unit of time and the capacity to meet market demand almost doubled; (3) delivery time of orders to customers decreased from 183 to 82 d; (4) production almost tripled the value of the initial situation, and (5) the level of service improved from 77% to more than 98%. In [7] a tool validated by experts and supported by digital transformation tools is proposed that is capable of quantifying the social impact of the activities generated by the organizations on their environment. In total, 28 indicators of the social implications of the organization on its stakeholders were measured.

- **Maturity models:** In [17] use the Three-Step Model for Industry 4.0 [11].This model considers different dimensions for its three main phases, which are:
  - View.
  - Enable.
  - Enact.

  For each of these phases, there are a series of factors to be evaluated, which show the path to follow within the digital transformation process. After the evaluation, the changes that an organization must make to evolve toward Industry 4.0 become evident.
- **No impact measurement:** Analyzing the selected primary studies, we found a set of research that did not consider impact measurement. [2,8,9, 20,25]. Although they do not specify reasons for not carrying out formal and empirical processes to measure the impact of the digital transformation process, they use conceptual models that allow them to analyze the process subjectively. We believe that as long as there are no formal guidelines to conduct this type of process, it is very difficult for empirical impact measurement to acquire a higher level of importance.

3.3 RQ3. How Are Agile Methods Integrated into Digital Transformation Processes in Industry 4.0?

When we designed this research, we felt that the concepts and practices coming from agility would play an important role. This hypothesis is based on the fact that the digital transformation processes for Industry 4.0 are centered on the people who make up organizations. That same concept is the one that drives agile methods through its manifesto [1]. In [29] design a holistic framework for Lean implementation [23].To achieve a systematic Lean assessment, a framework consisting of a three-dimensional hierarchy is proposed, consisting of main criteria, sub-criteria, and measures, respectively. In [13] propose to build an agile culture as an essential prerequisite for the effective implementation of digital transformation processes. This research does not follow a specific agile practice as it is the execution of a survey. However, the survey evaluates the factors and good practices that impact the implementation of agility in organizations.

4 Conclusions and Future Work

In this article, a literature review was conducted to get an overview of the digital transformation processes for Industry 4.0. Twenty-one primary studies were analyzed, from which valuable information was obtained from the experiences of companies. It was possible to verify that there is still a lack of a guideline or model to guide companies with less uncertainty. The people who make up the companies play an essential role in the digital transformation processes. Performing a holistic diagnosis before designing the digital transformation strategy is highly recommended. The use of questionnaires is still the most widely used method to assess the impact of these processes. Lean appears as the agile method that seems to be the most complementary to digital transformation processes. In future work, we want to continue advancing and deepening this topic and propose a model that can be applied and used in different companies. We visualize this new model with a solid diagnostic component and empirical impact evaluations.

References

1. Beck, K., et al.: Manifiesto por el desarrollo Ágil de Software. Obtenido de Agile Mani-festo: http://www.agilemanifesto.org/iso/es/manifesto.Html (2001)
2. Becker, S.J., Nemat, A.T., Lucas, S., Heinitz, R.M., Klevesath, M., Charton, J.E.: A Code of Digital Ethics: laying the foundation for digital ethics in a science and technology company. AI - SOCIETY, pp. 1–11 (2022)
3. Boneva, M.: Challenges related to the digital transformation of business companies. In Innovation Management, Entrepreneurship and Sustainability (IMES 2018), (pp. 101–114). Vysoká škola ekonomická v Praze (2018)
4. Björkdahl, J., Kronblad, C.: Getting on track for digital work: Digital transformation in an administrative court before and during COVID-19. J. Profess. Organization, **8**(3), 374–393 (2021)
5. Brozzi, R., D'Amico, R.D., Pasetti Monizza, G., Marcher, C., Riedl, M., Matt, D.: Design of self-assessment tools to measure industry 4.0 readiness. a methodological approach for craftsmanship SMEs. In: Chiabert, P., Bouras, A., Noël, F., Ríos, J. (eds.) PLM 2018. IAICT, vol. 540, pp. 566–578. Springer, Cham (2018). https://doi.org/10.1007/978-3-030-01614-2_52
6. Gallego-García, S., Groten, M., Halstrick, J.: Integration of Improvement Strategies and Industry 4.0 Technologies in a Dynamic Evaluation Model for Target-Oriented Optimization. Appl. Sci. **12**(3), 1530 (2022)
7. García-Muiña, F., Medina-Salgado, M.S., González-Sánchez, R., Huertas-Valdivia, I., Ferrari, A.M., Settembre-Blundo, D.: Social Organizational Life Cycle Assessment (SO-LCA) and Organization 4.0: An easy-to-implement method. MethodsX, **9**, 101692 (2022)
8. Girrbach, P.: Change management towards digitalization and innovation. In Innovation Management, Entrepreneurship and Sustainability (IMES 2018), (pp. 357–368). Vysoká škola ekonomická v Praze. (2018)
9. Gomes, S.B., Santoro, F.M., Da Silva, M.M., Iacob, M.E.A: reference model for digital transformation and innovation. In: 2019 IEEE 23rd International Enterprise Distributed Object Computing Conference (EDOC), (pp. 21–30). IEEE. (2019, October)
10. Guber, R. La etnografía: método, campo y reflexividad. Siglo XXI editores. (2019)
11. Jacquez-Hernández, M.V., Torre, V.G.L.: Modelos de evaluación de la madurez y preparación hacia la Industria 4.0: una revisión de literatura. Ingeniería Industrial. Actualidad y Nuevas Tendencias, **6**(20), 61–78 (2018)
12. Koryzis, D., Dalas, A., Spiliotopoulos, D., Fitsilis, F.: Parltech: Transformation framework for the digital parliament. Big Data Cogn. Comput. **5**(1), 15 (2021)
13. Kohnová, L., Stacho, Z., Salajová, N., Stachová, K., Papula, J.: Application of agile management methods in companies operating in Slovakia and the Czech Republic. Economic Research-Ekonomska Istraživanja, 1–16 (2022)

14. Lalband, N., Kavitha, D.: Software Development Technique for the Betterment of End User Satisfaction using Agile Methodology, TEM, vol. 9, no. 3, pp. 992–1002 (2020)
15. Matt, C., Hess T., Benlian, A.: Digital Transformation Strategies, Business and Information Systems Engineering, vol. 57, no. 5, pp. 339–343 (2015)
16. Mesa, D., Renda, G., Kuys, B., Cook, S.M.: Implementing a Design Thinking Approach to De-Risk the Digitalisation of Manufacturing SMEs. Sustainability **14**(21), 14358 (2022)
17. Moica, S., Ganzarain, J., Ibarra, D., Ferencz, P.: Change made in shop floor management to transform a conventional production system into an" Industry 4.0": Case studies in SME automotive production manufacturing. In: 2018 7th International Conference on Industrial Technology and Management (ICITM), (pp. 51–56). IEEE (2018, March)
18. Mora, H.L., Sánchez, P.P.: Transformación Digital en Instituciones de Educación Superior con Gestión de Procesos de Negocio - Modelo de Mediación de Automatización Robótica de Procesos, de Iberian Conference on Information Systems and Technologies (CISTI), Sevilla (2020)
19. Monereo, C.: La construcción virtual de la mente: implicaciones psicoeductivas, Interactive Educational Multimedia, no. 9 (2004)
20. Persson, M., Grundstrom, C., Väyrynen, K.: A case for participatory practices in the digital transformation of insurance (2018)
21. Petersen, K., Feldt, R., Mujtaba, S., Mattsson, M.: Systematic mapping studies in software engineering. In EASE **8**, 68–77 (2008)
22. Petersen, K., Vakkalanka, S., Kuzniarz, L.: Guidelines for conducting systematic mapping studies in software engineering: An update. Inform. Softw. Technol. **64**, 1–18 (2015). https://doi.org/10.1016/j.infsof.2015.03.007
23. Poppendieck, M., Cusumano, M.A.: Lean software development: A tutorial. IEEE Softw. **29**(5), 26–32 (2012)
24. Prensky, M. Enseñar A Nativos Digitales: Una propuesta pedagógica para la sociedad del conocimiento, Ediciones SM (2011)
25. Ramos, L.F.P., Loures, E.D.F.R., Deschamps, F.: An analysis of maturity models and current state assessment of organizations for industry 4.0 implementation. Proc. Manufact., **51**, 1098–1105 (2020)
26. Schumacher, A., Erol, S., Sihn, W.: A maturity model for assessing Industry 4.0 readiness and maturity of manufacturing enterprises. Procedia Cirp, **52**, 161–166 (2016)
27. Snyder, H.: Literature review as a research methodology: an overview and guidelines. J. Bus. Res. **104**, 333–339 (2019)
28. Suleiman, Z., Dikhanbayeva, D., Shaikholla, S., Turkyilmaz, A.: Readiness Assessment of SMEs in Transitional Economies: Introduction of Industry 4.0. In: 2021 The 2nd International Conference on Industrial Engineering and Industrial Management, (pp. 8–13). (2021, January)
29. Tayaksi, C., Sagnak, M., Kazancoglu, Y.: A new holistic conceptual framework for leanness assessment. Int. J. Math., Eng. Manage. Sci., **5**(4), 567 (2020)
30. Temel, A., Ayaz, M.: Digital Transformation Design of Banbury Mixing Unit in Tire Manufacturing. In: 2019 International Conference on Applied Automation and Industrial Diagnostics (ICAAID), (Vol. 1, pp. 1–6). IEEE. (2019, September)
31. Tortorella, G.L., Narayanamurthy, G., Thurer, M.: Identifying pathways to a high-performing lean automation implementation: an empirical study in the manufacturing industry. Int. J. Prod. Econ. **231**, 107918 (2021)

32. Ward, T., Day, A., Howells, K., Birgden, A.: The multifactor offender readiness model. Aggression Violent Behav. **9**(6), 645–673 (2004)
33. Weber-Lewerenz, B.: Corporate digital responsibility (CDR) in construction engineering-ethical guidelines for the application of digital transformation and artificial intelligence (AI) in user practice. SN Appl. Sci. **3**, 1–25 (2021)
34. Wilson, M.L., Hall, J.A., Mulder, D.J.: Assessing digital nativeness in pre-service teachers: Analysis of the Digital Natives Assessment Scale and implications for practice. Research on Technology in Education (2000)
35. Zaoui, F., Souissi, N.: A framework for a strategic digital transformation. In: 2020 6th IEEE Congress on Information Science and Technology (CiSt), (pp. 502–508). IEEE (2021, June)

Apply Natural Language Processing-Chatbot on Industry 4.0

Carlos Alexander Jarquin[1], Yicheng Cai[1], I Xuan Lu[1], and Yung-Hao Wong[1,2(✉)]

[1] Minghsin University of Science and Technology, Xinfeng 30401 Hsinchu, Taiwan
yvonwong@must.edu.tw

[2] National Yang Ming Chiao Tung University, 1001 University Road, 30010 Hsinchu, Taiwan

Abstract. NLP, or natural language processing, is an area of artificial intelligence that has been studied for more than 50 years and allows computers to comprehend human language. NLP interprets and makes sense of spoken or written natural language inputs using AI algorithms. Data preprocessing and algorithm development, which include tasks like tokenization, parsing, lemmatization, and part-of-speech tagging, are the two fundamental aspects of NLP. This break language down into smaller parts and make an effort to comprehend the connections between them. Improved documentation, better human-machine interaction, and personal assistants that can interpret natural language are all advantages of NLP.

In this paper, we will concentrate on one particular use of NLP: creating chatbots that can converse with people. NLP and programming languages like Python and JavaScript were used to create a chatbot. In order to build a better user interface, JavaScript was employed, while Python was used to implement the NLP algorithms and process the inputs in natural language. With this example, we want to show how NLP can be used to build engaging, user-friendly chatbots that can converse with people in a natural way.

Keywords: NLP · Natural Language Processing · AI · human-machine interaction · chatbots · conversation · Python · JavaScript · user interface · user-friendly · engaging

1 Introduction

Natural language processing (NLP) is a subfield of AI that works with the use of natural language in interactions between computers and people. NLP has been a field of study for over 50 years, with roots in linguistics, and has undergone significant development over time. The main objective of NLP is to make it conceivable for machines to understand, translate, and create spoken or written human language. This is accomplished through the decomposition of language into smaller parts, analysis of the relationships between them, and the use of AI algorithms to interpret the data [1, 2].

·The two main phases of NLP are data preprocessing and algorithm development, with tasks such as tokenization, parsing, lemmatization, and part-of-speech tagging playing critical roles in both phases. These efforts have led to improved documentation,

A. Coman and S. Vasilache (Eds.): HCII 2023, LNCS 14025, pp. 336–351, 2023.
https://doi.org/10.1007/978-3-031-35915-6_25

enhanced human-machine interaction, and advanced natural language processing for personal assistants [3, 4].

This paper focuses on the use of NLP in the creation of chatbots, a type of conversational agent that can communicate with people using natural language. The paper provides a step-by-step tutorial on how to build a chatbot that employs NLP, as well as an examination of its implementation in programming languages like Python and JavaScript, the latter of which can be especially useful in improving user interfaces. The aim of the paper is to provide a comprehensive introduction to NLP and its applications in chatbots so that academics and developers can have a better understanding of the advantages and drawbacks of this fascinating topic.

2 Literature Review

In the area of artificial intelligence, natural language processing (NLP) has grown in popularity recently (AI). In order to improve the algorithms for processing and comprehending human language, many researchers and professionals are investigating the applications of NLP. The development of chatbots, which are conversational agents capable of interacting with people in natural language, is one of the most promising uses of NLP.

The development of chatbots using NLP has been the subject of numerous studies, with the main goal of enhancing user experience and making conversational agents more human-like. For instance, the authors of "Building Chatbots with Python: Using Natural Language Processing and Machine Learning" The writers conduct experiments to evaluate the performance of chatbots built using Python, NLP, and ML, and the results show that these chatbots can provide accurate and relevant responses to user queries. In conclusion, the paper highlights the importance of using Python, NLP, and ML in the development of chatbots and presents it as a promising solution for businesses looking to improve customer engagement and satisfaction [5].

A different study, "Use of Chatbots in Website Navigation" by Boris Penko. In this study, the author investigated the potential use of chatbots for website navigation and the potential benefits that this technology offers. The author conducted a survey of users to gather their opinions and preferences on the use of chatbots for website navigation. The findings indicated that a substantial amount of users prefer using chatbots over traditional navigation methods and that chatbots can provide a more user-friendly and efficient way of navigating websites. The author concludes that chatbots have the potential to improve the user experience and suggests that they should be considered as a valuable tool for website navigation in the future [6].

The use of NLP in the creation of certain applications, such as e-commerce chatbots and personal assistant chatbots, has also been the subject of various studies. "A Comparative Study of Chatbots and Humans" and was published in the International Journal of Advanced Research in Computer and Communication Engineering. In this study, the writers compare the performance of chatbots and humans in terms of their ability to handle customer service inquiries. The authors conducted a survey and found that chatbots are able to handle a large volume of inquiries and can provide quick and accurate responses. However, they also found that chatbots have limitations in handling complex or emotional inquiries, which are better handled by human customer service representatives. The authors conclude that chatbots have the potential to enhance customer service operations, but they should be used in conjunction with human customer service representatives to provide a complete solution [7].

The literature study concludes that NLP plays a crucial role in the development of chatbots and conversational agents. The studies reviewed in this section have shown that NLP techniques can be used to create chatbots that are able to provide accurate and relevant responses to user inquiries, improve website navigation, and enhance customer service operations. However, while chatbots have the potential to improve customer engagement and satisfaction, they also have limitations in handling complex or emotional inquiries. These limitations suggest that chatbots should be used in conjunction with human customer service representatives to provide a complete solution. Overall, the results of these studies highlight the importance of using NLP in the development of chatbots and the potential benefits that this technology can offer.

3 Methodology

The term "Natural Language Processing" (NLP) refers to a field that is part of artificial intelligence (AI) that studies how computers and people communicate in natural language. Analyzing, comprehending, and creating the languages that people use to communicate with one another are all part of it. Chatbots, language translation, sentiment analysis, and text classification are just a few of the uses for NLP. To make it simpler for individuals to connect with computers and acquire information, NLP aims to develop computer programs that can communicate with people in a manner that resembles human-to-human conversation.

3.1 Applications of Natural Language Processing

- Voice Assistants and Chatbots
- Speech Recognition
- Automatic Summarization
- Chatbots
- Smart Assistant
- Text Summarization
- Recruitment
- Social Media Monitoring and Analytics
- Language Translation
- Advertisement to Targeted Audience
- Sentiment Analysis
- Email Filtering
- Online Searches
- Auto Correct and Auto Prediction
- Document analysis.

Fig. 1. NLP Applications

Here is an image of the most common scenarios (Fig. 1).

Let's start building your own AI chatbot from scratch!

The methodology of this paper involves the use of NLP to develop computer programs that can communicate with people in a way that resembles human-to-human conversation. The study of NLP involves analyzing, comprehending, and generating natural language. The study concludes by showing how NLP has a significant influence on the creation of chatbots and has the potential to enhance user interaction.

The next step is to deploy the chatbot on a website using Flask and JavaScript, where Flask is a simple and efficient framework for web applications and JavaScript is used to improve the user interface. This will make it easier for individuals to interact with the chatbot and access information.

The following steps will be taken in the process (Fig. 2):

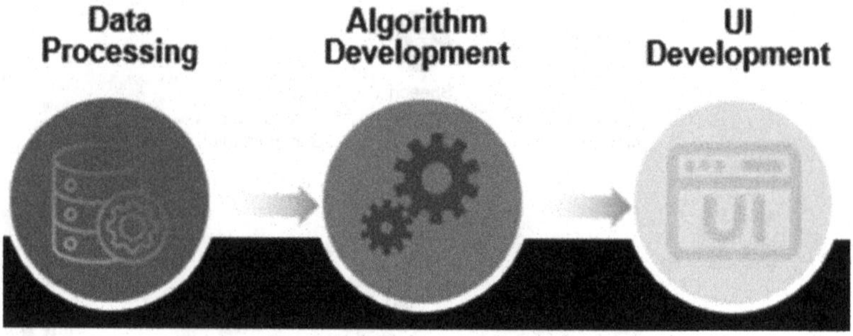

Fig. 2. Chatbot Development

3.2 Data Preprocessing

This involves cleaning and preparing the data to be used in the chatbot. The steps included are tokenization, stopword removal, lemmatization, and vectorization. I will explain this with more details in the following sentences.

3.2.1 Data Cleaning

This would include checking for any missing or inconsistent data in the JSON file and fixing it. Check how this.json file looks, this is an example of our data (Fig. 3 and Fig. 4).

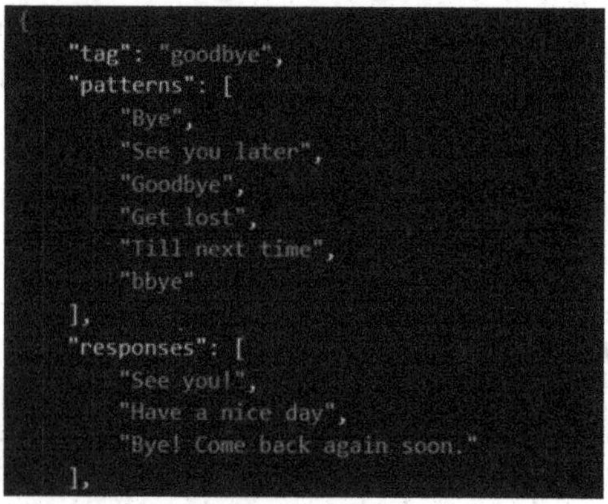

```
{
    "tag": "goodbye",
    "patterns": [
        "Bye",
        "See you later",
        "Goodbye",
        "Get lost",
        "Till next time",
        "bbye"
    ],
    "responses": [
        "See you!",
        "Have a nice day",
        "Bye! Come back again soon."
    ],
```

Fig. 3. JSON File

Here I am loading the.json file to our code.

3.2.2 Tokenization

Tokenization is the process of breaking up a long piece of text into tokens, which are smaller pieces of text. Depending on the job and the NLP model being utilized, tokens

```
# Load intents from intents.json file
with open('intents.json', 'r') as json_data:
    intents = json.load(json_data)
```

Fig. 4. Loading Data (.json)

might be words, sentences, symbols, or even subwords. To prepare text data for additional processing, such as text normalization, stopword removal, and feature extraction, tokenization is a key step in many NLP pipelines (Fig. 5).

```
def tokenize(sentence):
    """
    split sentence into array of words/tokens
    a token can be a word or punctuation character, or num
    """
    return nltk.word_tokenize(sentence)
```

Fig. 5. Tokenization

3.2.3 Stopword Removal

Stopword removal is a preprocessing step in Natural Language Processing (NLP) that eliminates common terms from the text, like "a," "an," "the," "and," etc. Stopwords are these words, and NLP tasks like sentiment analysis, document categorization, and topic modeling don't place much weight on them. When utilizing techniques like bag-of-words or TF-IDF, stopwords are commonly eliminated from the text because they occur frequently and do not have much meaning. This can result in a big and sparse matrix (term frequency-inverse document frequency). Stopword elimination can decrease the complexity of the data and boost the effectiveness of NLP models. [8, 9] (Fig. 6 and Fig. 7).

```
def bag_of_words(tokenized_sentence, words):
    """
    return bag of words array:
    1 for each known word that exists in the sentence, 0
    example:
    sentence = ["hello", "how", "are", "you"]
    words = ["hi", "hello", "I", "you", "bye", "thank", "
    bog   = [  0 ,    1 ,    0 ,   1 ,    0 ,     0 ,
    """
```

Fig. 6. Bag of Word Function Explanation

```
# stem each word        (variable) word: Any
sentence_words = [stem(word) for word in tokenized_se
# initialize bag with 0 for each word
bag = np.zeros(len(words), dtype=np.float32)
for idx, w in enumerate(words):
    if w in sentence_words:
        bag[idx] = 1

return bag
```

Fig. 7. Stopword removal

3.2.4 Lemmatization

When words are lemmatized, they are reduced to their root or fundamental form. The dataset's dimensions are decreased and the data are standardized. Lemmatization can be used to transform words like "running," "runner," and "ran" into their simplest form, "run." Words with the same root meaning are handled as the same word in text analysis tasks including sentiment analysis, document classification, and topic modeling. Lemmatization is distinct from stemming, which entails stripping words of all context and meaning before reducing them to their simplest form. Stemming algorithms frequently generate meaningless words and may yield outcomes that are challenging to understand. Lemmatization is commonly performed using libraries in NLP (Natural Language Processing) such as NLTK or Spacy in Python. [10, 11] (Fig. 8).

Here is an example of it:

```
def stem(word):
    """
    stemming = find the root form of the word
    examples:
    words = ["organize", "organizes", "organizing"]
    words = [stem(w) for w in words]
    -> ["organ", "organ", "organ"]
    """
    return stemmer.stem(word.lower())
```

Fig. 8. Lemmatization

3.2.5 Vectorization

Is the procedure of translating text data into numerical vectors or representations that can be processed by machine learning algorithms. The goal of vectorization is to represent text data in a format that is suitable for NLP tasks such as text classification, sentiment analysis, and topic modeling [12] (Fig. 9).

There are several vectorization techniques used in NLP, including:

1. **Bag of Words (BOW):** is a straightforward vectorization technique in which each document is represented as a collection of words, with the frequency of each word utilized as a feature.
2. **Term Frequency-Inverse Document Frequency (TF-IDF):** is a more cutting-edge vectorization strategy that contemplates both the rarity of terms over the whole corpus as well as their frequency in a given document. Words that are infrequent across the entire corpus but regularly appear in a document are given higher weight.
3. **Word Embeddings (Word2Vec, GloVe, BERT, etc.)**

Here is an example of it:

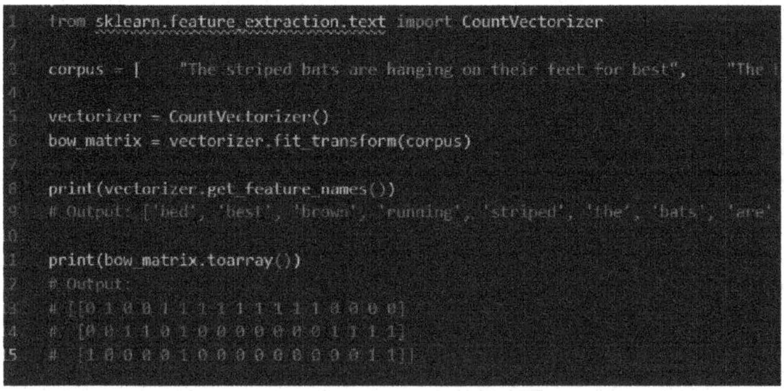

```
from sklearn.feature_extraction.text import CountVectorizer

corpus = [    "The striped bats are hanging on their feet for best",    "The

vectorizer = CountVectorizer()
bow_matrix = vectorizer.fit_transform(corpus)

print(vectorizer.get_feature_names())
# Output: ['bed', 'best', 'brown', 'running', 'striped', 'the', 'bats', 'are'

print(bow_matrix.toarray())
# Output:
# [[0 1 0 0 1 1 1 1 1 1 1 1 1 0 0 0 0]
#  [0 0 1 1 0 1 0 0 0 0 0 0 0 1 1 1 1]
#  [1 0 0 0 0 1 0 0 0 0 0 0 0 0 0 1 1]]
```

Fig. 9. Vectorization Example

Here we are not implementing this preprocessing step nevertheless this step is highly important in NLP to prepare text data for further processing.

3.3 Algorithm Development

This involves the creation of algorithms that can interpret the user input and generate a response. The algorithms will be implemented using the programming language Python.

We have a function called get response (msg), this function takes in a user message as input, tokenizes it into a sentence, converts the sentence into a bag of words representation, passes it through a pre-trained Neural Network model to make a prediction of the intent, and returns a response based on the prediction. The response could either be a random message associated with the predicted intent if the predicted probability is greater than 0.75, or a default message "I do not understand..." if the predicted probability is less than 0.75 (Fig. 10).

Following we have to train a PyTorch neural network for intent classification in a chatbot.

- First, the intents and the corresponding patterns are loaded from a JSON file (intents.json).
- The words in the patterns are tokenized and stemmed, and duplicates are removed.
- Then, a bag of words representation is created for each pattern sentence.

```
# If the predicted probability is greater than 0.75, retu
# associated with the predicted tag
if prob.item() > 0.75:
    for intent in intents['intents']:
        if tag == intent["tag"]:
            return random.choice(intent['responses'])

# If the predicted probability is less than 0.75, return
return "I do not understand..."
```

Fig. 10. Function to convert sentence to BOW

- The training data (inputs and outputs) are created from the bag of words and the corresponding tags.
- A PyTorch Dataset and a DataLoader are created for the training data.
- A neural network model is defined, with an input size equal to the size of the bag of words representation, a hidden size of 8, and an output size equal to the number of unique tags.
- The model is trained using the Adam optimizer and the CrossEntropyLoss criterion.
- Finally, the trained model is saved to a file (data.pth), along with related information such as the input/output sizes, the all words, and the tags.

Check the example below (Fig. 11):

```
# Train the model
for epoch in range(num_epochs):
    for (words, labels) in train_loader:
        words = words.to(device)
        labels = labels.to(dtype=torch.long).to(device)

        # Forward pass
        outputs = model(words)
        # if y would be one-hot, we must apply
        # labels = torch.max(labels, 1)[1]
        loss = criterion(outputs, labels)

        # Backward and optimize
        optimizer.zero_grad()
        loss.backward()
        optimizer.step()

    if (epoch+1) % 100 == 0:
        print (f'Epoch [{epoch+1}/{num_epochs}], Loss: {loss.item():.4f}')
```

Fig. 11. Train Model

Feed Forward Neural Net which will get our bag of words as an input and then we have one layer fully linked which has a sum of dissimilar patterns as an input size and the hidden layer, one more hidden layer and last but not least the output size must be the sum of different classes and then we apply Softmax.

Let's see this in our code to have a clear understanding but before I will add an image so you can have an idea of what is a feed forward neural net?

The linear information flow of a Feed Forward Neural Network is what distinguishes it from other artificial neural networks. A Feed Forward Neural Network's connections are linear and move from input to output in a single direction without loops or backwards flow, in contrast to a Recurrent Neural Network's connections, which create cycles. The most fundamental kind of neural network is this one. Although there are numerous intermediate nodes where the data must pass, the information flow is constant [13] (Fig. 12).

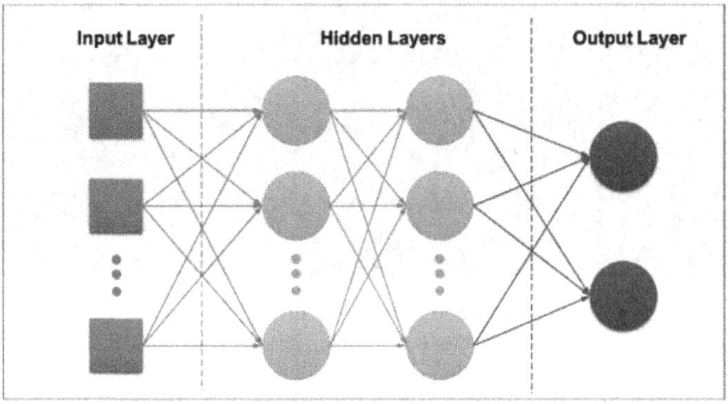

Fig. 12. Feed Forward Neural Network

A single layer perceptron is a simple example of a feed-forward neural network. In a feed-forward network, the data flows in only one direction, from input to output, through a series of interconnected nodes, called artificial neurons. Each neuron takes the inputs, applies weights to them, and passes them through a non-linear activation function, to produce an output. These outputs are then fed as inputs to the next layer of neurons, until the final output layer produces the desired result. This process of moving the inputs forward through the network to produce an output is known as "feeding the data forward." [14].

User Interface Design: The user interface was developed using the programming language JavaScript. This step is important for creating a user-friendly interface that can engage the user and make the chatbot more effective.

JavaScript plays a good role for the frontend because it provides a high level of interactivity and dynamic behavior on websites, making it ideal for creating user interfaces and web applications [14]. It is a widely used and well-supported language, making it easy to find resources and support when developing web applications. Additionally, JavaScript has a large and growing ecosystem of libraries and frameworks that can be leveraged to help speed up and simplify the development process.

Integration and Testing: The final step involves integrating the algorithms developed in step 2 with the user interface created in step 3. The chatbot will then be tested and evaluated to ensure that it is functioning as expected.

Our chatbot is built without a user interface at the moment, but it will be added later. Currently, Python is used to create the chatbot, but to use it in a more convenient way, we will need to deploy it on a website. Without a website, we can only access the chatbot through the terminal or command prompt (Fig. 13).

Here is an example:

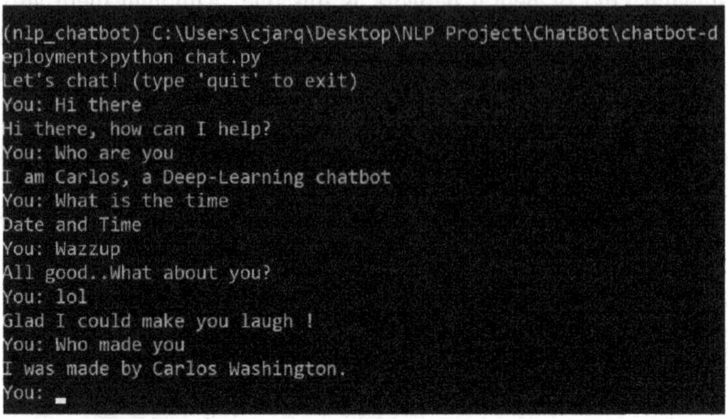
(nlp_chatbot) C:\Users\cjarq\Desktop\NLP Project\ChatBot\chatbot-d
eployment>python chat.py
Let's chat! (type 'quit' to exit)
You: Hi there
Hi there, how can I help?
You: Who are you
I am Carlos, a Deep-Learning chatbot
You: What is the time
Date and Time
You: Wazzup
All good..What about you?
You: lol
Glad I could make you laugh !
You: Who made you
I was made by Carlos Washington.
You:

Fig. 13. Chatbot from Command Prompt

This is an example of how it looks, it will look much better once we deploy it using JavaScript since it will be more friendly and easy to interact with.

This is pretty much everything related to the Natural Language Processing, from here you can execute the chat.py file to start chatting with the bot, once again, this needs to be executed in the Command Prompt or PowerShell since is not deployed on a website yet.

This is our next step, deploy it on a website to make it more attractive and easier to interact with, here is where Flask and JavaScript come in. First, I want to explain what is Flask?

Web Server Gateway Interface (WSGI) web application framework Flask is compact. It is designed to make getting started quick and easy, with the ability to scale up to complex projects. It began as a simple Werkzeug and Jinja wrapper but has now developed into one of the most popular Python web application frameworks. We are going to install it now:

First, we have to create a new environment, it is advised to handle your project's dependencies in a virtual environment for both development and production (Fig. 14).

> mkdir myproject.

> cd myproject.

> py -3 -m venv venv.

Now, it is time to activate the environment,

> C:\ > < *venv* > \Scripts\activate.bat.

These commands are for Windows users, you can visit the official website for the installation of different platform such as Linux and Mac https://flask.palletsprojects.com/en/2.2.x/installation/.

Fig. 14. Create Python Environment

Within the activated environment, use the following command to install Flask:

$ pip install Flask.

Now that Flask is installed, let's import some libraries we will use in our project, here is a snapshot (Fig. 15):

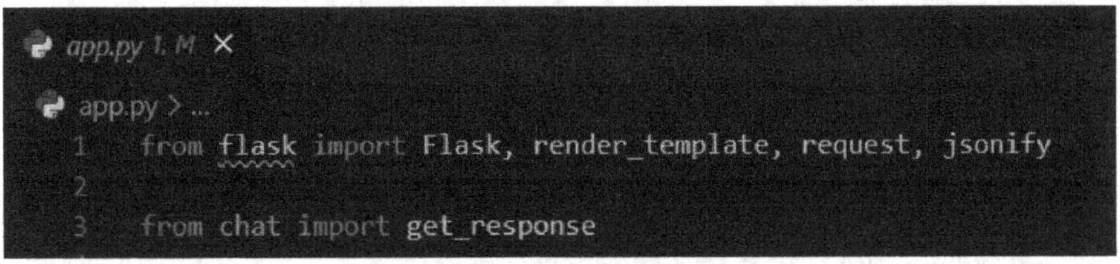

app.py 1, M ×
app.py > ...
from flask import Flask, render_template, request, jsonify
from chat import get_response

Fig. 15. Importing Flask

Ok, you might be asking what are those libraries that we imported, let me explain what those libraries do:

- **Render_Template:** Find the app by default in the templates folder. As a result, we only need to supply the template's name, not its complete path.
- **Request:** When a request is made, the context of the request is monitored to keep track of all the data associated with it. Rather than passing the request object to every function that is executed during the request, the request and session proxies are consulted instead. [3]

The Application Context, which manages the application-level data devoid of a request, is comparable to this. When a request context is pushed, a corresponding application context follows suit. [3]

- Jsonify: Flask jsonify is a Python feature that allows you to encapsulate a dumps() method and make enhancements to a json (JavaScript Object Notation) output to create a response object with the application/json mimetype (Fig. 16 and Fig. 17).

Let's take a look to the code:

This is all we need to render our website using Flask, let's see how it looks:

```
# Homepage to render the html template
@app.route("/")
def index_get():
    return render_template("base.html")

@app.post("/prediction")
def prediction():
    text = request.get_json().get("message")
    #Check if text is valid
    response = get_response(text)
    message = {"answer": response}
    return jsonify(message)

if __name__ == "__main__":
    app.run(debug=True)
```

Fig. 16. Rendering html template

```
(nlp_chatbot) C:\Users\cjarq\Desktop\NLP Project\ChatBot\chatbot-deployment>python app.p
y
 * Serving Flask app 'app'
 * Debug mode: on
WARNING: This is a development server. Do not use it in a production deployment. Use a p
roduction WSGI server instead.
 * Running on http://127.0.0.1:5000
Press CTRL+C to quit
 * Restarting with stat
 * Debugger is active!
 * Debugger PIN:
127.0.0.1 - - [24/Dec/2022 00:30:26] "GET / HTTP/1.1" 200 -
127.0.0.1 - - [24/Dec/2022 00:30:26] "GET /static/style.css HTTP/1.1" 304 -
127.0.0.1 - - [24/Dec/2022 00:30:27] "GET /static/images/chatbox-icon.svg HTTP/1.1" 304
-
127.0.0.1 - - [24/Dec/2022 00:30:27] "GET /static/app.js HTTP/1.1" 304 -
127.0.0.1 - - [24/Dec/2022 00:30:27] "GET /favicon.ico HTTP/1.1" 404 -
```

Fig. 17. Server up

4 Results

The results of combining NLP and programming languages like Python and JavaScript to create a chatbot can be seen in the final website. The user interface was improved with the use of JavaScript, while Python was used to implement the NLP algorithms and process natural language inputs. The end result is a chatbot that can engage in conversations with people in a natural way, demonstrating the capabilities of NLP in building user-friendly conversational agents.

The results of the project are a testament to the power of NLP in creating advanced conversational agents. By utilizing NLP algorithms and processing natural language inputs, the chatbot is able to interact with users in a way that resembles human-to-human conversation. The use of JavaScript in the user interface also highlights the importance of design in making chatbots appealing and accessible to users.

Overall, the project demonstrates the potential of NLP in building chatbots that can enhance human-computer interaction. The results obtained show that with the right combination of NLP algorithms and user interface design, it is possible to create chatbots that are both effective and enjoyable to use (Fig. 18).

This is how the website looks like after combining Python and JavaScript:

Fig. 18. Website

The results section of the website is the culmination of the integration between Python and JavaScript. Upon executing the app.py file in the command prompt, users can access the website by copying and pasting the generated IP address into their web browser of choice, including Google Chrome, Mozilla Firefox, Microsoft Edge, and Safari.

The website, though simple in design, serves as a demonstration of the potential applications of the integration, including small business websites, personal portfolios, blogs, e-commerce platforms, magazines, forums, and news websites, among others.

One notable feature of the website is the chat icon located in the bottom right corner. By clicking on this icon, a chat window will appear, allowing users to engage in conversation with the chatbot. The chatbot is capable of responding to user inquiries, though the quality of its responses will depend on the training data it was exposed to. If a user inputs an unfamiliar query, the chatbot will respond with "I do not understand."

In summary, the Results section showcases the functional integration of Python and JavaScript, presenting a simple but effective demonstration of the potential applications of this integration (Fig. 19 and Fig. 20).

Take a look to the following images.

The chatbot is initiated by clicking on the purple message icon located on the bottom right corner of the website. Once you click on it, a chat window will pop up, allowing you to start communicating with the bot.

Fig. 19. Chatbot interface

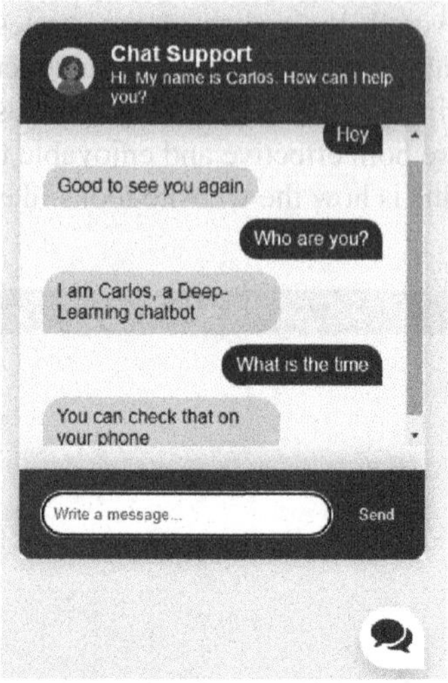

Fig. 20. Chatbot interactions

It is important to note that the responses you receive from the bot will be based on the training data provided. Therefore, if you ask a question that is not within the scope of the training data, you will receive a response indicating that the bot does not understand.

In conclusion, the results section provides a simple and user-friendly interface for you to communicate with the chatbot and get answers to your questions. The website has the potential to be used for a variety of purposes such as small business websites, portfolios, blogs, personal websites, e-commerce websites, magazines, forums, news, and more (Fig. 21).

Below you can see how the server shows every request:

127.0.0.1 - - [24/Dec/2022 01:02:23] "GET /favicon.ico HTTP/1.1" 404 -
127.0.0.1 - - [24/Dec/2022 01:05:55] "POST /prediction HTTP/1.1" 200 -
127.0.0.1 - - [24/Dec/2022 01:06:00] "POST /prediction HTTP/1.1" 200 -
127.0.0.1 - - [24/Dec/2022 01:06:09] "GET / HTTP/1.1" 200 -
127.0.0.1 - - [24/Dec/2022 01:06:09] "GET /static/style.css HTTP/1.1" 304 -
127.0.0.1 - - [24/Dec/2022 01:06:09] "GET /static/images/chatbox-icon.svg HTTP/1.1" 304 -
127.0.0.1 - - [24/Dec/2022 01:06:09] "GET /static/app.js HTTP/1.1" 304 -
127.0.0.1 - - [24/Dec/2022 02:16:18] "POST /prediction HTTP/1.1" 200 -
127.0.0.1 - - [24/Dec/2022 02:16:31] "POST /prediction HTTP/1.1" 200 -
127.0.0.1 - - [24/Dec/2022 02:16:44] "POST /prediction HTTP/1.1" 200 -
127.0.0.1 - - [24/Dec/2022 02:16:53] "GET / HTTP/1.1" 200 -
127.0.0.1 - - [24/Dec/2022 02:16:53] "GET /static/style.css HTTP/1.1" 304 -
127.0.0.1 - - [24/Dec/2022 02:16:53] "GET /static/images/chatbox-icon.svg HTTP/1.1" 304 -
127.0.0.1 - - [24/Dec/2022 02:16:53] "GET /static/app.js HTTP/1.1" 304 -

Fig. 21. Server requests on Command Prompt

5 Conclusion

A key component of artificial intelligence, natural language processing (NLP) has been studied for more than 50 years. It enables more natural communication between people and computers by helping computers comprehend human language. Data preparation and algorithm development are the two key stages of NLP development, and they are essential for enhancing human-machine interactions and building more sophisticated personal assistants. This study focused on the development of chatbots, which have grown in popularity across a range of applications, including e-commerce and personal assistant chatbots. The creation of an NLP-based chatbot using JavaScript and Python was explained step-by-step in the tutorial. According to the paper is findings, NLP has a substantial impact on chatbot development, has the potential to improve user interaction, and can make conversational agents more human-like. The focus of future research should be on enhancing the functionality of chatbots with NLP capabilities and identifying new NLP-related AI applications. The project's next stage is to install the chatbot on a website using JavaScript and Flask to make it more user-friendly.

References

1. Sun, T.-X., et al.: Paradigm shift in natural language processing. Mach. Intell. Res. **19**(3), 169–183 (2022)
2. Liu, P., et al.: Pre-train, prompt, and predict: A systematic survey of prompting methods in natural language processing. ACM Comput. Surv. **55**(9), 1–35 (2023)
3. Caucheteux, C., King, J.-R.: Brains and algorithms partially converge in natural language processing. Commun. Biol. **5**(1), 134 (2022)
4. Wu, L., et al.: Graph neural networks for natural language processing: A survey. Foundat. Trends® Mach. Learn. **16**(2), 119–328 (2023)
5. Lauriola, I., Lavelli, A., Aiolli, F.: An introduction to deep learning in natural language processing: Models, techniques, and tools. Neurocomputing **470**, 443–456 (2022)
6. Li, B., Hou, Y., Che, W.: Data augmentation approaches in natural language processing: A survey. AI Open **3**, 71–90 (2022)
7. Wu, C., et al.: Natural language processing for smart construction: Current status and future directions. Autom. Constr. **134**, 104059 (2022)
8. Tunstall, L., Von Werra, L., Wolf, T.: Natural language processing with transformers. O'Reilly Media, Inc. (2022)
9. Raina, V., et al.: Natural language processing. Building an Effective Data Science Practice: A Framework to Bootstrap and Manage a Successful Data Science Practice, pp. 63–73 (2022)
10. Khurana, D., et al.: Natural language processing: State of the art, current trends and challenges. Multimedia Tools Appli. pp. 1–32 (2022)
11. Klyuchnikov, N., et al.: Nas-bench-nlp: neural architecture search benchmark for natural language processing. IEEE Access **10**, 45736–45747 (2022)
12. Bayer, M., Kaufhold, M.-A., Buchhold, B., Keller, M., Dallmeyer, J., Reuter, C.: Data augmentation in natural language processing: a novel text generation approach for long and short text classifiers. Int. J. Mach. Learn. Cybern. , 1–16 (2022). https://doi.org/10.1007/s13042-022-01553-3
13. Heilbron, M., et al.: A hierarchy of linguistic predictions during natural language comprehension. Proc. Natl. Acad. Sci. **119**(32), e2201968119 (2022)
14. Regin, R., Rajest, S.S., Shynu, T.: An Automated conversation system using natural language processing (NLP) chatbot in python. Central Asian J. Med. Nat. Sci. **3**(4), 314–336 (2022)

Research on Store Evaluation in the Service Industry Through Analysis of Questionnaire Data on Employee Satisfaction

Akito Kumazawa[1](✉), Takashi Namatame[2], and Kohei Otake[3]

[1] Graduate School of Information and Telecommunication Engineering, Tokai University, 2-3-23, Takanawa, Minato-Ku, Tokyo 108-8619, Japan
9bjm2116@mail.u-tokai.ac.jp

[2] Faculty of Science and Engineering, Chuo University, 1-13-27, Kasuga, Bunkyo-Ku, Tokyo 112-8551, Japan
nama@kc.chu-o.ac.jp

[3] School of Information and Telecommunication Engineering, Tokai University, 2-3-23, Takanawa, Minato-Ku, Tokyo 108-8619, Japan
otake@tsc.u-tokai.ac.jp

Abstract. In recent years, the hair salon industry in Japan has seen an increase in the number of salons and a decrease in the number of customers, leading to intensified competition among salons for customers. To address this situation, salons are taking various measures, one of which is to improve employee satisfaction. In this paper, we examine whether employee satisfaction is related to customer purchasing behavior and identify factors that can improve employee satisfaction. Specifically, using data from a workplace satisfaction survey of employees, we select questionnaire items using factor analysis. Next, using the selected survey items, we performed basic tabulation to understand the characteristics of the data. Then, we examined a structural equation modeling to examine the causal relationship between employee satisfaction and latent factors, and the identification of factors that improve employee satisfaction using data on the number of all employees. In addition, we conducted a Multi group analysis was conducted to examine whether there were differences in response trends by job title. We divided frequency respondents into two categories with respect job titles that are stylist and assistant. Finally, we conducted RF analysis by using ID-POS data to evaluate the percentage of good customers for each store. We used the results of these analyses to examine the relationship between store satisfaction and customer purchasing behavior.

Keywords: Employee satisfaction · factor analysis · structural equation modeling

1 Introduction

In recent years, competition in the Japanese beauty salon industry has intensified. According to the Ministry of Health, Labor and Welfares 2020 Report on Health Administration [1], the number of beauty salons increased by approximately 15,000 over the

A. Coman and S. Vasilache (Eds.): HCII 2023, LNCS 14025, pp. 352–369, 2023.
https://doi.org/10.1007/978-3-031-35915-6_26

four years from 2016 to 2020, and the number of salons is expected to continue to increase every year without decreasing. On the other hand, according to the Ministry of Internal Affairs and Communications Population estimates [2], Japan total population has been declining year by year because of low birthrates and an aging population, decreasing by approximately 1.6 million people from 2015 to 2021. Against this backdrop, competition to attract customers is intensifying in the hair salon industry. As the results, each salon is making various efforts to attract customers. On each measure is the improvement of employee satisfaction. By improving employee satisfaction, employees feel that their work at the company is worthwhile, and it is expected that service will improve for individuals and the organization, and improved service is also expected to attract customers. According to Xu and Wakabayashi [3], they confirmed the tendency for factors that constitute employee satisfaction to have a positive impact on factors that constitute customer satisfaction, revealing a certain relationship between employees and customers. And Suzuki and Matsuoka [4], higher employee satisfaction leads to higher service quality, higher service quality leads to higher customer satisfaction, and higher customer satisfaction leads to higher financial performance. Therefore, this study will speculate on the relationship between employee satisfaction and customer purchasing behavior, and identify factors that improve employee satisfaction.

2 Purpose of This Study

In this study, we use ID-POS data and questionnaire data on employee satisfaction at hair salons to clarify whether employee satisfaction is related to customer purchasing behavior. Moreover, we also identify factors that are influenced by employee satisfaction.

To employee satisfaction we select questionnaire items by factor analysis and determine the causal relationship between the latent variables determined by factor analysis and the questionnaire items by structural equation modeling. We then use the results to identify factors that improve employee satisfaction. In this structural equation modeling, we also examine whether there is a difference in response difference between stylists and assistants in a hair salon chain due to differences in the job descriptions of the two jobs and discuss for each.

3 Definition of Employee Satisfaction

Employee Satisfaction (ES) can be broadly divided into two categories according to the motivational hygiene theory (two-component theory) proposed by Frederick Herzberg [5]. The first is motivators. Motivators are factors related to job content that directly motivate people to work, such as a sense of accomplishment, desire for recognition, promotion, responsibility, and the job itself, and are important factors in job satisfaction. It is said to be a factor that should be proactively improved to increase employee satisfaction.

The second is hygiene factors. Hygiene factors are also called dissatisfaction factors because they are factors related to job dissatisfaction, such as benefits, relationships with coworkers, salary, and management policies. Hygiene factors are said to have a preventive role but no positive effect on direct motivation to work [6]. However, since hygiene factors are factors related to the work environment, if employees work with a sense of dissatisfaction, it may lead to worsening of their work attitude and lower productivity. Since a decline in hygiene factors may affect employee satisfaction, it is believed that improving hygiene factors and increasing motivational factors will lead to higher employee satisfaction.

Based on the above ideas in this study, we will use these two factors in our analysis of employee satisfaction.

4 Dataset

In this study, we use id- point-of-sale data per customer provided by a national chain of hair salons with outlets, as well as survey data on employee workplace satisfaction.

4.1 ID-POS Data

In this study, we use ID-POS data for 10 stores in the same area. The data used a one-year period from April 1/2016 to March 31/ 2017 to match the implementation period of the survey data used in 4.2 below. The datasets for accounting history and accounting details are presented in Tables 1 and 2.

Table 1. Details of accounting history

Items	Contents
Account ID	Different IDs for each account
Store ID	10 stores from A to J
Accounting day	Date of accounting
Accounting time	hh:mm:ss
Customer ID	Classify by integer

Table 2. Details of accounting statements

Items	Contents
Account item ID	Different ID for each account, each treatment menu, and each product
Account ID	Different IDs for each account
Itemized product type	Product sales or treatment sales
Accounting details nomination classification	Nominated or not

4.2 Questionnaire Data on Workplace Satisfaction from Employees

In this study, we use data from a questionnaire survey conducted in July 2016 among 181 employees of 10 stores. The questions consisted of 52 items, rated on a 5-point scale: 5, exactly agree, 4, fairly agree, 3, neither agree nor disagree, 2, not really agree, 1, and not at all agree, respectively. In addition, we have four types of employee jobs: stylist, assistant, director, and store manager. However. The number of directors and store managers is small, we focused on stylist or assistant. Stylists are mainly responsible for customer satisfaction by providing technical services such as cutting. Assistants do not work directly with clients but assist the stylists. Tables 3 show the content and questions of the survey.

5 Analysis to Improve Employee Satisfaction

In this section, we identify the factors that contribute to employee satisfaction. First, we conducted a factor analysis to select our survey items. Then, based on the results we performed a basic tabulation. Next, we conducted a structural equation modeling to determine the causal relationship between the latent factors obtained from the factor analysis and employee satisfaction. Moreover, we then conducted a multiple population analysis to examine differences in response tendencies by job.

5.1 Selection of Questionnaire Items

First, we describe the results of our factor analysis. Here, we used promax rotation as the factor rotation method. We selected five latent factors based on the BIC and MAP criteria and extracted the top three question items with the highest factor loadings for each latent factor. The results of the factor analysis are shown in Table 4.

Using these results, we named each latent factor and used only the top three observed variables within the latent factor, as shown in Table 5.

We named ML1 Relation with boss because many of the questions in ML1 asked about the supervisor, such as whether the supervisor gives effective advice on the job and whether the supervisor takes in the opinions of the subordinates. ML 2 named Pride and Brand because many of the questions in ML 2 asked whether you feel that your work has a positive impact on the people around you and whether you feel that your work is valuable to society. ML 3 named Meeting because many of the questions in ML 3 were about Meeting, such as "Do you think the store conducts meaningful individual Meeting?" ML 4 named Organizational Understanding and Environment. Because many of the questions in ML 4 asked whether the employee understood the companies policies and the company environment, such as whether they understood and agreed with the company overall direction and decision-making, and whether they felt they could work in a secure environment in the future. ML5 named Compassion and Growth. The name Compassion and Growth was chosen because many of the questions asked whether the members of the store are making efforts and caring for the goal, such as whether they feel that they are all highly motivated to improve themselves and the organization, and whether they have consideration for their colleagues and try to take good care of them.

Table 3. Questionnaire Details

Items	summary
1. Clearly stated vision 2. Empathy with the vision 3. Specific plans 4. Clarification of jobs and responsibilities 5. Communication of information 6. Interest and concern 7. Attitude of listening 8. Effective advice 9. Consistency of words and actions 10. Trust	1 - 4 ask whether the boss has a vision 5 - 10 question the boss ability to empathize 11–25 asks about team and organizational understanding and organizational environment
11. Sense of purpose and goals 12. Consideration for customers 13. Consideration 14. Fellowship growth awareness 15. Understanding of company policy 16. Future security 17. Personal growth 18. Ability to think and speak for oneself 19. Ability to execute 20. Ability to continue 21. Climate that fosters strengths 22. Benchmark 23. Competitive salary 24. Environment of empowerment 25. Frequency of Meeting	11–25 asks about team and organizational understanding and organizational environment
26. Content of Meeting 27. Frequency of personal Meeting 28. Content of individual interviews 29. Job play frequency 30. Job play contents 31. Satisfaction	26–31 asks about Meeting and other initiatives

(continued)

Table 3. (*continued*)

Items	summary
32. Sense of accomplishment 33. Sense of growth 34. Sense of responsibility 35. Sense of self-determination 36. Meaningfulness 37. Sense of influence 38. Relationships 39. Appropriate evaluation 40. Mental and physical health 41. Hospitality 42. Pride 43. Growth mindset 44. Empathy for the brand	32–44 ask whether they are motivated by their job, such as pride in their job
45. Brand pursuit 46. Brand learning 47. Brand and customer satisfaction 48. Sense of belonging	45–48 asks about the brand
49. Sense of improvement 50. Suggestions 51. In-house evaluation 52. Job satisfaction	49–52 asks about making the company a better place to work and about job satisfaction

5.2 Summary Graphs

Next, we used the number of stylists and assistants in each store and the results from 5.1 to perform a basic tabulation of each latent factor for each store. The results are shown in Fig. 1 and Table 6.

Figure 1 shows the number of stylists and assistants in each store. The graph shows the number of stylists and assistants in each store. We can see that there are many assistants than stylists in Stores A, B, and J. The number of assistants differs significantly among stores. The number of employees differs greatly from store to store, with the largest store (D) having 30 employees and the smallest (H) having 3 employees.

Table 6 shows the mean satisfaction for each latent factor for each store: store F for ML1, ML2, and ML3, store E for ML4, and store I for ML5 showed high mean satisfaction. On the other hand, store C in ML1, store H in ML2, store D in ML3 and ML4, and store C in ML5 showed lower mean satisfaction. Store F had the highest mean satisfaction for all latent factors, while store F had the lowest mean satisfaction.

5.3 Causal Relationship between Employee Satisfaction and Latent Factors

Using the results of Sect. 5.1, we performed structural equation modeling. And we use a total of 21 variables: 15 observed variables obtained by factor analysis and 6 latent factors including employee satisfaction. The model used a quadratic factor analysis model, and

Table 4. Results of Factor Analysis

Question Items	Factor loading
Factor 1	
X8 Effective advice	0.954
X7 Attitude of listening	0.950
X10 Trust	0.941
X1 Clearly stated vision	0.892
X2 Empathy with the vision	0.882
X6 Interest and concern	0.824
X9 Consistency of words and actions	0.815
X3 Specific plans	0.727
X4 Clarification of jobs and responsibilities	0.645
X5 Communication of information	0.610
X38 Relationships	0.498
X39 Appropriate evaluation	0.448
X47 Brand and customer satisfaction	0.435
X24 Environment of empowerment	0.370
X40 Mental and physical health	0.304
X22 Benchmark	0.302
Factor 2	
X37 Sense of influence	0.827
X41 Hospitality	0.781
X36 Meaningfulness	0.760
X52 Job satisfaction	0.701
X33 Sense of growth	0.685
X42 Pride	0.676
X32 Sense of accomplishment	0.647
X49 Sense of improvement	0.587
X45 Brand pursuit	0.554
X46 Brand learning	0.523
X44 Empathy for the brand	0.411
X50 Suggestions	0.356
X31 Satisfaction	0.350
X34 Sense of responsibility	0.329

(continued)

Table 4. (*continued*)

Question Items	Factor loading
X35 Sense of self-determination	0.326
X18 Ability to think and speak for oneelf	0.099
Factor 3	
X28 Content of Individual Interviews	1.166
X29 Job play frequency	1.128
X26 Content of Meeting	0.744
X27 Frequency of personal Meeting	0.671
X25 Frequency of Meeting	0.465
X19 Ability to execute	0.292
Factor 4	
X15 Understanding of company policy	0.706
X30 Job play contents	0.585
X16 Future security	0.556
X17 Personal growth	0.382
X51 In-house evaluation	0.373
X23 Competitive salary	0.295
X43 Growth mindset	0.293
X48 Sense of belonging	0.288
Factor 5	
X14 Fellowship growth awareness	0.677
X11 Sense of purpose and goals	0.668
X13 Consideration	0.623
X12 Consideration for customers	0.559
X20 Ability to continue	0.332
X21 Climate that fosters strengths	0.314

covariate relationships were created to see the relationship between each latent factor. We tested covariate relationships for all latent factors, selected those with good values, and incorporated them into the model. The covariate relationships for the latent factors are shown in Table 7. We used GFI, CFI, and RMESEA as goodness-of-fit indices for the model, with values of GFI = 0.909, CFI = 0.952, and RMSEA = 0.070. The results of the structural equation modeling are shown in Fig. 2. The path coefficients for the structural equation modeling are standardized coefficients.

Table 5. List of latent factor naming

Factor	Survey items	Factor loading	Name
ML1	X8 Effective advice	0.954	Relation with boss
	X7 Attitude of listening	0.950	
	X10 Trust	0.941	
ML2	X37 Sense of influence	0.827	Pride and Brand
	X41 Hospitality	0.781	
	X36 Meaningfulness	0.760	
ML3	X28 Content of individual interviews	1.166	Meeting
	X29 Job play frequency	1.128	
	X26 Content of Meeting	0.744	
ML4	X15 Understanding of company policy	0.706	Organizational Understanding and Environment
	X30 Job play contents	0.585	
	X16 Future security	0.556	
ML5	X14 Fellowship growth awareness	0.677	Compassion and Growth
	X11 Sense of purpose and goals	0.668	
	X13 Consideration	0.623	

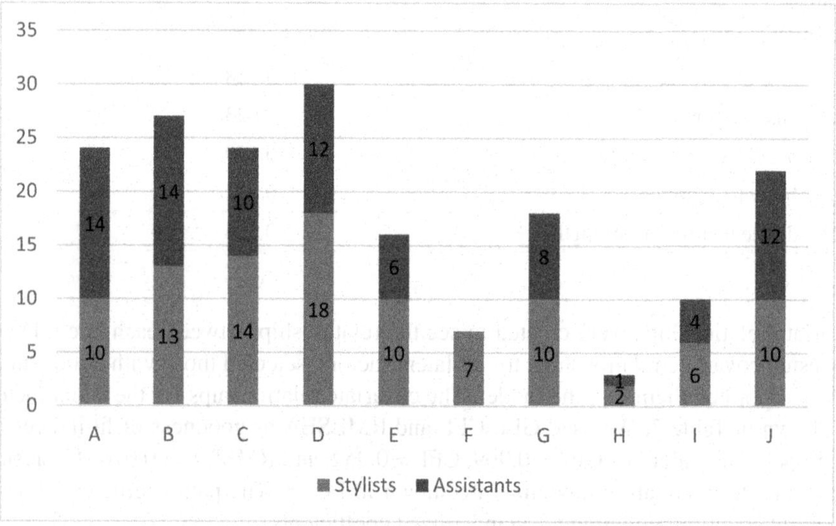

Fig. 1. Number of stylists and assistants in each store

Table 6. Questionnaire average of each latent factor per store

Store Factor	A	B	C	D	E	F	G	H	I	J
ML1	4.17	3.65	2.86	3.59	3.92	4.57	4.26	3.67	4.17	4.35
ML2	3.86	4.41	3.90	4.02	4.23	4.81	4.37	2.89	4.13	3.83
ML3	2.90	3.30	2.35	2.33	3.38	3.67	3.63	3.33	3.17	3.36
ML4	3.33	3.62	3.51	3.24	4.06	3.81	3.89	3.44	3.30	3.65
ML5	3.57	4.02	2.90	3.09	4.21	4.10	4.31	3.33	4.47	3.67
Average	3.57	3.80	3.11	3.26	3.96	4.19	4.09	3.33	3.85	3.77

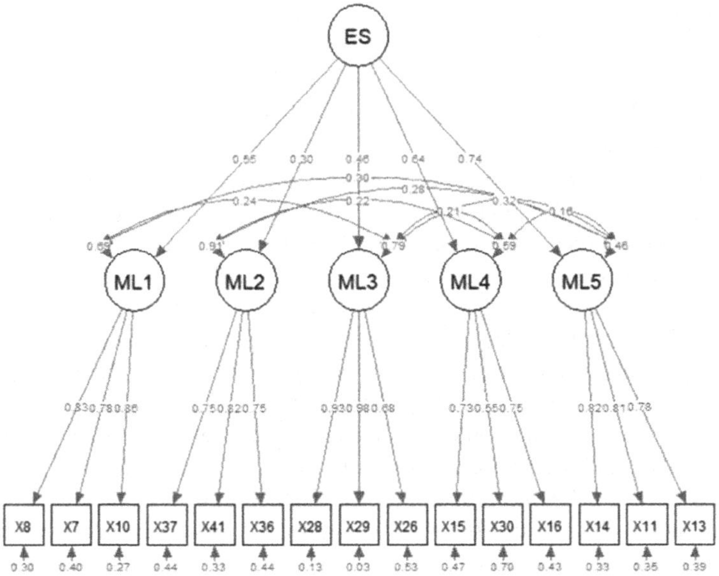

Fig. 2. Path diagram obtained by Structural Equation Modeling

Table 7 shows the good numerical values of the relationship between each latent factor. From these latent factors, we infer the relationship between each latent factor.

From Fig. 2, all five path coefficients for satisfaction (employee satisfaction) and the first-order latent factor have a causal relationship with a positive impact. Therefore, improving employee satisfaction is expected to improve each latent factor. The path coefficients from satisfaction to the latent factors in descending order are: ML5 (Compassion and Growth) 0.74 in first place, ML4 (Organizational Understanding and Environment) 0.64 in second place, ML1 (Relation with boss) 0.55 in third place, ML3 (Meeting) 0.46 in fourth place, ML2 (Pride and Brand) 0.30 were found to have a positive impact, in that order. This indicates that employee satisfaction has a strong causal relationship

Table 7. Some covariate relationships for each latent factor

covariance relation	
ML1 (Relation with boss)	ML3 (Meeting)
	ML5 (Compassion and Growth)
ML2 (Pride and Brand)	ML4 (Organizational Understanding and Environment)
	ML5 (Compassion and Growth)
ML3 (Meeting)	ML4 (Organizational Understanding and Environment)
	ML5 (Compassion and Growth)
ML4 (Organizational Understanding and Environment)	ML5 (Compassion and Growth)

with ML5 and ML4. Therefore, it can be said that improving employee satisfaction will significantly improve ML5 and ML4.

Next, we examine the covariate relationship of each latent factor: ML5 (Compassion and Growth) ↔ ML1 (Relation with boss), ML2 (Pride and Brand), ML3 (Meeting), and ML4 (organizational understanding and environment), ML5 shows a higher path coefficient than the other latent factors. ML1 was 0.30, ML2 was 0.28, ML3 was 0.32, and ML4 was 0.16, indicating that ML5 had an impact on all factors. This suggests that improving ML5 may affect other latent factors and improve other latent factors as well. Conversely, improving other latent factors may improve ML5. Therefore, we considered that ML5 is related to all the factors, and therefore, we found an influence of ML5 on all the factors. Next, focusing on the path coefficients of ML4 ↔ ML2 and ML3, we can see that ML2 and ML3 have a positive impact of 0.22 and 0.21, respectively. The impact of ML2 and ML3 was found in terms of understanding the content of one own work. The path coefficient of ML1 ↔ ML3 shows that ML3 has a positive impact of 0.24. This is because meeting is the place to communicate with superiors at work, and therefore, meeting influence the impression of superiors, and the higher impression of superiors leads to better "Meeting" with better contents.

This shows that each latent factor is not an independent entity. Each latent factor is composed of various elements. Therefore, we believe that it is important to look at employee satisfaction not only in terms of the items that we want to improve, but also in terms of other items from a bird eye view.

5.4 Multi Group Analysis by Employee jobs.

We conducted a Structural Equation Modeling on 100 stylists and 81 assistants. We hypothesized that because these two jobs have different job descriptions, the items on which they perceive satisfaction differ due to their influence, and thus there may be differences in response trends depending on the job. The values for each of the fit indices are GFI = 0.892, CFI = 0.970, and RMSEA = 0.049 for stylists. For assistants, GFI

= 0.849, CFI = 0.945, and RMSEA = 0.085. The results, respectively of the structural equation modeling for each job are shown in Fig. 3 and 4.

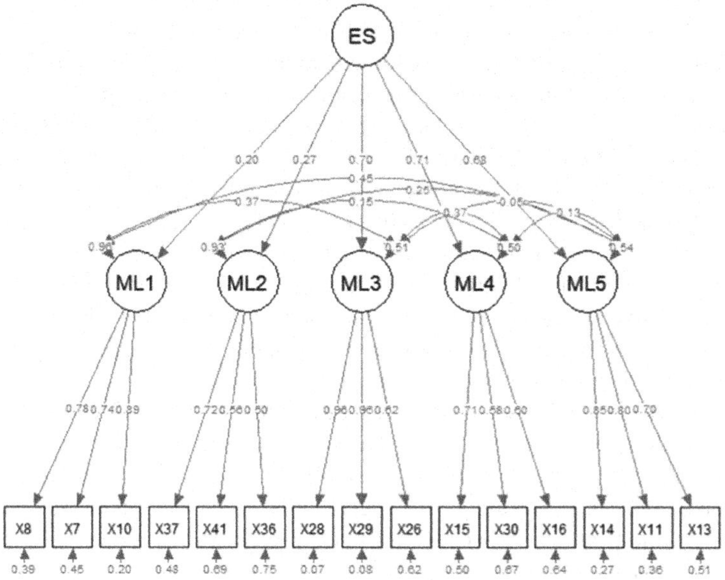

Fig. 3. Structural Equation Modeling by Stylist

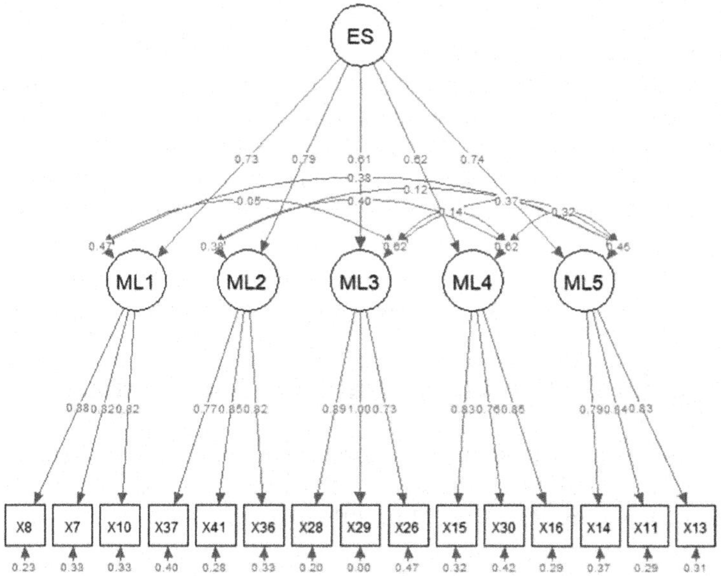

Fig. 4. Structural Equation Modeling with Assistant

From Fig. 3 and 4 show the results of the multi group analysis for stylists and assistants. Stylists showed high path coefficients for ML4 (Organizational Understanding and Environment), ML3 (Meeting), and ML5 (Compassion and Growth) based on employee satisfaction. On the other hand, ML2 (Pride and Brand) and ML1 (Relation with boss) showed low path coefficients. This may be since stylists have an important job in the store, such as styling for customers, and therefore employee satisfaction is directly related to their job, and ML4, ML3, and ML5 showed high path coefficients.

Covariate relationships showed large path coefficients for ML1 ↔ ML3, ML1 ↔ ML5, and ML3 ↔ ML4. ML1 and ML3 showed large path coefficients because the Relation with boss is easily formed in meeting where the stylist has many opportunities to speak.ML1 and ML5 showed large path coefficients because the boss concern for and communication with the subordinate led to the formation of an impression of the supervisor and the subordinate's feeling of consideration for the supervisor.ML3 and ML4 showed large path coefficients because we can conduct better meeting by learning organizational understanding and organizational environment, which leads to organizational understanding and organizational environment.

The assistants showed particularly large pass coefficients for ML2 (Pride and Brand), ML5 (Compassion and Growth), and ML1 (Relation with boss) based on employee satisfaction, but also large pass coefficients for ML4 (Organizational Understanding and Environment) and ML3 (Meeting). This suggests that employee satisfaction is strongly influenced by all latent factors because assistants oversee various tasks in the salon and have less years of service.

Covariate relationships showed large path coefficients for ML1 ↔ ML5, ML2 ↔ ML4, ML3 ↔ ML5, and ML4 ↔ ML5. ML1 and ML5 showed large path coefficients because, as with the stylists, the boss care and communication with the subordinate formed the Relation with boss, leading to the subordinates feeling of compassion. ML2 and ML4 showed large path coefficients because having pride in work and being brand-conscious of one work leads to better understanding of the organization and organizational environment, and learning about the organization and organizational environment leads to greater pride in one work and brand-consciousness of one work. ML4 and ML5 thought that the larger path coefficients were since the communication of caring and growth is formed by having meetings, and the better meetings can be held by improving the caring and growth. ML4 and ML5 showed larger path coefficients for having better meetings by improving organizational understanding and organizational environment and creating a more communicative and comfortable workplace by caring for coworkers.

6 Analysis for the Purpose of Identifying Good Customers

We used ID-POS data and performed basic tabulations to characterize the data. We then performed an RF analysis to determine the percentage of good customers per store. The data period used was 365 days from 04/01/2016 to 03/31/2017.

6.1 Basic Tabulation

We tabulated the number of transactions, the average number of transactions per person, and percentage of customers nominating stylist for each store. The results are shown in Table 8.

Table 8. Number of transactions, average number of transactions, and nomination rate for each store

Stores	Transactions	Average number of transactions	Nomination rate
A(24employees)	27,377	1140.71	97%
B(27employees)	32,970	1221.11	93%
C(24employees)	19,021	792.54	86%
D(30employees)	25,931	864.37	82%
E(16employees)	16,300	1018.75	87%
F(7employees)	12,852	1836.00	70%
G(18employees)	17,483	971.28	86%
H(3employees)	11,906	3968.67	81%
I(10employees)	9,371	937.10	82%
J(22employees)	20,889	949.50	92%
Average	19,410	1370.00	85%

Table 8 shows the number of transactions, average number of transactions per person, and nomination rate for each store. Store B has the largest number of transactions, store H has the largest average number of transactions, and store A has the largest nomination rate. On the other hand, store J had the largest number of transactions, store C had the largest average number of transactions, and store F had the lowest nomination rate.

6.2 RF Analysis

We performed an RF analysis to extract the percentage of good customers per store.

The reason why we chose RF analysis instead of RFM analysis is that we are dealing with a hair salon chain in this study. Since hair salon chains have a small difference in the amount of money that customers spend on purchases, we eliminated "M" and conducted RF analysis.

We used 04/01/2017, the day following 03/31/2017, the last day of the period, as the R indicator, and calculated the difference between the accounting date in the accounting history and the last purchase date during the period by the customer as a numerical value. We assign a value of 30 to each customer if the last purchase date was one month ago, and 365 to each customer if the last purchase date was one year ago. For the F indicator, the number of purchases was counted using customer IDs in the accounting history, and

Table 9. Ranking of each indicator

Rank	R	F
1	241 - 365	1
2	121 - 240	2 – 3
3	61 - 120	4 - 5
4	31 - 60	6 – 11
5	0 - 30	More than 12 times

the sum of the counts was used as the F indicator. The ranking criteria are shown in Table 9.

Based on this table we identify the best customers for each store. In this study we consider as good customers those whose R and F scores total more than 8 points.

6.3 Number of People per Rank in each Store

Using the rank criteria in Table 9, the total number of R and F customers for each store was expressed as a rank of 2–10. A rank of 8 or higher is then considered a good customer. The results are shown in Table 10.

Table 10. Number of people per rank overall and in each store.

Store Rank	Whole	A	B	C	D	E	F	G	H	I	J
2	938	93	111	147	178	105	80	98	46	74	68
3	2058	194	218	303	388	161	167	207	224	126	186
4	2185	190	238	287	417	182	161	204	213	153	239
5	1962	178	204	276	331	168	155	193	198	119	201
6	2109	212	236	275	354	187	165	203	194	131	220
7	2111	275	233	234	367	172	183	156	165	111	252
8	2104	288	288	220	325	168	162	180	131	128	227
9	2697	405	376	266	414	214	203	213	151	140	308
10	3206	478	583	298	382	269	199	293	171	153	351
	Total										
	19370	2313	2487	2306	3156	1626	1475	1747	1493	1135	2052
	Percentage of good customers										
	41%	51%	50%	34%	36%	40%	38%	39%	30%	37%	43%

Table 10 shows the number of people we determined for each rank overall and for each store. From this, we calculated the percentage of good customers overall and by store. Overall, the percentage of good customers was very large at 41%. Comparing the results for each store, store A and store B had particularly large rates of good customers, at more than 50%. On the other hand, store C and store H had low percentages of good customers, with store C at 34% and store H at 30%. Other stores had a good customer ratio close to 40%.

7 Relationship between employee satisfaction and customers

We considered employee satisfaction and customer purchasing trends in each store by using the results of basic aggregation of ID-POS data, factor analysis, aggregate results of average satisfaction using the results of structural equation modeling, and the rate of good customers obtained by RF analysis.

Table 11. Average satisfaction and customer purchase indicators for each store

Store Factor	A	B	C	D	E	F	G	H	I	J
ML1	4.17	3.65	2.86	3.59	3.92	4.57	4.26	3.67	4.17	4.35
ML2	3.86	4.41	3.90	4.02	4.23	4.81	4.37	2.89	4.13	3.83
ML3	2.90	3.30	2.35	2.33	3.38	3.67	3.63	3.33	3.17	3.36
ML4	3.33	3.62	3.51	3.24	4.06	3.81	3.89	3.44	3.30	3.65
ML5	3.57	4.02	2.90	3.09	4.21	4.10	4.31	3.33	4.47	3.67
	Average Satisfaction									
	3.57	3.80	3.11	3.26	3.96	4.19	4.09	3.33	3.85	3.77
	Average number of transactions									
	1141	1221	793	864	1019	1836	971	3969	937	950
	Nomination rate									
	97%	93%	86%	82%	87%	70%	86%	81%	82%	92%
	Percentage of good customers									
	51%	50%	34%	36%	40%	38%	39%	30%	37%	43%

Table 11 shows that the top three stores in terms of average satisfaction were F, G, and E, and the bottom three were C, D, and H. In terms of the average number of transactions, H, F, and B were the top three, and C, D, and I were the bottom three. In the nomination rate, A, B, and J were the top three, and F, H, D, and I were the bottom four with the same percentage. In the good customer rate, A, B, and J were in the top three, and H, C, and D were in the bottom three.

We found no effect of employee satisfaction on the number of transactions, the nomination rate, and the good customer rate in the stores with large employee satisfaction, but some negative effects on the average number of transactions and the good customer rate in the stores with low employee satisfaction. We therefore believe that low employee satisfaction affects customers purchasing behavior. Therefore, we can expect an increase in the number of transactions and the acquisition of good customers by creating and improving an environment with large employee satisfaction.

8 Conclusion

In this study, we used questionnaire data on workplace satisfaction of employees in a hair salon chain to identify factors that need to be improved to increase employee satisfaction, and ID-POS data to examine whether employee satisfaction affects customer purchasing behavior.

For the analysis, we used factor analysis to find common factors among the survey items and selected survey items. As a result, we obtained 5 latent variables and 15 observed variables, which we named ML1 (Relation with boss), ML2 (Pride and Brand), ML3 (Meeting), ML4 (Organizational Understanding and Environment), and ML5 (Compassion and Growth). We then used covariance structure analysis to create a path diagram to clarify the causal relationship with employee satisfaction. The results revealed that the potential factors influencing employee satisfaction are Compassion and Growth and organizational understanding and environment.

We also conducted a Multi group analysis for stylist and assistant jobs. Stylists indicated that the latent variables with large path coefficients from employee satisfaction were organizational understanding and environment, Meeting, and Compassion and Growth. Assistants showed that the latent variables with large path coefficients from employee satisfaction were Pride and Brand, which was particularly large, but all the path coefficients were large.

We then examined the relationship between employee satisfaction and customer purchase propensities using questionnaires and ID-POS data. We found that stores with large employee satisfaction did not affect the number of transactions, the nomination rate, or the good customer rate, while stores with low employee satisfaction had some negative effects on the average number of transactions and the good customer rate. From this result, we considered that increasing employee satisfaction would lead to an increase in the number of transactions and the acquisition of good customers.

Acknowledgment. We thank the hair salon for providing the data. This work was supported by JSPS KAKENHI Grant Number 21H04600 and 21K13385.

References

1. Ministry of Health, Labor and Welfare, Summary of Reports on Health Administration in FY 2020 .(2021)
2. Ministry of Internal Affairs and Communications, Population Projection (2022)
3. H. X., Wakabayashi, Y.: The Effect of Employee Satisfaction on Customer Satisfaction in the Retail Industry, An Empirical Analysis of a Food Supermarket Chain (2011)
4. Suzuki, K., Matsuoka, K.: The Relationship between Employee Satisfaction, Customer Satisfaction, and Financial Performance,An Examination of the Hospitality Industry (2014)

5. Herzberg, F.: Work and Humanity:Toyo Keizai Shinpousha (1968)
6. Takaya, K.: A Study on the Relationship between Employee Satisfaction, Good Customers and Corporate Performance (2012)

Investigating the Effect of Linguistic Features on Personality and Job Performance Predictions

Hung Le[1(✉)], Sixia Li[1], Candy Olivia Mawalim[1], Hung-Hsuan Huang[2], Chee Wee Leong[3], and Shogo Okada[1]

[1] Japan Advanced Institute of Science and Technology (JAIST), Nomi, Japan
{hungle,lisixia,candylim,okada-s}@jaist.ac.jp
[2] The University of Fukuchiyama, Fukuchiyama, Japan
hhhuang@acm.org
[3] Educational Testing Service, Princeton, USA
cleong@ets.org

Abstract. Personality traits are known to have a high correlation with job performance. On the other hand, there is a strong relationship between language and personality. In this paper, we presented a neural network model for inferring personality and hirability. Our model was trained only from linguistic features but achieved good results by incorporating transfer learning and multi-task learning techniques. The model improved the F1 score 5.6% point on the Hiring Recommendation label compared to previous work. The effect of different Automatic Speech Recognition systems on the performance of the models was also shown and discussed. Lastly, our analysis suggested that the model makes better judgments about hirability scores when the personality traits information is not absent.

Keywords: Personality Traits · Job Performance · Social Signal Processing · Natural Language Processing

1 Introduction

The way in which we perceive the world and how the world perceives us is largely influenced by our personality. Psychologists have studied human personalities for many decades, and the Big Five personality model is known as the best working hypothesis [17]. The Big Five model states that human personality differs across five dimensions: Openness, Conscientiousness, Extraversion, Agreeableness, and Emotional Stability (neuroticism). There are many situations where understanding one's personality is beneficial, such as in career coaching or in family conflict resolution. Prior research showed that there is also a strong relationship between a candidate's personality and their job performance [4,13]. Due to these advantages, companies are more and more interested in their candidates' personalities and projected job performance. However, the traditional method to evaluate

A. Coman and S. Vasilache (Eds.): HCII 2023, LNCS 14025, pp. 370–383, 2023.
https://doi.org/10.1007/978-3-031-35915-6_27

personality traits via filling out questionnaire forms is both subjective and time-consuming, so objective methods to automate this process are needed. To this end, machine learning (ML) models are developed for this task in recent years, for their ability to explore human multimodal behaviors.

Previous studies [7,19,21,24] have used both verbal and nonverbal behaviors to predict personality traits. Nonverbal behaviors features were found to be effective in predicting personality and hirability, however, data sets whose nonverbal features are predictive could be suffering from annotations bias (face attractiveness, perceived ages, etc.), and models could unintentionally learn the bias for making predictions [18]. As an attempt to overcome this problem, our work focuses on developing models for only linguistic features extracted from the videos. A neural network (NN) model is proposed to demonstrate that it is possible to simultaneously learn the personalities and job performance of an interviewee from the content of their speech. In addition, not much research [25] was dedicated to studying the relationship between the Big Five personality and the Hiring Recommendation label. In this work, we conducted experiments to show that when giving a model information about the speaker's personality, it could make better predictions about the Hiring Recommendation (hirability) label.

In the field of multimodal learning, Automatic Speech Recognition (ASR) systems are often used to convert speech from audio into text for processing. Different ASR systems may have different performance levels. Word Error Rate (WER), which is defined as the number of incorrectly recognized words divided by the total number of spoken words, is a common metric to evaluate ASR systems. ASRs errors influence NLP and personality trait modeling, but to what extent the influence affects post-processing tasks is not studied well [32]. Therefore, we also conducted experiments with transcriptions obtained from two different ASR systems (namely, Watson and Whisper) and discuss the results.

In summary, the main contributions are:

- A NN model for predicting personality traits and job interview performance is proposed. The model leverages a pre-trained large language model and the weighted linear sum of the losses function to carry out multi-task classification learning. Experimental results showed that the proposed model performed better than previous work when evaluated using the F1 score.
- The effect of two different ASR systems on the performances of different models was analyzed.
- This research is bridging the gap between computers and humans by improving computers' ability to predict human performance in job interview.

2 Related Work

The goal of multimodal machine learning can be defined as "to build models that can process and relate information from multiple modalities" [3]. There are many exciting works on multimodal learning such as works on visual question-answering systems [1,40] or image generation systems [36,37]. One of the fields that widely uses multimodal learning models is affective computing. In [27], the authors developed a framework to predict job interview performance using facial expressions, language, and prosodic information. [7] developed models to predict personality traits and hiring recommendation scores from monologue videos. [15] collected more than 7000 video job interviews for real positions and developed a hierarchical attention model (HireNet) to predict the hireability of the candidates.

One of the earliest research on computational hirability was conducted by [31]. This work found that it is possible to predict hirability scores from nonverbal features, and the interaction during the interview is more effective for the prediction than psychometric questionnaires data. Following work found that even nonverbal brief excerpts of interactions were still predictive of hirability impressions [29]. For many people, conducting job interviews is a stressful task. The authors of [11] explored the relationship between stress and hirability impressions, and individuals who are perceived as more stressful are more likely to get lower hirability scores. In [30], the authors collected a conversational video resumes dataset and developed a computational framework to predict first impressions, and the analysis showed that there are correlations between personality and hirability. A framework for improving the first impressions of hospitality students was proposed in [26]. Another feature-extraction framework was proposed in [33] to infer personality traits and hiring decisions.

The common features used to train predictive models are linguistic, acoustic, and visual features. Combining multiple modalities does not always mean much better results are obtained, though. In [7], fusing different modalities does not yield better results than models that only have text as the only modality. In [15], the authors stated that "more sophisticated fusion schemes are needed to improve on the monomodal results". One of the possible reasons is that by introducing more modalities, more noise is also introduced, making it more difficult for models to learn the useful signals. In this paper, we focus only on linguistic features to develop the models. This approach was also explored by [9], with the main difference being that our text comes directly from the speeches of interviewees and not from a chat-based interface.

Recent advances in machine learning come largely from the Transformer architecture [39] and its variants. The state of the art of many tasks was raised significantly by models built upon this architecture. In speech recognition, wav2vec2 [2] or Whisper models are approaching human accuracy and robustness. In NLP, large language models such as BERT [10], RoBERTa [23], or GPT-3 [6] do surprisingly well on the text classification task, along with other tasks. That being said, classical machine learning methods such as SVM [8] still have their place as a strong baseline, especially when the classes are clearly separated.

When developing models for large-corpus of conversational videos, it is not practical nor scalable to manually transcript the videos. Instead, an ASR system is usually used to convert speeches to text. In [32], three Japanese ASR systems were compared and their effects on the storytelling skill assessment were evaluated. To the best of our knowledge, no previous work has attempted to evaluate the effect of different ASR systems on personality traits and interview performance prediction models. Therefore, in this work, we extracted the text from two English ASR systems and analyzed the effect of the ASR error rate on the developed models.

3 Methodology

3.1 Predicting Personality from Linguistic Features

The Big Five traits theory was originally discovered by following the guidelines of the lexical hypothesis, which stated that we use language to encode the difference between people. Therefore, there is a strong relationship between language and personality traits [5]. Automatic personality recognition is one of the important tasks in the Personal Computing research field, as it has many implications in the emerging Human-Centered Artificial Intelligence scenarios.

Feature Representation. Two main approaches used to represent language are the closed-vocabulary approach and the open-vocabulary approach. In the closed-vocabulary approach, words are separated into predefined categories and the correlations between the number of words belonging to each category and personality are studied. The Linguistic Inquiry and Word Count (LIWC) [34] is one of the widely used lexicons in this approach. In the second approach, words and documents are usually converted into vector representations by a language model, and then the vector representations are inputted directly into machine learning models. In the proposed model, we used a large language model (LLM) named RoBERTa as the feature extractor. RoBERTa is an improved version of BERT [10], both of which are pre-trained LLMs based on the Transformer architecture [39]. Unlike the closed-vocabulary approach, where each word has only one concrete meaning, LLMs are capable of taking the word and its surrounding context into account when generating the embedding.

3.2 Dataset and ASR Systems

This work was conducted on the corpus shared by Chen el at. [7]. This corpus contains 1891 monologue videos from 260 interviewees, and each video was annotated with the perceived personality trait and holistic scores. A training set (1519 samples) and a test set (372 samples) were produced under the condition that no interviewee appears in both set. The original scores of the labels were in the 7-point Likert scale, but they are converted into two scores HIGH and LOW using the median scores as the thresholds. Figure 1 shows the training set score distributions of the labels before the conversion, and Table 1 shows the statistics of the labels after the conversion. One key observation from Fig. 1 is that the Hiring Recommendation scores follow the Gaussian distribution, while the Personality Traits scores follow the bimodal distribution.

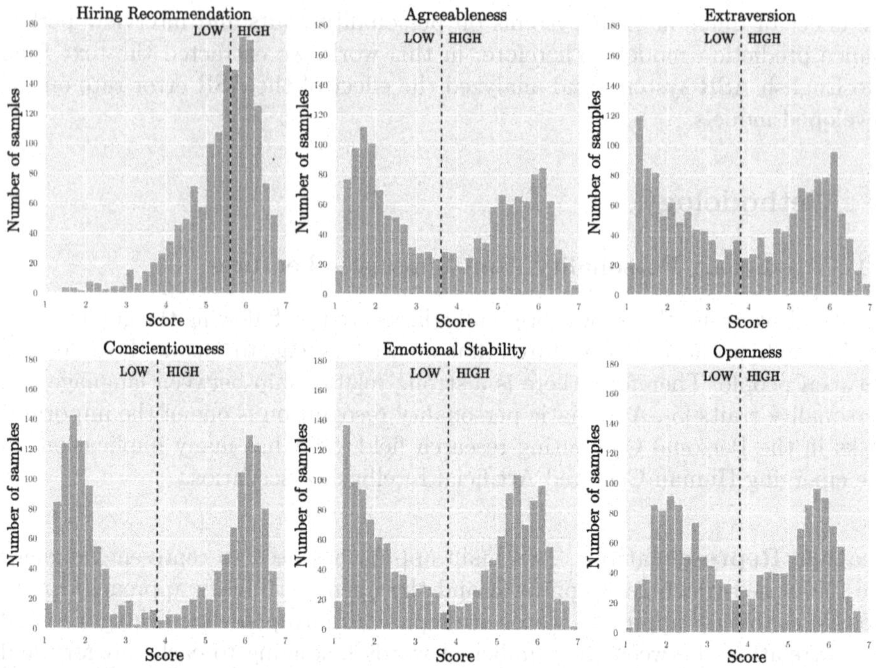

Fig. 1. The distributions of the labels on the training set before converting to HIGH and LOW classes. The dash lines indicate the median scores.

Table 1. The statistics of the labels after converted to HIGH and LOW classes

Label	Training Set		Test Set	
	HIGH	LOW	HIGH	LOW
Hiring Recommendation	773	746	191	181
Agreeableness	780	739	186	186
Extraversion	774	745	189	183
Conscientiousness	761	758	186	186
Emotional Stability	781	738	180	192
Openness	788	731	188	184

To convert the candidates' speech to text, two ASR systems were chosen: IBM Watson[1] (commercially available, transcription files were provided by the original authors of [7]), and OpenAI's Whisper system [35]. The WERs of the systems when calculated based on 22 manually transcribed random samples from the data set are 32.73% and 5.28%, and the average lengths of the transcriptions are 275 and 276 words, respectively.

[1] https://www.ibm.com/cloud/watson-text-to-speech.

3.3 Proposed Model: The Neural Network

In this paper, a neural network (NN) model was proposed as an alternative approach to the baseline model (the Support Vector Machine, to be introduced in Subsect. 3.4). Figure 2 shows the architecture of our model. Two main advantages of the neural network model compares to the baseline model are: more information can be encoded to the text embedding vector by the pre-trained language model, and only one model is trained for all six labels.

Since each candidate was given two minutes to answer a question, the answers came in form of a paragraph. We feed the paragraphs to RoBERTa [23] to obtain the paragraph embeddings. In this paper, we used the "roberta-base"[2] version, with the maximum input length set to 512 tokens. The output of this step is an embedding vector that has 768 dimensions. This embedding vector is then concatenated with the unique z-normalized numbers indicating the Speaker ID and the Question ID, resulting in a vector that has 770 dimensions (similar to the models proposed by [28]). The original (unnormalized) Speaker ID and Question ID are two unique integers indicating which speaker (interviewee) is answering which question. Since there are a total of 260 speakers and a maximum of 8 questions, the original Speaker ID ranges between 1 and 260, while the original Question ID ranges between 1 and 8. The Speaker ID and Question ID are inputted to the NN to provide the model with additional contextual information about the paragraph.

The 770 dimensions vector is then passed to four blocks of layers. Each of the first 3 blocks contains a Fully Connected (FC) layer, a LeakyReLU nonlinear activation layer, and a Dropout layer with a dropout probability of 0.5. The last block contains only a Fully Connected layer (FC_4). The first three FC layers are initialized using Kaiming initialization [14], while the FC_4 layer is initialized using Xavier initialization [12]. The final output is a vector that has 6 dimensions, corresponding to the six labels (the Hiring Recommendation and the Big Five personality traits).

The Loss Function. Since we formulated the problem as a multi-label classification problem, the Binary Cross-Entropy (BCE) loss is the natural choice for the loss function. However, the experiments showed that when BCE loss is naively applied, the model performs well on the Big Five labels, while performing poorly on the Hiring Recommendation label. The results suggest that the Hiring Recommendation label is more difficult to classify compared to other labels. Therefore, we modified the BCE loss to the weighted linear sum of the losses, which takes the formula:

$$\mathcal{L}_{total} = \sum_{i} w_i \mathcal{L}_i \tag{1}$$

where i is the label, $\mathcal{L}_i$ is the BCE loss with respect to label i, and w_i is the weighted parameter for $\mathcal{L}_i$. This loss function was previously used in multi-task

[2] https://huggingface.co/roberta-base.

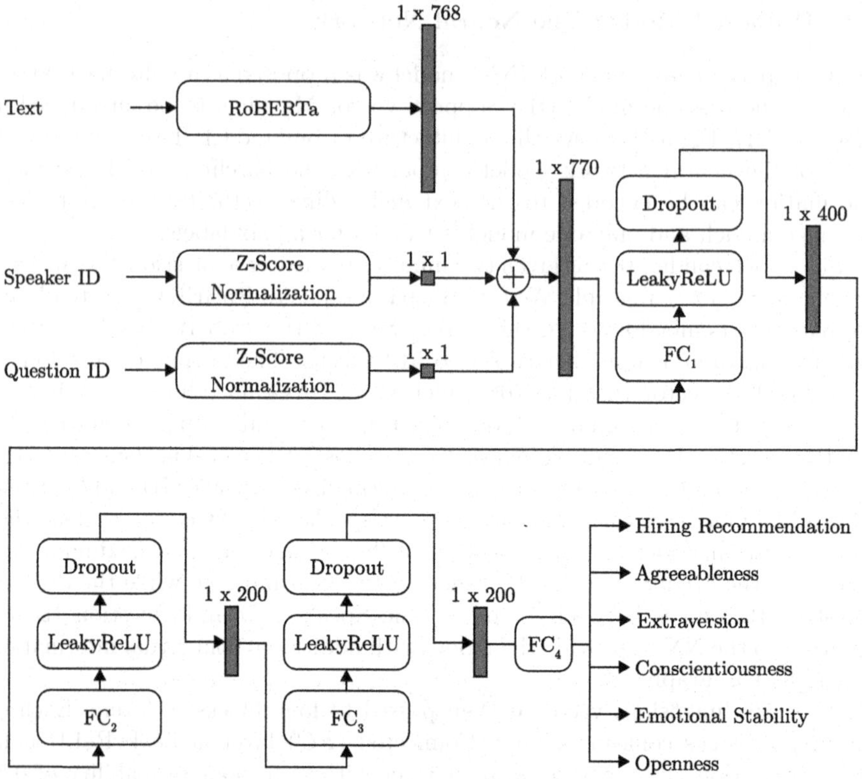

Fig. 2. The architecture of the neural network model ("FC" denotes the "Fully Connected" layer)

learning problems [20,22,38]. In our case, the concrete formula is:

$$\mathcal{L}_{total} = w_{hr}\mathcal{L}_{hr} + w_{ag}\mathcal{L}_{ag} + w_{ex}\mathcal{L}_{ex} + w_{co}\mathcal{L}_{co} + w_{em}\mathcal{L}_{em} + w_{op}\mathcal{L}_{op} \quad (2)$$

where the subscripts (*hr*, *ag*, *ex*, *co*, *em*, *op*) stand for the labels (hiring recommendation, agreeableness, extraversion, conscientiousness, emotional stability, openness), respectively.

Hyperparameters. Grid search was used for selecting the NN hyperparameters. To perform grid-search, roughly 20 percent of the original training set (298 samples) was separated to create the validation set. The separation was also performed under the condition that no speaker appears in both sets. Table 2 shows the best hyperparameters for the NN model.

Table 2. Training hyperparameters

Hyperparameter	Value
Batch Size	32
Optimizer	AdamW
β_1	0.9
β_2	0.99
ϵ	$1e-6$
Weight Decay	$1e-2$
AMSGrad	True
Training epoch	500
Max Learning Rate	$1e-2$
Learning Rate Scheduler	Cosine Annealing with Hard Restarts and Warm up
Number of restart cycles	2
Total training steps	24000
Warm-up steps	2400

3.4 Baseline Model: The Support Vector Machine

The Support Vector Machine (SVM) was chosen as the baseline model since this approach produced the best classifiers for this data set in previous work [7]. The general pipeline showed in [7] was followed: features are extracted from text using the Bag-of-Words model, then feed into the SVM. The Radius Basic Function (RBF) kernel was used in this study and grid-search was used for selecting the parameters C and γ from the following range [16]:

$$C \in \{2^{-5}, 2^{-3}, 2^{-1}, 1, 2^{1}, 2^{3}, 2^{5}, 2^{7}, 2^{9}\}$$

$$\gamma \in \{2^{-15}, 2^{-13}, 2^{-11}, 2^{-9}, 2^{-7}, 2^{-5}, 2^{-3}, 2^{-1}, 2^{1}, 2^{3}\}$$

The best parameters were chosen using 5-fold cross-validation on the training set, where the folds were separated under the same condition that the test set was separated.

4 Results

For the evaluation metric, the macro F1 measurement is reported (we found that the Precision and Recall scores are mostly equal to F1). Table 3 shows the experiment results of our methods. For the NN model, the table shows the average results of 5 runs with different random seeds.

Table 3. F1 scores on the test set

Label	Model			
	SVM		Neural Network	
	ASR System		**ASR System**	
	Watson (obtained from [7])	Whisper (ours)	Watson (ours)	Whisper (ours)
Hiring Recommendation	0.66	0.69	**0.716**	0.714
Agreeableness	0.84	0.85	0.838	**0.862**
Extraversion	0.78	0.80	**0.812**	0.802
Conscientiousness	0.86	0.86	0.85	**0.868**
Emotional Stability	0.83	0.84	0.85	**0.88**
Openness	0.81	0.83	0.828	**0.844**

5 Analysis and Discussion

Performance of the Proposed Model Compared to the Baseline Model. Table 3 shows that the performance of the proposed model is higher than the baseline models across all labels. The best results mostly come from the NN model trained on transcriptions from the ASR system with the lowest WER (Whisper). The highest F1 score for the Hiring Recommendation label is 0.716, which is a 0.056-point increment compared to previous work. For the Big Five personality trait labels, the gains range between 0.01 to 0.05 points.

Interpretation for the Improved Performance of the NN Model. When human annotators annotated the original videos, they did not watch the videos and annotated each of the labels separately. Instead, they watched a video once, and then annotated all the labels. Differing from the SVM models, the multi-label NN reassembled this process closely. In the SVM baseline, each model is separately trained with respect to each of the labels, so the Hiring Recommendation prediction model does not have access to the Personality Trait labels. On the other hand, the proposed NN model updated its weights from the feedback of all the labels at the same time, so the NN model can learn some relationships between the labels. To evaluate the effect of the Personality Trait labels on the model's ability to predict the Hiring Recommendation score, we conducted experiments with some changes to the weights of the loss function. In particular, we set the weights of the Personality Trait labels in Eq. 2 to zeros. We retrained the NN model on the Whisper's transcriptions and found that the 5-run average F1 score of the Hiring Recommendation label decreased to 0.696. This is similar to the results of the baseline model, where the Personality Trait labels also were not taken into account.

The Effect of ASR Systems on Models' Performance. With respect to different ASR systems, the results show that the SVM models benefited from the higher quality transcriptions, while it is not clear that the NN model received the same benefits. In the case of Hiring Recommendation and Extraversion labels, the NN model performed slightly worse when trained on higher-quality transcriptions. It is possible that the negative gains simply come from the randomization nature of NN models.

Sum of the BCE Losses. In Sect. 3.3, we mentioned that the weighted linear sum of the BCE losses function helped the model learn all labels efficiently. In this section, more details to support the claim are provided. By conducting parameter searches, our experiments show that when w_{hr} in Eq. 2 is 5 and w of each of the Big Five labels loss is 1, the model is able to learn all labels simultaneously. On the other hand, when all the weights in Eq. 2 are set to 1 (called the linear sum of the BCE losses function), the Hiring Recommendation label cannot be learned. Figure 3 shows the accuracy of the Hiring Recommendation label (the model was trained on Whisper's transcriptions) on the validation set when the weights are set in the two cases. The figure does not show the accuracy of the other labels since those are almost identical.

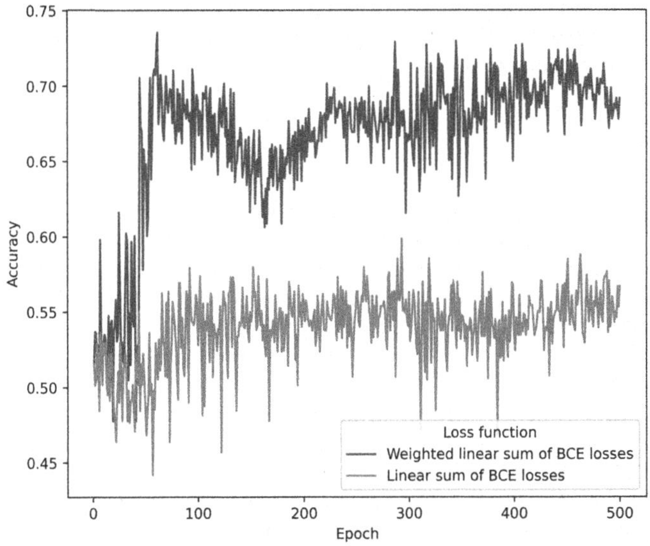

Fig. 3. The accuracy of the Hiring Recommendation label on the validation set when different weights are used for the loss function. The validation accuracy of the Big Five labels is omitted to simplify the figure.

6 Conclusion

In this work, we proposed a NN model for predicting personality traits and hiring recommendation scores. The experiment results showed that our NN architecture performs better than the baseline model. While the Big Five labels can be predicted quite accurately, predicting whether a candidate should be invited to an onsite interview is a much more challenging task. Our analysis showed that it is better to give the model can learn some relations between personality traits and the hiring recommendation labels. The effect of distinct ASR systems on the models' performances was also evaluated. We also found that the quality of the transcriptions only has little effect on the models' performance.

There are still some limitations to our approach. First, other modalities besides text were not considered. Secondly, our work is based on the assumption that the way people use their language in front of the camera is similar to real life. This is not always the case. In future work, we plan to incorporate other modalities such as visual and acoustic modalities into the NN model. Furthermore, in the context of HCI, more research is needed to understand how different types of people use their language differently in front of cameras.

Acknowledgements. This work was also partially supported by the Japan Society for the Promotion of Science (JSPS) KAKENHI (No. 22K21304, No. 22H04860 and 22H00536), JST AIP Trilateral AI Research, Japan (No. JPMJCR20G6) and JST Moonshot R&D program (JPMJMS2237-3). Hung is supported by the Japanese Government (MEXT) Scholarship.

References

1. Antol, S., et al.: Vqa: Visual question answering. In: Proceedings of the IEEE International Conference on Computer Vision, pp. 2425–2433 (2015)
2. Baevski, A., Zhou, H., Mohamed, A., Auli, M.: wav2vec 2.0: A framework for self-supervised learning of speech representations (2020). https://doi.org/10.48550/ARXIV.2006.11477
3. Baltrusaitis, T., Ahuja, C., Morency, L.P.: Multimodal machine learning: a survey and taxonomy. IEEE Trans. Pattern Anal. Mach. Intell. **41**, 423–443 (2019)
4. Barrick, M.R., Mount, M.K.: The big five personality dimensions and job performance: A meta-analysis. Pers. Psychol. **44**(1), 1–26 (1991). https://doi.org/10.1111/j.1744-6570.1991.tb00688.x
5. Boyd, R.L., Pennebaker, J.W.: Language-based personality: a new approach to personality in a digital world. Current Opinion in Behavioral Sciences **18**, 63–68 (2017). https://doi.org/10.1016/j.cobeha.2017.07.017, big data in the behavioural sciences
6. Brown, T.B., et al.: Language models are few-shot learners (2020). https://doi.org/10.48550/ARXIV.2005.14165
7. Chen, L., Zhao, R., Leong, C.W., Lehman, B., Feng, G., Hoque, M.E.: Automated video interview judgment on a large-sized corpus collected online. In: 2017 Seventh International Conference on Affective Computing and Intelligent Interaction (ACII), pp. 504–509 (2017). https://doi.org/10.1109/ACII.2017.8273646

8. Cortes, C., Vapnik, V.: Support-vector networks. Mach. Learn. **20**(3), 273–297 (sep 1995). https://doi.org/10.1023/A:1022627411411
9. Dai, Y., Jayaratne, M., Jayatilleke, B.: Explainable personality prediction using answers to open-ended interview questions. Front. Psychol. **13** (2022). https://doi.org/10.3389/fpsyg.2022.865841
10. Devlin, J., Chang, M.W., Lee, K., Toutanova, K.: Bert: Pre-training of deep bidirectional transformers for language understanding (2018). https://doi.org/10.48550/ARXIV.1810.04805
11. Finnerty, A.N., Muralidhar, S., Nguyen, L.S., Pianesi, F., Gatica-Perez, D.: Stressful first impressions in job interviews. In: Proceedings of the 18th ACM International Conference on Multimodal Interaction. pp. 325–332. ICMI '16, Association for Computing Machinery, New York, NY, USA (2016). https://doi.org/10.1145/2993148.2993198
12. Glorot, X., Bengio, Y.: Understanding the difficulty of training deep feedforward neural networks. In: Teh, Y.W., Titterington, M. (eds.) Proceedings of the Thirteenth International Conference on Artificial Intelligence and Statistics. Proceedings of Machine Learning Research, vol. 9, pp. 249–256. PMLR, Chia Laguna Resort, Sardinia, Italy (13–15 May 2010)
13. Goodstein, L.D., Lanyon, R.I.: Applications of personality assessment to the workplace: a review. J. Bus. Psychol. **13**, 291–322 (1999). https://doi.org/10.1023/A:1022941331649
14. He, K., Zhang, X., Ren, S., Sun, J.: Delving deep into rectifiers: Surpassing human-level performance on imagenet classification. In: 2015 IEEE International Conference on Computer Vision (ICCV), pp. 1026–1034 (2015). https://doi.org/10.1109/ICCV.2015.123
15. Hemamou, L., Felhi, G., Vandenbussche, V., Martin, J.C., Clavel, C.: Hirenet: A hierarchical attention model for the automatic analysis of asynchronous video job interviews. In: Proceedings of the AAAI Conference on Artificial Intelligence, vol. 33, pp. 573–581 (07 2019). https://doi.org/10.1609/aaai.v33i01.3301573
16. Hsu, C.W., Chang, C.C., Lin, C.J.: A practical guide to support vector classification. Tech. rep., Department of Computer Science, National Taiwan University (2003). http://www.csie.ntu.edu.tw/ cjlin/papers.html
17. John, O.P., Srivastava, S.: The big five trait taxonomy: History, measurement, and theoretical perspectives (1999)
18. Junior, J.C.S.J., Lapedriza, A., Palmero, C., Baró, X., Escalera, S.: Person perception biases exposed: Revisiting the first impressions dataset. In: 2021 IEEE Winter Conference on Applications of Computer Vision Workshops (WACVW), pp. 13–21 (2021). https://doi.org/10.1109/WACVW52041.2021.00006
19. Katada, S., Okada, S.: Biosignal-based user-independent recognition of emotion and personality with importance weighting. Multimedia Tools Appl. **81**(21), 30219–30241 (sep 2022). https://doi.org/10.1007/s11042-022-12711-8
20. Kendall, A., Gal, Y., Cipolla, R.: Multi-task learning using uncertainty to weigh losses for scene geometry and semantics (2017). https://doi.org/10.48550/ARXIV.1705.07115
21. Kwon, S., Choeh, J.Y., Lee, J.W.: User-personality classification based on the non-verbal cues from spoken conversations. Int. J. Comput. Intell. Syst. **6**, 739–749 (05 2013). https://doi.org/10.1080/18756891.2013.804143
22. Liao, Y., Kodagoda, S., Wang, Y., Shi, L., Liu, Y.: Understand scene categories by objects: A semantic regularized scene classifier using convolutional neural networks. In: 2016 IEEE International Conference on Robotics and Automation (ICRA), pp. 2318–2325. IEEE Press (2016). https://doi.org/10.1109/ICRA.2016.7487381

23. Liu, Y., et al.: Roberta: A robustly optimized bert pretraining approach (2019). https://doi.org/10.48550/ARXIV.1907.11692
24. Mawalim, C.O., Okada, S., Nakano, Y.I., Unoki, M.: Multimodal bigfive personality trait analysis using communication skill indices and multiple discussion types dataset. In: Meiselwitz, G. (ed.) Social Computing and Social Media. Design, Human Behavior and Analytics - 11th International Conference, SCSM 2019, Held as Part of the 21st HCI International Conference, HCII 2019, Orlando, FL, USA, July 26–31, 2019, IN: Proceedings, Part I. Lecture Notes in Computer Science, vol. 11578, pp. 370–383. Springer (2019). https://doi.org/10.1007/978-3-030-21902-4_27
25. Mujtaba, D.F., Mahapatra, N.R.: Multi-task deep neural networks for multimodal personality trait prediction. In: 2021 International Conference on Computational Science and Computational Intelligence (CSCI), pp. 85–91 (2021). https://doi.org/10.1109/CSCI54926.2021.00089
26. Muralidhar, S., Nguyen, L.S., Frauendorfer, D., Odobez, J.M., Schmid Mast, M., Gatica-Perez, D.: Training on the job: Behavioral analysis of job interviews in hospitality. In: Proceedings of the 18th ACM International Conference on Multimodal Interaction, pp. 84–91. ICMI '16, Association for Computing Machinery, New York, NY, USA (2016). https://doi.org/10.1145/2993148.2993191
27. Naim, I., Tanveer, M., Gildea, D., Hoque, E.: Automated prediction and analysis of job interview performance: The role of what you say and how you say it (05 2015). https://doi.org/10.1109/FG.2015.7163127
28. Nakano, Y.I., Hirose, E., Sakato, T., Okada, S., Martin, J.C.: Detecting change talk in motivational interviewing using verbal and facial information. In: Proceedings of the 2022 International Conference on Multimodal Interaction, pp. 5–14. ICMI '22, Association for Computing Machinery, New York, NY, USA (2022). https://doi.org/10.1145/3536221.3556607
29. Nguyen, L., Gatica-Perez, D.: I would hire you in a minute: Thin slices of nonverbal behavior in job interviews, pp. 51–58 (11 2015). https://doi.org/10.1145/2818346.2820760
30. Nguyen, L., Gatica-Perez, D.: Hirability in the wild: analysis of online conversational video resumes. IEEE Trans. Multimed. **18**, 1422–1437 (07 2016). https://doi.org/10.1109/TMM.2016.2557058
31. Nguyen, L.S., Frauendorfer, D., Mast, M.S., Gatica-Perez, D.: Hire me: computational inference of hirability in employment interviews based on nonverbal behavior. IEEE Trans. Multimedia **16**(4), 1018–1031 (2014). https://doi.org/10.1109/TMM.2014.2307169
32. Okada, S., Komatani, K.: Investigating effectiveness of linguistic features based on speech recognition for storytelling skill assessment. In: Mouhoub, M., Sadaoui, S., Ait Mohamed, O., Ali, M. (eds.) Recent Trends and Future Technology in Applied Intelligence, pp. 148–157. Springer International Publishing, Cham (2018)
33. Okada, S., Nguyen, L., Aran, O., Gatica-Perez, D.: Modeling dyadic and group impressions with intermodal and interperson features. ACM Trans. Multimed. Comput., Commun. Appl. **15**, 1–30 (01 2019). https://doi.org/10.1145/3265754
34. Pennebaker, J., Boyd, R., Jordan, K., Blackburn, K.: The development and psychometric properties of LIWC2015. University of Texas at Austin (2015). https://doi.org/10.15781/T29G6Z
35. Radford, A., Kim, J.W., Xu, T., Brockman, G., McLeavey, C., Sutskever, I.: Robust speech recognition via large-scale weak supervision (2022). https://doi.org/10.48550/ARXIV.2212.04356

36. Ramesh, A., et al.: Zero-shot text-to-image generation (2021) arxiv:2102.12092
37. Rombach, R., Blattmann, A., Lorenz, D., Esser, P., Ommer, B.: High-resolution image synthesis with latent diffusion models (2021)
38. Uhrig, J., Cordts, M., Franke, U., Brox, T.: Pixel-level encoding and depth layering for instance-level semantic labeling. In: German Conference on Pattern Recognition (2016)
39. Vaswani, A., et al: Attention is all you need. In: Proceedings of the 31st International Conference on Neural Information Processing Systems, pp. 6000–6010. NIPS'17, Curran Associates Inc., Red Hook, NY, USA (2017)
40. Wu, Q., Teney, D., Wang, P., Shen, C., Dick, A., Van Den Hengel, A.: Visual question answering: a survey of methods and datasets. Comput. Vis. Image Underst. **163**, 21–40 (2017)

Apply CNN Style Transformation on Industry 4.0

I Xuan Lu[1], Yicheng Cai[1], Boxu an Peng[1], Zhi-Xian Chen[1], Tai-Xiang Luo[1], and Yung-Hao Wong[1,2](✉)

[1] Minghsin University of Science and Technology, Xinfeng, 30401 Hsinchu County, Taiwan
yvonwong@must.edu.tw

[2] National Yang Ming Chiao Tung University, 1001 University Road ROC, Hsinchu 30010, Taiwan

Abstract. This project uses AI (artificial intelligence) rendering technology to realize how to present a photo in different forms of style. In a python environment, we establish a style transfer, inputting an original image for the software to recognize, then putting in a rendered style image for the software to perform the program. After 500 cycles are executed, the style will not have a stable form as the AI is evolving. By the time it reaches 1000 images, the algorithm has already remembered the common points of the images and grasped its own style, indicated by the gradual convergence of the loss function. The software will then produce different styles of rendered images.

Keywords: AI · style transfer · rendering technology

1 Introduction

AI is a product that aggregates data into a crystallization of wisdom, and the algorithm itself is a way of proving itself by learning wisdom. The final outcome is AI. By repeatedly aggregating vast amounts of data, it eventually becomes its own wisdom, with learning abilities far surpassing those of humans.

There has been a misconception in recent years that AI has been fully developed in a short period of time, but in fact, it has gone through three waves and taken nearly 50 years. The prototype of artificial intelligence was proposed by John McCarthy and three others on August 31, 1956, during a month-long conference at Dartmouth College, which sparked the first wave of enthusiasm. The first Perceptron was established in 1957, but it was ineffective. Due to a lack of funding, progress in AI was slow until 1980, when the problem of neural networks was solved and the second wave of excitement began. See Fig. 1

The Expert Systems in 1980 tied up the current hardware infrastructure and could not utilize AI effectively, leading to a gap between investment and results. By 1993, AI was once again put on hold.

The most critical moment was in 2012 when AlexNet neural network, developed by the University of Toronto, performed well in academic competitions and renewed interest in the possibilities of AI.

A. Coman and S. Vasilache (Eds.): HCII 2023, LNCS 14025, pp. 384–400, 2023.
https://doi.org/10.1007/978-3-031-35915-6_28

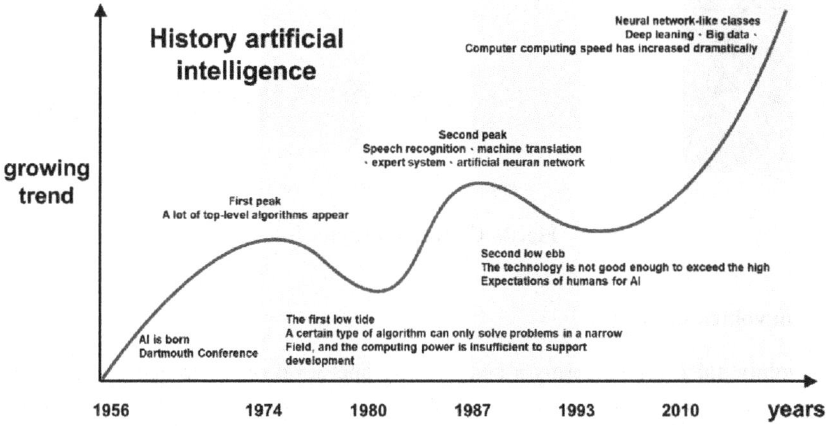

Fig. 1. The rise and fall of AI

Style transfer technology was proposed by Leon A. Gatys, Alexander S. Ecker, and Matthias Bethge in 2015. They described a method for using deep learning techniques to convert an image's style to another style in the paper "A Neural Algorithm of Artistic Style". The algorithm uses a Convolutional Neural Network (CNN)-deep learning model that extracts features of an image through convolution and pooling operations. By using two different CNN models, one for extracting the content features of the image and the other for extracting the style features, the algorithm can combine the two styles to create a new image.

2 Convolutional Neural Network, CNN

It is a deep learning model used for image processing [1, 2]. It has a structure similar to a traditional artificial neural network but with unique layers including convolution and pooling layers. The structure of a CNN usually includes an input layer, many combination of convolution layers, pooling layers and fully connected layers, etc., finally a output layer. See Fig. 2. During training, weights are continually adjusted through backpropagation algorithms so that the model can make accurate predictions. Its main advantage is its ability to capture local features in an image, making it particularly suitable for image recognition and classification tasks such as self-driving vehicles, face recognition, handwriting recognition, etc.

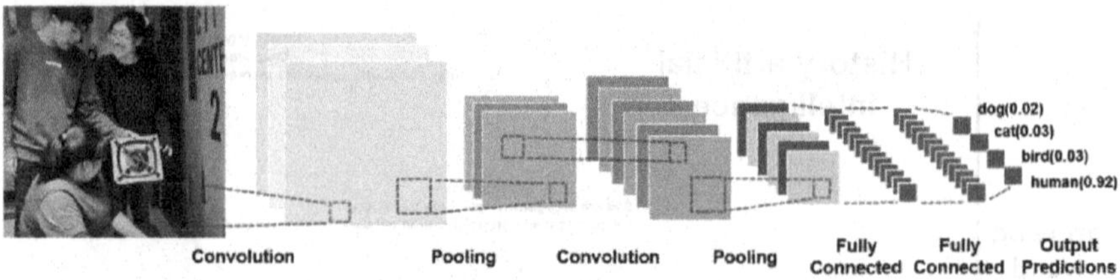

Fig. 2. CNN learning process

2.1 Convolutional Layer

A convolutional layer performs a convolution operation on an image using a weight matrix, filtering each sub region of the image, see Fig. 3. In one convolutional layer, each convolutional kernel is used to perform a convolution on different subregions of the image, capturing different features in the image. Convolutional layers are often shared between two models, one model being responsible for extracting local features from the original image, and the other being responsible for recombining these features into an image with a new style. By continually adjusting the weights of the model, the model can learn the mapping function needed to transform the style.

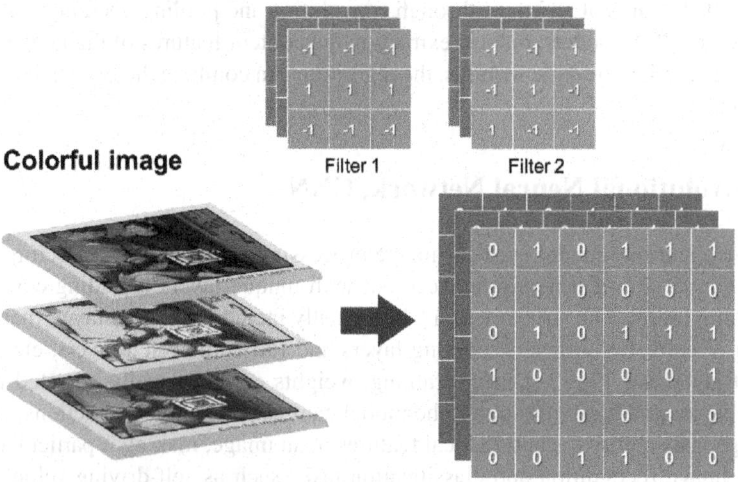

Fig. 3. Input image.

In a convolutional layer, the input image is divided into many small regions, each of which is called a receptive field. Each convolutional kernel has a corresponding receptive field and slides on the input image to perform convolutional operations on each receptive field, see Fig. 4.

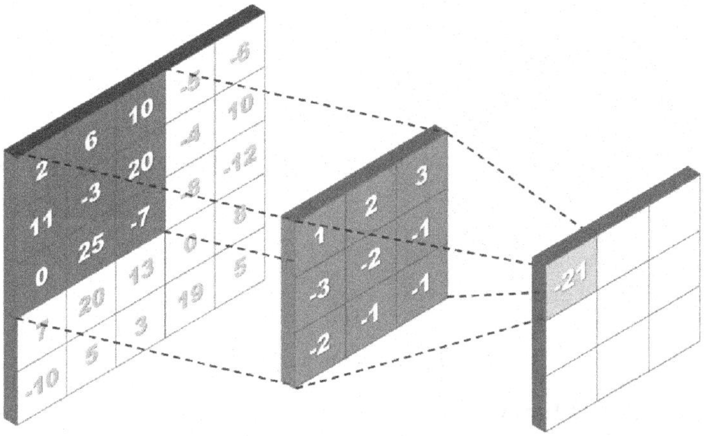

Fig. 4. Activation map.

In the convolution operation, each element of the convolutional kernel is multiplied with the corresponding element in the receptive field and then the products are added up to get the output of the convolutional layer. This output is a new matrix, where each element in it represents the presence or not of a specific feature in the receptive field.

The convolutional layer can be combined with other layers such as pooling layers and fully connected layers to build more complex models. In addition, the convolutional layer can also utilize residual structures or expand convolution structures to enhance the performance of the model.

2.2 Pooling Layer

In style transfer, the pooling layer is mainly responsible for compressing the image dimension by subsampling different regions of the image, reducing the image size. The most common pooling layers are the max pooling layer [3] and average pooling layer [4]. The max pooling layer takes the maximum value from each region of the input matrix, while the average pooling layer calculates the average value of each region.

The pooling layer takes a matrix as input and uses a small matrix, also known as a pooling window, to slide and traverse the input matrix. At each position, the pooling window captures a region and calculates the output value using the maximum or average value. This output value is stored in the output matrix and the size of the output matrix is smaller than the input matrix. See Fig. 5.

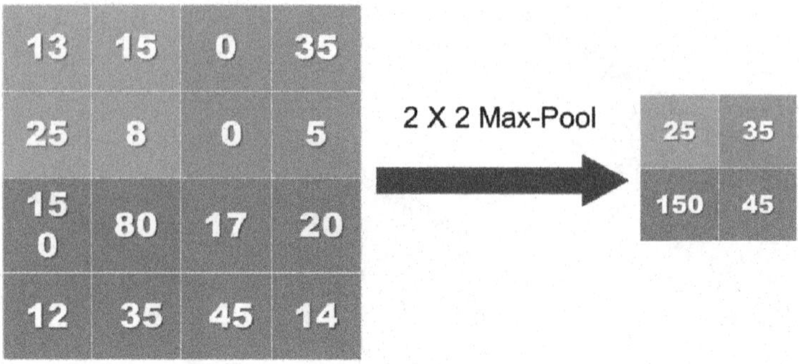

Fig. 5. Pooling Layer

2.3 Fully Connected Layer

The fully connected layer [5] is a common component of deep learning models that contains multiple neurons and each neuron in the current layer is connected to every neuron in the previous layer. The term "fully connected" refers to the fact that each neuron receives input from all neurons in the previous layer and produces an output that is used as input for all neurons in the next layer. These layers are typically used at the end of a CNN to make predictions based on the features extracted by the convolutional and pooling layers. The fully connected layers allow the network to learn complex, non-linear relationships between the features, and to make predictions based on those relationships.

In the fully connected layer, the input image undergoes a series of transformations to extract useful features and classify the image. These transformations are performed through the weights and biases of the neurons and are achieved by performing matrix multiplication and addition operations on the input image. See Fig. 6.

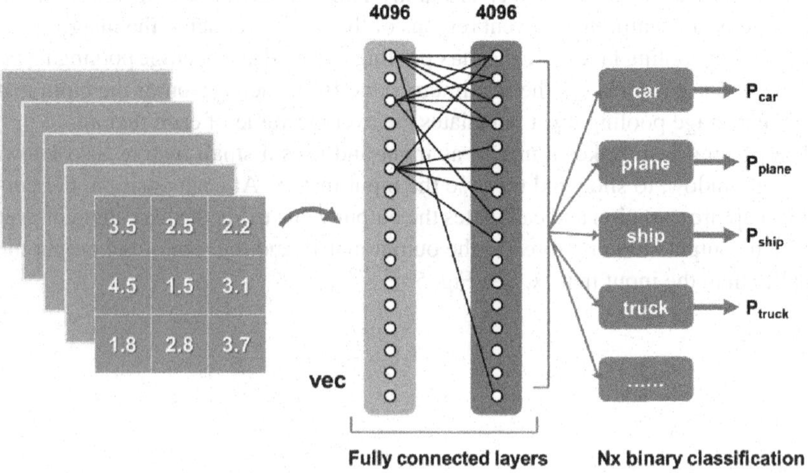

Fig. 6. Fully connected layer.

The output of a fully connected layer is typically a vector of length equal to the number of categories, where each element represents the probability that the image belongs to a specific category, and the final prediction of the image's category can be made using the maximum value in the output vector.

3 Featured Content

3.1 Introduction to Neural Network.

AI is composed of three parts, each part focuses on Artificial Intelligence, Machine Learning [6] and Deep Learning [7]. By reducing the scope of learning to a specific area and focusing on specific algorithms, artificial intelligence extends to machine learning and further extends to deep learning algorithms in machine learning. This project focuses on deep learning.

Deep learning itself is complex and consists of countless neurons. The neurons that transmit messages stand out with a thin, long axon that transmits electrical signals, and when the message touches the dendrite of another neuron, the dendrite receives the chemical message after which the axon continues to transmit the message. A few neurons cannot form artificial intelligence, only with tens of thousands or even more neurons can it be formed. See Fig. 7 and Fig. 8.

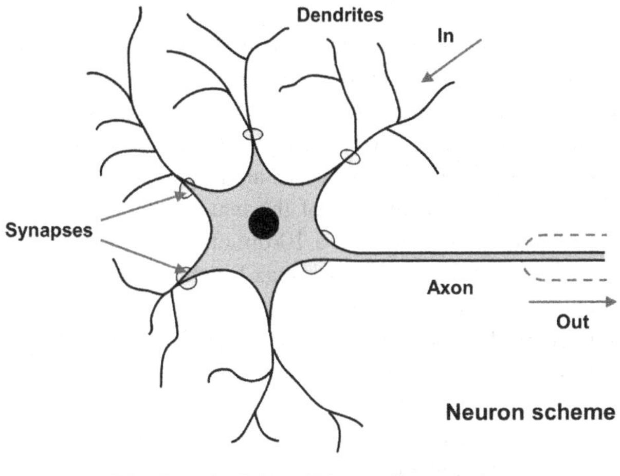

Fig. 7. Principles of Neuron Propagation

Using the image as an example, the number 3 is a 28x28 two-dimensional pattern that is transformed into 784 neurons using a matrix. There are only 10 output neurons at the bottom, and it is assumed that the answer to this number is within 0–9, with a total of 10 possible answers.

$H1 = \text{relu}(X \times W1 + b1)$ is the formula for creating the input layer and hidden layer. The input layer X is responsible for receiving messages and has 784 neurons, while the hidden layer h is an internal neuron with 256 neurons.

The weight w1 is the axon of the neuron responsible for input and output functions, that is, the transmission and transfer of information. $784 \times 256 = 200704$, to allow the

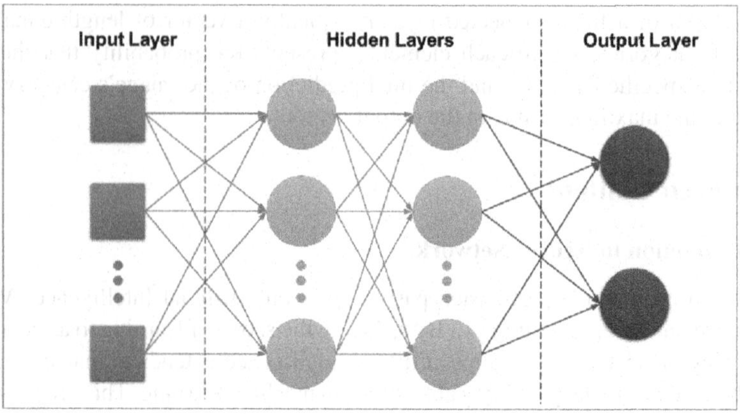

Fig. 8. How a multilayer perceptron works

two-layer neurons to connect with each other, 200704 axons are required, and the bias value b1 (bias) is at the end of the neuron, the more neurons, the better the message transmission, so the more biases there are. Since the hidden layer is composed of 256 neurons, the bias is a 256-dimensional vector, and after the relu function calculation, if it exceeds the expected value, it will transmit the electricity.

Y = softmax (h1 x W2 + b2) is the formula for creating the hidden layer and output layer.

The hidden layer h1 is an internal neuron with 256 neurons, and the output layer y simulates the output neuron. There are 0–9 results, with a total of 10 neurons, and the weight w2 is the axon of the neuron responsible for input and output functions, that is, the transmission and transfer of information. 256x10 = 2560, to allow the two-layer neurons to connect with each other, 2560 axons are required.

The bias value b2 (bias) is at the end of the neuron, the more neurons, the better the message transmission, and the bias is a 10-dimensional vector because the hidden layer is composed of 10 neurons, and the softmax function calculation will transmit the electricity if it exceeds the expected value.

The definition of the loss function for the original image. The loss function for the original image has various forms, but its main purpose is to make the transformed image as similar as possible to the original image. This part of the loss function can use forms such as (mean squared error) or (cross-entropy), which is the "difference in features between the original image and the synthesized image," as shown in the following formula, Eq. (1).

$$L_{content}(\vec{p}, \vec{x}, l) = \frac{1}{2}\sum_{i,j}(F_{ij}^{l} - P_{ij}^{l})^{2} \tag{1}$$

Equation (1), where P is the feature vector of the original image content and F is the feature vector of the composite image content.

Define the loss function for the style image, the loss function for the style image calculates the difference between the transformed image and the style image, that is, the "difference in features between the style image and the synthesized image", and the formula is as follows, Eq. (2)

$$E_t = \frac{1}{4N_1^2 M_1^2} \sum_{ij} (G_{ij}^l - A_{ij}^l)^2 \tag{2}$$

Equation (2), where A is the feature vector of the original image style and G is the feature vector of the composite image style.

Total loss function = Loss function for the original image + Loss function of the style image. Minimizing the "total loss function" can lead to obtaining the feature vectors of the synthesized image, and then it can be restored to the image by computing the partial derivatives of each using gradient descent method, the formula is as follows Eq. (3) and Eq. (4).

$$\frac{\partial \text{Lcontent}}{\partial F_{ij}^l} = \begin{cases} (F^l - P^l)_{ij} \; if \; F_{ij}^l > 0 \\ 0 \; if \; F_{ij}^l < 0. \end{cases} \tag{3}$$

Equation (3), the partial differential equation of the original image.

$$\frac{\partial E_l}{\partial F_{ij}^l} = \begin{cases} \frac{1}{N_l^2 M_l^2} \left((F^l)^T (G^l - A^l) \right)_{ji} & if \; F_{ij}^l > 0 \\ 0 & if \; F_{ij}^l < 0 \end{cases} \tag{4}$$

Equation (4), the partial differential equation of the original image.

3.2 Style Conversion Code

Let's get started. First, we'll use Jupyter Notebook to execute the entire network (project). Jupyter Notebook is an interactive environment that allows developers to write, test, run, debug, and record the process of coding and results (Fig. 9).

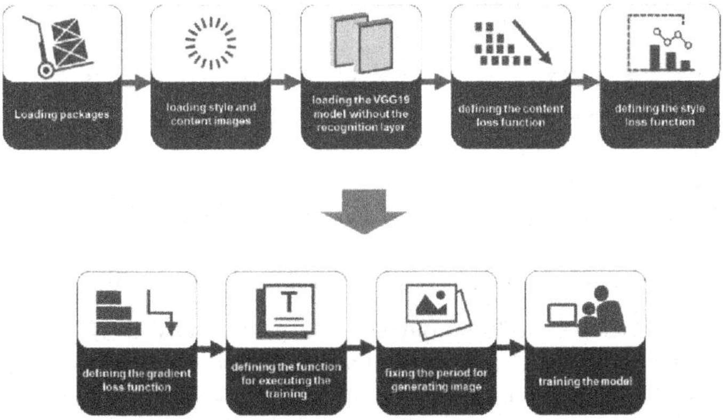

Fig. 9. Code Flowchart

Before we start the implementation, you need to first import all necessary libraries and packages. These libraries and packages allow you to use specific features in your code, which we will later use (Fig. 10).

```
import os
import time
import sys
import matplotlib.pyplot as plt
from PIL import Image
import numpy as np
import tensorflow as tf
from tensorflow.keras.applications.vgg19 import VGG19
from tensorflow.keras.preprocessing.image import load_img
from tensorflow.keras.preprocessing.image import img_to_array
```

Fig. 10. Load related packages. References and Citations [8]

Loading the content image refers to reading in an image and storing it in memory for further processing and analysis, which is a crucial step in style transfer because the content image is to be transformed into a new image with a different style (Fig. 11).

```
content_path = "Photosoflife.jpg"
content_image = load_img(content_path)
plt.imshow(content_image)
plt.axis('off')
plt.show()
```

Fig. 11. Load content image References and Citations [8]

Loading the style image involves reading in an image and storing it in memory for use during the style transfer process. This is a critical step in style transfer as the style image will be used to impart an artistic style to the content image (Fig. 12).

```
style_path = "TheStarryNight.jpg"
style_image = load_img(style_path)
plt.imshow(style_image)
plt.axis('off')
plt.show()
```

Fig. 12. Load style image References and Citations [8]

VGG19 [9] VGG19 is a deep convolutional neural network (CNN) architecture developed by the computer vision research team at the University of Oxford in 2014. VGG19 has 19 convolutional layers and 3 fully connected layers. Convolutional layers use 3x3 convolutional kernels with a constant stride of 1, and max pooling layers are added between each layer to reduce the size of the image and preserve important features. VGG19 uses smaller convolutional kernels and more convolutional layers, which allows it to better capture fine details in images. However, this also makes the training time of VGG19 longer. After training, VGG19 can distinguish up to a thousand objects. This paper uses a pre-trained VGG19 to extract the content and style of the user-inputted image, and then combines them to generate the stylized image. VGG19 is a pre-trained Convolutional Neural Network (CNN) model developed by the Visual Geometry Group at the University of Oxford. It is a 19-layer network trained on a large dataset of natural images, and it has been widely used for a variety of computer vision tasks, such as image classification, object detection, and semantic segmentation.

One of the main applications of VGG19 is transfer learning. This is a process where the pre-trained model is used as a base, and a new, smaller network is trained on top of it for a specific task. This allows the new network to benefit from the knowledge and features learned by the VGG19 network on the large dataset, reducing the amount of data and computational resources needed for the new task. Another application of VGG19 is feature extraction. The intermediate layers of a CNN can be used to extract meaningful features from an image, which can then be used for other tasks, such as image classification or object detection. VGG19 has been shown to produce high-quality features that can be used for a variety of computer vision tasks. Overall, the VGG19 model has proven to be a highly effective tool for various computer vision tasks, and its pre-trained network and features have been widely used in research and industry (Fig. 13).

```
from tensorflow.python.keras import models
def get_model():
    vgg = tf.keras.applications.vgg19.VGG19(include_top=False, weights='imagenet'
    vgg.trainable = False
    for layer in vgg.layers:
        layer.trainable = False

        style_outputs = [vgg.get_layer(name).output for name in style_layers]
        content_outputs = [vgg.get_layer(name).output for name in content_layers]
        model_outputs = style_outputs + content_outputss
        return models.Model(vgg.input, model_outputs)
```

Fig. 13. Build the VGG19 model. References and Citations [8]

The square root of the sum of the squares of the differences between the feature vectors of the content image and the generated image (Fig. 14).

```
def get_content_loss(base_content, target):

    return tf.reduce_mean(tf.square(base_content - target))
```

Fig. 14. Defining the content loss function. References and Citations [8]

First, defining the Gram Matrix calculation function, then defining the style loss function (Fig. 15).

A loss function in a Convolutional Neural Network (CNN) is a mathematical function that measures the difference between the predicted output and the actual output of the network. The goal of training a CNN is to minimize the value of the loss function, so that the network's predictions are as close as possible to the actual outputs. The choice of loss function depends on the specific task being performed by the CNN. For example, in a binary classification task, the common loss function used is binary

```python
def gram_matrix(input_tensor):
    # We make the image channels first
    channels = int(input_tensor.shape[-1])
    a = tf.reshape(input_tensor, [-1, channels])
    n = tf.shape(a)[0]
    gram = tf.matmul(a, a, transpose_a=True)
    return gram / tf.cast(n, tf.float32)


def get_style_loss(base_style, gram_target):
    # Get the height, width, and number of colors of the style map
    height, width, channels = base_style.get_shape().as_list()

    # Calculate the Gram Matrix
    gram_style = gram_matrix(base_style)

    # Compute style Loss
    return tf.reduce_mean(tf.square(gram_style - gram_target))
```

Fig. 15. Defining the style loss function References and Citations [8]

cross-entropy, which measures the difference between the predicted probability of the positive class and the actual label. In a multi-class classification task, the commonly used loss function is categorical cross-entropy, which measures the difference between the predicted probabilities of the classes and the actual label. In regression tasks, mean squared error is a common loss function, which measures the average squared difference between the predicted output and the actual output. In other tasks, such as semantic segmentation, custom loss functions can be designed to reflect the specific objectives of the task. Overall, the loss function plays a crucial role in the training process of a CNN, as it guides the optimization algorithm to find the best parameters for the network that minimize the difference between the predictions and the actual outputs (Fig. 16).

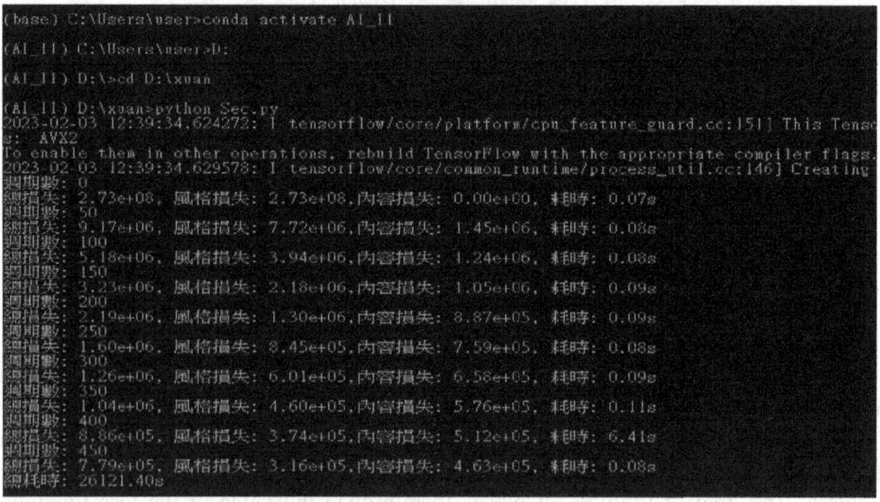

Fig. 16. Code conversion process.

4 Results and Discussion

It's time to take a look at the process of transforming the style of one image to another. This process is usually achieved through training a deep learning model and using two images as input. We use a classmate's life photo as the "source image" and another picture, The Starry Night by Van Gogh, as the "style image". The source image is the image that retains its shape and structure, while the style image is used to convey style information. The algorithm generates a new image by combining the features of these two images, with the shape and structure of the source image and the style of the style image (Figs. 17 and 18).

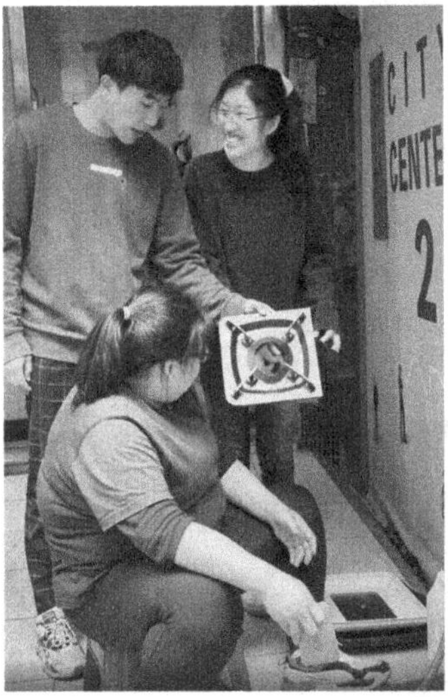

Fig. 17. Photos of life

Fig. 18. The Starry Night

Translated to English: The first image produced in style transfer, the effect of the style transfer is not yet strong, compared to the original image, total loss: 9.17e + 06, style loss: 7.72e + 06, content loss: 1.45e + 06 (Fig. 19).

This is the fourth image produced in style transfer, at this point the style transfer effect is complete 40% to 50%, total loss: 2.19e + 06, style loss: 1.30e + 06, content loss: 8.87e + 05. This value is the loss value calculated by the machine learning model during the style transfer, the lower the loss value, the better the model results (Fig. 20).

This is the final completed image in the style transfer, total loss: 7.79e + 05, style loss: 3.16e + 05, content loss: 4.63e + 05, total time elapsed: 26121.40S. At this point, the style transfer effect is complete. Here we can see that the transformed image is more colorful, rich, or has a more unique appearance (Fig. 21).

These are the images produced in the style transfer, we can see that as the style loss function changes, different synthesized images were generated. By transforming the image into an oil painting style through style transfer, the transformed image may have a more natural color gradient and rich texture (Fig. 22).

This time, we choose a picture style with a stronger atmosphere and consider the following important factors:

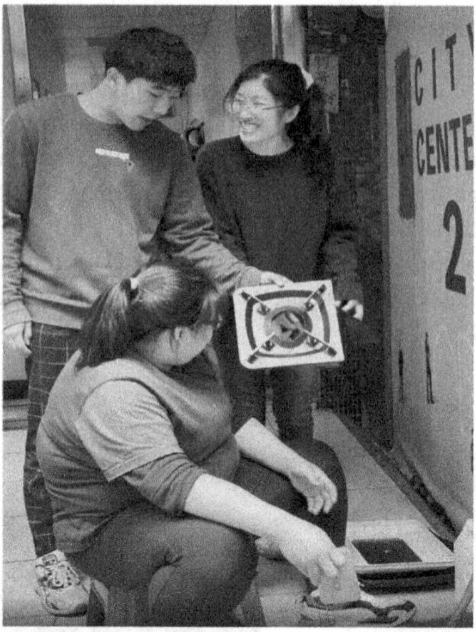

Fig. 19. .

Fig. 20. .

Color: Color is one of the important elements in presenting the style of the picture. Choosing bright and eye-catching colors can make the picture show a stronger style. For

Fig. 21. .

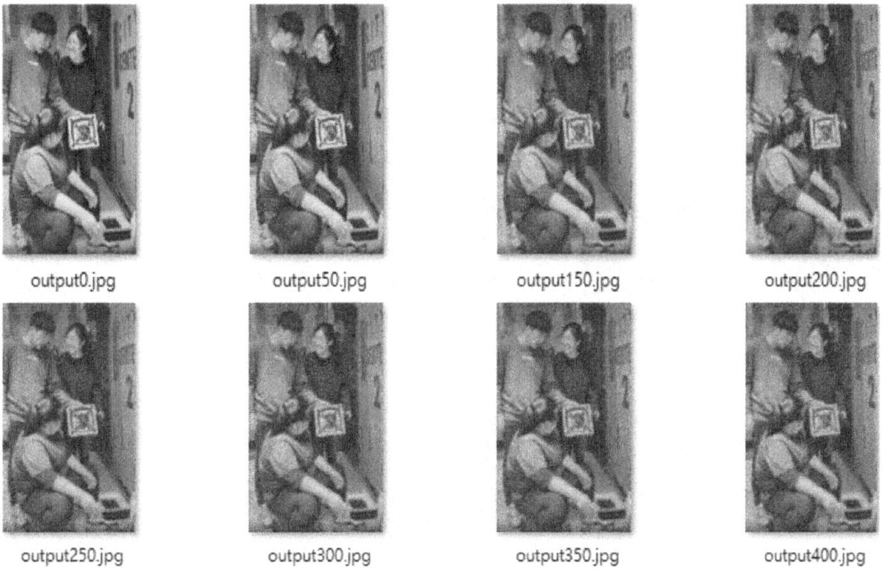

Fig. 22. Style Transfer Process Image

example, when choosing color, you can choose bright red, green or blue, etc. to show a strong style.

Lines: Lines are also an important element in presenting the style of the picture. Simple lines or strong curves can make the picture show a stronger style. For example, when choosing lines, you can choose straight lines or curves to show a strong style.

Elements: Choosing special elements in the picture, such as special shapes, objects, etc., can also make the picture show a stronger style. For example, when choosing elements, you can choose different objects or shapes to show a strong style.

Contrast: Choosing powerful contrasts in the picture, such as black and white contrasts or bright and dark contrasts, can also make the picture show a stronger style. For example, when choosing contrast, you can choose a bright white and black contrast, as these two pictures have a strong style and are different, so the conversion process takes longer (Figs. 23, 24 and 25).

Fig. 23. Landscape

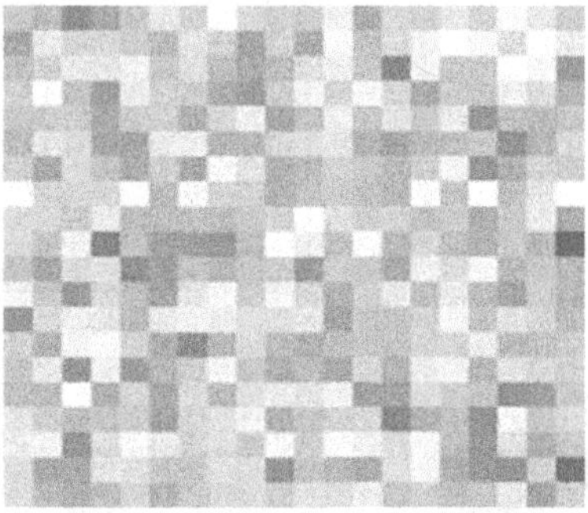

Fig. 24. Mosaic.

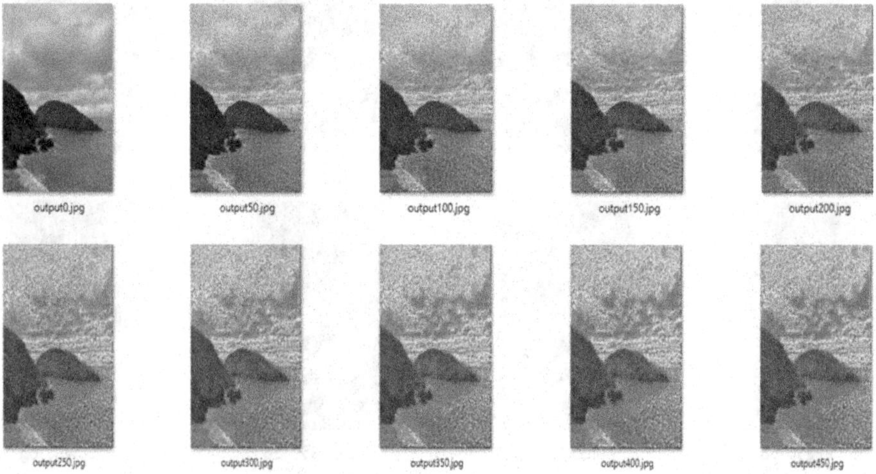

Fig. 25. Style Transfer Process Image

During our trip, we took several photos and finally chose these two because they have the following characteristics that make them highly attractive: This landscape picture has beautiful scenery that can capture the viewer's attention. It has artistic value: This landscape picture has high-quality artistic value that can enhance the overall atmosphere of the place. It has a strong stylistic effect that can enhance the overall effect of the stylistic change. These characteristics make this landscape picture an ideal choice that can bring a positive effect to the place (Figs. 26 and 27).

Fig. 26. Night view.

Fig. 27. Feature wall.

These two photos have similar styles and took 13530.70 s to complete, which is less time compared to the previous groups and the completion is more ideal. The following ten pictures are the process and result of the style transfer (Fig. 28).

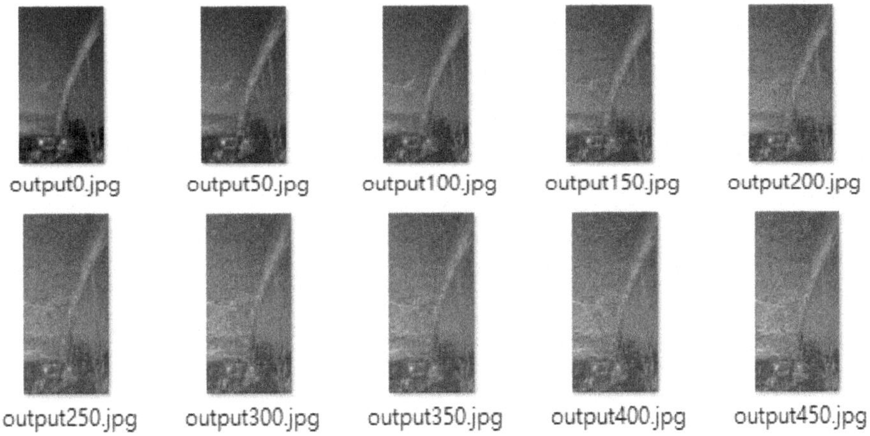

Fig. 28. Style Transfer Process Image

5 Conclusion

Currently in 2022, we are in the midst of a peak and are deeply interested in AI's computational abilities beyond human capabilities, influenced by this trend, we have invested in research, initially choosing the direction of image recognition. When AI learned the method of recognizing images, we were not satisfied. At this time, a passionate photography team member proposed using images to improve image proposals, merging two different styles of landscapes, not just simply beautifying the images, but even recreating the styles of dead greats, expanding the modern aesthetics of artists and photographers.

References

1. Hakim, W.L., et al.: Convolutional neural network (CNN) with metaheuristic optimization algorithms for landslide susceptibility mapping in Icheon, South Korea. J. Environ. Manage. **305**, 114367 (2022)
2. Whig, P.: More on Convolution Neural Network CNN. Int. J. Sustain. Dev. Comput. Sci. **4**(1) (2022)
3. Rodriguez-Martinez, I., et al.: Replacing pooling functions in Convolutional Neural Networks by linear combinations of increasing functions. Neural Netw. **152**, 380–393 (2022)
4. Skourt, B.A., El Hassani, A., Majda, A.: Mixed-pooling-dropout for convolutional neural network regularization. J. King Saud Univ. Comput. Inf. Sci. **34**(8), 4756–4762 (2022)
5. Abu-Jamie, T.N., et al.: Six Fruits Classification Using Deep Learning (2022)
6. Wu, X., et al.: A survey of human-in-the-loop for machine learning. Future Gener. Comput. Syst. **135**, 364–381 (2022)
7. Matsuo, Y., et al.: Deep learning, reinforcement learning, and world models. Neural Netw. **152**, 267–275 (2022)
8. MING, C.Z.: 深度學習 DEEP LEARNING最佳入門邁向AI專題實戰. 2021: 深智數位股份有限公司.
9. Karacı, A.: VGGCOV19-NET: automatic detection of COVID-19 cases from X-ray images using modified VGG19 CNN architecture and YOLO algorithm. Neural Comput. Appl. **34**(10), 8253–8274 (2022)

Causal Inference of Direct Email Advertising Effects Using ID-POS Data of an Electronics Store

Yujun Ma[1(✉)], Kohei Otake[2], and Takashi Namatame[3]

[1] Causal Inference of Dire and Engineering, Chuo University, 1-13-27, Kasuga, Bunkyo -ku, Tokyo 112-8551, Japan
a18.ajcx@g.chuo-u.ac.jp
[2] School of Information and Telecommunication Engineering, Tokai University, 2-3-23, Takanawa, Minato-ku, Tokyo 108-8619, Japan
otake@tsc.u-tokai.ac.jp
[3] Faculty of Science and Engineering, Chuo University, 1-13-27, Kasuga, Bunkyo -ku, Tokyo 112-8551, Japan
nama@kc.chuo-u.ac.jp

Abstract. In this study, we estimate the causal effect of direct promotional email advertising when an RCT could not be performed by only using observational data from a Japanese electronics store. To do so, we build two models for two different types of direct promotional email under a causal inference framework and estimate the treatment effect using the traditional method like propensity score weighting and framework combined with machine learning estimators like meta-learner. The estimated results in our two models show the positive advertising effects of two kinds of direct promotional emails sent by the electronics store. We find that the targeting policy may affect the success of causal inference modeling due to the different difficulties in identifying confounder variables during modeling between the targeting strategy is clear and not. We also find that the electronics store could increase its direct email advertising effects by changing its targeting strategy.

Keywords: Advertising Measurement · Digital Advertising · Causal Inference · Email Direct Marketing

1 Introduction

There are generally two approaches to advertising and promotion: mass marketing and direct marketing. The former uses mass media to promote the product indiscriminately, whereas the latter studies customers' needs and selects specific customers as a target for promotion. Compared to the former method, the latter seems more effective in today's overwhelming products and highly competitive marketing environment

As a medium for advertising, there are also generally two approaches: traditional marketing uses traditional media like television and newspaper, and digital

A. Coman and S. Vasilache (Eds.): HCII 2023, LNCS 14025, pp. 401–417, 2023.
https://doi.org/10.1007/978-3-031-35915-6_29

marketing uses digital media like email and websites. Although digital marketing was established early in the 1990s, with the expansion of devices capable of accessing the Internet like smartphones, it is still growing in the 2010s [2]. Also, during the current covid-19 pandemic, digital marketing shows potential to mitigate the harmful effect of the pandemic on revenue by strengthening customer relationship management [3,4].

With the backdrop of direct marketing's important position and the high growth potential of digital marketing mentioned above, direct email marketing, which effectively utilizes the advantages of both methods, seems to be used more in the future. Therefore, the evaluation of its advertising effects would receive more attention. However, measuring advertising effectiveness in direct email marketing can be challenging for advertisers since finding the causal effect of sending a promotional email on the outcome, such as the increase in revenue, is difficult. That is, although the gold standard to estimate the causal effect is to conduct an RCT (randomized controlled trial), running an RCT is not always feasible in direct email marketing due to RCT may force the advertisers to forgive maximization of their campaign's reach in the control group [5]. In some cases, RCT can even be impossible to implement [6]. As a result, the advertiser may need to evaluate the advertising effect of direct email just by observational data. However, such observed data is biased by correlations and unobserved confounding. To make the correct causal inference, such correlations and confounding need to be removed from the observational data [7]. In this study, we investigate to estimate the causal effect of direct email advertising using data from a Japanese electronics store, where precisely the same scenarios mentioned above — only biased observed data are available.

The rest of the paper proceeds as follows. Section 2 describes the details of the data and how we do the data preprocessing. Section 3 details how we make the causal inference and check the robustness of the estimated result, including the causal framework and the python libraries and the algorithm behind them we used. Section 4 details the causal inference model we built. Section 5 shows the empirical estimate result we gained. Section 6 discusses the result. Section 7 concludes.

2 Data

In this study, we used the two datasets provided by a Japanese electronics store: One consists of POS (point of sale) data with customer attributes, also called "ID-POS" data. The other shows the recipient' s reactions after receiving a direct promotional email. In the data preprocessing, we aim to figure out and extract the pretreatment (before direct email was sent) covariates and the outcome after treatment. The following subsection will cover more details about the two datasets.

2.1 ID-POS Data

POS data is point-of-sale data collected from transactions made at a point of sale. The data associated with the customer' s ID to the "POS" is called "ID-POS" data. There are 56 items in our dataset, consisting of "POS" information, including products sold, time of sale, location etc., and ID information such as customers' demographic information like sex and age. Data was recorded from January 2017 to August 2021.

2.2 Recipient's Reactions Data

There are generally four following items in the reactions data:

- Hashing customer number: This item identifies the customer uniquely.
- Status of emails and recipient' s actions: This item shows whether the email was sent successfully and whether the recipient opened the email or clicked the promotion link.
- Time of actions: This item shows when the above actions happen.
- Type of promotional email: This item shows what direct promotional email was sent.

Table 1 summarizes the number of deliveries, open rate, and click rate of all and two types of promotional emails we used in our study (they will be detailed in the Model section).

Table 1. Summary of recipient's reactions data.

Type of promotional email	Number of deliveries	Open rate	Click rate
All	903,876	0.125	0.003
1	123,706	0.153	0.003
2	568,828	0.101	0.003

3 Method

In the three subsections, we will briefly review the general causal inference framework, then detail how we make the causal inference based on the framework and check the robustness of the estimated result, including the python libraries we used and the algorithm behind them.

3.1 Causal Inference Framework

In this subsection, we will describe the causal inference framework using the notation developed by Heckman and Vytlacil (HV) [8]. Following the HV setup, we define the outcome corresponding to treatment state for individual ω as $Y(s, \omega), \omega \in \Omega$. The details of treatments and outcomes in our study will be covered in Sect. 4. By setup above, suppose we want to find the causal effect of taking an action A on the outcome Y, individual treatment effect (ITE) for individual ω is given by

$$Y(A = 1, \omega) - Y(A = 0, \omega) \tag{1}$$

where $A = 1, A = 0$ stands for whether the treatment is conducted or not. The average treatment effect (ATE), which stands for the treatment effect for all individuals respectively in Ω is given by

$$\text{ATE}(A = 1, A = 0) = E(Y(A = 1, \omega) - Y(A = 0, \omega)) \equiv \tau \tag{2}$$

To estimate the ATE, the gold standard is to conduct an RCT where a randomized subset of units is acted upon ($A = 1$), and the other subset is not ($A = 0$) [7]. However, as mentioned in Sect. 1, it is not always feasible to do that, which leads to only observed data being available — exactly the same case in our study. Since correlations and unobserved confounding bias in such observed data, there are systematic differences in which units were acted upon and which units were not [7]. In this case, instead of calculating ATE directly, we can consider such pretreatment correlations and unobserved confounding as X, so the treatment effect conditions on X, *conditional average treatment effect* (CATE) can be defined as

$$\text{CATE}(A = 1, A = 0) = E(Y(A = 1, \omega) - Y(A = 0, \omega) \mid X = x) \equiv \tau(x) \tag{3}$$

We aim to calculate the causal effect by estimating the CATE using methods details in the following subsection.

3.2 Estimation Approach

We use propensity score matching [9] and Meta-Learner [10] to estimate the above CATE.

Propensity Score Matching. The propensity score, $e\left(X_i\right)$, is the conditional probability of treatment given features X_i,

$$e\left(X_i\right) \equiv \Pr\left(\mathrm{A} = 1 \mid X_i = x\right) \tag{4}$$

Under strong ignorability, treatment assignment, and the potential outcomes can be considered independent, conditional on the propensity score [11],

$$\left(Y_i(A = 0), Y_i(A = 1)\right) \perp\!\!\!\perp \mathrm{A} \mid e\left(X_i\right) \tag{5}$$

equation (5) shows that estimating CATE in (3), instead of conditioning on covariate X, we now can condition on the propensity score $e\left(X_i\right)$

$$\text{CATE}(A=1, A=0) = E\left(Y(A=1,\omega) - Y(A=0,\omega) \mid e\left(X_i\right)\right) \equiv \tau(x) \quad (6)$$

Based on the idea of equation (6), the propensity score matching method tries to find one (or more) users without treatment ($A = 0$) with the closest propensity score to each user with treatment ($A = 1$) to estimate the CATE. We use the python library "DoWhy" [12] to perform the propensity score matching.

Meta-Learner. A meta-learner is a framework to estimate the CATE in (3) using any machine learning estimators (we use XGB [eXtreme Gradient Boosting] in our study) [10]. The meta-learner uses either a single base learner with the treatment indicator as a feature (e.g., S-learner) or multiple base learners separately for each treatment (e.g., T-learner, X-learner, and R-learner). We will use the python library "Causal ML" [16], which provides a meta-learner framework to conduct causal inference. S-learner, T-learner, X-learner, and R-learner will be detailed below.

S-Learner: S-learner estimates the treatment effect using a single machine learning model as follows:

1. Using a machine learning model to estimate the average outcomes $\mu(x)$ with covariates X and an indicator variable for treatment W:

$$\mu(x,w) = E[Y \mid X = x, W = w] \quad (7)$$

2. The CATE estimate is defined as

$$\hat{\tau}(x) = \hat{\mu}_1(x) - \hat{\mu}_0(x) \quad (8)$$

The drawback of the S-learner is that when the control and treatment groups are very different in covariates, a single linear model may not encode the different features for the control and treatment groups [13].

T-Learner: T in T-Learner [14] stands for two, which consists of two stages as follows:

1. Using the machine learning models to estimate the average $\mu_0(x)$ and $\mu_1(x)$:

$$\begin{aligned} \mu_0(x) &= E[Y(0) \mid X = x] \\ \mu_1(x) &= E[Y(1) \mid X = x] \end{aligned} \quad (9)$$

2. The CATE can be defined similarly to S-learner as equation (8).

The drawback of the T-Learner is that it may suffer from the problem of double-model error accumulation; also, when the data discrepancy is too large (such as data volume and sampling bias), it significantly impacts the accuracy rate [14].

X-Learner: X-learner, an extension of T-learner, utilizes the total amount of data for prediction, mainly addressing the situation where the amount of data varies significantly between Treatment groups [14]. X-learner consists of three stages as follows:

1. Using the machine learning models to estimate the average $\mu_0(x)$ and $\mu_1(x)$ same as T-learner in (9):
2. Impute the user-level treatment effects, D_i^1 and D_j^0 for user i in the treatment group based on $\mu_0(x)$, and user j in the control groups based on $\mu_1(x)$:

$$\begin{aligned} D_i^1 &= Y_i^1 - \hat{\mu}_0\left(X_i^1\right) \\ D_i^0 &= \hat{\mu}_1\left(X_i^0\right) - Y_i^0 \end{aligned} \tag{10}$$

   then estimate $\tau_1(x) = E\left[D^1 \mid X = x\right]$, and $\tau_0(x) = E\left[D^0 \mid X = x\right]$ using machine learning models.
3. Define the CATE estimate by a weighted average of $\tau_1(x)$ and $\tau_0(x)$:

$$\tau(x) = g(x)\tau_0(x) + (1 - g(x))\tau_1(x) \tag{11}$$

R-Learner: The idea of the R-Learner is to train learning by transforming the problem into a defined R-loss function. It consists of two stages as follows:

1. Using the cross-validation out-of-fold estimates of outcomes $\hat{m}^{(-i)}\left(x_i\right)$ and propensity scores $\hat{e}^{(-i)}\left(x_i\right)$

$$\begin{aligned} \hat{e}(x) &= E[W = 1 \mid X = x] \\ \hat{m}(x) &= E[Y = 1 \mid X = x] \end{aligned} \tag{12}$$

2. Estimate treatment effects by minimizing the R-loss, $\hat{L}_n(\tau(x))$:

$$\hat{L}_n(\tau(x)) = \frac{1}{n}\sum_{i=1}^{n}\left(\left(Y_i - \hat{m}^{(-i)}\left(X_i\right)\right) - \left(W_i - \hat{e}^{(-i)}\left(X_i\right)\right)\tau\left(X_i\right)\right)^2 \tag{13}$$

   where $\hat{e}^{(-i)}\left(X_i\right)$ and $\hat{m}^{(-i)}\left(X_i\right)$ denote the out-of-fold held-out predictions made without using the i-th training sample. R-Learner is relatively flexible, but the model effect depends on the estimation accuracy of $\hat{m}$ and $\hat{e}$.

3.3 Validation of Estimated Result

We obtained estimates using the approaches in Sect. 3.2 under the causal inference framework mentioned in Sect. 3.1. Next, we validate the estimated result since it may be wrong for many reasons, such as unsuitable modeling. However, validation of the estimated treatment effect is challenging since the actual value, except for the experimental data, is not available as conventional machine learning predictions [17]. In this study, we validate the result by using two internal validation methods, assuming the unconfoundedness of potential outcomes and the treatment status conditioned on the feature set available to us. Two methods will be detailed below.

Method 1: Validation with Multiple Estimates. We can validate the estimated treatment result by comparing the estimates with other approaches and checking the consistency of estimates across different levels. Since meta-learner uses different underlying algorithms, and the confidence intervals of estimates in meta-learner can be calculated based on the lower bound equation (7) from [18], we validate the result by checking the consistency of estimates within 95 intervals across different learners.

Method 2: Validation with Refutation Tests. We do the three refutation tests provide by "DoWhy" library [12], which aim to refute the correctness of the complete causal analysis, including modeling and estimation. Three *refutation* tests include:

1. Adding a random common cause variable:
   If the causal analysis is correct, the estimated result should not change after adding an independent random variable as a common cause to the dataset.
2. Replacing treatment with a random (placebo) variable:
   If the causal analysis is correct, the estimated result should go to zero when replacing the true treatment variable with an independent random variable.
3. Removing a random subset of the data:
   If the causal analysis is correct, the estimated result should not change significantly when replacing the given dataset with bootstrapped samples from the same datasets.

4 Model

The framework of our causal inference model is shown in Fig. 1 below:

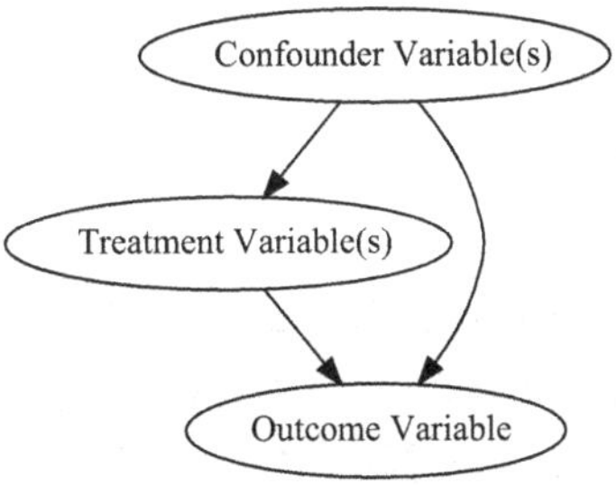

Fig. 1. Causal inference model framework.

The model has three variables: confounder variable(s), treatment variable(s), and outcome variable.

- Confounder variable(s): These variables cause both the treatment and the outcome. Any observed correlation between the treatment and the outcome may be due to the confounder variables but not any causal relationship between the treatment and the outcome itself. So, our goal is to eliminate the influence of confounder variables by using the methods and tools mentioned in the previous section.
- Treatment Variable(s): In our study, this variable indicates whether the customers are the target of the direct promotional email.
- Outcome Variable: This variable shows the advertising effect of the direct promotional email.

In this study, we build 2 models based on the above framework to estimate the advertising effects of the two types of direct emails mentioned in Sect. 2.2.

4.1 Model 1

The first type of direct promotional email consists of a discount offering of Microsoft Surface products. Model 1 determines if that direct email can increase the Surface related product sales. The electronics store decided that less engagement in PC-related product-purchased customers[1] as their first type of email promotion target. We consider that such a targeting policy will not only directly influence the treatment but also indirectly influence the outcome, as the engagement level may be highly related to their purchase intention. So we selected customers' purchase amount and frequency of PC-related products in the past year before sending promotional emails as the covariates. Besides, though it seems that the influence of purchasing behavior of general products is not as strong as specific PC-related products, we think that would somehow influence both treatment and outcome. Therefore, as indicators representing customer purchasing behavior, RFM (Recency, Frequency, and Monetary) is chosen as covariates. Finally, customers' demographic variables (sex and age) are also selected. Model 1 is shown in Fig. 2 below:

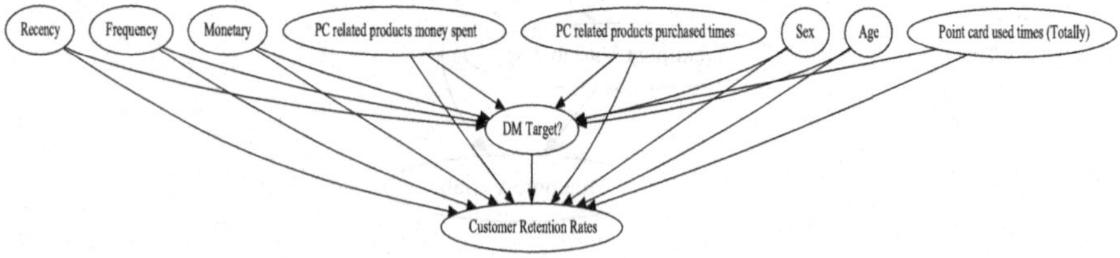

Fig. 2. Model 1: Causal inference of Surface promotional email advertising effects.

[1] Customers who had not bought any PC-related product in the past year before sending the promotional email.

Finally, we use the traditional method like propensity score weighting and framework combined with machine learning estimators like meta-learner mentioned in Sect. 3.2 to estimate the conditional average treatment effect (CATE).

4.2 Model 2

Contrary to the first type of direct promotional email, the targeting strategy of the second type is unclear. The second type is a premium membership[2] promotion email for a part of the randomly selected member. Model 2 determines if that direct email can increase the customer retention rate. We choose customer retention rate as the outcome variable in model 2 for the following two reasons:

1. There is room to improve the customer retention rate.
   As Fig. 3 shows below, only around 12% of new customers monthly are kept after one month except for June 2020, and the numbers even decrease to 7% after five months. Considering that the average customer retention rate in the retail industry is around 63% [19], the customer retention rate seems to have room for growth.
2. Direct promotional email of the second type seems to be somehow effective in increasing the customer retention rate.

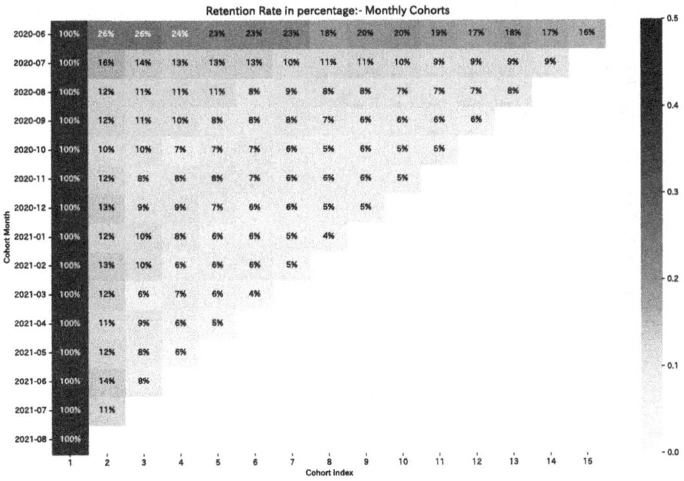

Fig. 3. Monthly customer retention rate (all customers).

[2] Compared to regular membership 1% more extra points for purchases. The annual average fee is 1,078 yen, but it will be free if you make a purchase once a year.

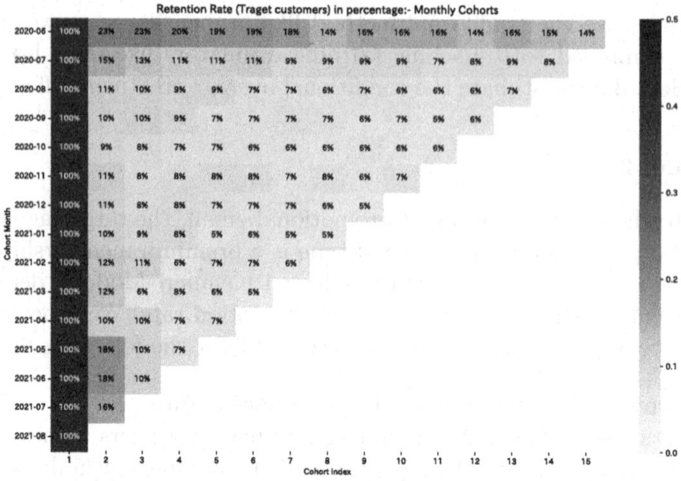

Fig. 4. Monthly customer retention rate (promotional email target customers).

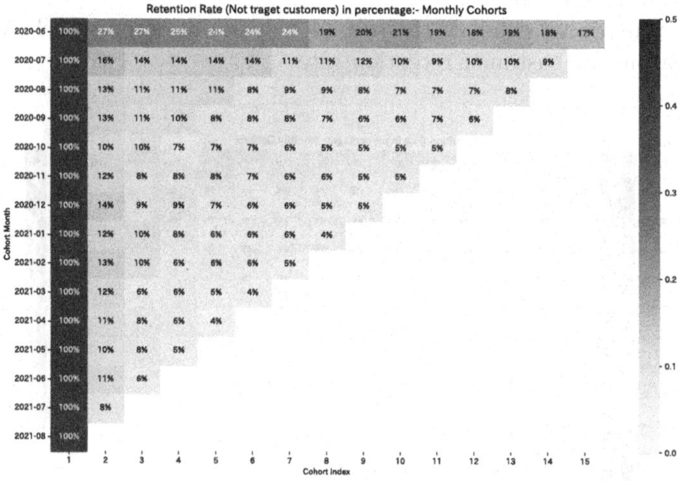

Fig. 5. Monthly customer retention rate (not promotional email target customers).

Given that premium membership promoted by the second type of promotional email offers extra points on purchases and no membership fee for at least one purchase per year, it seems to aim to promote customer purchasing behavior. How about the exact number? Figs. 4 and 5 show the customer retention rate of direct promotional email target customers not, respectively. Figure 6 shows the difference between them. In Fig. 6, compared to non-target customers, we can see target customers seems to have higher customer retention rates after receiving promotional email (June 2021) from November 2020 to June 2021.

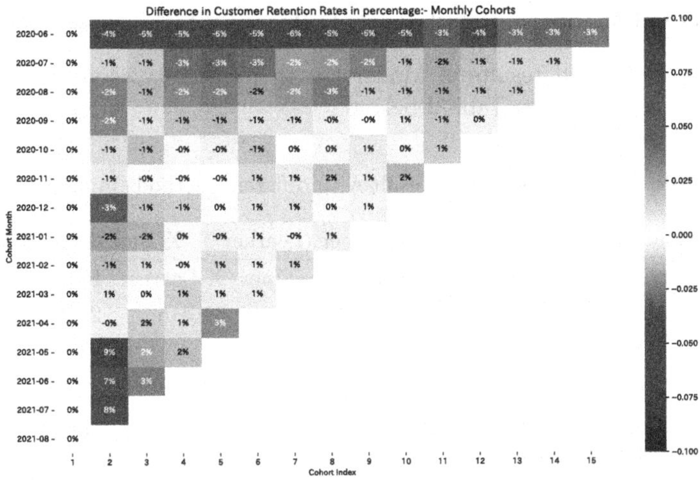

Fig. 6. Difference in customer retention rates between targets and non-target customers.

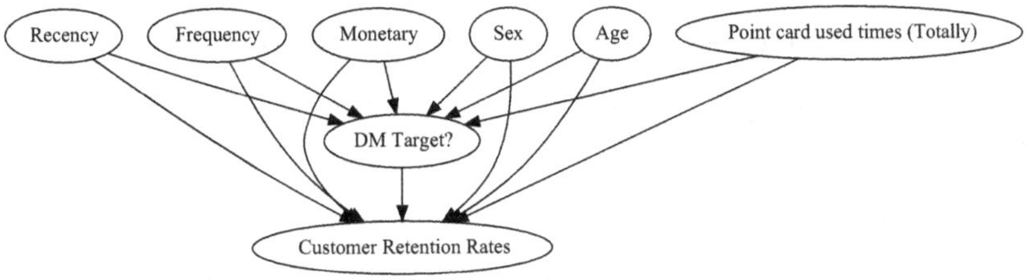

Fig. 7. Model 2: Causal inference of premium membership promotional email ad effects.

After defining the treatment and outcome variable, we will select the confounder variables in model 2. However, identifying the confounder variables is challenging in model 2 due to the indecisive targeting policy in the second type of email. Finally, as indicators representing engagement level on customer purchasing behavior, RFM and the number of times point cards' usages are selected as covariates. Also, customers' demographic variables (sex and age) are chosen. Model 2 is shown in Fig. 7.

5 Result

This section presents the results of the two models mentioned in the previous quarter.

5.1 CATE Estimated Result with Different Methods in Model 1

The CATE estimated results of Model 1 with propensity score matching and Metalearner are shown in Table 2 below:

Table 2. CATE estimated result with different methods in model 1.

Traditional Method:	Meta-Learner (Learner T, X, and R using XGB):			
Propensity Score Matching	S-Learner	T-Learner	X-Learner	R-Learner
21.450	−4.283	17.415	17.415	28.351

To check the robustness of the estimated results, we use the two methods in Sect. 3.3. Firstly, we use the technique mentioned in Sect. 3.3.1 to plot the outcome of each meta-learner' s estimated result falling in a 95% confidence interval in the Fig. 8:

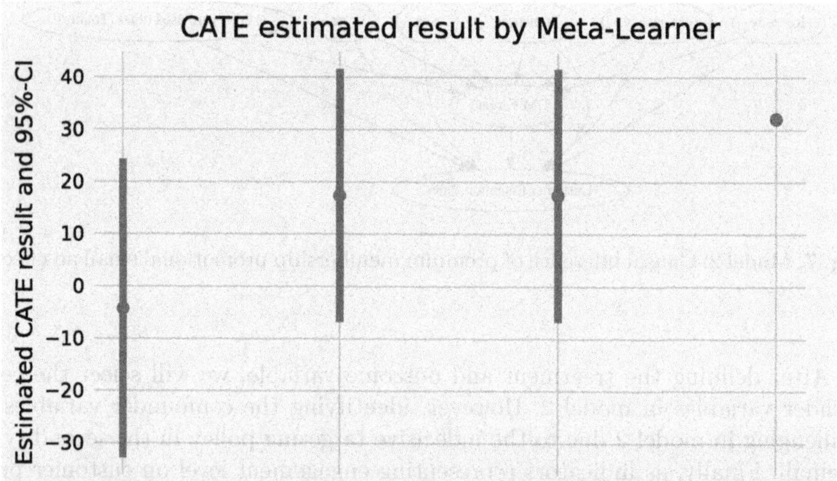

Fig. 8. Each meta-learner's estimated result's variation in 95% in model 1.

Also, we do the three refutation tests detailed in Sect. 3.3.2. To determine how the covariates influence the outcome, we plot the feature importance and shape value in Figs. 9 and 10.

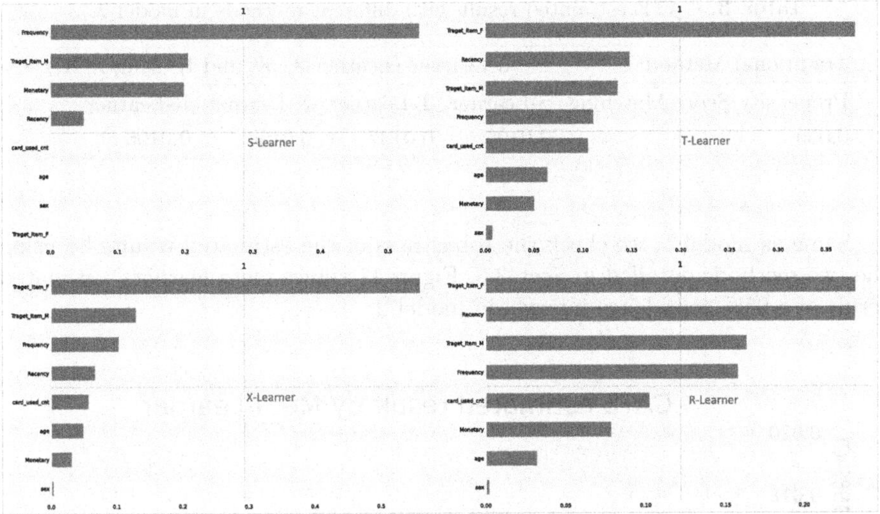

Fig. 9. Covariates' feature importance of each learner in the meta-learner method in model 1.

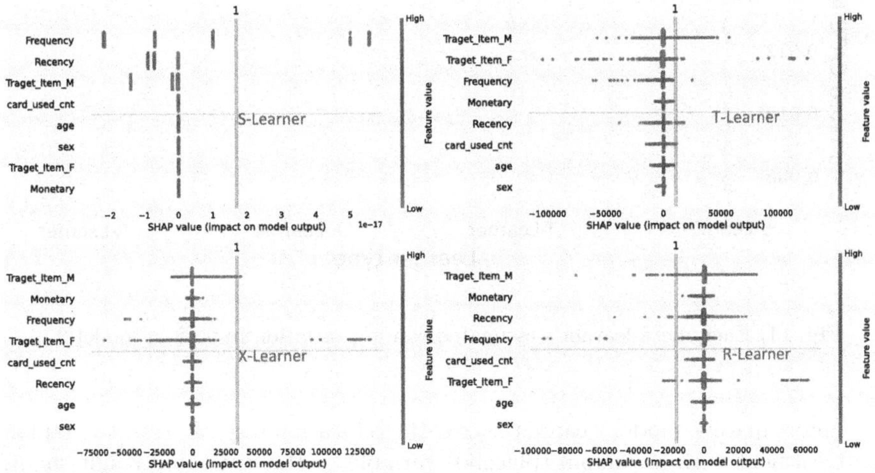

Fig. 10. Covariates' shape value of each learner in the meta-learner method in model 1.

5.2 Result of Model 2

The CATE estimated results of Model 2 with propensity score matching and Metalearner are shown in Table 3 below:

Table 3. CATE estimated result with different methods in model 2.

Traditional Method:	Meta-Learner (Learner T, X, and R using XGB):			
Propensity Score Matching	S-Learner	T-Learner	X-Learner	R-Learner
0.059	0.0106	0.0137	0.0137	0.0196

Same as model 1, we check the robustness of the estimated results by using the two methods detailed in Sect. 3.3. Figure 11 shows meta-learners' estimated result of a 95% confidence interval in model 2.

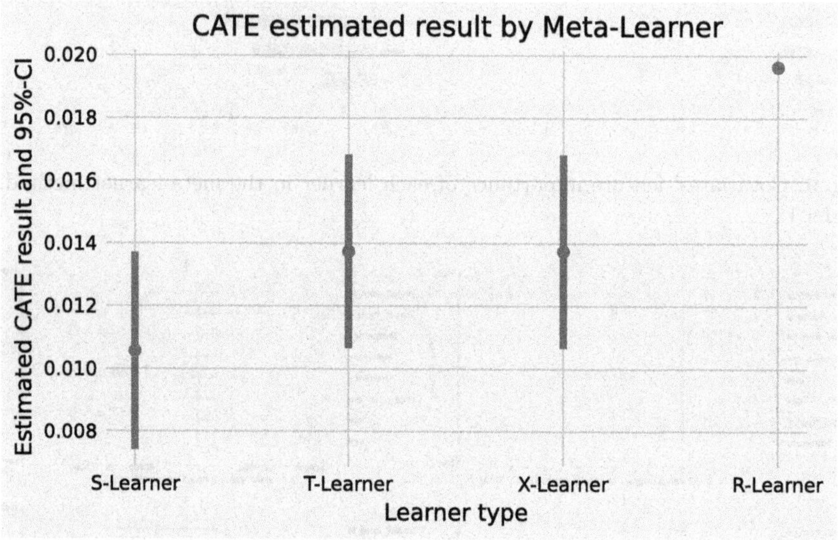

Fig. 11. Each meta-learner's estimated result's variation in 95% in model 2.

Unfortunately, model 2 cannot accept the refutation tests. In test 2 — replacing treatment with a random (placebo) variable — the estimated result should go to zero when replacing the valid treatment variable with an independent random variable. However, the new estimated result in propensity score matching and meta-learner became a minus number (between −0.015 to −0.007).

6 Discussion

The values in Table 1 mean comparing to those who are not promotion target customers, how many more estimated purchases (Japanese yen) in Surface made per customer in 1 month by those who are targeted. Although the amount is small, we can see that except for S-Learner, all positive return values indicate that the direct promotional email positively affects the purchasing behavior for Surface products. Fortunately, the estimated results pass the refutation tests mentioned in Sect. 3.3.2. Although passing these tests does not necessarily prove that the results are correct, given the stable estimated result by different estimators except learner S shown in Fig. 8, learner T, X, and R's estimated results seem to have a high degree of robustness.

In Fig. 9, we can see in the learners that believed to have high robustness estimate results (Learner T, X, and R), "target_item_M" and "target_item_F" features in covariates, which represent customers' purchase amount and frequency of PC-related products, have a high-level influence on the outcome. Given that this electronics store targets the Surface promotional mail by customers' engagement on PC-related products, we estimate the target strategy itself strongly influences Surface sales. Figure 10 details how individuals in features "target_item_M" and "target_item_F" are influenced by their shape value. We can see the "target_item_M" feature in learner T, X, and R that when the feature value goes high (the dots turns pink), although the shape values are both increasing and decreasing, the increasing part is more than the decreasing part. The same tendency can observe in "target_item_F". The above tendencies indicate high engaged customers of PC-related products tend to purchase Surface. It suggests that if the electronics stores change their target strategy — from low to high engagement customers on PC-related products as Surface promotional direct email target — they may gain better advertisement effects.

Table 2 shows that in model 2, after receiving premium membership promotional emails, the customer retention rates for target customers are estimated to be higher than those not about 0.5% to 2%. However, given that model 2 failed the refutation test and the inconsistent estimates shown in Fig. 11, the estimated results in Table 2 may be incorrect, and the modeling may be inappropriate. The failure in modeling is probably due to the difficulty in identifying covariates in model 2 since the targeting policy is unclear.

7 Conclusion

This study was conducted to estimate the causal effect of direct email advertising when an RCT could not be performed by only using observational data from Japanese electronics stores with traditional and machine learning based approaches. We have two findings in this study. Firstly, when the targeting strategy is clear, it may be easier to construct a model with highly robust estimation results due to the ease of identifying confounding factors. Secondly, it was suggested that reversing the target strategy may be more effective in advertising. As their promotional email target, the electronics store selected less engagement in PC-related product-purchased customers. However, Fig. 10 suggests that the advertising effect may increase when they change their target strategy to those more engaged in PC-related product-purchased. Further experiments are needed to confirm that.

Although model 1 shows high robustness in its estimates by validating the two methods detailed in Sect. 3.3, its accuracy remains questionable for three reasons. First, conducting the two validation methods can only increase the estimated result's robustness but cannot prove it is correct. Second, whether the preconditions for causal inference are met has not been adequately discussed. That is, the causal inference should be conducted under the two key assumptions comprising strong ignorability: unconfounded assignment and sufficient overlap [11]. Although the unconfounded assignment condition seems to be satisfied due to the firm's algorithmic targeting policy [5], whether our data satisfy the sufficient overlap condition still needs further discussion. Third, Brett et al.'s research shows that the treatment result estimated by the non-experimental methods may be poor [20].

In the future, we aim to do three works. First, verify if our data fulfill the sufficient overlap condition. Secondly, review if the modeling failure in model 2 is due to the inappropriate covariates selected; if so, try to figure out the appropriate one. Finally, we aim to verify the accuracy of our causal inference modeling by comparing the result estimated by our model with those measured by RCT.

Acknowledgment. We thank an electoronical retail campany of Japan for permission to use valuable datasets. This work was supported by JSPS KAKENHI Grant Number 21H04600 and 21K13385.

References

1. Ling, C.X., Li, C.: Data mining for direct marketing: Problems and solutions. In: Proceedings of the Fourth International Conference on Knowledge Discovery and Data Mining, pp. 73–79. AAAI Press (1998)
2. Desai, D.M.: Digital marketing: A review. International Journal of Trend in Scientific Research and Development Special Issue(Special Issue-FIIIIPM2019), pp. 196–200 (2019)
3. Mehralian, M.M., Khazaee, P.: Effect of digital marketing on the business performance of msmes during the covid-19 pandemic: The mediating role of customer relationship management. SSRN Electronic Journal (2022), https://ssrn.com/abstract=4195985
4. Corona disaster's digital marketing implementation effectiveness revealed - adobe survey (Dec 2021). https://japan.zdnet.com/article/35180445/ Accessed 2 May 2022
5. Ellickson, P.B., Kar, W., Reeder, J.C.: Estimating marketing component effects: Double machine learning from targeted digital promotions. Marketing Science 0(0) (2022). https://doi.org/10.1287/mksc.2022.1401
6. Johnson, G.: Inferno: A guide to field experiments in online display advertising. SSRN Electronic Journal (2020). https://ssrn.com/abstract=3581396
7. Tutorial on causal inference and its connections to machine learning (using dowhy+econml). https://www.pywhy.org/dowhy/v0.8/tutorial-causalinference-machinelearning-using-dowhy-econml.html, Accessed 2 May 2022
8. Heckman, J.J., Vytlacil, E.J.: Chapter 70 econometric evaluation of social programs, part i: Causal models, structural models and econometric policy evaluation. Handbook of Econometrics, pp. 4779–4874 (2007)

9. Dehejia, R.H., Wahba, S.: Propensity score-matching methods for nonexperimental causal studies. Rev. Econ. Stat. **84**(1), 151–161 (2002)
10. Künzel, S.R., Sekhon, J.S., Bickel, P.J., Yu, B.: Metalearners for estimating heterogeneous treatment effects using machine learning. Proc. Natl. Acad. Sci. **116**(10), 4156–4165 (2019)
11. Rosenbaum, P.R., Rubin, D.B.: The central role of the propensity score in observational studies for causal effects. Biometrika **70**(1), 41–55 (1983)
12. Sharma, A., Kiciman, E.: Dowhy: An end-to-end library for causal inference (2020). https://arxiv.org/abs/2011.04216
13. Alaa, A., van der Schaar, M.: Limits of estimating heterogeneous treatment effects: Guidelines for practical algorithm design. In: Dy, J., Krause, A. (eds.) Proceedings of the 35th International Conference on Machine Learning. Proceedings of Machine Learning Research, 80, pp. 129–138 (10–15 Jul 2018), https://proceedings.mlr.press/v80/alaa18a.html
14. Künzel, S.R., Sekhon, J.S., Bickel, P.J., Yu, B.: Metalearners for estimating heterogeneous treatment effects using machine learning. Proc. Natl. Acad. Sci. **116**(10), 4156–4165 (2019)
15. Nie, X., Wager, S.: Quasi-oracle estimation of heterogeneous treatment effects (2017), https://arxiv.org/abs/1712.04912
16. About causal ml. https://causalml.readthedocs.io/en/latest/about.html Accessed 2 May 2022
17. Validation. https://causalml.readthedocs.io/en/latest/validation.html Accessed 2 May 2022
18. Imbens, G.W., Wooldridge, J.M.: Recent developments in the econometrics of program evaluation. J. Econ. Lit. textbf47(1), pp. 5–86 (March 2009). https://www.aeaweb.org/articles?id=10.1257/jel.47.1.5
19. CustomerGauge: NPS&CX BENCHMARK REPORT (2018)
20. Gordon, B.R., Moakler, R., Zettelmeyer, F.: Close enough? a large-scale exploration of non-experimental approaches to advertising measurement. Marketing Science 0(0) (2022), https://doi.org/10.1287/mksc.2022.1413

Visualization of Community Structure Using Follower Data on Twitter and Comparison Between Stores

Ryo Morooka[1(✉)], Takashi Namatame[2], and Kohei Otake[3]

[1] Graduate School of Information and Telecommunication Engineering, Tokai University, 2-3-23, Takanawa, Minato-ku, Tokyo 108-8619, Japan
2cjnm019@mail.u-tokai.ac.jp

[2] Faculty of Science and Engineering, Chuo University, 1-13-27, Kasuga, Bunkyo-ku, Tokyo 112-8551, Japan
nama@kc.chuo-u.ac.jp

[3] School of Information and Telecommunication Engineering, Tokai University, 2-3-23, Takanawa, Minato-ku, Tokyo 108-8619, Japan
otake@tsc.u-tokai.ac.jp

Abstract. In recent years, social networking services (SNS) have become widespread and have become an essential communication tool for all of us. Accordingly, companies are using SNS as a communication and marketing platform with consumers. We believe that it is important to focus on the consumer community and understand the characteristics of consumers to effectively conduct SNS marketing. In this study, we use follower data obtain from Twitter to visualize the community structure. Specifically, we conduct a network analysis to visualize the network structure of each store. Then, we comparisons between stores and detect the consumer community of each store. Finally, we suggest product promotion methods based on the characteristics of the communities.

Keywords: Social Media Marketing · Network Analysis · Community Structure

1 Introduction

In recent years, social network services (SNS) have become much more widespread. According to the 2nd year of Reiwa Survey on Information and Communication Media Usage Time and Information Behavior, the percentage of users of LINE and Twitter have been increasing since 2012, and for Instagram since 2015 in Japan (Fig. 1) [1]. This indicates that SNS have become essential communication tools for us.

In addition, the percentage of companies utilizing social media services is increasing according to the results of the 30th year of Heisei Communications Usage Trends Survey released by the Ministry of Internal Affairs and Communications (Fig. 2) [2]. A high percentage of companies use social media services for the purpose of "introduction and promotion of products and events" and "providing regular information" based on the same results of the 30th year of Heisei Communications Usage Trends Survey (Fig. 3) [2].

A. Coman and S. Vasilache (Eds.): HCII 2023, LNCS 14025, pp. 418–428, 2023.
https://doi.org/10.1007/978-3-031-35915-6_30

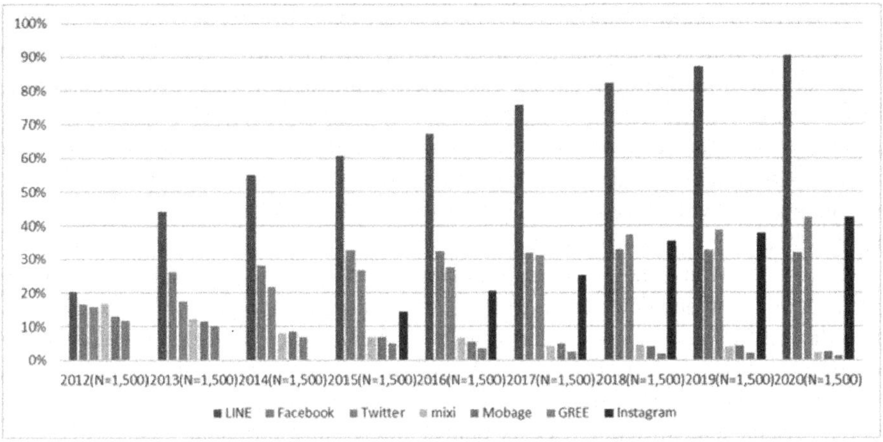

Fig. 1. Use of major social media services/applications in Japan

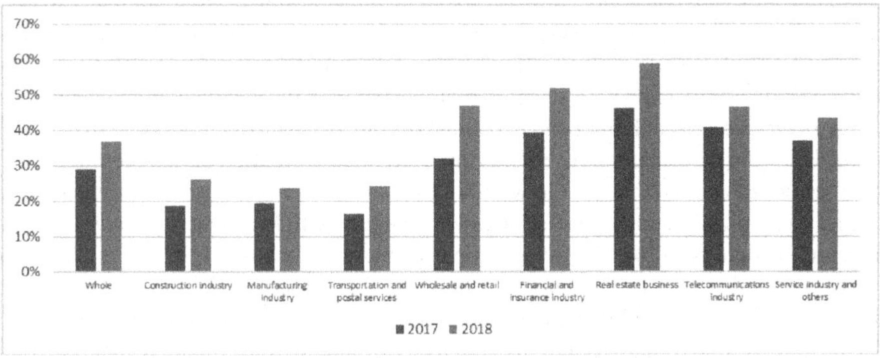

Fig. 2. Utilization of Social Media Services by Industry

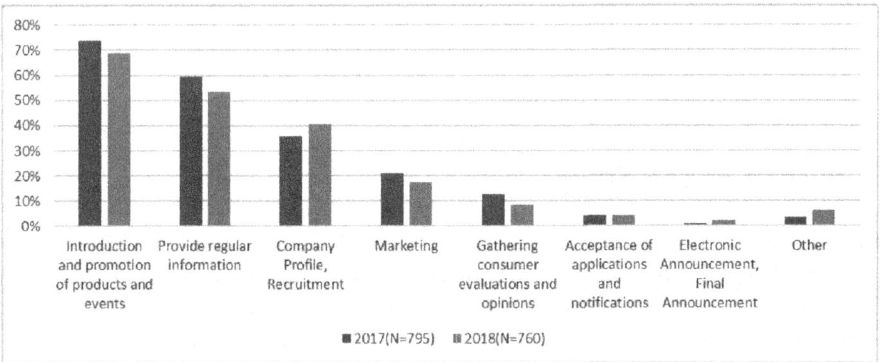

Fig. 3. Purpose and usage of social media services

Based on the above, companies are presumably using SNS as an important place to communicate with consumers and conduct marketing activities. However, most studies on social media marketing focus on consumers (influencers), and not enough studies focus on communities generated among consumers. In this case, the community refers to a group of consumers who share common values and interests on social network services. Consumers have a wide variety of values, and we believe it is important to focus on communities with shared values and understand the characteristics of consumers to make SNS marketing more effective.

In some previous study focusing on communities, Miyake et al. [3] targeted a certain fashion brand and detected consumer communities composed of SNS. In addition, they utilized the frequency of tweets posted by consumers belonging to the communities to understand the characteristics of each community. As a result, they found that the content of tweets posted differed by community. Moreover, they found that consumer's preference characteristics influence the connection within a community. Ishida [4] set up the hypotheses leading to the relationship between brand and community and conducted confirmatory factor analysis and causal model testing. He found that when a company communicates with consumers through social media, consumers are more likely to perceive individuality in the content of posts when the personality of the person in charge or a fictitious character is set up. In addition, he found that consumers become more attached to the store and have a stronger relationship with the company brand when they receive an impression of humor and friendliness from social media posts. Suzuki et al. [5] studied how the personality of users was involved in the formation of SNS communities. As a result, they found that people with high sociability, sincerity, and clarity tended to connect with people with high sincerity, while people with low sincerity tended to connect with people with low sincerity (people with common attributes were more likely to connect with each other). Hato [6] examined the influence relationship among the frequency of the community members interactions and their relationship with the brand. As a result, he found that it is not the frequency of interactions, but their identification with the community that strengthens their relationship with the brand.

These studies provided several important knowledge about communities on SNS. However, the history of research on SNS is short, and it is necessary to accumulate case studies on a variety of subjects. In particular, we believe it is important to discover communities and understand their structure by using the actual follower information of companies that conduct SNS marketing.

2 Purpose of This Study

The purpose of this study is to examine effective product public relations (PR) methods for stores based on the characteristics of their network structure using follower data from SNS accounts of companies operating multiple electronics retail stores in the same region. In particular, we collect follower data of stores from Twitter to visualize the network structure on SNS. Furthermore, we detect communities from the network structure and compare them among stores. Then, we suggest effective product PR methods for the analyzed stores based on the characteristics of their communities.

3 Summary of Data to Analysis

In this study, we used Twitter API to extract user's information who were followers of company's account operating multiple electronics retail stores in the same region. Here, we excluded accounts of stores in the same family, etc., from the perspective of investigating the community structure of the stores alone. Next, we obtained information on all accounts that follow the followers of company's account. In this study, we selected the accounts of stores located in Akihabara, Tokyo (Store A and Store B). Store A account has 1,484 followers and Store B account has 3,702 followers. Store A mainly sells consumer electronics products and Store B sells mainly anime-related goods.

4 Analysis to Characterize the Network Structure of Each Store

In this section, we attempt to visualize the network structure of the stores. Concretely, we conduct a network analysis to identify the characteristics of the network structure of stores based on degree centrality. In addition, we use Modularity [7] to detect communities of stores and compare each store.

4.1 Visualization of the Network Structure of Each Store

First, we conducted a network analysis to visualize the network structure of users based on the follower relationships of followers of the stores analyzed. Social network analysis is an analysis that focuses on relationships (connections) among people, teams, organizations, regions, political parties, and so on. Based on graph theory, relationships are mathematically described and visualized as a graph with nodes and edges. In this study, we defined a node as a follower of a store, and an edge as a common follower or follow relationship among nodes. Then, we removed any node when there was no edge existed. In addition, the number of common users and node-to-node connections that follow the follower was set as a weight. Next, we calculated degree centrality to determine the extent to which followers of each store are connected through their own followers (Eq. (1)).

$$degree\ centrality = \frac{d_i}{N-1} \tag{1}$$

where

d_i *Degree of node i*

N *Number of all nodes*

Figures 4 and 5 show histograms of the degree centrality at stores A and B.

The x-axis of the figure represents the value of degree centrality, and the y-axis represents the number of users. In Figs. 4 and 5, the degree centrality values for many users are near 0, indicating that users are not connected to each other. In addition, focusing on the areas where the degree centrality is above 0.5, more than half of users are accounted for in Store A, indicating that users are strongly connected to each other through followers. On the other hand, there are almost no users with degree centrality

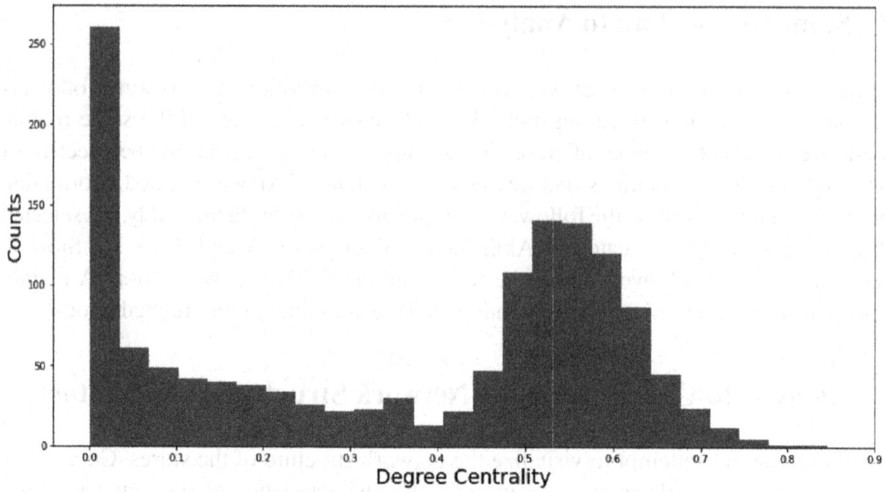

Fig. 4. Histogram of degree centrality (Store A)

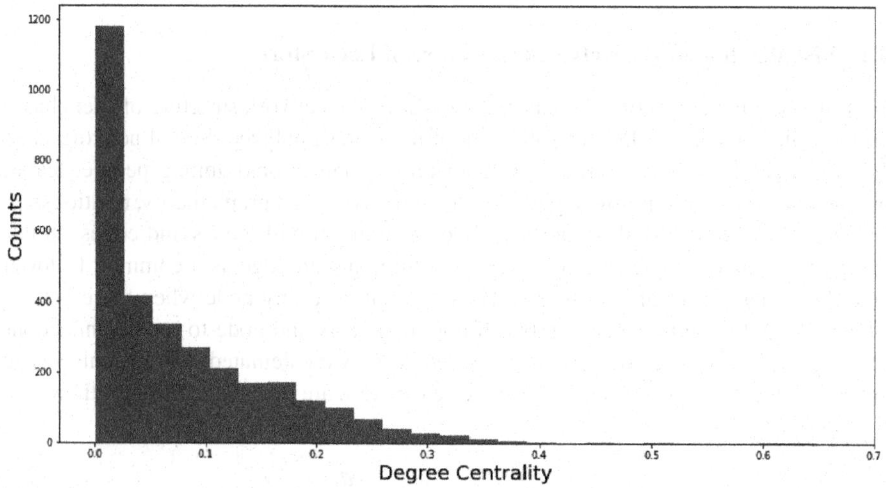

Fig. 5. Histogram of degree centrality (Store B)

of 0.5 or higher in Store B, indicating that the connection between users is weaker than in Store A.

Based on these results, we removed nodes with small degree to easy to understand the strongly connected relationships. In particular, we removed nodes with degree less than 100 for Store A and nodes with degree less than 200 for Store B. Thus, the number of nodes in store A went from 1391 to 1065, and in store B from 3144 to 1378.

To understand the relationship between the network structure of each store and the connections of each node, we visualized a network where the node size is proportional to the degree value. The degree represents the number of edges connected to a node.

Concretely, we created a network graph using python based on a list of edges and the weights of each edge. We considered a node to be related if there was a common follower or follow relationship between the nodes. The number of common followers was then used as the edge weight. Next, we visualized the network structure of the created graphs using matplotlib. The network graphs are shown in Figs. 6 and 7.

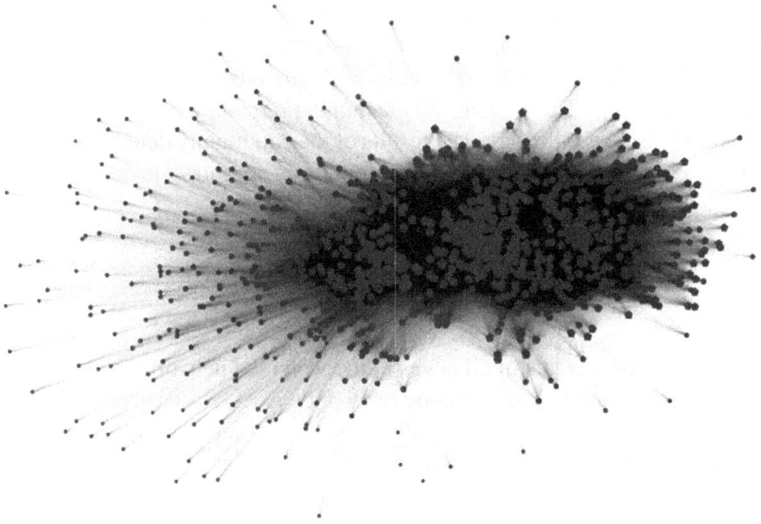

Fig. 6. Network graph representing follower relationships for store A

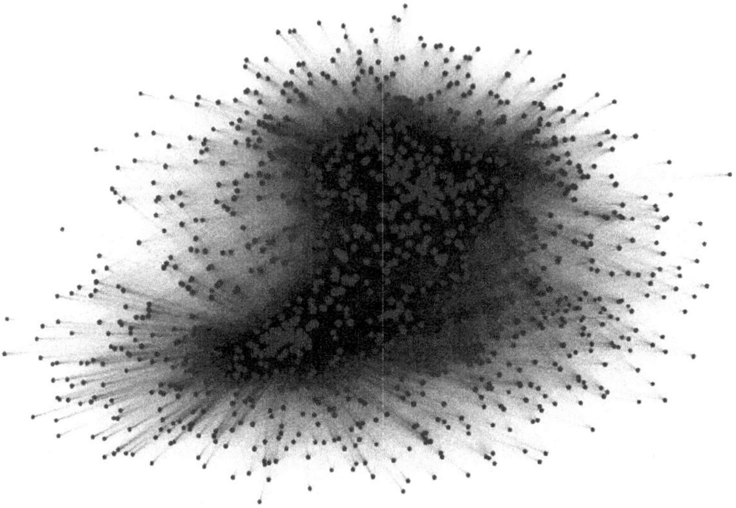

Fig. 7. Network graph representing follower relationships for store B

From Figs. 6 and 7, the larger the node size, indicates that there are more connections among users who follow the store.

We found that both stores A and B have many connections. Comparing stores A with B, the network in store A is more crowded with nodes. In addition, no nodes with strong connections were clearly identified in either store.

4.2 Detecting Communities Using Modularity

After constructing a network of each store, we attempt to detect communities to understand the community characteristics of each store. Based on the edge list and weights that indicate the node connections in each store, community detection is performed using Modularity Q (Eq. (2)). The weights are the number of common user and node-to-node connections that follow followers. The results of the community detection for each store and the number of users belonging to each community are shown in the following figure and table.

$$Q = \frac{1}{2W}\sum\nolimits_{ij}\left(W_{ij} - \frac{w_i w_j}{2W}\right)\delta(C_i, C_j) \tag{2}$$

where

W the sum of the weights of all edges in the weighted network,
W_{ij} the sum of weights between node i and node j,
$w_i w_j$ the sum of the weights of the edges adjacent to each of node i and node j,
$C_i C_j$ the community to which node i and node j belong,
δ Kronecker delta.

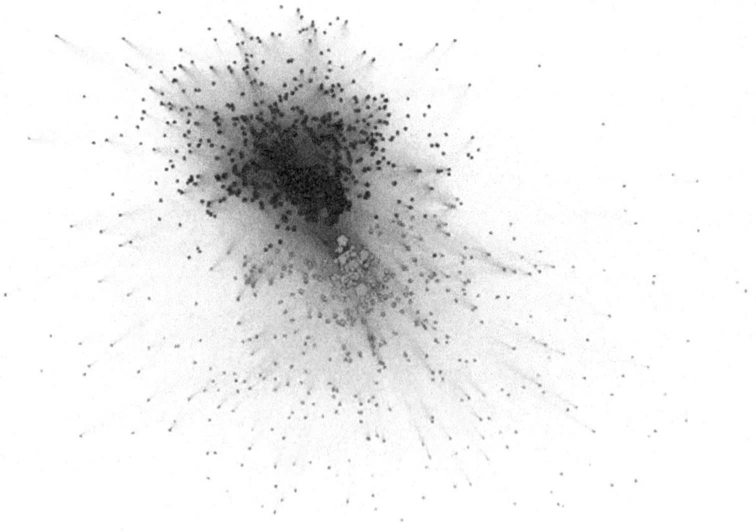

Fig. 8. Detecting Communities (Store A)

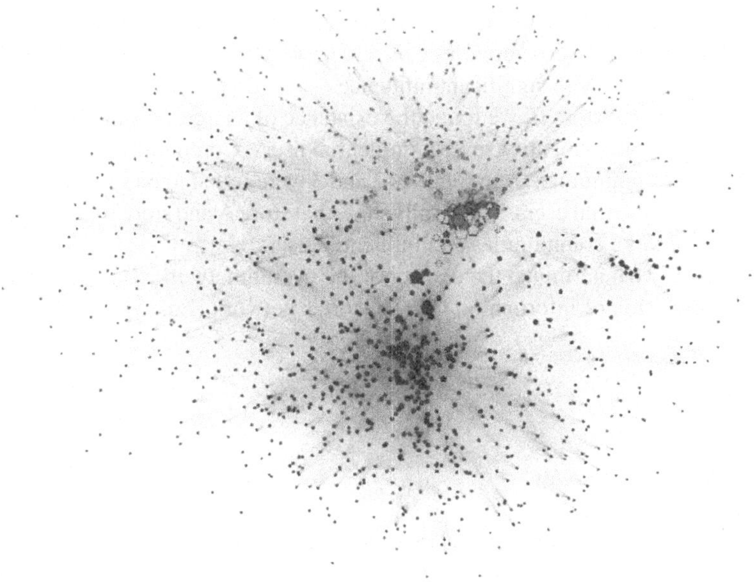

Fig. 9. Detecting Communities (Store B)

Table 1. Number of users for each community (Store A)

Community name	Number of users	Community color
Community0	576	Blue
Community1	338	Green
Community2	47	Brown
Community3	80	Gray
Community4	24	Light blue

Table 2. Number of users for each community (Store B)

Community name	Number of users	Community color
Community0	987	Blue
Community1	317	Orange
Community2	47	Violet
Community3	27	Gray

Node size in Figs. 8 and 9 is proportional to PageRank [8]. It represents the influence on the surrounding nodes. Tables 1 and 2 also show the naming and color of each community. From these, 5 communities for Store A and 4 communities for Store B could be detected. In the network of Store A, we found that there were 2 large communities, Communities 0 and 1. In communities 2, 3, and 4, we identified several users with small community sizes, but with significant influence.

In the network of store B, we found the existence of a large community, community 0. We were also able to identify several influential users. Community 1 was found to be a medium-sized community. Communities 2 and 3 were found to be small communities, but with many influential users. The results show that store A and store B have in common the presence of large communities and influential users.

In addition, we determined the density of the overall network after node deletion to capture the diffusion of information in each store's network (Eq. (3)).

$$density = \frac{2m}{n(n-1)} \tag{3}$$

where

n Total number of nodes

m Total number of edges.

As a result, we found that the density of the network for store A was about 0.59, and for store B, about 0.30. This confirms that the network of store A is superior to that of store B in terms of information diffusivity. We also obtained the overall Modularity in the network, which was 0.45 for store A and 0.32 for store B.

5 Consideration of Product PR Methods

We use the results of the community detection to consider the characteristics of the communities in each store. We also referred to some of the accounts of users belonging to each community to understand the characteristics of the communities.

We checked some of the accounts of each community in store A. Communities 0 and 2 were mostly sweepstakes accounts. It refers to accounts that frequently enter Twitter giveaway contests. These accounts may have shared retweets of posts about the giveaway project within the community. Community 1 had many individual accounts related to games and amine. In this community, it can be expected that individual accounts interacted with each other by posting about games and anime. In Communities 3 and 4, there were many store accounts related to multi-store electronics retailers and consumer electronics products.

In the same way, we identified several accounts belonging to each community in Store B as well. As a result, Community 0 included news accounts, such as accounts about anime and manga, and accounts that post information about their hobbies. These were influential accounts with high PageRank. From this, it can be expected that community 0 is a community composed of users who refer to that information mainly through news accounts. In Community 1, there were many accounts related to individuals who like anime. Other accounts included those of artists and hobbyists, including those who play games. This suggests that this community has a wide variety of users, and that many of them post about a wide range of topics related to their hobbies. In Community 2, there were many consumer electronics retail store accounts. In community 3, there were retail accounts for a variety of products, such as accounts selling electronics and stationery.

Next, we compare the stores based on the characteristics of each store. One of unique feature that store A has been the presence of 2 communities of sweepstakes accounts. Among these, community 0 occupies many nodes on the network. This means that if there is a post about a campaign or a gift, there is a high likelihood that the post will be instantly spread. Thus, it can be said that store A has a network structure with excellent information diffusion through the connections of many users.

On the other hand, Store B is characterized by the community to which accounts transmitting information on anime and hobbies belong. Since this community is large, if a product handled by Store B becomes a topic of conversation, the information will be shared with many users. Thus, it can be said that store B has a network structure with excellent information dissemination through a single news account.

Based on the above, we consider the product PR method of each store. Store A has a community of 0 and 2, which is excellent for information diffusion. We believe that product PR through a gift plan utilizing the SNS function of retweeting would be effective. This allows the postings to be spread by many sweepstakes accounts and deliver product information to many users. This will also spread the information to users outside the network, making the product known to many users. Thus, we believe that for store A, the present project on SNS is an effective method of product PR.

Store B has a community 0 with excellent information transmission capabilities, and we believe that having influential users conduct product PR is an effective method. Specifically, store B provides the products it wants to promote to influential users and asks them to evaluate their items. Next, they are invited to act as an influencer for Store B and post comments and evaluations of the products on a social networking service to spread the words to followers. This is a way to have followers become aware of the product and its appeal. Since information can be sent out from multiple accounts, including store accounts, this can be expected to have a large advertising effect. In addition, by transmitting honest evaluations from a consumer's point of view, it is expected to stimulate follower's willingness and interest in purchasing. Furthermore, since Community 1 is a collection of accounts related to hobbies, including animation, it is possible to promote products to users who have high expectations of being interested in the products. Thus, we believe that it is effective for Store B to request highly influential users to promote its products by taking advantage of its strong information transmission capabilities.

6 Conclusion

This study used follower data from the accounts of companies operating multiple electronics retail stores to visualize the network structure of the stores and perform community detection. We conducted a network analysis using follower data from the stores under analysis. Furthermore, we set the number of followers in common as a weight and used the Modularity to detect community. From the results, we identified the characteristics of the stores. Then, based on these characteristics, we examined each store's product PR methods.

Our future works include community detection of other stores, extraction of the content of each community's postings, and analysis of what topics are being shared. This will enable us to understand the characteristics of each store network, clarify the detailed characteristics of each community, and make suggestions on how to effectively promote specific products.

Acknowledgment. We thank an electronic retail store of Japan for permission to use valuable datasets. This work was supported by JSPS KAKENHI Grant Number 21H04600 and 21K13385.

References

1. National Institute of Information and Communications Policy, Ministry of Internal Affairs and Communications, The 2nd year of Reiwa Survey on Information and Communication Media Usage Time and Information Behavior. https://www.soumu.go.jp/main_content/000765258.pdf. Author Checked 10 Feb 2023
2. Ministry of Internal Affairs and Communications, the 30th year of Heisei Communications Usage Trends Survey. https://www.soumu.go.jp/johotsusintokei/statistics/data/190531_1.pdf. Author Checked 10 Feb 2023
3. Mitake, S., Otake, K., Namatame, T.: Detection and characterization of consumer communities using tweet data. In: The 82nd National Convention of Information Processing Society Japan, 2ZG-01, pp. 4-609–4-610 (2020). (in Japanese)
4. Ishida, M.: The influence of Social Media accounts personality traits on brand community. J. Bus. Adm. **98**, 67–78 (2021). (in Japanese)
5. Suzuki, G., Ochi, M., Sakaki, T., Sakata, I.: Analyzing the influence of human personality on SNS community formation. In: The 32nd Annual Conference of the Japanese Society for Artificial Intelligence, 1B3-02, pp. 1c–4 (2018). (in Japanese)
6. Hatou, M.: Factors connecting interaction and brand commitment - media effects of identification with the community. Jpn. Soc. Mark. Distrib. **1**(1), 11–17 (2017). (in Japanese)
7. Newman, M.E.J.: Fast algorithm for detecting community structure in networks. Phys. Rev. E **69**(066133), 1–5 (2004)
8. Page, L., Brin, S., Motwani, R., Winograd, T.: The PageRank citation ranking: bringing order to the web. Technical report, Stanford Digital Library Technologies Project, SIDL-WP-1999-0120 (1999)

New Product Development (NPD) - Staying Competitive in an Ever-Changing Business Environment

Marc Oliver Opresnik(✉)

Technische Hochschule Lübeck, Public Corporation, Mönkhofer Weg 239, 23562 Lübeck, Germany
Marc.Oliver.Opresnik@TH-Luebeck.de

Abstract. Given the rapid changes in customer tastes, technology and competition, companies must develop a steady stream of new products and services. A company can create new products in two ways. One is through acquisition – by buying another company, a patent or a license to produce someone else's product. The other is through new product development (NPD) in the company's own research-and-development (R&D) department.

The traditional new product development models involve the following stages in product development: idea generation, screening, concept development and testing, business analysis, product development and testing, test marketing, commercialization or launch.

An effective commercialization strategy relies upon marketing management making plain choices regarding the target market, and the development of a marketing strategy that provides a differential advantage.

Keyword: Social Media Marketing AI NPD New Product Development Innovation Internet of Things Artificial Intelligence Marketing Management Web 2.0 Marketing 5.0 Social Computing Social Media

1 Strategic Product and Service Decisions

Essentially, a product can be defined as anything that can be offered to a customer for attention, acquisition, use, or consumption and that might satisfy a want or need. Product is a core element in the marketing mix as it provides the functional requirements sought by customers. Careful management of the product offering is essential if your company is to produce the desired responses from customers but the product is only part of the story. In an age of intense competition where it is of critical importance to differentiate one's offerings from competitors.

In creating an acceptable product offer for international markets, it is necessary to examine first what contributes to the 'total' product offer. In the product dimensions, we include not just the core physical properties, but also additional elements such as packaging, branding and after-sales service that make up the total package for the purchaser. We can look at three levels of a product [1]:

A. Coman and S. Vasilache (Eds.): HCII 2023, LNCS 14025, pp. 429–438, 2023.
https://doi.org/10.1007/978-3-031-35915-6_31

Core product benefits: Functional features, performance, perceived value, image and technology.

Product attributes: Brand name, design, packaging, price, size, color variants, country of origin.

Support services: Delivery, installation, guarantees, after-sales service (repair and maintenance), spare part services.

Products and services can be seen on at least four main levels. These levels are the core product, the expected product, the augmented product and the potential product [1].

Differentiation is possible in all these respects.

At the centre of this model is the core, or generic, product. This is the central product or service offered. The core benefit addresses the following question: What is the buyer really buying? When designing products, marketers must first define the core, problem-solving benefits or services that consumer want.

Beyond the generic product, however, is what customers expect in addition, the expected product. When buying petrol, for example, customers expect the possibility of paying by credit card, the availability of screen wash facilities, and so on. Since most petrol forecourts meet these expectations, they do not serve to differentiate one supplier from another.

At the next level, there is the augmented product. This constitutes all the additional features and services that exceed customer expectations to convey added value and hence serve to differentiate the offer from that of competitors. Product planners must build an augmented product around the core benefit and expected product by offering additional customer services and benefits. The petrol station where one attendant fills the car with petrol while another cleans the windscreen, head-lamps and mirrors, is going beyond what is expected. Over time, however, these means of distinguishing can become copied, routine, and ultimately merely part of what is expected.

Finally, the potential product can be described as all those further additional features and benefits that could be offered. At the petrol station these may include a free car wash with every fifth fill up.

While the model shows the potential product bounded, in reality it is only bounded by the imagination and ingenuity of the supplier.

In the past, suppliers have concentrated on attempts to differentiate their offerings on the basis of the core and expected product that convergence is occurring at this level in many markets. As quality control, assurance and management methods become more widely understood and practiced, delivering a performing, reliable, durable, conforming offer (a 'quality' product in the classic sense of the word) will no longer be adequate. In the future, there will be greater emphasis on the augmented and potential product as ways of adding value, creating customer delight and hence creating competitive advantage.

The key decisions in the development and marketing of individual products and services include product attributes, branding, packaging, labelling and product support services.

Beyond decisions about individual products and services, product strategy also calls for building a product line. A product line is a group of products that are closely related because they function in a similar manner, are sold to the same customer groups, are marketed through the same types of outlets, or fall within given price ranges. For example, Samsung produces several lines of telecommunication products.

The major product line decision involves product line length – the number of items in the product line. The line is too short if the manager can enlarge profits by adding items and the line is too long if the marketer can increase profits by dropping items. Product line length is influenced by company objectives and resources. For example, one goal might be allowing for upselling. Thus, BMW wants to move customers up from its 3-series models to 5- and 7-series models. Another objective might be to allow cross-selling: Hewlett-Packard sells printers as well as cartridges.

A firm can lengthen the product line in two ways: by line stretching or by line filling. Product line stretching occurs when a company lengthens its product line beyond its current range. The firm can stretch its line downward, upward, or both ways. Mercedes-Benz, for example, stretched its Mercedes line downward because of the following reasons: Facing a slow-growth luxury car market and attacks by Japanese automakers on its high-end positioning, it successfully introduced its Mercedes C-Class cars.

Product line filling involves adding more items within the present range of the line. Reasons for this approach include reaching for extra profits, satisfying dealers, using excess capacity and being the leading full-line company. Sony, for example, filled its Walkman line by adding solar-powered and waterproof Walkmans, ultra-light models for exercises, and the Memory Stick Walkman. Line filling is overdone if it results in cannibalization and customer confusion [2].

An organisation with several product lines has a product mix. A product mix (or product assortment) consist of all the product lines and items that a particular company markets. A company's product mix has four important dimensions [1]:

Product mix width refers to the number of different product lines the company carries. For example, Procter & Gamble markets a wide product mix consisting of 250 brands organized into five major product lines: personal and beauty, house and home, health and wellness, baby and family, and pet nutrition and care products.

Product mix length refers to the total number of items the firm carries within its product lines. P&G carries many brands within each line. For example, its house and home lines include seven laundry detergents, six hand soaps, five shampoos, and four dishwashing detergents.

Product line depth refers to the number of versions offered for each product in the line. P&G's Crest toothpaste comes in 16 varieties.

Consistency: The consistency of the product mix refers to how closely related the various product lines are in end use, production requirements, distribution channels, or some other way. P&G's product lines are consistent insofar as they are consumer products that go through the same distribution channels. The lines are less consistent insofar as they perform different functions for customers.

Services have grown dramatically in recent years. It is seen from the definition of a product that services often accompany products. Increasingly it is accepted that because buyers are concerned with benefits or satisfactions this is a combination of both tangible 'products', and intangible 'services'.

Services are characterized by the following features [1]:

Intangibility means that services cannot be seen, tasted, felt, heard, or smelled before they are bought. For example, as ser-vices like air transportation or education cannot be touched or tested, the buyers or services cannot claim ownership or anything tangible in the conventional sense. Payment is for use or performance. Tangible elements of the ser-vice, such as food or drink on airlines, are used as part of the service in order to confirm the benefit provided and to enhance its perceived value. Against this background, a service marketing strategy consistently tries to 'make the intangible tangible' and send the right signals about the quality. This is called evidence management, in which the service organisation presents its customers with organized, honest evidence of its capabilities.

Perishability means that services cannot be stored for future usage – for example, unfilled airline seats are lost once the aircraft takes off. This characteristic causes considerable problems in planning and promotion in order to match supply and demand. To maintain service capacity constantly at levels necessary to satisfy peak demand will be very expensive. The marketer must therefore attempt to estimate demand levels in order optimise the use of capacity.

Heterogeneity implies that services are rarely the same because they involve interactions between people. Furthermore, there is high customer involvement in the production of services. This can cause problems of maintaining quality, particularly in international markets where there are quite different attitudes to-wards customer service. For example, within a given Marriott hotel, one registration-desk employee may be cheerful and highly efficient, whereas another standing just a few feet away may be un-pleasant and slow. Even the quality of a single Marriott employee's service varies according to his or her energy at the time of each customer encounter. Consequently, the management of staff is of supreme importance in the framework of service marketing.

Inseparability means that services cannot be separated from their providers. The time of production is very close to or even simultaneous with the time of consumption. The service is provided at the point of sale. This means that economies of scale and experience curve benefits are difficult to achieve, and supplying the service to scattered markets can be expensive, particularly in the initial setting-up phase. If a service employee provides the service, then the employee is a part of the service. Because the customer is also present, provider-customer-interaction is a special feature of services marketing and both the provider and the customer affect the service outcome.

All products, both goods and services, consist of a core element that is surrounded by an array of optional supplementary elements. If we look first at the core service products, we can assign them to one of three broad categories depending on their tangibility and the extent to which customers need to be physically present during service production as shown in Fig. 1.

Categories of service	Charactetistics	Examples
People processing	Customers become a part of the production process. The service needs to maintain local geographic presence	Education Healthcare Food service Hotel service
Possession processing	The object needs to be involved in the production process, but the owner of the object (the customer) does not. Involve tangible actions to physical objects to improve their value for the customers	Car repair
Information based services	Collecting, interpreting and transmitting data to create value to others. Minimal tangibility. Minimal customer involvement in the production process	Banking Internet services

Fig. 1. Categories of Service (Source: Opresnik and Hollensen, 2020)

2 New Product Development (NPD)

Given the rapid changes in customer tastes, technology and competition, companies must develop a steady stream of new products and services (question marks in the terminology of the BCG matrix). A company can create new products in two ways. One is through acquisition – by buying another company, a patent or a license to produce someone else's product. The other is through new product development (NPD) in the company's own research-and-development (R&D) department.

The traditional new product development models involve the following stages in product development: idea generation, screening, concept development and testing, business analysis, product development and testing, test marketing, commercialization or launch [3].

An effective commercialization strategy relies upon marketing management making plain choices regarding the target market, and the development of a marketing strategy that provides a differential advantage.

A useful starting point for choosing a target market is an understanding of the diffusion of innovation process which explains how a new product spreads throughout a market over time. Figure 2. Shows the diffusion of innovation curve which categorizes people or organisations according to how soon they are willing to adopt the innovation [1].

The graph shows that those actors (innovators and early adopters) who are willing to purchase the new product soon after launch are likely to from a minor part of the total number of actors who will eventually be willing to buy it. As the new product is accepted and approved by these customers, and the decision to purchase it becomes less risky, the customers that make up the bulk of the market, comprising the early and late majority, begin to try the product themselves. Finally, after the product has gained full acceptance, a group describes as the laggards adopt the new product.

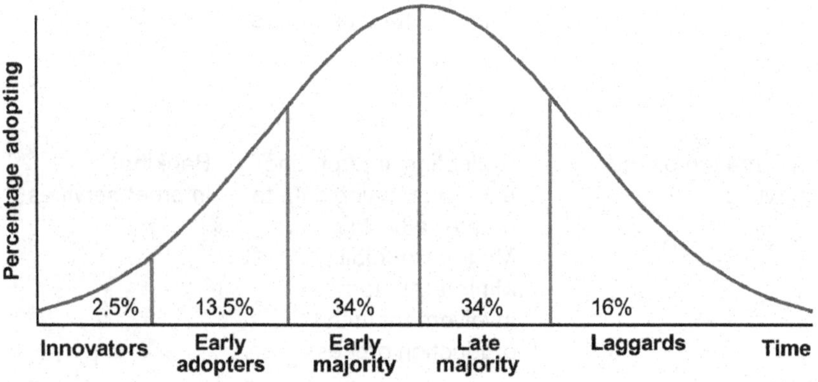

Fig. 2. The diffusion of innovation process (Source: Opresnik and Hollensen, 2020)

3 Degrees of Product Newness

A new product can have several degrees of newness. A product may be an entirely new invention (new to the world) or it may be a slight modification of an existing product (cost reductions).

Let us briefly discuss the main categories [1]:

New to International Markets: These represent a small proportion of all new products introduced. Most new products modify and improve a company's existing products. They are inventions that usually contain a significant development in technology such as a new discovery or manipulation of existing technology in a very different way leading to revolutionary new designs, such as the Sony Discman. Other examples include Polaroid Instamatic camera and 3M's Post-it.

New to the Company: Although not new to the marketplace, these products are new to the particular company. They provide an opportunity for the company to enter an established market for the first time. For ex-ample, Microsoft will be able to enter the games console market, when it launches X-box, ready to compete head-on with Sony and Nintendo.

Line Extensions: In this situation, the company already has a line of products in the market. For example, Virgin energy drink was an addition to its established line of cola-brands.

Reposition Existing Products: This has more to do with new customer perception and branding than technical development. Therefore, this alternative may be new to the market (new perception) but not new to the company itself.

4 The Multiple Convergent Process Model

Baker and Hart [3] have suggested the so-called multiple convergent process model, which has been derived from the idea of parallel processing.

In the multiple convergent approach, there are tasks that must be carried out in different internal departments (research and development, marketing, engineering/design, manufacturing), and carried out in co-operation with external partners (suppliers and customers). The tasks have to be carried out simultaneously and the results must converge at some juncture, which is likely to happen several times due to the iterations in the process.

Consequently, there are multiple convergent points that link the activity-stage model to the decision-stage models. The extent of involvement of internal and external players will be determined by the firm's specific needs in the product development process.

One of the advantages of this model is that it recognizes the involving of external partners in the product development process. There is growing interest in the need for supplier and customer involvement in the NPD. From the customers, the firm can benefit in form of new product ideas and product adaptations to specific customer needs. The supplier can contribute with supplier innovation and just-in-time techniques [1].

5 Product Platform and Modularity in NPD

The modular approach to product development is an important success factor in many markets. By sharing components and production processes across a product platform, companies can develop differentiated products efficiently, increase the flexibility and responsiveness of their manufacturing processes, and take market share away from competitors that develop only one product at a time.

The modular approach is also a way to achieve successful mass customization – the manufacture of products in high volumes that are tailored to meet the needs of individual customers. It allows highly differentiated products to be delivered to the market without consuming excessive resources [1].

Product modularity consists of designing a platform that is a collection of assets which are shared by a set of products. These assets can be divided into four categories [1]:

Components – the part designs of a product, the fixtures and tools needed to make them, the circuit designs, and the pro-grammes burned into programmable chips or stored on disks.

Processes – the equipment used to make components or to assemble components into products and the design of the associated production process and supply chain.

Knowledge – design know-how, technology applications and limitations, production techniques, mathematical models, and testing methods.

People and relationship – teams, relationships among team members, relationships between the team and the larger organization, and relationships with a network of suppliers.

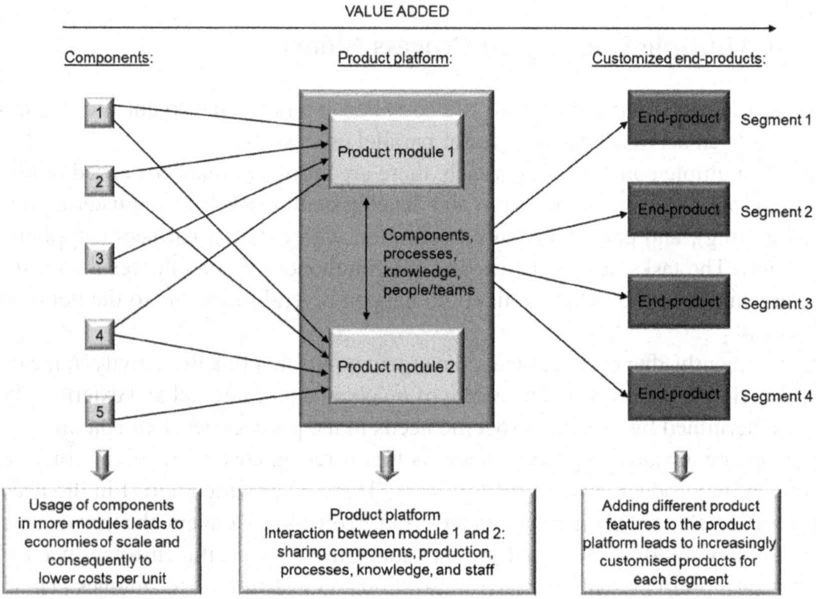

Fig. 3. Principle of using modularity in creating product platforms (Source: Opresnik and Hollensen, 2020)

This general product platform should then be used for tailoring end products to the needs of different market segments or customers. The platform approach reduces the incremental cost of addressing the specific needs of a market segment or of an individual customer. See also Fig. 2. as an example of the modularity approach in new product development. For the sake of simplicity only the interaction between two product modules is illustrated.

The firm's advantages of using product modularity are [1]:

Reduction of development cost and time: Parts and assembly processes developed for one end product can be used for other products.

Reduction of variable costs: When producing larger volumes of common components, companies achieve economies of scale, which cut costs in materials management, logistics, distribution, inventory management, sales and service and purchasing.

Reduction of production investments: Machinery, equipment, tooling and the engineering time needed to create them, can be shared across higher production volumes.

Reduction of risks: The lower investment required for each product, developed from a platform, results in decreased risk for each new product. Sharing components across products allows companies to stock fewer parts in their production and service parts inventories, which translates into better service levels and/or lower service costs.

6 New Products For The International Market

Customer needs are the starting point for product development, whether for domestic or global markets. In addition to customer needs, conditions of use and ability to buy the product form a framework for decisions on new product development for the international market.

As a consequence of increasing international competition, speed is be-coming a key success factor for an increasing number of companies that manufacture technologically sophisticated products.

This speed of change in the environment is accelerating, leading to greater complexity and added 'turbulence', or discontinuity. Technological developments are combining to shorten product life cycles and speed up commercialization times.

The increasing turbulence in the market makes it particularly difficult to predict. As a result, planning horizons have been shortened. Where long-range plans in relatively predictable markets could span 10–15 years, very few companies today are able to plan beyond the next few years in any but the most general terms.

In parallel to shorter product life cycles (PLCs), the product development times for new products are being greatly reduced. This applies not only to technical products in the field of office communication equipment, but also to cars and consumer electronics. In some cases, there have been reductions in development times of more than half.

Similarly, the time for marketing and selling, and hence also to pay off R & D costing has gone down from about four years to only two years and less for a number of products like printers and computers, over a period of ten years [1].

For all types of technological products, it holds true that the manufactured product must be as good as required by the customer (i. e. as good as necessary), but not as good as technically feasible. Too frequently, technological products are over-optimized and therefore too expensive from the customer's point of view.

Today product quality is not enough to reach and to satisfy the customer. Quality of design and appearance play an increasingly important role. A highly qualified product support and customer service is also required.

7 Conclusion

Competitive advantage and how one gains it have changed much over the years. In lesser-developed markets advantage can be gained through simple market mechanisms such as achieving distribution where none existed before. As markets mature, competitive advantage becomes increasingly difficult to attain. Many factors contribute to these, including increases in sophistication of competitors and consumers, consumer mobility, distribution intensity, and flow of product and market information. At a macro level, such things as the structural nature of industries, networking, alliances and governmental interventions contribute to difficulties in achieving competitive advantage in a mature market.

NPD is a key element of time-based competition which in essence focuses on gaining advantage by being faster than competitors – faster in responding to market changes, faster with product development and introductions, faster in integrating new technology into products and faster in distribution and customer service.

Ultimately, NPD is a customer-focused strategy. Speed and variety are the means by which a company can do more for its clients. However, succeeding at this requires a coordinated company effort. A time-based competitor develops the high degree of internal responsiveness and co-ordination among different parts of the company that allows it to discern differences among key customers and customize the products and services delivered to each. Thus, the ultimate purpose of NPD is not maximizing speed and variety, but owning the customer.

References

1. Hollensen, S., Opresnik, M.: Marketing: Principles and Practice. 4th edition. Lübeck (2020)
2. Armstrong, G., Kotler, P., Opresnik, M.: Marketing: An Introduction. 14th ed., Harlow (2019)
3. Baker, M., Hart, S.: Product Strategy and Management, Prentice Hall (1999)

Implementing RFID Technologies for Automated Guided Vehicles in Industry 4.0

Alkriz Zahir M. Reyes[1], Russel Aldrei D. Hernandez[1], Justice Maverick L. Cruz[1], Elija Gabriel Padre Juan[1], John Albert L. Marasigan[1], Ian Kristof P. Balboa[1], Michelangelo Barroga[1], and Yung-Hao Wong[1,2](✉)

[1] Minghsin University of Science and Technology, 30401 Xinfeng, Hsinchu County, Taiwan
yvonwong@must.edu.tw

[2] National Yang Ming Chiao Tung University, 1001 University Road, Hsinchu 30010, Republic of China (Taiwan)

Abstract. Advancement is an integral aspect of society that has been driving humanity forward for centuries. The Fourth Industrial Revolution, as we know, is not just about the current trend in automation and manufacturing industries, but also, a new way of life. As such, this study had determined the advantages, disadvantages, potential, and challenges of implementing Radio Frequency Identification (RFID) technologies for Automated Guided Vehicles (AGV) in Industry 4.0 using Kolb's Experiential Learning Theory (ELT) to share up to date information on the latest technological trends in the 21st century. This study is a Qualitative type of research that incorporates a Descriptive Research Design using the Experiential Research Method (ERM). The results were garnered from the participants of the Top International Robotics Tournament (TIRT) 2022 held in Taoyuan Arena, Taiwan (ROC). In conclusion, results show that even though huge advancements were made in this aspect of technology, further problems arise to these developments and will require a lot of time and effort from like-minded individuals to harness its full potential.

Keywords: AGV · Industry 4.0 · Arduino · RFID · Line following Robot

1 Introduction

While the future is never certain in the aspect of technology, there are some emerging trends in Engineering that provide solutions to these needs. Robot technology is becoming a more significant part of our evolving society, particularly in the industrial sector. The 1950s marks the beginning of industrial robot history when the first robots were created for utilization in manufacturing and other industrial settings. The Unimate, a robotic arm used for activities including spot welding and die casting, was considered the first industrial robot and it was created by John Devol in the early 1950s [12]. According to Ullrich [26], Barrett Electronics of Northbrook, Illinois, USA introduced the first known Automated Guided Vehicles. They were mainly used in manufacturing and logistics operations through following predetermined paths using wires or reflective tapes stuck in the floor. Industrial robots continued to advance and change in the

A. Coman and S. Vasilache (Eds.): HCII 2023, LNCS 14025, pp. 439–456, 2023.
https://doi.org/10.1007/978-3-031-35915-6_32

1960s and 1970s as new sensors and control systems were created. During this time, a wider number of industries and applications started to use robots, such as material handling, assembly, and packaging. In 1973, the first AGV project was implemented in the Volvo Kalmar Assembly plant in Sweden and were used to transport car bodies between different stages of the assembly process and were able to navigate using wires embedded in the floor as an alternative to traditional conveyor assembly lines [27]. This project was a significant milestone in the development and commercialization of AGVs and helped to pave the way for the widespread adoption of AGVs in manufacturing and logistics operations. After which, many businesses started to invest in industrial robots to increase productivity and save labor costs, enabling industrial robots to start to take off in the 1980s. KUKA, a previously German-based company, moved from using Unimate robots to developing their own robot, the Famulus, which was the first robot to have six electromechanically driven axes [5]. Programming and controlling robots became simpler with the introduction of computer-aided design (CAD) and computer-aided manufacturing (CAM) technologies. Nonlinear guidance techniques like laser and inertial guidance were introduced in the late 1980s to improve the system's adaptability and precision in wireless steering [27]. AGVs became more sophisticated and versatile in the 1990s as they started to incorporate new technologies such as lasers, cameras, and sensors for navigation and guidance. With this, industrial robot use has steadily increased in recent years as a result of technological advancements that have enabled robots to become more advanced and versatile. Today, there are numerous industries that use industrial robots, and they are becoming more and more connected with other advanced technologies like artificial intelligence (AI) and the Internet of Things (IoT). According to a recent statistical study conducted by McCain [1] in 2022, there are about 2.7 million industrial robots currently used around the globe, with 88% of companies planning to invest in robotics for their own use. In April 2022, Grand View Research [13] reported that the market for AGVs was estimated to be worth around USD 3.81 billion in 2021, and from 2022 to 2030. AGV demand is expected to grow as a result of an increase in industry automation, particularly in the logistics and warehousing sector, which currently accounts for over 40% of industrial robots' market revenue.

In 2008, Bosien, Venzke, & Turau [8] mentioned that creating algorithms that allows an AGV to follow a designated path without getting lost is the main problem. Even when crossings are brought about by loops or intersecting pathways, the mechanism must function consistently. With this, they concluded with the idea of "single RFID reader does not enable smooth movements" and mentioned that "It is thus unsuitable for manufacturing scenarios." Additionally, they suggested the idea of equipping additional sensors, particularly configurations with two or more RFID readers that could potentially outperform their previous works. Moreover, Zou and Zhong [28] showed that AGVs equipped with RFID technology could have improved intelligence through the addition of obstacle detection and infrared sensors which enables them to have a better sight of the workplace. They advised future researchers to have an autonomous system through creating path planning algorithms that incorporate robots having the ability to grab and move objects though various locations.

With this, the researchers had chosen the topic "Implementing RFID Technologies for Automated Guided Vehicles in Industry 4.0" not just to report their participation in the Top International Robotics Tournament (TIRT) AGV Challenge, but also to present up to date information on the new technologies that are being associated with AGVs and provide strategies to implement RFID technology efficiently (Fig. 1).

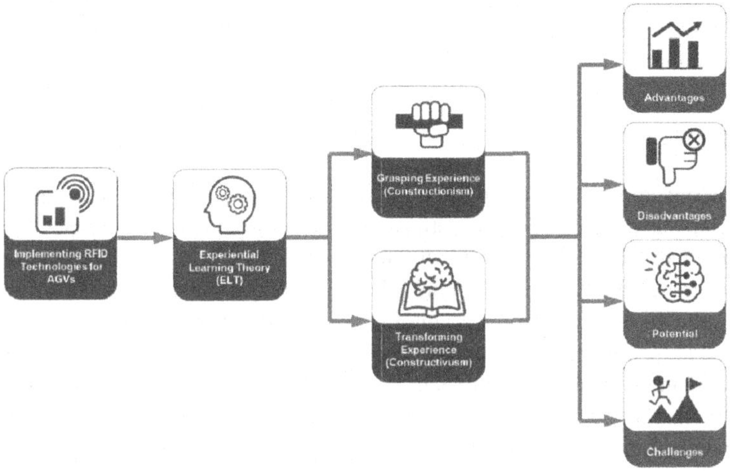

Fig. 1. Theoretical Framework

This study utilized Kolb's Experiential Learning Theory (ELT) to acquire, process and relay information because according to a study conducted by Reyes et al. [21], students, specifically Mechatronics students, can learn, experience, and make useful learning discoveries using the experiential learning approach.

In a deeper examination of the study, this research had obtained data through theoretical and practical approaches in a way of grasping and transforming experiences, accordingly, to provide more accurate and meaningful results. Specifically: Advantages, Disadvantages, Potential, and Challenges.

2 Background

2.1 Industry 4.0

With the emerging innovation of the manufacturing industry in the 21st century, Industry 4.0 plays a huge part in providing wide development such as usage of artificial intelligence and cloud computing on different aspects of advanced technologies, which makes imagination easily turn into an actual product. Originated in 2011 from the German government, its main objective is to promote the usage of advanced computers in the field of manufacturing and was considered as the continuation of Industry 3.0 where computers were introduced in the world of manufacturing process. This manufacturing era is mostly known for the boom of internet, cyber concepts, automation, and robotics. According to Erboz [11], Industry 4.0 focuses on increasing network integration and digitized system development through smart systems that could potentially replace humans in some duties and improve the working environment. This provides an evolution of technologies; developing more products and machines that may be useful in creating more innovative concepts. With this, Industry 4.0 also extends its purpose as these benefits in world manufacturers and suppliers became an investment among big companies across different competitive countries, and the ability for a company to integrate automation with seamless and wireless control will surely give them an edge in the competitive industrial manufacturing field.

2.2 Robotics

The increased appeal towards the use of robots in industry is evident, and although commercially available robots are still expensive today, many companies would still prefer to put the technology to use due to the ability of robots to be fully automated to perform repetitive tasks. Companies that have benefited the most from the use of robotics have mostly been from the automotive industry, with almost 900,000 robots in 2017 alone [1], adding more to that number every year since. Apart from the industrial sector, companies involved with restaurants, hotel management, education, agriculture, and medicine, among many others, have had increased involvement with robots [24]. As more robots are manufactured, the technology and manufacturing process is further developed, which can lead to the decrease of initial capital investment cost of acquiring such a technology. Withal, the robotics industry is predicted to advance at a relatively high rate in years to come, with a CAGR (Compound Annual Growth Rate) of 11.7% from years 2021–2030 [1].

2.3 Automatic Guided Vehicles

Automated Guided Vehicles or AGVs are mobile programmed robots that navigate with the guidance of tapes, markers, and wires which utilize various kinds of sensors including vision, proximity, and infrared sensors to provide its function. This autonomous electrically powered vehicle is commonly used in industrial factories which lessens the workforce inside the workplace, such as delivering raw materials, tools, and finished products. In this generation, AGVs are used in transporting in different industries, like automotive, food and beverage, paper and pulp, pharmaceuticals and more [10]. This device becomes more user dependent as it utilizes user-made programs to provide certain tasks. Previous research of Iqbal and Omar [17] stated that AGVs standardly have actuators for movement, sensors for navigation, processors for its programming, power source, and communication systems which perform the device's functionality using path-planning algorithms in the environments where it will be utilized (Fig. 2).

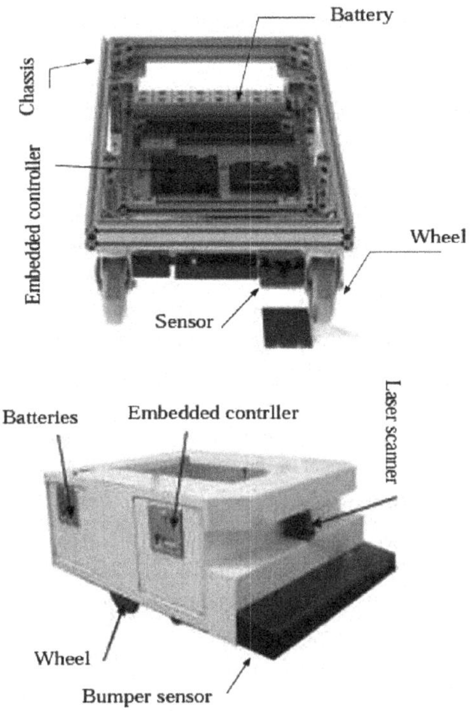

Fig. 2. AGV parts [9]

Aside from AGVs, there are also automated robots that can also be utilized inside the workplace. Autonomous Mobile Robots, also known as AMRs, are robots that can adapt to the environment [15]. It has a huge similarity with the AGVs however, AMRs are more focused on flexibility and adaptability in the workspace [22]. They can be programmed to perform a wide range of tasks and can be integrated with various sensors, cameras, and other technologies to enable them to perceive and understand their environment. These robots can be utilized in various industries such as manufacturing, logistics, and healthcare. Li [16] discussed the comparison between the two products to provide a clearer understanding of their capabilities. Attached in Table 1 is the explication of AGV and AMR (Table 2).

Table 1. Comparison Table of Automated Guided Vehicles (AGV) and Autonomous Mobile Robots (AMR) [16]

AGV vs AMR Comparison	Automated Guided Vehicle (AGV)	Autonomous Mobile Robot (AMR)
Navigation	Dependent on markers and lines such as magnetic and colored tapes	Utilize Global Positioning System (GPS) that can detect and observe the environment of the robot
Environment Flexibility	Can be more flexible since its routes can be programmed and modified by a user	Easier to create new paths and modify certain changes in directions
Obstacles	Distracts the movement of the AGV which stops the movement of the vehicle	The robot will observe the area of the obstacle and identify the best way to reroute the path
Cost	less expensive	More expensive
Usage and Installation	Requires more time due to creation of paths and installation of different sensors	Easy to use
Dependability	Very dependent with the path which results to less reliability	Independent, however, this may vary depending on the environment and the work area
Safety	B56.5–2019 in US / ISO 3691–4:2020 in UE	ANSI/RIA R15.08–1-2020

According to Mehami, Nawi, and Zhong [19], AGVs can work in two separate guidance methods. Specifically: Fixed route and free route methods. The fixed route method follows a specific path inside the workspace where the AGV detects and relies on lines such as magnetic lines or black tapes. On the other hand, the free route method becomes dependent on the coordinates stored in the device using GPS and visual sensors. In comparison, the fixed route method has low cost of materials however, it requires high maintenance in re-taping the line guides for accurate movement of the robot. In contrast with the first guidance method, the free route method is considered less maintenance vehicles which can provide exact location of the AGV once it started to run since there is an installed GPS within the device. However, this method requires expensive materials to be built at the same time, can be disturbed by some environmental situations.

2.4 RFID Application

RFID (Radio Frequency Identification) according to Amsler and Shea [6], RFID is a wireless communication technology that uses electromagnetic radio frequency in an RFID tag which stores data encoded for specific actions specifically for the RFID reader installed in the AGV or in other devices. As stated by Rajiv [20] and Thrasher [25] there are many applications of RFID technology such as:

- **Supply Chains and Retail Stores:** With this technology, supply chains and retail stores can now manage their stocks efficiently, which is also an advantage for the customers since they can now also access the store's stock information and find their desired product from the store and checkout the product with ease. Another advantage of RFID in retail stores is the reduction of theft since there are installed RFID readers along the exit and entrances of the stores which would be detected whenever there is an item that is not yet paid for.
- **Patients in Hospital:** RFID can be used to make tags that are suitable for patients to wear which gives the medical staff an efficient way to handle patients and give them their procedures and treatment. The implementation of RFID tags in hospitals would increase the hospital's efficiency in treating their patients and avoiding errors in providing medication since RFID tags could store data which would help in providing the patient's past medical records certain conditions, and other personal information.
- **Access and Security:** With this application of RFID technology, employers can assign each person to the office environment where they could only get access to which would provide more security, especially in places that require a high level of protection. In addition, RFID would provide more information on where the employee has gained access and the employees would be more traceable inside the building if ever there is a breach in security.
- **Logistics and Shipping of Products and Goods:** RFID tags are utilized in shipping and logistics due to added improvement in efficiency since it is much more reliable and considerably faster than manual recording. RFID would make the updating of the inventory faster and more precise since RFID readers can accurately scan hundreds of tags in a day.
- **Automation of Manufacturing:** Many smart factory concepts have shown the use of RFID technology due to its given efficiency in the production line and in the inventory field since manually updating the inventory may sometimes cause errors and miscalculations while entering the data and monitoring the status of the products same with its information and the whereabouts of hundreds of products and can be recorded in real-time.
- **Baggage Handling in Airlines and Airports:** With the help of RFID technology, it would give airline companies fewer costs due to mishandling issues and be more efficient since the pieces of baggage are more traceable because of the RFID and are more organized since there are no barcodes yet would only need to attach the RFID to the baggage and the RFID reader would be the one to organize and save the data on where the specific bag needs to go.
- **Animal Tracking:** RFID tags can help farmers in updating and tracking their livestock since manually updating their data may cause errors and is not an easy task. RFID technology is helpful for veterinary doctors since owners could buy RFID tags for

their pets that could store data like the vaccination dates, weight, and age of their pet which lessens the workload for veterinary doctors in going through records.

- **Toll Gates:** Some of the toll gates around the world have been using RFID technology to charge payments for entry into a certain area since RFID is traceable and can store data, it can help in making more efficient ways of charging the people rather than the manual toll gates that are troublesome.

3 Materials and Methodology

This study is a Qualitative type of Research that incorporates a Descriptive Research Design using the Experiential Research Method (ERM) that was introduced by Grant et al. [14] that focuses on the experiences and perceptions of individuals in a particular situation. Furthermore, the participants for this research will also be the researchers as they were the ones who participated in the tournament. The themes of this research were based on previous studies and subjective experiences of the researchers from the event.

The Top International Robot Tournament (TIRT) was introduced by Xiangyi Enterprise, alongside the Taoyuan Municipal Government in 2018 to aid the transformation of domestic industries and give momentum to the development of the economy by creating a space that promotes a deeper understanding in robotics. Creating an avenue to share ideas between different core clusters that are known for creating innovations in the industry. The 5th TIRT was held in the Taoyuan Arena on October 15–16, 2022, where the researchers participated in the AGV competition to understand more about AGVs and exhibit skills in strategy planning, problem solving, and create programs that are appropriate to the given tasks.

3.1 Hardware Used: InnoAGV by Niche Applied Technology

(See Fig. 3)

Fig. 3. InnoAGV by Niche Applied Technology

- The AGV Robot measures 35 cm in length, 28 cm in width, and 12 cm in height.
- It moves by utilizing 2 bevel gearbox motors with silicone tires and 2 servo wheels.
- The 12 V power system is powered by a 12 V 15000 mAh lithium battery.
- It has line-sensing, RFID reading, and ultrasonic obstacle avoidance modules for obstacle circumvention.
- The control panel includes an LCD display, power switch, emergency stop button, and 4 × 4 keypad.
- It also has Bluetooth and LoRa transmission modules.
- The robot has light and voice alert functions.
- It is suitable for both industrial and educational use as a basic AGV vehicle platform.

3.2 Software Used

During the competition, the AGV was programmed using a block-program called innoBlockly Path Editor. It is specifically designed for AGVs developed by Niche Applied Technology. It allows the programmer to use RFID cards as input, and program the output into the AGV to control its speed, direction at intersections, and control the level of the platform.

This makes it easy for even non-technical users to program the AGV without having to know how to write code. With innoBlocklyAGV, the user can simply drag and drop blocks representing various actions, such as changing speed or direction, and connect them to create a program.

3.3 Relay of Information From Input to Output

Step 1: Pre-programming the AGV: Before the competition, the AGVs are pre-programmed with a set of instructions or "path" for how it should behave when it reads a specific RFID card.
Step 2: Program selection: At the beginning of the competition, 'Path Mode' is selected on the AGVs built-in user interface via keypad. This determines the path that the AGV will take.
Step 3: Reading RFID Cards: As the AGV moves along the competition course, it uses its RFID reader to detect and read the numbered RFID cards.
Step 4: Interpreting Information: The AGV reads the RFID card and recognizes its number as an instruction.
Step 5: Implementing Information: Once the RFID card is read, the AGV implements the instruction immediately. If the information dictates a change in speed, the AGV adjusts accordingly. If the information dictates a change in direction, the AGV takes the appropriate turn at the next intersection.
Step 6: Repeating the Process: The AGV continues to repeat this process of reading RFID cards, interpreting information, and implementing instructions until the end of the competition or until it is instructed or forced to stop (Fig. 4 and Fig. 5).

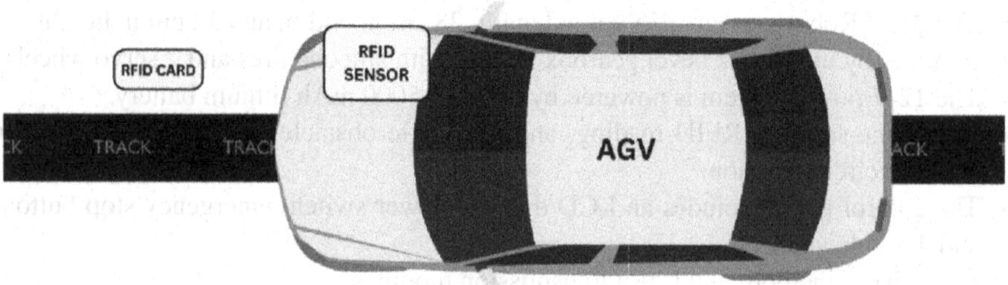

Fig. 4. Information *Processing*

The competition area is 700 cm by 400 cm in size. The background is black with white lines, and the width of the white lines is 2 cm.

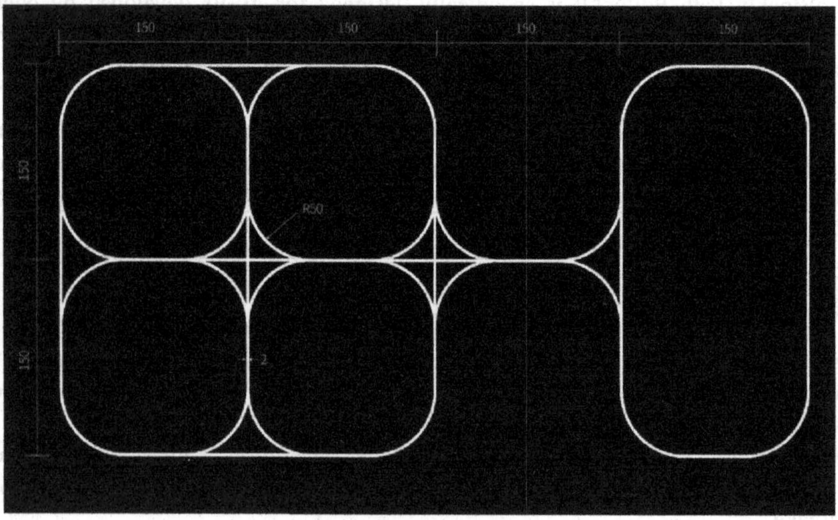

Fig. 5. TIRT Map

In order to complete the mission, each team must complete all given tasks using two (2) AGVs provided by the company. Specifically:

Task A: The vehicle will move to A1 to retrieve the shelf, and then move the shelf to A2 to receive the goods that will drop from the side conveyor. The player must manually activate the conveyor to allow the goods to fall onto the shelf. Finally, the vehicle will place the shelf in the A3 area.

Task B: The vehicle will move to B1 to retrieve the shelf, and then move the shelf to B2 for precise placement. A laser dot will shine on the circular target on the shelf from above in the B2 area checkpoint.

Task C: The vehicle will move to C1 to retrieve the shelf, which will have 8 bottles of 600 ml bottled water placed above it. The vehicle will then smoothly move the shelf to the C2 area, and the score will be based on the state of the cargo (Fig. 6).

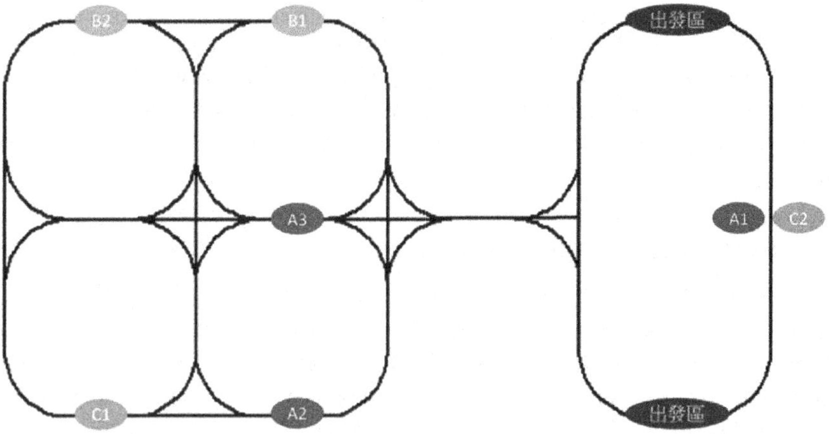

Fig. 6. Tasks A, B, and C

4 Results and Discussions

Entering the TIRT competition has given insights for the researchers in both the results of the performance of the AGV robot, and further suggestions for improving it. The competition rules include tasks for the robots to accomplish which are given by sensing RFID cards placed in designated positions. The route for the AGV robots to follow is shown in the Fig. 7:

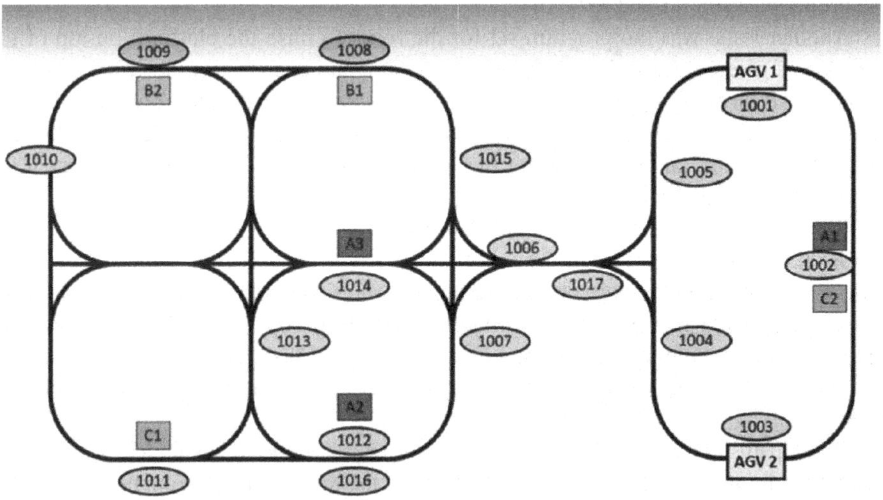

Fig. 7. AGVs' Path

Each group will use two AGV robots both following different paths and tasks which are to be programmed and determined by the competitors. The AGV robots that can finish all the tasks the fastest win. The numbers indicated in the figure starting from 1001 to 1017 are the designated positions of RFIDs set by the competitors. Each RFID will tell the AGV either to change its speed or to do a certain task which is programmed by the competitors. The black line indicates the route of the robot, while labels A2, A3, B1, B2, C1 are positions where a task is to be done and labels A1 and C2 are starting points.

4.1 Advantages and Disadvantages

In this part of the research, the researchers did not only present the advantages of implementing RFID technologies for AGVs, but also the disadvantages to give a more neutral and objective impression of the discussion. The data obtained to make these given samples in this research were derived from two approaches that were present in Kolb's Experiential Learning Theory (ELT). Specifically: grasping and transforming. The first part would be the researcher's own experiences in operating the AGV (Grasping Experience), and the second part would tackle various articles and literature of the same topic (Transforming Experience) [2, 3, 7].

4.2 Challenges

During the competition, the researchers encountered certain challenges with the AGV robot. The program on the AGV robot created by the researchers has proved to be flawed. One of them being the speed input to be too fast resulting the robot to move too quickly through the guideline and overshoots from the designated stop position wherein the RFID is found. The robot is then unable to detect the RFIDs once it overshoots through the proper position it is set to be in.

Another issue was the program set for the robot to raise the platform on top of it. A task was given to raise the platform on the robot and carry a cart that was on top of it and move through the guideline. This task is to be done after the robot detects the RFID card set underneath the cart. The program has been inaccurate which resulted in the platform being raised too low for the robot to lift the cart and unable to carry it to the next designated position.

Creating algorithms that allow an AGV to follow a specified path without getting lost is one of the main problems. The mechanism must function consistently even when crossings are brought by loops or intersecting pathways. Dealing with the limited storage space in RFID tags presents another difficulty. Therefore, sophisticated algorithms must reduce the amount of memory they use. One strategy is focused on predicting the course that will be taken. Another quality that must be addressed is the ability to offer multiple paths.

When paths are tagged during production, it is preferable to design a type of aging that allows for the forgetting of previous paths and the release of tags from previous data. For actively erasing outdated pathways, algorithms are necessary as an alternative. Age obviously must not affect permanently necessary pathways. Enabling fault-tolerance in the event of RFID tag failures and smooth motions are requirements that will be discussed in the following requirements. Additionally, to enable AGVs to operate at a high pace, the number of read and write operations should be minimized.

Table 2. Advantages and Disadvantages in forms of Grasping and Transforming Experiences

Advantages	*Grasping Experience*	• Follows pre-determined task: Since AGVs have the capacity to store and receive data, the operator can send the ready-made programs to the AGV to perform anticipated results. • Can store different paths or modes: AGVs can keep paths that you can program according to what you envision the AGV would do. • Programmability: The AGV's software is written in blocks where you can program codes with ease and without the need for advanced knowledge of different programming languages. • Numerous applications: Since AGVs can store data/paths that are made by the programmer, the AGV can do different tasks such as carrying packages, delivering tools, etc. • Improvement opportunities: In our present time, the AGV is still in its early age and because of this, there are a few rough spots that need to be smoothened in programming and making the AGV do specific tasks.
	Transforming Experience	• Increased Safety: AGVs have sensors and guidance systems that allow them to read and analyze their way through factories and other facilities without the problem of them colliding with things in the environment.
		• Increased Inventory Efficiency: Since AGVs can be programmed to do specific tasks, they can offer good quality in handling materials inside the warehouse. • Can work for long hours non-stop: AGVs use battery packs as the main source of electricity and because of this an AGV can work for longer hours if the battery is sufficient. • Ability to work in extreme conditions: In industries that have products that are kept in low temperatures or in places that are hazardous, human personnel tends to be outfitted with proper safety equipment and clothes and may sometimes cause side effects in the long run. Unlike AGVs, they can operate under any type of condition as long as it is designed well to fit in with the environment. • Transparency of Operations: since AGVs are programmed to do particular tasks, they can offer transparency and security since it reduces the personnel that would be requiring access to highly secured areas and is traceable due to its single workload and route.
Disadvantages	*Grasping Experience*	• Has no backward motion or reverse: The software that was provided has no reverse codes. Consequently, the time to reach certain stops has increased and planning involved timing and positioning of AGVs. • Interference: Though Bluetooth could provide connection to the AGV and the source, it posed as an unreliable source to the researchers because of the connectivity issues that were faced. • Connection Security: Having a Bluetooth module enables anyone to connect to your machine, and with the right software, it could also control/hack it. • Costly: Setting up a workplace/path for an AGV could also pose a disadvantage because it defeats the purpose of having a machine that is not too expensive.
	Transforming Experience	• Lack of flexibility: Since AGVs are only programmed to do the task and are designed to work in a repetitive manner, they can't react to certain changes in the working environment and can't adjust on their own. • Maintenance costs: Since AGVs are considered a machine they would undergo preventive maintenance every once in a while, to prevent further damage. As such, this would give operational downtime to the workplace and would cost the workplace more if the AGV would require parts to be changed. • Floor requirements: AGVs are not designed to go through terrains and floor flatness is one factor that needs to be considered.

Another problem experienced first-hand by the researchers is the inability of the AGV to move into two different locations, i.e., move backwards after passing through an RFID which tells the AGV to move forward. Furthermore, sensors also pose an issue as less sensors can lead to inaccurate path detection while more sensors will cause the AGV to be more expensive.

4.3 Potential

The market for AGV is ever more booming in the industry 4.0. According to Maxon [18], a report by Research and Markets predicts that the global market for AGVs would increase by 10.8% by 2026. The fields of application are manifold, one industry where AGVs are widely used is in manufacturing. AGVs help in manufacturing as they carry heavy loads and transfer products and/or equipment automatically with ease and having no manpower needed, providing more efficiency, safety, and cost effectiveness. AGVs are also slowly being adopted to many other industries as their potential is being realized in other sectors, some of the following include [4]:

Medical Industry: AGVs are also used in hospitals to simplify the work of medical personnel and fully eliminate the possibility of contamination in the event of an outbreak. Robots are proving handy for lifting big objects and are capable of hauling food, laundry, or rubbish, as well as providing patients with medication. They have been contacted by numerous hospitals throughout the world during the Covid-19 issue.

Aeronautical Industry: Using AGVs, aviation businesses have automated their assembly lines. Recently, Airbus put into operation a highly automated digital assembly line for the A320, A321 and A321R planes' fuselages. Automated guided vehicles can deliver heavy load items like fuselage pieces in this high added value industry. They also offer a solution for automating the inspection of aviation engine assembly to speed up procedures and prevent adverse body postures, which can pose issues for the technicians.

AGVs are particularly helpful in the maintenance industry for pinpointing the cause of a malfunction or breakdown. An AGV used by Thalès DMS France can move on its own underneath an aircraft and produce electromagnetic waves. A mechanic can arrange various maintenance procedures by using this AGV to check cabin parameters and assess sensor damage. Other, more creative ideas are also being developed and implemented.

Automotive Industry: The automotive industry is flooded with pusher robots, shelf extensions, automated pallet trucks and other intelligent mobile shelving systems. At Audi's factory in Bavaria, assembly stations with two or three operators have taken the place of the assembly line. During the assembly process, the vehicle is moved from one station to the next while mounted on an AGV. The AGV then selects the best path using an algorithm. All manufacturing data are analyzed in a control room where the entire operation is coordinated.

The development of crawler AGVs, which can slip underneath a cart or a rolling cabinet before grabbing it with a hook mechanism and transferring it, has also been seen in the automobile industry and large marketplaces. The crawler AGV efficiently handles the difficulties of confined places because it can fit into smaller spaces by maximizing the length of the AVG and the cart.

Food Industry: The food industry is one of the largest markets in the world providing new and unique experiences to its customers. As such, AGVs are also being utilized by some fast-food chains and restaurants in ordering and serving food to their customers. In a study conducted by Shimmura et al. [23], a Japanese cuisine restaurant introduced AGVs as a service robot to enhance labor productivity and to improve service quality. The results showed that the introduction of AGV in the restaurant has decreased the work hours that the staff must do and improved the labor productivity in terms of sales/labor hour.

4.4 Limitations

- The AGV that the researchers used in the competition had unique specifications and they are not allowed to change and modify the hardware and firmware of the provided machine.
- The tasks that the AGV did were limited to what was specified in the competition.
- The responses that were derived from the constructionist side of learning were limited to the subjective thoughts and experiences of the researchers.

4.5 Recommendations

- Add the right number of sensors to an AGV. Sensors enable precise movements.
- Plan the machine's specific tasks way ahead.
- Plan the placement of RFIDs. Make sure that the RFIDs can still be read by the RFID reader during the turns that the AGV will make on certain task/s.
- Apply the right speed for particular tasks since RFID readers sometimes cannot detect the RFID if the AGV is going too fast and might get away from its designated path.
- Apply appropriate speeds for different path types. Slow during curves and downhill and fast during straights and uphill.

5 Conclusion

In conclusion, this paper aims to add to the growing discourse about the new industrial revolution trend. It encourages using tools and/or aids to make some tasks significantly easier for humans rather than advocating their replacement in the workforce. Furthermore, it discussed how Industry 4.0 needs are being met by modifying current production machinery and manufacturing processes using RFID implementation approaches. The works on the implementation of RFID technologies for AGVs that are discussed in this paper serve as convincing evidence that, as RFID becomes more technologically accessible, a full implementation of the technology in our current manufacturing processes will quickly enable us to complete the transition into the next industrial revolution.

After compiling and organizing the information used for this study, it became clear regarding future work and the best course of action that, despite the advantages and potential of RFID in AGV technologies as seen in the competition and discussed in this paper, RFID generally has reliability and stability issues and presents challenging aspects when it comes to large-scale implementation, requiring careful consideration, especially in terms of programming. Therefore, to handle RFID deployment in AGV properly, people with a high set of skills and knowhow would be needed. As such, more study and testing of the technology's application are still needed to realize its full potential.

Appendix: Pictures Taken From Tirt 2022

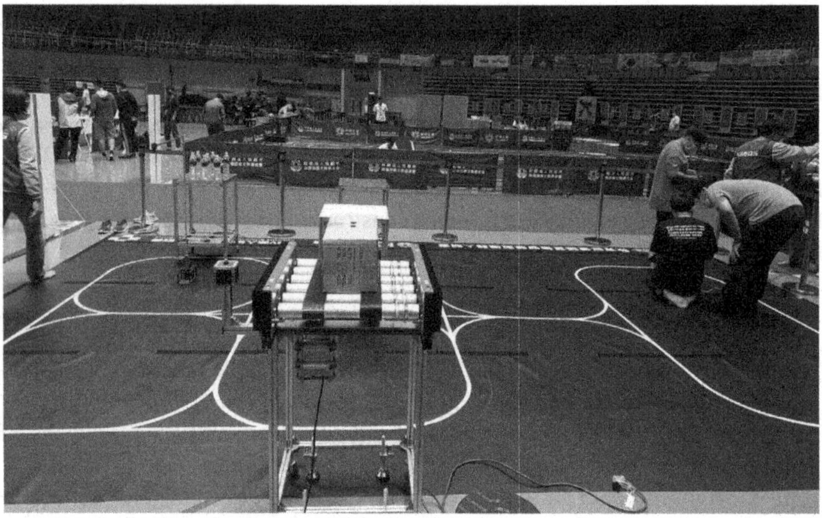

References

1. Abby McCain. 25 Revolutionary Robotics Industry Statistics (2022): Market Size, Growth, and Biggest Companies Zippia.com. https://www.zippia.com/advice/robotics-industry-statistics/. Accessed Oct 5 2022
2. Adams, H.: The advantages & disadvantages of Automated Guided Vehicles. Manufacturing Digital (24 December 2021). https://manufacturingdigital.com/ai-and-automation/advantages-and-disadvantages-automated-guided-vehicles. Accessed 7 Feb 2023
3. AGV - Advantages and disadvantages. Handling Specialty. (n.d.). https://www.handling.com/agv-advantages-and-disadvantages. Accessed 7 Feb 2023
4. Åkerman, M., Fast-Berglund, Å., Ekered, S.: Interoperability for a dynamic assembly system. Procedia CIRP **44**, 407–411 (2016)
5. Amend, J., Cheng, N., Fakhouri, S., Culley, B.: Soft robotics commercialization: jamming grippers from research to product. Soft Rob. **3**, 213–222 (2016). https://doi.org/10.1089/soro.2016.0021
6. Amsler, S., Shea, S.: What is RFID and how does it work? IoT Agenda (31 March 2021). https://www.techtarget.com/iotagenda/definition/RFID-radio-frequency-identification. Accessed 30 Jan 2023
7. Benevides, C.: The advantages and disadvantages of Automated Guided Vehicles (agvs). Conveyco (5 Jan 2021). https://www.conveyco.com/blog/advantages-disadvantages-automated-guided-vehicles-agvs/. Accessed 7 Feb 2023
8. Bosien, A., Venzke, M., Turau, V.: A rewritable RFID environment for AGV navigation. In: Proceeding of the 5th International Workshop on Intelligent Transportation (WIT 2008) (2008, March)
9. Building a Magnetic Track Guided AGV. https://www.roboteq.com/index.php/home/100-applications/how-to/278-building-a-magnetictrack-guided-agv. Accessed 06 Feb 2023
10. De Ryck, M., Versteyhe, M., Debrouwere, F.: Automated guided vehicle systems, state-of-the-art control algorithms and techniques. J. Manuf. Syst. **54**, 152–173 (2020). https://doi.org/10.1016/j.jmsy.2019.12.002

11. Erboz, G.: How to define industry 4.0: the main pillars of industry 4.0. Manager. Trends Dev. Enterpr. Globalization Era, Nitra, 761–767 (2017). https://www.researchgate.net/publication/326557388_How_To_Define_Industry_40_Main_Pillars_Of_Industry_40
12. Gasparetto, A., Scalera, L.: From the unimate to the delta robot: the early decades of industrial robotics. In: Zhang, B., Ceccarelli, M. (eds.) Explorations in the History and Heritage of Machines and Mechanisms. HMMS, vol. 37, pp. 284–295. Springer, Cham (2019). https://doi.org/10.1007/978-3-030-03538-9_23
13. Grand View Research. Automated Guided Vehicle Market Size, Share & Trends Analysis Report By Vehicle Type, By Navigation Technology, By Application, By End Use Industry, By Component, By Battery Type, And Segment Forecasts, 2022 – 2030 (2022 April). https://www.grandviewresearch.com/industry-analysis/automated-guided-vehicle-agv-market
14. Grant, K., Gilmore, A., Carson, D., Laney, R., Pickett, B.: Experiential research methodology: an integrated academic-practitioner team approach. J. Cetacean Res. Manag. **4**, 66–75 (2001). https://doi.org/10.1108/13522750110388563
15. Intel Corporation.: Autonomous Mobile Robot (AMR) overview: Types and use cases. Intel (2023). https://www.intel.com/content/www/us/en/robotics/autonomous-mobile-robots/overview.html
16. Li, J.: 睿揚創新科技RealPlus. RealPlus (2022)
17. Iqbal, M., Omar, R.: Automatic guided vehicle (AGV) design using an IoT-based RFID for location determination. In: 2020 International Conference on Applied Science and Technology (iCAST), Padang, Indonesia, pp. 489–494 (2020). https://doi.org/10.1109/iCAST51016.2020.9557700
18. Maxon. The future is AGV. The Robot Report (3 May 2021). https://www.therobotreport.com/the-future-is-agv/. Accessed 7 Feb 2023
19. Mehami, J., Nawi, M., Zhong, R.Y.: Smart automated guided vehicles for manufacturing in the context of industry 4.0. Procedia Manuf. **26**, 1077–1086 (2018). https://doi.org/10.1016/j.promfg.2018.07.144
20. Rajiv. Components of RFID technology and applications. RF Page (31 July 2022). https://www.rfpage.com/components-of-rfid-technology-and-applications/. Accessed 30 Jan 2023
21. Reyes, A.Z.M., et al.: The age of mechatronics: a phenomenological study of students' utilization of educational robots in class. **5**(2) (2020)
22. Romaine, E.: Types and applications of Autonomous Mobile Robots (AMRS). Conveyco (31 July 2022). https://www.conveyco.com/blog/types-and-applications-of-amrs/
23. Shimmura, T., Ichikari, R., Okuma, T., Ito, H., Okada, K., Nonaka, T.: Service robot introduction to a restaurant enhances both labor productivity and service quality. Procedia CIRP. **88**, 589–594 (2020). https://doi.org/10.1016/j.procir.2020.05.103
24. Some, K.: 8 Industries That Will Increase Adoption of Robots In Five Years. Analytics Insight (2019). https://www.analyticsinsight.net/8-industries-that-will-increase-adoption-of-robots-in-five-years/. Accessed 1 Oct 2022
25. Thrasher, J.: How is RFID used in the real world. atlasRFIDstore (22 August 2013). https://www.atlasrfidstore.com/rfid-insider/what-is-rfid-used-for-in-applications/. Accessed 30 Jan 2023
26. Ullrich, G.: The history of automated guided vehicle systems. In: Automated Guided Vehicle Systems, pp. 1–14. Springer, Heidelberg (2015). https://doi.org/10.1007/978-3-662-44814-4_1
27. Zhu, M.: The history of the AGV(automatic guided vehicle) (20 April 2021). https://www.linkedin.com/pulse/history-agvautomatic-guided-vehicle-ava-mao
28. Zou, O., Zhong, R.Y.: Automatic logistics in a smart factory using RFID-enabled AGVs. In: 2018 IEEE/ASME International Conference on Advanced Intelligent Mechatronics (AIM), Auckland, New Zealand, pp. 822–826 (2018). https://doi.org/10.1109/AIM.2018.8452349

A Research on Innovation and Benefit of Interactive Design Method of Smartphone Digital Social Media Advertising

Sheng-Ming Wang[1] and Yi-Han Wang[2](✉)

[1] Department of Interaction Design, National Taipei University of Technology, Taipei, Taiwan
[2] College of Design, National Taipei University of Technology, Taipei, Taiwan
yihanwang0210@gmail.com

Abstract. Social media design is directly affected by social changes, media development, and advances in hardware devices, and there is a long-term relationship between devices and human-computer interaction design. With widespread use and technological evolution, it has become an interesting research issue and has important substantive applicability to research. Investing in this research topic can produce diverse and very practical research results, and help improve the current inefficient digital advertising pricing method and improve the design method of social media advertising, so as not to be interfered by negative design product. The research results provide positive design and positive use experience. The research outcomes should be able to solve the long-term problem that the delivery benefits of social media advertising pricing in the electronic market are not equal to the actual advertising benefits.

Keywords: Social Media Design · CPC: Cost per Click · CPA: Cost per Action · CPM: Cost per 1000 Impression

1 Introduction

1.1 A Subsection Sample

Social media design is directly affected by social changes, media development, and advancements in hardware equipment. The correlation between each other has become an interesting research direction with the wide application and technological evolution and has the importance of research. This research topic could produce a very practical research results and help improve the current inefficient digital advertising pricing method. In addition, the research finding maybe improve the design method of social media advertising. The research is used to solve the long-standing social problems in the electronic market. The delivery efficiency of group media advertising pricing is not the same as the real advertising efficiency. The digital environment is based on the evolution of hardware equipment. What is the relationship and influence between the design of social media advertisements for commercial activities, the effectiveness of related advertisements, and users, designers, and owners? As far as the relevant design level and

A. Coman and S. Vasilache (Eds.): HCII 2023, LNCS 14025, pp. 457–469, 2023.
https://doi.org/10.1007/978-3-031-35915-6_33

the development of effective advertising are concerned, the above should be the main axis of future related development, and it is actually a research topic that needs to be discussed and researched. This study focuses on the above motivation, and finds that it is possible to do the effective cross-field research on social media design in combination with the current situation and future development, so as to improve the improvement model of social media advertising design and pricing methods, in order to In the future, social media advertising design can improve users' positive emotions and reduce negative emotions. The creative value of design and the practical operation of design are sometimes not the same. However, the practical value of design can only be brought into full play after being tested in the actual use environment and market value. Based on the actual commercial market review, Interpretation of Brand Communication (2022): The reasons for the common failure of advertising are roughly divided into the following five points:

1. Not putting in enough time.
2. Not paying attention to the quality of advertising content.
3. No strategy, plan, tracking analysis.
4. No ads were tested.
5. No reasonable budget was allocated. (Interpretation of Brand Communication, 2022)

The research purpose of this study is divided into the following three points:

1. **The research explores the current status and possible future development of social media advertising design.**
2. **The study explores whether the pricing method of social media advertising design is in line with the actual effectiveness of advertising.**
3. **Research to explore the user-friendly design methods of social media advertisements.**

2 Literature Review

2.1 Definition and Development of Social Media

Social media (social media) is a virtual network platform used by people to create, share, and exchange opinions. Users can release information through text, pictures, music, and videos, and form a community of reading audiences. Social media usually It has three functions: virtual interpersonal network, information sharing and dissemination, and a platform for gathering people. From the perspective of Internet development history, since Swiss researchers sent the first e-mail in 1970, the earliest social media may be called "Open Diary" Internet social media proposed by Bruce and Abelson in 1998. Group services, which bring together Internet users to write online diaries together on a website. In 2000, Jimmy Wales and Larry Sanger launched Wikipedia. In 2004, Facebook was established. It was originally a social network platform for students. In 2005, Youtube came out, allowing users to upload and share videos for free. Until now, everyone can be a creator Those who become Internet celebrities. Duffett, R., Petrosanu, D. M.,, Negricea, IC & Edu, T. (2019) point out: The widespread use of YouTube has generated billions of dollars in marketing communications revenue, but in developing economies Academic research is very limited, possibly due to usage and population effects. The emergence of Twitter in 2006, the establishment of Spotify, users can share music, and the Pinterest community in 2012. So far, social media has continued to innovate, making us use social media longer and longer, which has become an inseparable trend. In recent years, the age group using social media has also gradually increased and expanded. From Bui, HT (2022) pointed out: middle-aged and elderly people are a big market for social media sales, and research related middle-aged and elderly people in social media shopping behavior and motivation. Therefore, there is still a huge room for development in the placement of social media advertisements, which can correspondingly enhance the growth of e-commerce.The blog type for decades, and has gradually accumulated to the current relatively mature stage. A social media platform that is widely used today. However, its influence has an absolute dependence on users and corporate advertising sponsors, and will affect the usage and popularity of social media products in the future. With the change of users' usage habits, even the same user has different usage habits and self-categorization purposes for different social media. However, whether the current social media pricing relationship can actually be close to the consumer demand and the owner's demand will produce positive results. The impact of advertisements directly affects the future design and sustainable development of related social media.

Since 2020, under the impact of the COVID-19 epidemic, many industries in the world have been severely affected, but social media has increased the use of the market. Dubbelink, SI, Herrando, C., & Constantinides, E. (2021) proposed: After the epidemic, how business owners can adjust their social media marketing strategies to create positive brand equity, which targets social media marketing, brand elements, marketing activities Time to do a consideration and evaluation. Yost, E., Zhang, TT, & Qi, RX (2021) research shows that effective release time, type, label and social media with high participation rate can effectively promote company performance. Michopoulou, E. & Moisa, DG (2019) Findings: Return on Investment (ROI) is understood as an umbrella concept where engagement rate, customer response, and number of likes and comments are the most important, while hotel managers A variety of strategies are employed for social media deployment, but the focus on the effectiveness of these strategies is questionable, especially in light of financial metrics. The point of view questioned by the above research is one of the most powerful motivations for the study of performance costs. The same point of view looks at the effectiveness of social media advertising, whether it is in recent research data, or in the use experience of all social media users: to increase users' positive emotions and reduce negative usage emotions, It is a general consensus to get better advertising effect. This study is not only focused on the design point of view, but also a prospective study on the effect of design. The results of this study can effectively solve the benefits of social media advertising, reduce the negative usage emotions of users who are disturbed by advertising when using social media, and improve the positive advertising benefits. Looking at the content of the above research, this study is unique and future-oriented, and can also make up for the blind spots of the above research and make up for the lack of academic theory. Combining social media advertising design practices with effective social media advertising pricing methods, the research results can make up for the shortcomings and shortcomings of current social media advertising pricing methods.

2.2 Research on Issues Related to Electronic Pricing of Social Media Advertisements

The past, social media was priced based on CTR advertising click-through rate and CVR advertising conversion rate. The following is an introduction to the current pricing method:

1. **CPC** (Cost Per Click) cost per click:
2. **CPM** (Cost Per 1000 Impression) cost per thousand impressions:
3. **CPA** (Cost Per Action) cost per action:

However, **the current social media advertising pricing method does not take into account the positive and negative receiving emotions of actual users, which means that positive conversion, stickiness, and advertising time may all produce different advertising benefits, which in turn affect social media advertising The effectiveness of personal delivery.** These related issues and content are worthy of in-depth exploration. The current situation of digital products, which is not in line with actual benefits in theory and practice, highlights the importance and forward-looking of this research. The following issues are discussed based on the journal literature related to social media in the past five years:

Duan, WJ & Zhang, J. (2021) pointed out: the effectiveness, dynamics, and dependence among search engines, social media, and third-party websites are studied. The research results show that search engines have a great impact on sales, but social media recommendations have the strongest direct and cumulative impact on conversion rates of e-commerce sites. The argument of the above research happens to be very interesting to support the importance of the relevant research hypotheses of this study and the developability of the research results. Regarding the positive or negative benefits related to social media advertising, there is indeed a need for discussion and exploration, which exists in future research on social media advertising design. In addition, Huang, TC, Zaeem, RN & Barber, KS (2019) pointed out: social media provides a lot of information, but the source of information may come from untrustworthy users, so the first thing to solve is to solve the problem of polluted data, advertising or filter out credible and trustworthy messages. The above research content shows that some researchers have done relevant time-sensitive research on the effectiveness and credibility of social media advertising. The argument of polluted data is a very unique insight, emphasizing the importance of social media. The importance of media advertising efficiency also points out the fact that the high exposure rate of social media advertising today does not equate to the actual situation of high efficiency rate. However, solving the design method of social media advertisements today and enhancing users' positive emotions in order to obtain better positive advertising benefits highlights the importance of this research. Iannelli, L., Giglietto, F., Rossi, L. & Zurovac, E. (2020) Research Notes: A Marketing Tool for Targeting Ads by Demographics, Behaviors, and Interests of the Facebook Advertising Platform to Evaluate an Innovative The efficiency and effectiveness of the method. Although the above research has differentiated the demographics, behaviors, and interests of the advertising platform to retarget Facebook advertising marketing tools to evaluate the efficiency and effectiveness of an innovative approach, compared with the content of this research, it still does not show the positive benefits of advertising.

Incorporating negative benefits into it has produced an effectiveness evaluation model that is more in line with actual advertising benefits. The insufficiency of the results of this research highlights the importance and future of my research. I can try to solve the problem of evaluating the effectiveness of advertising received positively or negatively by users, so as to achieve better advertising effects in social media advertising design. Our research can make up for the lack of research assumptions above, and develop social media advertising design and placement into a better design product and a more cost-effective pricing method. Jalali, N. Y. & Papatla, P. (2019) pointed out: Writing articles is to increase followers. When articles are forwarded, followers can be increased and a large number of audiences can be quickly attracted. The research results propose a social media how to Ways to write tweets based on our findings to get the most retweets and generate more viewers and readers. Although the assumption of the above research is that forwarding is a positive form of advertising. But for today's different age groups, the forwarding of some age groups is a negative spreading mode. For example, in Taiwan's presidential election, a candidate's illustrations and texts were widely reposted. However, during the Taiwan presidential election, such reposting was a negative advertising benefit. The facts afterwards also proved that there was no possibility of one of the final losing factors. (The above example is James Soong's candidate in the 2000 Taiwan presidential election.) There is also a possibility that in the social media environment, negative advertisements may also be forwarded, and negatively forwarded, and negatively forwarded again. Therefore, the findings of the research and the actual negative advertising benefits of the actual case are the focus of discussing the actual benefits of advertising. Khan, G., Mohaisen, M. & Trier, M. (2020) pointed out that the purpose of the study was to model two different returns on investment (ROI) measures: networked ROI, which captures Network Effects of Media Investments, and Discrete ROI, focuses on the discrete returns of social media from individual users. The above research can provide relevant research considerations and appropriate research methods that may be required for this study, so as to obtain the relevant evaluation of the actual advertising effectiveness of the current social media advertising pricing methods.

Papa, A., Santoro, G., Tirabeni, L. & Monge, F. (2018) pointed out that social media is a tool to promote knowledge creation and innovation in SMEs, and social media contributes to three quarters of knowledge The creative process has a positive impact, and they help to facilitate the innovation process. From a management perspective, the study recommends that managers implement and engage social media in their business and innovation processes. Therefore, the existence of social media is still necessary, but this study will discuss how to exert great benefits. Keegan, BJ & Rowley, J. (2017) used six stages in their research: setting evaluation objectives, determining key performance indicators (KPI), determining indicators, data collection and analysis, report generation and management decision-making to explore relevant research hypotheses. An evaluation of such technologies as organizations increases their investments in social media marketing (SMM). The purpose of this study was to contribute to knowledge about SMM strategies by developing a stage model of SMM assessment and revealing the challenges in this process. Research by Zhou, YY, Calder, B. J., Malthouse, EC & Hessary, YK (2021): This study attempts to analyze data from three news websites and shows that these disaggregated clickstream variables, compared to the original, Undisaggregated clickstream data is more predictive of a website's willingness to pay. Based on the above research points of view, in the research of related fields in academia, real inspections and attempts have been made to evaluate and explore: whether the related benefits of social media advertising are really like the actual advertising costs, and bring back positive advertising benefits.

The above literature discussion discusses the definition and development of social media, issues related to the electronic pricing of social media advertising, and makes a basic and recent research related literature discussion, in order to seek the relevant required literature content of this study and the possibility of research way, and highlights the necessity and practical importance of this study in theory. The discussion of the above research literature is enough to prove that this research is a very necessary and forward-looking research. It can try to solve the long-term research. The positive and negative advertising benefits of social media advertising have not been formally evaluated in social media advertising. Valuation in progress. In addition, how to effectively design a social media advertisement design with positive advertising effects to achieve the actual effect of actual advertisement placement.

3 Research Methods

3.1 Research Design

According to statistics from Taiwan Network Information Center, 94.2% of the social media use Facebook the most, followed by Instagram with 39.2% and Line with 35%. Therefore, this research will use Facebook as the social media with the most people. Research target of group media advertising.

The proposed research steps are as follows, and the analysis methods are described as follows:

1. According to the results of the questionnaire survey, the user's satisfaction with the current social media advertising design methods in the process of using social media is collected.
2. Analyze and design social media advertising design patterns that meet user expectations.
3. Exploring the effectiveness of social media advertising design prototype mode through users and advertising owners.

3.2 Research Methods

Variance, also known as analysis of variance, analysis of variance (Analysis of Variance, ANOVA) is divided into single-factor analysis of variance (One-way ANOVA), two-way analysis of variance (Two-way ANOVA), is for multiple the test method for the significance of the difference in the mean of the parent group can be used to know the F value. The F value is to compare the average difference between the groups. If the value is larger, it means that the difference in the average of these groups is greater.

1. The degree of dispersion of all samples: summed up by the sum of squares (SS, Sum of Square).

$$SS_{T(\text{Sum of Square})} = \sum_{\text{all samples}} \left(Xi - \overline{X}_{\text{total average}}\right)^2$$

2. Between-group variation: the sum of the squares of the difference between the group mean and the total mean.

$$SS_{B(\text{Between-group variation})} = \sum_{\text{each group}} n_{\text{The number of samples in each group}} \times \left(\overline{X}\text{group average} - \overline{X}_{\text{total average}}\right)^2$$

3. Intra-group variation: The samples in the group minus the squares of the group squares are summed up, and then the sum of the squares of the intra-group deviations from the mean square of all groups is added.

$$SS_{W(\text{within-group variation})} = \sum_{\text{All groups}} \sum_{\substack{\text{All samples} \\ \text{Vin the group}}} \left(X_{gi(\text{gample of the group})} - \overline{X}_{\text{The group average}}\right)^2$$

Sum of mean squares: divided by degrees of freedom (df)

$$MS_{W(\text{between-groupsumofmeansquares})} = SS_{B(\text{Between-group variation})}/df_B$$

$$MS_{W(\text{within-groupsumofmeansquares})} = SS_{W(\text{within-group variation})}/df_B$$

4 Research Analysis and Discussion

4.1 Statistics of the Basic Data of the Subjects

162 valid questionnaires were statistically sorted out as shown in Table 1.

4.2 Statistics of Users' Satisfaction with the Evaluation of the Current Design Mode of Advertising in Social Media Facebook

This study conducted a reliability analysis on the satisfaction of 15 items in the questionnaire, and the analysis results showed that the internal consistency coefficient of Cronbach's alpha was .947, which was acceptable reliability, so there was no factor to be considered for deleting items. The results of independent sample t -test analysis is shown in Table 2 below. This study found that there are four items above: there are

Table 1. Distribution statistics of the basic information of the subjects (sorted out in this study)

item	topic	Sample size (person)	percentage
gender	male	76	46.9
	female	86	53.1
	total	162	100
age	10 years old	0	0
	11–20 years old	5	3.1
	21–30 years old	42	25.9
	31–40 years old	65	40.1
	41–50 years old	40	24.7
	51–60 years old	10	6.2
	61–70 years old	0	0
	over 70 years old	0	0
	total	162	100
education level	elementary school	1	0.6
	secondary	1	0.6
	high school	twenty one	13
	University	102	63
	master	34	twenty one
	PhD	3	1.9
	total	162	100

significant differences, and the rest have no significant differences. Therefore, we must consider avoiding: "In Facebook, avoid designing ads that friends like to appear on the page." , "In Facebook, avoid designing content that has been searched on other web pages to appear on the page.", "In Facebook, avoid designing to repeatedly see similar or the same Advertisement content." And make good use of "the video advertisement designed in Facebook is dynamic and dynamic, which will help the advertisement attract more users' attention in the news feed." Better advertising efficiency can be obtained.

The single-factor independent sample ANOVA was used to analyze the effects of different ages on various items. The results are shown in Table 3 below. The results of the study found that the design that must be considered to avoid is: "In **Facebook, avoid designing advertisements that friends like Appear on the page."**, **"Advertisements searched in Facebook appear more than your friends' posts."**, **"Adverts videos in Facebook will automatically play and become the next relevant ad to appear "Content"** and **"Facebook design to avoid repeating similar or identical advertising content."**, the above four social media advertising design methods should be avoided as much as possible to avoid negative advertising benefits.

Table 2. Satisfaction statistics and significance of users of different genders for the evaluation of the current design model of social media Facebook advertisements (compiled in this study)

item	Boys (N = 76)		Girls (N = 86)		freedom df	t -value	P
	average value	standard deviation	average value	standard deviation			
5. In your fb, the ads that your friends like will appear on your page. Are you satisfied with this design?	2.97	1.21	2.41	1.16	160	3.03	.003
8. The content you searched on other web pages appears on the fb page. Are you satisfied with this design method?	3.12	1.22	2.60	1.09	151.384	2.811	.006
9. In fb, you see similar or the same advertisement content repeatedly, are you satisfied with this design method?	2.66	1.22	2.23	1.07	150.503	2.35	.020
12. The video advertisement in fb injects dynamic vitality into the advertisement, which helps the advertisement attract more attention in the dynamic news. Are you satisfied with this design method?	3.36	1.09	3.00	1.04	160	2.113	.036

Table 3. Satisfaction statistics and significance of users of different ages for the evaluation of the current design model of social media Facebook advertisements (compiled in this study)

item	mean (standard deviation)					SS	df	MS	f	p	ηp 2
	11–20 years old (N = 5)	21–30 years old (N = 42)	31–40 years old (N = 65)	41–50 years old (N = 40)	51–60 years old (N = 10)						
2. In your fb, the number of advertisements you have searched for appears more than the number of posts posted by your friends. Are you satisfied with this design method?	2.6 (1.14)	2.29 (1.24)	1.85 (1.15)	2.6 (1.26)	2.3 (1.06)	15.746	4	3.937	2.76	.03	.066
4. In your fb, there are many types of related advertisements that you have liked, which will appear repeatedly on your page. Are you satisfied with this design method?	4.0 (1.22)	2.76 (1.36)	2.4 (1.17)	2,85 (1.17)	2.6 (.966)	15.281	4	3.82	2.6	.038	.062
7. In your fb, the advertising video will automatically play for you, and become the content of the next relevant advertisement. Are you satisfied with this design method?	3.6 (1.67)	2.47 (1.25)	2.09 (1.18)	2.62 (1.21)	2.60 (1.35)	16.022	4	4.006	2.632	.036	.063
9. In fb, you see similar or the same advertisement content repeatedly, are you satisfied with this design method?	2.20 (0.837)	2.74 (1.23)	2.12 (1.038)	2.75 (1.235)	2.000 (0.817)	16.319	4	4.08	3.212	0.014	0.076

The research results obtained after the research test analysis are shown in the following Fig. 1:

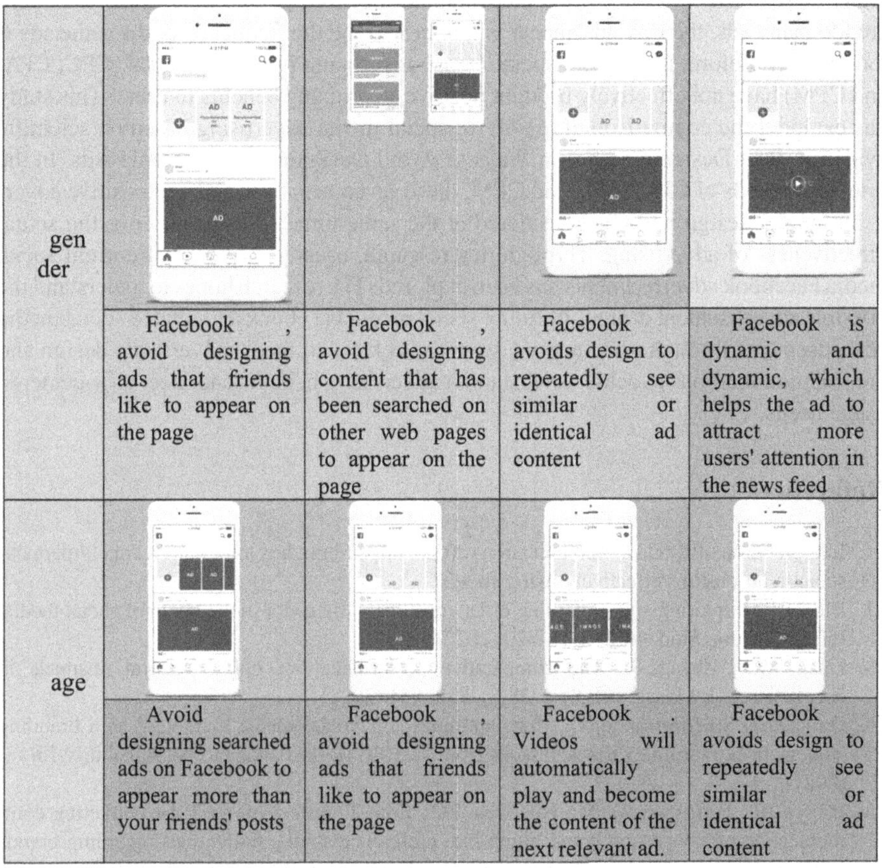
gen der
Facebook , avoid designing ads that friends like to appear on the page
Facebook , avoid designing content that has been searched on other web pages to appear on the page
Facebook avoids design to repeatedly see similar or identical ad content
Facebook is dynamic and dynamic, which helps the ad to attract more users' attention in the news feed
age
Avoid designing searched ads on Facebook to appear more than your friends' posts
Facebook , avoid designing ads that friends like to appear on the page
Facebook . Videos will automatically play and become the content of the next relevant ad.
Facebook avoids design to repeatedly see similar or identical ad content
AD

Fig. 1. Seven Negative Advertising Design Methods and One Positive Advertising Benefit Design Method of Facebook Social Media Advertising Design Blue represents negative emotions Orange represents positive emotions design

5 Conclusions

This study takes Facebook, the social media most used by the most people, as the research target of social media advertising design and innovative design and effectiveness, to understand the current users' satisfaction with Facebook advertising design for research and analysis, and to understand the current Facebook advertising owners' pricing way, to find more suitable advertisements to be placed in users' social media, so that users can receive the advertisement information they want to receive, and avoid unnecessary advertisement design and placement, so as to improve users' time when using social media of positive emotions. Relatively speaking, with this design method, advertisers can also obtain better advertising effects and profitable advertising when placing social media advertisements. The results of the study found that users are generally dissatisfied with the current presentation of Facebook ads. Users think that there are too many ads, the way ads appear is too messy, and the frequency of the same ads is too high. Therefore, the current social media advertising pricing methods (CPC, CPA, and CPM) have not effectively brought positive advertising benefits to users. This study has explored the comparison of the above social media advertising based on scientific evidence. Best Design, and Seven Ways to Avoid Designing Social Media Ads. In the pricing methods of CPC, CPA, and CPM, these seven negatives and one positive advertising model design must be considered at the same time, so as to improve the actual effectiveness of advertising. Through this research, users' evaluation of current social media Facebook advertisements has been explored. The research hopes to understand the possible advertisement designs of future social media Facebook and related social media advertisements through user surveys, so as to Seek social media advertising design and presentation methods to achieve substantial advertising benefits and meet user-centered usage needs.

References

1. Interpretation of Brand Communication (2022). https://branding-now.com/martech/martech-social-relationships/effectively-using-fb-ads/
2. Bui, H.T.: Exploring and explaining older consumers' behavior in the boom of social media. Int. J. Consum. Stud. **46**(2), 601–620 (2022)
3. Duan, W.J., Zhang, J.: The comparative performance of online referral channels in E-commerce. J. Manag. Inf. Syst. **38**(3), 828–854 (2021)
4. Dubbelink, S.I., Herrando, C., Constantinides, E.: Social media marketing as a branding strategy in extraordinary times: lessons from the COVID-19 Pandemic. Sustainability **13**(18) (2021)
5. Duffett, R., Petrosanu, D. M., Negricea, I.C., Edu, T.: Effect of YouTube marketing communication on converting brand liking into preference among millennials regarding brands in general and sustainable offers in particular. Evid. South Africa Rom. Ustainability **11**(3) (2019)
6. Huang, T.C., Zaeem, R.N., Barber, K.S.: It is an equal failing to trust everybody and to trust nobody: stock price prediction using trust filters and enhanced user sentiment on Twitter. ACM Trans. Internet Technol. **19**(4) (2019)
7. Iannelli, L., Giglietto, F., Rossi, L., Zurovac, E.: Facebook digital traces for survey research: assessing the efficiency and effectiveness of a Facebook ad-based procedure for recruiting online survey respondents in niche and difficult -to-reach populations. Soc. Sci. Comput. Rev. **38**(4), 462–476 (2020)
8. Jalali, N.Y., Papatla, P.: Composing tweets to increase retweets. Int. J. Res. Mark. **36**(4), 647–668 (2019)
9. Keegan, B.J., Rowley, J.: Evaluation and decision making in social media marketing. Manag. Decis. **55**(1), 15–31 (2017)
10. Khan, G., Mohaisen, M., Trier, M.: The network ROI: concept, metrics, and measurement of social media returns (a Facebook experiment). Internet Res. **30**(2), 631–652 (2020)
11. Michopoulou, E., Moisa, D.G.: Hotel social media metrics: the ROI dilemma. Int. J. Hosp. Manag. **76**, 308–315 (2019)

12. Papa, A., Santoro, G., Tirabeni, L., Monge, F.: Social media as tool for facilitating knowledge creation and innovation in small and medium enterprises. Balt. J. Manag. **13**(3), 329–344 (2018)
13. Yost, E., Zhang, T.T., Qi, R.X.: The power of engagement: understanding active social media engagement and the impact on sales in the hospitality industry. J. Hosp. Tour. Manag. **46**, 83–95 (2021)
14. Zhou, Y.Y., Calder, B.J., Malthouse, E.C., Hessary, Y.K.: Not all clicks are equal: detecting engagement with digital content. J. Media Bus. Stud. (2021)

Dysfunctional User States in Interface Use and Their Dependency on Work Environment and Task Complexity

Alexandr V. Yakunin(✉) and Svetlana S. Bodrunova

St. Petersburg State University, St. Petersburg 199004, Russia
{a.yakunin,s.bodrunova}@spbu.ru

Abstract. Usability testing today comprises quantitative and qualitative approaches. Within the former, factors that shape test results include four major ones put together within the 'contextual fidelity' model. These factors include product features, task complexity, user traits (including cultural belonging and gender), and experiment settings. However, most usability tests only consider one or two, not four of them. Our earlier research [1] has shown that, when four factors are assessed in parallel, cumulative impact of all of them makes test results highly diverge. Our current study complements this research by showing how usability tests diverge when task complexity varies highly. Another gap in usability research is that they miss the point in their final target, as they measure relative efficiency of interfaces for various groups of users but do not study formation of dysfunctional psychological states that critically prevent efficient Internet use and task performance. This happens despite the growing evidence of mental harm brought by interfaces to, e.g., youngsters' health or office workers. By testing 60 assessors in either groups or individually on tasks that induce dysfunctional states, namely monotony and anxiety, and introducing tasks of varying complexity, we show that excessive cognitive load leads to rapid rise of user dysfunctionality. Our results suggest that anxiety reduction in real-world tasks may not be reached by reducing task complexity. We recommend group performance on monotonous tasks and individual performance on anxiety-inducing tasks. By that, we illustrate our doubt of the possibility to reach any 'objective' results of usability tests; the latter need to be treated as fundamentally conditioned by the contextual fidelity factors. This has two consequences: First, usability testing needs to be conducted in accordance with prospective goals of interface use; second, multi-functional interfaces of general use need to pass through multiple usability tests that would combine contextual fidelity factors in various ways.

Keywords: usability · usability testing · contextual fidelity model · user states · dysfunctional state · monotony · anxiety · interface · human-computer interaction

1 Introduction

Usability testing today comprises quantitative and qualitative approaches. Quantitative studies use objective measurements and aim at assessing both objective user performance and subjective user satisfaction, also measured by standardized instruments, unlike in

A. Coman and S. Vasilache (Eds.): HCII 2023, LNCS 14025, pp. 470–485, 2023.
https://doi.org/10.1007/978-3-031-35915-6_34

qualitative studies where assessment is often based on user narratives about human-computer interaction (HCI) experience.

Quantitative usability research has gradually accumulated knowledge on factors that critically affect (and, thus, may highly distort) the results of usability tests. Beside the qualities of the tested product itself (say, more or less harmonious interface design or more or less efficient navigation), task features, user traits, and experiment settings have been shown to highly influence test results. Several scholars have urged the research community to take these factors into account [1–5], as they were seen as key in the search for the optimal usability testing model. The four factors – product features (including web aesthetics), task features (especially task complexity), user traits (including socio-demographic features and cultural belonging), and experiment conditions (especially individual/group testing) – have been united in the so-called 'contextual fidelity' model [6] which we will below describe in more detail. However, this model, despite being formulated over a decade ago, has not gained proper popularity among the usability researchers. Most quantitative studies of usability, including those utilizing eye tracking and other instrumental facilities, have ignored the complex character of impact of the 'contextual fidelity' factors and habitually use research designs that employ only one or two factors and disregard their potential cumulative impact.

Another research gap that is extremely wide in usability testing in both academe and industry is the ultimate goal of testing. Most research aims at detecting some optimal features of interfaces that would allow for optimal, most efficient interface use (the best objective performance), as well as for the best levels of subjective user satisfaction. However, the other end of the quality spectrum is rarely taken into consideration. This other end is manifested via user states of critically low functional efficiency. Meanwhile, the theory of user states that comes from psychology of professions [7–11] has already formulated the concept of dysfunctional user states that critically prevent efficient work performance. Despite the growing evidence of negative impact of interface use upon mental states of younger audiences, office workers, or high-risk interface-dependent professionals (like military pilots), dysfunctional user states have not been the major focus of usability studies.

In 2022, we have contributed to today's usability research by uniting these two research gaps and showing that certain combinations of 'contextual fidelity' factors could lead, first, to significant differences in testing results and cumulative effects that arose from those combinations of influences and, second, to formation of dysfunctional user states [1]. However, in our previous research pipeline, tasks only varied one-dimensionally, as they induced two opposing dysfunctional states, namely monotony and anxiety. Today, we expand this research by making tasks vary multi-dimensionally. The second dimension will be task complexity, which will vary significantly, while the tasks will still aim at inducing dysfunctional states. To this, we add variations in experiment conditions, setting either individual or group test conditions for our assessors, as our previous research suggested that group conditions could compensate for or diminish the level of dysfunctionality that formed during the tests. Combining these two factors would better explain how task complexity relates to user dysfunctionality in various conditions of interface use.

To reach this goal, we test 60 assessors in either group or individual setting on tasks that induce dysfunctional states, namely monotony and anxiety. We provide the assessors with three tasks of varying complexity for each of the potential dysfunctional state.

The remainder of the paper is organized as follows. Section 2 provides an account on the 'contextual fidelity' model and on dysfunctional user states. Section 3 describes our methodology and the research pipeline. Section 4 demonstrates our results, and Sect. 5 discusses them. We conclude by posing the questions on future prospects of usability studies being conditioned by the 'contextual fidelity' factors.

2 User Dysfunctionality and Factors that Condition It in Usability Testing

2.1 The Concept of Dysfunctional User State and Its Application to Usability Research

Conceptualization of user states has mostly developed within Russian psychology of professions, but some works have also been published in English and have gained international recognition. We find them useful for detection of types of interfaces and tasks that critically affect user efficiency.

According to Leonova [7, 10, 11], the impact of functional states on the emotional-volitional and cognitive sphere of a person is complex. Under the influence of certain activities, the most important mental processes and phenomena undergo significant changes. The sensitivity threshold of sensory systems and the tone of the sympathetic nervous system change [9], as well as stable changes are observed in the ability to memorize information, longer-term memory, reactions to stimuli, and the dynamics of intellectual-representative systems [12]. In particular, according to [8], the growth of mental fatigue or subjective anxiety causes changes in the whole spectrum of psychophysiological characteristics of a given user. Not only the sensitivity of analyzers changes, but also the ability to concentrate, to search in long-term memory, and to manipulate memorized objects.

According to the systemic approach in studying the functional systems of the human psyche, such changes in psychophysiological characteristics are part of a complex systemic reaction of an individual to factors that condition his/her activity during the work process [8: 1133]. Such an understanding of functional changes as reactions formed under external impact requires consideration of deviations from the state of operational rest as a response of functional systems on different levels to the factors/conditions of the activity performed by a worker (in our case, an interface user). As a rule, in studies based on theory of activity, the following factors are named that shape functional states: The content of the activity, conditions for its implementation, working person's functions, and its individual psychological traits [13, 14]. These factors, as we will see below, correspond well to the 'contextual fidelity' factors that have been studied in usability research, regretfully unrelated to wider psychology.

Due to the integral, systemic nature of functional states, the nature of the changes they cause in the psychophysiological state of users gains specific, recognizable, and stable shape. Via assessing psychophysiological indicators of the dominant user state in a particular moment *and* the factors that caused them, the researcher can accurately identify functional states, differentiate them both functionally and qualitatively, and describe them through combinations of indicators. For instance, as it follows from the results of several studies including our own, qualitative differences in the states of anxiety and monotony cause different effects on the user state. According to [9], the development of anxiety entails a change in the sense of time, transformation of the structure of intellectual operations, decrease in control over the performance quality, and a shift motivation [13]. The development of monotony is accompanied by subjective (boredom, apathy, drowsiness) and objective (decrease in the level of wakefulness and in the tone of the sympathetic nervous system) manifestations [15, 16].

Attempts to formulate conceptual foundations for detection of functional states in modern research have been made repeatedly. The first stream of studies is represented by the research dedicated to more general issues in the physiology of formation and development of functional states in human-machine interaction and methodological support for their diagnostics. In these studies, formation of (dys)functional states depends on both fundamental factors of their genesis [10] and external conditions of professional activity [14, 15]. Within the framework of such a universal perspective, approaches to classifying (dys)functional states are also presented, and their main types (operational rest, anxiety, monotony, fatigue, and psycho-emotional stress) are identified. Attempt were even made to characterize changes in psychophysiological traits specific to particular functional states [9]. However, these studies employ too general, universal indicators of functional states without taking into account the dynamics of user activity and without connection with task features. They do not pay much attention to shifts in functional states potentially brought by changes in intensity of influencing factors. The model they provide is static and, thus, less relevant to web interaction.

The second, smaller stream consists of studies that focus upon to the typology of affective and communicative states in human-computer interaction. This approach, based on detection and analysis of behavioral cues, attempts to identify persistent types of behavioral responses depending on user states [17]. In such works, the goal of the study is, as a rule, determining the behavioral patterns that accompany certain user states, e.g., the state of 'technological addiction' [18] or consumer behavior [19]. A special place in this group is occupied by studies on patterns of navigational behavior [20–22]. The design of these studies that aim at modeling user preferences in choosing a path through the website architecture best reflects the methodological flaw inherent in the entire group: The typology of user states and behavioral patterns is built upon machine processing of datasets of behavioral data, while external and internal factors in the formation of behavioral reactions and states are not considered.

Thus, as our review shows, neither of the research streams pays enough attention to.

the relationship between the intensity of exposure to factors that foster dysfunctionality and the intensity of experiencing dysfunctional states, which we see as a significant gap in word dysfunctionality studies. One of the promising directions in this regard is the study of the relationship between the degree of cognitive load and the intensity of the experienced dysfunctional state. The level of cognitive load is of decisive importance for the development of dysfunctions in one's cognitive-representative system [12].

2.2 The 'Contextual Fidelity' Model and Functional State Patterns

As we stated above, in usability studies, the concept of dysfunctional user states may be seen as consistent with the 'contextual fidelity' model, as the latter assesses similar variables, including user traits, product features, task complexity, and experimental settings. The model was proposed in 2011 and further developed in 2018 [16] and 2019 [2]. According to this model, various parameters related to product quality, user traits, and the test task may significantly affect the accuracy of testing. In this case, the user's functional state derives from the combined impact of the product, task, and testing environment, and is further conditioned by the user him-/herself.

Assessing the process of activity via the model, we get a flexible tool that allows for determining the external and internal factors affecting the workflow, at the intersection of which, a certain type of 'interaction experience' forms. Such combinations that link independent variables (e.g., the intensity of task plus the impact of the testing environment) and target variables (e.g., the level of user performance plus changes in the user's functional state) can be called *functional state patterns.* Such patterns describe stable linkages between combinations of 'contextual fidelity' factors, user performance, and user's functional state. The patterns are actually a sort of cumulative effects that persist and affect user performance. Finding them may be one of the goals of usability studies, as they show that interfaces need to be checked against formation of such patterns of inefficiency – that is, against particular combinations of 'contextual fidelity' factors.

In 2021–2022, we explored the impact of web aesthetics upon the dynamics of user experience as two different adverse functional states developed, namely monotony and anxiety. We have shown that functional state patterns critically affect the results of usability testing; we have detected three cumulative effects that were playing both for and against higher quality of user performance [1, 23, 24]. In these works, however, the 'contextual fidelity' factors were fixed in a binary way – e.g., aesthetic/non-aesthetic design, individual/group performance, Western/Eastern provenance of assessors, and monotony-/anxiety-inducing tasks. Thus, the intensity of each parameter was not taken into account. Moreover, in creating the tasks, we oriented them to being inductive in terms of a particular dysfunctional state but did not deal with actual task complexity which is another task feature that is, by common sense, to additionally induce dysfunctionality as task complexity grows. At the same time, today's research (including our own earlier works) suggests that, of the whole four-factor 'contextual fidelity' model, the main factors that regulate the users' cognitive load are the task complexity (to a greater extent) and the impact of the testing environment (to a lesser extent). We will check user performance against the two 'contextual fidelity' factors, thus adding to discovery of dysfunctional state patterns.

2.3 The Research Questions and Hypotheses

Given all stated above, we have formulated the following simple research questions:

RQ1. How does task complexity affect formation of the dysfunctional states of monotony and anxiety in usability tests?

RQ2. How does individual/group regimes of testing affect user performance on the tasks of varying complexity? What are the dysfunctional state patterns that we can see under the combined impact of testing environment and task complexity?

In accordance with these questions and with our previous findings, we put forward a range of hypotheses, on the basis of which we developed the design of the experiment. The hypotheses on individual testing correspond to RQ1, while those on group testing open up the RQ2.

Individual testing:

H1a. In individual testing, intellectual lability drops the deeper, the higher task complexity for both types of tasks.

H1b. In individual testing, emotional stress rises in accordance with the growth of task complexity via the rise of indicators respective to each of the two dysfunctional states. Thus, fatigue and anxiety will steadily grow for the monotony- and anxiety-inducing tasks, respectively.

H1c. In individual testing, full-fledged dysfunctional states that combine low intellectual lability and high fatigue/anxiety (respective to the conditions of task completion) will develop for the tasks of middle-range and high complexity.

Group testing:

H2a. In group testing of monotony, in line with our previous results [1], intellectual lability does not drop significantly for easy tasks, as group-based distraction compensates for the impact of cognitive load. However, it drops for mid-range and complex tasks for similar percentages.

H2b. In group testing of anxiety, the group environment does not compensate for the drop of intellectual lability.

H2c. In group testing of emotional stress for both types of tasks, drops in the respective indicators will be smaller than in individual testing.

H2d. In group testing, full-fledged dysfunctional states only form for complex tasks.

3 The Research Method

In order to study in more detail the relationship between the intensity of the impact of 'contextual fidelity' factors (in particular, task complexity that induces varying cognitive load) and the intensity of experiencing dysfunctional states, we have developed an experiment that includes tasks of various levels of complexity fulfilled by assessors in two formats, namely the group one and the individual one.

3.1 The Experimental Design

According to a number of studies, the level of cognitive load that varies due to varying task complexity, is crucial for performance and productivity in solving interactive communication problems in human-computer interaction [25, 26]. At the same time, the correlation between the complexity of the task and the efficiency of its solution is inversely proportional: As the complexity of the task decreases, the accuracy and speed of its execution increase, and as the complexity grows, they fall [27].

In usability testing, the most common and relevant practice is to analyze the complexity of a task at three levels, namely structural, semantic, and cognitive.

The structural complexity defined by the information architecture of a web interface refers to the potential range of alternative paths to the target information in the hierarchical structure of a website. As studies in this area show, there is a relationship between the depth of target information, patterns of user behavior in the search process, and the subjectively perceived complexity of the search task [28]. The depth of the path to the target information is, thus, one of the key factors that affect the users' cognitive states.

The semantic complexity of the task is determined by the obviousness of the path to the target information, as stated in the task description. The formulation of the search goal in this case either indicates the optimal path to solving the problem or masks it making the task more difficult. At the same time, the relevance of the path is measured by the degree of semantic closeness between the description of the search goal and the wording of the headings of navigation links [29].

The cognitive complexity of a task is determined by the number of components involved simultaneously in the process of intellectual activity. Tasks like comparison or classification imply the achievement of goals based on several criteria and places higher demands on the user's cognitive resources. In experimental research, the Miller criterion is widely used as a metric for cognitive complexity [30], according to which the efficiency of intellectual operations depends upon the number of objects that the assessor is able to simultaneously manipulate in his/her short-term memory [31]. The threshold value here is 5 ± 2, and, beyond this value, the task becomes very difficult for most representatives of the online audience.

Thus, task complexity of the turns out to be a function of the interaction of the structural (depth), semantic (relevance), and cognitive aspects of the navigation path. Low task complexity is characterized by small depth, high relevance, and the number of objects of intellectual activity less than seven, while high complexity implies significant depth (long path to target information), low relevance of the goal description, and the number of objects of intellectual activity exceeding the threshold value.

In accordance with this approach, we have identified three types of complexity for our prospective tasks, with three corresponding levels of cognitive load on the user:

- 'Easy' tasks with the minimal and fairly comfortable level of cognitive load;
- 'Medium-level' tasks with a threshold level of cognitive load, close to the psychophysiological limit, beyond which the efficiency of decisions should drop sharply;
- 'Complex' tasks of a high level of complexity, implying mobilization of maximum user's cognitive resources in the process of task solving.

For more accurate monitoring of changes in the user states, we have chosen the method of sequential complication of the task based on increasing the values of a discrete parameter with a minimum step according to the formula $(n + 1)$ as the basis for measuring structural complexity. In particular, the number of levels of website architecture that needs to be passed to the target content acts as a metric. As a criterion of semantic complexity, the ratio of the wording of the search goal and menu headings was chosen, and, for cognitive complexity, the number of criteria in intellectual operations that had to be operated simultaneously was fixed.

As a result, three tasks with different expected cognitive load were compiled, the complexity criteria for which are presented in detail in Table 1.

In essence, the task itself for inducing monotony and anxiety is of the same type; it aims at information search. However, an essential part of the task is how it is to be

Table 1. Tank complexity as part of the research design

Complexity level	Level of cognitive load	Structural complexity (the number of website layers)	Cognitive complexity (the number of criteria in smart operations)	Semantic complexity (goal statement vs. the menu headings)
easy	minimum	2	1	complete match
medium	threshold	3	2	non-complete match
complex	excessive	4	3	

Table 2. Assessor groups based on the research design, 5 assessors per group

Test format	Dysfunctional state	Task complexity level		
		Easy	Medium	Complex
Individual test	Monotony	sub-group1	sub-group5	sub-group9
	Anxiety	sub-group2	sub-group6	sub-group10
Group test	Monotony	sub-group3	sub-group7	sub-group11
	Anxiety	sub-group4	sub-group8	sub-group12

performed. Via additionally conditioning the tasks, we made them be more monotony-inducing or anxiety-inducing (see below).

As a task, we offered the assessors to evaluate and sort Master programs offered by Syracuse University, USA according to a range of criteria. The university website was chosen due to its recent redesign and high usability qualities. The target information bits that had to be found and evaluated by the assessors were the following:

1. Presence/absence of GRE (Graduate Record Examination) results in the admission requirements.
2. Presence/absence of GPA/TOEFL exam results in the admission requirements.
3. The minimum eligible amount of credit hours.
4. Presence/absence of final essay in the requirements for completion of the study program.
5. A requirement to present an official transcript of achievement as undergraduate.
6. The number of training trajectories.
7. The amount of financial support available via the scholarship program (in %).

In accordance with what is stated above, the differences between the tasks were determined by the website 'layer' on which the entry point for navigation situated, as well as by the number of sorting criteria. The 'easy' task meant searching for curricula according to the first three criteria to the depth of no more than two levels of architecture, while the criteria were clearly defined by the task statement. The task of medium complexity implied comparison of programs within the architecture of three levels of immersion, based on five criteria. In the high-complexity task, the search was carried out four levels deep and across the entire list of criteria. In the 'medium' and 'complex' tasks, the formulations of the criteria were identical and did not correspond to particular page headings.

Just as in our previous studies, we aimed at checking the formation of two dysfunctional states, namely monotony and anxiety. The former is to appear in the conditions of repetitive completion of a large number of typical operations with an insignificant creative component. The main factors that induce monotony, in our task, were the unawareness of the fixed time for task completion and a significant number of repetitive operations of comparing educational programs in order to sort them. The dysfunctional state of anxiety is formed in conditions of lack of time and information when solving a problem. Also, the development of this state may be associated with unforeseen changes in operating modes: for example, with a sharp complication of the task or a sudden change in its conditions combined with an unforeseen reduction in the time to solve. The induction of the anxiety mode was fostered by an unexpected reduction in timing and a change in the goal three minutes after the start of the test.

3.2 Measurements and Instruments

To measure the quality of user experience, we have chosen the following indicators for tracking the dynamics of assessors' (dys) functional states.

Intellectual Lability. This metric characterizes the ability to switch attention, that is, the ability to quickly move from solving one problem to solving another one without making mistakes. According to the theory of functional states, high levels of anxiety provoke impulsivity and an excessively high rate of reactions; in the case of monotony, the rate decreases down to apathy. We measure this indicator using the so-called Gorbov – Schulte table [32], a short test of attention switching before and after the experiment.

Emotional Condition. Here, we use four metrics that, taken together, make up the integral indicator of a user's emotional state. In accordance with the method of self-assessment of emotional states by Wessman and Ricks [33], we intend to measure the level of anxiety (calmness/anxiety scale), fatigue (energy/ fatigue scale), arousal (excitement/depression scale), and confidence (self-confidence/helplessness scale).

Experimental Design. To test the hypotheses, we developed the 4x3 study design. Test tasks were performed in twelve subgroups of assessors, 5 assessors per group. Each group worked with a task of a certain level of complexity in one of the two testing formats (either group or individual) and in one of two cognitive modes of ac-tivity, that is, in conditions that fostered either anxiety or monotony. Thus, our exper-iment included 60 assessors and had the following design (see Table 2).

The experiment had the following steps.

1. Input testing for the cognitive and emotional state, used to fix the initial state of cognitive efficiency and emotional stress in 'operational comfort' of each assessor:
   - assessment of the current level of emotional stress (self-assessment of emotional conditions by Wessman and Ricks);

- test on intellectual lability (via the Gorbov – Schulte table).

2. Performing tasks of one of three levels of complexity that form dysfunctional states (either anxiety and monotony) in a group/individual test.
3. Output testing for the cognitive and emotional state, used to fix changes in the indicators of cognitive efficiency and emotional stress of each user.

Data Analysis and Interpretation. For each assessor, the results of input and output testing were fixed. Then, in each group, mean values and standard deviations for them were calculated for each indicator. After that, the difference between the indicator values before and after task completion (delta, or Δ) was calculated, and its mean and its standard deviation were, too. The deltas are the secondary indicator that allows for comparing individual and group testing, as well as the very assessment of the user cognitive and emotional states. As the emotional indicators were measured from 10 (the best state) to 1 (the worst state), drops in values indicate the growth of dysfunctionality. The same is true for intellectual lability, though it is measured in points that combine time and precision of finding the targets on the Gorbov – Schulte table.

4 Results

The results of our experiment are shown in Table 3 (for the individual testing environment) and Table 4 (for the group one).

RQ1. As the results show, the changes in assessors' functional states vary depending on the level of task complexity. This is especially noticeable in reactions to the cognitive load from attention and intellect via the intellectual lability indicator. However, the results for indicators of emotional stress point to multi-directional effects caused by combinations of testing settings and task complexity.

Individual task completion. In line with expectations, for both monotony and anxiety, intellectual lability decreases least intensely when the 'easy' task is solved. In particular, intellectual lability drops by ~ 15% (187.15 to 171.13, $\Delta = -16.02$) for the anxiety-inducing task and by ~ 8.5% (from 187.05 to 182.93, $\Delta = -4.12$) for the monotony-inducing one. It is worth noting that the anxiety-inducing task has caused twice as big a drop in lability than the monotonous task. For mid-range task complexity, expectedly, lability drops more significantly but nearly equally for both task types – for ~ 23% for anxiety and for ~ 27% for monotony. This pattern continues for the complex tasks: Lability drops for ~ 45% anxiety and for ~ 44% for monotony, thus making users lose nearly a half of their initial multi-tasking capacity. This confirms **H1a** and hints that, for more complex tasks, complexity plays a bigger role in defining the user states than the nature of the task; with growth of complexity, anxiety- and monotony-inducing task solving becomes equally dominated by cognitive load, rather than by testing conditions.

H1b, though, cannot be confirmed, as the results for indicators of emotional stress differ from those expected. Thus, there is no pattern of steady growth of fatigue/anxiety with the growth of task complexity; in neither case (including the group results) emotions 'responsible' for a given dysfunctional state grow in relation to task complexity. For monotony, fatigue, indeed, grows on average, but, for 'easy' and mid-range tasks, the results are within the standard deviation interval, which tells that the assessors' results

Table 3. The results of individual testing

User state	Indicator		Task complexity level								
			Easy			Medium			Complex		
			before task	after task	*delta (Δ)*	before task	after task	*delta (Δ)*	before task	after task	*delta (Δ)*
Monotony	Intellectual lability		187,05 (1,057)	182,93 (1,228)	***-4,12 (1,504)***	188 (1,00)	132,2 (1,300)	***-50,8 (2,167)***	188,54 (0,756)	105,6 (1,148)	***-82,94 (1,357)***
	Emotional stress	Calmness/ anxiety	7 (0,471)	7 (0,471)	*0 (0,666)*	6,8 (0,447)	7 (0,707)	*0,2 (0,836)*	7 (0)	7 (0,707)	*0 (0,707)*
		Energy/ fatigue	6,9 (1,197)	5,5 (0,527)	*-1,4 (1,505)*	6,6 (1,513)	5,4 (0,547)	*-1,2 (1,923)*	7 (0,707)	5,2 (0,447)	***-1,8 (0,836)***
		Excitement/ depression	6,9 (0,567)	6,9 (316)	*0 (0,816)*	7,2 (0,447)	6,8 (0,447)	*-0,4 (0,894)*	8 (0)	7 (0,707)	***-1 (0,707)***
		Self-conf./ helplessness	6.8 (1,475)	7,1 (1,100)	*0,3 (1,766)*	6,8 (1,095)	6,8 (1,303)	*0 (0,707)*	6,6 (1,140)	6,6 (1,140)	*0 (0,707)*
Anxiety	Intellectual lability		187,15 (1,285)	171,13 (3,067)	***-16,02 (2,791)***	194,2 (3,193)	149,4 (2,073)	***-44,8 (2,049)***	191 (2,549)	105,05 (2,132)	***-85,94 (3,112)***
	Emotional stress	Calmness/ anxiety	7,1 (0,875)	6,1 (0,875)	***-1 (0,471)***	7,2 (1,095)	6,2 (1,095)	***-1 (0)***	7,2 (1,095)	6,2 (1,095)	***-1 (0)***
		Energy/ fatigue	6 (0,666)	6 (0,666)	*0 (0,666)*	5,6 (0,547)	5,8 (0,836)	*0,2 (0,447)*	5,7 (0,447)	5,7 (0,670)	*0 (0,353)*
		Excitement/ depression	6,9 (0,567)	7 (0,471)	*0,1 (0,567)*	7 (0,707)	7,2 (0,447)	*0,2 (0,447)*	6,4 (0,547)	7,4 (0,547)	***1 (0,707)***
		Self-conf./ helplessness	7,1 (0,370)	7,3 (0,251)	*0,2 (0,788)*	6,8 (1,095)	6,8 (1,303)	*0 (0,707)*	6,8 (1,095)	6,8 (1,303)	*0 (0,707)*

were too divergent to form a stable pattern. Fatigue significantly grows only for the 'complex' task. In case of anxiety, calmness drops equally for all the levels of complexity; this pattern also repeats for the group performance, however, with nearly two times higher rise of anxiety. Such stable drops of calmness could be induced by the very fact of task completion; however, this does not seem to be true, as the figures for group work are stably bigger than those for individual task solving, and are non-significant for monotonous tasks. More probably, the rises of anxiety are induced by the task conditions, and, in this case, it is anxiety that dominates over complexity in shaping the users' state. Due to worse performance in groups, as judged by the level of anxiety, we recommend that the tasks potentially leading to high anxiety are performed in the individual regime.

Thus, it is for 'complex' tasks only that full-fledged dysfunctional states may be detected; this is why they were not discovered in our previous studies which did not offer complex enough tasks to the assessors. Moreover, in each case, the dysfunctional states not only combine low lability and high stress by the corresponding indicator (either fatigue or anxiety) but is also complemented by changes in one other emotional indicator. For monotony, depression also rises in both individual and group testing, which is quite understandable intuitively. For anxiety, though, a counter-intuitive rise in excitement is observed (which is also noticeable for 'easy' and mid-range tasks but is not significant), and this pattern does not repeat for group testing (see below). Thus, **H1c** is confirmed for high-complexity tasks but not for borderline cognitive load.

Table 4. The results of group testing

User state	**Indicator**		**Task complexity level**								
			Easy			**Medium**			**Complex**		
			before task	after task	*delta (Δ)*	before task	after task	*delta (Δ)*	before task	after task	*delta (Δ)*
Monotony	Intellectual lability		190,2 (0,836)	188,2 (6,906)	*-2 (6,442)*	185 (4,527)	127,5 (1,581)	***-57,5 (3,640)***	183,4 (3,189)	86,2 (2,196)	***-97,2 (3,701)***
	Emotional stress	Calmness/ anxiety	6 (0)	6 (0,707)	*0 (0,707)*	6 (0,547)	6 (0,707)	*0 (0,547)*	6 (0,707)	6 (0,707)	*0 (0,707)*
		Energy/ fatigue	6,4 (0,547)	6,2 (0,447)	*-0,2 (0,836)*	7 (0,707)	6 (0,707)	*-1 (1,224)*	7,6 (0,547)	6 (0,707)	***-1,6 (0,894)***
		Excitement/ depression	7,2 (0,836)	7 (0)	*-0,2 (0,836)*	7,2 (0,836)	7 (0)	*-0,2 (0,836)*	7,8 (0,447)	6,6 (0,547)	***-1,2 (0,447)***
		Self-conf./ helplessness	6,6 (0,894)	7,4 (0,547)	*0,8 (0,836)*	7 (0)	7 (0)	*0 (0)*	7,4 (0,547)	7,4 (0,547)	*0 (0,707)*
Anxiety	Intellectual lability		188,64 (1,499)	159,1 (3,398)	***-29,54 (4,450)***	189,2 (1,303)	132,4 (5,594)	***-56 (6,140)***	193 (2,915)	96,5 (2,179)	***-96,5 (3,240)***
	Emotional stress	Calmness/ anxiety	7 (1,870)	5,2 (1,788)	***-1,8 (0,836)***	7 (1,870)	5,2 (1,788)	***-1,8 (0,836)***	6,8 (1,303)	5,2 (1,483)	***-1,6 (1,140)***
		Energy/ fatigue	6,4 (0,547)	7,2 (0,447)	*0,8 (0,836)*	7 (0)	7 (0)	*0 (0)*	6,4 (0,894)	6,4 (1,140)	*0 (1,870)*
		Excitement/ depression	7 (0,707)	7,6 (0,547)	*0,6 (0,894)*	7 (0,707)	8 (0,707)	*1 (1,224)*	6,6 (0,894)	7,6 (0,547)	*1 (1,224)*
		Self-conf./ helplessness	6,8 (0,447)	7,4 (0,547)	***0,6 (0,547)***	6,8 (0,447)	7,8 (0,836)	***1 (0,707)***	6,8 (0,447)	5,6 (0,894)	***-1,2 (0,836)***

RQ2. The group testing has, in general, demonstrated similar dysfunctional state patterns. In both individual and group testing, emotional stress indicators mostly responded in an expected way: Thus, for monotony, there was growth of fatigue and no changes in anxiety; for anxiety, there was growth of anxiety and no changes in fatigue.

Group Testing Environment. Here, we juxtapose the results of individual and group testing. First, intellectual lability for the ‘easy’ task solved in groups is the only case of insignificant lability change, in line with our previous research [1]. If for individual testing, intellectual lability dropped by ~ 15% for anxiety and by ~ 8.5% for monotony, for the group test, the decrease in intellectual lability was very similar (~15.6%) for anxiety but insignificant for monotony (~1%; Δ = -2, SD = 6.442). For the ‘easy’ task, we see that group testing compensates for pressures created via insignificant cognitive load; however, this is only true for monotony-, not for anxiety-inducing performance procedures. For mid-range and ‘complex’ tasks, lability drops sharply and similarly for both monotony and anxiety (~31%/ ~ 30% and ~ 53%/50%, respectively). This fully confirms **H2a.** This is why we here repeat our recommendation for group-based completion of monotonous tasks, as group-based distraction compensates for the impact of cognitive load. This, however, may not work for more complex tasks. One more consequence of our study is the following: We could test any given task for complexity and identify whether this or that task is easy enough if group testing compensates for intellectual lability drops, and lability remains unchanged.

For anxiety, as we have just stated, no compensation happens, and lability drops in a notable way even for 'easy' tasks (~15,6%), and this drop intensifies with the growth of complexity. Thus, **H2b** is also confirmed.

As to the emotional stress, we had expected that group testing would compensate for negative emotions and allow for lower indicator values. However, **H2c** has to be rejected. We could only assess the emotional stress indicators for high-complexity tasks where they have shown significant drops; the changes of emotional states are multi-directional. There are only two stable patterns that we could detect. First, as already stated above, for the anxiety-inducing task, group values on anxiety are nearly two times worse than those for the monotonous task, contrary to expectations. Second, in both individual and group testing, excitement slightly (and insignificantly) rises for the anxiety task, while self-confidence behaves highly unpredictably. Thus, for individual testing, it remains completely unchanged, and in group testing it first rises significantly (allegedly, group support allows for better self-confidence when the task is solved), but then sharply drops. This result is not counter-intuitive, as successful solution of 'easy' and 'mid-range' tasks may foster a rise of self-confidence, while the excessive task complexity may leave people irritated and dissatisfied.

Just as in individual testing, in group testing, full-fledged dysfunctional states only form under the impact of tasks of maximum complexity. This shows that group testing does not fully compensate for drops in performance efficiency, and complex enough tasks may eventually destroy functionality of web users. **H2d** is confirmed.

5 Discussion and Conclusion

After our research, one may say that stable patterns of emotional-cognitive reactions are observed that are specific for tasks of different levels of complexity. However, accumulation of dysfunctionality is non-linear, and certain dysfunctional state patterns deserve special attention.

Monotonous tasks cause relatively less dysfunctionality on low and middle levels of complexity. When solving an 'easy' task in both group and individual conditions, cognitive functions are close to operational rest in both individual and group regimes of testing. On medium levels of complexity, only intellectual capacities diminish in a notable way (approximately one fourth of initial capacity), while emotional stress grows insubstantially. But as soon as the level of complexity grows beyond a certain level, the dysfunctional state forms, with a nearly half loss of brain lability and growth of fatigue and depression. Here, the sharp break in performance beyond the threshold load points an area for future research in the field of managing the formation of dysfunctions.

Anxiety-inducing tasks cause somewhat bigger drops of intellectual lability, which also stably increases with the growth of task complexity. What differs the anxiety-inducing tasks from monotonous ones is immediate rise of emotional stress exactly via loss of calmness; anxiety remains on the same level in both individual and group environments regardless of task complexity, which may mean that anxiety reduction in real-world HCI cannot be reached by reducing task complexity and introducing simpler, less complex tasks. This deserves immediate attention by education professionals and interface developers. However, as anxiety in groups is nearly two times higher on average than that registered for individual performance, it is not that assessors' anxiety reaches its maximum from the very beginning; individual format allows for lesser growth of anxiety, as well as prevents the feeling of helplessness. This is a counter-intuitive finding, as, usually, group task solution is characterized by lesser helplessness due to potential mutual help of participants and lesser expression of helplessness in front of fellow assessors. However, here, we see that group performance enhances helplessness even for low- and mid-range task complexity.

For anxiety-inducing tasks, the pattern of sharp formation of dysfunctionality is less evident for individual testing, where brain lability gradually diminishes with the growth of complexity but anxiety remains stably higher than in rest. However, for group performance, the rise and then sharp fall of self-confidence reveals that sharp drops of functionality may also happen for anxiety tasks.

Thus, the formation of dysfunctional states is shaped by a combination of inner conditions of task solving and task complexity, as, both types of dysfunctionality sharply rise in any external conditions of task solving. Along with that, group performance may compensate for the drops of intellectual lability for monotonous tasks, while enhances helplessness for anxiety-inducing tasks. Thus, our recommendations that aim at harm reduction call for group performance on monotonous tasks and, vice versa, individual performance on anxiety-inducing tasks.

To conclude, we need to state one thought that derives from our studies of the 'contextual fidelity' model. As 'contextual fidelity' factors are multiple and their combinations affect testing results, this poses a simple question: What do we see as the 'objective' result of quantitative usability testing? Is it the result of individual or group testing? Perceiving usability test results as objective might be misleading. What is needed instead is conduction of target-oriented usability research, where the usability test model would correspond to prospective uses of a given interface. E.g., if an interface implies office work or use in school class, group tests need to be compulsory, while interfaces for personal use need to pass testing in individual regimes. This also implies that multi-function interfaces, for which one cannot easily predict preferential modes of use need to pass multiple testing with various combinations of 'contextual fidelity' factors, in order to detect the threshold cognitive loads and find out how and when dysfunctionality arises.

Acknowledgements. . This research has been supported in full by the project 'Center for International Media Research' of St. Petersburg State University, year 3, #94033584.

References

1. Yakunin, A.V., Bodrunova, S.S.: Cumulative impact of testing factors in usability tests for human-centered web design. Future Internet **14**(12), 359 (2022)
2. Sauer, J., Sonderegger, A., Heyden, K, Biller, J., Klotz, J., Uebelbacher, A.: Extra-laboratorial usability tests: An empirical comparison of remote and classical field testing with lab testing. Appl. Ergon. **74**, 85–96 (2019)

3. Doi, T., Doi, S., Yamaoka, T.: The peak-end rule in evaluating product user experience: the chronological evaluation of past impressive episodes on overall satisfaction. Hum. Fact. Ergon. Manufact. Serv. Indust. **32**(3), 256–267 (2022)
4. Cha, S.S., Lee, S.H.: The effects of user experience factors on satisfaction and repurchase intention at online food market. J. Indust. Distribut. Bus. **12**(4), 7–13 (2021)
5. Holden, R.J., et al.: Human factors engineering and human-computer interaction: supporting user performance and experience. Clin. Inform. Study Guide: Text Rev., 119–132 (2022)
6. Sauer, J., Sonderegger, A.: The influence of product aesthetics and user state in usability testing. Behav. Inf. Technol. **30**(6), 787–796 (2011)
7. Leonova, A.B.: Functional status and regulatory processes in stress management. In: Hockey, G. R.J., Gaillard, A.W.K., Burov, O., (Eds.) Operator functional state: the assessment and prediction of human performance degradation in complex tasks, pp. 36–52. IOS Press, Amsterdam (2003)
8. Ushakov, I.B., Bogomolov, A.V., Kukushkin, Y.A.: Psychophysiological mechanisms of formation and development of functional states. Russian J. Physiol. (Formerly I. M. Sechenov Physiol. J.) **100**(10), 1130–1137 (2014)
9. Ushakov, I.B., Bogomolov, A.V., Kukushkin, Y.: A: Patterns of operator functional states [Patterny funktsional'nyh sostoyaniy operatora]. Nauka, Moscow (2010)
10. Leonova, A.B., Medvedev, V.I.: Functional states of a person in labor activity: A textbook [Funktsional'nye sostoyaniya cheloveka v trudovoy deyatel'nosti]. Lomonosov Moscow State University Publishing House, Moscow (1981)
11. Leonova, A.B.: The concept of human functional state in Russian applied psychology. Psychol, Russia: State of the Art **2**, 517–538 (2009)
12. Chuprikova, N.I.: Human reaction time: Physiological mechanisms, verbal-semantic regulation, connection with intelligence and properties of the nervous system [Vremya reaktsiy cheloveka: Fiziologicheskie mehanizmy, verbal'no-smyslovaya regulyatsiya, svyaz' s intellektom i svoystvami nervnoy systemy]. Yask Publishing House, Moscow (2019)
13. Suvorova, G.A.: Psychology of activity [Psihologiya deyatelnosti]. PER SE Publishing House, Moscow (2003)
14. Kaptelinin, V., Nardi, B.: Activity Theory in HCI: Fundamentals and Reflections. Morgan & Claypool Publishers, San Rafael (2012)
15. Bodrov, V.A.: Psychological foundations of professional activity [Psihologicheskie osnovy professional'noy deyatel'nosti]. PER SE / Logos, Moscow (2007)
16. Ilyin, E.P.: Psychophysiology of human states [Psihpfiziologiya sostoyaniy cheloveka]. Piter, St. Petersburg (2005)
17. Scherer, S., et al.: A generic framework for the inference of user states in human computer interaction. J. Multimodal User Interf. **6**, 117–141 (2012)
18. Laor, T., Galily, Y..: In WAZE we trust? GPS-based navigation application users' behavior and patterns of dependency. PLoS ONE **17**(11), e0276449 (2022)
19. Li, X., Zhao, X., Pu, W.: Measuring ease of use of mobile applications in e-commerce retailing from the perspective of consumer online shopping behaviour patterns. J. Retail. Consum. Serv. **55**, 102093 (2020)
20. Diwandari, S., Hidayat, A.T.: Comparison of classification performance based on dynamic mining of user interest navigation pattern in e-commerce websites. J. Phys. Conf. Ser. **1844**(1), 012025 (2021)
21. He, Q., Borgonovi, F., Suárez-Álvarez, J.: Clustering sequential navigation patterns in multiple-source reading tasks with dynamic time warping method. J. Comput. Assist. Learn. (2022). https://doi.org/10.1111/jcal.12748
22. Gao, Y., Cui, Y., Bulut, O., Zhai, X., Chen, F.: Examining adults' web navigation patterns in multi-layered hypertext environments. Comput. Hum. Behav. **129**, 107142 (2022)

23. Yakunin, A.V., Bodrunova, S.S.: Website aesthetics and functional user states as factors of web usability. In: Ahram, T., Taiar, R. (eds.) IHIET 2021. LNNS, vol. 319, pp. 394–401. Springer, Cham (2022). https://doi.org/10.1007/978-3-030-85540-6_51
24. Yakunin, A.V., Bodrunova, S.S.: Cumulative distortions in usability testing: combined impact of web design, experiment conditions, and type of task and upon user states during internet use // design, user experience, and usability: ux research, design, and assessment. In: 11th International Conference, DUXU 2022, Held as Part of the 24th HCI International Conference, HCII 2022, Proceedings, pp. 526–535. Springer Nature, Cham (2022)
25. Campbell, D. J.: Task complexity: A review and analysis. Academy of Management Review, 13(1), 40–52 (19880
26. Hong, W., Thong, J.Y., Tam, K.Y.: The effects of information format and shopping task on consumers' online shopping behavior: A cognitive fit perspective. J. Manag. Inf. Syst. **21**(3), 149–184 (2004)
27. Byström, K.: Information and information sources in tasks of varying complexity. J. Am. Soc. Inform. Sci. Technol. **53**(7), 581–591 (2002)
28. Gwizdka, J., Spence, I.: What can searching behavior tell us about the difficulty of information tasks? A study of web navigation. In: Proceedings of the 69th Annual Meeting of the American Society for Information Science and Technology (ASIS&T), vol 43. Information Today, Inc, Medford (2006), asistdl.onlinelibrary.wiley.com/doi/pdf/https://doi.org/10.1002/meet.14504301167, (Assessed 23 Feb 2023)
29. Van Oostendorp, H., Ignacio Madridb, R., Carmen Puerta Melguizo, M.: The effect of menu type and task complexity on information retrieval performance. Ergonom. Open J. **2**(1), 64–71 (2009)
30. Jiang, Z., Benbasat, I.: The effects of presentation formats and task complexity on online consumers' product understanding. MIS Q. **31**(3), 475–500 (2007)
31. Michailidou, E., Harper, S., Bechhofer, S.: Visual complexity and aesthetic perception of web pages. In: Proceedings of the 26th Annual ACM International Conference on Design of communication, pp. 215–224. ACM (2008)
32. Mashin, V.A.: Analysis of heart rate variability based on the graph method. Hum. Physiol. **28**, 437–447 (2002)
33. Wessman, A.E., Ricks, D.F.: Mood and personality. Holt, Rinehart and Winston, New York (1966)

Consumer Behavior in Social Computing and Social Media

Behavior of Current Consumers of Nintendo Video Game Consoles

Cristobal Fernandez-Robin[1(✉)], Diego Yañez[1], Maria Ignacia Müller[1], and Scott McCoy[2]

[1] Departamento de Industrias, Universidad Técnica Federico Santa María, Av. España 1680, Valparaíso, Chile
{cristobal.fernandez,diego.yanez}@usm.cl, ignacia@wenuwork.cl
[2] Mason School of Business, Williamsburg, VA, USA
scott.mccoy@mason.wm.edu
https://www.industrias.usm.cl/

Abstract. The gaming industry is part of a niche market of consumers who invest their time and money in interactive audiovisual experiences that are based on platforms, such as computers, arcade machines, consoles, and mobile devices. The research creates a questionnaire that includes questions about demographic information, user behavior, and theoretical constructs proposed by the TCT model, reaching 253 people. SPSS Statistics v.28 was employed to assess the reliability of each construct through Cronbach's alpha. Subsequently, a structural equation analysis was conducted using SPSS Amos v.28. The results confirm that the intention to continue using Nintendo Switch is explained by Attitude (b = 0.441) and Perceived Usefulness (0.288). In turn, Confirmation and Subjective Norm are not significant for Intention to Use, which is explained by the fact that in an early technology adaptation stage, the concept of social pressure and fulfillment of expectations may be relevant, but not in a stage at which users have already assimilated the use of a technology (Weng et al., 2017). Likewise, Attitude is explained by Expectation Confirmation, Perceived Usefulness of the console and the opinion of people important to the user in the form of Subjective Norm. In summary, if the consoles meet user expectations (confirmation), and an interface that is easy to use (perceived ease of use) and socially attractive (subjective norms), the probability that users will continue to use the console will increase, since that the user's attitude towards the console and the perceived usefulness it generates will experience a positive impact.

Keywords: Gaming · Attitude · Continuance intention

1 Research Problem

Consumption is an economic problem associated with a satisfaction of desires and needs. It occurs in all economic systems due to the purchasing power of

A. Coman and S. Vasilache (Eds.): HCII 2023, LNCS 14025, pp. 489–505, 2023.
https://doi.org/10.1007/978-3-031-35915-6_35

consumers. The current consumption era can be interpreted as a cycle from functionalism to post-modernism that focuses on individual and mass consumption (Alonso L, 2005). The socioeconomic concept of a consumption society denominates the states with an industrial or productive capitalist development-in which, as a consequence of the mass production of goods and services, there exists a massive consumption of the same, as well as a broad offering that is in some cases greater than the demand (Carosio, 2008).

Consumer behavior is a factor that influences decision-making when searching for, buying, using, assessing and discarding a good and/or service, i.e., what? how? when? and where to buy something? (Schiffman & Kanuk, 2005). In decisions that are affected by physical and mental factors, analyses serve as a basis for the creation of efficient strategic marketing plans in which the needs and attributes valued by the public are understood to increase the utility and positioning of a brand (Alonso & Grande, 1997).

The video game industry is part of a niche of consumers who invest their time and money in interactive audiovisual experiences through platforms such as computers, arcade machines, consoles or mobile devices. Every year, hundreds of video games are developed, and consoles are designed that are constantly adapting to the new technologies in the market. As a reference, in 2005 and only in Europe, there were already 255 video game studios in a growing market (Benito, 2005). The misidentification of factors or attributes relevant to consumers using technology then becomes a problem. This, together with individual consumer behavior in decision-making, becomes a fundamental aspect for the creation of an assertive marketing plan.

Through the study of consumption habits, a product that satisfies the needs of users can be designed and delivered. In the case of technology consumption, behavior is expected to be explained through use and user acceptance models, identifying product attributes and individual perceptions that increase the interest of consumers in purchasing a good based on its added value. In the video game market, Nintendo Co has a presence as a large company. Since 1990, it focuses on the creation of its own consoles, and has developed a wide product portfolio, including video games from diverse genres, different accessories and a total of 12 consoles, namely 5 desktop, 6 portable and 1 hybrid (Wagner, 2019). But what makes consumers prefer new consoles over previous models and those from competing companies?

2 Objectives of the Study

2.1 General Objective

To determine factors influencing the consumption habits of Nintendo video game consoles, applying a technology acceptance model to identify opportunities to improve products and commercial strategies.

Specific Objectives

1. To gather information about consumer motivations when purchasing video game consoles through a qualitative study on a population sample to create hypotheses.
2. To identify technology acceptance models and determine the one that best applies to the present case.
3. To carry out quantitative studies to create conceptual models of factors influencing consumer decision-making according to the hypotheses formulated in the qualitative phase.
4. To reach conclusions on the relationship between various factors and acquisition by users through the testing of the hypotheses formulated.

3 Theoretical Framework

3.1 Literature Review

Since the 1960s,s, the video game industry has been evolving into a complex market. In addition, specializations have been created, budgets have grown, new technologies have been developed and society has evolved. Video game developers usually adapt cultural factors to create virtual experiences, expecting to have a good reception from the consumer once the product is launched in the market (Egenfeldt-Nielsen, 2018).

This industry experienced strong growth during the 20th century, maintaining a relatively constant annual growth rate of 7.8%, currently presenting annual global revenues of around 129 billion euros, of which 31% corresponds to the acquisition of video games for traditional consoles (Egenfeldt-Nielsen, 2018). In turn, the competing brands of Sony, Nintendo and Microsoft not only compete in hardware production, but also have strong incentives to acquire exclusive title licenses and spend large amounts of money on developing their own titles, since most of the industry's revenue originates from the games themselves (Egenfeldt-Nielsen, 2018).

The historical evolution of the market can be classified into "console cycles", which on average last 5 years, after which a new cycle begins with the launch of a new generation of consoles and the development of titles specifically designed for them, generating a temporary burst in sales. With the passing of time, revenue begins to slowly decline, prompting manufacturers to develop new consoles and start a new cycle (Egenfeldt-Nielsen, 2018). In this industry, developers compete to achieve leadership in sales, because if a product that is developed does not have the expected reception in the market, it implies a downturn that is difficult to recover from.

In the last identified cycle, Sony led the market with cumulative sales of its PlayStation 4 console, released in 2013. Microsoft, until 2018, followed in second place with its Xbox One console, released in 2013, but far below in number of sales, as shown in Fig. 1. In last place, until a couple of years ago, was Nintendo with the Nintendo Switch console, which was launched 4 years later (2017) than its competitors. In March 2021, the Nintendo Switch increased its sales, and experienced an accelerated reception growth within the market (Orus, 2021).

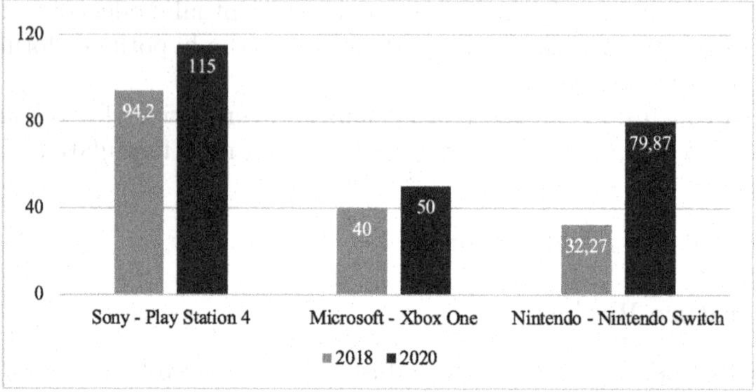

Fig. 1. Cumulative sales by consoles in millions of units Source: (Egenfeldt-Nielsen, 2018); (Orus, 2021)

3.2 The Video Game Industry Value Chain

The value chain is the breakdown that an organization makes of its strategically relevant activities to understand their costs and existing differentiation paths. Firms that use value innovation strategies, such as those participating in technology markets, focus their resources on creating distinguishing product characteristics and increasing consumer perceived value (Gonzáles- Piñero, 2017). From this perspective, W. Chan Kim and Reneé Mauborgne suggested a process that seeks to create value through innovation in 4 stages:

1. Eliminate what is not valuable.
2. Reduce what is less valued.
3. Increase what is most valued.
4. Create what others are offering.

The concept of user empowerment determines what customers give real value to; therefore, their opinion and perception becomes essential when launching new products (Gonzáles-Piñero, 2017). In the video game industry, 5 critical stages are identified in the creation of value for the final product.

In Fig. 2, the value chain begins with the design and production of physical consoles or devices (hardware) capable of processing video games. Here Sony, Nintendo and Microsoft are identified as the main manufacturers in the industry.

Fig. 2. Value chain in the video game industry Source: (Egenfeldt-Nielsen, 2018)

Game development plays a key role in the chain and has various phases, starting with concept development, continuing with design, and ending with production and testing, carried out by a team of multidisciplinary specialists (Egenfeldt-Nielsen, 2018). This work is limited by the technical specifications of the console; thus, hardware development is fundamental to users' gaming experience, and innovating or incorporating next-generation technologies can be crucial for the reception of the console and its titles (Gonzáles-Piñero, 2017).

Distributors play an intermediary role between publishers (companies that pay commissions for the rights to publish video games and hire developers to produce them, responsible for manufacturing, distribution and advertising) and retail, where final consumers can purchase the products (Egenfeldt-Nielsen, 2018). However, there is a trend towards the purchase of video games in digital format, through direct acquisition via console platforms (Gonzáles-Piñero, 2017).

3.3 Nintendo in the Industry

Nintendo is one of the most recognized firms in the industry. Since 1980 it has been dedicated to the manufacture and development of video game consoles, having popularly recognized consoles such as Gameboy, Nintendo DS and Nintendo Wii as part of its catalog. The firm has developed different video game franchises since its beginnings in the industry. The development of titles has evolved from arcade machines to current consoles (Takeda, 2020), and some popular franchises that have accumulated millions of units sold have been identified, such as Mario Bros (752.43 million), Pokémon (380 million), The Legend of Zelda (127.91 million) and Donkey Kong (82.88 million) (Nintendo, Dedicated Video Game Sales Units, 2021).

The evolution of franchises goes hand in hand with the development of consoles, since through new technologies, they generate innovative gaming experiences to maintain the interest and loyalty of users (Takeda, 2020). Figure 3 shows the development of consoles by Nintendo since 1980.

Nintendo maintained a constant market share until the release of Nintendo GameCube (Egenfeldt-Nielsen, 2018). Its sales failure was a hard loss for the Japanese corporation, which was in direct competition at that time with Sony and its launch of PlayStation 2 (PS2), which accumulated more than 155 million units sold (Sony, 2021).

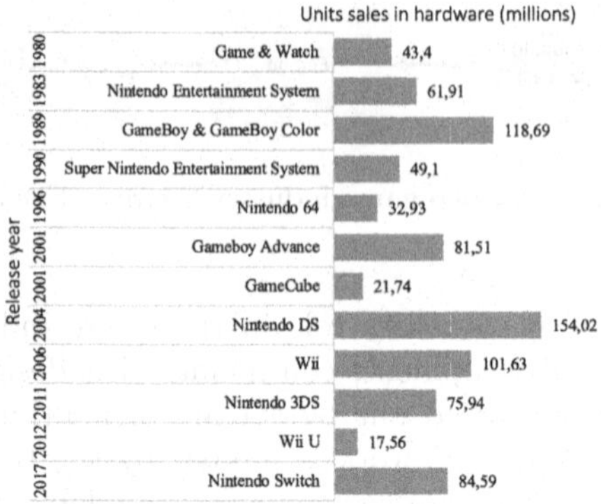

Fig. 3. Console sales through March 2021 in millions of units Source: Nintendo, Dedicated Video Game Sales Units, 2021

After the failure of Nintendo GameCube, in 2004, they opted for a 100% portable console under the name of Nintendo DS, which became the second best-selling console in history, surpassed only by PS2 (Nintendo, Dedicated Video Game Sales Units, 2021), repositioning the brand. After the success of the console, its sales rose again thanks to the launch of Nintendo Wii, a console with a technology that increased user interaction through an infrared control with a motion reader, allowing for a more dynamic video game experience (BusinessWeek, 2006). In this way, the Wii marked a milestone by being the first console to exceed the sales of its direct competition at that time, PlayStation 3 from Sony (Nintendo, Dedicated Video Game Sales Units, 2021) (Sony, 2021). However, despite the popularity that Nintendo was reaching, the next generation, Nintendo Wii U, had a poor reception from the public, with unprecedented losses for the corporation and making it the worst console launched in its history (Nintendo, Dedicated Video Game Sales Units, 2021).

Four years after the fall in the market, the firm announced the development of a new hybrid console, which drew the attention of followers. In 2017, at its premiere, Nintendo Switch managed to sell a total of 2.7 million units worldwide, and accumulated a total of 84.6 million units sold by 2021 (Nintendo, Dedicated Video Game Sales Units, 2021).

3.4 The Strategy of Nintendo Switch

Understanding the success of the console is crucial to understanding Nintendo's current situation and strategies as a company, as well as to identifying the factors that led to past business failures.

One of the causes to which the success of the new console is attributed is its innovative technology, since having a console in which users can play from the comfort of a television or transform it to a handheld device with a single click was unprecedented. The biggest reason behind the console's success was its clear marketing strategy and value proposition (Wagner, 2019). Contrary to its predecessor, which gave the feeling of being just a Wii update rather than a new console, the Switch from the beginning had a clear and concise proposal: play it wherever, whenever and with whomever. Clearly communicating to the user how easy the new technology is to understand and what this implies for its use is key to creating a friendly and attractive concept for users. They carried out campaigns in which rather than explaining how the console worked, they showed people using it on a daily basis, generating a sense of familiarity with the equipment and a strong incentive to acquire it (Ngoc, 2018).

The firm shortened the cycles of releases and product notifications, showing evidence of the importance of conducting studies about consumer preferences and essential attributes in the design of new products, in addition to understanding what the factors are that influence consumers to generate a desire to purchase new technologies.

3.5 Consumer Behavior in the Face of New Technologies

The adoption of innovations is the process in which consumers go from awareness to full acceptance of a new product, procedure or idea, applicable to contact with new technologies (López-Bonilla, L., and López-Bonilla, J. 2011).

There are relatively recent studies on the individual acceptance of the use of information and technologies. Diverse technology acceptance models (TAM) based on psychological and sociological theories have been proposed to explain the acceptance and use of technology, which converge in the unified theory of acceptance and use of technology (Unified Theory of Acceptance and Use of Technology; UTAUT) (Venkatesh, Morris, Davis, & Davis, 2003). The UTAUT model employs the critical factors and contingencies for the prediction of consumer behavior and their intentions towards the use of technologies (Vankatesh, Thong, & Xu, 2012).

In turn, the TCT (Technology Continuance Theory) model combines the two main constructs of attitude and satisfaction in a continuous model, being applicable for the entire life cycle of technology adoption, i.e., from initial users to long-term use and use confirmation (Liao, 2009). The biggest advantage of the TCT model is that the satisfaction and attitude constructs are merged in the TCT model, keeping utility and ease of use constructs as predecessor constructs (Liao, 2009).

3.6 Model Under Study

In the proposed model in Fig. 4, diverse constructs previously proposed in applications of TCT models are used. The concepts of attitude, confirmation, perceived ease of use and perceived usefulness are considered influential in continuance intention to use according to several studies (Weng, 2017), and therefore have been included in this model.

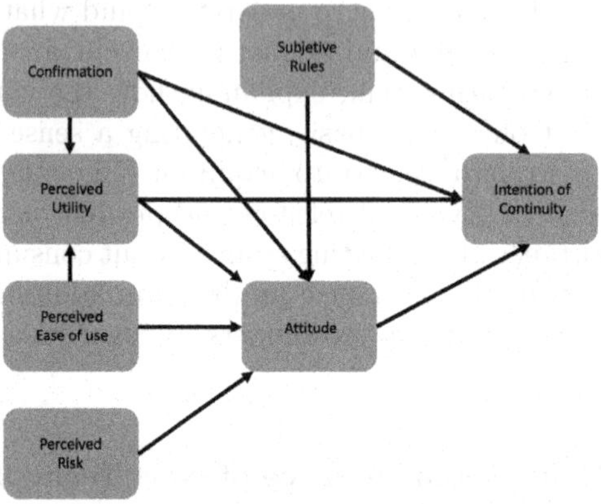

Fig. 4. TCT model proposed for the intention to continue using the Nintendo Switch.

The model also includes the constructs of perceived risk and subjective norms because previous studies suggested adding them as significant factors for user attitude and continuance intention to use technologies (Weng, 2017).

Therefore, technology acceptance models expect to predict, in the most accurate possible way, consumer behavior towards the consumption of various types of technology, including video games, considering the factors of performance expectations, user effort, social influence, ease of understanding and user demographic information.

3.7 Definition of Constructs and Hypotheses

For the formulation of hypotheses in the model, the constructs under study are defined. Attitude is understood as the degree of positivity or negativity that a person perceives about the performance of a specific object (Davis, 1989).

- **H1**:The attitude towards the use of the Nintendo Switch is directly related to the continuance of its use.

The perceived usefulness refers to the perception that people have about how much the object or technology helps in a task or objective. In turn, perceived ease of use indicates the degree to which a person adapts to technologies without much effort. There is literature in which both terms can influence the user's attitude and intent to use (Weng, 2017). Thus, the following hypotheses are proposed:

- **H2**: The perceived usefulness of the Nintendo Switch is directly related to the continuance of its use.
- **H3**: The perceived usefulness of the Nintendo Switch is directly related to the user attitude towards the console.
- **H4**: The perceived ease of use of the Nintendo Switch is directly related to its perceived usefulness.
- **H5**: The perceived ease of use of the Nintendo Switch is directly related to the user's attitude towards the console.

Confirmation as such is considered the cognitive notion of the user about the actual console use experience versus the expected one, i.e., what happens after the user makes effective use of the technology in question (Bhattacherjee, 2001). Use confirmation is expected to reflect user satisfaction with technologies by meeting expectations, which is the reason why it is considered a factor that positively influences user attitude and interest in continued use of technologies. (Weng, 2017). In addition, the concept of confirmation can be related to perceived usefulness, since the user's confirmatory experience is useful in adjusting usefulness when there is uncertainty in the user's use expectations (Bhattacherjee, 2001). Thus, the following hypotheses are proposed:

- **H6**: The confirmation of expectations in the use of the Nintendo Switch is directly related to the continuance of its use.
- **H7**: The confirmation of expectations in the use of the Nintendo Switch is directly related to its perceived usefulness.
- **H8**: The confirmation of expectations in the use of the Nintendo Switch is directly related to the user's attitude towards the console.

The concept of risk is defined as the consequences and uncertainty related to consumer decisions (Bauer, 1960). It is expected that if a technology does not meet the expected results, it will result in a loss for the user; therefore, perceived risk affects people's trust in the perceived usefulness of technologies (Weng, 2017)

- **H9**: The perceived risk in the use of the Nintendo Switch is inversely related to the user's attitude towards the console.

Subjective norms are interpreted as the existing perceived social pressure whether or not to perform a certain behavior (Ajzen, 1991). Subjective norms have a great influence on the intentions and attitudes of individuals towards their behavior, since the use of a type of technology is expected to be greater if the individual's social circle accepts this technology as such (Weng, 2017).

- **H10**: The subjective norms regarding the use of the Nintendo Switch are directly related to the continuance of its use.
- **H11**: The subjective norms regarding the use of the Nintendo Switch are directly related to the user's attitude towards the console.

4 Methodology

In order to identify the factors that influence the consumption habits of users, a technology use model is expected to explain their behavior.

From the literature and secondary sources, the factors influencing the behavior of the technology's user are identified and, according to the research problem, a model is selected that explains the behavior of the current user of Nintendo consoles; in this case, the model is based on the TCT. To identify product improvements or effective business strategies, the analysis needs to be complemented with a quantitative study that demonstrates consumer behavior with empirical evidence.

Based on the research problem and model selected for the study, a questionnaire composed of 34 items is built, which includes demographic questions about user behavior and the theoretical constructs proposed by the TCT model. Demographic questions include age, sex and occupation, while questions concerning the model are formulated based on existing studies to ensure its validity. A Likert scale was used to assess answers, which have been compiled in Fig. 5.

The study employs a representative sample of the universe of video game console users. Convenience sampling is used for data collection. The questionnaire is disseminated through the Internet in communities of Nintendo users, reaching 253 people in a period of one month.

The first filter question is whether or not a person is actually a Nintendo Switch user, ending the survey if the answer is negative. Of the 253 people who started the survey, only 89.72% responded positively to the filter question, of which only 189 completed the questionnaire.

To validate the questions, the SPSS program is used. Specifically, the reliability of the constructs is calculated through Cronbach's alpha, which should have a minimum value of 0.6 to be acceptable (Hair, 2009). In addition, questions are grouped by construct since this is a confirmatory factor analysis.

To identify the structural relationships between constructs and the weight of the variables that compose them, structural equation models (SEM) are used, analyzing the significance and value of the results obtained. Subsequently, how well the data fit the model is evaluated through a goodness-of-fit analysis to confirm whether the model is correct.

5 Results

5.1 Sample Characteristics

Of 187 people who completed the survey, 47 (25.13%) identify themselves with the female gender, 137 (73.26%) with the male gender and 3 (1.06%) with another gender. Most people are aged 23 to 27 (45.45%), followed by people aged 18 to 22 (20.86%), 28 to 32 (18.72%), 33 to 37 (8.56%), 38 years and above (4.28%) and less than 17 years (2.14%). Regarding occupation, 80 people (42.78%) answered that they were students, 74 (39.57%), identified themselves as dependent workers, 22 (11.76%) as independent workers and 11 (5.88%) as none of the above.

Construct	Item
Perceived usefulness (PU)	1. The console is good for playing video games
	2. The console is the most convenient for playing video games
	3. Having the console helps me acquire video games easily
	4. Having the console grants me quick access to play video games
	5. The console allows me to access video games at a lower cost
	6. In general, I find the console useful for playing video games
Perceived ease-of-use (PEU)	7. Interacting with the console does not require a high mental effort
	8. I find the console interface easy to use
	9. Learning to use the console would be easy for me.
	10. The console interface is manageable enough to interact with it.
	11. I find the console easy to use
Perceived risk (PR)	12. I think that payment within the console platform may be risky
	13. I don't feel safe about my data on the console platform
Attitude (ATT)	14. Having the Nintendo Switch console over another console is a good idea
	15. Having the Nintendo Switch console over another console is a wise idea
	16. I like the idea of having a Nintendo Switch console over another console
Confirmation (CON)	17. My experience with the console was better than I expected
	18. The service provided by the console platform was better than expected
	19. The information delivered about the console was better than expected
	20. The cost associated with using the console and my experience was better than expected
	21. In general, my experience with the console confirmed what I expected.
Subjective norms (SN)	22. My family would be happy if I had a Nintendo Switch console
	23. My friends would be happy if I had a Nintendo Switch console
	24. My coworkers would be happy if I had a Nintendo Switch console
Continuance intention (CI)	25. I intend to continue using the console rather than discontinue its use
	26. I intend to continue using the console rather than other consoles on the market
	27. If I could, I would like to use the console as much as possible.

Fig. 5. Measurement model

5.2 Mathematical Validation

A reliability analysis similar to Cronbach's alpha is performed. The reliability of the items is verified through values higher than 0.6 for each one, as observed in Fig. 6a below. Therefore, a priori questions are not removed from the questionnaire in the formulated model. After verifying data reliability, the proposed structural equation model is analyzed using the SPSS Amos software.

First, the model presents an error when estimating a negative variance in the risk construct, specifically with a value of –27.166. Therefore, tests are carried out to solve this problem. A negative variance that is far from zero is the reason for inverse parallelism, i.e., in a model, small values of X correspond to large values of Y and vice versa (Roldán, 2020). The scales of the questions are inverted, together and then separately, to verify that it is not a scale error of the question and the model yields a feasible result. However, since no changes are obtained in the results, it is decided to remove the construct from the model, which results in a mathematically feasible model.

Construct	Cronbach's alpha
Perceived usefulness	0.755
Perceived ease of use	0.82
Perceived risk	0.763
Attitude	0.904
Confirmation	0.832
Subjective norms	0.735
Continuance intention	0.701

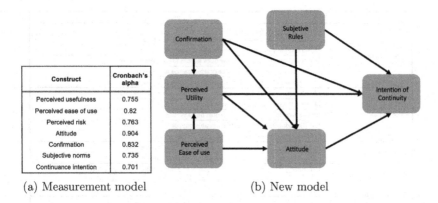

(a) Measurement model

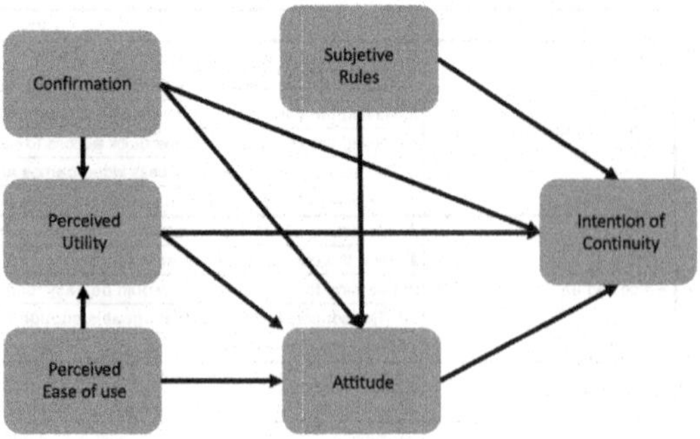

(b) New model

Fig. 6. Model

By analyzing the p-value of the new model, we can confirm whether the variables are significant for the model using the criterion of $p < 0.05$. Figure 7 contains values obtained for each proposed hypothesis, noting that H5, H6 and H10 do not meet the established criteria, and therefore are not mathematically supported in the model.

Hypotheses	Relationships	P-value	Decision
H1	ACT $\xrightarrow{+}$ IC	***	Supported
H2	UP $\xrightarrow{+}$ IC	0.044	Supported
H3	UP $\xrightarrow{+}$ ACT	0.002	Supported
H4	FUP $\xrightarrow{+}$ UP	0.006	Supported
H5	FUP $\xrightarrow{+}$ ACT	0.867	Non-supported
H6	CON $\xrightarrow{+}$ IC	0.254	Non-supported
H7	CON $\xrightarrow{+}$ UP	***	Supported
H8	CON $\xrightarrow{+}$ ACT	0.023	Supported
H9	RP $\xrightarrow{-}$ ACT	-	Removed
H10	NS $\xrightarrow{+}$ IC	0.124	Non-supported
H11	NS $\xrightarrow{+}$ ACT	0.007	Supported

Fig. 7. P-value and hypothesis tests with *** when $p < 0.001$

Therefore, according to the present model, it cannot be verified that the construct of perceived ease of use is related to the user's attitude towards the console. In addition, it cannot be established that the constructs of confirmation and subjective norms are linked directly to continuance intention of use by the user.

In turn, if the values obtained for the standardized coefficients are observed, the construct with the strongest direct influence on the continuance intention of use of users can be identified. In this case, this is useful to conduct a cross-sectional analysis. The values obtained are presented in Fig. 8.

Relationship			Coefficient
ACT	→	**IC**	**0,441**
UP	→	**IC**	**0,288**
UP	→	ACT	0,413
FUP	→	UP	0,235
FUP	→	ACT	0,012
CON	→	**IC**	**0,139**
CON	→	UP	0,689
CON	→	ACT	0,271
NS	→	**IC**	**-0,13**
NS	→	ACT	0,204

Fig. 8. Weightings of standardized regressions of the model

5.3 Model Adjustment

As a result of the model, a degree of freedom value equal to DF = 265 is obtained. As this is a value far from 0, it is interpreted that the model is generalizable and does not exclusively represent the data sample. In turn, the value of chi-squared, CMIN = 567.404, together with degrees-of-freedom, indicates that the model presents an acceptable adjustment, as the value for CMIN/DF = 2.140 ranges from 2 to 3 (Escobedo, 2016).

Regarding the index of goodness-of-fit of the model, a value of CFI=0.856 is obtained, which by being lower than 0.9 indicates a slightly poor model adjustment. Additionally, if the value of the mean square approximation error is analyzed, RMSEA=0.067, this result is above the acceptable value of 0.05, and therefore the model does not satisfy the minimal adjustment conditions (Escobedo, 2016).

The adjustment results, despite not meeting the acceptable ranges in the literature, are within the normal range, since they are close enough to assert that the model has an acceptable fit. This can be explained since the model under study uses data collected from surveys, in which external variables that may be influencing the responses of the interviewees cannot be controlled.

6 Discussion and Analysis

The objective of the study is to determine the continuance intention to use Nintendo Switch through the TCT model. The advantage of this model lies in its synthesis of user attitude and satisfaction, preserving perceived usefulness and the ease of use as its constructs at the same level (Weng, 2017). Despite the fact that all the hypotheses proposed for the model are supported except for H10, the risk construct should be removed due to inconsistencies in the model.

When analyzing the impact of the model's constructs (Appendix, Fig. 9), it is observed that despite the fact that the influence of perceived ease of use (PEU) on attitude (ATT) and on subjective norms (SN), together with the influence of confirmation (CON) on continuance intention (CI), were not supported, these continue to be related to other constructs of the model, specifically to attitude and perceived usefulness.

If the effects of the constructs supported by CI are considered, those that generate the strongest impact are precisely attitude (b = 0.441 and $p < 0.001$) and perceived usefulness (b=0.288 and p=0.044). This is supported by previous studies, since the continuance intention to use applied to an e-learning system was studied, obtaining that perceived usefulness, satisfaction and attitude have an important effect on the users (Liao, 2009). It is established that attitude is based on cognitive beliefs, which can be unlearned, in which the individual in question forms his ideas based on information from his environment, people, media, advertising and others (Lee, 2010).

In turn, some relationships were not directly supported by continuance intention, such as subjective norms (b = –0.13 and p = 0.124) and confirmation (b = 0.139 and p = 0.254). The above is explained on the basis that in a phase of premature adaptation of technologies, the concept of social pressure and the fulfillment of expectations may be relevant, but not in a stage at which the user has already assimilated the use of a technology (Weng, 2017).

The attitude construct is explained, in decreasing order, by perceived usefulness (b = 0.413 and p = 0.002), confirmation (b = 0.271 and p = 0.023) and subjective norms (b = 0.204 and p = 0.007). Therefore, despite the fact that the relationship between confirmation and subjective norms versus continuance intention are not supported by the model, they are antecedents that are indirectly relevant to the model, but cannot be directly associated to the same.

In turn, as above mentioned, the effects of perceived ease of use and perceived risk on the attitude of users were not mathematically supported. This is explained in the way users obtain more knowledge of the technology and with the generation of perceived usefulness, i.e., its use becomes routine and its features will be familiar to them, such that perceived ease of use will lose weight in the attitude equation with the passing of time (Weng, 2017).

The effect of subjective norms on the attitude of users implies that they feel some social pressure to acquire this technology, and suggests that they will prefer opinions from their social circles over information from the media or from experts (Weng, 2017).

Given the results of the weightings explained, one of the first things that should be considered is the necessity of efforts to design technologies that provide a positive use experience for users, rather than just devoting these efforts to marketing campaigns (Hsu, 2014).

Likewise, the perceived usefulness construct is represented in its measure, in decreasing order, by confirmation (b=0.689 and $p < 0.001$) and perceived ease of use (b=0.235 and p=0.006), which confirms that the confirmation construct cannot be directly related to continuance intention but rather does have a strong indirect influence on the final variable. In addition, perceived ease of use is not removed from the model since it is also an antecedent of the construct under study.

Some studies find that perceived ease of use should score higher than confirmation in terms of influence on perceived usefulness (Weng, 2017), which is the contrary in this case. This is explained by the fact that users are already used to employing the console and its features. Therefore, it can be assumed that they have been dealing with this technology for some time, which could be included in subsequent surveys to confirm it. However, it is suggested that the technologies have a user-friendly system that can be easily adapted to from the beginning.

This study has demonstrated, through empirical information, not only the intention of users to continue using technology, but also the importance of factors such as attitude and perceived usefulness, proving the effectiveness of using the proposed TCT model. This work confirmed the versatility of the model's application to explain user behavior in a post-adaptation stage, with fruitful results for cases of technology use in hospitals, online games, e-learning, mobile applications, and in this case, video game consoles (Weng, 2017).

In addition to empirically verifying the adaptation of the model to the case, there are glimpses of opportunities to improve the user's experience with the product. By being clear about the factors that influence the perception of users, more assertive strategies can be generated that target the attitude and usefulness generated in the user, thereby allocating resources more efficiently in the development of the product and in the way that it is launched on the market. A focus on the user's environment could also be considered, since subjective norms have been demonstrated to directly influence the user's perception when acquiring the technology, which makes it a factor to consider when designing an advertising plan. In summary, if consoles are presented that meet the expectations generated by the user (confirmation), with an easy-to-use interface (perceived ease of use) and socially attractive to acquire (subjective norms), the probability that users continuously employ the console during a period after adaptation will increase, because user attitude towards and the perceived usefulness the console will generate will be positively impacted. In this case, the risk is considered insignificant, which can be explained by the nature of console technology, in which it is difficult to identify any source of risk a priori.

In the future, adding the satisfaction construct to the model would be useful to gather more information, since this has been regularly used in TCT models with positive results. The incorporation of this construct could be a key complement to the development of continuous improvements in soon-to-be-released technologies, thereby directly identifying the user's reception of the technology per se.

7 Conclusions

In the video game industry, specifically in the development of consoles by the Nintendo firm, influential factors have been found in the habits of consumers that use the Nintendo Switch console. Within the universe of existing technology acceptance models, the TCT model positively adapts to the study, finding relevant information on user acceptance of this technology, also proving the versatility of the model. Gathering information quantitatively has enabled the successful conduction of the study and the verification of its hypotheses, which found that the factors that most influence users' continued use of this console in a post-adaptive phase are attitude and perceived usefulness.

8 Anexos

			Estimate	S.E.	C.R.	P label
PU	<---	CON	0,523	0,084	6,239	***
PU	<---	PEU	0,382	0,14	2,74	0,006
ATT	<---	SN	0,324	0,12	2,701	0,007
ATT	<---	PEU	0,032	0,191	0,167	0,867
ATT	<---	PU	0,656	0,217	3,031	0,002
ATT	<---	CON	0,327	0,144	2,277	0,023
CI	<---	SN	-0,116	0,076	-1,538	0,124
CI	<---	ATT	0,249	0,065	3,843	***
CI	<---	PU	0,258	0,128	2,015	0,044
CI	<---	CON	0,094	0,083	1,14	0,254

Fig. 9. Result of the model obtained by SPSS Amos

References

Ajzen, I.: The theory of planned behavior (1991)

Alonso, J., Grande, I.: Comportamiento del Consumidor: Planes y Estrategias de Marketing (1997)

Alonso, L.: La Era del Consumo (2005). https://www.redalyc.org/pdf/3232/323227828011.pdf

Bauer, R.: Consumer Behavior as Risk Taking (1960)

Benito, J.: El Mercado del Videojuego: Unas Cifras. Retrieved from Revista de comunicación y tecnologías emergentes (2005). https://www.redalyc.org/pdf/5525/552556595003.pdf
Bhattacherjee, A.: Understanding Information Systems Continuance: An Expectation-Confirmation Model (2001)
BusinessWeek, Obtenido de (2006).https://n9.cl/sy8ao
Carosio, A.: EL Género del Consumo en la Sociedad de Consumo. SciELO. Retrieved from Scientific Electronic Library Online (julio de 2008)
Davis, F.: Perceived Usefulness, Perceived Ease of Use, and User Acceptance of Information Technology (1989)
Egenfeldt-Nielsen, E.H.: Video Games: The Essential Introduction (2018)
Escobedo, M.H.: Modelos de ecuaciones estructurales: Características, fases, construcción, aplicación y resultados (2016). https://n9.cl/aiu0r
Gonzáles-Piñero, M.: Redifining The Value Chain of the Video Games Industry (2017)
Hair, J.F.: Multivariate Data Analysis (2009)
Hsu, C.Y.: Exploring the continuance intention of social networking websites: an empirical research (2014). https://n9.cl/ldt2dp
Lee, M.: Explaining and predicting users' continuance intention toward e-learning: An extension of the expectation-confirmation model (2010)
Liao, C.P.: Information technology adoption behavior life cycle: Toward a Technology Continuance Theory (TCT). Obtenido de International Journal of Information Management **29**(4) (Agosto de 2009). https://n9.cl/ghgdl
Ngoc, L.: Nintendo vs ITS competitors in marketing efforts: From the point of view of customers (Abril de 2018). https://n9.cl/iyi38
Nintendo, Dedicates Video Games Sales Units (30 de junio de 2019). https://n9.cl/odzi8
Nintendo, Dedicated Video Game Sales Units (2021). https://n9.cl/odzi8
Orus, A.: Ranking de las videoconsolas con el mayor volumen de ventas a nivel mundial a fecha de febrero de 2021. Statista (2021)
Roldán, A.: Estadística Práctica (2020)
Schiffman, L., Kanuk, L.: Comportamiento del Consumidor (Octava Edición ed.) (2005)
Silverman, B.: Wii U sales improve, but are still historically terrible. Retrieved from Yahoo Finance (Mayo de 2015). https://n9.cl/hs1ey
Sony (2021). https://n9.cl/hvyvb
Takeda, L.: The History of Nintendo: the Company, Consoles And Games (2020)
Vankatesh, V., Thong, J., Xu, X.: Consumer Acceptance and use of Information Technology: Extending the Unified Theory of Acceptance and Use of Technology (2012)
Venkatesh, V., Morris, M., Davis, G., Davis, F.: User Acceptance of Information Technology: Toward a Unified View (2003)
Wagner, E.: A strategic Audit of Nintendo Co., Ltd (2019)
Weng, G.S.: Mobile taxi booking application service's continuance usage intention by users (2017)

A Preliminary Methodology for Information Consumer Experience Evaluation

M. Godoy[1(✉)], C. Rusu[2], and J. Ugalde[1]

[1] Universidad de Valparaíso, Valparaíso 2340000, Chile
mariapaz.godoy@uv.cl
[2] Pontificia Universidad Católica de Valparaíso, Valparaíso 2340000, Chile

Abstract. In recent years, information has become one of the most important goods for organizations as it brings insights about customer preferences and internal processes that could help to improve organizational performance, decrease costs, improve customer engagement, among other benefits. The consumption of information within an organization has been studied in the literature under several approaches associated to information system success nor information management, but the Information Consumer eXperience (ICX) has not been evaluated following a formally defined methodology. In this work, a methodology to formalize the ICX evaluation process within the organization is proposed. The main goal of this methodology is to improve ICX into the organization by generating recommendations based on information consumers perceptions under a customer experience CX approach. The proposed methodology consists of 3 sequential stages: Characterization, Experimentation and Analysis. In The Characterization Stage an exploratory diagnosis is performed, including the experimental setup planification, consumers behavior exploration, and a preliminary version of the customer Journey Map. The Experimentation Stage is focused on data collection using different instruments such as surveys, interviews, questionnaire, and a mixed qualitative and quantitative instrument to generate data about consumers expectations and perceptions. In the third stage of Analysis, the collected data is analyzed to generate a definitive Customer Journey Map, through quantitative and qualitative data analysis. Our proposed ICX evaluation methodology is the first formally described methodology for information consumer perceptions analysis and experience evaluation. Which could be used to face ICX analysis into any kind of organization that works with information.

Keywords: Information Consumer Experience · Customer Experience · Evaluation Methodology

1 Introduction

In modern organizations, access to information is crucial for employees to carry out their duties effectively and make informed decisions. As a result, many organizations have established informatics or analytics departments with the purpose

A. Coman and S. Vasilache (Eds.): HCII 2023, LNCS 14025, pp. 506–519, 2023.
https://doi.org/10.1007/978-3-031-35915-6_36

of collecting, storing, and making data accessible to other departments. These departments provide employees with a range of information products, systems, and services, including reporting systems, data management systems, analytics tools, data extraction tools, data visualization services, and communications services. These tools and services play a vital role in helping employees from several departments such as sales, people management, financial, operations, executive, among others, to access and use the information they need to perform their work competently.

As can be seen in Fig. 1, the utilization of information products, systems, and services by consumers is influenced by various factors that modify their perception. External factors, such as social relationships with information or technology and literacy rates in the local area, have a bearing on their views. Additionally, organizational factors, such as official protocols for information access and usage, can also impact information consumers' behavior. Importantly, internal factors, such as personal preferences for specific information products, systems, or services, can result in ineffective or non-utilization of these resources. It is crucial to consider these factors in the evaluation of information consumer needs, pains, gains, and experiences.

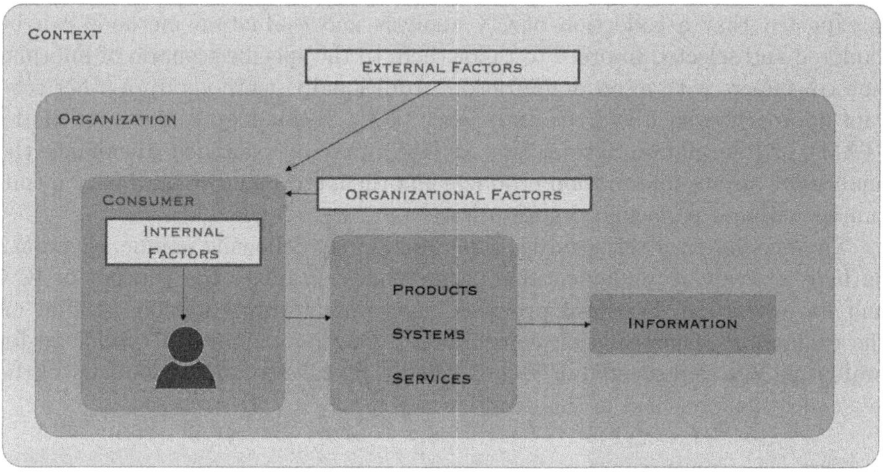

Fig. 1. Diagram that describes the Information Consumer Context into an organization.

Every information product, system, and service provided by an organization constitutes a potential point of interaction with its information consumers, from the moment of access to its use in their work tasks. Previous research on information systems success [34] and user experience [22] has largely focused on evaluating user satisfaction with a single system. However, at the organizational level, information consumers interact with multiple systems, products, and services, making it challenging to address these interactions through a broader approach. For this reason, in this work we aim to look forward User Experience and Information System Success to cover the major variety of interactions between information consumers and information products, systems and services. With our preliminary methodology proposal we aim to offer of a novel tool to organizations and researchers for analyze and evaluate ICX, which could allows them to obtain ICX diagnosis and insights for generating strategic plans in order to improve ICX and working climate within the organization.

In order to address the analysis of information consumption within an organization from an experience-based perspective, this study presents a preliminary methodology utilizing a Customer Experience (CX) approach for evaluating Information Consumer Experience (ICX). The methodology seeks to analyze the needs, pains, and gains of information consumers within the organization and evaluate their experience in consuming different information products, systems, and services. This methodology endeavors to comprehensively assess the interactions of consumers with information, taking into account all aspects of information generation, management, application, and sharing. The ultimate goal of this methodology is to conduct a thorough analysis of the overall experience of information consumers.

Given that the concept of ICX can be considered a specific case of CX, it is expected that a collection of CX analysis and evaluation methods can be explored and selected in order to tailor them to the specific scenario of information consumers with in an organization. Additionally, methods from other relevant approaches, such as User Experience (UX), Technology Acceptance Model (TAM), or Information System Success (ISS), may be examined to enhance the analysis of various information products and the interactions of information consumers within a particular organization.

The remainder of this study is structured in the following manner. Section 2 outlines a series of fundamental concepts that pertain to the concept of ICX and its evaluation. Section 3 provides an examination of previous studies on the evaluation of information consumption. Our preliminary methodology for evaluating ICX is presented in Sect. 4. Finally, Sect. 5 contains a summary of the key conclusions reached in this study.

2 Theoretical Background

In this section, a set of key concepts regarding the Information Consumer Experience (ICX) are presented. These concept are related to the most important approaches that have been preliminary selected to be used in the proposed methodology. For each concept, a brief description is given.

2.1 Costumer eXperience (CX)

Although the Customer eXperience (CX) has been widely studied in the literature, it does not have a formal definition. CX is referred to customer's perception produced by his interactions with all products, systems and services offered by a company or organization [16]. As a complex concept, authors have given different definitions of CX in the literature. In [8] six dimensions of CX are described: Emotional: associated to consumers feelings and emotions. Sensorial: that involves the stimulation of different senses of the customer produced by his interaction with the company. Cognitive: related with the conscious mental and thinking processes of the costumers. Pragmatic: involved with the practical act of doing a job within a company's product or service. Lifestyle: related with consumers values and the beliefs. Relational: associated with the social contexts of the costumer and his relationships with other customers or people.

CX involves the customers perception produced by his interaction with one or more touchpoints, which are fundamental components in the elaboration of the Customer Journey Map (CJM). CJM is a strategic management instrument that allows to represent CX in a company on a graphical way, where all touchpoints are identified together with their channels, expectations and emotions associated during the customer interaction [32]. Although there is no unique definition of the CJM structure, in [19] four key elements of CJM are defined: (i) Persona: The central element of the CJM which describes the behavior, motivations, habits, interests and needs patterns of the customer. (ii) Touchpoints: Represent the interactions points between the costumer and the products and services of the companies. Into the CMJ, touchpoints describe a logical sequence, in some cases grouped by stages, of actions performed by the costumer during the usage of the product or the consumption of the service. (iii) Channels: Involves the medium, physical or logic, through the customers interacts with the company's touchpoints. (iv) Emotions: The customer perceptions, feelings and moods during his interactions in each touchpoint, reflecting which are the critical points of the customer journey where the customer is satisfied or not, and need to be improved.

2.2 Touchpoints

As it has been mentioned before, CX involves the interactions between a costumer and the products or services offered by a brand or company. These interactions are called touchpoints and in [30] are defined as the moments when costumer's experiences occur as the costumer "touch" a brand or company through the interaction of any piece of their products or services, across a medium or channel in a certain point of time. On this sense, in [16] four categories of touchpoints are proposed: Brand-owned touchpoints: interactions which are designed and managed and controlled by the company. Partner-owned touchpoints: interactions which are designed, managed, and/or controlled by the company together with one or more of its partners. Customer-owned touchpoints: those which are not managed or controlled by the company or any of its partners. Social/external touchpoints: Touchpoints that take place outside the company domain but can be associatedto the brand or company products or services.

On other hand, [30] identifies a set of touchpoints components such as atmospheric, technological, communicative, process, employee-customer interaction, customercustomer interaction, and product interaction elements. With all these touchpoints categories and components, is possible identify and understand several touchpoints instances in the analysis of the relationship between the costumer and the products and services of a company.

2.3 Customer Journey Map (CJM))

The CX involves the customers perception produced by his interaction with one or more touchpoints, which are fundamental components in the elaboration of the Customer Journey Map (CJM). CJM is a strategic management instrument that allows to represent CX in a company on a graphical way, where all touchpoints are identified together with their channels, expectations and emotions associated during the customer interaction [32]. Although there is no unique definition of the CJM structure, [19] defines at four key elements of CJM: Persona, Touchpoints, Channels, and Emotions. The Persona element describes the type of customer that is interacting with the products and services. A consumer can by characterized by his behavior, motivations, habits, interests and needs patterns. The Touchpoints elements corresponds to the interactions between the costumer and the products and services of the companies previously described in Sect. 2.2. The Channels represent the medium (physical or virtual), where the interactions occurs. And the Emotions elements represents the customer perceptions, feelings and moods during his interactions in each touchpoints. An emotion is used to express if the customer is satisfied or not at a certain touchpoint, and helps to identify where improvements are needed. With all the elements described above, a CJM represent an important tool for the understanding of the CX and costumers' perception about the set of touchpoints of the company.

2.4 Information Consumer eXperience (ICX)

The concept of Information Consumer Experience (ICX) encompasses all the interactions between employees, who are considered information consumers, and the information products, systems, and services within an organization. This encompasses activities such as information usage, information generation, inter-department information sharing, team collaboration, and decision-making. These interactions represent the touchpoints between the information consumers (employees or departments) and the information provider departments within the organization.

Therefore, ICX can be viewed as a specific instance of the Customer Experience (CX) concept, and can be analyzed using analytical methods from the CX domain. This allows for a deeper understanding of the ICX within an organization, the identification of various touchpoints, representation of the ICX through a Customer Journey Map, and evaluation using well-established CX evaluation techniques such as SERVQUAL [24].

3 Related Works

The information consumption within the organization has been addressed in the literature through several studies related with different approaches. A perspective has been oriented to analyze the dimensions of the information systems success model proposed [4], has also been studied how user satisfaction is an important factor which affects the use of information systems through the analysis of a set of factors that are involved in as use of the system, system quality, information quality and performance of the user [13].

Regarding to information quality, many authors have proposed definitions for this concept, describing the quality as set of characteristics such as useful, current, and accurate [27]. Later, [3] was addressed the information quality with focus in the improvement of decision making On the other hand, through an auditable information approach, [17] addressed the value generation through information-intensive services (IISs) use, they identified nine key factors that characterize this data-based value generation. Also other approach to address the information consumption into an organization has been assessed since [25] discusses Personal Information Management (PIM) in different perspective.

Other authors [11] have also analyzed discusses the information consumer needs into the design of software tools about information management and archiving systems, [31] also examined the perceived impacts of information technology use on firm marketing organization performance. Also, Some works have addressed the employee experience in various job types, including non-information based roles [1,5,33]. Other works have focused on information management and sharing within organizations [10,20,26,36]. Furthermore, other studies have addressed the acceptance and success of information systems [12,21,28,29].

Different analysis and evaluation methods for ICX related approaches have been used in the literature [9]. Most of these methods are based on the implementation of a custom questionnaire [12,29], designed to gather data on employee or information consumer perceptions concerning specific measurement constructs or factors that may impact said perceptions. These questionnaires are largely derived from existing ones, such as the ACRL Questionnaire [36], the WEIS-SR Questionnaire [6], the Job Satisfaction Survey [5], among others. After data collection, various statistical techniques such as multiple and hierarchical regression, PLS, SEM, and LGM modeling have been employed to validate the authors' approaches and determine perceptions metrics and correlations [12,29].

These approaches are highly favored due to their adaptability to specific organizations, departments, and consumer samples. In contrast, other methods such as Social Network Analysis [7,26] and theoretical modeling [26] lack the same degree of flexibility. However, due to the vast array of custom methods, constructs, and factors employed, it is necessary to validate the security of these methods through complementary methods. To this end, alternatives such as semi-structured and open interviews [2,10,15,18] have been utilized.

These alternatives offer a complementary approach by providing explanations and, in our opinion, illuminating the underlying causes of quantitative results.

It has been noted that no formal or informal definition of the Information Consumer Experience (ICX) has been discovered in the systematic review. However, there are several concepts or approaches related to ICX that have been widely studied in the literature, including Employee Experience [14,33], understanding and learning to use information products, systems, and services [36], information management [10], information sharing [20,23,26,36], intention to use information systems [12,29], and user experience [10,26,37]. Additionally, job satisfaction [1,5] and qualitative approaches [15] have also been studied in order to analyze the interactions between employees and the resources and regulations within an organization.

4 ICX Evaluation Methodology Proposal

As a preliminary approach, we propose a methodology to formalize the ICX evaluation process within the organization. This methodology has been inspired from the findings presented in [9]. In order to address ICX analysis and evaluation, we propose three sequential stages: A Characterization Stage, followed by an Experimentation Stage, and ending with an Analysis Stage. All the evaluations tasks involved with every stage can be seen in Fig. 2.

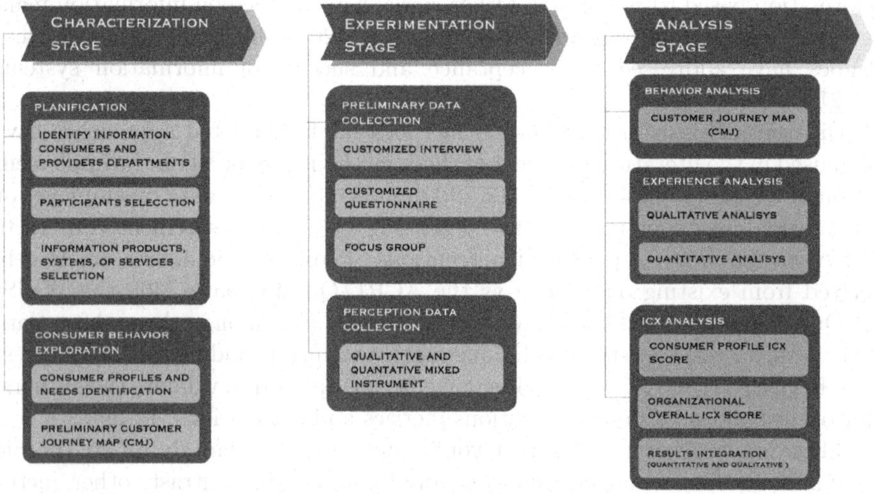

Fig. 2. Detailed proposal of evaluation methodology for ICX.

4.1 Characterization Stage

The objective of the initial stage, called the Characterization Stage, is to perform an exploratory diagnosis. In the first sub-stage called Planification, the information must be chosen and selected from three fundamental elements to use in further stages: Departments (that may be the entire organization), participants (Sample) and information products, systems or services. Thise elements need to be well-defined in order to applied the methodology correctly. Then, in the second sub-stage called Consumer Behavior Exploration, a behavioral diagnosis will be performed, identifying the needs and profiles of consumers, generating a preliminary version of the customer Journey Map to be improved in the third stage of analysis.

Planification

- **Identify Consumers of Information and Supplier Departments**
  The objective of this is to identify the information provider departments within the organization or levels that are dedicated to providing information at the core of the organization and to identify information consumers.
- **Selection of Participants.**
  The purpose of this is to define and select the users who will be the participants. in the experiments to be carried out in the next stage of the methodology. Recommended have a diversity and a significant number of participants, considering at least 20 participants from the different consumer departments identified in the previous stage, in order to have a better representation of those involved.
- **Information Products, Systems or Services Selection**
  The objective of this sub-stage is to select the information products, systems or services that are used within the organization. It is recommended to cover a reasonable number of products, systems or services, to allow on performing an analysis at the organizational level in later stages.

Consumer Behavior Exploration

- **Consumer Profiles and Needs Identification**
  The objective of this sub-stage is to explore the preliminary behavior of the information consumer, identifying the needs and profiles of the consumers of the organization described in the previous sub-stage called planification.
- **Preliminary Customer Journey (CMJ)**
  According to the information collected in the previous sub-stages of the characterization, a preliminary version of the customer journey map must be made. where this strategic management instrument allows us to represent ICX in a company in a graphic way, where all the points of contact are identified along with their channels, expectations and associated emotions during the interaction with the client. [32]

4.2 Experimentation Stage

The objective of the second stage, called the experimentation stage, is to generate data through the different instruments that will be carried out in the different experiments. Initially, in the sub-stage called Preliminary Data Collection, a preliminary information survey must be carried out, with an interview and a personalized questionnaire according to the characterization made in the previous stage, ending with a focus group to get deeper insights about consumers needs. In the next sub-stage called Perception Data Collection, it is intended to carry out a mixed qualitative and quantitative instrument to generate data about consumers expectations and perceptions.

Preliminary Data Collection.

- **Customized Interview**
  In this sub-stage we apply a personalized interview that is built from the information collected in the previous stage of characterization, where based on certain characteristics of the organization, a personalized interview will be made to a sub-selection of the participants selected in the stage of characterization.
- **Customized Questionnaire**
  In this sub-stage we apply a personalized survey that is built from the information collected in the Customized Interview sub-stage, and is applied to 60 of the selection of participants made in the previous stage.
- **Focus Group**
  The evaluation and experience with products and services.remains a substantial area of focus group research. therefore, a focus group should be carried out to carry out the preliminary data collection stage since focus groups have been used as a complement to other methods, as part of an investigation [35].

Perception Data Collection.

- **Qualitative and Quantitative Mixed Instrument**
  From the two instruments applied in the previous sub-stages, an ICX adaptation of questionnaires used in the literature is going to be explored in order to collect the expectations and perceptions data of different information consumer measurement dimensions, which would be related to the factors founded in the Consumer Behavior Exploration activities from the Characterization stage. Also, this questionnaire will include open questions, in order to complement the quantitative data collection with qualitative data, obtained from consumers explanations of their expectations, perceptions and opinions about the information consumption experience. This qualitative data can be important to identify causes or explanations for the quantitative data collected.

4.3 Analysis Stage

The objective of the third stage, called the Analysis stage, is to carry out several analysis according to the behavior and perception of information consumers. Initially generating a definitive customer journey maps and carrying out a quantitative analysis from which ICX indicators by profiles will be derived and at the organizational level. And a qualitative analysis to identify the causes that could explain quantitative results. Finally, an integration of the results of these two analyzes will be performed in order to generate recommendations to improve the ICX of organizations.

Behavior Analysis.

- **Customer Journey Map (CMJ)**
  The previous results must be collected and analyzed, one of these analyzes is taken to the customer journey map, with the data collection it was possible to establish the points of contact and the experience in each of them. A map must be generated for each profile identified in the previous stages of the analysis, considering the preliminary version of the customer journey maps.

Experience Analysis In order to perform a complete analysis of the information consumption experience, a quantitative and qualitative mixed approach has been selected because our preliminary idea is to complement quantitative results, which indicates a diagnosis evaluation of the information consumption (i.e. bad experience or good experience in a score questionnaire score [24]), with the explanations of that diagnosis in terms of causes that origins good or bad information consumption experiences from qualitative instruments.

- **Quantitative Analisys**
  In this activity, a quantitative analysis of the data collected from the mixed instrument for data collection to be elaborated in the Perception data collection activity from the Experimentation stage. This analysis will be performed using a combination of statistical methods used in the literature [12,24,29] yet to explore.
- **Qualitative Analisys**
  In this activity, a qualitative analysis of the data collected from the mixed instrument for data collection. This qualitative analysis will be performed examinins the answers to the open questions included in instrument by using some of the method yet to explore from the literature [10,15].

ICX Analysis.

- **Consumer Profile ICX Score**
  Is spected to generate a personal score to evaluate the experience in information consumption from a group of consumers that belongs to a specific information consumer profile identified in the Consumer Behavior Exploration

activities from the Planification stage. The objective of this score is to give a customized diagnosis for a certain information consumer profile, and perform an analysis for their specific needs and experience satisfactions or pains.

- **Organizational Overall ICX Score**
  An organizational level ICX score will be formulated, in a preliminary approach, from the aggregation of the different Consumer Profile Scores. The main objective is to give a general diagnosis of the information consumption experience in all the organization or the specific unit studied, and perform an analysis for the general level needs and experience satisfactions or pains of the organization members.
- **Results Integration**
  Finally, for both Consumer Profile ICX Score and Organization Overall ICX Score a set of recommendations will be elaborated by using the quantitative analysis performed in the previous Experience Analysis stage. The main objective of every recommendation elaborated is related to address poorly-evaluated or enhancing well-evaluated elements of the information consumption experience, with the ultimate goal of improve the information consumption experience in the organization.

5 Conclusions

Most of the methods found in the literature have addressed the information consumption within an organization are limited in their focus to the analysis and evaluation of the interaction between a single information consumer and a particular information system [10,26], or information sharing [20,23,36]. These approaches fail to take into account the fact that information consumers interacts with multiple others consumers and specific organizational scenarios. Additionally, an organization does not operate with one information system only, but typically offers a suite of information products, systems, or services to its employees. Hence, the phenomenon of information consumption within the organization must be analyzed with a more comprehensive approach that considers its complexity when evaluating the Information Consumer Experience (ICX).

In this regard, in this work we have proposed a preliminary methodology for ICX evaluation, describing all the stateges and major tasks that need to be accomplished in order to analyze and evaluate ICX into an organization. Also we proposed a preliminar set of instruments and methods that are available in the literature that could be adapted in order to assess ICX. All those instruments are expected to enhance the CX analysis approach, which has been the inspiration for the ICX concept.

For future works we have planned to refine and validate this preliminary methodology proposal, including further details about the data collection, data analysis, and evaluation instruments to explore, in order to define the structure of the first ICX evaluation methodology.

References

1. Ahmad, K.Z.B., Jasimuddin, S.M., Kee, W.L.: Organizational climate and job satisfaction: do employees' personalities matter? Manag. Decision **56**(2), 421–440 (2018). https://doi.org/10.1108/md-10-2016-0713
2. Aljuwaiber, A.: Technology-based vs. face-to-face interaction for knowledge sharing in the project teams. Int. J. Project Organisat. Manag. **11**(3), 227 (2019). https://doi.org/10.1504/ijpom.2019.102943
3. Azemi, N.A., Zaidi, H., Hussin, N., et al.: Information quality in organization for better decision-making. Int. J. Acad. Res. Bus. Social Sci. **7**(12), 429–437 (2018)
4. DeLone, W.H.: Mclean. 1992. Information systems success: The quest for the dependent variable. Inf. Syst. Res. **3**(1), 60–95 (2003)
5. Dhamija, P., Gupta, S., Bag, S.: Measuring of job satisfaction: the use of quality of work life factors. Benchmarking: An Internat. J. **26**(3), 871–892 (2019). https://doi.org/10.1108/bij-06-2018-0155
6. Dorsey, J., et al.: Using the WEIS-SR to evaluate employee perceptions of their college work environment. Work **54**(1), 103–111 (2016). https://doi.org/10.3233/wor-162281
7. Fabbri, T., Mandreoli, F., Martoglia, R., Scapolan, A.C.: Employee attitudes and (digital) collaboration data: A preliminary analysis in the HRM field. In: 2019 28th International Conference on Computer Communication and Networks (ICCCN). IEEE (July 2019). https://doi.org/10.1109/icccn.2019.8846957
8. Gentile, C., Spiller, N., Noci, G.: How to sustain the customer experience: An overview of experience components that co-create value with the customer. Eur. Manag. J. **25**(5), 395–410 (2007)
9. Godoy, M.P., Rusu, C., Ugalde, J.: Information consumer experience: A systematic review. Appli. Sci. **12**(24) (2022). https://doi.org/10.3390/app122412630, https://www.mdpi.com/2076-3417/12/24/12630
10. Gunadham, T., Thammakoranonta, N.: Knowledge management systems functionalities enhancement in practice. In: Proceedings of the 5th International Conference on Frontiers of Educational Technologies - ICFET 2019. ACM Press (2019). https://doi.org/10.1145/3338188.3338213
11. Hepworth, J.B., Griffin, E., Vidgen, G.A., Woodward, T.: Adopting an information management approach to the design and implementation of information systems. Health Serv. Manage. Res. **5**(2), 115–122 (1992)
12. Hossain, M.E., Mahmud, I., Idrus, R.M.: Modelling end users' continuance intention to use information systems in academic settings: Expectation-confirmation and stress perspective. Interdisc. J. Information, Knowl. Manag. **16**, 371–395 (2021). https://doi.org/10.28945/4841
13. Igbaria, M., Tan, M.: The consequences of information technology acceptance on subsequent individual performance. Inf. Manag. **32**(3), 113–121 (1997)
14. Kabicher-Fuchs, S., Mangler, J., Rinderle-Ma, S.: Experience breeding in process-aware information systems. In: Salinesi, C., Norrie, M.C., Pastor, Ó. (eds.) CAiSE 2013. LNCS, vol. 7908, pp. 594–609. Springer, Heidelberg (2013). https://doi.org/10.1007/978-3-642-38709-8_38
15. Klesel, M., Mokosch, G., Niehaves, B.: Putting flesh on the duality of structure: The case of it consumerization (Jan 2015)
16. Lemon, K.N., Verhoef, P.C.: Understanding customer experience throughout the customer journey. J. Mark. **80**(6), 69–96 (2016)

17. Lim, C., Kim, K.H., Kim, M.J., Heo, J.Y., Kim, K.J., Maglio, P.P.: From data to value: A nine-factor framework for data-based value creation in information-intensive services. Int. J. Inf. Manage. **39**, 121–135 (2018)
18. Malik, N., Tripathi, S.N., Kar, A.K., Gupta, S.: Impact of artificial intelligence on employees working in industry 4.0 led organizations. Int. J. Manpower **43**(2), 334–354 (2021). https://doi.org/10.1108/ijm-03-2021-0173
19. Marquez, J.J., Downey, A., Clement, R.: Walking a mile in the user's shoes: Customer journey mapping as a method to understanding the user experience. Internet Ref. Serv. Q. **20**(3–4), 135–150 (2015)
20. Meske, C., Kissmer, T., Stieglitz, S.: Bridging formal barriers in digital work environments – investigating technology-enabled interactions across organizational hierarchies. Telemat. Inform. **48**, 101342 (2020). https://doi.org/10.1016/j.tele.2020.101342
21. Molino, M., Cortese, C.G., Ghislieri, C.: Technology acceptance and leadership 4.0: A quali-quantitative study. Int. J. Environ. Res. Public Health **18**(20), 10845 (2021). https://doi.org/10.3390/ijerph182010845
22. Morales, J., Rusu, C., Botella, F., Quiñones, D.: Programmer experience: A systematic literature review. IEEE Access **7**, 71079–71094 (2019)
23. Ostermann, U., , Holten, R., Franzmann, D., and: The influence of private alternatives on employees' acceptance of organizational IS. Commun. Associat. Inform. Syst. **47**(1), 764–786 (2020). https://doi.org/10.17705/1cais.04735
24. Parasuraman, A., Zeithaml, V.A., Berry, L.: Servqual: A multiple-item scale for measuring consumer perceptions of service quality, vol. 64(1), pp. 12–40 (1988)
25. Peters, R.: Exploring the design space for personal information management tools. In: CHI 2001 Extended Abstracts on Human Factors in Computing Systems, pp. 413–414 (2001)
26. Pigg, S., Lauren, B., Keller, E.J.: Designing for learning experiences. In: Proceedings of the 35th ACM International Conference on the Design of Communication. ACM (Aug 2017). https://doi.org/10.1145/3121113.3121127
27. Rieh, S.Y.: Judgment of information quality and cognitive authority in the web. J. Am. Soc. Inform. Sci. Technol. **53**(2), 145–161 (2002)
28. Sanda, M.-A.: Employees perception of the implementation of information technology systems in the ghanaian public sector. In: Nunes, I.L. (ed.) AHFE 2020. AISC, vol. 1207, pp. 148–155. Springer, Cham (2020). https://doi.org/10.1007/978-3-030-51369-6_20
29. Shamsi, M., Iakovleva, T., Olsen, E., Bagozzi, R.P.: Employees' work-related well-being during COVID-19 pandemic: An integrated perspective of technology acceptance model and JD-r theory. Int. J. Environm. Res. Public Health **18**(22), 11888 (2021). https://doi.org/10.3390/ijerph182211888
30. Stein, A., Ramaseshan, B.: Towards the identification of customer experience touch point elements. J. Retail. Consum. Serv. **30**, 8–19 (2016)
31. Stone, R.W., Good, D.J., Baker-Eveleth, L.: The impact of information technology on individual and firm marketing performance. Behav. Inform. Technol. **26**(6), 465–482 (2007)
32. Temkin, B.D.: Mapping Customer J. Forrester Res. **3**, 20 (2010)
33. Vasilieva, E., Tochilkina, T.: Design thinking and process transformation: Synergy of these approaches. In: CEUR Workshop Proceedings (2020)

34. Watungwa, T., Pather, S.: Identification of user satisfaction dimensions for the evaluation of university administration information systems. In: ICICKM 2018 15th International Conference on Intellectual Capital Knowledge Management & Organisational Learning, p. 346. Academic Conferences and publishing limited (2018)
35. Wilkinson, S.: Focus group methodology: a review. Int. J. Soc. Res. Methodol. **1**(3), 181–203 (1998)
36. Wu, M.S.: Information literacy, creativity and work performance. Inform. Develop. **35**(5), 676–687 (2018). https://doi.org/10.1177/0266666918781436
37. Zeiner, K.M., Laib, M., Schippert, K., Burmester, M.: Identifying experience categories to design for positive experiences with technology at work. In: Proceedings of the 2016 CHI Conference Extended Abstracts on Human Factors in Computing Systems. ACM (May 2016). https://doi.org/10.1145/2851581.2892548

Shopee Affiliates: How is the Pattern of Using Hashtags on Twitter in Promoting Sales Products

Devira Ailen Indrasari(✉) and Firly Annisa

Department of Communication, Faculty of Social and Politics, Yogyakarta, Indonesia
devira.ailen.isip19@mail.umy.ac.id, firly@umy.ac.id

Abstract. The internet has changed the transaction of buying and selling. Product promotion uses the internet because many people use space to share information. Social media is one of the means to convey information from companies to consumers. Each social media has a different form of content and characteristic. This study aims to analyze the pattern of using hashtags on Twitter by Shopee Affiliates for product promotion. This research uses a qualitative analysis approach to hashtags used by Shopee Affiliates, with Wordstat as an analysis tool. This research answers that the pattern of product promotion carried out by Shopee Affiliates on Twitter is categorized as a collection of recommendation tweets. Tweets from Shopee Affiliates predominantly promote women's products, thus using language specifically for women. There is a practice of Neoliberalism in promotions by Shopee Affiliates because digital marketing deliberately depicts successful and empowered individuals when they engage in consumption activities.

Keywords: Shopee affiliates · social media · promoting sales products · hashtags

1 Introduction

Through online marketing, which enlists internet users to market and sell goods and services, the business sector uses the internet for purchasing and selling transactions [1]. Because demographic data may be calculated based on objectives and can be used to contact customers directly, online marketing benefits businesses in terms of time efficiency when generating promotions and reaching a larger and more significant target market [2]. Partnerships that can encourage customers to make purchases are essential to the effectiveness of internet marketing. Affiliation is a type of relationship that involves working with bloggers and other online content producers to drive traffic to a company's website [3].

Technological advancements impact how people buy and sell things in society. E-commerce refers to transactions made over electronic networks that include buying, selling, exchanging, and distributing products and services [4]. Furthermore, according to Sudiwijaya & Ambardi [4], e-commerce facilitates community interaction because anybody may engage as a seller or a customer. Since its launch in 2015, Shopee has established itself as Indonesians' go-to online retailer [5]. Shopee will be the most popular

A. Coman and S. Vasilache (Eds.): HCII 2023, LNCS 14025, pp. 520–529, 2023.
https://doi.org/10.1007/978-3-031-35915-6_37

e-commerce service via social media between July and September 2022, according to statistics from Similar Web [6]. At first, not many individuals were eager to purchase anything on Shopee. However, the relentless marketing campaign involving advertisements and alluring television commercials has caused people to consider Shopee's existence [7]. Shopee uses technology by running online marketing to reach more customers [8]. One of Shopee's partnering initiatives, Shopee Affiliates, gives consumers a chance to boost their revenue by recommending products on social media. Marketers advertise by publishing text and inserting URL links that they have copied from product pages. The marketer will get paid a commission if customers buy something after clicking this link.

Twitter is the only social media outlet that Shopee Affiliates use as a means of promotion due to its simple method of using the site's text, audio, and video features. Utilizing a hashtag relevant to the post's purpose can make it easier for shoppers to find posts and increase brand exposure [9]. Shopee Affiliates use the hashtag #shopeeaffiliate in their tweets, and recommendations for various products will appear if it is selected. According to the data collected using the hashtag #shopeeaffiliate, most of the promoted products are goods for women. Thus, any promotions carried out are done to improve women's feelings about dating. According to research from Dataindonesia.id, Shopee will account for around 53% of all personal consumer e-commerce purchases in 2021. The employees are constantly being directed to engage in business transactions because excessive consumption is regarded as a sign of a failing economy [10]. In other words, women's shopping habits are treated like a commodity [11]. Additionally, promotions run by Shopee Affiliates influence the micro-celebrity industry, which employs personal image as a form of emotional labour [12].

Some previous research related to social media and Shopee Affiliates, namely research Nurazizah et al. [13], explains that the use of Tik Tok social media for marketing fashion products by Shopee Affiliates has a positive effect on hedonistic shopping motivation and impulsive purchases. Research from Sutarman et al. [14] explains that Instagram Shopee Affiliates' content analyzed using the AIDA communication model (Attention, Interest, Desire, Action) influences consumer buying interest. Other research from Oryza & Nilowardono [15] confirms that digital marketing, reviews, and ratings also influence consumer buying interest through Shopee. Meanwhile, Fauziah and Nurochani [5] explains that product information obtained from Shopee Affiliates affects student consumption.

It is clear from this justification that past research on social media and Shopee Affiliates continues to emphasize the impact of promotions on consumer purchasing interest. However, the trends that show up in social media advertising postings from Shopee Affiliates have not been the subject of any study. As a result, the uniqueness of this study focuses on the trends that come from Shopee Affiliates' use of hashtags to promote their products on Twitter. Therefore, this study aims to describe how Shopee Affiliates use hashtags on Twitter for promotional purposes.

2 Overview of Literature

2.1 Digital Marketing

The practice of advertising products online is known as digital marketing [16]. People who have easy access to the internet are more likely to be in a position to use their influence to market things online [17]. Social media marketing is one method of online product promotion. The numerous social media platforms, like Instagram, Facebook, and Twitter, can be utilized to update customers about a company's offerings. Nevertheless, each social media platform undoubtedly has content that sets it apart from the others. Due to this, digital marketing is done while taking into account social media characteristics to ensure promotions run as smoothly as possible [18]. Consumers' propensity to purchase through digital channels is influenced by efficient time management, competitive pricing, high-quality products, and interactive features [19].

According to the promotion's objective from Puspita & Nuraeni [20], there are three goals. First, the promotion aims to inform how to use the product, how they work, the services offered, and the prices of goods/services. Second, promotions aim to remind them what products are sold and selling locations so that they become top-of-mind consumers. Third, promotions aim to influence consumers' decisions not to buy other brands and make purchases on the spot. Engagement is crucial to the success of digital marketing on social media [21].

2.2 Promosi di Twitter

Social media enables businesses to interact with customers, build brand awareness, shape consumer attitudes, gather feedback, enhance current products and services, and boost sales [22, 23]. Twitter is a powerful social media platform for promotional efforts since it enables people to send website links, provide information, and even respond to questions [24–26]. Promotional messages that are appealing and use clear, concise, and organized wording can capture the reader's attention, increasing the likelihood that they will make a purchase [27]. Users on Twitter have the option of following or being followed. Users with large followings typically have more valuable information [25, 28] stressed that a social media campaign is successful if the message or content generated attracts plenty of followers, resulting in increased exposure to the content.

Some tools on Twitter can be utilized to maximize promotional efforts [29]. First off, tweets can include text, images, videos, and links. Retweet, or tweeting back, is the second action. Third, mention or bring up an instance. Fourth, to be searchable, hashtags take the form of the "#" symbol followed by a string of words that refer to a specific subject [30]. Due to Twitter's informal nature, businesses can be regarded as actual individuals rather than impersonal brands, products, or organizations [31]. User profiles on Twitter are linked together by a network. Individuals can view the tweets of other users they follow and reply to them if they like [32]. This style enables users to communicate instantaneously, which increases the likelihood that brands will be remembered by users longer and be seen as more open and approachable [33, 34].

3 Methods

This study employs a computer-assisted tool called Wordstat and a qualitative methodology. Textual data is analyzed using Wordstat. The frequency of words or phrases in text is known as textual data. Wordstat translates data from Twitter and is used to identify word or phrase patterns on social media [35]. Because Shopee sponsored a promotional event called "Shopee 10.10 Brand Festival" during this time, data from September to October 2022 is used in this study to explain the trend of tweets from Shopee Affiliates on Twitter.

The keyword selection step, specifically "shopee affiliate," generates textual data in the form of words and phrases based on the analysis, making it possible to gather information on the frequency of these words and similar words [36]. Then, phrases and terms connected to Shopee Affiliates show together with topic-based categorization as a result of the correlation between the data in the form of tweet text and user ID and tweets. The third stage involved text exploration and analysis to identify a promotion classification based on the hashtag usage pattern.

4 Result and Discussion

4.1 Analysis of Shopee Affiliates Product Promotion

See Table 1; promotional tweets by Shopee Affiliates contain information about the products being sold. The promoted Tweet mentions the product name, rating, and price. Apart from using the hashtag #shopeeaffiliate, other hashtags include in promotional posts that mention the e-commerce name where the product comes from, such as #racunshopee, #shopeehaul, #shopeeID, and #rekomendasishopee. Shopee Affiliates accounts have more than 100 followers and friends, and tweets reach tens of thousands.

Shopee Affiliates utilize Twitter's services for their product advertising [29]. The tweet feature aids Shopee Affiliates in educating customers about product facts and images so that they may understand the benefits and drawbacks of the product in full. Additionally, Shopee Affiliates' affiliate marketing method, which entails giving a product URL link, makes it simpler for customers to buy right from the product page. As other accounts repost promotional tweets, the retweet feature enables Shopee Affiliates to reach a wider audience than just their followers. The hashtag tool, meanwhile, makes it simpler for customers to locate additional promotional tweets.

Twitter can be used as a promotional tool to introduce products by using user influence over followers [17]. As a result, Tunca et al. [24] believes that Twitter promotion is successful. Not every Shopee Affiliates account has a sizable following. However, owners of accounts with a small following can still work as Shopee Affiliates. The feature offered by Shopee to users demonstrates that anyone may start a business in the digital arena as a vendor or a buyer [4]. Promotions run by Shopee Affiliates can persuade other users to follow them by comparing their followers, friends, and tweets. Nigel & Lilleker [25] analyze the desire to follow an account due to its informative content.

Table 1. Example Tweet

Tweet	Followers	Friends	Tweets
RT @skyieev: Recommended tartan model tops #shopeeaffiliate #racunshopee #shopeehaul #rekomendasishopee #racunbelanja	689	844	5474
Oval fashion sunglasses (8 warna). Rating 5, price 19k #racunbelanja #racunshopeemurah #rekomendasishopee #ShopeeID #shopeeaffiliate #pinterest #shopeefinds #kacamatahitam #fashionstyle #ootd #Aesthetic #AmericanGirl	805	218	15763
Check housedress maura, housedress latest models, women's clothing, women's dresses, jumbo housedress, cheapest housedress, cheap housedress, retail housedress Get it on Shopee now! #shopeepay #shopeepayTHR #shopeeaffiliate	207	5000	35735
Elegant women's bag recommendations, but very suitable for daily use #shopeeaffiliate #racunshopee #shopeehaul #rekomendasishopee #racunbelanja	194	243	1192

4.2 Hashtag Shopee Affiliates Content

As shown in Table 2, several subjects are covered in the search results for tweets about Shopee-related products. The topics of women's apparel recommendations, self-development book recommendations, product link collections, and Korean fashion recommendations are all covered in tweets with the hashtag #shopeeaffiliate. Because it has the lowest eigenvalue across all themes, 3.71, the topic of Korean fashion tips is typical or typical of Shopee Affiliates promotional postings. The tweets that Shopee Affiliate promotes the most discuss recommendations for women's clothing.

Women's fashion items are promoted in most Shopee Affiliates' tweets. The Shopee Affiliates marketing strives to satisfy the demands of women as a result. Women are a prospective target market for online business, so women's fashion is a product that receives much promotion [10]. As can be observed, nearly every topic category contains the word "recommendations," making the promotional tweets from Shopee Affiliates appear to be a compilation of recommendation tweets. According to Abrahan et al. [30], hashtags can be used to categorize tweets.

Several terms are utilized in the Shopee Affiliates promotional tweet (see image 1). The phrase "recommend" is most frequently used in promotional lines, followed by phrases that describe the product's benefits, give instructions on how to click on the provided link, explain how to utilize the goods, and request that readers place an order right away. Users of linked social media are the target audience for promotion on these platforms. As 280 characters are the maximum posting length on Twitter, tweets must be concise and straightforward for users to understand. The terms "recommendations," "product advantages," and "product benefits" are employed to describe details about products that customers should be aware of. The phrases "click the link below" and "buy

Table 2. Topic Category

Topic	Keywords	Coherence	Eigenvalue	Frequency
Women's Clothing Recommendations	Pants, viashop, women, recommendations, https	0,967	10,96	2276
Self-Development Book Recommendations	Books, bookstore, improvement, book recommendations, selfimprovement, spilloutfitshop, recommendation, thread, shopeeaffiliate	0,808	9,16	1706
Product Link Collection	Transitlove, backpack, village women, shootingstarjkt, shopeehaul, recommendation, thread, shopeeaffiliate	0,540	5,41	1147
Product Link Collection	Cfykqcunzs, dcpun, nbehnvwb, voitgg, white	0,564	7,50	938
Korean Fashion Recommendations	Blackpink, shopee, cardigan, jennie, shopeeaffiliate, recommendations	0,169	3,71	581

now" are used in advertisements to influence consumers' decision-making and persuade them to make purchases immediately. According to [14, 27], promotional content needs to grab consumers' attention and persuade them to purchase (Fig. 1).

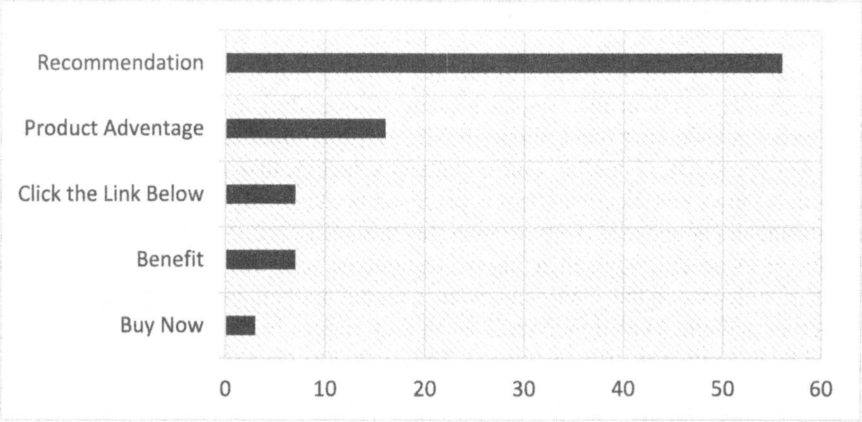

Fig. 1. Frequency of Phrase

See Fig. 2. According to the tweets from Shopee Affiliates that contain the hashtag #shopeeaffiliate, some fascinating terms frequently appear, like suggestions, women, improvement, book recommendations, self-development, Blackpink, and rural women. Shopee Affiliates leverages influence to persuade audiences when making product recommendations. A person might increase his sense of self-worth through this buying activity, just as the term "self-improvement" came into existence. Success will come more easily to those with more aptitudes and accomplishments. This circumstance exemplifies the neoliberal idea that the powerful can dominate the market [12]. Because women have such high economic value, they are treated as commodities together with their buying interests. The rise of the prominent music group Black Pink, which is well-known worldwide, depicts successful women. As a result, shopping actions continuously inspire women who want to succeed and be appreciated.

Fig. 2. Frequency of Words

5 Conclusion

This result reveals that the pattern of product promotion practised by Shopee Affiliate through Twitter social media using the hashtag #shopeeaffiliate is classified as a collection of recommendation tweets. Shopee Affiliates' promotions emphasize the promotion of women's products; hence they employ language specific to women. Shopee Affiliate's promotion shows that Neoliberalism is practised because only those with the aptitude and credentials can succeed. Thus, women are constantly encouraged to boost their sense of value to succeed through engaging in consumerist activities. Consumption takes on greater significance in this environment since digital marketing purposefully portrays a prosperous and empowered individual when they engage in the consumption activities offered by e-commerce, such as Shopee. This study also demonstrates that Wordstat, a data analysis tool, can describe data in graphs and tables by mapping data sets from the hashtag #shopeeaffiliate.

References

1. Bala, M., Verma, D.: A critical review of digital marketing paper type: - review and viewpoint. Int. J. Manag. IT Eng. **8**(10), 321–339 (2018)
2. Chaffey, D., Ellis-Chadwick, F.: Digital Marketing. Pearson (2019)
3. Sandeep Prabhu, T.S.: Affiliate Marketing's Furute in India. Indian J. Sci. Technol. **8**(2), 83–89 (2015). https://doi.org/10.17485/ijst/2015/v8i
4. Sudiwijaya, E., Ambardi, K.: E-Commerce strategy in driving sharing economy in culinary industry. Komunikator **13**(1) (2021). https://journal.umy.ac.id/index.php/jkm/article/download/9226/6306
5. Fauziah, G.U., Nurochani, N.: The influence of shopee'S E-commerce features on islamic consumption behavior: a case study of Stei Student Ar-Risalah Ciamis. Syari'ah Econ. **6**(1), 53 (2022). https://doi.org/10.36667/se.v6i1.1171
6. Similarweb (2022). https://www.similarweb.com/website/shopee.co.id/#outgoing-links (Accessed 20 Oct. 2022)
7. Pratama Afrianto, A., Irwansyah, I.: Eksplorasi Kondisi Masyarakat Dalam Memilih Belanja Online Melalui Shopee Selama Masa Pandemi Covid-19 Di Indonesia. J. Teknol. Dan Sist. Inf. Bisnis 3(1), 10–29 (2021). https://doi.org/10.47233/jteksis.v3i1.181
8. Mardiana, A.P., Haryanto, B.: Purchasing decisions in the new normal period: implementation of digital marketing, brand awareness, and viral marketing at shopee e-commerce on the use of spaylater. J. Econ. Bus. **5**(3) (2022). https://doi.org/10.31014/aior.1992.05.03.447
9. Yocevina, S., Rumapea, P., Pasandaran, C., Juliadi, R.: Jurnal komunikasi profesional social network analysis about brand awareness of shopee indonesia on twitter. J. Komun. Prof. **6**(5), 516–534 (2022)
10. Raman, P.: Understanding female consumers' intention to shop online: The role of trust, convenience and customer service. Asia Pacific J. Mark. Logist. **31**(4), 1138–1160 (2019). https://doi.org/10.1108/APJML-10-2018-0396
11. Khairiyah, A., et al.: Homo Digitalis: Manusia dan Teknologi di Era Digital, May. Yogyakarta: Penerbit Elmatera (2018)
12. Annisa, F.: Performance of Micro Celebrities : from digital meritocracy to neoliberalism. J. Contemp. Islam. Commun. Media **2**(2) (2022)
13. Nurazizah, R., Eka Saputri, M., Rubiyanti, N., Rustandi Kartawinata, B., Indra Wijaksana, T.: The effect of tiktok social media marketing on impulsive purchases of fashion products in the shopee affiliate campaign with hedonic shopping motivation as the intervening variable. In: Proceedings of the International Conference on Industrial Engineering and Operations Management, pp. 1324–1335 (2022). https://ijafibs.pelnus.ac.id/index.php/ijafibs/article/view/62
14. Sutarman, A., Oxcygentri, O., Kusumaningrum, R.: Pengaruh Unggahan Dari Content Creator Program Afiliasi E-Commerce Shopee Terhadap Minat Beli (Analisis Regresi Linear Berganda pada Konsumen Shopee Indonesia di media sosial Instagram) Mahasiswa Ilmu Komunikasi Universitas Singaperbangsa Karawang Dosen. J. Ilm. Wahana Pendidik. **8**(23), 70–80 (2022)
15. Oryza, G.A., Nilowardono, S.: The effect of digital marketing, online customer reviews and ratings on consumer buying interest through shopee. J. Ekon. **22**, 13–22 (2022). https://ejournal.worldconference.id/index.php/eko
16. Minculete, G., Olar, P.: "pproaches to the modern concept of digital marketing. Sciendo **XXIV**(2), 63–69 (2018). https://doi.org/10.1515/kbo-2018-0067
17. Mangiò, F., Di Domenico, G.: All that glitters is not real affiliation: How to handle affiliate marketing programs in the era of falsity. Bus. Horiz. **65**(6), 765–776 (2022). https://doi.org/10.1016/j.bushor.2022.07.001

18. Tresnawati, Y., Prasetyo, K.: Pemetaan Konten Promosi Digital Bisnis Kuliner kika's Catering di Media Sosial. PRofesi humas. J. Ilm. ilmu Hub. Masy. **3**(1), 102 (2018). https://doi.org/10.24198/prh.v3i1.15333
19. Erlangga, H., et al.: Effect of digital marketing and social media on purchase intention of smes food products. Turkish J. Comput. Math. Educ. **12**(3), 3672–3678 (2021). https://doi.org/10.17762/turcomat.v12i3.1648
20. Puspitarini, D.S., Nuraeni, R.: Pemanfaatan Media Sosial Sebagai Media Promosi (Studi Deskriptif pada Happy Go Lucky House). J. Common **3**(1), 71–80 (2019). https://doi.org/10.34010/COMMON.V3I1.1950
21. Edlom, J.: The engagement imperative: experiences of communication practitioners' brand work in the music industry. Media Commun. **10**(1), 66–76 (2022). https://doi.org/10.17645/mac.v10i1.4448
22. Dwivedi, Y.K., et al.: Setting the future of digital and social media marketing research: Perspectives and research propositions. Int. J. Inf. Manage. **59**, 102168 (2021). https://doi.org/10.1016/j.ijinfomgt.2020.102168
23. Lee, D., Hosanagar, K., Nair, H.S.: Advertising content and consumer engagement on social media: evidence from facebook. management science published online in articles in advance. Manage. Sci., 1–27 (2018)
24. Tunca, S., Sezen, B., Balcioğlu, Y.S.: Twitter Analysis for Metaverse Literacy. Researchgate.Net (January 2022). https://www.researchgate.net/profile/Sezai-Tunca-2/publication/358045545_TWITTER_ANALYSIS_FOR_METAVERSE_LITERACY/links/61ee6aed8d338833e38f33f5/TWITTER-ANALYSIS-FOR-METAVERSE-LITERACY.pdf
25. Nigel, J., Lilleker, D.: Microblogging, constituency service and impression management: uk mps and the use of twitter. J. Legis. Stud., 414–433 (2020). https://doi.org/10.1080/13572334.2011.545181
26. Hanifa Madina, I., Sukmono, F.G., Junaedi, F.: Micro-influencer marketing beauty brand on social media. Commun. Comput. Inf. Sci., vol. 1655. CCIS, pp. 40–47 (2022). https://doi.org/10.1007/978-3-031-19682-9_6
27. Susanti, S., Erwina, W.: Pesan Promosi Program Televisi dalam Akun Twitter @netmediatama. Komuniti J. Komun. dan Teknol. Inf. **12**(1), 1 (2020). https://doi.org/10.23917/komuniti.v12i1.9634
28. Muliasari, N., Sahrir, V.A., Hartaman, N.: disaster communication campaign via instagram and twitter palang merah Indonesia. J. Audiens **3**(3), 141–148 (2022). https://doi.org/10.18196/jas.v3i3.14010
29. Talalu, T.R., Valentine, F.: Interaksi Pendengar dan Promosi Program Siaran Radio 'Polemik Trijaya' di Twitter. J. Dakwah dan Komun. **6**(2), 237 (2021). https://doi.org/10.29240/jdk.v6i2.3757
30. Abraham, J., et al.: SMU data science review cryptocurrency price prediction using tweet volumes and sentiment analysis cryptocurrency price prediction using tweet volumes and sentiment analysis. SMU Data Sci. Rev. **1**(3) (2018)
31. Charlesworth, A.: An introduction to social media marketing, vol. 52(11). Routledge, New York (2015)
32. Sari, R.P., Putra, F.K.K., Maemunah, I.: The Use of Twitter in Social Media Marketing: Evidence from Hotels in Asia. In: APMBA, Asia Pacific, vol. 1, pp. 59–74 (2022). https://doi.org/10.21776/ub.apmba.2022.011.01.4
33. Swani, K., Brown, B.P., Milne, G.R.: Should tweets differ for B2B and B2C? an analysis of fortune 500 companies' twitter communications. Ind. Mark. Manag. **43**(5), 873–881 (2014). https://doi.org/10.1016/j.indmarman.2014.04.012
34. Allgeyer, T.: The Importance of Twitter to Destination Marketing Organizations. Theses Diss. (2019)

35. Silver, C., Lewins, A.: QDA Miner 3 . 2 (with WordStat & Simstat) Distinguishing features and functions. Database **2** (2007)
36. Brown, R.L.: Media review: wordstat version 5.1. J. Mix. Methods Res. **1**(2), 201–203 (2007). https://doi.org/10.1177/1558689806297372

Identification of Evaluation Items in Consumer Reviews Using Natural Language Processing Models with Social Media Information

Emi Iwanade[1](✉), Takashi Namatame[2], and Kohei Otake[3]

[1] Graduate School of Information and Telecommunication Engineering, Tokai University, 2-3-23, Takanawa, Minato-Ku 108-8619, Japan
9bjm2106@mail.u-tokai.ac.jp

[2] Faculty of Science and Engineering, Chuo University, 1-13-27, Kasuga, Bunkyo-Ku 112-8551, Japan
nama@kc.chuo-u.ac.jp

[3] School of Information and Telecommunication Engineering, Tokai University, 2-3-23, Takanawa, Minato-Ku 108-8619, Japan
otake@tsc.u-tokai.ac.jp

Abstract. In recent years, customer reviews have been attracting attention as data representing real consumer feedback. On the other hand, it is said that it is difficult to identify the detailed contents from the text. In this study, we aim to understand the detailed contents of customer reviews from the data of customer reviews of accommodation facilities. Specifically, we collected tweets using keywords related to accommodation reviews as search queries, and used them to create a sentence classification model by fine-tuning a previously developed Japanese version of BERT model. Sentence classification was conducted by applying this model to the customer review data, which was separated into sentences. In addition, sentiment analysis was conducted to identify whether the sentences were positive or negative.

Keywords: Review Data · Natural Language Processing · Bidirectional Encoder Representations from Transformers

1 Introduction

In recent years, there are many travel sites that use OTA (Online Travel Agents) with the spread of internet. OTA is travel agencie that handle travel products only on the Internet, and some of the most popular ones worldwide are Booking.com [1] and expedia [2]. In Japan, Rakuten Travel [3] and Jalan.net [4] are representative examples of OTA. According to a survey by JTB Research Institute [5], booking and purchasing travel products via smartphones is on the rise and exceed the majority by 2019 (Fig. 1). This means that OTA use is on the rise.

With the increase in the use of OTA, customers also review through the Internet. These reviews via the Internet are attracting attention in marketing activities as data representing the reality of consumers, which was previously unknown. Yamashita et al. [6] analyzed

A. Coman and S. Vasilache (Eds.): HCII 2023, LNCS 14025, pp. 530–541, 2023.
https://doi.org/10.1007/978-3-031-35915-6_38

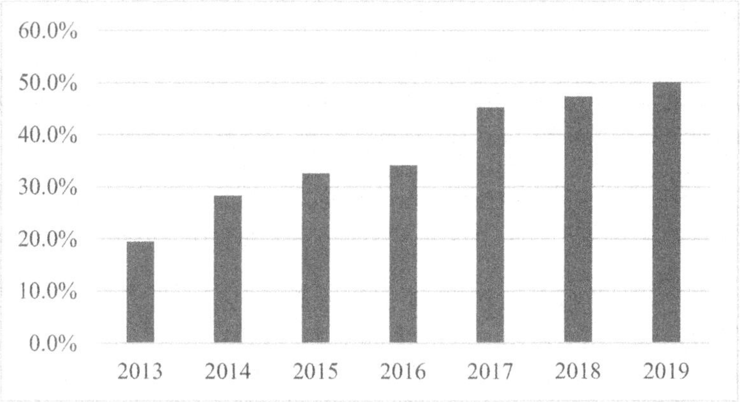

Fig. 1. Used a smartphone to booking or purchasing travel products (most recent trip)

product review data and proposed a method for understanding the overall trend of review data and extracting unique reviews. They conducted pre-training using review data that had already been labeled, created a binary classifier for multiple categories of unlabeled review data, and created a model to assign new labels to the unlabeled review data.

Other studies on review data that attempt to identify review content have been actively conducted. NAILA et al. [7] proposed a deep learning-based approach for classifying the content of app reviews in application stores. Ichikawa et al. [8] proposed a review classification method that reduces the cost of preparing training data by using them categorized forum topics. However, some reviews do not have categorized forums. Therefore, it is difficult to apply this method to all reviews. In addition, for those with a large amount of text, it is difficult to correctly estimate the content because many elements are included in the document. In order to understand more detailed behavior, we believe that it may be possible to analyze individual review texts by dividing them into sentences.

2 Purpose

In this study, we analyze textual customer review data with the aim of understanding in detail what the data say and what kind of evaluation the customers give to the content. We think that by understanding the content of customer review data, it is possible to identify the highest and lowest rated categories for each lodging facility. Specifically, we attempt to understand the content of each sentence by using BERT(Bidirectional Encoder Representations from Transformers) [9] that has recently attracted attention in natural language processing analysis. We identify the content of these sentences by classifying them into sentences, and evaluate the content by analyzing the sentiment of the sentences.

3 Datasets

In this study, we used the "Rakuten Dataset" (https://rit.rakuten.com/data_release/) [10] provided by Rakuten Group, Inc. Through the IDR dataset provision service of the National Institute of Informatics. This is the review data of the guests who stayed at the facilities of Rakuten Travel. We used a total of 25,111 items extracted for the period from July 31, 2016 to July 31, 2018, hereafter referred to as customer review data. Table 1. shows the data items and their contents related to the customer review data.

Table 1. Summary of Customer Review Data

Data Content	Data Item Description
Contributor ID	A numeric string of reviewer
Posting Date	Date and time the review was submitted
Facility ID	A numeric string of lodging facilities
Plan ID	A numeric string of lodging facilities plan
Plan Title	A character string of lodging facilities plan
Room Type	A character string of lodging facilities room
Room Name	A character string with the name of the lodging facilities room
Purpose	A character string describing the purpose of using the lodging facilities
Companions	A character string describing the people with whom you used the lodging facilities
Evaluation 1 (location)	Reviewer's rating of the location (5-point scale)
Evaluation 2 (room)	Reviewer's rating of the location (5-point scale)
Evaluation 3 (meal)	Reviewer's rating of the location (5-point scale)
Evaluation 4 (bath)	Reviewer's rating of the location (5-point scale)
Evaluation 5 (service)	Reviewer's rating of the location (5-point scale)
Evaluation 6 (facility)	Reviewer's rating of the location (5-point scale)
Evaluation 7 (total)	Comprehensive evaluation (5-point scale)
Posted Text for Customer	A character string of reviewer's comments
Replied Text for Facilities Employees	A character string of replied text for facilities employees to reviewer's comments

4 Estimation of Customer Review Data Content

In this study, we conducted analyses using the text data in the customer review data. Specifically, we first created a sentence classification model by performing fine tuning on the Japanese version of the BERT model. We applied the classification model to the text data of the customer review data, which was separated into sentences. We also performed sentiment analysis using the BERT model for calculating sentiment values. Finally, we combined our estimates of the category and sentiment values for each sentence with the ratings given by the user. Figure 2 shows the analysis flow in this study.

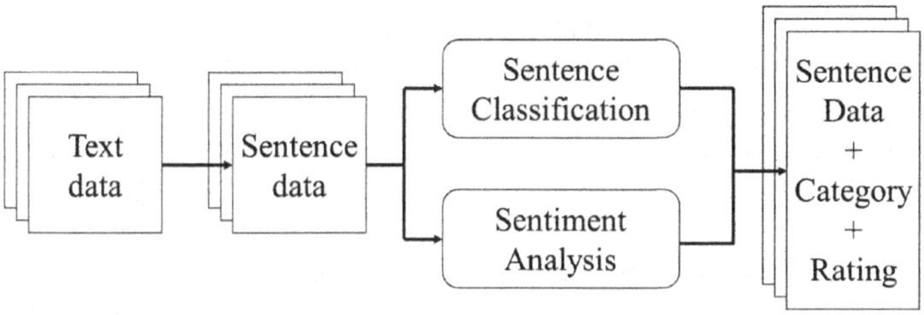

Fig. 2. Analysis flow of content estimation

4.1 Creating a Sentence Classification Model

In this study, we created a text classification model for lodging facilities by performing fine tuning on the Japanese version of the BERT model created by the Inui Lab. at Tohoku University [11]. The corpus was created using text data from Twitter, a social networking service. First, we created a crawler using Twitter API and collected 15,000 Japanese tweets (2,500 each) from the most recent tweets using "立地"**(Location)**, "部屋"**(Room)**, "食事"**(Meal)**, "風呂"**(Bath)**, サービス"**(Service)**, "施設"**(Facilities)**(Facilities) as search queries. Retweets were not included.

Next, we formatted the collected text data. We removed English, numbers, and symbols that we considered unnecessary for linguistic analysis. Then, all tweets that were text were separated by sentences based on "。"for Japanese punctuation and deleted sentences that did not contain a search query. Finally, all sentences were tagged with the search query word as a classification category. Location was set to 0, rooms to 1, meals to 2, baths to 3, services to 4, and facilities to 5. Table 2 shows an excerpt of the corpus dataset.

Here, we decided that the names of the categories would have a significant impact on the model itself if we used the corpus as is, we removed the names of the categories from the sentences.

In fine-tuningwe used 13,500 documents (90% of the total 15,000 documents) as training data and 1500 documents (10% of the total 15,000 documents) as validation data, and the number of epochs was set to 4. As a result, we were able to create a sentence classification model with an accuracy of approximately 78%.

Table 2. Part of the corpus created using tweet information

Sentence	Category
駅利用可能の使い勝手の良い立地です (Easy to use location with access to stations)	0
ついに全ての部屋に扇風機を設置完了 (Finally finished installing fans in all rooms)	1
今朝の食事は、いつものアジの干物と昨日の残りの味噌汁 (This morning's meal was the usual dried horse mackerel and miso soup left over from yesterday.)	2
なので私はビジネスホテルも内湯や露天風呂のあるところを探してゆく (So I am going to look for a business hotel with an indoor or outdoor bath)	3
サービス運営する側はそれを売りにしてほしい (I hope the service operators will make it a selling point.)	4
館内にはレストラン、バー、コンビニなど多数の設備あります (There are numerous facilities in the hotel, including a restaurant, bar, and convenience store)	5

4.2 Sentence Extraction Through Data Formatting of Customer Review Data

In order to use the created text classification model for customer review data, we extracted data from the customer review data. We analyzed the text posted by users in the customer review data, and formatted the data. First, we formatted the review data, which are documents, into sentence units by separating them with "。" to separate them into sentence units. In addition, we removed English, numbers, and symbols that we considered unnecessary for natural language processing analysis, as we did when we created the corpus for the sentences. In this study, only sentences with more than 10 characters were extracted. The number of sentences extracted from all 25,111 customer reviews was 85,073. Table 3 shows a part of the dataset of customer review sentences created.

Table 3. Part of the Customer Review Sentence

User No.	Sentence
1	フロントの方たちも親切でしたしとても気持ちよく宿泊できました (The people at the front desk were friendly and made our stay very pleasant)
2	外観は古いが部屋の内装は綺麗 (The exterior is old, but the interior of the room is beautiful)
2	銀座に徒歩圏内で便利です (Conveniently located within walking distance to Ginza)
3	次の機会も泊まりたいと思います (I would like to stay here again next time)

4.3 Sentence Classification Using a Creation Model for Extracted Sentences

We used our document classification model on customer review sentences to perform sentence classification. Sentence classification is the classification of sentences into given categories. Table 4 shows some of the results of the document classification for the customer review sentences.

Table 4. Part of the results of the text classification of customer review sentences

User No.	Sentence	Predict label
4	駅から近くて便利でした (It was conveniently close to the station)	0
5	景色も良く朝食がとても美味しかったです (The view was great and the breakfast was very good)	2
6	フロントは清潔感があり応対も丁寧で次回も利用したいと思います (The front desk was clean and courteous and I would use it again next time)	4

Table 5 shows the number and percentage of sentences belonging to each of the above categories. Note that if a category name was found in a sentence, we included it in that category, regardless of the results of the sentence classification model we used.

Table 5. The Number and percentage of sentences belonging to each category overwritten by words

category	The Number of sentences	percentage
立地(Location)	18,202	21.40%
部屋(Room)	18,573	21.83%
食事(Meal)	13,628	16.02%
風呂(Bath)	9,829	11.55%
サービス(Service)	14,462	17.00%
設備(Favility)	10,379	12.20%
合計(Total)	85,073	100.00%

Tables 5 show that there are many sentences categorized as location or room, while there are few sentences categorized as bath than in the other categories. We can think that this is due to the fact that reviews on baths themselves are not written in the reviews on day-trip use. On the other hand, there are many reviews about the location and the rooms, suggesting that we tend to consider the location and the rooms as important in choosing a facility.

4.4 Frequent Words in Each Category by Sentence Classification

We performed morphological analysis to determine the extent to which categorical trends emerged in the classified customer review sentences, and extracted the frequency counts of the words. Table 6 shows the top 10 words extracted by frequency analysis in each category.

Table 6. Top 10 most frequently appearing words in each category

Rank	立地 (Location)	部屋 (Room)	食事 (Meal)	風呂 (Bath)	サービス (Service)	設備 (Facility)
1	立地 (location)	部屋 (room)	朝食 (breakfast)	風呂 (bath)	利用 (utilization)	ホテル (hotel)
2	ホテル (hotel)	快適 (comforta-ble)	食事 (meal)	へや (room)	サービス (service)	対応 (correspond-ence)
3	便利 (convenient)	宿泊 (lodging)	宿泊 (lodging)	バス (bus)	フロント (front)	設備 (Facility)
4	近く (near)	利用 (utilization)	ホテル (hotel)	朝食 (breakfast)	対応 (correspond-ence)	フロント (front)
5	駅 (station)	泊 (staying)	満足 (satisfac-tion)	露天風呂(open-air bath)	ホテル (hotel)	宿泊 (lodgind)
6	利用 (utilization)	今回 (this time)	パン (bread)	洗面 (toilet)	出張 (business trip)	スタッフ (staff)
7	コンビニ (convenience store)	予約 (reserva-tion)	朝 (moning)	タブ (tub)	お世話 (care)	利用 (utilization)
8	宿泊 (lodging)	満足 (satisfac-tion)	種類 (kind)	ホテル (hotel)	際 (when)	充実 (repletion)
9	満足 (satisfaction)	ホテル (hotel)	利用 (utiliza-tion)	温泉 (spa)	スタッフ (staff)	バス (bus)
10	大変 (very)	清掃 (cleaning)	バイキング (buffet-style)	朝 (moning)	機会 (opportunity)	清掃 (cleaning)

Table 6 shows that the location category contains words related to distance and buildings such as "near," "utilization," and "convenience store". In other categories, words such as "comfortable" and "cleaning" in the room category, "breakfast" and "bread" in the meal category, "open-air bath" and "spa" in the bath category, "utilization" and "correspondence" in the service category, and "front" and "repletion" in the facilities category also appear frequently in each category. Therefore, we believe that the sentences are appropriately classified by this sentence classification model.

4.5 Emotional Analysis of the Extracted Sentences Using a Pre-created Model

We performed sentiment analysis on each sentence to grasp whether the content of the sentence was a good or a bad review of each category. Sentiment analysis is a task to judge whether the input sentences are positive or negative. In this study, we used a model called daigo/bert-base-japanese-sentiment, which is based on BERT published on Hugging Face [12]. Table 7 shows some of the results of sentiment analysis using the above model for all sentences.

Table 7. Part of the results of the emotional analysis

User No.	Sentence	Classification	Score
7	スタッフへの教育が不十分であると思いました (I thought the training of the staff was inadequate)	Negative	0.7955
8	駅にも近く朝食も満足しています (Close to the station and satisfied with the breakfast)	Positive	0.9888
9	アメニティも充実していました (Amenities were also well stocked)	Positive	0.9836

The results of the sentiment analysis showed that of the total 85,073 sentences of customer reviews, 74,454 (87.52%) were classified as positive and 10,619 (12.48%) were classified as negative. We can see that many sentences are judged as positive. This suggests that reviews in lodging facilities tend to have more positive sentences.

Table 8 shows the number and percentage of positive and negative sentences for each category of sentences.

Table 8. Number and percentage of total emotion analysis results for each category

	立地 (Location)	部屋 (Room)	食事 (Meal)	風呂 (Bath)	サービス (Service)	設備 (Facility)
Positive (Number)	16,589	16,035	12,116	7,974	13,387	8,353
Negative (Number)	1,613	2,394	1,573	1,831	1,190	1,982
Positive (Percentage)	91.14%	87.01%	88.51%	81.33%	91.84%	80.82%
Negative (Percentage)	8.86%	12.99%	11.49%	18.67%	8.16%	19.18%

Table 8 shows that there are many positive reviews regarding service. There are also many positive reviews about the location. We believe that this is due to the fact that customers consider the location of the lodging facility when choosing a lodging facility in the first place. Reviews about baths and facilities have fewer positive reviews than the other categories. We think that one of the reasons for the negative reviews about baths is that it is difficult to keep the baths clean because of the water supply. In fact, negative reviews about the baths included, "It's a pity that the bath smelled a little damp." We believe that the level of facilities required by each customer and the facilities needed by each user may differ. The negative review regarding facilities, "The only complaint for women who wear makeup is that there is no mirror in front of the table in the room," indicates that different individuals require different facilities.

4.6 Model Evaluation Used for Sentiment Analysis

We evaluated the appropriateness of the model used in this study for judging positivity or negativity by sentiment analysis in the review of lodging facilities. We used the data items Rating 1 (Location) to Rating 6 (Facilities) from the customer review data to conduct this evaluation. First, we extracted the customer evaluation values corresponding to each category classified by document classification. For example, a sentence classified as "Location" uses the customer's rating of 1 (Location). If the value is 4 or 5, it is positive, if it is 1 or 2, it is negative, and if the value is 3, the sentence is not used in the model evaluation. We assumed that a sentence was correctly assessed by the model used if the assessment using the model and the assessment using the customer review data were in agreement. As a result, 59,025 sentences (85.70%) were answered correctly and 9,848 (14.30%) incorrectly.

Table 9 shows the number and percentage of correct or incorrect sentences in each category.

Table 9. Number and percentage of correct and incorrect sentences in each category

	立地 (Loca-tion)	部屋 (Room)	食事 (Meal)	風呂 (Bath)	サービス (Service)	設備 (Facility)
Correct (Number)	14,920	13,386	7,722	5,926	11,012	6,059
Incorrect (Number)	1,528	2,510	1,432	1,535	1,244	1,599
Correct (Percentage)	90.71%	84.21%	84.36%	79.43%	89.85%	79.12%
Incorrect (Percentage)	9.29%	15.79%	15.64%	20.57%	10.15%	20.88%

Table 9 shows that the correct response rate for the location and service categories is high, exceeding 90% for location. On the other hand, the correct response rate for sentences classified in the bath and service categories tends to be low.

5 Result and Discussion

In this study, we attempted to estimate the content of text data in customer reviews at lodging facilities. First, this section summarizes the results of the text classification and sentiment analysis and evaluation of customer reviews conducted in this study. Table 10 summarizes the overall results of this analysis.

Table 10. Categories extracted by the analysis

Item	Category
Categories with the most reviews	立地，部屋 (location, room)
Categories with few reviews	風呂 (bath)
Categories with many positive reviews	立地，サービス (location, service)
Categories with many negative reviews	風呂，設備 (bath, facility)
Categories with high percentage of correct responses	立地 (location)
Categories with high percentage of incorrect responses	風呂，設備 (bath, facility)

Table 10 shows that the location category not only has a large number of reviews, but also a large number of positive reviews, indicating that location tends to be highly rated in reviews of lodging facilities. We expected this to be because the location can be known in advance when choosing an lodging facilities facility. While other categories tend to show differences between what is actually used and what is seen in photos, it is thought that negative impressions are difficult to form about the location because it does not change when the user uses the facility. Although there are as many reviews in the room category as in the location category, positive reviews are harder to come by than those in the location category, suggesting the above reasons. On the other hand, there are many positive reviews for the service category, even though the number of reviews is not large. This indicates that the service level of Japanese lodging facilities is high.

Next, in terms of the percentage of correct responses, categories with a high percentage of positive reviews also had a high percentage of correct responses, while categories with a high percentage of negative reviews had a lower percentage of correct responses than the other categories. In other words, positive reviews were more likely to be judged correctly, but negative reviews were more likely to be judged incorrectly than positive reviews.

In the following, we describe our estimates of customer review sentences for a specific facility.

Luxury hotel A in Japan had the highest number of positive reviews in the review sentences for the service category. This hotel has a long history in Japan and has a very good reputation for its service. In fact, the Forbes Travel Guide, one of the world's leading travel guides that rates first-class hospitality based on strict criteria, awarded Executive House Zen the highest rating of five stars for three consecutive years and The Maine the four-star rating for two consecutive years in the hotel category for its 2022 rating [13].

On the other hand, business hotel B, one of the most famous business hotels in Japan, received many positive review sentiments regarding its location. This may be due to the fact that business hotels are often used for business trips and are located closer to urban areas. Room was the most frequent negative review sentiment. We consider this to be a characteristic of business hotels, which are designed with the minimum number of rooms required. We believe that even business hotels can improve their reputation and sales by differentiating themselves from common business hotels, such as by providing better beds in the rooms so that guests can relax after a long day of work.

6 Conclusion

In this study, we conducted research using customer review data on lodging facilities. Specifically, we conducted sentence-by-sentence classification and content estimation using sentiment analysis. For sentence classification, we created a sentence classification model for lodging facilities by fine-tuning a Japanese version of the trained BERT model created by Inui Lab. at Tohoku University. To create the dataset for fine tuning, we created a crawler using the Twitter API. The search queries were location, room, meal, bath, service, and facilities in the lodging facilities reviews, and 2,500 tweets were collected for each. By tagging all 15,000 sentences with the name of the search query, we created a sentence classification model with six categories. The result was a model with 78% accuracy. By applying this model to customer review data separated into sentences, we were able to estimate the content of each sentence.

We also performed sentiment analysis on each sentence to determine whether the review was about positive or negative sentence. As a result, many of the reviews about the location and the room were positive. This may be due to the fact that the location and room can be predicted to some extent at the stage of choosing an lodging facilities facility. On the other hand, there were more negative reviews about the baths than in the other categories. One of the reasons for this is that there are few reviews about the baths due to the fact that guests stay overnight without a bath, and that baths deteriorate more quickly than rooms, making it easier to see the difference between the pictures on the homepage and the baths.

Through this study, we have been able to understand the detailed contents of customer reviews of lodging facilities by performing sentence-by-sentence content and sentiment estimation on text reviews. In the past, it was only possible to understand the detailed opinions of customers by reading the entire text of customer reviews. It is also difficult to identify what the review is about when using the analysis method, because each document contains various elements, such as information on both rooms and baths in one document. However, by using this analytical model, it is possible to estimate the review contents and evaluation of many customer reviews without reading all the documents. The model developed in this study can be used for lodging facilities review data. By creating models for other categories, we believe it will be possible to create models for estimating review contents other than lodging facilities. However, in dividing the review text into sentences, only "。" Therefore, sentences that end with symbols such as exclamation marks are not correctly separated into sentences. We believe that methods for correctly delimiting sentences need to be studied in detail. We believe that there is still room for improvement in the sentence classification model. The sentence categorization model was classified into six categories, but there are some reviews that do not belong to any of the six categories, such as those related to customer service. In addition, it is not clear whether the service category refers to services related to amenities, etc., or services related to how employees respond to customers. We believe that further refinement of the categories would improve the results. As for sentiment analysis, only positive or negative judgment results were used in this study, and scores were not used.

Acknowledgment. In this paper, we used "Rakuten Dataset"(https://rit.rakuten.com/data_release/) provided by Rakuten Group, Inc. Via IDR Dataset Service of National Institute of Informatics. This work was supported by JSPS KAKENHI Grant Number 21H04600 and 21K13385.

References

1. Booking.com official site. https://www.booking.com/index.ja.html (2 Aug 2023 author checked)
2. Expedia official site. https://www.expedia.co.jp/ (2 Aug 2023 author checked)
3. Rakuten Travel official site. https://travel.rakuten.co.jp/ (2 Aug 2023 author checked)
4. Jalan net official site. https://www.jalan.net/ (2 Aug 2023 author checked)
5. JTB Tourism Research & Consulting Co. Survey on Smartphone Use and Travel Consumption (2019)
6. Yamashita, K., Kumoi, G., Hasumoto, K.: Masayuki Goto a study of analytical model of product review data based on features extracted by BERT". Inf. Process. Soc. Japan **1**, 841–842 (2022)
7. Aslam, N., Ramay, W.Y., Xia, K., Sarwar, N.: Convolutional neural network-based classification of app reviews. IEEE Access **8**, 185619–185628 (2020)
8. Classification Model for Application Review Training with Forums," The Institute of Electronics, Information and Communication Engineers. D, pp 669–678 (2022)
9. Devlin, J., Chang, M., Lee, K., Toutanova K.: BERT: Pretraining of deep bidirectional transformers for language understanding. In: Proceedings of Conference North American Chapter of the Association for Computational Linguistics: Human Language Technologies, pp. 4171–4186 (2019)
10. Rakuten Group, Inc. Rakuten Dataset. Informatics Research Data Repository, National Institute of Informatics (2014). https://doi.org/10.32130/idr.2.0 (2 Aug 2023 author checked)
11. Pretrained Japanese BERT models released | Tohoku NLP Lab https://www.nlp.ecei.tohoku.ac.jp/news-release/3284/(2023/2/08 author checked)
12. Hugging Face:https://huggingface.co/daigo/bert-base-japanese-sentiment (2 Aug 2023 author checked)
13. Forbes Travel Guide Star Rated Hotels, Restaurants & Spas https://www.forbestravelguide.com/ (2 Aug 2023 author checked)

Analysis of Purchasing Behavior Based on Discount Rates Using Home Scan Data

Takaaki Mimura[1(✉)] and Takashi Namatame[2]

[1] Graduate School of Science and Engineering, Chuo University, 1-13-27, Kasuga, Bunkyo-Ku, Tokyo 112-8551, Japan
a19.7yx6@chuo-u.ac.jp

[2] Faculty of Science and Engineering, Chuo University, 1-13-27, Kasuga, Bunkyo-Ku, Tokyo 112-8551, Japan
nama@kc.chuo-u.ac.jp

Abstract. In this study, we analyzed the relationship between purchasing behavior and discount rates using a home scan data provided by a research company. We conducted pLSA to cluster the monitors and discount rates, correspondence analysis to reveals the relationship between product and business categories, and association analysis to reveal relationships among categories. The results of the clustering allowed us to classify the data into 10 classes. The results showed that convenience store frequenters did not respond well to the discount policy, while supermarket frequenters responded differently to the discount policy. The impact of discount policies on frozen foods was significant and discounts on beverages will encourage these consumers to buy more in supermarkets.

Keywords: Home Scan Data · Purchase Behavior · pLSA · Correspondence Analysis · Association Analysis

1 Introduction

In Japan, it is now possible to obtain the same products through various channels, such as supermarkets, convenience stores, and drugstores. Currently, it is necessary to differentiate products from those in other channels. One of the perspectives for marketing activities to achieve differentiation is the marketing mix (4Ps) proposed by McCarthy in the 1960s [4].

Existing studies, [1–3], used ID-POS data and focused on purchases at a single store or a single company for analysis. In this study, we use a home scan data to analyze purchases across stores, focusing on purchases by each monitor.

In this study, we focus on "price", one of the 4Ps of the marketing mix, and evaluate the impact of product discounts. The purpose of this study is to analyze store usage patterns based on product discount rates of purchased products, and to clarify the effects of discounts.

A. Coman and S. Vasilache (Eds.): HCII 2023, LNCS 14025, pp. 542–553, 2023.
https://doi.org/10.1007/978-3-031-35915-6_39

2 Datasets

Table 1. The Summery of Datasets

Period	2014/04/01–2015/03/31
Number of monitors	40,025
Number of data	41,198,853
region	All Japan
Number of categories	331 categories
Number of products	323,595 products
Business Categories	Supermarket, Convenience Store, Home Center/Discount Store, Pharmacy/Drugstore, Vending Machine (in workplace/school), 100/99 Yen Stores, Home Delivery/Mail Order (Internet order), General Grocery Stores, Vending Machines (in facilities), Vending Machines (street and roadside), Home Electronics Store,,Department Store, Discount Liquor Store, General Merchandise Store, Home Delivery/Mail order (catalog, telephone and other orders), Cosmetics Store, Door-to-door Sales, Station Kiosks, Pet Goods Store, Coffee Store, Beauty Salon, Bread and Confectionery Store, General Liquor Store, aby Specialty and Toy Store, Butcher/Fish/Grocery Store, University co-op Store, Animal Hospital, Others

In this study, we analyze purchasing behavior using home scan data provided by INTAGE Inc, which one of the most famous Japanese research company that records the daily purchases of specific monitors, excluding fresh food and prepared foods. An overview of the data is as follows.

3 Method

In this section, we explain the analysis methods used in this study. In this study, all analyses were conducted using Python.

First, data for 1,000 monitors were randomly sampled from all data and used in the analysis of this study. Second, after removing items that the product name is "unknown" or "other", then the highest price among all unit prices in the datasets for each product was defined as the list price of that product. Then, the discount rate (%) for each product at each purchase was calculated and using this study. Third, we defined a main user as a customer who uses one business category for more than 60% of all purchases.

3.1 Probabilistic Latent Semantic Analysis (pLSA)

Probabilistic latent semantic analysis (pLSA) is a statistical technique for the analysis of two-mode and co-occurrence data. In effect, one can derive a low-dimensional representation of the observed variables (x, y) in terms of their affinity to certain hidden variables (z), just as in latent semantic analysis [5] (Fig. 1).

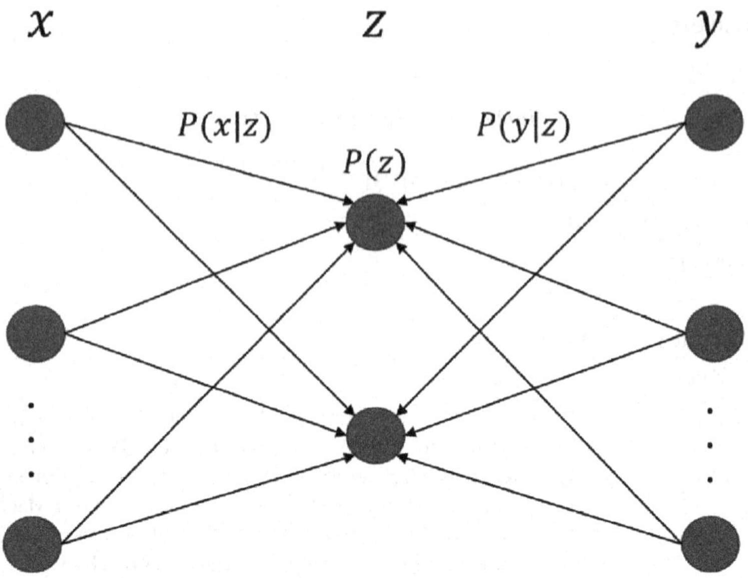

Fig. 1. Image of pLSA

In this study, pLSA was conducted using monitor ID and category3. The calculated discount rates were used in the analysis in 11 levels: "0%", "1% to less than 10%", "10% to less than 20%", ..., and "90% to less than 100%". A matrix of the number of monitors (1000) × discount rate (11) was created and used in the analysis.

3.2 Correspondence Analysis

Correspondence analysis is a multivariate analytical technique that maps multidimensional aggregated data into a low-dimensional space to visually express the relationship between data elements, visualizing the relationship between row and column elements in a cross-tabulation table. In the visualized figure, it can be grasped that data points that are close to each other are deeply related, and data points that are far from each other are less related [6].

In this study, "mca", a Python library for correspondence analysis, was used for the analysis.

Four correspondence analyses were conducted in this study: 1) category2 (18 categories) and business categories using all data, 2) category3 (65 categories) and business categories using all data, 3) category2 (18 categories) and business categories using main users of supermarkets, 4) category3 (65 categories) and business categories using main users of supermarkets.

3.3 Association Analysis

Association analysis is a method of analyzing customer purchase patterns by receipt unit, and can reveal patterns of purchase behavior among products and categories, such as simultaneous purchases. In this study, association analysis was conducted with a focus on lift values. The formulation of the lift value is as follows [7].

$$lift(A \Rightarrow B) = \frac{confidence(A \Rightarrow B)}{support(B)} \tag{1}$$

In this study, we used "mlxten" in the "apriori" module, an algorithm for association analysis in Python.

Association analysis was conducted for all data using category3 and for the main users of the supermarket data using category3, dividing them into two groups: those who responded to the discount and those who did not. The lift values were calculated based on the support values of 0.01 or more. The top 50 lift values or those with a lift value of 1 or more were created in the network diagram. In addition, the lift values are higher for products with low approval ratings when the same selling behavior is frequently observed. Therefore, the lift values were calculated and the top 50 lift values were created on the network diagram for the median or higher support level among the products with support level of 0.01 or higher.

4 Result

In this section, we present the results of the analysis.

4.1 Probabilistic Latent Semantic Analysis (pLSA)

Using the Akaike's information criterion (AIC), the number of classes was determined to be 10. The following graph shows the change in the value of the AIC for each number of classes.

Next, the characteristics of each class when data divided into 10 classes are shown in the Table 2. The number of persons is shown after determining which class each person has the highest probability of belonging to. As for the discount rates, as well as the number of persons, we show which class has the highest probability of belonging to each discount rate (Table 1).

We defined a main user as a person who uses one business category for more than 60% of all purchases. Using the results of this clustering, we examined classes for each main user. Table 3 and Table 4 show the number of people in each class who are main users of convenience stores and supermarkets.

4.2 Correspondence Analysis

First, we conducted a correspondence analysis of all data using category2 and business categories as a variable. The results are shown Fig. 3.

Second, we conducted a correspondence analysis of all data using category3 and business categories as a variable. The results are shown Fig. 4.

Next, we focus on the main users of supermarkets, whose responses to discounts varied from person to person, and show the results of a correspondence analysis by category2 and business categories. The results are shown Fig. 5.

Finally, we conducted a correspondence analysis of main users of supermarkets data using category2 and business categories as a variable. The results are shown Fig. 6.

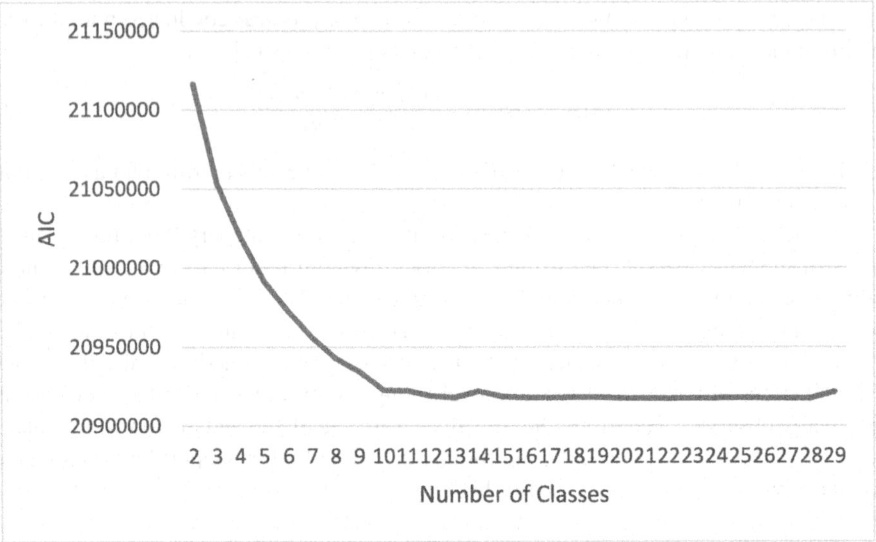

Fig. 2. The Change in the Value of the Akaike Information Criterion for Each Number of Classes

Table 2. The Characteristics of Each Class

Class	The Number of People	Discount Rate	Characteristics
0	72	20–30	male
1	133		female, married, part-time worker
2	111	79–80, 80–90, 90–100	self-employed/sole proprietor
3	131	0	male, unmarried, full-time worker
4	84	10–20	60's, full-time worker
5	66	50–60	40's
6	99	60–70	married
7	132	1–10	male, 10's, 20's, unmarried, full-time worker, homemaker/student
8	62	30–40	temporary worker
9	110	40–50	married

4.3 Association Analysis

First, we conducted an association analysis of all data using category3. A network diagram was created for the top 50 lift values. The results are shown Fig. 7.

Table 3. The Number of People in Each Class who are Main Users of Supermarkets

Class	The Number of People
0	44
1	97
2	56
3	29
4	28
5	42
6	68
7	40
8	39
9	64

Table 4. The Number of People in Each Class who are Main Users of Convenience Stores

Class	The Number of People
3	21
6	1
7	14

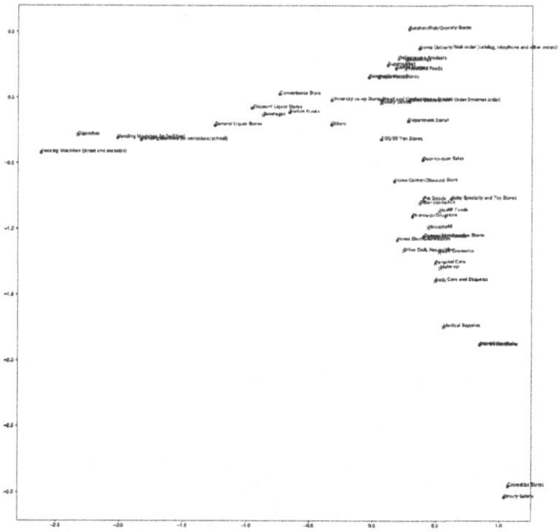

Fig. 3. Correspondence Analysis Using Category2 and Business Categories

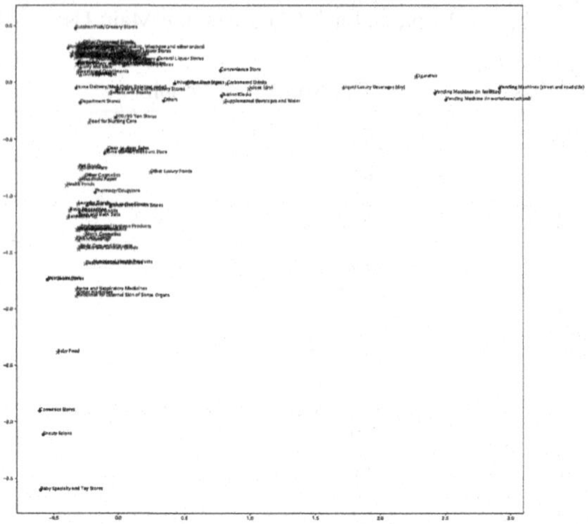

Fig. 4. Correspondence Analysis Using Category3 and Business Categories

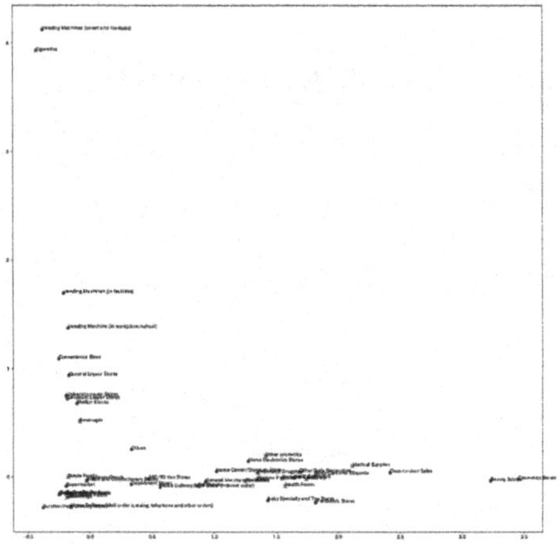

Fig. 5. Correspondence Analysis Using Category2 and Business Categories (Main users of supermarkets)

Second, we conducted an association analysis of the top 100 support values (above the median) using all data. A network diagram was created for the top 50 lift values. The results are shown Fig. 8.

Third, we conducted an association analysis of the main users of the supermarket data using category3 those who did not respond to the discount. A network diagram was created for the top 50 lift values. The results are shown Fig. 9.

Forth, we conducted an association analysis of the top 109 support values (above the median) among the main users of supermarkets who did not respond to discounts. A network diagram was created for the top 50 lift values. The results are shown Fig. 10.

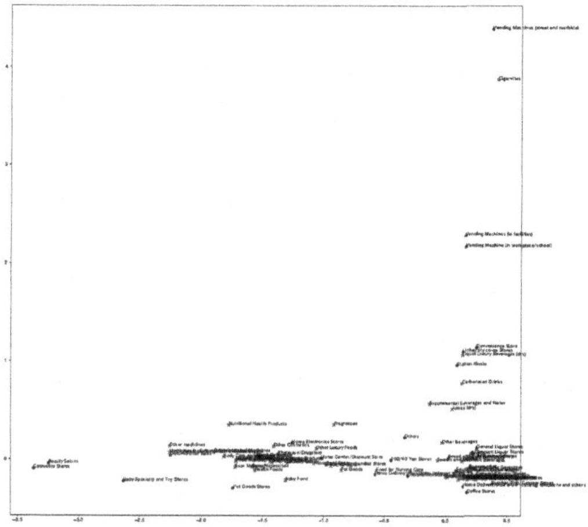

Fig. 6. Correspondence Analysis Using Category3 and Business Categories (Main users of supermarkets)

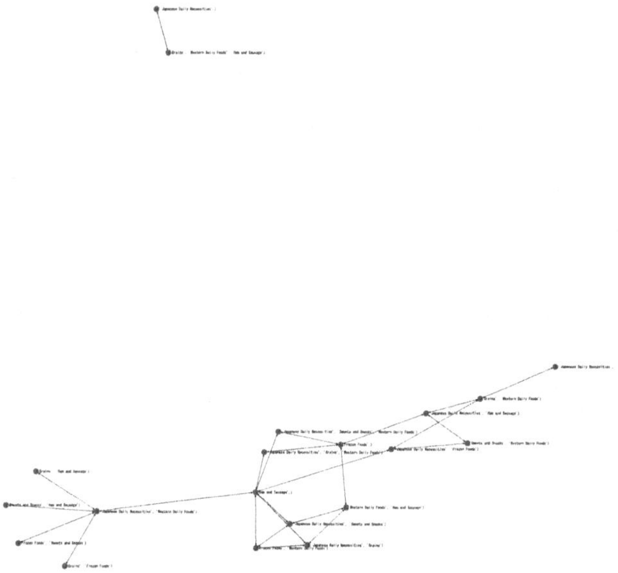

Fig. 7. Association Analysis of All Data

Fifth, we conducted an association analysis of the main users of the supermarket data using category3 those who responded to the discount. A network diagram was created for the top 50 lift values. The results are shown Fig. 11.

Sixth, we conducted an association analysis of the top 158 support values (above the median) among the main users of supermarkets who responded to discounts. A network diagram was created for the top 50 lift values. The results are shown Fig. 12.

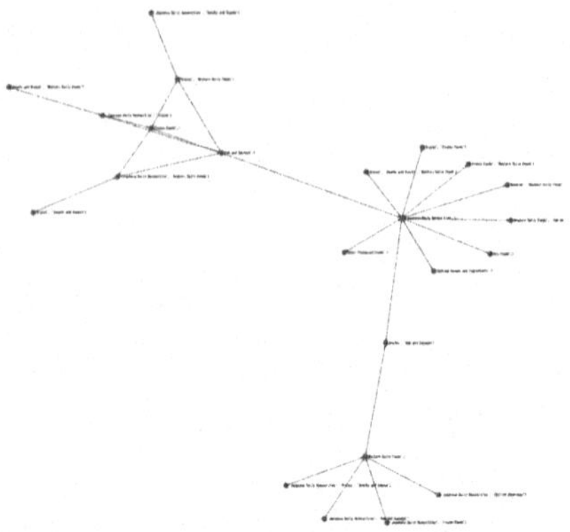

Fig. 8. Association Analysis of the Top 100 Support Values

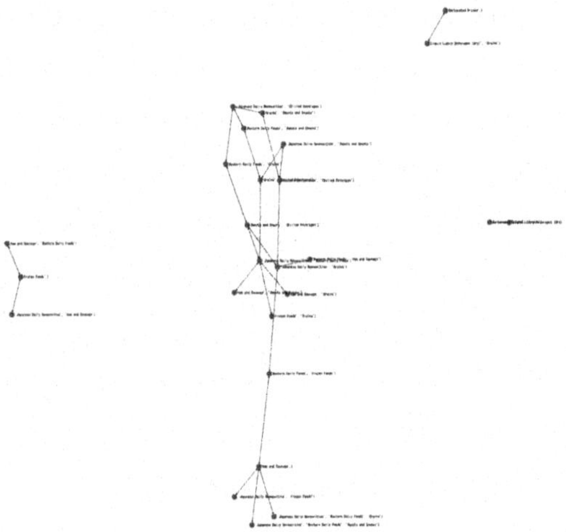

Fig. 9. Association Analysis of the Main Users of the Supermarket Data Using Category3 those who did not Respond to the Discount

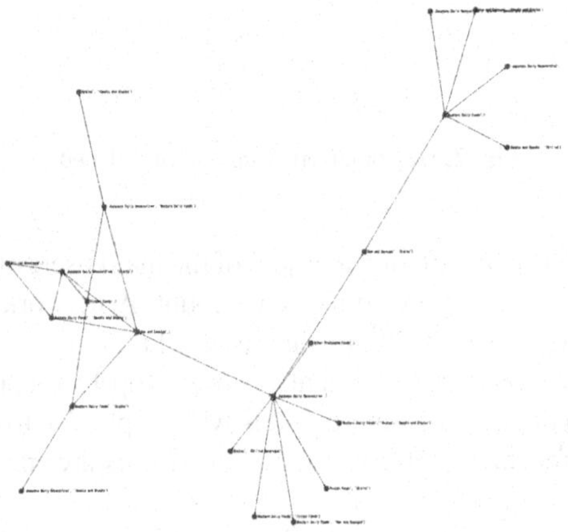

Fig. 10. Association Analysis of the Main Users of the Supermarket Data Using Category3 those who did not Respond to the Discount (above the median)

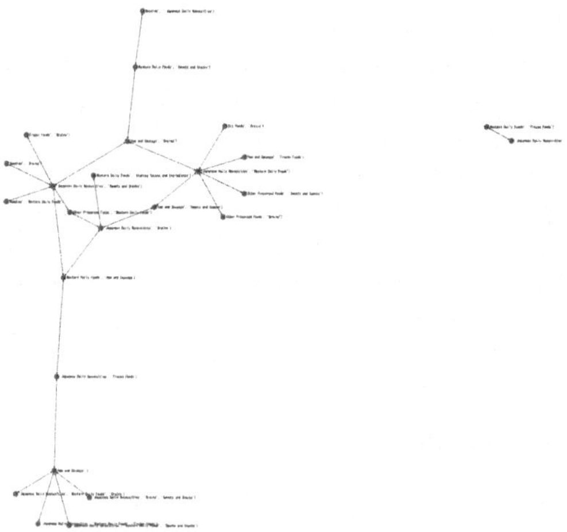

Fig. 11. Association Analysis of the Main Users of the Supermarket Data Using Category3 those who Responded to the Discount

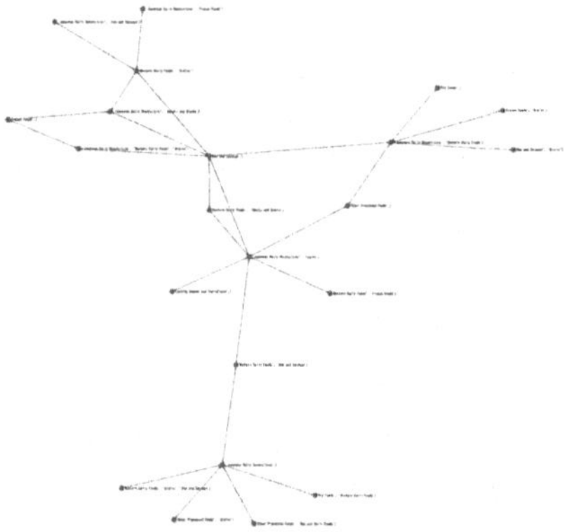

Fig. 12. Association Analysis of the Main Users of the Supermarket Data Using Category3 those who Responded to the Discount (above the median)

5 Discussion

In this section, we discuss each result of analysis.

5.1 Probabilistic Latent Semantic Analysis (pLSA)

The results of the pLSA revealed that users who mainly purchase at convenience stores do not respond well to discounting services, and purchase items at regular prices when they need them. Users who mainly shop at supermarkets were classified into all classes.

The reason for this is when supermarkets are analyzed together, monitors who mainly use supermarkets that rarely offer discounts, such as high-end supermarkets and EDLP (every-day low price) supermarkets, and monitors who mainly purchase private brand products that do not offer discounts, are included in the analysis. This is thought to be because the analysis of the data includes monitors who mainly use supermarkets that rarely offer discounts, such as high-end supermarkets and EDLP supermarkets, and monitors who mainly purchase private brand products that do not offer discounts. In addition, since the price of private brand products is generally fixed, it is considered difficult to examine purchasing behavior in terms of discount rates. The inclusion of these monitors may have led to the emergence of monitors classified in the low discount rate class. The data did not allow us to confirm the name of the supermarket store because the supermarkets were grouped together, but we confirmed that the monitors frequently bought private brand products by checking the product names.

5.2 Correspondence Analysis

The results of the correspondence analysis (Figs. 2 and 3) of all the data for business category and category indicate that processed foods, seasonings, and daily necessities are located near the data points for supermarkets, and beverages are located near the data points for convenience stores. It is considered that supermarkets tend to purchase items that are planned, while convenience stores tend to purchase items that are urgently needed.

The results of the correspondence analysis of the supermarket main users' data for business category and category for business category and category (Figs. 4 and 5) indicate that supermarket main users tend to buy beverages relatively often in convenience stores.

5.3 Association Analysis

The results of the association analysis of all data (Figs. 6 and 7) showed that "Western daily delivery", "Japanese daily delivery", and "ham and sausage" products were frequently purchased. This is thought to be due to the short shelf life of these products, which provides many opportunities to purchase them.

"Frozen food" and "processed food" appear more frequently in the network diagram in Figs. 10 and 11 than in Figs. 8 and 9. Therefore, it can be assumed that discounts on these products have a large impact on purchasing. In addition, there is a category of beverages that appears in Figs. 8 and 9, but not in Figs. 10 and 11. Therefore, in order to encourage more purchases from those who belong to supermarkets that respond to discounts, it is considered necessary to implement discount measures in the beverage category.

6 Conclusion

In this study, we conducted pLSA to cluster the monitors and the discount rate, correspondence analysis to reveals the relationship between categories and business category, and association analysis to reveal relationships among categories.

The main users of convenience stores did not respond well to discounts. Therefore, it can be said that the effect of implementing a discount policy for main users of convenience stores is limited.

The main users of supermarkets reacted differently to discounts. The impact of discount policies on frozen foods was significant. If discounts could be offered on "carbonated beverages", "chilled beverages", "dry liquid beverages" and "supplemental beverages/water", it would further promote purchases at supermarkets.

Acknowledgments. We were able to use valuable data by providing data free of charge through the educational support activities by INTAGE Inc.. This work was supported by Chuo University Grant for Special Research (2021–2022).

References

1. Ishigaki, T., Takenaka, T., Motomura, Y., et al.: Customer behavior prediction system by large scale data fusion on a retail service. Trans. Jpn. Soc. Artif. Intell. **26**(6), 670–681 (2011). (in Japanese)
2. Sakurai, N.: Market segmentation using latent class analysis. Trans. Jpn. Soc. Comput. Stat. 21–30 (2004). (in Japanese)
3. Seki, Y.: Extraction of customer behavior patterns from ID-POS data. Trans. Oper. Res. Soc. Japan, pp.75–82 (2003). (in Japanese)
4. Persol Career CO., LTD.. What is the marketing mix?. https://biz.hipro-job.jp/column/corporation/marketing-mix/
5. Analytics Design Lab Inc. Summary of PLSA. http://www.analyticsdlab.co.jp/column/plsa.html
6. NTTCom Online Marketing Solutions Corporation, Correspondence analysis is explained in an easy-to-understand manner with examples of its use. https://www.nttcoms.com/service/research/dataanalysis/correspondence-analysis/
7. ALBERT Inc. Methods of product analysis (ABC analysis, association analysis). https://www.albert2005.co.jp/knowledge/marketing/customer_product_analysis/abc_association

Virtual Reality, Augmented Reality and Metaverse: Customer Experience Approach and User Experience Evaluation Methods. Literature Review

Jenny Morales[1(✉)], Héctor Cornide-Reyes[2], Pedro O. Rossel[3,4], Paula Sáez[1], and Fabián Silva-Aravena[1]

[1] Facultad de Ciencias Sociales y Económicas, Departamento de Economía y Administración, Universidad Católica del Maule, Talca, Chile
{jmoralesb,pfsaez,fasilva}@ucm.cl

[2] Facultad de Ingeniería, Departamento de Ingeniería Informática y Ciencias de La Computación, Universidad de Atacama, Copiapó, Chile
hector.cornide@uda.cl

[3] Facultad de Ingeniería, Departamento de Ingeniería Informática, Universidad Católica de La Santísima Concepción, Concepción, Chile
prossel@ucsc.cl

[4] Centro de Investigación en Biodiversidad y Ambientes Sustentables (CIBAS), Universidad Católica de La Santísima Concepción, Concepción, Chile

Abstract. Currently, the technologies associated with the web and telecommunications have an essential role in different areas, such as education, medicine, tourism, commerce, among others. The coronavirus pandemic (COVID-19) accelerated the process of adopting these technologies. The announcement of the metaverse and its large number of opportunities, immersive experiences, scenarios, contexts, and possibilities have generated much expectation. This has increased interest in technologies such as Virtual Reality (VR), Augmented Reality (AR), and the mixture of both, which are not new technologies, but now taking advantage of the opportunities for better performance offered by communication networks such as 5G. Thus, user and/or customer experiences can be changed. This paper presents a literature review related to two concepts which are the user experience (UX) and customer experience (CX) in VR, AR, and metaverse, and their evaluation methods. We follow a review protocol and consult five representative databases. We found studies related to the user experience in virtual reality and augmented reality but not related to the metaverse. Regarding the evaluation methods of the user experience found, it is possible to identify heuristic evaluations and user tests that include data collection through questionnaires and the use of brain and body signals. In future work, we pretend to extend this literature review in a systematic review and intend to create guides to evaluate virtual environments applied to VR, AR, or metaverse.

Keywords: User experience · customer experience · evaluation methods · virtual reality · augmented reality · Metaverse

A. Coman and S. Vasilache (Eds.): HCII 2023, LNCS 14025, pp. 554–566, 2023.
https://doi.org/10.1007/978-3-031-35915-6_40

1 Introduction

Today, technology has taken an important position in different areas of daily life. It promises to make changes in areas of everyday life by incorporating virtual environments, for example in education, work, medicine, art, or commerce [1–3]. The announcement of metaverse has generated expectations of new immersive experiences for users, considering virtual, augmented, and mixed reality, among other technologies, and the development of communication networks such as 5G. Thus, the user and customer experience aspects can vary or migrate to new concepts and incorporate other elements. In this sense, it is interesting to identify the methods used to evaluate the user/customer experience in VR and/or AR and metaverse.

This article reviews the literature related to two concepts: the customer experience (CX)/user experience (UX) and the evaluation methods in VR, AR, and metaverse. For this, a review protocol was developed with five stages: identification of research questions, selection of data sources, selection of articles, classification of articles, and results. The results showed that there are studies related to evaluation methods to the user experience (not about customer experience) in virtual and augmented reality (mainly oriented to corporeality, presence, and interactivity), but it did not find studies about metaverse. Regarding the user experience evaluation methods found, it is possible to identify heuristic evaluations and user tests that include data collection through questionnaires and the use of brain and body signals collected through wearables.

The paper is organized as follows: Sect. 2 introduces the related work; Sect. 3 presents the methodology and the results obtained; finally, in Sect. 4, we offer conclusions and future work.

2 Related Work

In this section, we addressed concepts used during the development of this work, which cover the topics of the information searches carried out in this literature review.

2.1 Customer Experience and User Experience

The concept of customer experience (CX) addresses several elements related to the interaction of the customer with any part of a company or organization. This interaction can be intentional or casual, and the results of this interaction involve personal and emotional elements which influence the decision to purchase that the customer may have [4, 5].

The authors have defined dimensions that make up the customer experience, which are [6]: (i) sensorial component, which is related to sensations that provide good sensory experiences, such as taste and touch, (ii) emotional component that is related to feelings and emotions that can generate emotional experiences, (iii) cognitive component, that focused on connecting conscious thoughts or mental processes, (iv) pragmatic component that comes from the practice of doing something. This Includes usability but involves life cycle stages, (v) lifestyle component, that is associated to people's lifestyles and beliefs, and (vi) relational component, this involves the person beyond their social context, relationship with others, and ideal self.

Similarly, to the CX, the user experience (UX) is directly related to the perceptions of expectations of use or use of a product, system, or service, which considers personal and emotional aspects [7]. For our study, we consider that CX is a broader and more inclusive concept than UX, in which various interactions with companies, products and/or services are involved [8].

2.2 Evaluation Methods

As the concept of customer experience is complex due to the variety of elements that compose it together with the subjectivity of each person, its evaluation becomes complex to carry out. However, works were found that have addressed the challenge, for example [9] addressed two case studies of the perception of the customer experience through the data available on websites. On the other hand and considering that the evaluation of the customer experience must be carried out constantly [9], several of the methods to evaluate the user experience contribute to the evaluation of the customer experience, such as satisfaction surveys, interviews, focus group among others.

Regarding user experience evaluations, various methods are already established and widely known. More than 80 evaluation methods can be consulted [10], being able to filter methods according to type of study, development phase, period of experience, types of evaluators, type of data (qualitative, quantitative) among others.

In general terms, two types of evaluation methods can be distinguished: one that requires experts (inspection methods) and others that require users (user testing). Among the most widely used in the case of inspections are heuristic evaluations, which are carried out following usability principles and standards of compliance with these principles on the interface [11]. More recently, heuristics have not only referred to aspects of usability, but also to UX factors [12]. Regarding the tests with users, one or several activities with the users are prepared for them to use and carry out activities with the system under evaluation.

Generally, after users use it they are asked to complete a survey to collect data. These surveys are instrumentalized by means of a widely known questionnaire [13] and/or with questionnaires made to measure according to the needs of the person evaluating [14].

2.3 Virtual Reality, Augmented Reality and Metaverse

Virtual and augmented reality concepts have been known for over two decades and have contributed to and challenged those studying interfaces and human-computer interaction.

Virtual reality, from its beginnings, also generated significant challenges, such as the necessary software and hardware, the related human factors, and the need for high-speed networks [15]. Nowadays, VR offers three-dimensional experiences in a virtual environment through computer technologies. It requires devices such as glasses, gloves, or other controls, which allow people to feel and visualize virtual reality, and obtained the immersion experience [16].

Augmented reality was considered a variation of virtual reality because AR users can see the real world. In contrast, in VR, the user is immersive in a digital world [17].

AR is then considered a technology that allows some devices to overlap digital objects to the real world, in real-time, thus allowing the enhancing user experience [16].

The conjunction of augmented reality and virtual reality has been called mixed reality, which allows interaction in real time and improves the experience and perception of those who use them [18]. Through these and other technologies, metaverse promises to be a completely immersive 3D space [19], including interactions through avatars that bring us closer to an authentic experience of sharing with others, such as the ability to make visual contact or manipulate objects. It will also create spaces like the one we know today for commerce, art, and education. Studies in this regard have already been published [20, 21]. In this context, many elements remain to be addressed and worked on, such as data law, security, and legal regulations, among other things that affect people in real life [22].

Other vital challenges arise from the evaluations of the experiences in metaverse and how those who study the area approach this evaluation with specific and standardized instruments.

3 Methodology

Five stages were carried out for doing this literature review: establishing the research questions, determining the data sources, selecting the articles, classifying the articles found, and finally, analyzing the results.

3.1 Research Questions

Because we are interested in collecting information about the evaluation methods to evaluate the user experience and/or customer experience in virtual reality, augmented reality, and/or metaverse, the following research questions were posed:

(1) What methods are used to evaluate the user and/or customer experience in the metaverse, virtual reality, or augmented reality?
(2) What aspects does the evaluation method focus on?

3.2 Data Sources

To plan the search for scientific articles and consider the research questions, the following concepts were used: User experience, customer experience, metaverse, virtual reality, augmented reality, and evaluation methods.

Finally, the search string obtained was:

- ((“*user experience*” OR “*customer experience*”) AND “*evaluation method*”) AND (*metaverse* OR “*virtual reality*” OR “*augmented reality*”)

With this, we could find the evaluation methods used to evaluate the user experience and customer experience in different contexts, such as virtual reality, augmented reality, and metaverse, if any.

Five representative databases associated with the subject under study were selected to find an adequate number of scientific articles for further analysis. The search was performed in Web of Science (WoS), Scopus, IEEE Xplore, ACM Digital Library, and Science Direct. The investigation was initially carried out in November 2022, and its last update was carried out in mid-December 2022.

3.3 Selection Articles

The search in the previously indicated databases was carried considering the use of search for abstract with limited to 10 years from publication was used. This search was available in all the databases considered in the review and where, finally 28 articles were obtained. The results are shown in Table 1, considering the data sources.

Table 1. Papers found in data source.

Data source	Abstract selection and limited to 10 years
WoS	1
Scopus	24
IEEE Xplore	0
ACM Digital Library	1
Science Direct	2
Total	28

The results were consolidated into a single file and duplicates (4 papers) were removed. Then, the literature review articles were eliminated and selected by type of documents considering only those that were paper conference and article (8 papers were removed). Also, only papers in English were selected (1 paper was removed), leaving 15 papers for the complete reading of the group of researchers.

Finally, in the reading process, only one of the articles was eliminated from the analysis because, although it contained the keywords searched for in the abstract, it was only limited to showing a virtual reality platform to try to improve the user experience without indicating how they do it, and how they address evaluations, which is the focus of interest of this work (Fig. 1).

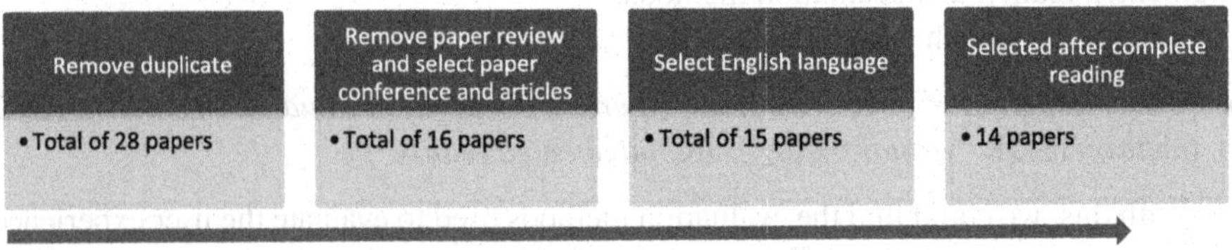

Fig. 1. Results of selection process.

3.4 Articles Classification

Of the articles found and considering the ten years that the search covered, the number of articles per year seems similar (one per year) except for 2019 and 2020 (with three articles), in addition to 2021 (with two articles), which presents a slight increase. In Fig. 2. The percentage of the number of papers per year is given.

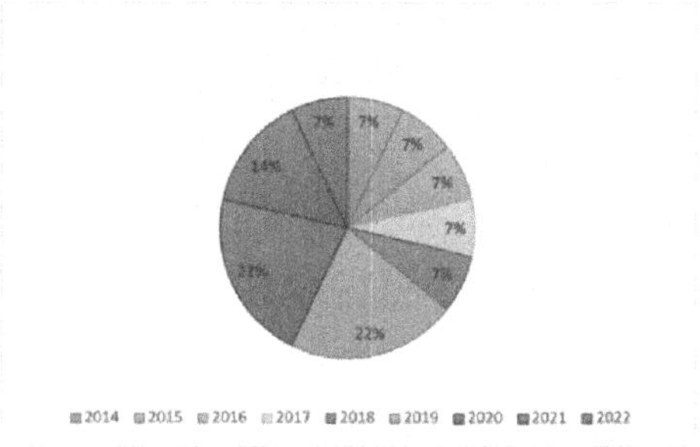

Fig. 2. Selected articles per year.

Considering the document type, we select conference articles and journal articles per review. Among the papers found, 9 corresponding to 64%, are conference articles and 5 journal articles (see Fig. 3). It is essential to indicate that although the data sources were 5 different, all the selected papers have Scopus indexing, regardless of whether they have also been indexed in the other databases.

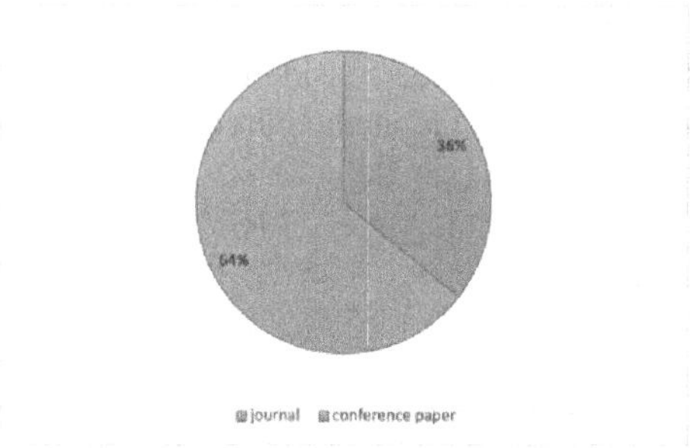

Fig. 3. Document type found.

Even though we were searching for articles that evaluated the user and/or customer experience, none of the articles found addressed the evaluation of the customer experience. On the other hand, considering that the evaluations sought could have augmented reality, virtual reality, and metaverse as objects of study, no evaluation related to metaverse was found.

Considering the object of study, all the selected papers addressed the evaluation of the user experience in virtual reality or augmented reality. Figure 4 shows the percentage of studies associated with each, with a more significant number of studies evaluating the user experience of different aspects of virtual reality (10 articles, representing 71%) and a smaller number of augmented reality (4 articles, representing 29%).

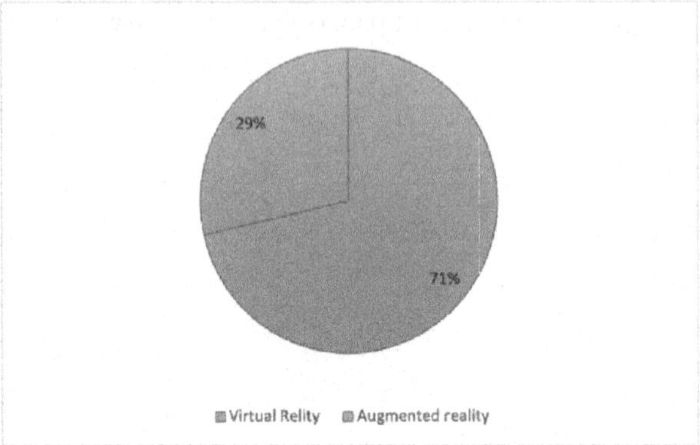

Fig. 4. Number articles about UX evaluation in virtual reality and augmented reality.

In relation to the types of evaluations found, most of them include quantitative studies (6 out of 14, 43%) followed by mixed (5 out of 14, 36%) and to a lesser extent qualitative (3 out of 16, 21%).

In another aspect, we consider essential to mention that we found just one article that separates its evaluation study considering some gender aspects [23]. Although it is not the subject of this work, it is interesting to consider that gender studies could make the results of the evaluations more intriguing, especially if one group or another is to be explicitly addressed.

The articles' classification was made considering the subject evaluated, in this case, virtual reality or augmented reality, the method used, the type of study, and the aspects or elements evaluated in each case (see Table 2).

3.5 Answer Research Questions

Considering the previous classification shown in Table 2 and the research questions defined in Sect. 3.1, we present the responses associated with the articles found and analyzed.

(1) *What methods are used to evaluate the user and/or customer experience in the metaverse, virtual reality, or augmented reality?* Within the articles found and analyzed, it is essential to indicate that two concepts of the searched ones are not present, such as the evaluation of the customer experience and evaluations for metaverse. Concerning the evaluations that used surveys (6 out of 14 articles, 42%), among them, some widely known ones can be mentioned, such as SUS, CSUQ, and UEQ, to name a few. In addition, inspections (4 out of 14, 29%) were used, including heuristic evaluations with adaptations of the very widely known Nielsen heuristics and other more specific sets, such as heuristics for augmented reality applications

Table 2. Papers classification.

Cite	Evaluation of	Methods used	Kind of study	Aspect or attributes evaluated
[24]	Virtual Reality	Survey. Questionnaire Modified embodiment; Questionnaire Presence aspects	Mixed	Embodiment questionnaire, and presence aspects, control and sensory factors
[25]	Virtual Reality	Survey. System Usability Scale (SUS); Computer System Usability Questionnaire (CSUQ); User Experience Questionnaire (UEQ), Communicability evaluation method (CEM)	Mixed	Usability SUS; information quality, interface quality, overall satisfaction CSUQ; UEQ, attractiveness, perspicuity, efficiency, dependability, stimulation, and novelty
[26]	Augmented Reality	Inspections, Heuristic evaluation	Qualitative	Evaluate usability with adapted Nielsen heuristics
[27]	Virtual Reality	Vital or body signs, physiological signals, photoplethysmogram (PPG), electrodermal activity (EDA), eye tracking, Questionnaire for evaluation of the experience and for emotional feedback	Mixed	UX and Emotions
[28]	Virtual Reality	User simulation and response time test about object interaction	Quantitative	Interactive experience features to improve the positive feeling UX
[29]	Augmented Reality	Survey. Technological Acceptance Model, bipolar laddering assessment (BLA)	Mixed	First, characterizes users in terms of technology. The second part evaluates AR, understanding, motivation, usefulness, and ease of use

(*continued*)

Table 2. (*continued*)

Cite	Evaluation of	Methods used	Kind of study	Aspect or attributes evaluated
[30]	Virtual Reality	Visual fatigue study with electroencephalogram (EEG)	Quantitative	UX
[31]	Virtual Reality	Heuristic evaluation; Mile +; user test and interview	Qualitative	Usability and UX
[32]	Virtual Reality	Adaptive bucket algorithm based on dead Reckoning (DR); Mean Opinion Score (MOS), to assess the quality of experience	Mixed	Evaluate immersion, synchronization, fluency visibility
[33]	Virtual Reality	Survey. User experience evaluation questionnaires in virtual reality environments	Quantitative	Evaluate presence, immersion, visual aesthetics, behavioral interaction, user impression
[34]	Augmented Reality	User test, Thinking aloud; inspection Heuristic evaluation	Quantitative	Evaluate usability considering Nielsen heuristics and heuristics for augmented reality applications
[23]	Virtual Reality	Survey	Quantitative	The questionnaire incorporates novelty, sickness effects, satisfaction, perception of duration, surprising elements, and what would add to the VR experience
[35]	Augmented Reality	User test; inspections	Qualitative	Usability, effectiveness of the guide

(*continued*)

Table 2. *(continued)*

Cite	Evaluation of	Methods used	Kind of study	Aspect or attributes evaluated
[36]	Virtual Reality	Survey. VR UX questionnaire; NASA Task Load Index (TLX); neurophysiological recording of the brain signals using electroencephalography (EEG)	Quantitative	UX, presence, engagement, immersion, flow, emotion, judgement, experience consequence (VR- related sickness), and technology adoption

and heuristics for virtual reality. The user experience evaluations considering virtual or body signals, with the use of PGG, EDA, EGG (3 out of 14 studies, 21%), and the studies considering algorithms and response times without real users (2 of 14, 14%) emerge as interesting elements. An element to highlight is that these studies incorporate one or more methods, which makes the evaluation results more reliable. Due to the above, the counts and percentages described are also not exclusive or add up to 100%.

(2) What aspects does the evaluation method focus on? We separated the elements evaluated for virtual and augmented reality to answer this question. For the first case, usability and user experience are essential. These studies mainly consider the aspects of immersion or embodiment and other elements related to the interaction with objects in a virtual space, such as synchronization and visualization. The study of the effects of the disease is also the object of study in the VR UX. Regarding augmented reality, the studies focus on usability and UX regarding aspects, such as, understanding, motivation, usefulness, and ease of use.

4 Conclusion and Future Work

We carried out the literature review related to two concepts that are the user experience (UX) and the customer experience (CX) in VR, AR, and metaverse, and their evaluation methods. Considering the above, the following elements can be indicated: (i) We did not find articles that addressed the evaluation of the customer experience, in VR, AR or metaverse. This may be because the customer experience is complex to evaluate due to its characteristics, subjectivity, and need for constant evaluation. We found a recent study that establishes a preliminary version of the scale for Tourist Experience (TX), which is a particular case of CX [37]. (ii) In turn, we also did not find evaluation studies on metaverse user experience, which appears as a future research opportunity.

From the articles found, we answered the research questions, considering that: most of the UX evaluations were carried out through surveys and using some widely known questionnaires; in the case of inspections, heuristic evaluations are identifiable. It is interesting to consider that most of the articles found include quantitative and mixed studies, in turn, the use of body signals to complement perception surveys, for example.

Regarding the aspects evaluated in virtual reality, immersion and interaction with objects stand out. For augmented reality, usability and some elements of the UX utility and understanding were identified.

For future work, we consider conducting a systematic literature review and developing user/customer experience evaluation guides for virtual and/or augmented reality to advance into metaverse aspects.

References

1. Akçayır, M., Akçayır, G.: Advantages and challenges associated with augmented reality for education: a systematic review of the literature. Educ. Res. Rev. **20**, 1–11 (2017)
2. Baghaei, N., Chitale, V., Hlasnik, A., Stemmet, L., Liang, H.N., Porter, R.: Virtual reality for supporting the treatment of depression and anxiety: scoping review. JMIR Mental Health **8**(9), e29681 (2021)
3. Emmelkamp, P.M., Meyerbröker, K.: Virtual reality therapy in mental health. Annu. Rev. Clin. Psychol. **17**, 495–519 (2021)
4. Meyer, C., Schwager, A.: Understanding customer experience. Harv. Bus. Rev. **85**(2), 116 (2007)
5. Alfaro, E., Velilla, J., Brunetta, H., Navarro, B., Molina, C.: Customer experience. Una visión multidimensional del marketing de experiencias. La experiencia del cliente, un marco para el marketing del futuro, Libro colaborativo, 12–19 (2012)
6. Gentile, C., Spiller, N., Noci, G.: How to sustain the customer experience: an overview of experience components that co-create value with the customer. Eur. Manag. J. **25**(5), 395–410 (2007)
7. UX-definition ISO9241–210:Ergonomics of human-system interaction-Part11:Usability: Definitions and concepts, International Organization for Standardization, Geneva (2018)
8. Rusu, V., Rusu, C., Botella, F., Quiñones, D.: Customer experience: is this the ultimate experience?. In: Proceedings of the XIX International Conference on Human Computer Interaction, pp. 1–4 (2018)
9. Rusu, V., et al.: Assessing the customer experience based on quantitative data: virtual travel agencies. In: Marcus, A. (ed.) DUXU 2016. LNCS, vol. 9746, pp. 499–508. Springer, Cham (2016). https://doi.org/10.1007/978-3-319-40409-7_47
10. Experience Research Society. UX Evaluation Methods. https://experienceresearchsociety.org/ux/evaluation-methods/. Accessed 30 Dec 2022
11. Nielsen Norman Group. 10 usability heuristics for user interface design. https://www.nngroup.com/articles/ten-usability-heuristics/. Accessed 30 Dec 2022
12. Quiñones, D., Rusu, C., Arancibia, D., González, S., Saavedra, M.J.: SNUXH: a set of social network user experience heuristics. Appl. Sci. **10**(18), 6547 (2020)
13. Brooke, J.: SUS-aquick and dirty usability scale. Usability Eval. Ind. **189**(194), 4–7 (1996)
14. Morales, J., Rojas, G., Cerda, G.: Towards a methodology to evaluate user experience with personalized questionnaires for the developments of custom systems. In: HCI International 2022-Late Breaking Papers. Design, User Experience and Interaction: 24th International Conference on Human-Computer Interaction, HCII 2022, Virtual Event, June 26–July 1, 2022, Proceedings, pp. 267–281. Cham: Springer International Publishing (2022). https://doi.org/10.1007/978-3-031-17615-9_19
15. Zheng, J.M., Chan, K.W., Gibson, I.: Virtual reality. IEEE Potentials **17**(2), 20–23 (1998)
16. Kardong-Edgren, S.S., Farra, S.L., Alinier, G., Young, H.M.: A call to unify definitions of virtual reality. Clin. Simul. Nurs. **31**, 28–34 (2019)

17. Azuma, R.T.: A survey of augmented reality. Pres. Teleoper. Vir. Environ. **6**(4), 355–385 (1997)
18. Bekele, M.K., Pierdicca, R., Frontoni, E., Malinverni, E.S., Gain, J.: A survey of augmented, virtual, and mixed reality for cultural heritage. J. Comput. Cult. Heritage (JOCCH) **11**(2), 1–36 (2018)
19. Metaverso- Suzuki, S.N., et al.: Virtual experiments in metaverse and their applications to collaborative projects: the framework and its significance. Procedia Comput. Sci. **176**, 2125–2132 (2020)
20. Barráez-Herrera, D.P.: Metaversos en el Contexto de la Educación Virtual. Rev. Tecnol. - Educativa Docentes 2.0 **13**(1), 11–19 (2022)
21. E-commerce Meta-Jeong, H., Yi, Y., Kim, D.: An innovative e-commerce platform incorporating metaverse to live commerce. Int. J. Innov. Comput. Inf. Control **18**(1), 221–229 (2022)
22. Ball, M.: Metaverso. Cosa significa, chi lo controllerà e perché sta rivoluzionando le nostre vite. Garzanti. Milano (2022)
23. Alaguero, M., Checa, D., Bustillo, A.: Measuring the impact of low-cost short-term virtual reality on the user experience. In: De Paolis, L.T., Bourdot, P., Mongelli, A. (eds.) AVR 2017. LNCS, vol. 10324, pp. 320–336. Springer, Cham (2017). https://doi.org/10.1007/978-3-319-60922-5_26
24. Fröhner, J., Beckerle, P., Endo, S., Hirche, S.: An embodiment paradigm in evaluation of human-in-the-loop control. IFAC-PapersOnLine **51**(34), 104–109 (2019). https://doi.org/10.1016/j.ifacol.2019.01.036
25. Barricelli, B.R., De Bonis, A., Di Gaetano, S., Valtolina, S.: Semiotic framework for virtual reality usability and UX evaluation: a pilot study. In: GHItaly@ AVI (2018)
26. Rambli, D.R.A., Irshad, S.: UX design evaluation of mobile augmented reality marketing products and services for Asia pacific region. In: Proceedings of the Asia Pacific HCI and UX Design Symposium, pp. 42–45 (2015). https://doi.org/10.1145/2846439.2846450
27. Pei, W., Guo, X., Lo, T.: Pre-evaluation method of the experiential architecture based on multidimensional physiological perception. J. Asian Arch. Build. Eng. 1–25 (2022). https://doi.org/10.1080/13467581.2022.2074019
28. Song, H., Yue, Z.: Research on user experience evaluation of man-machine interaction interface based on virtual reality technology. Int. J. Inf. Commun. Technol. **19**(4), 356–370 (2021)
29. Navarro, I., et al.: Heritage augmented reality applications for enhanced user experience. In: Zaphiris, P., Ioannou, A. (eds.) HCII 2021. LNCS, vol. 12785, pp. 302–312. Springer, Cham (2021). https://doi.org/10.1007/978-3-030-77943-6_20
30. Yue, K., Wang, D.: EEG-based 3D visual fatigue evaluation using CNN. Electronics **8**(11), 1208 (2019). https://doi.org/10.3390/electronics8111208
31. Videva, J., Marchiori, E., Cantoni, L.: Assessing usability and user experience of immersive web VR platforms for tourism destinations. E-review Tour. Res. **17**(2) (2019)
32. Zhang, X., Hu, Y., Huang, T.: A multiplayer MR application based on adaptive synchronization algorithm. In: 2020 7th International Conference on Control, Decision and Information Technologies (CoDIT) , vol. 1, pp. 628–632. IEEE (2020)
33. Gan, B., Xia, P.: Research on automatic generation method of virtual reality scene and design of user experience evaluation. In: 2020 International Conference on Information Science, Parallel and Distributed Systems (ISPDS), pp. 308–312. IEEE (2020). https://doi.org/10.1109/ISPDS51347.2020.00071
34. Giraldo, F.D., Arango, E., Cruz, C.D., Bernal, C.C.: Application of augmented reality and usability approaches for the implementation of an interactive tour applied at the University of Quindio. In: 2016 IEEE 11th Colombian Computing Conference (CCC), pp. 1–8. IEEE (2016). https://doi.org/10.1109/ColumbianCC.2016.7750798

35. Chippendale, P., et al.: Personal shopping assistance and navigator system for visually impaired people. In: Agapito, L., Bronstein, M.M., Rother, C. (eds.) ECCV 2014. LNCS, vol. 8927, pp. 375–390. Springer, Cham (2015). https://doi.org/10.1007/978-3-319-16199-0_27
36. Škola, F., et al.: Virtual reality with 360-video storytelling in cultural heritage: study of presence, engagement, and immersion. Sensors **20**(20), 5851 (2020). https://doi.org/10.3390/s20205851
37. Rusu, V., Márquez, L., González, P., Rusu, C.: Evaluating the post-pandemic tourist experience: a scale for tourist experience in Valparaíso, Chile. in: social computing and social media: applications in education and commerce. In: 14th International Conference, SCSM 2022, Held as Part of the 24th HCI International Conference, HCII 2022, Virtual Event, June 26–July 1, 2022, Proceedings, Part II, pp. 331–343. Cham: Springer International Publishing (2022). https://doi.org/10.1007/978-3-031-05064-0_25

Evaluation of Consumer Behavior Focusing on the Change in Flow Line Impacted by Floor Renovation in a Fashion Department Store

Jin Nakashima[1(✉)], Takashi Namatame[2], and Kohei Otake[3]

[1] Graduate School of Information and Telecommunication Engineering, Tokai University, 2-3-23, Takanawa, Minato-Ku, Tokyo 108-8619, Japan
9BJM1203@cc.u-tokai.ac.jp

[2] School of Science and Engineering, Chuo University, 1-13-27, Kasuga, Bunkyo-Ku, Tokyo 112-8551, Japan
nama@kc.chuo-u.ac.jp

[3] School of Information and Telecommunication Engineering, Tokai University, 2-3-23, Takanawa, Minato-Ku, Tokyo 108-8619, Japan
otake@tsc.u-tokai.ac.jp

Abstract. The spread of COVID-19 has led to a slump in consumer market sales in real stores such as department stores and shopping centers. Under this situation, marketing measures to take advantage of the strengths of actual stores are strongly required. In this study, we conduct an experiment on consumer behavior in a department store and collect flow line data. Specifically, we attempted to understand consumer behavior by conducting social network analysis using flow line data acquired with an eye tracking device. The purpose of this study is to evaluate the changes in consumer behavior in real stores in response to changes in the store structure, and to propose marketing measures for real stores that are in line with consumer behavior.

Keywords: Consumer Behavior · Social Network Analysis · Fashion Department Store

1 Introduction

The consumer market in real venues such as department stores and shopping centers has been hit hard by the spread of the new coronavirus that has been endemic in Japan since 2020. According to the Japan Department Stores Association, annual sales in 2021 increased 5.8% (4,418.2 billion yen), the first year-on-year increase in four years, but annual sales fell 21.5% compared to 2019, the year before the corona disaster, and inbound sales, which had supported department store performance, declined 86.7% [1]. In 2021, the number of shopping center openings will be 24, the smallest ever, and the number of openings is declining, stores, especially clothing and restaurants, is declining due to sluggish sales and business restrictions [2]. In addition, the size of the BtoC EC market in the field of goods sales has been increasing year after year, influenced by

A. Coman and S. Vasilache (Eds.): HCII 2023, LNCS 14025, pp. 567–580, 2023.
https://doi.org/10.1007/978-3-031-35915-6_41

nest egg demand, and the market is expected to continue to expand in the future [3]. As described above, consumers purchasing behavior has changed significantly after the corona disaster, and it is necessary to consider measures unique to brick-and-mortar stores that are in line with consumer behavior.

Although the use of e-commerce has increased due to the impact of the voluntary curfew due to the spread of the new coronavirus, a consumer trend survey conducted in 2021 revealed some surprising results. First, a survey conducted under the theme of How do you choose between real stores and online stores? [4], the most consumers in all categories of products purchased their purchases mainly in physical stores, mainly online, and half in physical stores and half online, especially in the category of clothing and fashion accessories, which is a key item in department stores. The percentage of respondents who purchase clothing and fashion accessories, which are the key items in department stores, was very high at 46.5%. As for the reason for purchasing clothing and fashion accessories in actual stores, 56.8% of the respondents chose to see the product in person, followed by to see the entire product on the display shelf (27.2%). The Retail DX Survey [5], which conducted a survey of the actual situation of consumers in the corona disaster, revealed that reasons for returning to actual stores (department stores) after the corona convergence include to enjoy the world view and atmosphere of the store and to expect new encounters with various products as the experience value sought. The results revealed that the respondents wanted to enjoy the world view and atmosphere of the store and to have new encounters with various products.

From these consumer trend surveys, it seems that what consumers who have experienced the corona disaster seek from actual stores are certainty and unexpectedness through the experience of picking up and touching actual products. The former is an experience value that consumers have been seeking for a long time: I want to see the actual product and buy it, while the latter is an experience value unique to actual stores, such as a place as an experience and an encounter with a new product. The insights of consumers in actual stores can be further explored by investigating their actual store usage and purchasing behavior, and practical implications can be obtained. For this purpose, it is necessary to investigate how consumers use and search for products in department stores and shopping centers, and to gain insight into the process leading up to purchase (experience value). Based on these results, quantitative analysis and consideration of stores that are easy to stop by and easy to purchase and the relationships among stores will enable us to propose measures for shopping centers and department stores as a whole.

In this study, we investigate consumers migratory behavior in department stores, and propose marketing measures that are unique to actual stores based on consumer behavior using the collected data. Specifically, we use an eye tracking device to collect a series of data on the flow of consumers in a department store from entry to exit. Using the collected data, we evaluate the changes in migratory behavior before and after the remodeling using social network analysis (SNA) techniques.

2 Previous Study

In recent years, it has become possible to obtain highly accurate data on consumer flow lines by using IT devices such as RFID technology and GPS devices in flow line research. The research by Miyazaki [6] uses RFID technology attempted to visualize migratory behavior by attaching IC tags to shopping carts in supermarkets and identifying the in-store flow lines based on the probability density of customer present lotation and the vector field. The results showed that the locations with high probability density of customer presence in a store are important locations for sales promotion because they are relatively long-stayed, and that the understanding of flow lines by vector fields helps to determine the direction of POP displays and the location of digital signage. Moreover, it was clarified that visualization of consumer flow lines is useful for architectural planning and marketing strategies. Another study using GPS technology is that of Nagai et al. [7]. They conducted a GPS survey of actual consumers in an urban outlet mall and examined the relationship between behavioral characteristics such as migratory behavior distance, range of behavior, and tendency to stop and shop. The results showed that neither purchase amount nor unplanned purchases were significantly correlated with the length of the flow line, but there was a significant negative correlation between the length of the flow line and the intention to reuse. It remains to be examined the specific behavioral characteristics of consumers considering the shape of the mall and the relationship between stores. There are still few examples of traffic flow studies targeting such commercial complexes.

There have been attempts to clarify the structural relationships among actors in real space using SNA methods. Matsumura et al. [8]. The results of degree centrality and flow centrality suggest that core stores such as supermarkets and drugstores have a strong ability to attract customers, while small and medium-sized stores such as retailers selling clothing and food have a role in encouraging visitors to move between stores. This study points out that while the structured method based on SNA is effective as an approach to revitalizing shopping areas, it has limitations when referring to stores with a low number of visitors. In this study, SNA is also used to verify the importance of each store in a department store and the ties between stores, with the aim of obtaining suggestions for practical application.

3 Experiments on Flow Line Observation

The flow line observation experiment in this study was conducted in a large multi-story department store located in the center of Tokyo. The experiment was conducted over three days on October 4, 5, and 8, 2022, using an eye tracking device to observe the subjects viewpoints and extract flow line data.

3.1 Department Stores Included in the Experiment

The department store in the experiment consists on 11 floors from B2 to 8F, where various categories of stores such as fashion, sundries, and food stores are located. Since the 7th and 8th floors are restaurant floors, they were excluded from this experiment, which focused on the subjects migratory behavior, and the floors from B2 to 6F were used for analysis. Table 1 shows a list of the product categories offered in the stores on the target floors.

Table 1. List of product categories

Product Categories			
fashion	womens fashion	mens fashion	shoes
womens shoes	bag	accessory	glass
hat	watch	innerwear	lingerie
socks	suit	kimono	contact
wig	sundries	cosmetics	perfume
art supplies	sweets	ticket	event space

3.2 Experimental Equipment and Software

In this experiment, we asked subjects to wear Tobii Pro Glasses2 (Fig. 1: left) [9] and Tobii Pro Glasses3 (Fig. 1: right) [10], eye tracking devices manufactured by Tobii, to observe their viewpoints. The devices were portable, allowing the subjects to walk freely around the museum while wearing them, and to collect gaze data that they were looking. The recorded data obtained from the point-of-view observations can be used with Tobii Pro Lab [11], a dedicated analysis software program, to extract motion-line data.

Fig. 1. Tobii Pro Glasses2 (left), Tobii Pro Glasses3 (right) from https://www.tobii.com/products/eye-trackers/wearables/tobii-pro-glasses-2, https://www.tobii.com/products/eye-trackers/wearables/tobii-pro-glasses-3.

3.3 Experimental Procedure

Since women are the main target of the experimental stores, subjects were recruited so that more than half of them were women. A total of 63 subjects (32 female and 31 male) participated in the experiment, and data were collected on 38 of them. Of the 36 valid pairs of subjects used in the analysis, 13 were alone, 9 were female participants,

8 were male participants, 5 were male-female participants, and 1 was a total of three participants, one female and two males. In order to reproduce the same situation as in everyday shopping, the subjects were asked to shop freely by themselves or in pairs (one of them wearing a device), taking into account their intentions. The duration of the experiment was one hour for each pair, and the subjects were allowed to purchase items. Since the participants were wearing eye tracking devices, they were not allowed to use the fitting rooms. To prevent the experiment staff from losing track of the subjects, the use of elevators was prohibited, and only escalators and stairs were allowed to move around the floor. On the day of the experiment, we conducted the following steps 1 through 8 for each subject.

1. Subjects were asked to gather at a rented space near the experimental store.
2. At the reception desk, the outline of the experiment is explained, and the subjects are asked to fill out a consent form, a receipt, and a preliminary questionnaire, and are given an honorarium.
3. The subject is asked to wear the eye tracking device and calibrate it (correction of the gazing point).
4. The experimental staff guides the subject to the experimental store.
5. After arriving at the experimental site, the staff will confirm the precautions again.
6. The experiment begins, and the subjects are free to shop around in the experimental store.
7. After the experiment, the eye tracking device is collected and the subjects are asked to fill out a questionnaire after the experiment.
8. The experiment staff returns to the rental space and backs up the recorded data stored in the collected eye tracking device.

3.4 Experimental Equipment and Software

In this study, we used the viewpoint observation data obtained from the experiment to extract the flow line data for each subject. As a condition for extraction, this study defined store entry and exit in a department store as follows.

- A store is entered when the user stops in front of the store and gazes at the products, or when the floor tiles change to an aisle.
- A store exit is defined as the time when the visitor's gaze is removed from the product or when the floor tiles change from the inside of the store to the aisle.

Based on the above definitions, we used Tobii Pro Lab, a dedicated analysis software program, to flag subjects as they entered or left a store, and to extract data on the time spent by each subject and on their movement between stores. Figure 2 shows the Tobii Pro Lab data.

Fig. 2. Screenshot of Data Extraction with Tobii Pro Lab.

4 Dataset

In this study, we extracted data on subjects flow line data between stores in a department store from the recorded data collected by an eye tracking device. We created a node list representing the stores where they stayed and an edge list representing their movement lines between stores.

4.1 Node List - Stores Stayed

The stores where the subjects stayed are represented as a node list consisting of store IDs, store names, and store floors (Table 2).

Table 2. Example of Node List

Store ID	Store Name	Floor
1F_01	Store A	1F
1F_02	Store B	1F
1F_03	Store C	1F

4.2 Edge Listings - Store-to-Store Flow Line

The subjects movement between stores is represented as an edge list, consisting of the store ID before the move (from) and the store ID at the destination (to) (Table 3). Here,

Table 3. Example of Edge List

From	To	Weight
1F_01	1F_02	1
1F_02	1F_03	1
1F_03	1F_04	1

the number of moves is given as a weight for each from-to record that represents a move between stores.

In this study, we conduct SNA using these node and edge lists. From the result of SNA, we evaluate the changes in the behavior before and after the remodeling.

5 Centrality Indicators

SNA is performed using network objects created from the aforementioned dataset. In this study, the network was constructed by considering nodes as stores and edges as the number of movement between stores, and analyzed using two types of centrality indices: degree centrality and betweenness centrality.

5.1 Degree Centrality

Degree centrality is an index that evaluates the importance of a node based on the number of relations(edges) connecting nodes. Let $A = (a_{ij})$ be the adjacency matrix of a graph, and $C_d\ (i)$, the total degree of the input degree $C_{id}\ (i)$ and the output degree $C_{od}\ (i)$ of node i, is formulated as follows [12].

$$C_d(i) = C_{id}(i) + C_{od}(i) = \sum_{j=1}^{n} a_{ji} + \sum_{j=1}^{n} a_{ij}$$

In the SNA using order centrality, the order centrality of each node was calculated for each group and reflected in the size of the node in order to compare before and after the renovation. The number of moves between stores is reflected in the thickness of the edges.

5.2 Betweenness Centrality

Betweenness centrality is an index of the degree to which a node is the shortest path for another node. The standardize betweenness centrality of a node v in a graph is formulated as follows [13].

$$C_b(v) = \frac{1}{(n-1)(n-2)} \sum_{v \neq i \neq j} \frac{g_{ij}(v)}{g_{ij}}$$

The standardized edge-betweenness centrality of an edge e in a graph is then formulated as follows [13].

$$C_b(e) = \frac{1}{n(n-1)} \sum_{e \neq i \neq j} \frac{g_{ij}(e)}{g_{ij}}$$

Here, n is the number of nodes in the graph and g_{ij} is the number of shortest paths between nodes i and j, $g_{ij}(v)$ is the number of shortest paths between nodes i and j that pass through node v and $g_{ij}(e)$ is the number of paths that pass through edge e.

SNA using betweenness centrality reflects betweenness centrality in the size of nodes and edge-betweenness centrality in the thickness of edges.

6 Result and Discussion

6.1 Evaluation of Consumer Behavior Before and After Renovation

A comparison of the networks before and after the remodeling is conducted to examine consumers migratory behavior in department stores. A summary of the networks is shown in Table 1. Figures 3 and 4 show the results of the SNA of degree centrality, and Figs. 5 and 6 show the results of the SNA of betweenness centrality. The top 10 stores in terms of degree centrality and betweenness centrality are shown in Tables 5 through 8. Fruchterman Reingold, a force-directed algorithm, was used to draw the networks in this analysis.

Table 4. Overview of network graphs

Group	Number of subjects	Number of nodes	Average number of moves
Before renovation	20	93	21.8
After renovation	36	91	13.9

From Fig. 3, 4 and Table 5, 6, a network comparison of degree centrality before and after the renovation, we infer the following.

- Before the renovation, the node sizes were particularly large on the 2nd, 5th, and 6th floors, whereas after the renovation, the node sizes are relatively even from the 1st to 6th floors, although there is some variation.
- Both before and after the renovation, the node sizes of the stores on the lower floors, such as B1F and B2F, are very small.
- Before the renovation, the nodes were accessory T (2F accessories), sundries B (5F furniture and interior goods), cosmetics R (5F cosmetics), and sundries S (5F sundries), after the renovation, sundries P (M2F sundries), sundries FF (sundries), and so on were commonly located in the same area. The node sizes of stores handling

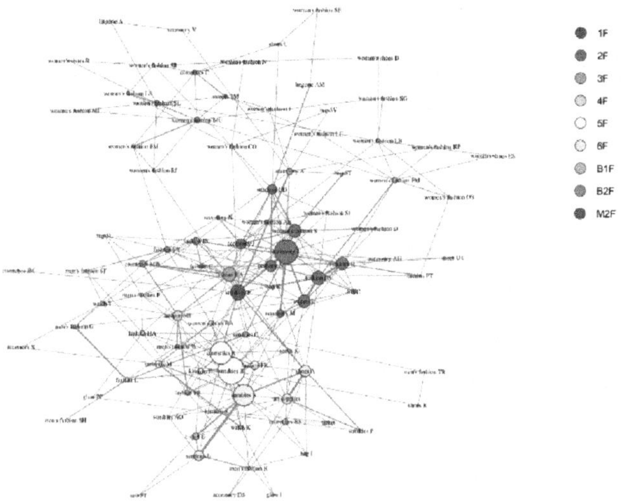

Fig. 3. SNA Results before Renovation - Degree Centrality

Table 5. Degree Centrality before renovation

Floor	Shop	Degree centrality
5F	sundries B	0.113
2F	accessory T	0.099
5F	cosmetics R	0.092
6F	sundries S	0.087
M2F	sundries P	0.062
3F	fashion UA	0.057
2F	fashion FS	0.055
2F	womens fashion S	0.053
2F	sundries H	0.051
2F	sweets L	0.051

cosmetics and accessories are large, and the edges connecting them to other stores are thick.

The following were inferred from Figs. 5 and 6 and Tables 7 and 8 as network comparisons of mediating centrality.

- While before the renovation, stores were scattered throughout many floors, after the remodeling, stores with high centrality tended to be concentrated.

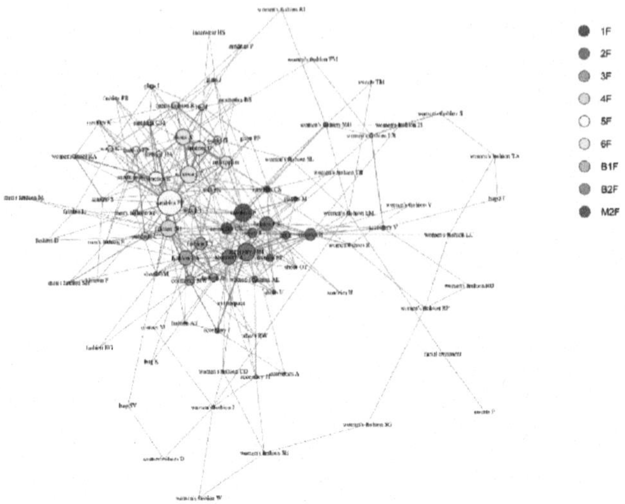

Fig. 4. SNA Results after Renovation - Degree Centrality

Table 6. Degree Centrality after renovation

Floor	Shop	Degree centrality
5F	sundries FF	0.104
M2F	sundries P	0.072
2F	accessory MM	0.072
6F	accessory T	0.070
4F	fashion SH	0.068
6F	shoes A	0.064
2F	accessory A	0.060
3F	fashion UA	0.060
5F	cosmetics R	0.058
6F	sundries U	0.056

- After the renovation, sundries P (M2F general merchandise), sundries FF (5F general merchandise), cosmetics CK (1F cosmetics), and sundries H (2F accessories) have particularly large node sizes and play an important role as relay points.

These results suggest that subjects stopped by stores on more floors after the renovation compared to before the renovation, and that the range of subjects circulation has expanded. In addition, stores that serve as relay points are concentrated, and stores on the first floor, which were hardly noticeable before the remodeling, are highly evaluated, indicating that the frontage of the pavilion itself has expanded. In common, the centrality of stores selling sundries and accessories is high for all indicators, and these stores are

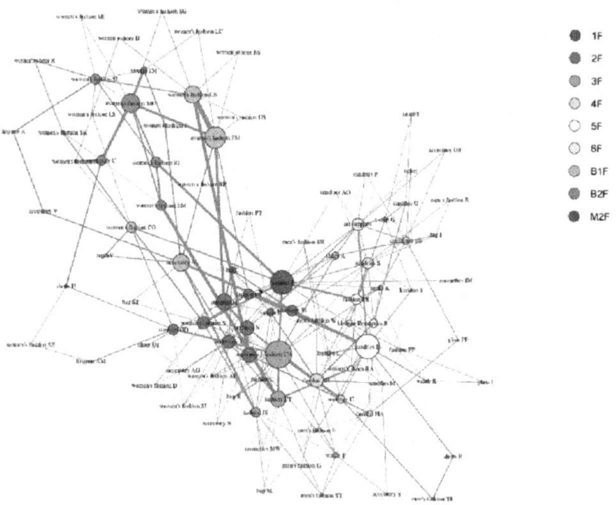

Fig. 5. SNA Results before Renovation - Betweenness Centrality

Table 7. Betweenness Centrality before renovation

Floor	Shop	Between centrality
3F	fashion UA	0.112
5F	sundries B	0.100
M2F	sundries P	0.097
B1F	womens fashion FM	0.088
B2F	womens fashion MU	0.079
B1F	womens fashion LB	0.072
B1F	accessory A	0.071
2F	sundries H	0.067
3F	fashion UT	0.065
2F	accessory J	0.060

strongly connected to each other, while the number of drop-ins at stores on the lower floors is low. Table 4 shows that while there is no significant difference in the number of nodes representing the number of stores visited, the number of times subjects moved between stores decreased, suggesting that the time spent in each store increased and that the importance of each store increased.

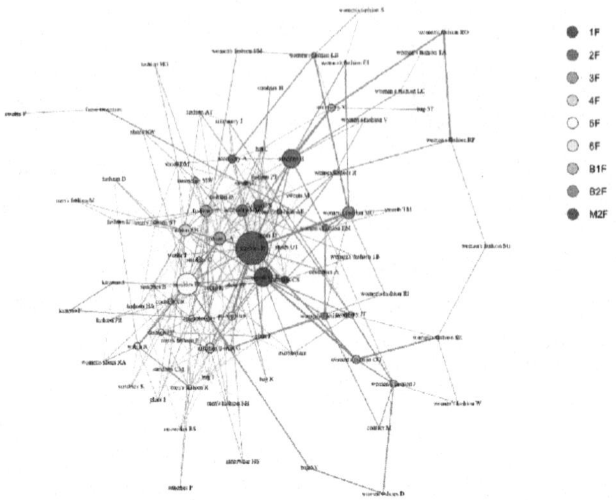

Fig. 6. SNA Results after Renovation - Betweenness Centrality

Table 8. Betweenness Centrality after renovation

Floor	Shop	Between centrality
M2F	sundries P	0.136
5F	sundries FF	0.090
1F	cosmetics CK	0.078
2F	sundries H	0.076
B2F	womens fashion MU	0.051
3F	fashion UA	0.051
4F	fashion SH	0.048
2F	accessory MM	0.048
3F	fashion UT	0.047
2F	fashion FS	0.046

6.2 Store Evaluation Based on Centrality Index

The results of the analysis and discussion focused on stores on the 2nd, 5th, and 6th floors, which were the floors where people were most likely to stop by and stay, and the following characteristics were observed.

- Stores selling sundries, accessories, and cosmetics can be key stores on a floor, making it easy for people to stop by and stay.
- These key stores also tend to play an important role as relay points between stores.

- Compared to other floors, many of the stores on this floor sell a various of product categories, such as sundries, accessories, and cosmetics.

Based on the above, and taking into consideration the fact that the main target of the experimental store is women, it is considered important to construct a layout that encourages customers to stay and purchase by placing sundries, accessories, and cosmetics stores, which play a role as relay points, on each floor in more conspicuous locations. It is considered important to construct a layout that encourages customers to stay and purchase. In other words, the placement of sundries, accessories, and cosmetics stores as relay points is an effective measure to increase the number of connections between stores and to construct a floor that encourages people to stop by the stores. Furthermore, the fact that the cosmetics store on the first floor after renovation serves as a relay point, making it a grand floor that expands the frontage of the building itself, suggests the importance of such key stores.

7 Conclusion

In this study, we conducted a flow line observation experiment in a Fashion department store using an eye tracking device, and evaluated consumers migratory behavior. Specifically, we visualized consumer flow lines using a SNA technique and compared migratory behavior before and after remodeling to capture a store structure that encourages people to stop by and stay. The results of the analysis and discussion suggest that sundries, accessories, and cosmetics stores play the role of key stores on the floor that induce people to stop by the stores. This study evaluated consumer migratory behavior before and after the renovation, but this study only confirmed migratory behavior between stores within the building, and did not address detailed product-seeking behavior such as in-store circulation and approaches to products. Therefore, a more detailed analysis focusing on specific stores is needed. This is an issue to be addressed in the future. Furthermore, the findings obtained in this study cannot be easily generalized to other shopping centers and department stores. Therefore, repeated experiments in various types of stores other than the department stores that are the subject of this study and the accumulation of findings provide a means of proposing optimal marketing measures suited to each type of store.

Acknowledgment. We thank the department stores for their cooperation in the experiment. This work was supported by JSPS KAKENHI Grant Number 21H04600 and 21K13385.

References

1. Ministry of Economy, Trade and Industry (METI), Market Research on Electronic Commerce, April 2021. https://www.meti.go.jp/press/2022/08/20220812005/20220812005-h.pdf. Accessed 05 Feb 2023
2. Japan Department Store Association (JDSA), Summary of Department Store Sales in Japan, December 2021. https://www.depart.or.jp/store_sale/files/202112zenkokup.pdf. Accessed 05 Feb 2023

3. Japan Department Store Association (JDSA), Summary of Department Store Sales in Japan, December 2019
4. https://www.depart.or.jp/store_sale/files/a2933dfa6818c84fd76e1fc5e03b216f1480e6cb.pdf. Accessed 05 Feb 2023
5. PR TIMES, Inc., How do you choose between real stores and online stores?, October 2021. https://prtimes.jp/main/html/rd/p/000000240.000003149.html. Accessed 05 Feb 2023
6. Dentsu Digital Inc., Retail DX Survey (2021, 6 business categories), December 2021. https://www.dentsudigital.co.jp/news/release/services/2021-1202-001123. Accessed 05 Feb 2023
7. Miyazaki, S.: Visualization of customer shopping-path using RFID techniques. AIJ J. Technol. Des. **18**(40), 1033–1037 (2012)
8. Nagai, R., Onzo, N., Oshima, T.: Consumers shopping around behavior and emotions: through a GPS survey at Minami-Machida granberry mall. Japan Mark. J. **35**(4), 90–104 (2016)
9. Matsumura, N., Miyake, N.: The Study of the Relations Between the Shopping District Stores by the Visitor's Action, Civil Engineering Society Proceedings D3, vol. 68, no. 5, pp. I_445-I_452 (2012)
10. Tobii Pro Glasses 2. https://www.tobiipro.com/product-listing/tobii-pro-glasses-2/. Accessed 05 Feb 2023
11. Tobii Pro Glasses 3. https://www.tobiipro.com/product-listing/tobii-pro-glasses-3/. Accessed 05 Feb 2023
12. Tobii Pro Lab. https://www.tobiipro.com/product-listing/tobii-pro-lab/. Accessed 05 Feb 2023
13. Suzuki T., Data Science in R 8: Network Analysis, 2nd Edition, Kyoritsu Publishing, pp. 2–71 (2017)
14. Brandes, U.: On variants of shortest-path betweenness centrality and their generic computation. Soc. Netw. **30**(2), 136–145 (2008)

Customer Review Classification Using Machine Learning and Deep Learning Techniques

Nikhil Sunil and Farid Shirazi(✉)

Toronto Metropolitan University, Toronto, Canada
{nikhil.sunil,f2shiraz}@ryerson.ca

Abstract. The online e-commerce industry has become very competitive today and continues to increase. Companies generate a lot of data that contain customer feedback data like reviews about their products and services. In addition, online customer reviews play a significant role in helping the company improve its sales and increase its customer base.

Customer reviews are feedback given to businesses and Retailers based on the customer's experience with their organization. Companies use them to improve upon their existing service or the product they are selling. For example, in an e-commerce-driven world, where people have no physical access to the goods they wish to purchase, many customers will turn to online reviews to get an opinion on what to buy.

E-commerce is changing how people buy products and services. For example, many businesses look at past data to increase customer count. In this context, companies can use customer reviews on their products to promote their high sales and gain a competitive edge in the market. This paper focuses on classifying the sentiment of customer reviews using machine learning approaches. The models are evaluated using various metrics like confusion matrix, AUROC curve, and classification report.

Keywords: Text Classification · Logistic Regression · AdaBoost · Decision Tree · Random Forest · LSTM · Bi- LSTM · GRU

1 Introduction

The online e-commerce industry has become very competitive today, and it continues to increase. Companies generate a lot of data that contain customer feedback data like reviews about their products and services. In addition, online customer reviews play a significant role in helping the company improve its sales and increase its customer base.

Customer reviews are feedback given to businesses and Retailers based on the customer's experience with their organization. Companies use them to improve upon their existing service or the product they are selling.

In an e-commerce-driven world, where people have no physical access to the goods they wish to purchase, many customers will turn to online reviews to get an opinion on what to buy.

A. Coman and S. Vasilache (Eds.): HCII 2023, LNCS 14025, pp. 581–597, 2023.
https://doi.org/10.1007/978-3-031-35915-6_42

E-commerce is changing how people buy products and services. To move up in the corporate world, many businesses are finding ways to increase their customer count by looking at past data. For example, companies can use customer reviews on their products to promote their high sales and gain a competitive edge in the market. This paper focuses on classifying the sentiment of customer reviews using modeling techniques, and the results vary with each method.

We first start by briefly explaining the dataset, defining the research question, and then the literature review and an exploratory data analysis to gain insights into the data.

The methodology section talks about the experimental design, i.e., how the data is processed before they are used to train the models for classification. We then review the modeling results and compare them with appropriate metrics to select the best-performing model.

Our primary research questions include the following:

RQ1: What patterns may help analyze the company's clothing sales performance in each department and customer ratings on those products?

RQ2: What is the best method for correctly selecting the best-performing classifier using machine learning and deep learning?

To do so, we take different customer reviews on women's clothing and classify them as good or bad, which can help decide whether the product/service is doing well in the market. To achieve this, we will use various classification models in deep learning and machine learning to classify the customer reviews and compare their accuracies and other parameters to decide which model best fits this task. The machine learning models proposed here are Logistic Regression, AdaBoost, Decision Tree, Support Vector Machine, Random Forest, and deep learning models like LSTM, Bi-LSTM, and GRU.

The models are evaluated using various metrics like confusion matrix, AUROC curve, and classification report.

2 Related Works

To better understand customer reviews, we started by reviewing articles on online reviews' impact on the market. A 2019 paper on the impact of online consumer reviews on hotel Booking explained the influence that reviews have on the decision of customers. They explained that online reviews are like an 'electronic word of mouth' that has changed how people buy stuff with more internet usage. Customers are more inclined to purchase products if the advertisements and reviews are realistic. The paper has stressed that businesses need to understand the importance of online reviews and use them to devise strategies, to improve sales [1]. Another article in 2020 on Sentiment Analysis on an e-commerce product, using an Indonesian dataset, explained how different techniques in machine learning could be used to classify reviews. The paper concluded that the best accuracy was achieved by applying the TF-IDF and Backward Elimination in SVM, which performed well with a score of 85.97%, which goes up by 7.91% after using feature selection [2]. Iqbal et al. [3] conducted a sentimental analysis on a SNAP dataset containing Amazon reviews. This paper aimed to use a popular machine learning algorithms such as Multinomial Naive Bayes (MNB), Support Vector Machine (SVM), and deep learning based long short-term memory (LSTM). Their experiments concluded that LSTM classifiers performed better than other algorithms, making them suitable for classifying large data [3]. Another paper talks about a proposed amazon web analysis app that uses ML models to classify reviews as negative or positive different models were used in combination with different feature extraction methods, which were tested on data from the dataset. The researchers concluded from their experiments that the logistic regression model, combined with the count vectorizer, gave the best performance with an accuracy of 0.9339 [4].

Two papers on Exploratory and Sentiment Analysis on Netflix data [18] give a detailed overview of how to review data from Netflix is used to get insights and also perform sentiment analysis on them. This 2021 paper on the study of covid-19 tweets using sentimental analysis aims to analyze tweets by Indians during the Covid-19 lockdown. The text from the tweets has been put into four categories: fear, sadness, anger, and joy. Data analysis was conducted using four models (Bert, Logistic Regression, Support Vector Machine, and LSTM) to predict the sentiment of these tweets. The Bert Model surpassed the other models in terms of performance (89%). The researchers concluded that the government needs to perform fact-checks to avoid spreading false information. Using the findings from this research, public authorities can work to overcome needless anxiety during pandemics [5]. The paper 'Determinant Factors of E-commerce Adoption by SMEs in Developing Country' investigates factors influencing SMEs in developing countries to adopt e-commerce. In this study, 11 variables, namely, perceived benefits, compatibility, cost, technology readiness, Firm size, Customers/suppliers pressure, competitor pressure, external support, Innovativeness, IT ability, IT experience, were studied to see if they are relevant to an SME's success in business. Finally, they were grouped into four groups: technological contexts, organizational contexts, environmental contexts, and individual contexts, which were identified as factors that affect the Indonesian SMEs in their adoption of E-commerce. The paper concludes that various factors like technology readiness, innovative ability, IT experience, and IT ability are substantial to the success of SMEs in developing countries like Indonesia [6]. This paper briefly talks about the various methods for sentiment analysis on tweets to give us a good overview of the field. The article covers topics like sentiment monitoring, Twitter opinion retrieval over time, emotion recognition, irony recognition, and other issues related to sentiment analysis. It also discusses using supervised learning techniques like Maximum Entropy, Support Vector Machines, Random Forest, Naive Bayes, Logistic Regression, and Conditional Random Field [7].

Twitter is a platform that is widely used by people all over the world. Twitter data(tweets) is widely used to analyze the sentiments of various tweets. The paper on the study of Twitter sentimental analysis gives an excellent overview of how tweets are collected and processed before they're used with machine learning models for feeding data to train them [19]. Another 2016 paper on "Techniques for Sentiment Analysis of Twitter" discusses the different techniques used to conduct sentiment analysis on Twitter data. The fundamental methods to prepare the data are as follow. Firstly, the collected data is pre-processed to remove noise. After this, we extract essential features from the data. The data is then labeled as positive or negative to prepare the dataset, which goes as input to the model classifier for training. A small part of the dataset is kept aside for testing purposes. The writers also applied supervised machine learning based on identified parameters [10]. This paper implemented a sentiment classification approach using deep learning algorithms such as LSMT and CNN and hybrid CNN and LSTM models to predict the sentiment of reviews. Deep learning networks like CNN, LSTM, and other hybrid models of CNN and LSTM were applied to data from the IMDB dataset. The results have shown that the hybrid CNN_LSTM model has outperformed the MLP and singular CNN and LSTM networks with a high accuracy rate of 89.2% [8]. Another paper on movie review classification by [17] focused on using feature-based opinion mining, speech tagging, and supervised machine learning techniques to perform sentiment analysis of movie reviews [17]. The 2020 paper on Sentiment Analysis in E-Commerce-review of methods and algorithms tackles a comprehensive overview of sentiment analysis and relevant techniques in the e-commerce industry that is always keen to find out about the consumers' opinions of their goods and services. The writers talk about how companies nowadays use social media to analyze sentiments to find various trends to achieve business value, such as customer satisfaction and reputation while attaining high revenue and revenue. One of the challenges with sentiment analysis is that sometimes, exaggeration by users in reviews cannot be easily picked by the models, and they tend to classify them in one way. In reality, the sentiment is the opposite [9].

To explore other sentiment analysis methods, I came across a technique known as Lexicon Sentimental analysis used by companies, which is another helpful way of classifying the sentiment. This method uses a predefined list of words, where each word is associated with a particular sentiment [11]. The paper on "Lexicon-based methods for Sentiment Analysis" by [12] proposed the Semantic Orientation Calculator to extract sentiment from text using dictionaries of words annotated with polarity and strength. The strength/intensity of sentiment word groups in a dictionary can be expressed as a number [12]. Another 2016 paper on lexicon feature extraction for emotion text classification presented a unigram mixture model (UMM) based DSEL through the usage of labeled & weakly-labeled emotion text to get essential features for emotion classification [13]. A 2016 paper on Lexicon-enhanced Sentiment Analysis using rule-based classification came up with the idea to combine emoticons, modifiers, and domain-specific terms to find some trends in the reviews posted in online communities [14]. A 2001 paper on Sentiment parsing from small talk on the Web, written by [15], proposes a technology for extracting investor sentiment from web sources. The method uses different classification algorithms for analyzing the sentiment of any message posted on the chat board [15].

The 2018 paper on Sentiment Analysis for Election Results followed a step-by-step approach to data collection, pre-processing of data, and machine learning analysis to predict the result of the 2020 US presidential Election using Twitter emotional analysis. They use a random forest classifier to predict users' sentiments from tweets. They achieved an accuracy of 83.22% with trump's tweets and 85.73% with Biden's tweets [16].

3 Exploratory Data and Analysis

The selected dataset[1] contains reviews written by customers purchasing a different type of clothing. It has nine important features and will instantiate a perfect way to classify the reviews for further analysis. The data has been anonymized, and credit has been given to the company since the data is commercial. The reference to the company in the review text and body has been replaced with the 'retailer.'

This dataset has 23486 rows and ten feature variables. Each row corresponds to a customer Review and includes the variables. As the data is filled with noise, I will perform intensive data cleaning to filter out the unwanted data to make it ready for model testing.

Below are the features of the dataset:

Clothing ID: reference for the clothing being reviewed (categorical variable).

- **Age:** variable depicting the reviewer's age(Positive Integer variable).
- **Title:** the heading sentence for the review (String variable).
- **Review Text:** a review of the customer (String variable).
- **Rating:** rating score on a scale of 1(worst) to 5(best) (Positive Ordinal Integer variable)
- **Recommended IND:** customer recommendation of a product between 1 and 0.(Binary variable) 1- recommended, 0- not recommended
- **Positive Feedback Count:** keeps count of the customers that found this review to be helpful
- **Division Name:** Description of the high-level product division (Categorical variable).
- **Department Name:** product dept name (Categorical variable).
- **Class Name:** product class name (Categorical variable).

The data is first loaded from the.csv file into a dataframe using the pandas' library. Then, before we perform EDA, we do some data cleaning by removing duplicate and null values from the dataframe.

4 Customer Analysis

a. The proportion of customer recommendations.

To get an idea about how the customers are giving recommendations, Fig. 1 shows that more than 80% of the customers are satisfied and have highly recommended the products they have purchased.

While training our model, the proportion of 1(recommended) to 0 (non-recommended) must be very high. According to [21], many machine learning models, like logistic regression, face performance issues whenever the ratio difference between the number of data points is imbalanced. To resolve this, we go with the upscaling process to balance the data.

After upscaling, the data appears well-balanced, as seen in Fig. 2.

[1] The link to dataset is: https://www.kaggle.com/datasets/nicapotato/womens-ecommerce-clothing-reviews.

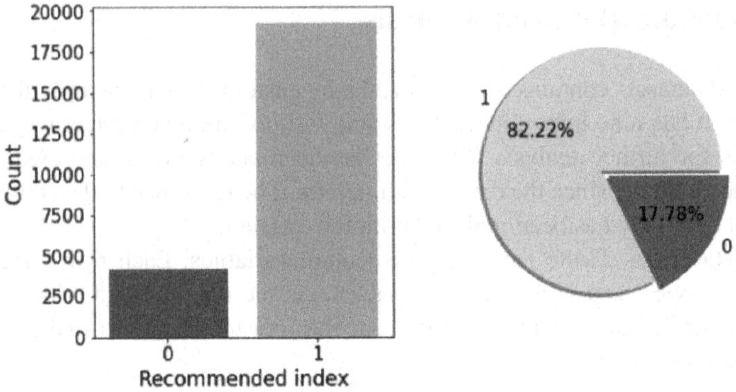

Fig. 1. Proportion of customer recommendations before upscaling

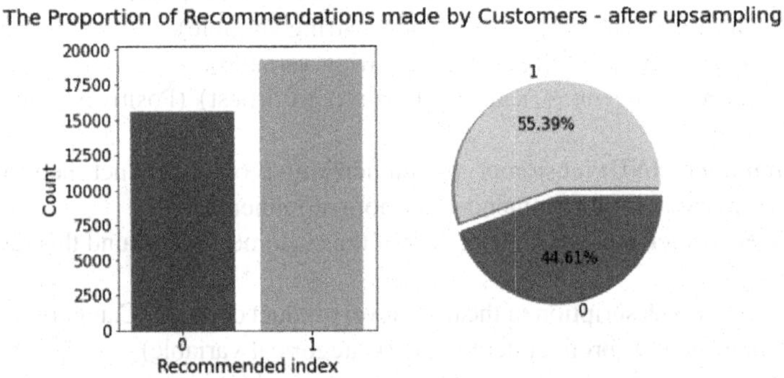

Fig. 2. Proportion of customer recommendations after upscaling

b. The proportion of customer Ratings on all products.

Ratings provided by customers play a significant role in predicting customers' sentiments. Based on this info, companies can offer their customers reasonable offers and discounts to promote more sales.

In the donut chart in Fig. 3, more than 50% of the customers have given a 5-star rating for all the products, up to 35% of the customers have given 3 and 4-star ratings, while the remaining 10% have given a lower rating.

c. Age distribution of customers.

From the graphs in Fig. 4, we can identify the age group of the company's customers. A higher concentration of customers is between the age group of 30 and 50. As the age value increases, the customer count keeps declining.

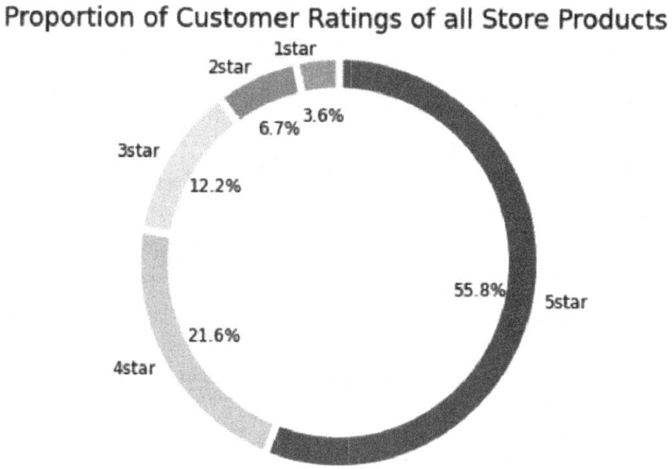

Fig. 3. Proportion of customer ratings on all store-bought products

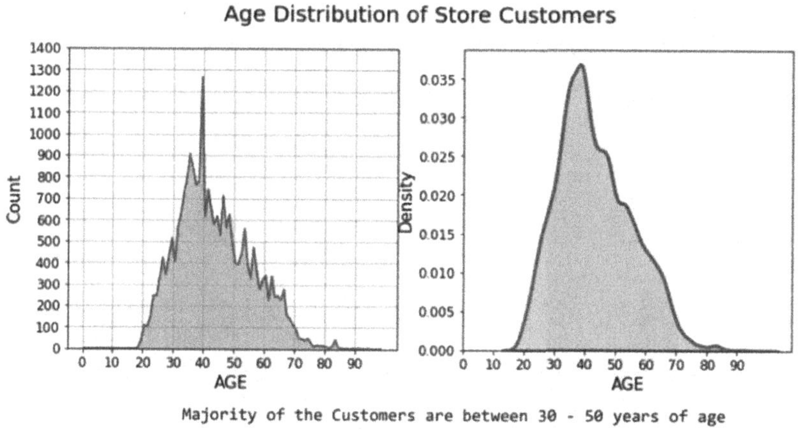

Fig. 4. Age group of customers making purchases

4.1 Product Trend Analysis

a. Products purchased from each department.

The clothing store has three departments- namely, the general department, the Intimate clothing department, and the General petite department. According to the pie chart in Fig. 5, almost 60% of the store purchases have been made from the general department, making it the popular choice among the customers. The general petite department comes second in clothes sold with a customer base of almost 35%, while the intimate department sells under 7%.

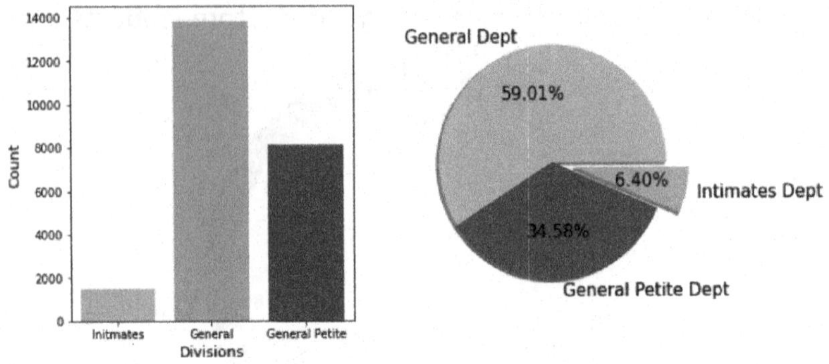

Fig. 5. Proportion of purchases made in each product division in the store

b. Popular choice of clothing among the customers.

As shown in Fig. 6, clothing like Tops and Dresses are the top choices among customers, with just 70% of clothes sales. Very few customers have opted to buy Trendy clothes and jackets, making them the least sought-out clothes at just under 7%. Intimate clothing and Bottoms make up about 25% of the total store sales.

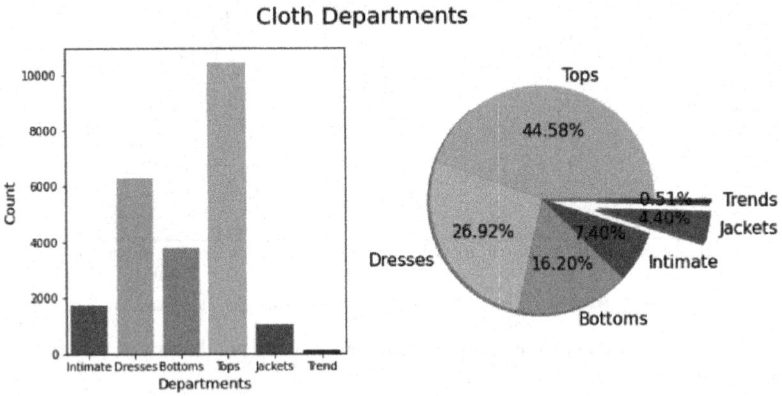

Fig. 6. Different types of clothes purchased by customers

c. Clothing recommendations made by customers.

As shown in Fig. 7, it is confirmed that almost all of the products have been highly recommended by customers between the age of 20 and 70; the scatterplot shows a high concentration of 1's(good) and a lower amount of 0's (bad).

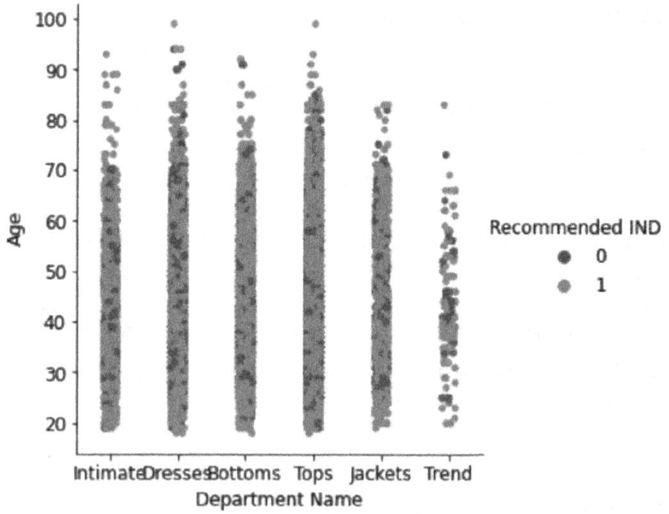

Fig. 7. Recommendations made by the customer of different age groups on different clothing

d. Ratings vs. Recommendations.

As depicted in Fig. 8, ratings 4 and 5 have been highly recommended, while products of ratings 1–3 have comparatively lower positive recommendations. This plot shows us the relationship between the ratings and the recommendation data.

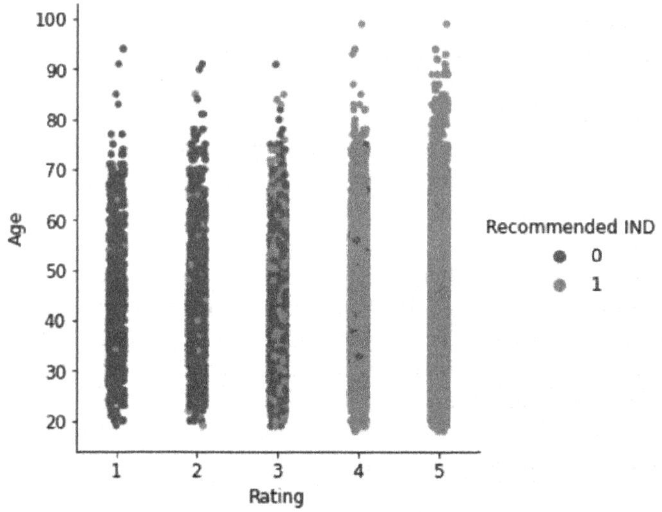

Fig. 8. Ratings vs. Recommended ID

5 Methodology and Experiments

As mentioned before, the study aims to perform sentiment analysis to predict whether the product is recommended by the customer based on the reviews. To find out the prediction, five machine learning models and three deep learning models were trained, tested, and compared to determine the best fit for this process. These methods include Logistic regression, Linear Support Vector Machine, Decision Tree, Random Forest, AdaBoost, Long short-term memory(LSTM), Bidirectional LSTM, and Gated Recurrent Unit (GRU).

Also, as mentioned before, the dataset has 23,486 rows and ten columns. It is based on the e-commerce marketplace that contains reviews written by the customers and is supported by nine other extra features that give us a little more insight into the pattern of reviews. Before the text processing, we removed missing and null values from the dataset using the dropna() function.

5.1 Text Processing

To remove unnecessary symbols and other noise in the reviews, we need to perform the following techniques to attain the best model performance.

- **Removing Punctuations**: Characters that exist in the text apart from alphabets and whitespaces are removed. The "n't" in words like "wouldn't" are also removed. We use the regex function substitute(re.sub) to remove the punctuation marks from the comments.
- **Tokenization**- It is the process of splitting a large text sample into several words or substrings. This is a common practice in Natural Language processing for classifying a particular sentiment.
- **Removing numbers**- We use a common function in python called 'isalpha()' to differentiate the numbers from the text. Removal of numbers can help models focus on more important words.
- **Filtering stop words**- While analyzing texts or performing NLP operations, stop-words like 'the', 'is', 'in', 'for'... etc. may not add much meaning to the reviews. Some of the key advantages of doing this are as follows:
- Dataset size decreases
- The accuracy of results is better.
- **Lemmatization** is the process of obtaining the root words from a particular word. This method is applied to reduce the number of unique words in the Reviews, which reduces the model training time. We use the WordNetLemmatizer() to perform the lemma operation in our processing.

5.2 Randomization and Stratification

The dataset was randomly divided into two sets. 80% of the data is used for training the model, while the remaining 20% is used for testing. We use the stratify parameter to ensure that the data is evenly split between the training and test set. Finally, it ensures that data is split evenly between each class in training and testing data.

The dataset contains 11 columns. For this experiment, we will use the 'Reviews Text' and 'Recommended IND' columns to train our models and predict the recommendation index using the review.

As mentioned before. For predicting the sentiment of the reviews, we will be using five machine learning models, namely Logistic Regression, Support vector machine classifier, Decision Tree classifier. In addition, we will be using primarily Recurrent neural networks for predicting customer reviews' sentiment, as these models are appropriate for text or sentence learning. The models used in this research are LSTM, GRU, and BI-LSTM.

5.3 The Metrics

To compare the performances of the models, the best metrics proposed are as follows.

- **Confusion Matrix.** It is a table used to visualize a model's performance on a set of test data. The confusion matrix provides four different combinations of Predicted and Actual values [23]. We will evaluate four different parameters to compare the model performance
- **True positive.** It is the number of times that the model predicts the positive class correctly.
- **True negative**. It is the number of times that the model predicts the negative class correctly.
- **False positive**. It is the number of times that the model mispredicts the positive class.
- **False negative**. It is the number of times the model predicts the negative class wrongly
- **AUROC curve** is the area under the Receiver operating characteristics that tell us how much the model can distinguish between classes. Higher the area, the better the model is at predicting the sentiment.
- **Roc-probability curve** is calculated by using the actual results and the predicted results. We calculate the true positive rate values and the false positive rate values from them to plot the curve. The formula for them is as below.
- *True positive rate = True positive/ (True positive + False negative).*
- *False positive rate = False positive/ (False Positive + True Negative).*
- **Auc-degree of measure of separability** is a perfect metric for measuring the performance of any model. A higher value of Auc means that the model has done well in classification.
- **Classification report**. The classification report gives us a detailed report of the model scores, such as accuracy, precision, recall, f1-score, and support.

5.4 Experimental process/implementation

Data – Preprocessing

To fit the data into the model, it needs to be cleaned to remove noise and other anomalies to get accurate modeling results. Then, we remove punctuations and numbers that are irrelevant to the review comment and then use tokenization to get the list of tokens(words) from a comment and further simplify them by lemmatizing them(converting words to their root words based on the dictionary).

Training the models
We have divided the data into 80–20 train-test ratios to allow the model to learn well.

Using TF-IDF with the models
Once the data is prepared, we convert the data into a vector form using the TF-IDF vectorizer, which transforms the words in the comment into a vector matrix.

TF-IDF(term frequency-inverse document frequency) is a vectorizer that converts words into a vector matrix, where each row represents the frequency of words in all the comments [22]. The formula (1) for TF-IDF is as below.

$$W_{i,j} = tf_{i,j} \text{ x } \mathrm{idf_i} \tag{1}$$

Where $w_{i,j}$ is the TF-IDF score for a word 'i' in a doc 'j'. Words with a higher TF-IDF score have higher occurrence than those with a lower score.

5.5 Measuring Classifier Performance

We use various model performance measuring methods like confusion matrix, AU-ROC curve, and classification table.

Any model with a higher true positive and negative probability count will have performed the best out of the rest. For example, a model with a larger area of the *auroc* curve has a higher accuracy rate.

We'll use the classification table to look at the accuracy, precision, and recall values that will give us better insight into how the models differ in performance.

6 Results and Discussion

6.1 Exploratory Analysis Results

The exploratory data analysis on the customer review data provided some impactful insights into how the company is doing regarding clothes sales. For instance, more than 50% of the customer have given a 5-star rating for their products, while only less than 15% have given 1 or 2 stars. This confirms that most of the company's products are very popular with their customers and are in line with the current fashion trends that are popular these days.

An analysis of the customer data confirmed that most of the buyers were 30–50, and their preferred choice of clothing was Tops and dresses. Under 25% of the purchases included bottoms and intimate clothing and very few customers purchased jackets and trendy clothing.

The company needs to work on providing more options, to improve its sales in this category.

The company sells clothing in 5 categories: tops, Dresses, intimate, Bottoms, Jackets, and trendy clothing. As per the catplot in the ED analysis, almost all the products have high recommendations from customers of all age groups. This is a sign that the company is doing a good job overall with product selection by following the current trends in the design/fashion industry.

Since the recommendation count is unevenly balanced, we have tested our models with the original and the up-sampled data to show the difference in performance. Modeling results with upsampled data performs slightly better than the original data.

6.2 Modeling Experiment Results

Before predicting outcomes using modeling techniques, the data needed to be cleaned properly to fit the model, therefore, we performed the following experiments below.

a) Experiment 1

While performing EDA, I noticed an imbalance in the number of recommendations made. The number of good recommendations was significantly more than the number of negative recommendations. It is known that upsampling the data would be the right move to improve the model's accuracy [20]. To test this, we performed modeling with both types of datasets, and we found an increase in accuracy when working with up-sampled data. In Fig. 9, we have highlighted the scores of the model working with usampled data.

	Train_Score	Test_Score	Precision_Score	Recall_Score	F1_Score	accuracy
logisitc regression	0.918018	0.893633	0.908071	0.895092	0.901535	0.893633
lr for data without upscaling	0.910280	0.891564	0.904451	0.970065	0.936109	0.891564
Support Vector Machine	0.94076	0.913146	0.938626	0.899137	0.918457	0.913146
SVM on data without upscaling	0.844247	0.833922	0.831966	0.998921	0.907843	0.833922
Decision Tree	1.0	0.910065	0.981038	0.851133	0.911480	0.910065
Decision Tree for data without upscaling	1.0	0.812279	0.884760	0.886192	0.885476	0.812279
Random Forest Tree	1.0	0.970217	0.978172	0.966628	0.972467	0.970217
random forest for data without upscaling	1.0	0.847836	0.846932	0.993797	0.914506	0.847836
AdaBoost	0.901181	0.870745	0.876632	0.887271	0.881919	0.870745
Adaboost for data without upscaling	0.864013	0.858436	0.884818	0.950917	0.916677	0.858436

Fig. 9. Modeling scores after working with and without upscaled data

b) Experiment 2

To get optimal results with modeling, we need to ensure that our data is cleaned correctly. After researching, we found the most suitable methods for performing text cleaning. Many reviews are often filled with unnecessary numbers, punctuation marks, and other common stop words, which would only make the modeling processes much longer. Therefore, the following methods in the methodology section were implemented to achieve this.

After implementing the proposed models, we concluded that the random forest model had outperformed most other models in certain aspects. The data was evenly passed to the models using the stratified method, which ensures an equal ratio of imbalance in the model error if any.

c) Model hyperparameters

For certain models, hyperparameter testing has been done to reach the expected accuracy rates. For the SVM model, we set the kernel to radial basis function (rbf), random states are set to 0, the regularization parameter 'C' is set to 0.2, and the probability parameter is set to true to enable probability estimates. For example, in the AdaBoost classifier, the hyperparameter n_estimates is set to 100 initially and was increased gradually to see a change in performance. The best result was achieved with n_estimators set to 500 with a random_state of 0.

d) Performance Metrics

We used the confusion matrix to review the number of correct and wrong classifications made by all the models. The classification table was examined to check the model scores on test and training data, and the auroc curve will be checked to compare the area under the curve score and the roc curve for every model.

The True positive (TP) is the number of bad review recommendations that have been correctly classified by the model, and the True Negative is the number of good review recommendations that the model correctly classified. On the other hand, false positives and false negatives are the opposite, where the first is the number of bad review recommendations that were wrongly classified, and the latter is the number of improperly categorized good review classifications.

We have normalized the values between 0 and 1 to compare the values of all models.

Although all the models have done reasonably well, Random Forest has edged out the models in terms of parameter values. It has the second highest value of True positive (0.44) and highest value of True negative (0.53) while also having the lowest value of False negative (0.012) and False positive (0.018). On the other hand, models like AdaBoost, Decision Tree, and Logistic Regression have fared low in classification, having marginally low True positive values, but have a good True negative value. Though the decision Tree has a higher True positive value than the Random Forest model, it still has better values than other parameters.

Recurrent neural networks have also performed reasonably well in classifying classes as they are just below random forest in confusion matrix parameter scores. Table 1, below shows the classification of all modeling techniques used in this study.

Based on the above scores, we can see that Random Forest Tree has just marginally edged out other models. The accuracy and the test data score (0.9710) are much higher than the remaining models. The Recurrent neural networks (LSTM, GRU, BI-LSTM) are the second best in the list and have performed reasonably well in classifying the data. The AdaBoost ml classifier is placed last as it has the lowest scores compared to the rest.

Table 1. Classification scores of all the modeling techniques

	Train_Score	Test_Score	Precision_Score	Recall_Score	F1_Score	accuracy
Random Forest Tree	1.000000	0.971097	0.979514	0.967098	0.973266	0.971097
BI-LSTM	0.990023	0.947330	0.964494	0.937702	0.950909	0.947330
LSTM	0.994645	0.941755	0.976129	0.915318	0.944746	0.941755
GRU	0.970435	0.933979	0.946057	0.931769	0.938859	0.933979
Support Vector Machine	0.940760	0.913146	0.938626	0.899137	0.918457	0.913146
Decision Tree	1.000000	0.907424	0.981534	0.845739	0.908590	0.907424
logisitc regression	0.918018	0.893633	0.908071	0.895092	0.901535	0.893633
AdaBoost	0.901181	0.870745	0.876632	0.887271	0.881919	0.870745

6.3 AUC-ROC Curve

The AUC-ROC graph is the best for measuring any model's performance in the graph presented in Fig. 10. Random Forest classifier has once again achieved the best performance as it has the highest AUC value of 99.6% and its ROC curve is higher than that of other models. LSTM and BI-LSTM are very close in terms of AUC values (LSTM AUC = 0.976, BI-LSTM AUC = 0.977), and their ROC curves are almost on a similar trajectory. The GRU model sees a slight dip with an AUC value of 0.978 and a similar RUC curve trajectory. The remaining ML models produced the three bottom ROC curves (SVC, Logistic Regression, AdaBoost, and Decision Tree), which fared worse than the RNN models with low AUC scores and no upward incline of ROC curves.

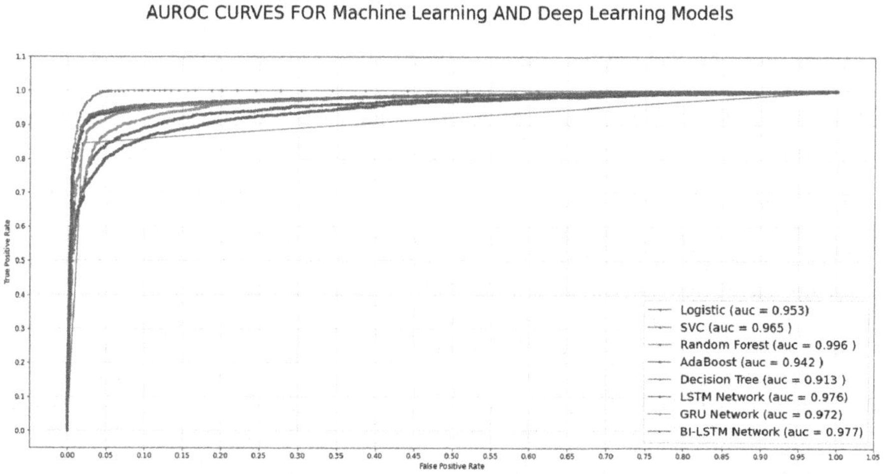

Fig. 10. AUROC curve for all the modelling techniques

7 Conclusion and Future Works

In this research paper, we predict the sentiment of customer reviews using five machine learning models and three deep learning models. For the ML models, we trained them with the help of a TF-IDF vectorizer. The experiments we carried out helped us study the models' performance based on their accuracy while predicting testing data, and comparing their confusion matrix and AU-ROC curves.

Among all the models, The Random Forest Classifier with TF-IDF vectorizer seemed to predict sentiments with the highest accuracy and better AU-ROC curve than the rest. However, based on overall performance, it can be concluded that the Deep learning models have a better overall score than the machine learning models.

For future works, consider adding emojis to the dataset, which helps the models better predict sentiments. For example, reviews may contain many stop words that remain even after processing, which can be classified as positive sentiment, even though the overall sentiment is negative. We can also look further to fine-tune the hyperparaters of the deep learning networks to perform better predicting sentiments.

References

1. Danish, R.Q., Hafeez, S., Ali, H.F., Shahid, R., Nadeem, K.: Impact of online consumer reviews on hotel booking intentions: the case of Pakistan. Europ. Sci. J. ESJ **15**(7), 144–159 (2019)
2. Willianto, T., Wibowo, A.: Sentiment analysis on E-commerce product using machine learning and combination of TF-IDF and backward elimination. Int. J. Electr. Comput. Eng. (IJECE) **8**(6), 2862–2867 (2020)
3. Iqbal, A., Amin, R., Iqbal, J., Alroobaea, R., Binmahfoudh, A., Hussain, M.: Sentiment analysis of consumer reviews using deep learning. Sustainability **14**(17), 10844 (2022)
4. Mane, V., Patil, S., Awale, R., Pisal, V.: An Efficient Sentiment Analysis Based on Product Reviews. SAMRIDDHI: A J. Phys. Sci., Eng. Technol. **13**(SUP 2), 203–208 (2021)
5. Chintalapudi, N., Battineni, G., Amenta, F.: Sentimental analysis of COVID-19 tweets using deep learning models. Infect. Disease Reports **13**(2), 329–339 (2021)
6. Rahayu, R., Day, J.: Determinant factors of e-commerce adoption by SMEs in developing country: evidence from Indonesia. Procedia Soc. Behav. Sci. **195**, 142–150 (2015)
7. Giachanou, A., Crestani, F.: Like it or not: a survey of twitter sentiment analysis methods. ACM Comput. Surv. (CSUR) **49**(2), 1–41 (2016)
8. Ali, N.M., Abd El Hamid, M.M., Youssif, A.: Sentiment analysis for movies reviews dataset using deep learning models. In: International Journal of Data Mining & Knowledge Management Process (IJDKP) vol. 9 (2019)
9. Marong, M., Batcha, N. K., & Mafas, R. (2020). Sentiment Analysis in E-Commerce: A Review on The Techniques and Algorithms. J. Appl. Technol. Innov. (e-ISSN: 2600–7304), **4**(1), 6 (2020)
10. Desai, M., Mehta, M.A.: Techniques for sentiment analysis of Twitter data: A comprehensive survey. In: 2016 International Conference on Computing, Communication and Automation (ICCCA), pp. 149–154 IEEE (2016)
11. Almatarneh, S., Gamallo, P.: A lexicon based method to search for extreme opinions. PLoS ONE **13**(5), e0197816 (2018)
12. Taboada, M., Brooke, J., Tofiloski, M., Voll, K., Stede, M.: Lexicon-based methods for sentiment analysis. Comput. Linguist. **37**(2), 267–307 (2011)

13. Bandhakavi, A., Wiratunga, N., Padmanabhan, D., Massie, S.: Lexicon based feature extraction for emotion text classification. Pattern Recogn. Lett. **93**, 133–142 (2017)
14. Asghar, M.Z., Khan, A., Ahmad, S., Qasim, M., Khan, I.A.: Lexicon-enhanced sentiment analysis framework using rule-based classification scheme. PLoS ONE **12**(2), e0171649 (2017)
15. Das, S.R., Chen, M.Y.: Yahoo! for Amazon: Sentiment parsing from small talk on the web. For Amazon: Sentiment Parsing from Small Talk on the Web (August 5, 2001). EFA (2021)
16. Bhaskar, N., Sandeep, P., Amarnath, N., Thankachan, J.: A study: sentimental analysis for election results by using twitter data. Turkish J. Physiother. Rehab. **32**, 3 (2021)
17. Brar, G.S., Sharma, A.: Sentiment analysis of movie review using supervised machine learning techniques. Int. J. Appl. Eng. Res. **13**(16), 12788–12791 (2018)
18. Tripathi, A., Singh, A.K., Singh, K.K., Choudhary, P., Vashist, P.C.: Machine learning architecture and framework. In: Machine Learning and the Internet of Medical Things in Healthcare, pp. 1–22. Academic Press (2021).
19. Gupta, B., Negi, M., Vishwakarma, K., Rawat, G., Badhani, P., Tech, B.: Study of Twitter sentiment analysis using machine learning algorithms on Python. Int. J. Comput. Appl. **165**(9), 29–34 (2017)
20. Kumar, S.: 5 Techniques to work with Imbalanced Data in Machine Learning. https://www.towardsdatascience.com/5-techniques-to-work-with-imbalanced-data-in-machine-learning-80836d45d30c (2021)
21. Verma, Y.: Why Data Scaling is important in Machine Learning & How to effectively do it. https://www.analyticsindiamag.com/why-data-scaling-is-important-in-machine-learning-how-to-effectively-do-it/23. Library containing all the regex functions https://www.docs.python.org/3/library/re.html (2021)
22. Scikit-learn developers Convert a collection of raw documents to a matrix of TF-IDF features. https://www.scikit-learn.org/stable/modules/generated/sklearn.feature_extraction.text.TfidfVectorizer.html (2022)
23. Narkhede, S.: Understanding Confusion Matrix. https://www.towardsdatascience.com/understanding-confusion-matrix-a9ad42dcfd62 (2022)

Evaluating Differences in Consumer Behavior With and Without Planning and Predicting Unplanned Purchases

Hiromi Tanabe[1], Kohei Otake[2], and Takashi Namatame[3](✉)

[1] Graduate School of Science and Engineering, Chuo University, 1-13-27, Kasuga, Bunkyo-Ku, Tokyo 112-8551, Japan
a19.e7x3@g.chuo-u.ac.jp

[2] School of Information and Telecommunication Engineering, Tokai University, 2-3-23, Takanawa, Minato-Ku, Tokyo 108-8619, Japan
otake@tsc.u-tokai.ac.jp

[3] Faculty of Science and Engineering, Chuo University, 1-13-27, Kasuga, Bunkyo-Ku, Tokyo 112-8551, Japan
nama@kc.chuo-u.ac.jp

Abstract. In this study, we conducted an experiment in an actual store and used the data to analyze the characteristics of consumer behavior. First, consumers were grouped into two patterns: with or without plan and with or without unplanned purchases. Next, we compared differences in consumer behavior between groups using t-tests and Wilcoxon rank sum tests. Eleven consumer behaviors were listed, which were obtained from the eye gaze and traffic line data. Then, we conducted logistic regression analysis to analyze how each consumer behavior correlates with presence of unplanned purchases. The results showed that there was a difference in behavior outside the tenant with and without a plan, and a difference in post-experiment satisfaction with and without unplanned purchases. However, we did not obtain clear differences in consumers' in-store behavior with and without unplanned purchases.

Keywords: Marketing Science · Logistic Regression · Planned or Unplanned Purchase

1 Introduction

Marketing research has shown that the effectiveness of corporate advertising leads to visits to physical stores and online sites, which in turn leads to purchases. However, "Unplanned purchases", in which consumers make purchasing decisions impulsively in stores, are said to account for 50–90% of all consumer purchases. In other words, in-store sales promotions that induce consumers to make impulse purchases will become more important. Furthermore, after the pandemic of COVID-19, the number of e-commerce site user increased as they refrained from going out. Accordingly, the frequency of use of

A. Coman and S. Vasilache (Eds.): HCII 2023, LNCS 14025, pp. 598–610, 2023.
https://doi.org/10.1007/978-3-031-35915-6_43

shopping centers has also decreased. Specifically, in front of the pandemic of COVID-19, more than 60% of the respondents visited store more than twice a month, but after the pandemic of COVID-19, that consumers decreased to 40%. This indicates that it is more important than ever before for physical stores such as shopping centers to develop strategies to encourage each and every consumer to purchase their products.

2 Purpose of This Study

In this study, we conduct the purchasing experiment in an actual store and we use the data obtained from the experiment. To compare the data from a statistical point of view, we perform t-tests and Wilcoxon rank sum tests on the two aspects of "Planned vs. Unplanned" and "Unplanned purchases vs. Other" to find differences in consumer behavior in each group. Logistic regression analysis will then be performed to evaluate which behavioral characteristics have the greatest impact. Then, we will find the important factors that tend to induce unplanned purchases and propose marketing strategies to induce unplanned purchases.

3 Datasets

In this study, we conducted an experiment in a real store. The store is a commercial facility with many tenants, mostly fashion brands. And we use the data obtained there for the analysis (Table 1).

Table 1. The summary of Datasets

Date of experiment	2022/10/4, 5, 8
Number of subjects	38
Store Type	Department store type large store

However, two sets of gaze data were lost due to equipment trouble, so 36 sets of data were used in this study.

Next, the experimental method is described.

4 Experimental Methods

To obtain data on consumer gaze and flow lines, we asked participants to wear Tobi Pro Glasses 2 and 3, eyeglass-type gaze observation devices by Tobii Corporation. We instructed participants to wear Tobii Pro Glasses 2 and Tobii Pro Glasses 3 and to look around a large commercial facility, primarily fashion brands, to obtain data on consumer gaze. From this, data on lines of flow were obtained (Fig. 1).

The experiment was conducted as follows.

1. Ask the subjects to gather to the rental space at the scheduled time.

Fig. 1. Tobii Pro Glasses 3

2. The experiment staff will explain the flow of the experiment and precautions to the subjects, ask them to fill out the experiment participation consent form, preliminary questionnaire, and gratuity, and give them the gratuity.
3. The subject wears the eye tracking device and calibrates it so that the viewpoint is corrected
4. Experiment staffs will guide the subject to the experiment location.
5. Start the experiment and ask the subject to shop in the experimental store.
6. Announce the end of the experiment, remove the eye tracking device, and ask the subject to move to a location where he/she will not be disturbed by other users.
7. Ask the subjects to fill out the post-experiment questionnaire via the QR code.
8. The staff collects the data from the eye tracking device and prepares for the next subject's experiment.

The figure below is a screen capture of "Tobii Pro Lab", tool for analyzing gaze data (Fig. 2).

Fig. 2. Screenshot of the Tobii Pro Lab control panel

Questionnaires were administered before and after the experiment to investigate the usual shopping situation and the day of the experiment.

4.1 Pre-experiment Questionnaire

A pre-experiment questionnaire surveyed the participants about their usual shopping situation, their purchasing plans for the day, and their values when shopping. In it, the following items are used.

- Purchase plan on the day of the experiment
- Amount of budget available per month

"Purchase plan on the day of the experiment" was used to group the participants according to whether they planned to make a purchase. It was also used to group the participants according to whether they made unplanned purchases or not.

"Amount of budget available per month" is used as one of the consumer behaviors to make comparisons.

The following table shows the breakdown of plans with and without plans, as well as a breakdown of budgets (Tables 2 and 3).

Table 2. Number of people with or without plan

	Subjects
Planned	15
Unplanned	21

Table 3. Amount of budget available per month

Monthly budget	Subjects
10,000 ~ 19,999	3
20,000 ~ 29,999	11
30,000 ~ 39,999	11
4,0000 ~ 49,999	1
50,000 ~ 59,999	7
60,000 ~	3

4.2 Post-experiment Questionnaire

A post-experiment questionnaire was used to survey the purchase status on the day of the experiment and the level of satisfaction with the facility and tenants. In it, the following items are used.

- Evaluation of facilities and tenants

- Whether or not merchandise was purchased
- The category of merchandise purchased

A total of 11 evaluations of facilities and tenants were prepared, and respondents were asked to rate each on a 5-point scale. Specific details are shown below.

- Did you finding attractiveness products in the tenants you stopped by?
- Assortment of products of the tenants you stopped by.
- Ease of understanding the features (e.g., prices) of the products of the tenants you stopped by.
- Prices of the products of the tenants you stopped by.
- Customer service of the tenants you stopped by.
- Overall cleanliness of the facility.
- Air-conditioning environment in the facility.
- Ease of understanding of the facility's information and floor guide.
- Familiarity with other customers in the facility.
- Rest area in the facility.
- Would you like to use this store again?

"Whether or not merchandise was purchased" and "The category of merchandise purchased" were used to categorize whether an unplanned purchase was made. Those who did not plan to purchase and those who purchased product categories not included in the planned product categories were classified as "Unplanned purchases". The number of unplanned purchases and the number of persons who did not make an unplanned purchase are shown below.

The numbers of those who made non-planned purchases and those who did not are shown in the Table 4 below.

Table 4. Non-planned purchases or not

	Subjects
Unplanned purchases	14
Other	22

5 Analysis Method

5.1 T-test

The t-test is a method of testing whether there is a difference in the means of samples drawn for two independent populations.

In this study, comparisons are made under two conditions. "Planned group" and "Unplanned group", and the "Unplanned purchase group" and "Other group" will be compared under the two conditions.

The consumer behavior items for which t-tests will be conducted are as follows.

- Time spent in each tenant

- Number of tenants visited
- Total number of tenants visited
- Average time spent in the tenants (= Time spent in tenants/Total number of tenants visited)
- Maximum time spent in tenant
- Time spent in store aisles
- Number of visits to store aisles
- Average time spent in store aisles (= time spent in store aisles/Number of times spent in store aisles)
- Number of times the floor was moved
- Overall Survey Score (Overall score based on a 5-point scale of 11 questions in a questionnaire about the facility and tenants)
- Budget for the month.

The significance level was set at 10% for this test.

Before doing the t-test, we checked if the variances were different and changed the method of the t-test accordingly. To check for equal variances, the F test was performed. The null and alternative hypotheses are set as follows.

In this study, when the p-value is less than 10%, the null hypothesis is rejected, the variance is judged to be different between the two groups, and a Welch's t-test is conducted, which is a t-test without the assumption of equal variances. When the p-value is greater than 10%, the null hypothesis is accepted, the variance is determined to be no difference between the two groups, and a two-sample t-test without correspondence is performed assuming equal variances.

When the p-value is less than 10%, the null hypothesis is rejected and it is judged that there is a difference in the mean of the characteristics of consumer behavior, and when the p-value is greater than 10%, the null hypothesis is accepted, and it is judged that there is no difference in the mean of the characteristics of consumer behavior.

5.2 Wilcoxon Rank-um Test

Since the data may not be normally distributed, we also performed the Wilcoxon rank sum test. The Wilcoxon rank sum test is a nonparametric test that does not assume a distribution and is a method for comparing the distributions of two groups. The null and alternative hypotheses are listed below.

If the p-value was less than 10%, the null hypothesis was rejected and it was determined that there was a difference in the variance of the consumer behavior characteristics; if the p-value was greater than 10%, the null hypothesis was adopted, and it was determined that there was no difference in the variance of the consumer behavior characteristics. For consumer characteristics, the same items as in the t-test were used.

5.3 Logistic Regression

Logistic regression is one of general linearized model, a method that predicts the probability of an event in the objective variable from the explanatory variables. The logistic regression is shown in the following equation.

$$p_i = \frac{1}{1 + \exp\left\{-\left(\beta_0 + \sum_{j=1}^{p} \beta_j x_{ij}\right)\right\}}$$

In this study, the predicted value is set to 0 when it is less than 0.5 and 1 when it is greater than 0.5. In this study, the objective variable p_i is the probability that customer i has a plan and makes an unplanned purchase (the objective variable), x_{ij} is the factor affecting the objective variable (the explanatory variable), and β_j is the parameter of each explanatory variable (β_0 is the intercept). In this study, the objective variables were "Planning a purchase" and "Unplanned purchases", and the explanatory variables were the items of consumer behavior dealt with in the t-test.

6 Result

Before starting the analysis, we grouped the respondents by whether they had a purchase plan or not, and whether they had unplanned purchases or not. The mean values for each group are listed in the Table 5 below (Table 6).

Table 5. Average with and without purchasing plan

variables	Planned	Unplanned
Time spent in each tenant	2124.34	2144.72
Total number of tenants visited	12.86	14.61
Average time spent in the tenants	14.40	15.80
Maximum time spent in tenant	155.38	155.25
Time spent in store aisles	533.18	675.77
Number of visits to store aisles	1453.17	1418.73
Average time spent in store aisles	14.93	17.14
Number of times the floor was moved	104.45	101.36
Number of tenants visited	9.86	11.76
Overall Survey Score	42.53	44.47
Budget for the month	29333.33	35952.38

6.1 Comparison with and Without Purchase Plans

First, we note the results of the t-test (Table 7).

The two variables, "Number of times spent in store aisles" and "Number of times the floor was moved" were less than 10% of p-value. The group with a plan had a lower average number of store aisle visits and a lower average number of floor trips.

Table 6. Average with and without unplanned purchases

variables	Unplanned	Others
Time spent in each tenant	2234.52	2073.67
Total number of tenants visited	13.57	14.09
Average time spent in the tenants	14.35	15.77
Maximum time spent in tenant	166.17	148.39
Time spent in store aisles	693.48	580.92
Number of visits to store aisles	1340.2	1492.14
Average time spent in store aisles	15.71	16.54
Number of times the floor was moved	94.91	107.56
Number of tenants visited	10.64	11.18
Overall Survey Score	45.92	42.22
Budget for the month	30714.28	34772.72

Table 7. T-test with and without plan

variables	t-value	p-value
Time spent in tenants	−0.1261	0.4502
Number of tenants visited	−1.2523	0.1097
Total number of tenants visited	−0.8630	0.1972
Average time spent in tenants	0.0067	0.4973
Maximum time spent in tenant	−1.2859	0.1041
Time spent in store aisles	0.2210	0.4132
Number of times spent in store aisles	−1.3480	0.0934
Average time spent in store aisles	0.1443	0.4431
Number of times the floor was moved	−1.5196	0.0692
Overall Survey Score	−1.0202	0.1574
Monthly budget	−1.2200	0.1152

Next, the results of the Wilcoxon rank sum test are presented (Table 8).

"Average time spent in store aisles" was significant at 10%. This indicates that there is a difference in "Average time spent in store aisles" depending on the presence or absence of a plan.

Next, we share the results of the logistic regression (Table 9).

The only "Time spent in store aisles", was significant at the 10% significance level.

Table 8. Wilcoxon rank sum test with and without plan

variables	p-value
Time spent in tenants	0.4371
Number of tenants visited	0.1332
Total number of tenants visited	0.3308
Average time spent in tenants	0.3286
Maximum time spent in tenants	0.3144
Time spent in store aisles	0.3878
Number of times spent in store aisles	0.1553
Average time spent in store aisles	0.0664
Number of times the floor was moved	0.1469
Overall Survey Score	0.1754
Monthly budget	0.3450

Table 9. Logistic regression with and without plan

data items	Partial regression coefficients	p-value
Time spent in tenants	0.0068	0.129
Number of tenants visited	−0.4293	0.276
Total number of tenants visited	0.5916	0.293
Average time spent in tenants	0.0097	0.756
Maximum time spent in tenants	−0.0340	0.178
Time spent in store aisles	0.0083	0.042
Number of times spent in store aisles	−0.8342	0.170
Average time spent in store aisles	0.2910	0.400
Number of times the floor was moved	−0.1873	0.316
Overall survey score	0.1628	0.137
Monthly budget	-2.4×10^{-5}	0.410

6.2 Comparison with and Without Non-planned Purchases

First, we note the results of the t-test (Table 10).

"Overall survey score" was significant at the 10% level of significance. From this, we can see that those who made non-planned purchases had higher overall scores on the questionnaire.

Next, the results of the Wilcoxon rank sum test are presented (Table 11).

Table 10. T-test with and without unplanned purchases

data items	t-value	p-value
Time spent in tenants	0.9981	0.1626
Number of tenants visited	−0.3308	0.3712
Total number of tenants visited	−0.7829	0.2196
Average time spent in tenants	0.9049	0.1859
Maximum time spent in tenants	1.0437	0.1520
Time spent in store aisles	−0.9741	0.1679
Number of times spent in store aisles	−0.4518	0.3271
Average time spent in store aisles	−0.5284	0.3003
Number of times the floor was moved	−0.3789	0.3536
Overall survey score	2.0015	0.0267
Monthly budget	−0.6536	0.2589

Table 11. Wilcoxon rank sum test with and without unplanned purchases

data variables	p-value
Time spent in tenants	0.1344
Number of tenants visited	0.3408
Total number of tenants visited	0.8014
Average time spent in tenants	0.2254
Maximum time spent in tenants	0.0998
Time spent in store aisles	0.1199
Number of times spent in store aisles	0.6472
Average time spent in store aisles	0.7842
Number of times the floor was moved	0.6777
Overall Survey Score	0.0275
Monthly budget	0.6642

"Maximum time spent in tenants" and "Overall survey score" were significant at 10%. This indicates that there is a difference in "Maximum time spent in tenant" and "Overall survey score" depending on the presence or absence of unplanned purchases.

Next, we show the results of the logistic regression (Table 12).

The variables that were significant at the 10% level of significance were "Total Number of tenant visits" and "Overall survey score".

Table 12. Logistic regression with and without unplanned purchases

variables	Partial regression coefficients	p-value
Time spent in tenants	0.0023	0.457
Number of tenants visited	0.0401	0.902
Total number of tenants visited	−0.9168	0.073
Average time spent in tenants	−0.0432	0.159
Maximum time spent in tenants	0.0008	0.638
Time spent in store aisles	−0.0020	0.422
Number of times spent in store aisles	0.4459	0.318
Average time spent in store aisles	−0.0002	0.991
Number of times the floor was moved	0.1268	0.468
Overall survey score	0.1876	0.051
Monthly budget	-3.2×10^{-6}	0.911

7 Discussion

7.1 Comparison with and Without Plans

The t-test results showed that consumers with a plan stayed in the aisles of the store less frequently and moved around the floor less frequently. One possible reason for the reduced number of aisle stays is that consumers have a specific product or tenant they are interested in, so they waste less time moving around to achieve their goal in the limited time of one hour. It is also possible that the number of trips within the floor was reduced because the presence of the desired product or tenant allowed consumers to move around the floor more efficiently. The results of the Wilcoxon rank-sum test showed that there was a difference in the average time spent in store aisles between consumers with and without a plan. The average time spent in store aisles was longer for consumers with a plan. In other words, consumers with a plan tended to spend more time on average in store aisles.

Considering the results of the t-test, it can be inferred that consumer with a plan tend to spend less time in the aisles than consumers without a plan, although there is no difference in the time spent in the aisles, resulting in a longer average length of stay. In addition, when we checked the eye movement videos, we found that many consumers who had a plan stopped at the aisles and checked the floor map. This behavior seems to indicate that they were checking the floor map to see where the tenants with the brand and product categories they were interested in were located on the floor. This behavior may have led them to spend more time in the aisles at one time than consumers without a plan.

The logistic regression results also confirmed that there was a difference in the time spent in the store aisles depending on whether a plan was in place or not. In the eye movement video, it was confirmed that those with a purchase plan tended to look at the floor map more often. This behavior is to see where the desired tenant is located. This behavior is thought to have caused the difference in time spent in the aisles. The analysis showed differences in time spent in store aisles, number of times spent in store aisles, and number of trips between floors. This suggests that the presence or absence of a plan influences behavior outside the tenant.

7.2 Comparison with and Without Non-planned Purchases

The results of the t-test showed that unplanned purchases scored higher on the overall questionnaire. The questionnaire asked respondents to rate the store environment, tenant abundance, product assortment, and price on a 5-point scale. This suggests that satisfaction with assortment and price leads to unplanned purchases, but further experimentation is needed to clarify this, as it is possible that the respondents rated assortment and price satisfaction as good because they purchased the merchandise.

The results of the Wilcoxon rank-sum test indicate that there is a difference in the maximum time spent in the store and the overall score of the questionnaire depending on the presence or absence of unplanned purchases. Since the t-test also confirmed a significant difference in the overall questionnaire score, it seems that there is a clear difference in the overall questionnaire score. As for the maximum time spent in stores, we found that the maximum time spent in the store who made unplanned purchases tended to be the maximum time spent in the store which made unplanned purchases. This tendency is thought to be since tenants have time to look at the entire tenant and to think about whether to purchase a product or not. In addition, the time spent in the store who made unplanned purchases may have been longer because of the time required to pay for the goods purchased.

The logistic regression results predicted that a decrease in the number of tenant visits would increase the likelihood of making an unplanned purchase. However, it is unclear whether a decrease in tenant visits makes tenants more likely to make unplanned purchases or whether tenant visits decrease because of unplanned purchases, which also requires further investigation. In this study, we find clear differences in consumer behavior with and without plan. However, it was not possible to specify differences in consumer behavior with and without non-planned purchases.

8 Conclusion

In this study, we conducted an experiment in a real store and used the data to evaluate the differences in consumer behavior with and without a purchase plan and with and without unplanned purchases, and to propose strategies in stores that induce unplanned purchases. In this study, we find clear differences in consumer behavior with and without plan. However, it was not able to explicitly state the difference in consumer behavior with and without unplanned purchases, and it did not go as far as to come up with a strategy that would induce unplanned purchases. Therefore, we believe it is necessary to experiment with new stores in order to develop a strategy to induce unplanned purchases.

Acknowledgments. We thank a large size retail store of Japan for permission to use valuable datasets. This work was supported by JSPS KAKENHI Grant Number 21H04600 and 21K13385.

References

1. Kato, R.: Institute of Economics and Business Research. Kobe University, RIEB Newsletter, No.196, March 2019
2. https://www.rieb.kobe-u.ac.jp/research/publication/newsletter/column_back-issues/file/column196.pdf
3. Ohigasi, K.: From general linear model to the generalized linear model. Weed Sci. Soc. Japan **12**, 268–274 (2010)
4. Fujiwara, M.: The determinants of consumption behavior in fast fashion -from the point of view of SNS, smartphone technology and consumption values. J. Japan Res. Assoc. Textile End-uses **61**(4), 299 (2020)
5. Nonaka, M.: A study on product search behavior using traffic line and viewpoint data. Master's thesis, Graduate School of Research Engineering, Chuo University (2022)
6. Sugiyama, Y., Tone, R., Imamura, S., Yatani, K.: Behavioral characteristics of unplanned buyers in front of merchandise shelves. IPSJ SIG Tech. Rep. **UBI-62**(10) (2019)
7. Makino, K., Takagi, O., Hayashi, H.: Effects of whether consumer's having some purchase plans or not and a condition of POP advertising presentation on in-store consumer behaviors: a field experiment using image type POP and price type POP. Res. Soc. Psychol. **10**(1), 11–23 (1994)
8. Tobii Pro Glasses2. https://www.tobiipro.com/product-listing/tobii-pro-glasses-2/
9. Tobii Pro Glasses3. https://www.tobii.com/ja/products/eye-trackers/wearables/tobii-pro-glasses-3
10. Tobii Pro Lab. https://www.tobiipro.com/product-listing/tobii-pro-lab/

Audiovisual Content Consumer Behavior Regarding Advertising on Online Streaming Platforms

Diego Yáñez(✉), Cristóbal Fernández-Robin, and Fabián Vásquez

Departamento de Industrias, Universidad Técnica Federico Santa María, Av. España 1680, Valparaíso, Chile
{diego.yanez,cristobal.fernandez}@usm.cl,
fabian.vasquez@sansano.usm.cl

Abstract. The industry that has benefited the most from consumers seeking to satisfy their entertainment needs is streaming. By 2022, the consumption of Internet video streaming in Chile is estimated to reach 741 PBs (Petabytes) [5], considering viewing of videos on YouTube and other streaming platforms. Therefore, this study aims to analyze and model consumer behavior in the online streaming industry, specifically towards the advertisement presented on the YouTube and Twitch TV platforms. To achieve this objective, a methodology is proposed, which attempts to identify the factors influencing the attitude of users when they see ads during the use of online streaming platforms and how this may influence their intention to purchase the product advertised. To this end, a model that causally relates the latent variables of Information, Entertainment, Invasiveness, Advertisement Value, Consumer Attitude and Purchase Intention, is proposed. To obtain the data necessary for the analysis of the structural equation model proposed, a questionnaire was developed through the SurveyMonkey platform during June and July 2022, obtaining 243 complete responses. Data analysis consisted of a descriptive statistic and a subsequent reliability assessment of each construct with Cronbach's alpha. Then, the structural equation model was carried out. Results indicate that information about products and services in advertisements on an online video streaming platform, in addition to being entertaining and fun, have a positive impact on the attitude and consequent purchase intention of the product or service advertised shown by users of these platforms. Finally, the theoretical and practical implications are discussed.

Keywords: Streaming · Attitude · Advertising

1 Introduction

The internet has brought about endless benefits that help consumers satisfy their needs. However, this technology impacts consumers and generates new cultural and social schemes due to the lifestyle changes it implies. Several factors define how users consume different services, such as occupation, economic status, perception, learning, needs and desires [21].

A. Coman and S. Vasilache (Eds.): HCII 2023, LNCS 14025, pp. 611–621, 2023.
https://doi.org/10.1007/978-3-031-35915-6_44

In recent years, the industry that has benefited the most from the attempts of consumers to fulfill their need for entertainment is streaming. According to [6] in 2014, only 2.4% of the Chilean population reported subscribing to streaming services, a number that grew to 4.4% in 2022, with two platforms hired per household on average. User satisfaction with streaming is very high and reached 80% during 2021. This is in stark contrast with the satisfaction reported with open television, which is only 24%. Meanwhile, cable and satellite television present 42%, whereas local or regional TV have only 20% of user satisfaction [6].

YouTube and Twitch TV are among the most influential platforms in the streaming industry. YouTube, the largest video storage platform, focuses on promoting hours of video consumption to generate revenues based on the advertisement within them. In turn, Twitch TV is the most popular platform in terms of live streaming. Streaming content is varied, but the category of videogames stands out. The business model of this category is based on subscriptions (SVoD), advertisement in streaming and direct donations from consumers [24]. Therefore, the streaming system has offered users great flexibility, as they do not need to leave their homes to buy or rent movies, documentaries or seasons of series and can rather stay home and watch them online [14].

A key attribute of advertisement within these platforms is interactivity [26]. This is considered one of the main features that make these platforms an important advertising channel [25]. In interactive terms, there is consensus that the communication of traditional marketing changes from a unidirectional to a bidirectional process [32]. In this process, first, advertisers have the advantage of identifying their customers and differentiating them, thereby personalizing their content [25]. Second, consumers have higher participation in advertisement, being able to choose when and how to interact with ads [23]. In this context, this study aims to analyze and model the behavior of consumers in the online streaming industry towards advertising in the YouTube and Twitch TV platforms.

2 Literature Review

The growth of the internet and the increased access people have to it has made this network one of the most important tools for searching information, expressing opinions, conducting social interactions, or seeking audiovisual entertainment. In terms of internet access by individuals, there are three influencing factors, namely capacity, interest, and expectations. Capacity refers to the user having access to a computer or connection to use the internet [28]. In Chile, smartphones have become practically universal, with 90% of homes having at least one. In addition, 74% of households report having a Smart TV and 61%, a laptop. Furthermore, 61% of the population reports watching audiovisual content on smartphones [6].

The entertainment industry, formed by television, radio, movies, music, and videogames, is experiencing the digital transformation generated by the Internet. According to [16], the accelerated development of smartphones, tablets and music and video platforms has produced changes in consumer preferences, increasing the demand for music, video, television, and games distributed on the Internet and its technological devices, both for periodical subscriptions and specific payments for events. Streaming originates as part of this transformation. The word streaming refers to the system used to watch videos or listen to music without the need to previously download the content, since fragments of this are issued and sequentially sent through an Internet connection [7]. Streaming can be live, in which the audio or video is broadcasted while the event is taking place, or on demand, in which the user selects the content to watch or listen to, having the option to pause, fast forward or rewind.

Subscription video on demand (SVoD) became popular in the late 2000s [1]. This system offers the possibility of watching movies, series, documentaries, reality shows, short films, and children's content without advertisement on any device with a screen and internet connection (internet browsers on computers, smartphones and Smart TVs, tablets and video game consoles) in exchange for a monthly paid subscription.

Thanks to streaming, the content offered has broadened to the extent that diverse Internet distributed digital platforms such as OTT (Over the Top)—i.e., systems for managing audiovisual content on demand and free online broadcasting such as YouTube, Netflix or Twitch—host third party content or their own content [11]. Linked to the growth in streaming content is the breadth of content offered. Although in the beginning streaming services were only distributors, they also became producers of original audiovisual content cover time, starting with Netflix in 2013 [20]. The reasons behind this vertical integration into a supplying industry include reinforcing their strength in the market [15], the high cost of acquiring series and movie licensing, the termination of contracts with suppliers [1], the search for self-sufficiency and the need to eliminate licensed content in advance because suppliers joined the industry as new competitors, as in the case of Disney [34]. In addition, streaming platforms also take advantage of the high degree of knowledge they have about their subscription profiles, producing content based on users' tastes and preferences, increasing their probability of success, and attracting more subscriptions [22].

According to [31], the streaming industry, considering only services of subscription video on demand (SVoD), had revenues of approximately US$ 70.845 billion in 2021. Together with this value, the user penetration of the industry also stands out, with a value of 14.3% in 2021. Regarding data, by 2025, the industry expects a growth (considering only SVoD) of US$ 108.508 billion and a user penetration of 18.2%.

With respect to SVoD consumers, in 2021, there were 1.0786 billion users, which is expected to reach 1.423 billion for the different platforms offering SVoD by 2025 [31]. According to the users, streaming is popular because it allows for watching content whenever a user wants, different family members can watch different content on multiple devices simultaneously, as well as several consecutive episodes in the case of series, it is comfortable and easy to use, it has a wide variety of content [27], there are no interruptions because there is no advertising, and personal profiles allow for regulating consumption and obtain recommendations from the platforms [19]. With the increase in offerings, more and more users are deciding to subscribe to more than one streaming platform, and they can cancel their subscriptions if they do not use the service frequently [4]. However, if consumers decided not to subscribe to various platforms simultaneously, the industry could become more competitive [15]. One of the segments most favored by the growth of the live streaming service industry is videogames. [18] states that Twitch is the platform with the highest number of concurrent spectators on average, reaching 2.62

million concurrent viewers. Regarding market participation, in 2022, according to [18] the number of hours watched per consumer by platform was led by Twitch with 78.6% of total watched hours, which is equivalent to a total of 5.7 billion hours, followed by YouTube Gaming with 16.2% [18].

To understand how the streaming industry operates, it is necessary to differentiate between services that have a business model defined as subscription—such as Netflix, Amazon prime video and Crunchyroll—which specialize in offering movie and series streaming, and streaming services that obtain revenues based on advertisement within videos and that target the preference of consumers—denominated "viewers"—thereby allowing the creator of the advertisement and the platform to obtain benefits proportional to the number of visualizations or income for clicking "pay per view" ads. This last category includes Twitch, YouTube, Spotify free, and Facebook Gaming.

The TAM model initially formulated by [8] has the main objective of seeking the best variables for predicting and somehow explaining the use intention of information systems. The model proposes the existence of two main constructs that can explain the acceptance of a technology by users, which are perceived usefulness and perceived ease of use. [35] expands the construct of Perceived Enjoyment, which is considered a dominant variable over Perceived Usefulness in the context of hedonic information systems. This extension of the TAM model has the main objective of explaining the current use of hedonic information systems and is because consumers are both passive and active entities [12, 29], i.e., consumers of live streaming services are people who participate by watching videos (passive) or commenting on them (active).

The unified theory of acceptance and use of technology (UTAUT) is the combination of eight models and theories of individual acceptance (among which is TAM), each with different key constructs that model the behavior of target people in different but related contexts [36]. To improve the model proposed through UTAUT, this is extended to UTAUT2, which in addition to being applicable to information technologies, can be also applied in consumption technologies [37]. This study is based on the model proposed by [13], shown in Fig. 1, which studies the factors influencing consumer behavior towards the broadcasting of advertising on online streaming platforms. The factors are defined below.

Attitude is understood as the predisposition of consumers to favorably respond to a specific stimulus. Studies have explored the differences between web users classified as heavy, medium, and light in terms of their beliefs about web advertisement, purchase patterns and demography [15]. These factors generate a more positive attitude towards web advertisement, which probably leads to more frequent web purchases and higher amounts spent.

Online entertainment has become a new medium for advertisement, which is characterized by its easy access to consumers as a product with a relatively low cost of installation, time independence and interactivity [3]. Therefore for advertisements to be effective in this medium, the user perception of web media usability and the effect of using these media on attitude towards individual announcements need to be considered [2].

Information for the user works as a positive effect in advertising. It allows consumers to get to know new products and brands and provides information to make comparisons as a purchase decision tool. The information element of the ad within an online video has motivated consumers to purchase the products advertised [30].

Invasiveness in the online medium became a barrier that affects the privacy of consumers, considering that, by nature, online video advertisements tend to interrupt and distract humans, as well as disrupt the behavior of consumers towards an objective [17]. Regarding invasiveness in social network websites, consumers report concerns about privacy, generating a significant and negative impact on their attitude towards social network ads. In this sense, entertainment, consistency with the brand and peer influence have a significant effect and positive impact on the attitude towards advertising in social networks [33].

The value of advertising tends to directly influence buying behavior. New media technology will make audiences more selective when processing advertisements [10].

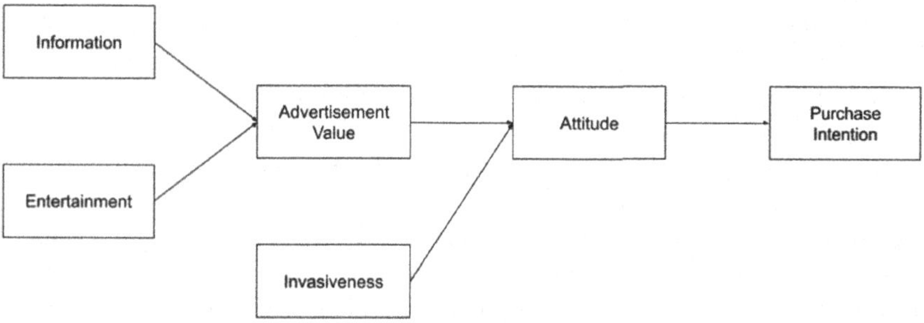

Fig. 1. Proposed model

Based on the above, the following hypotheses are proposed:

H1: Information has a significant and positive impact on the advertisement value in online video streaming.

H2: Entertainment has a significant and positive impact on the advertisement value in online video streaming.

H3: Invasiveness has a significant and negative impact on the attitude of users towards advertisements in online video streaming.

H4: Advertisement value has a significant and positive impact on attitude towards advertisements in online video streaming.

H5: Attitude towards advertising in online video streaming has a positive impact on purchase intention.

3 Methodology

To obtain the data necessary for the structural equation model proposed in Fig. 1, a questionnaire was created, which included both the observable variables [13] —measured on a 5-point Likert scale—and some characterization questions about use behavior and demographic information. The questionnaire was disseminated through the SurveyMonkey platform during the months of June and July 2022, with a total of 243 complete responses.

The analysis of the surveyed sample was performed using IBM SPSS Statistics v.28 to first conduct a descriptive analysis of data and then a reliability assessment of each construct through Cronbach's alpha. Subsequently, a structural equation analysis is carried out using IBM SPSS Amos v.28 to validate the proposed hypotheses about consumers and their purchase intention after watching ads on online streaming platforms. The model contains 6 latent variables and 23 observable variables that will be analyzed below.

4 Results

First, the profile of the sample is analyzed. Regarding gender, 55.1% of participants identified themselves with the masculine gender, 42.8% with the female gender, and the remaining 2.1% preferred not to specify their gender. In turn, the predominant age range of respondents was 19-to-24 years old for 43.6% of the total sample, followed by 25-to-30 and 36 and above, with 20.6% and 21%, respectively, 31-to-35 years of age with 9.1% and finally respondents with ages under or equal to 15 years and aged 16-to-18, accounting for 2.1% and 3.7%, respectively. The results are consistent since most survey dissemination focuses on students and young adults that consume content in diverse online streaming platforms.

Subsequently, to confirm the internal consistency of each construct, a reliability analysis was conducted. Table 1 presents the Cronbach's alpha of each construct; all of them are reliable since their Cronbach's alpha is above 0.6, with invasiveness as the lowest value, at 0.752. In general, results show that values range between 0.7 and 0.95, which indicates that constructs have an acceptable reliability. However, when observing the change of this indicator by construct and removing some of its observable variables, it is revealed that, if the item "Online video advertisements are believable" is eliminated, the Cronbach's alpha for consumer attitude improves to 0.876. This will leave the construct with four items, which is recommended, and therefore, the model analysis continues with a total of 22 observable variables.

Regarding the values obtained, most are considered acceptable or close to acceptable, which indicates a tolerable model fit, as shown in Table 2. The CMIN/DF ratio has a value close to 2, which is within the parameters for acceptability. In the case of GFI and AGFI, values are observed to be above 0.83, close to the value considered to represent a reasonable fit [9]. CFI, NFI and TLI exhibit values equal to or above 0.9, which are within the range proposed by most authors. Finally, the parsimony normed fit index is considered acceptable as its value is above 0.5.

The results from the model reveal that purchase intention has a R^2 of 0.67. This implies that 67% of the error variance of this endogenous variable is explained by the other variables. In the case of attitude, it is observed that 94% of error variance is explained by the invasiveness exogenous variable and the advertisement value endogenous variable. The latter has a R^2 of 0.87, which means that 87% of error variance is explained by the exogenous variables of entertainment and information.

As for the structural relationships among variables shown in Table 3, four out of the five proposed hypotheses were significant for a p-value below 0.05. The positive effect of entertainment on advertisement value (H1) was confirmed, while information also has

Table 1. Cronbach's alpha associated with the model constructs.

Construct	Cronbach's Alpha	Item	Cronbach's Alpha if item deleted
Information	0.852	INF1	0.769
		INF2	0.751
		INF3	0.855
Entertainment	0.927	ENT1	0.899
		ENT2	0.914
		ENT3	0.899
		ENT4	0.905
Invasiveness	0.752	INV1	0.198
		INV2	0.309
		INV3	0.413
		INV4	0–396
		INV5	0.380
Advertisement Value	0.805	ADV1	0.765
		ADV2	0.676
		ADV3	0.758
Attitude	0.864	ATT1	0.818
		ATT2	0.835
		ATT3	0.821
		ATT4	0.876
		ATT5	0.823
Purchase Intention	0.923	PI1	0.908
		PI2	0.863
		PI3	0.895

a positive effect on advertisement value (H2). Regarding the latter variable, its positive and significant effect on attitude (H4) was validated, and attitude was confirmed to have a positive effect on purchase intention (H5). In turn, the effect of invasiveness on attitude is not significant in the studied sample.

The results reveal that information about advertisement value, in addition to be significant, has a factor load of 0.57. This implies that the information variable is explaining 57% of advertisement value; in the case of entertainment, this variable is significant as it exhibits a factor load of 0.41. In turn, advertisement value has a factor load of 0.97 over attitude and the latter presents a factor load of 0.82 over purchase intention. Both relationships are significant with a p-value below 0.001. Therefore, it is concluded that the consumer attitude towards advertisements broadcasted on online streaming platforms

Table 2. Model fit index.

Index	Value
Chi squared	399.91
CMIN/DF	2.01
GFI	0.869
AGFI	0.834
RMR	0.119
RMSEA	0.065
CFI	0.946
NFI	0.900
TLI	0.938
PNFI	0.775

Table 3. SEM results.

Item	Standardized Estimate	P-Value
PI ← ATT	0.82	***
ATT ← INV	−0.01	0.627
ATT ← ADV	0.97	***
ADV ← INF	0.57	***
ADV ← ENT	0.41	***

are closely related to the advertisement values. In turn, the advertisement value that consumers attribute is mostly explained by the information delivered, without neglecting the entertainment this may bring users. Finally, a positive attitude from the consumer towards these advertisements tends to generate purchase intention from users.

5 Conclusions

After analyzing the results, it is possible to successfully determine the influence of audiovisual advertisements broadcasted on online video streaming platforms on purchase intention, noting the importance of the entertainment and information factors as key determinants of advertisement effectiveness.

Additionally, according to the analysis of the model studied, it is noteworthy that although the invasiveness factor is negatively related to consumer attitude, advertisement value has a stronger relationship with attitude than advertisement. This finding indicated that advertisement value plays an important role in the attitude adopted by consumers towards advertisements broadcasted on online video streaming platforms. As the use of ads on online video streaming increases day by day on different websites such as Twitch,

YouTube and Facebook, a growing need for understanding the different factors influencing consumer attitude towards advertising in this type of content has been generated, which seeks to achieve more efficacy in increasing the purchase intention of consumers. This study provides detailed knowledge on the different attitude factors that affect the purchase intention of consumers after watching ads on online video streaming platforms. It should be noted that information has a greater impact on the value perceived from advertising compared to entertainment. It is also observed that invasiveness negatively affects consumer attitude; however, this hypothesis is rejected as it is not significant in the study. Consequently, marketing specialists can design their online video ads in such a way that these are more visible by increasing information content, which in turn would enhance acceptance by users. Entertainment has a positive influence on consumer attitude; therefore, advertisers should ensure that their advertising format on online video streaming platforms is creative to maintain the attention flow from the audience.

In summary, advertisers or marketing experts on these platforms should develop ads with an emphasis on the quantity of information provided to users, balancing this variable with creativity so the advertisement value perceived by consumers has a positive effect on their attitude, since a good attitude from users was demonstrated to have a close relationship with their future purchase intention, resulting in an effective implementation of advertising.

References

1. Acuña Alegre, C., Huamán Vilchez, L., Taddey García, C.: Caso Netflix: planeamiento estratégico 2015–2019 (2015)
2. Alwitt, L.F., Prabhaker, P.R.: Identifying who dislikes television advertising: not by demographics alone. J. Advert. Res. **34**(6), 17–30 (1994)
3. Berthon, P., Pitt, L.F., Watson, R.T.: The World Wide Web as an advertising medium. J. Advert. Res. **36**(1), 43–54 (1996)
4. Bolaños, D.: Plataformas de streaming: este es el secreto de su éxito. Consumer (2020). https://www.consumer.es/tecnologia/internet/plataformas-streaming-secreto-exito.html, Accessed 26 Jan 2023
5. Cisco: Chile Cisco VNI 2017–2022. (2018). http://ciscovnilatam.com/chile/. Accessed 7 Nov 2022
6. CNTV Estudio CNTV revela que la TV abierta pierde audiencia mientras se consolida el consumo de servicios de streaming. Consejo Nacional de Televisión (2022). https://www.cntv.cl/2022/09/estudio-cntv-revela-que-la-tv-abierta-pierde-audiencia-mientras-se-consolida-el-consumo-de-servicios-de-streaming/. Accessed 26 Jan 2023
7. Cuevas Cárdenas, J.: Apropiación de las plataformas OTT entre las audiencias audiovisuales de Cali (2019)
8. Davis, F.D.: Perceived usefulness, perceived ease of use, and user acceptance of information technology. MIS Quart., 319–340 (1989)
9. Doll, W.J., Xia, W., Torkzadeh, G.: A confirmatory factor analysis of the end-user computing satisfaction instrument. MIS Quart., 453–461 (1994)
10. Ducoffe, R.H., Curlo, E.: Advertising value and advertising processing. J. Mark. Commun. **6**(4), 247–262 (2000)
11. García, M.M.: Innovación en formatos audiovisuales. El uso de herramientas de live streaming en Antena 3 y Univision. Miguel Hernández Commun. J. (7) (2016)

12. Heinonen, K.: Consumer activity in social media: Managerial approaches to consumers' social media behavior. J. Consum. Behav. **10**(6), 356–364 (2011)
13. Jain, G., Rakesh, S., Chaturvedi, K.R.: Online video advertisements' effect on purchase intention: an exploratory study on youth. Int. J. E-Bus. Res. (IJEBR) **14**(2), 87–101 (2018)
14. Kenworthy, A.D.: The Streaming Wars: The Future of Entertainment (2020)
15. Korgaonkar, P., Wolin, L.D.: Web usage, advertising, and shopping: relationship patterns. Internet Res. (2002). https://doi.org/10.1108/10662240210422549
16. Laudon, K.C., Guercio Traver, C.: E-commerce: Negocios, Tecnología, Sociedad (Novena Edi) (2013)
17. Li, H., Edwards, S.M., Lee, J.H.: Measuring the intrusiveness of advertisements: scale development and validation. J. Advert. **31**(2), 37–47 (2002)
18. Streamlabs and Stream Hatchet Q3 2022 Live Streaming Report. Streamlabs (2022). https://streamlabs.com/content-hub/post/streamlabs-and-stream-hatchet-q3-2022-live-streaming-report#:~:text=Viewers%20broadcasted%2010.4%20billion%20hours,billion%20hours%20in%20Q3%202021. Accessed 26 Jan 2023
19. Mejia Wille, N.: Usos, hábitos, actitudes y experiencias usuario de jóvenes universitarios en el consumo audiovisual de Netflix. Revista Aportes de la Comunicación y la Cultura **25**, 49–62 (2018)
20. Millán: Lluvia de millones: esto es lo que están gastando las plataformas de streaming en su contenido original. Hipertextual (2022). https://hipertextual.com/2020/10/gasto-plataformas-streaming-contenido-original, Accessed 26 Jan 2023
21. Moreno, O.C., Andrade, J.G., Ramírez, M.C., Quiñones, R.V.: El comportamiento del consumidor en internet bajo el modelo psicológico social de Veblen. Revista Global de Negocios **3**(5), 101–112 (2015)
22. Ordonez, K., Suing, A., Ramón, M., Ramirez-Coronel, R.: The internet and the content audiovisual's. Netflix in Latin America. In: 2018 13th Iberian Conference on Information Systems and Technologies (CISTI), pp. 1–5. IEEE (2018)
23. Pavlou, P.A., Stewart, D.W.: Measuring the effects and effectiveness of interactive advertising: a research agenda. J. Interact. Advert. **1**(1), 61–77 (2000)
24. Pires, K., Simon, G.: YouTube live and Twitch: a tour of user-generated live streaming systems. In: Proceedings of the 6th ACM Multimedia Systems Conference, pp. 225–230 (2015)
25. Roberts, M.S., Ko, H.: Global interactive advertising: defining what we mean and using what we have learned. J. Interact. Advert. **1**(2), 18–27 (2001)
26. Rodgers, S., Thorson, E.: The interactive advertising model: how users perceive and process online ads. J. Interact. Advert. **1**(1), 41–60 (2000)
27. Saavedra Chau, C.D.J., Vera Chaparro, A.P.: Perfil del consumidor de servicios Over-The-Top por internet de la ciudad de Trujillo (2019)
28. Salzman, R., Albarran, A.B.: Internet use in Latin America. Palabra Clave **14**(2), 297–313 (2011)
29. Shao, G.: Understanding the appeal of user-generated media: a uses and gratification perspective. Internet Res. (2009)
30. Shavitt, S., Lowrey, P., Haefner, J.: Public attitudes toward advertising: more favorable than you might think. J. Advertis **38**(4), 7–22 (1998)
31. Statista: Video Streaming (SVoD) - Worldwide. Statista (2021). https://www.statista.com/outlook/dmo/digital-media/video-on-demand/video-streaming-svod/worldwide Accessed 26 Jan 2023
32. Stewart, D.W., Pavlou, P.A.: From consumer response to active consumer: measuring the effectiveness of interactive media. J. Acad. Mark. Sci. **30**(4), 376–396 (2002)
33. Taylor, D.G., Lewin, J.E., Strutton, D.: Friends, fans, and followers: do ads work on social networks?: How gender and age shape receptivity. J. Advert. Res. **51**(1), 258–275 (2011)

34. Towler, L.: Netflix during COVID: More reliant on older, acquired content. Ampere Analysis (2020). https://www.ampereanalysis.com/insight/netflix-during-covid-more-reliant-on-older-acquired-content. Accessed 29 Oct 2021
35. Van der Heijden, H.: User acceptance of hedonic information systems. MIS Q., 695–704 (2004)
36. Venkatesh, V., Morris, M.G., Davis, G.B., Davis, F.D.: User acceptance of information technology: toward a unified view. MIS Q., 425–478 (2003)
37. Venkatesh, V., Thong, J.Y., Xu, X.: Consumer acceptance and use of information technology: extending the unified theory of acceptance and use of technology. MIS Q., 157–178 (2012)

Analysis of Loyal Customers Considering Diversity of Customers

Tomoki Yoshimi[1], Kohei Otake[2(✉)], and Takashi Namatame[3]

[1] Graduate School of Science and Engineering, Chuo University, 1-13-27, Bunkyo-Ku, Kasuga 112-8551, Tokyo, Japan
a19.pb66@g.chuo-u.ac.jp

[2] Faculty of Science and Engineering, Chuo University, 1-13-27, Bunkyo-Ku, Kasuga 112-8551, Tokyo, Japan
otake@tsc.u-tokai.ac.jp

[3] School of Information and Telecommunication Engineering, Tokai University, 2-3-23, Minato-Ku, Takanawa 108-8619, Tokyo, Japan
nama@kc.chuo-u.ac.jp

Abstract. In recent years, the Japanese electronics retail store business has continued to develop, and sales promotion activities tailored to customer preferences have become necessary. This study analyzes the relationship between customers and products using ID-POS data of an electronics retail stores. We use pLSA, a clustering method, since it can cluster customers and products at the same time, it is easy to grasp the relationship between them. Based on the result of pLSA sales promotion activities for representative products are discussed using the indicators of loyal customers and recurring purchase.

Keywords: pLSA · probabilistic Latent Semantic Analysis · POS data

1 Introduction

Recently, electronics retail business for consumer has continued to develop in Japan, according to the report of the Ministry of Economy, Trade and Industry [1], the sales value of products has been on an upward trend since 2017. In this data, the sales price of information appliances has increased significantly, especially with the introduction of remote working due to the pandemic of COVID-19. However, in 2021, the sales value has turned to a slight decline due to reaction reduction. As shown in the above situations, it is possible that the global condition will continue to affect the sales of home electronics stores in the future. In particular, as customer preferences are said to be diversifying, it is necessary to understand the characteristics of each customer segment and conduct sales promotion activities in line with their needs.

A. Coman and S. Vasilache (Eds.): HCII 2023, LNCS 14025, pp. 622–634, 2023.
https://doi.org/10.1007/978-3-031-35915-6_45

2 Purpose

In previous studies, pLSA, a latent class analysis, has often been used to examine the relationship between customers and products. Specifically, the relationship between customers' purchasing behavior and products has been studied on supermarket data [2]. It is also used a study that examined the relationship between membership stage and products purchased [3]. However, pLSA has never been used to analyze ID-POS data of electronics retail stores. The range of each product category in this data is wide. In addition, the amount of money spent per purchase is large, and recurring purchases occur to certain extent in the data. The purpose of this study is to understand the relationship between customers and products and to propose specific sales promotion activities using POS data from electronics retail stores.

3 Datasets

3.1 Datasets Summary

In this study, we use the sales data with IDs of a company which sales electronic products. This store mainly treats PCs, software, digital products like video games, and anime goods. Table 1 is the summary of the data which we used.

Table 1. The summary of Datasets

Period	2020/1/1-2021/6/30
Number of product groups	226
Number of sales transactions	3,463,425
Used columns	Customer ID, product group, Number of units purchased, Purchase price, Return flag

We use the above information to capture customer characteristics from the data. The data contains information on returns, so it has been deleted and handled. The names of some categories have been changed in accordance with the wishes of the data providers.

3.2 Data Description

Changes in Sales Amount. First, we calculated the total sales for each of the six months in the analysis period (Fig. 1).

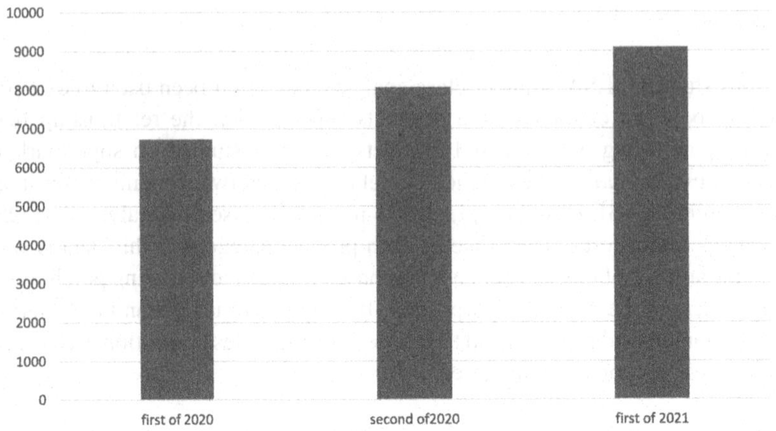

Fig. 1. Changing in sales amount

The unit is one million yen. Figure 2 shows that total sales have been increasing steadily and will exceed 9 billion yen in the first half of 2021.

Summary of Product Categories. We analyzed the number of products sold by product category. Table 2 summarizes the 10 product categories with the highest total number of sales for each six-month period.

Rank	First of 2020	Second of 2020	First of 2021
1	PC game software	PC game software	Plastic models
2	Plastic models	Plastic models	PC game software
3	Anime goods	TV game software	BD software
4	TV game software	BD software	TV game software
5	BD software	DVD software	DVD software
6	Used PC software	Used PC software	PC parts
7	PC parts	CD software	Used PC software
8	Books	Books	Books
9	DVD software	PC parts	CD software
10	CD software	Educational toy	TV game console

The main products are related to various types of software.

Purchase Price. We calculate the per person purchase amount for the entire analysis period.

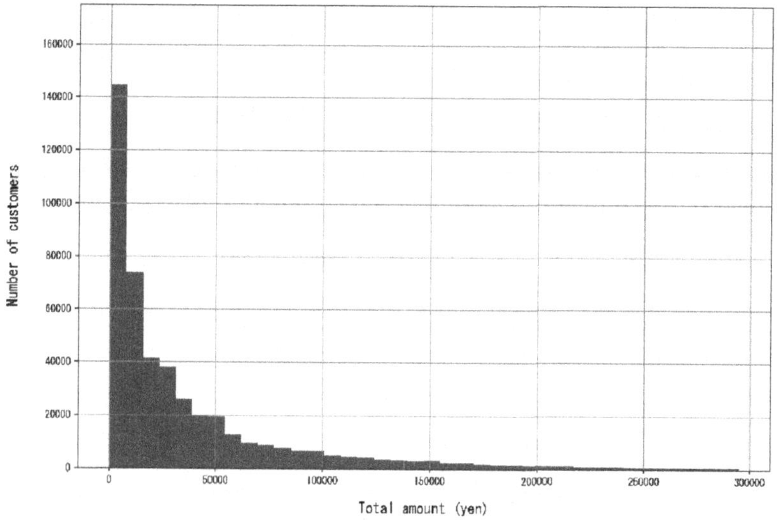

Fig. 2. Histogram of purchase amounts

Most customers spent less than 50,000 yen for their purchases during the analysis period. The median purchase amount was 18,838 yen and the mean purchase amount was 50,459 yen.

4 Analytical Method

First, we performed probabilistic latent semantic analysis to cluster customers and products in order to determine which product group and how many products each customer purchased in a given time period. The data for consecutive periods of time were used to show how customers moved from one cluster to another using a Sankey diagram. Second, we analyzed loyal customers.

4.1 pLSA (Probabilistic Latent Semantic Analysis)

In this study, the analysis was conducted using probabilistic Latent Semantic Analysis "pLSA" [4], one of the clustering methods, as a method of dividing customers into certain segments. pLSA is a soft clustering method originally used for text analysis, and is capable of simultaneously segmenting customers and products into segments for the obtained data [5]. Specifically, it has the following characteristics. First, it can handle high-dimensional data. In pLSA, high-dimensional data is compressed to a lower dimension and then clustered, so it can handle high-dimensional data. Second, by assuming that there is a common latent class for the row and column elements of the matrix data, it is possible to cluster the row and column elements simultaneously. In the marketing field, clustering customers and products simultaneously facilitates class interpretation.

We assume that there is a common latent class z for row element x and column element y. By using the latent class z to expand the co-occurrence probability $P(x_i, y_j)$ of x_i and y_j, $P(x_i|z_k)$, $P(y_j|z_k)$, and $P(z_k)$ are calculated. The co-occurrence probability is as in Eq. (1).

$$P(x_i, y_j) = \sum_k P(x_i|z_k)P(y_j|z_k)P(z_k) \tag{1}$$

where $P(x|z)$, $P(y|z)$, and $P(z)$ are determined by the EM algorithm that maximizes the log-likelihood. And the log-likelihood function L is as in Eq. (2).

$$L = \sum_i \sum_j n(i, j) \log P(x_i, y_j) \tag{2}$$

where $n(i, j)$ is the co-occurrence frequency of x_i and y_j (Fig. 3).

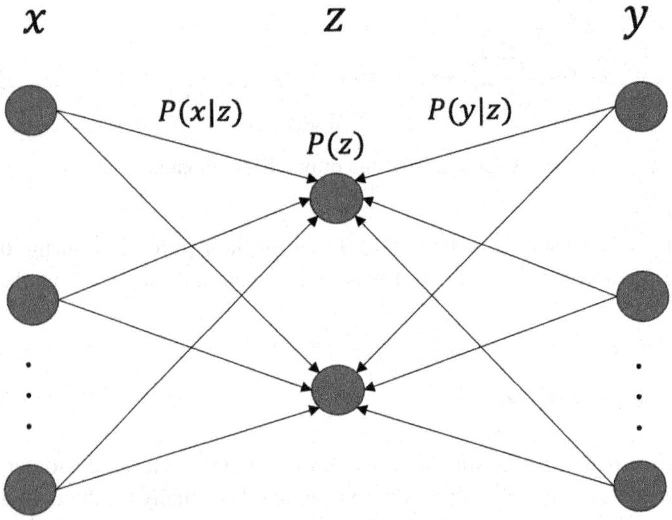

Fig. 3. Concept of pLSA

5 Analysis and Results

5.1 Data Processing

ID-POS data of the electronics retail store is processed into a form used for pLSA. Specifically, the data were processed as shown in the Table 2 that are co-occurrence matrices for rows and columns.

The rows are assigned to customers and the columns are assigned to product categories, and the co-occurrence matrix is the number of products purchased in each

Table 2. 1.1Data Processing

	Category 1	Category 2	Category 3	…
Customer 1	1	0	3	…
Customer 2	0	0	1	…
Customer 3	1	2	3	…
…	…	…	…	…

period. Since there are 226 product categories in this case, the total matrix is 473,113 (customers) × 226 (products). We also split the data every six months in order to check for differences in each period. The number of customers who purchased in each period is 198,645 in the first half of 2020, 216,835 in the second half of 2020, and 209,446 in the first half of 2021, when the split was conducted.

5.2 Determining the Number of Latent Class

In pLSA, we have to determine the number of classes ourself in pLSA, so we determined it based on the Bayesian Information Criterion (BIC) and interpretability of each latent class (Fig. 4).

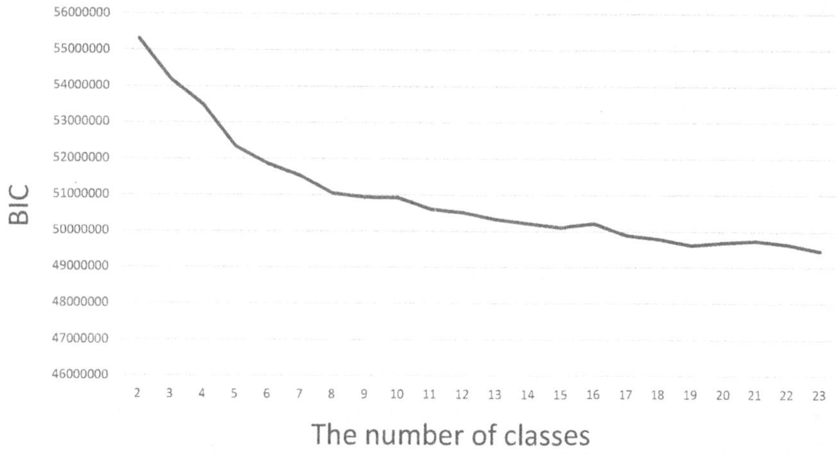

Fig. 4. BIC with increase in number of classes

Generally, the number of classes is determined by the minimum in BIC. However, the BIC keeps decreasing but, the slope is decreasing, so we decided to divide data into eight classes in consideration of interpretability and class size. The results of the pLSA and representative products for the first half of 2021 are shown below. In really, pLSA is a soft clustering method, so membership in each class is determined probabilistically. Although, in this study, we assume that the customers belong to the class of the highest probability.

5.3 Results of pLSA

In order to examine changes in customer purchasing behavior over a period of time, we divided analysis period into every six months and use pLSA method.

Table 3. Results of the pLSA for the first half of 2020

Class	Customer ratio (%)	Typical Products
1	4.5	Anime goods
2	10.2	BD DVD Software, Used PC software
3	16.9	PC games software, TV game software
4	15.7	CD Software
5	17.9	PC parts, Used game software
6	20.2	Educational Toys, TV game console
7	7.4	Books
8	1.5	Plastic models

Table 4. Results of the pLSA for the second half of 2020

Class	Customer ratio (%)	Typical Products
1	14.2	TV game software, Used game software
2	16.5	Books, PC parts
3	11.5	PC game software, Used PC software
4	7.8	Anime goods
5	9.5	Plastic models
6	18.6	Educational toys, TV game console
7	5.3	BD DVD software
8	16.2	CD software

The above Tables 3, 4 and 5 shows the customer ratio clustered into each class and the typical products of each group. We use a time-series Sankey diagram to illustrate how customers moved between clusters over the three periods (Fig. 5).

From the left node, the first half of 2020, the second half of 2020, and the first half of 2021. The figure above shows how customers move between classes. While many customers are moving to the same product class, we can also read some strongly related products such as anime BD software and DVD software.

5.4 Survey of Loyal Customers

In this study, we define a loyal customer as a customer with a high purchase amount, and the customers with the top half of purchase amounts in the three periods are defined

Table 5. Results of the pLSA for the first half of 2021

Class	Customer ratio (%)	Typical Products
1	11.5	Anime goods
2	13.1	Plastic models
3	16.0	PC games, TV game consoles
4	14.1	PC Parts, CD Software
5	13.2	Used PC Software
6	12.6	TV game software
7	18.0	BD DVD Software, Books
8	1.4	Educational Toys

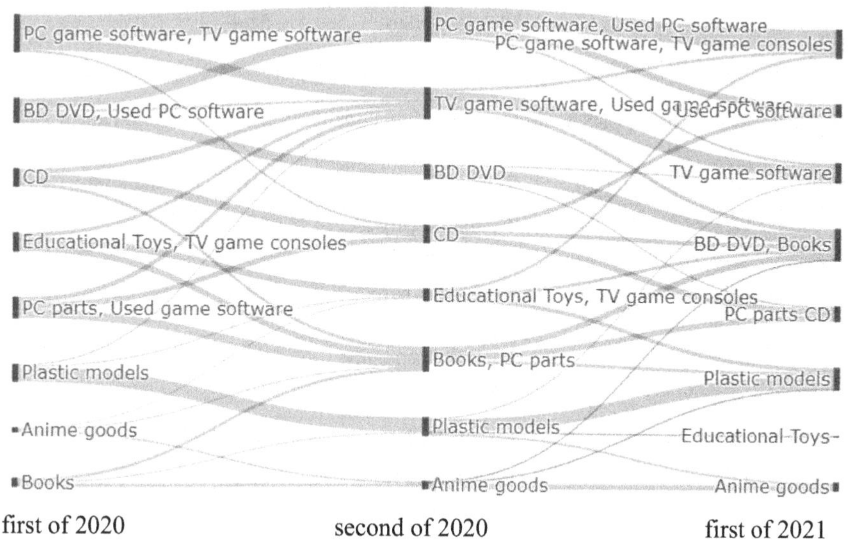

Fig. 5. Customer class transitions during seasonal changes

as loyal customers. A Table 6 showing the results of the clustering and the percentage of loyal customers is shown below.

The table above shows that the PC games and TV game consoles classes attract a large number of loyal customers. On the other hand, the percentage of loyal customers ratio is lower for anime goods and plastic models.

5.5 Survey of Recurring Customers

Next, we analyze the customer's continued purchases. As in the previous section, for each period pLSA results are used to determine the percentage of recurring customer

Table 6. Results of the pLSA and loyal customers distribution for the first half of 2020

Class	Customer ratio (%)	Typical Products	Loyal customers ratio (%)
1	4.5	Anime goods	42.5
2	10.2	BD DVD Software, Used PC software	59.3
3	16.9	PC games software, TV game software	56.5
4	15.7	CD Software	55.8
5	17.9	PC parts, Used game software	54.5
6	20.2	Educational Toys, TV game console	63.0
7	7.4	Books	20.9
8	1.5	Plastic models	51.4

Table 7. Results of the pLSA and loyal customers distribution for the second half of 2021

Class	Customer ratio (%)	Typical Products	Loyal customers ratio (%)
1	14.2	TV game software, Used game software	55.2
2	16.5	Books, PC parts	52.2
3	11.5	PC game software, Used PC software	72.4
4	7.8	Anime goods	17.5
5	9.5	Plastic models	45.6
6	18.6	Educational toys, TV game console	71.2
7	5.3	BD DVD software	73.3
8	16.2	CD software	55.4

in the next period. This analysis is not performed for the second half of 2021, because there are no data available for that period and beyond.

The above tables show that anime goods, PC parts, and video game consoles are less likely to be purchased recurringly while PC game software, BD software, DVD software, and plastic models tend to be purchased recurrently.

Table 8. Results of the pLSA and loyal customers distribution for the first half of 2021

Class	Customer ratio (%)	Typical Products	Loyal customers ratio (%)
1	11.5	Anime goods	18.3
2	13.1	Plastic models	43.1
3	16.0	PC games, TV game consoles	62.9
4	14.1	PC Parts, CD Software	51.9
5	13.2	Used PC Software	45.0
6	12.6	TV game software	46.0
7	18.0	BD DVD Software, Books	53.7
8	1.4	Educational Toys	41.7

Table 9. Results of the pLSA and recurring customer ratio for the first half of 2021

Class	Customer ratio (%)	Typical Products	Recurring customer ratio (%)
1	4.5	Anime goods	28.8
2	10.2	BD DVD Software, Used PC software	50.4
3	16.9	PC games software, TV game software	46.7
4	15.7	CD Software	31.2
5	17.9	PC parts, Used game software	27.3
6	20.2	Educational Toys, TV game console	23.0
7	7.4	Books	28.7
8	1.5	Plastic models	51.8

6 Discussion

As shown is Tables 6, 7, 8, loyal customers ratio varies widely by class. In particular, the loyal customers ratio for PC game software is large. The results show that loyal customers are those who purchase BD software, DVD software, PC parts, PC game software, TV game consoles, etc. On the other hand, loyal customers are less likely to purchase anime goods, the number of loyal customers is low among those who purchase anime goods. In addition to the analysis of Recurring purchases, we can see that there are differences in the classes to which loyal customers belong (Tables 9 and 10).

Table 10. Results of the pLSA and recurring customer ratio for the second half of 2021

Class	Customer ratio (%)	Typical Products	Recurring customer ratio (%)
1	14.2	TV game software, Used game software	33.6
2	16.5	Books, PC parts	27.2
3	11.5	PC game software, Used PC software	49.9
4	7.8	Anime goods	19.3
5	9.5	Plastic models	38.2
6	18.6	Educational toys, TV game console	20.1
7	5.3	BD DVD software	52.8
8	16.2	CD software	25.0

Specifically, customers who purchase BD software, DVD software, PC game software, etc. purchase recurrently, while those who purchase TV game consoles and PC parts are less likely to do. This result is considered to be a strong reflection of the two characteristics of each product. BD software, DVD software, and PC game software have a large number of products and relatively low unit prices. On the other hand, the unit price of TV game consoles and PC parts is high and the number of products is small, so consumers often do not purchase until they find a product they like, which makes purchase difficult (Fig. 6).

The above figures are for Loyal customer ratio and Recurring purchasing ratio. From here we consider specific promotional activities.

The first group includes BD software, DVD software, and PC game software, etc. The high number of loyal customers in this product group and the high rate of recurring purchasing ratio suggest a high level of product satisfaction. In this product group, Recurring purchase by customers in the same class leads to higher sales and retention of loyal customers. Therefore, it is appropriate to recommend the same class of products to this group of customers.

The second group products are TV game consoles. These are characterized by high unit prices and are unlikely to be purchased repeatedly. Therefore, it is effective to recommend products that are related to Group 2 products, such as TV game software, and are likely to be purchased repeatedly.

The third group, A typical products are a plastic models. Although the percentage of loyal customers is not high, they are likely to purchase recurrently. The Sankey diagram in the Fig. 5 shows that plastic models are likely to be purchased independently of other products. Therefore, we infer that it is appropriate to have customers continue to purchase this category, since they are satisfied with the recurring purchase and are unlikely to move to other product classes.

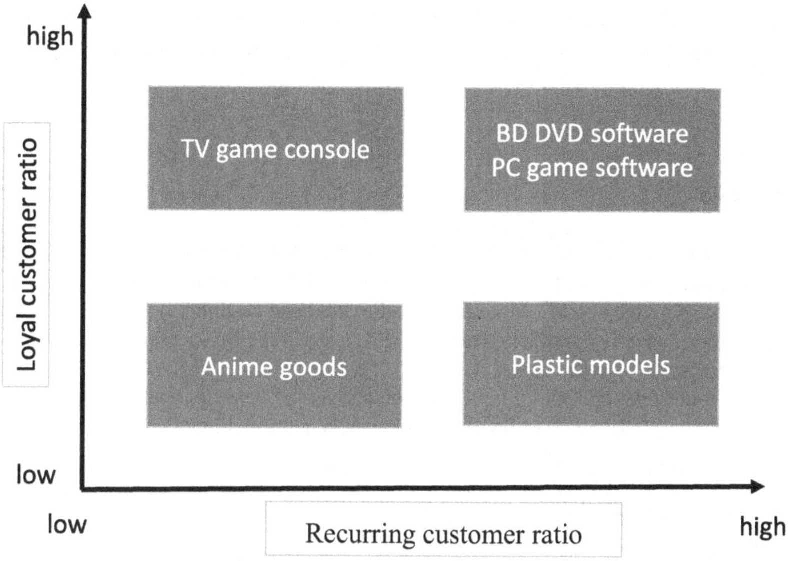

Fig. 6. Product map of typical products

The fourth group, major products are anime goods. This group of products is less likely to be purchased recurringly. As a result, they are less likely to be judged as loyal customers. It can be inferred that customers who purchase anime goods tend to visit the store only when their favorite anime goods are on sale. Therefore, it is necessary to implement measures to encourage customers to move to a different group for each purchased item. For example, BD and DVD software and plastic models of anime are good products to recommend.

7 Conclusion

The purpose of this study was to analyze the relationship between customers and products using POS data with ID from a large electronics retail store, and to examine sales promotion activities for each representative product. The analysis method used was pLSA, a latent class model, to analyze the relationship between customers and products by clustering customers and products at the same time. In addition, we analyzed the characteristics of customers for each product by using the indicators of the percentage of loyal customers and the percentage of repeat purchases, and proposed sales promotion activities.

However, since pLSA performs clustering based on two axes, it could not handle more than three axes simultaneously. Therefore, we believe that more detailed understanding of customer segments can be achieved by adding seasonal differences and differences in purchase patterns to the analysis. In addition, in this study, loyal customers were judged only on the basis of monetary value, but it is also possible to use RFM indicators, and it would be possible to propose different sales promotion activities by using these perspectives.

Acknowledgment. We thank an electronical retail company of Japan for permission to use valuable datasets. This work was supported by JSPS KAKENHI Grant Number 21H04600 and 21K13385.

References

1. Ministry of Economy, Trade and Industry in Japan, "Sales by product at large electronics specialty stores and year-on-year (degree, same period, same month) comparison"
2. Kawashima, K., Yoshida, M., Motomura, Y.: Probabilistic customer behavior modeling with latent class explanatory model extracted by PLSA. Behaviometric Soc. Jpn. **42**, 228–231 (2014) (in Japanese)
3. Yang, T., Yamashita, H., Goto, M.: A study on purchasing behavior analysis method by comparing difference in latent class distributions between membership stages. J. Jpn. Ind. Manage. Assoc. **73**, 54–69 (2022). (in Japanese)
4. Hofman, T.: Probabilistic latent semantic analysis. In: Uncertainity in Artificial Intelligence, UAI 1999, Stockholm (1999)
5. Murayama, K.: A case study of big data application using probabilistic latent semantic structure model ~data modeling by bayesian network and pLSA utilization. In: Proceedings of the Japanese Society for Artificial Intelligence Basic Problems in Artificial Intelligence, 96th, pp. 17–22 (2015). (in Japanese)

Correction to: Implementing Digital Transformation Processes in Industry 4.0

Héctor Cornide-Reyes, Jenny Morales, Fabián Silva-Aravena, Alfredo Ocqueteau, Nahur Melendez, and Rodolfo Villarroel

Correction to:
Chapter 24 in: A. Coman and S. Vasilache (Eds.): *Social Computing and Social Media*, LNCS 14025, https://doi.org/10.1007/978-3-031-35915-6_24

In the original version of this paper one affiliation of the authors Jenny Morales and Fabian Silva is missing. The correction for the two authors is as follows: Facultad de Ciencias Sociales y Económicas, Departamento de Economía y Administración, Universidad Católica del Maule, Talca, Chile

The updated version of this chapter can be found at
https://doi.org/10.1007/978-3-031-35915-6_24

A. Coman and S. Vasilache (Eds.): HCII 2023, LNCS 14025, p. C1, 2024.
https://doi.org/10.1007/978-3-031-35915-6_46

Author Index

A. Coman and S. Vasilache (Eds.): HCII 2023, LNCS 14025, pp. 635–637, 2023.
https://doi.org/10.1007/978-3-031-35915-6

Printed in the United States
by Baker & Taylor Publisher Services